Towards a Cultural Political Economy

For Constance and Stanley Jessop

Towards a Cultural Political Economy

Putting Culture in its Place in Political Economy

Ngai-Ling Sum

Senior Lecturer, Department of Politics, Philosophy and Religion, Lancaster University, UK

Bob Jessop

Distinguished Professor of Sociology, Lancaster University, UK

Edward Elgar
Cheltenham, UK • Northampton, MA, USA

© Ngai-Ling Sum and Bob Jessop 2013

All rights reserved. No part of this publication may be reproduced, stored in a retrieval system or transmitted in any form or by any means, electronic, mechanical or photocopying, recording, or otherwise without the prior permission of the publisher.

Published by
Edward Elgar Publishing Limited
The Lypiatts
15 Lansdown Road
Cheltenham
Glos GL50 2JA
UK

Edward Elgar Publishing, Inc.
William Pratt House
9 Dewey Court
Northampton
Massachusetts 01060
USA

A catalogue record for this book
is available from the British Library

Library of Congress Control Number: 2013944943

This book is available electronically in the ElgarOnline.com
Economics Subject Collection, E-ISBN 978 0 85793 071 2

ISBN 978 1 84542 036 9 (cased)

Typeset by Servis Filmsetting Ltd, Stockport, Cheshire
Printed and bound in Great Britain by T.J. International Ltd, Padstow

Contents

Boxes and figures	vii
Preface	viii
Abbreviations	xiv
Acknowledgements	xvii
Introduction	1

PART I THE LOGOS, LOGICS AND LIMITS OF INSTITUTIONAL AND CULTURAL TURNS: CHALLENGES AND RESPONSES

1	Institutional turns and beyond in political economy	33
2	Cultural turns and beyond in political economy	72
3	Semiotics for cultural political economy	96

PART II TOWARDS A POST-DISCIPLINARY CULTURAL POLITICAL ECONOMY

4	Between Scylla and Charybdis: locating cultural political economy	147
5	Elaborating the cultural political economy research agenda: selectivities, dispositives and the production of (counter-) hegemonies	196

PART III REIMAGINING AND INSTITUTIONALIZING COMPETITIVE GOVERNANCE: NARRATIVES, STRATEGIES AND STRUGGLES

6	A cultural political economy of variegated capitalism	233
7	A cultural political economy of competitiveness and the knowledge-based economy	261

8 The production of a hegemonic knowledge brand:
   competitiveness discourses and neoliberal developmentalism   296

9 Competitiveness clusters, Wal-Martization and the
   (re)making of corporate social responsibilities   324

10 Competitiveness knowledge brands and service governance:
   the making of Hong Kong's competitiveness–integration
   (dis)order   352

PART IV FINANCIALIZATION, FINANCIAL CRISIS AND
         REIMAGINATIONS

11 Crisis construals and crisis recovery in the North Atlantic
   financial crisis   395

12 The North Atlantic financial crisis and crisis recovery:
   (trans-)national imaginaries of 'BRIC' and subaltern groups
   in China   440

PART V CONSOLIDATING CULTURAL POLITICAL
        ECONOMY: FROM PRE-THEORETICAL
        INTUITION TO POST-DISCIPLINARY
        PRACTICE

13 Implications for future research in and on cultural political
   economy   467

References   484
Name index   549
Subject index   553

Boxes and figures

BOXES

0.1	Cultural political economy as a social science	2
0.2	Six distinctive features of the present CPE approach	23
5.1	The seven discursive–material moments in the production of hegemonies	220
6.1	Some commonalities of capitalism	237
6.2	The 'law of value' in capitalism	242
6.3	Spatio-temporal fixes	248
7.1	Six social–epistemic functions of trans-discursive terms	278

FIGURES

1.1	Structure–agency beyond structuration theory	50
1.2	A strategic-relational approach to spatio-temporality	63
3.1	A strategic-relational approach to dialogical heteroglossia	106
4.1	Complexity reduction through enforced selection	151
4.2	Dialectical relations among the basic concepts	160
4.3	The improbability of complexity reduction via enforced selection	192
5.1	An encounter between Gramsci, Marx and Foucault	206
5.2	A preliminary mapping of the seven material–discursive moments in the selectivity space	225
8.1	Porter's diamond model of national advantage	300
9.1	Mapping and making visible clusters in the Pearl River Delta	327
9.2	The glocal partnership of Wal-Mart in China	332
9.3	Articulation of 'new constitutionalism' and 'new ethicalism'	348
10.1	The emergence of a service bloc in Hong Kong between 1997 and 2004	366
11.1	Schematic representation of variation, selection and retention	403

Preface

This volume is a companion to our co-authored *Beyond the Regulation Approach: Putting Capitalist Economies in their Place* (2006) and an earlier book by Bob Jessop, *State Theory: Putting the Capitalist State in its Place* (1990). It adopts the same critical-realist, strategic-relational approach as these two works but elaborates our response to various institutional and cultural turns in political economy. This response was implicit in *State Theory* and more fully developed in *Beyond the Regulation Approach*. Through a critical interrogation and recontextualization of different regulation schools, our previous joint text placed the profit-oriented, market-mediated logic of the capitalist economy and some of its instantiations in their wider political and socio-cultural context.

This work focuses on the semiotic dimensions of political economy considered both as a field of inquiry and as an ensemble of social relations. Introducing semiosis is not intended to replace, but to deepen, critical political economy. The principal referent of 'semiosis', which we develop, refine and re-specify throughout the book, is sense- and meaning-making. Integrating semiosis provides crucial concepts and analytical tools to interpret and explain even more powerfully the logic of capital accumulation and its relation to the social formations in which it is embedded. This focus explains the sub-title of our book: putting culture in its place in political economy. Consistent with our definition of semiosis, culture can be defined in preliminary terms as 'the ensemble of social processes by which meanings are produced, circulated and exchanged' (Thwaites et al. 1994: 1). This definition indicates the overlap between culture and semiosis and, importantly, does not reduce culture to language or discourse. We develop and move beyond this initial definition in Part II of the book and apply these elaborations in Parts III and IV. Overall, we present a research programme that responds to the cultural turn without losing sight of the specificity of the economic categories and economic dynamics typical of capitalist formations. Although cultural political economy (hereafter CPE) is applied mainly, as its name implies, in political economy, the general propositions about semiosis and its grounded heuristics can be applied elsewhere by combining the same semiotic analysis with concepts appropriate to other social forms and institutional dynamics.

The background to this work is easily summarized. For some 18 years now the authors have been working individually and together on an approach to political economy that does not fit into standard disciplinary ways of thinking. We describe our approach as pre-disciplinary in inspiration, trans-disciplinary in practice, and post-disciplinary in its aspiration. We are not alone in refusing disciplinary boundaries and decrying some of their effects. Indeed, there are many signs of increasing commitment among scholars in the arts, humanities and social sciences (and, indeed, natural sciences) to transcend such boundaries in order to better understand the complex interconnections within and across the natural and social worlds. We argue that CPE can productively transform understandings of recent developments in political economy both as a discipline and as a changing field of social relations.

The present book retraces the development of CPE in our individual and collective writings and, more importantly, offers a joint view of its current status and prospects. When we refer to CPE, therefore, it is sometimes a metonym for our work; but, more often, it refers to a broader current with which we identify. The chapters reflect our intellectual trajectories. Ngai-Ling Sum worked on the approach in the early 1990s and initially applied it to East Asia. She began to integrate sense- and meaning-making, at first implicitly, then explicitly, into her work on the discursive and substantive dimensions of the 1997 transfer of Hong Kong to Mainland China (Sum 1995) and East Asian economic strategies (Sum 1996, 2000), drawing particularly on Foucault. Bob Jessop became interested in the regulation approach *and its limits* in the 1980s and explored the potential of a return to Marx and Gramsci to reinvigorate and move beyond it. This informed his response to various institutional and cultural turns in the late 1990s. Over the last few years, we have worked intermittently on various aspects of the emerging approach (for an early statement, see Jessop and Sum 2001).

While it would be tempting to narrate how CPE evolved mainly in response to the cultural turn, this would be far too simple. This still developing approach is grounded in a general interest in the philosophy of science, efforts to reconstruct historical materialism, and developments in state theory. We also addressed the explosive interest in institutions, especially political science, which is reflected in various institutional turns and institutionalisms (see Chapter 1). The next chapter assesses the heuristic potential and limits of cultural turns in political economy, focusing, for the sake of presentation, on the work of Gramsci, neo-Gramscian international political economy, and the regulation approach. Our responses in both cases rest on two important paradigms: one is a 'critical realist' view of the social world (including the nature of science); the other is the strategic-relational approach to structure-agency (see the Introduction). Both paradigms put sense- and meaning-making at the heart of their social science research programmes. *Sense-making* refers to the role of semiosis in the *apprehension of the natural and social world* and highlights the referential value of semiosis, even if this is to as-yet-unrealized possibilities, the 'irreal' (or 'irrealis'), immaterial or virtual entities (see the Introduction). *Meaning-making* refers to processes of signification and meaningful communication and is more closely related, but not restricted, to *the production of linguistic meaning*. The fact that sense- and meaning-making are already part of critical realism and the strategic-relational approach nullifies the need for a belated cultural turn. Indeed, these paradigms provide important resources to respond to one-sided cultural turns and, as a favourite phrase goes, 'to put them in their place'. One of our main goals below is to show how this can be done and to develop a more rounded account of the relation between semiosis and structuration in political economy. We describe the basic structure of the book in the Introduction.

Just as there are many kinds of cultural turn, there are many currents in political economy. Our approach draws mainly on Marxism, supplemented by the German Historical School, modern heterodox economics, and Foucauldian analyses of discourses, technologies and power/knowledge relations. However, in contrast to orthodox Marxism, which, like orthodox economics, tends to reify and essentialize the different moments of capital accumulation, treating them as objective forces, a historical materialist CPE stresses their contingent and always tendential nature.

Bob Jessop's starting point for this long-term project was the problem of understanding the British state and his dissatisfaction with prevailing theoretical approaches in the 1970s. This was also the time of crisis in Atlantic Fordism and of the mobilization not only of old but also of new social movements – raising in part the question for many public employees of how to work in and against the state. He developed an approach to the state that has subsequently been labelled the 'strategic-relational approach', through his reading of German legal and state theory (especially work in the historical materialist tradition but also other schools), the work of Nicos Poulantzas, the *Prison Notebooks* of Antonio Gramsci, and a critical reading of the work of Louis Althusser and his collaborators and disciples. He then turned to the regulation approach as a complement to the strategic-relational approach to the state and, more recently, has developed an interest in critical historical semiotic analyses. These interests are combined in the present book.

Ngai-Ling Sum's starting points were Hong Kong as a colonial social formation and the critique of western-centric theoretical approaches in political economy. The results were presented in *Beyond the Regulation Approach* (Jessop and Sum 2006). The 'war of words' around the transfer of Hong Kong to the People's Republic of China in 1997 stimulated her interest in critical discourse analysis. Together with a growing concern with competitiveness, Wal-Martization and issues of corporate social responsibility, this led to engagement not only with Marx and Gramsci but also with Foucault's work on disciplinarity and governmental powers. This explains her interest in governmentalizing Gramsci and Marxianizing Foucault (see Chapter 5). Together with her work on exportism and the world market (Jessop and Sum 2006) and the 'new ethicalism' (see Chapter 9), these are important entry-points into CPE.

All chapters have been freshly written but most draw on earlier work. A monograph with the breadth of the present text is even more prone to uneven development and non-contemporaneity than most, and the contingency of our key reference points and citations reflects our shifting interests. If one comes to new ideas, concepts and insights through a particular author or school, this will be more influential than when one encounters similar ideas elsewhere and later. This may explain why some celebrated scholars receive less attention than their place in one or more canons might lead dedicated followers or informed readers to expect, and why others are given more prominence than is normal. It also explains why we have not given equal weight to debates in all the disciplines and trans-disciplines that bear on our main arguments.

Ngai-Ling Sum is identified as the senior author of this volume because the majority of the primarily sole-authored chapters are revisions of her pioneering studies in CPE and because this recognizes her decisive contributions to the new research agenda in CPE over two decades.

Our analysis is inspired by our cooperation and discussions with many scholars from around the world and, in particular, with colleagues at Lancaster University. Among other forums, this occurred in the 'Language, Ideology, and Power' research group at Lancaster, run first by Norman Fairclough and more recently by Ruth Wodak, in the 'Complexity Network' mediated by John Urry, and the 'Cultural Political Economy' workshop organized by Ngai-Ling Sum and funded by Lancaster University's Institute for Advanced Studies (2004–2006). We have also tested the CPE approach in a European Union Framework 6 Project, directed by Frank Moulaert, on socio-economic models of development (acronym: DEMOLOGOS); and, more recently, in the EU-COST programme on World Financial Crisis: Systemic Risks, Financial Crises and Credit (COST Action IS0902), in which we have been involved in the working group on cultures of finance. We have also benefited from general discussions with Norman Fairclough and Andrew Sayer over many years.

Our approach to CPE has been influenced at different times by discussions with Andrew Baker, Florian Becker, Mats Benner, Robert Boyer, Neil Brenner, Michael Brie, Ulrich Brand, Ian Bruff, Mario Candeias, Carolyn Cartier, Roger Dale, Charlie Dannreuther, Judith Dellheim, Alex Demirović, Frank Deppe, Heather Ellis, Michael Farrelly, Frank Fischer, Benoît Godin, Eva Hartmann, Jerzy Hausner, Colin Hay, Mathis Heinrich, Antony Hesketh, Ray Hudson, Joo-Hyoung Ji, Martin Jones, Oliver Kessler, Michael Krätke, Amelie Kutter, Thomas Lemke, Reijo Miettinen, Pun Ngai, Henk Overbeek, Jamie Peck, Kees van der Pijl, Katharina Puehl, Hugo Radice, Susan Robertson, Thomas Sablowski, Andrew Sayer, Christoph Scherrer, George Steinmetz, Rob Stones, Peter Utting, Bastiaan van Apeldoorn, Brigitte Young, Beat Weber and Alexander Ziem. Participants in the CPE Seminar at Lancaster have included Sara Gonzales, Ramón Ribera-Fumáz, Santiago Leyva Botero, Stijn Oosterlynck, Ralph Guth, Raphaël Ramuz and Nana Rodaki. Our colleagues in the DEMOLOGOS project included Abid Mehmood, Frank Moulaert, Andreas Novy, Stijn Oosterlynck, Jamie Peck, Pun Ngai, Alvin So, Erik Swyngedouw, Nik Theodore and Pasquale Tridico. The usual disclaimers apply.

Bob Jessop received financial support from Lancaster University Research Committee for a pilot study on the CPE of economic crisis and, later, from the Economic and Social Research Council (UK) for a three-year Professorial Fellowship (RES–051-27-0303) on the cultural political economy of crises of crisis management. Ngai-Ling Sum received a British Academy Research Development Award for a project on 'Changing Cultures of Competitiveness: A Cultural Political Economy Approach' (BARDA-48854). This research compared the Pearl River Delta and India, 2008–2010. She also secured funding from the quondam Institute for Advanced Studies at Lancaster University (now closed) for a three-year post-disciplinary research seminar series on CPE. Both authors also benefited from a major EU grant for participation in the European Union Framework 6 Project on models of socio-economic development (DEMOLOGOS); from funding under the European Union's EU-COST World Financial Crisis: Systemic Risks, Financial Crises and Credit (COST Action IS0902); and from short-term senior fellowships from the Rosa Luxemburg Foundation to visit the Institut für Gesellschaftsforschung, directed in this period by Professor Michael Brie. Indeed, the manuscript was finished during our stay at the Rosa Luxemburg Foundation – a cause for particular pleasure. We are grateful to all these bodies for facilitating our research on this new theoretical project. We express our gratitude to Elizabeth Teague for her careful, scrupulous and judicious reading and copy-editing of the final text. We want to thank Audrey Nolan for providing the space to read and write in Berlin. And, in our trips to Hong Kong, Lo Mo Kwan, Slamet Sowiyah, Anita Pak, Virginia Pak, Pauline Yip, Anna Lam, Jane Che, Paula Chung, Siu Shuk Ngor, Chau Lai Ha, Diana Yim and Maria Yu provided help, assistance and friendship.

Ngai-Ling Sum
Bob Jessop
Lancaster and Berlin
1 May 2013

Abbreviations

ACI	Asia Competitiveness Institute
ADB	Asian Development Bank
ADBI	Asian Development Bank Institute
ALBA	Bolivarian Alliance for the Americas
ASEAN	Association of South East Asian Nations
BCI	Business Competitiveness Index
BRIC	Brazil, Russia, India, China
BRICS	Brazil, Russia, India, China, South Africa
BSPU	Business and Services Promotion Unit (Hong Kong)
CE	chief executive
CDA	critical discourse analysis
CEO	chief executive officer
CEPA	Closer Economic Partnership Arrangement
CEPAL	La Comisión Económica para América Latina
CPE	cultural political economy
CSR	corporate social responsibility
DHA	discourse historical approach
FDI	foreign direct investment
FS	financial secretary
GATS	General Agreement on Trade in Services
GATT	General Agreement on Tariffs and Trade
GFC	global financial crisis
GCI	Global Competitiveness Index
GDP	gross domestic product
GES	Growth Environmental Scores
GSCP	Global Social Compliance Programme
GVC	global value chain
HBS	Harvard Business School
HKCER	Hong Kong Centre for Economic Research
HKCSI	Hong Kong Coalition of Service Industry
HKSAR	Hong Kong Special Administration Region
IDeA	Improvement and Development Agency (UK)
IMD	Institute for Management Development
IFI	independent financial institution

IMF	International Monetary Fund
IADB	Inter-American Development Bank
IPE	international political economy
IPR	intellectual property right
IVS	Individual Visit Scheme (China)
JICA	Japan International Cooperation Agency
KBE	knowledge-based economy
MIT	Massachusetts Institute of Technology
MNC	multi-national corporation
MSME	micro, small and medium enterprise
NAFC	North Atlantic financial crisis
NAFTA	North Atlantic Free Trade Agreement
NGO	non-governmental organization
NIEs	newly industrializing economies
OECD	Organisation for Economic Co-operation and Development
OBM	original brand manufacturing
ODM	own-design manufacturing
OEM	original equipment manufacturing
POS	point-of-sale
PRD	Pearl River Delta
RA	regulation approach
R&D	research and development
RMB	renminbi (Chinese currency)
SACOM	Students and Scholars Against Corporate Misbehaviour
SAR	Special Administration Region
SARS	Severe Acute Respiratory Syndrome
SCMP	*South China Morning Post*
SDR	special drawing right
SME	small and medium enterprise
SRA	strategic-relational approach
STF	spatio-temporal fix
TDC	Trade Development Council
TRIMS	Agreement on Trade Related Investment Measures
TRIPS	Agreement on Trade Related Intellectual Property Rights
UNCTAD	United Nations Commission on Trade and Development
UNECE	United Nations Economic Commission for Europe
UNESCO	United Nations Educational, Scientific and Cultural Organization
UNIDO	United Nations Industrial Development Organization
USA	United States of America
USAID	US Agency for International Development

USD	United States dollar
WB	World Bank
WEF	World Economic Forum
WTO	World Trade Organization

Acknowledgements

The publishers wish to thank the following who have kindly given permission for the use of copyright material.

Edward Elgar for material in Chapter 11 drawn from Jessop (2013d).

John Benjamins Publishing Company in Chapter 10 from Sum (2010a).

Palgrave-Macmillan for material in Chapter 8 drawn from Sum (2010b).

Pion for material in Chapter 1 drawn from Jessop (2001a).

SAGE Publications for material in Chapters 4 and 8 drawn from Jessop (2009) and Sum (2009) respectively.

SENSE Publishers for material in Chapter 7 from Jessop (2008a).

Taylor and Francis for material in Chapters 8 and 12 from Sum (2009, 2013a).

ORIGINAL SOURCES OF THE CHAPTERS

All the chapters have been freshly written but some draw in part on previously published work. We list these below.

Chapter 1 derives in part from Bob Jessop (2001a), 'Institutional (re)turns and the strategic-relational approach', *Environment and Planning A*, **33** (7), 1213–37.

Chapter 6 derives in part from Bob Jessop (2013e), 'Revisiting the regulation approach: critical reflections on the contradictions, dilemmas, fixes, and crisis dynamics of growth regimes', *Capital & Class*, **37** (1), 5–24.

Chapter 7 derives in part from Bob Jessop (2008a), 'A cultural political economy of competitiveness and its implications for higher education', in Bob Jessop, Norman Fairclough and Ruth Wodak (eds), *Education and the Knowledge-Based Economy in Europe*, Rotterdam: Sense Publishers, 11–39.

Chapter 8 derives in part from Ngai-Ling Sum (2009), 'The production of hegemonic policy discourses: "competitiveness" as a knowledge brand and its (re-)contextualizations', *Critical Policy Studies*, **3** (2), 184–203.

Chapter 9 derives in part from Ngai-Ling Sum (2010b), 'Wal-Martization and CSR-ization in developing countries', in Peter Utting and José Carlos Marques (eds), *Corporate Social Responsibility and Regulatory Governance*, London: Palgrave and Geneva: UNRISD, 50–76.

Chapter 10 derives in part from Ngai-Ling Sum (2010a), 'A cultural political economy of transnational knowledge brands: Porterian "competitiveness" discourse and its recontextualization in Hong Kong/Pearl River Delta', *Journal of Language and Politics*, **9** (4), 546–73.

Chapter 11 derives in part from Bob Jessop (2013d), 'Recovered imaginaries, imagined recoveries', in Mats Benner (ed.), *Before and Beyond the Global Economic Crisis*, Cheltenham UK and Northampton, MA, USA: Edward Elgar, 234–54.

Chapter 12 derives in part from Ngai-Ling Sum (2013a), 'A cultural political economy of crisis recovery: (trans)national imaginaries of "BRIC" and the case of Subaltern Groups in China', *Economy & Society*, **42** (4), in press.

Introduction

Cultural political economy is an emerging and still developing transdisciplinary approach oriented to post-disciplinary horizons. It is concerned with the semiotic and structural aspects of social life and, even more importantly, their articulation. It combines concepts from critical, historically sensitive, semiotic analyses and from critical evolutionary and institutional political economy. In this context, cultural political economy refers both to an increasingly 'grand theory' and to an expanding field of empirical study. Theoretically, it has six features (see 23–25) that, together, distinguish it from other approaches with similar theoretical ambitions. In brief, it combines the analysis of sense- and meaning-making with the analysis of instituted economic and political relations and their social embedding. More expansively, it aims to produce a consistent 'integral' analysis of political economy from the perspective of the interaction of its specific semiotic and structural features at the same time as it embeds this analysis into a more general account of semiosis and structuration in wider social formations. Thus, as a grand-theoretical project, its insights can be applied far beyond its home domain in political economy.

Cultural political economy (CPE) builds on our earlier work on state theory and political economy and our critical engagement with Marx's prefigurative contributions to language and discourse analysis (see Höppe 1982; Fairclough and Graham 2002). It also confirms the importance of Gramsci's elaborate philological and materialist studies of hegemony and Foucault's work on discursive formations and dispositives (see Chapters 3 and 4). On this basis, CPE posits that the economic field (or, better, political economy) is always-already meaningful as well as structured. Thus, whether or not meaning-making provides the initial entry-point, it must be included sooner or later to ensure the descriptive and explanatory adequacy of the analysis. The same holds for the need sooner or later to bring structural factors in. We now set out the rationale for this and other claims about CPE, beginning with some philosophical preliminaries that ground our subsequent remarks on critical realism.

SOME PHILOSOPHICAL PRELIMINARIES

It is conventional to distinguish four modes of philosophical inquiry: ontology, epistemology, methodology and ethics. Ontology concerns the nature and properties of being or existence and the categorial structure of reality. A derivative meaning, more important for our purposes, is 'the set of things whose existence is acknowledged by a particular theory or system of thought' (Lowe 1995: 634). Epistemology concerns knowledge (or belief), its very possibility, its defining features and scope, its substantive conditions and sources, its limits and its justification. Methodology deals with general rules for gaining and testing (scientific) knowledge, including analytical strategies, assuming such knowledge is possible. It is more practical and technical than epistemology, being concerned with the logic of discovery and methods of scientific inquiry. Finally, ethics concerns the good or right, that which should be. It has two main branches: deontological (concerned with the duties and obligations of individuals, focusing on their will and intention without much regard, if any, to the consequences of good conduct); and consequential (which defines proper conduct in terms of consequences rather than intentions). Cultural political economy can be considered from all four perspectives (see Box 0.1).

BOX 0.1   CULTURAL POLITICAL ECONOMY AS A SOCIAL SCIENCE

Four modes of philosophical inquiry

- ontology: nature of being, existence, meaning
- epistemology: nature of knowledge
- methodology: rules for gaining, testing knowledge
- ethics: nature of the good, that which should be

Placing CPE as social science

- complexity and its reduction through semiosis and structuration
- intransitive and transitive dimensions interact in scientific inquiry
- pluralistic logic of research, logical–historical presentation
- commitment to critique of ideology and domination

Ontology

Our approach posits that the world is too complex to be grasped in all its complexity in real time (or ever) and for all permutations of social relations to be realizable in the same time-space. This is self-evidently and trivially true, of course, yet it has important implications for social science and everyday life. In particular, CPE does not aim to theorize or model complexity as such but to explore how complexity is reduced (but not thereby mastered) through sense- and meaning-making (semiosis)[1] and through limiting compossible social relations (structuration). In this sense, semiosis and structuration are both equally real, even though their character, generative mechanisms and effects differ. We deal with each in turn.

Regarding semiosis, this enforced selection occurs as individuals and other social agents adopt, wittingly or not, specific entry-points and standpoints to reduce complexity and make it calculable (if only to ease muddling through) so that they can participate within it and/or describe and interpret it as disinterested observers. This produces the paradox that the current complexity of the real world is also in part a path-dependent product of past and present efforts to reduce complexity. This holds both for the social world and the effects of social action in and on the natural world (e.g. the built environment, 'second nature', etc.). In this sense, attempts at complexity reduction may increase overall complexity; and the efforts of some forces (or systems) to reduce complexity may increase it for other forces (or systems). While the real world pre-exists current efforts at complexity reduction, actors/observers have no direct access to it. The 'aspects' that they regard as significant are not pre-given but depend on the meaning systems that frame its significance for them. Sense-making, to repeat the definition given in the Preface, refers to the role of semiosis in the *apprehension of the natural and social world* and highlights the referential value of semiosis, even if this is to as-yet-unrealized possibilities, to the 'irreal' (or 'irrealis'), to immaterial or virtual entities or to inexistent but culturally recognized entities (cf. Eco 1976; Graham 2001). *Meaning-making* refers in turn to processes of signification and meaningful communication and is closely related to *the production of linguistic meaning* but also includes non-linguistic modes of signification and communication. Thus sense- and meaning-making not only reduce complexity for actors (and observers), but also give meaning to the world.[2] They are foundational to all social relations in both senses of ontology as presented above.[3] In other words, CPE posits that the social world is always-already meaningful by nature and that its analysis must acknowledge the importance of sense- and meaning-making. This further implies that social explanation must be adequate at the level of meaning as well as of 'material' causation (see Chapter 4). In fact, as we argue below, semiosis is causally effective and not a mere supplement to causal analysis.

For the sake of clarity, in this context, meaning does not denote 'linguistic meaning' as analysed by specialists in 'core linguistics'[4] who study how meaning emerges from the composition of linguistic units (e.g. Frege 1984; Grice 1989). Instead it denotes the 'sense meaning' involved in the apprehension (e.g. cognitive, normative or appreciative significance) of the world and which, when translated into intersubjective meaning-making, has important intertextual, contextual and pragmatic aspects. In this respect our approach to CPE is closer to the pragmatic tradition of Charles Sanders Peirce (1992) and Charles W. Morris (1946) without being located within it (see Chapter 3). Viewed thus, to make sense of the world is also to make sense of ourselves (Møller 2006: 65–8). In addition, construals may shape the natural and social world in so far as they guide a critical mass of self-confirming actions based on more or less correct diagnoses of unrealized potentials. In this sense construals become a 'material force', that is, have durable transformative effects in the natural and social world. It is the role of some, if not all, construals in constructing the world that justifies, indeed requires, an ontological cultural turn. Conversely, because not all construals lead to durable changes in the natural and social world, semiosis must also be linked to the extra-semiotic.[5] Recognizing that only some construals have constructive effects ensures, in the words of Andrew Sayer (2009: 423), that discourse analysis is not merely 'sceptical' (because all ideas or discourse are deemed equally ideational), but critical (because some discourses undermine the conditions for human flourishing). Indeed, underpinning CPE's contribution to *Ideologiekritik* is recognition that the effects of semiosis are not just internal to semiosis but also affect the natural and social world.

Structuration (or structure-building) is also included in 'the set of things whose existence is acknowledged by a particular theory or system of thought'. It is a form of enforced selection that sets limits to compossible combinations of relations among relations within specific time-space envelopes. The core concept here is compossibility. For not everything that is *possible* is *com*possible. Compossibility is, as indicated, relative to specific time-space structures and horizons of action. To illustrate, several 'varieties of capitalism' coexisted in the European Union before the Economic and Monetary Union was established and, indeed, its heterogeneity had increased with each round of expansion. This prompted a turn from integration measures based on coordination and indicative planning towards greater reliance on market forces to facilitate mutual adjustment. In addition to increased trade, investment, and a more extensive division of labour, another result was intensified centre–periphery relations. The formation of the eurozone removed key sources of flexibility. What was previously compossible (a relatively benign co-evolution of varieties of capitalism) became hard to maintain, leading to increasing crises and, more importantly, crises of crisis management. This situation can be contrasted with the pathological co-dependency of the USA and China (sometimes known as 'Chimerica'),[6] where growing interdependence has not yet produced a ruptural incompossibility (see Jessop 2007c; and Chapters 6 and 11).

Structuration (or structure-building) is subject to processes of variation, selection and retention in the same way as semiosis. In other words, even where agents try to limit the covariation of relations among relations, these attempts rarely fully succeed. Indeed, there are many efforts at many scales to structure social relations and, if structural coherence and a strategic line do emerge, even in a provisional, partial and unstable way, this result cannot be attributed to a single master subject. It is a contingently necessary outcome of the asymmetrical interaction of competing structuration attempts and, most importantly, of blind co-evolution (Jessop 2007b; cf. Foucault 2008a, 2008b; Poulantzas 1978).

The ontological distinction between semiosis and structuration is crucial to our approach. Since our arguments are first developed in Parts I and II, we refer here to the renowned cultural anthropologist, Clifford Geertz, who defines culture as 'an historically transmitted pattern of meanings embodied in symbols' (1975: 89). Given this definition, he might be expected to privilege semiosis over structuration. But he argues that the study of society must explore the articulation between cultural and social structures, without superimposing one on the other (via the metaphor of a mirror) or implying that one mechanically generates the other (1975: 142–69). Geertz adds that, if one studies only cultural symbols, the social dissolves into the meanings attributed to it by social agents via their theoretical or practical knowledge of it. But social structure has hidden depths due to the hierarchical layering of different kinds of social relations. Thus, as Luhmann might say, social agents 'cannot see what they cannot see'. This clearly raises epistemological questions.

Epistemology

Inspired by the Marxian critique of political economy and Foucault's analyses of truth regimes (among other sources), CPE assumes that knowledge is always partial, provisional and incomplete. 'Knowledging' activities can never exhaust the complexity of the world. On this basis, against a universal, trans-historical account of the 'economy', we emphasize the inevitable contextuality and historicity of knowledge claims about historically specific economic orders. The same holds for other positivist social science analyses that take for granted their respective research objects. The basis for our understanding of (scientific) knowledge production is critical realism (see next section) with its distinction between the intransitive and transitive moments of scientific investigation. The intransitive moment refers to the external world as the object of observation and, in many cases, intervention; the transitive moment refers to the practices of science and scientific communities as a set (or sets) of observers and, perhaps, interveners.

Critical realists analyse knowledge as the fallible result of interaction of the intransitive and transitive moments and view its production as a continuing but discontinuous process. Of course, one can also study science as a set of social practices. In this case, scientists remain 'located' in the intransitive world (which varies across the natural and social sciences) and those who observe them act *as if* they operate outside it, at least for observational purposes. In good recursive fashion, one could also study the science of science studies (and so on) as well as the history of science and scientific disciplines – including their relationship to other kinds of social practice. Interesting topics here include how disciplines are distinguished from each other and from other forms of knowledge production. There is much work on the scientific practices, scientific communities and scientific knowledge that considers how knowledge production is mediated through scientific imaginaries, the structure of communities of scientific practice, scientific methods and techniques, and, of course, the ability of certain scientists or teams to produce 'scientific revolutions'.

Because not all knowledge is produced through scientific practices (even science is embedded in other practices and its practitioners may have mixed motives), other modes of knowledge production and knowledge claims also affect social practices and how they get structured. A useful entry-point into knowledge production and its effects is Foucault's concept of 'truth regimes'. Later chapters explore situated knowledge production, its reception by social agents, and its long-term social effects within and beyond its sites of production (for example, Chapter 5 considers intellectuals, Chapter 4 treats reception and societal effects, Chapter 7 considers the genealogy and impact of alternative post-Fordist imaginaries, and Chapter 12 explores the genealogy and impact of changing views about the BRIC economies). Of interest is how 'knowledge' enters strategic calculation, policy formulation and implementation, and, in some cases, becomes the basis for 'knowledge brands' that are marketed as patent remedies to solve socially diagnosed problems and to realize socially constructed objectives (on knowledge brands, see Chapter 8).

Methodology

CPE works with a critical-realist and strategic-relational approach that relies on a pluralistic logic of discovery and a logical–historical method of presentation. Pluralism can be justified deontically and/or pragmatically in many ways, but it is grounded ontologically in the complexity of the world, which entails that it cannot be fully understood and explained from any one entry-point. Nonetheless, this does not exclude well-grounded critiques of individual entry-points as an important part of scientific practice. It is not a recipe for an 'anything-goes' relativism.

The logical–historical method entails the movement from abstract–simple analytical categories to increasingly complex–concrete ones. Whereas this movement initially relies more on elaborating and articulating analytical categories and identifying basic mechanisms, tendencies and counter-tendencies, later steps consider their historical and conjunctural actualization, with due attention paid to the interaction of different causes and conditions. Nonetheless, as our comments on complexity imply, this process of discovery and method of presentation cannot culminate in the exhaustive reproduction of the real world (or, as Marx put it, the 'real-concrete') in all its complexity (for Marx, as a 'concrete-in-thought'). Positing such an outcome contradicts the foundational ontological postulate of the complexity of the real world. Thus the same method of presentation can be used for a wide range of research programmes that start from different entry-points, mark out some aspects of the world as objects of investigation, and pursue multiple lines of inquiry. The aim is to provide adequate explanations for these research problems as they are posed with different degrees of concreteness–complexity. We discussed these epistemological issues in *Beyond the Regulation Approach* (2006) and will shortly consider their implications for pre-disciplinary, disciplinary, multi-disciplinary, trans-disciplinary and post-disciplinary research. Chapter 4 presents the analytical tools for CPE in more detail, after we introduce concepts for structural (especially institutional) analysis in Chapter 1 and some crucial concepts for the study of semiosis in Chapter 3.

Ethics

CPE can be extended to include ethics in both senses (deontological and consequential) as part of its subject matter. Within the broad church of CPE this is the set of pews reserved for the study of moral economy (Thompson 1971; Sayer 1995, 2002, 2005, 2009; Scott 1977). This is concerned with revealing and evaluating the often implicit ethical and moral values, sentiments, commitments, feelings, temporal horizons, attitudes to the environment and judgements that shape everyday life, organizational practices, institutional orders and societal self-understandings. It examines capitalist as well as pre-capitalist social formations. Within a CPE framework, moral economy involves the critique of ideology and the ways in which morality and ethics are enrolled in reproducing domination. In this sense, by virtue of its commitment to the critique of ideology and domination, CPE also rests on certain ethical convictions on the part of its adherents (for an incisive account of moral economy consistent with the broader CPE project, see Sayer 2002). This does not commit cultural political economists to (1) a utopian belief in a social world with no traces of ideology or domination or (2) a relativist position that all sets of social relations are equally bad, neutral or good. Within these limits, convictions are contestable and must be justified.

Missing from these observations is the substantive character of CPE. This concerns how these general philosophical principles are reflected and refracted in a particular theoretical programme. This question can be answered by identifying the positive heuristic of the CPE research agenda, that is, the concepts, assumptions, guidelines and theoretical models with which it operates. The present volume, like its predecessor, is an exercise in elaborating a substantive CPE research programme that is consistent with the ontological, epistemological and methodological principles that we have set out. We present the six basic features of this research programme below (see 23-35) and develop them in the rest of the book.

This approach can also be applied to itself. It can assess the place of CPE in the social sciences and compare its practices and achievements, if any, with others. It can compare its philosophical presuppositions, that is, its ontological, epistemological, methodological and ethical horizons, with other approaches. It can inquire into its own conditions of possibility, the distinctiveness of its knowledge, its particular modes of inquiry, and the normative commitments of CPE scholars. These are interesting meta-analytical questions but will not be explored at length here.

ON CRITICAL REALISM

We now briefly introduce critical realism as the philosophy of science that has informed our development of CPE. Critical realism has an important 'underlabouring' role in the natural and social sciences. In other words, it examines, critiques, refines and reflects on the ontological, epistemological, methodological and substantive presuppositions of different theoretical traditions, disciplines, schools and so forth. This 'underlabouring' role also implies that critical realism in general cannot provide the substantive concepts and methods necessary to develop particular critical-realist theoretical approaches. These have to be produced through other means – but can then be subject to further critical-realist reflection as one among several ways to elaborate their substantive implications.

In general terms, adherents of critical realism posit the existence of real but often latent causal mechanisms that may be contingently actualized in specific conjunctures but may also, thanks to diverse factors or actors, remain latent. On this basis, critical realists distinguish among real mechanisms, actual events and empirical observations. Specifically, the real comprises the defining emergent features, causal properties, affordances (i.e. the possibilities of action afforded, or offered by, a given material object or social network)[7] and vulnerabilities of a given set of relations – which may or may not be actualized. The empirical concerns evidence about the actual, that is, those inherent potentials that are actualized. Together the empirical and the actual provoke questions about the nature of the real (for introductions to critical realism, see Bhaskar 1972; Archer et al. 1998; and Sayer 2000; and on its relevance to the regulation approach, Jessop and Sum 2006: 259–78).

This approach invalidates the naïve positivist method of inferring causation from empirical regularities, as if these could reveal cause–effect relations without prior or later theoretical work. The existence of the real world is a crucial 'regulative idea' in critical realism but its adherents do not claim to have direct access to this reality. Instead they rely on a method known as retroduction. This asks 'what must the world be like for "x" to happen?' This is an open process that switches among concept-building, retroductive moments, empirical inquiries, conceptual refinement, further retroduction and so on. Theory-building and testing are never final and complete: they are always 'under construction' based on a movement between more theoretical and more empirical phases. For critical realists, then, science involves a continuing, spiral movement from knowledge of manifest (empirical) phenomena to knowledge of the underlying structures and causal mechanisms that generate them.

Knowledge of and/or about the real world is never theoretically innocent. This implies, as cultural political economists, among others, would insist, that the starting point for inquiry is discursively constituted. The movement is one from a research problem that is defined in more or less simple and, perhaps, one-sided, superficial or, worse, chaotic, terms to an account that is more complex and has greater ontological depth. This kind of problematization synthesizes multiple determinations, identifies the underlying real mechanisms, and connects them to actual and empirical aspects of the explanandum. As the spiral of scientific inquiry continues, the explanandum is defined with increasing complexity and concreteness.

Thus, as Michel Aglietta, a pioneer regulation theorist, noted, 'concepts are never introduced once and for all at a single level of abstraction but are continually redefined in the movement from abstract to concrete – acquiring new forms and transcending the limits of their previous formulations' (1979: 15–16). He added, 'the objective is the development of concepts and not the "verification" of a finished theory' (ibid.: 66).

Critical realists also posit that the real world is stratified into different layers and regions that require different concepts, assumptions and explanatory principles corresponding to their different emergent properties. Obviously, while philosophical argument can justify a 'critical-realist ontology and epistemology in general', it cannot validate a 'critical-realist ontology and epistemology in particular'. The latter depends, as indicated above, on specific analyses of a specific object rather than on a simplistic and generic application of the critical-realist approach. We illustrated this for the regulation approach (RA) in our earlier book and do so for semiosis in Chapter 4.

PRE-DISCIPLINARITY, EMERGING DISCIPLINES AND RESEARCH CHALLENGES

Concerns with big questions and grand theory emerged well before disciplinary boundaries were established and have continued without much regard for them. Examples in the modern epoch include classical political economy, Hegelian philosophy, the German Historical School, other 'old institutionalisms' and some versions of CPE. Relevant here is Marxism, considered as a family of approaches rather than a single unified system. It originated in a creative synthesis of German philosophy, classical English economics and French politics (and more besides), and has remained open (in its non-ossified, undogmatic variants) to other influences – witness the impact at different times of psychoanalysis, linguistics, structuralism, post-structuralism,[8] 'cultural turns', feminism, nationalism and post-colonialism. Among important developments in the last 25 years or so are the RA and trans-national historical materialism (Jessop and Sum 2006; see also Chapter 2). Marxism offers a *totalizing perspective* on social relations as a whole in terms of the historically specific conditions of existence, dynamic and repercussions of the social organization of production. This does not commit this approach (although it is often assumed that it does) to the claim that the world comprises a closed totality that is unified and governed by a single principle of societal organization (e.g. accumulation). CPE explicitly rejects this. It insists on a plurality of competing principles grounded in different sets of social relations associated with different grammars (codes, programmes, orders of discourse) and different social logics (systemic, institutional, organizational) and competing efforts and struggles to make one or other of these principles of societalization hegemonic and/or dominant. The very existence of competing principles and their uneven instantiation at different sites and scales of social organization invalidates attempts to understand societies or social formations as closed totalities (see Chapter 6).

Another important pre-disciplinary intellectual tradition is the so-called *Staats-* or *Polizeiwissenschaften* (state or 'police' sciences) approach that developed in the eighteenth-century German-speaking world and elsewhere in Europe. This was a hybrid theoretical and policy science that explored the nature and obligations of the state with a view to promoting economic development and good governance. This has been revived in the concern (whether Foucauldian or non-Foucauldian in inspiration) with governance and governmentality. It is particularly relevant to the articulation of the economic and political in institutional, organizational and practical terms – especially to the political economy of state policy. It is also reflected in recent work on global governance in international political economy and in the practices of international agencies such as the World Bank.

More orthodox forms of political economy began the retreat from these wide-ranging concerns in the early nineteenth century; and pure economics as a distinct discipline degenerated further as it became increasingly rigorous (mathematical and formal) at the expense of real-world relevance. More generally, only in the mid-nineteenth century did more specialized disciplines emerge, corresponding to the growing functional differentiation of modern societies in this period and to struggles to establish a hierarchized division of mental labour within and across expanding academic and technocratic communities. Political economy was separated into disciplines: economics; politics, jurisprudence and public administration; and sociology and/or anthropology (see Wallerstein 1996). These coexisted with history (typically subdivided in terms of distinctive historical periods, areas and places, and borrowing many concepts from other branches of the humanities and social sciences) and geography (which has an ambivalent identity, employs eclectic methods due to its position at the interface of nature and society, and is prone to spatial fetishism). At the turn of the nineteenth century two other major disciplines emerged: linguistics and semiotics – one focusing on language, the other on signs more generally (linked to Ferdinand de Saussure and Charles S. Peirce respectively).

These more specialized disciplines tend to reject philosophical anthropology (a concern with the essential, trans-historical character of the human species or its alleged subtypes) as pre-modern, unscientific, or overtly normative – although neoclassical economics retains a touching faith in *homo economicus*. In other cases they tend to work with attenuated assumptions about functionally specific rationalities (modes of calculation) or logics of appropriateness that provide no real basis for a more general critique of contemporary societies. These disciplinary boundaries are now breaking down in a period when space and time are seen as socially constructed, socially constitutive relations rather than mere external parameters of disciplinary inquiry. To clarify these points we now distinguish forms of disciplinarity, indicating how they affect the study of economic rules and institutions, and noting their implications for a political and ethical critique of economic activities.

It is impossible to return to the pre-disciplinary age[9] that existed before specialized disciplines were institutionalized in the mid- to late nineteenth century in Europe and North America. But this does not require us to think and act in terms set by mainstream disciplines and correspond to often outdated epistemic concerns, ideological biases and ontological realities. Indeed the dominance of disciplinary thinking has prompted many scholars to attempt to escape or transcend the limited horizons of disciplines. To understand what is at stake here we now consider the nature of disciplines and different approaches to escaping from disciplinary straitjackets (for some different positions on disciplinarity, see Table 0.1).

A narrow disciplinary approach to a given topic explores themes identified in terms of a single discipline. For example, in mainstream economic analysis, this would entail focusing on themes that are identified in terms of vulgar political economy and its subsequent development as a specialized, mathematized discipline concerned with economizing behaviour. It would also correspond to the naïve, positivist belief that the market economy exists and can be studied in isolation from other spheres of social relations. This naturalization of the economy is linked to top–down pedagogic practices that reproduce an unreflecting and fetishistic approach to the laws of the market and the basic tendencies of the market economy. It also neglects the ethico-political dimensions of the economic field. Instead it would be better to develop and combine pluri-, trans- and post-disciplinary analyses of economic activities that not only draw on different disciplines and research traditions but also elaborate new concepts and methodologies to transcend disciplinary boundaries.

A pluri- or multi-disciplinary approach proceeds from a problem located at the interface of different disciplines and mechanically combines the inherently valid understandings and knowledge of different disciplines about their respective objects of inquiry to produce the 'complete picture' through 'joined-up thinking'. Whilst this is better than a one-sided disciplinary analysis of complex problems, inter- and/or trans-disciplinary

Table 0.1 From pre-disciplinarity to post-disciplinarities

	Thematic concerns	Methodological approach	Epistemic and ontological outlook	Extent and form of scientific reflexivity
Pre-disciplinary period	Focuses on holistic, multi-faceted themes. Analyses pre-date the rise of distinct academic disciplines	Polymathic, holistic and integrative methodologies, often with humanistic as well as positivistic aspects	Tied to a world with low functional differentiation. So society–nature–cosmos often seen as integrated under God or by natural laws	Tends to naturalize a holistic world and hence tends to assert need to study it from all available perspectives
Disciplinary	Focuses exclusively on themes that are identified in terms of categories of a given discipline; ignores all other aspects of an entity and other possible themes	Approach to any theme is based on categories of a given discipline. Can prompt efforts to colonize other disciplines via disciplinary imperialism	Distinct disciplines correspond to the structure of the real world – each set of ontological entities has its own discipline	Tends to naturalize respective disciplinary objects of analysis as real-world entities and so does not reflect on the constructed nature of disciplines
Multi- or pluri-disciplinary	Focuses on themes located at intersection of the categories of two or more conventional disciplines	Combines approaches from these disciplines to produce a simple *additive* account of the chosen topic	Conventional disciplines correspond to simple and/or emergent entities in the real world. Joining them helps to understand a complex world	Aware of *epistemic* limits of disciplines and of resulting need to combine them to get a 'complete' account

13

Table 0.1 (continued)

	Thematic concerns	Methodological approach	Epistemic and ontological outlook	Extent and form of scientific reflexivity
Inter- or trans-disciplinary	Focuses on selected topics or themes that are compatible with categories of several disciplines	Combines approaches from these disciplines to produce a more complex account	Objects are always complex and cannot be understood just by adding together a series of given disciplines	Aware of *ontological* limits of disciplines and of resulting need to combine them to get better accounts
Post-disciplinary	Identifies and studies specific problems independently of how different disciplines would classify them, if at all	Draws on/develops concepts and methodologies suited to problem(s) without regard to specific disciplinary proprieties. Often develops new concepts not rooted in any 'discipline'	World is descriptively inexhaustible and nomically complex. Study it in terms of problems that are constructed for specific research purposes	Critically self-aware of epistemic and ontological limits of inherited disciplines and of resulting need to follow problems
Anti-disciplinary	Reject the idea that there are clearly identifiable themes open to discipline-based research	'Anything goes'	Real world is one of largely unstructured complexity, chaos and even catastrophe	Disciplines are socially constructed and arbitrary

approaches are preferable. These focus on complex problems that can be approached in terms of the categories of two or more disciplines and combines these categories to produce a more complex, non-additive account. They recognize the ontological as well as the epistemic limits of different disciplines, that is, that they do not correspond to distinct objects in the real world; and therefore accept the need to combine disciplines to produce a more rounded account of specific themes.

Rejecting the legitimacy of disciplinary boundaries is not a licence to engage in an anti-disciplinary conceptual free-for-all in which, as Paul Feyerabend (1978) suggests, 'anything goes' and the most likely outcome of which is eclecticism and/or incoherence. It is a commitment to a problem-oriented rather than discipline-bounded approach and, indeed, a move towards the most advanced form of such problem-orientation, that is, post-disciplinarity.

Post-disciplinarity requires further steps. These are to recognize the conventional nature and inherent limitations of individual disciplines and disciplinarity as a whole and to remain open to new ideas that may be inconsistent or incommensurable with any or all established disciplines. This approach refuses historically contingent disciplinary boundaries. Instead, post-disciplinary analyses begin by identifying specific problems independent of how they would be classified, if at all, by different disciplines; and they then mobilize, develop and integrate the necessary concepts, methodologies and knowledge to address such problems without regard to disciplinary boundaries. In sum, this research orientation is critically self-aware of both the epistemic and ontological limits of inherited disciplines and is explicitly problem-oriented rather than tied to disciplinary blinkers. As such, this is a research programme that should be discursively and structurally resistant to disciplinary institutionalization, that is, to becoming another discipline alongside others.

This creates the space for looser-textured, more concrete and more complex analyses that may also be more relevant to political and ethical issues. It also leads to more critical pedagogic practices and presents us with a constantly moving target as disciplines and their relations are reorganized. In an age when established disciplines still dominate higher education and the intellectual division of labour, trans-disciplinarity is often sufficient for many purposes and is also easier to deliver.

RESPONSES TO DISCIPLINARITY STRAITJACKETS

While the origins of classical political economy were pre-disciplinary, contemporary political economy is becoming trans-disciplinary and, in some cases, has post-disciplinary aspirations. Classical political economy was a pre-disciplinary field of inquiry for two reasons. First, it developed in the early modern period of Western thought, when the market economy was not yet fully disembedded from other societal spheres and when, in particular, the commodity form had not been fully extended to labour power (cf. Tribe 1978). Second, it was formed before academic disciplines crystallized and began to fragment knowledge in the mid- to late nineteenth century. Thus it was pioneered by polymaths who regarded political economy as the integrated study of economic organization and wealth creation, good government and good governance, and moral economy (including language, culture and ethical issues). They examined how wealth was produced and distributed, and explored the close connection between these processes and the eventual formation of civil society and the modern state. Exemplars include John Locke, Adam Smith, Adam Ferguson, John Millar, Montesquieu and Hegel. A potential downside to this approach was its penchant for philosophical anthropologies (i.e. sets of assumptions about human nature and its development) that were often linked to ethico-political considerations.

New intellectual currents have emerged that are pertinent to political economy. Here we mention just five. First, political ecology transcends the nature–society dichotomy and associated disciplinary boundaries to better understand, explain and critique the complex interconnections in and across the natural and social worlds (Altvater 1993; Gorz 1980; Harribey 1998; Lipietz 1995; Peet et al. 2010). Second, semiotics, critical linguistics and discourse analysis have partly shifted from specific disciplines focused on particular objects of inquiry (signification, language, discourse respectively) to become, for some scholars, analytical strategies for developing 'grand theories' about social order (see Chapter 4). They have moved beyond text analysis to study pragmatics, that is, the use of language (and other forms of signification) as an important moment of social practices in different social contexts. This current is reflected in diverse 'cultural turns': narrative, rhetorical, argumentative, linguistic, metaphorical, translational and so on (see Chapter 3). Concern with semantic conceptual history, the analysis of discursive formations, and, more recently, historical genre analysis also have major implications for the discursive constitution and regularization of the capitalist economy and the national state as imagined entities and their cultural as well as social embeddedness (see Chapter 4).

A third, related, trend is the massive expansion of cultural and/or media studies. This is a wide-ranging field defined by its thematic focus (or foci) rather than by agreed ontological, epistemological and methodological assumptions. Indeed, as one authority notes, cultural studies are marked by significant ontological and methodological differences, ranging from a more macro-historical, dialectical cultural materialism concerned with everyday life through to a more micro-analytical, constructivist concern with power/knowledge relations (Babe 2009: 61–88; on cultural studies, see also Bowman 2003; Chen and Morley 1996; Hartley 2003; Gregg 2006; Grossberg 2006, 2010).

A fourth current, less significant as yet but with obvious import for political economy, is 'queer theory'. This aims to subvert the heteronormative assumptions of feminism as well as malestream theory, stresses the ambivalence and instability of all identities and social entities, and aims to create a space for marginalized voices. In this sense, it, too, is an imperial, potentially unbounded project (on queer theory, see Butler 1990, 1993; Duggan 1994; Halley and Parker 2007; Sedgwick 1990; Warner 1993; for partial applications to political economy, Gibson-Graham 1995; Cornwall 1998; Gibson and Graham 2008; see also Hearn 1996; Jacobsen and Zeller 2008; and Winnubst 2012). This current partly overlaps with intersectionalist approaches. These emphasize the semiotic and material interdependence of different forms of exploitation, oppression or disadvantage and tend to reject (or be agnostic about) the primacy of any given identity, set of interests or type of domination (see Degele and Winker 2009; and Chapter 4). The fourth current is critical geo-politics and critical security studies. This applies various new intellectual currents to deconstruct and redefine the nature of international relations (e.g. Deudney 2000; Farrell 2002; Campbell 1992; O'Tuathail 1996; Wæver 2004).

ON THE AMBIVALENCE OF CULTURAL TURNS

The case for trans-disciplinarity against disciplinarity (especially when it takes the form of disciplinary imperialism) can be strengthened by developing two main lines of argument. The first concerns the continued relevance of Marxism as a pre-disciplinary intellectual tradition committed to the critique of political economy and the continuing scope for its creative development. This remark needs less defence and merits less defensiveness in the last decade than some deemed prudent during the boom years of the 'new economy' in the 1990s and early 2000s (heralded by some as 'the great moderation'; see Chapter 11). We illustrate the continued relevance of historical materialism, especially its concern with basic social forms and fundamental contradictions, at many points below (notably in Chapters 6 and 11). The second line concerns the significance of diverse 'cultural turns' for rethinking political economy. These have been instrumental in directing political economy away from neoclassical economics, rational-choice institutionalism and realism in international political economy. In this sense, as turns, they are important. But they can prove counterproductive if they encourage neglect of the materiality of political economy as regards its objects of analysis and its methods of inquiry.

To clarify and qualify this remark, we note that there are many cultural turns with diverse denotations, connotations and significance depending on their intended contribution to the social sciences and humanities.[10] Four main types can be observed: thematic, methodological, ontological and reflexive. These occur in many disciplines but our focus is political economy. In this context, the first type highlights hitherto neglected themes (e.g. the political economy of art); the second suggests a new entry-point into the analysis of economic subjectivity, activities, institutions or dynamics (e.g. constructivist accounts of the financialization of everyday life); the third claims that economic order always involves meaningful action and that a valid explanation of economic phenomena must be adequate at the level of meaning as well as of causality (e.g. analysis of the ideational as well as institutional foundations of catch-up competitiveness); and the fourth applies one or more of these turns to economic analysis itself (e.g. the critique of economic categories in classical political economy, in neoclassical economics, or of rhetoric in economic debate; see respectively Marx 1972; Häring and Douglas 2012; and McCloskey 1998). We discuss these turns in greater detail in Chapters 2 and 3.

Given the range of recent cultural turns and of their starting points as well as the widely different definitions of political economy (and its critique), contemporary scholars disagree about the nature of CPE. We have identified five projects, besides the present one, that self-designate as 'cultural political economy' or 'cultural economy'; and another eight that invoke some kind of cultural turn to advance the critique of political economy and/or identify significant shifts in capitalism. Others undoubtedly exist. Those that we have noted comprise:

1. An eclectic interest in the broad field of study constituted by 'the cultural dimensions of the economy, the economic aspects of culture, and the political character of both' (Best and Paterson 2010b: 2; also Best and Paterson 2010a).
2. Studies of the relation between cultural production and political struggle by developing CPE as a 'bridging concept at the intersections of anthropology, sociology, economics, political theory, and literary and cultural studies' (Sheller 2006, discussing recent work on the Caribbean region).
3. The addition of cultural anthropology to economic and political history as proposed by Wickramasinghe and Hopper (2005) in their account of cultural political economy.

4. An argument that political economy should be studied at the level of everyday experience as well as in terms of elite practices and projects (Aitken 2007; Langley 2008; Hobson and Seabrooke 2007).
5. Efforts to overcome the stultifying base–superstructure dichotomy inherited from orthodox Marxism and to develop cultural studies as a trans-disciplinary enterprise that shows the intricate connections and reciprocal determinations of these spheres (e.g. Thompson 1963; Williams 1980; Jones 2004; Hall 1980; Chen and Morley 1996; Grossberg 2006, 2010).
6. Proposals to reintegrate cultural studies and the study of political economy by returning to the cultural materialism of Harold Innis, Theodor Adorno, Raymond Williams, Richard Hoggart and E.P. Thompson (e.g. Babe 2009: 3).
7. Interest in the political economy of culture on the grounds that the economy 'contains' culture, that is, that material provisioning touches all major belief systems and modes of understanding and acting (cf. Calabrese 2004).
8. Arguments about the culturalization, or aestheticization, of the economy and the economization of culture, sometimes with an emphasis on the declining significance of 'material' use-values relative to the importance of 'sign-value' (e.g. du Gay and Pryke 2002; Lash and Urry 1994; for a critique, see Bryson and Ruston 2010).
9. Privileging the soft features of the lifeworld, such as aesthetics, affect or consumption, over the hard logic of economic and political systems (for critiques of this, see Sayer 2001).
10. Applying the insights of social studies of science to issues in political economy (e.g. Callon 1988; MacKenzie 2006, 2009).
11. Applying 'cultural theory' as a useful tool in policy analysis or, indeed, in shaping cultural policies for development and competitiveness (see, e.g. Bennett 1998; and, for critiques, Craik 1995; Barnett 1999).
12. Examining culture in terms of norms and values and how they influence economic institutions and growth (de Jong 2009).
13. Extending and deepening the regulation approach by integrating the economics of conventions and/or through appropriating cultural and sociological insights from Gramsci or Bourdieu (see Jessop and Sum 2006; and Chapter 3).

These approaches can all contribute to multi- or trans-disciplinary studies in political economy but they are not central to CPE as we develop it. This is especially true of the vague notion that CPE is a broad field of study located at the intersection of cultural, political and economic analysis. In contrast, our concern is to reconstruct critical political economy in the light of the cultural turn. Thus, arguing that the social world has semiotic (cultural) *and* structural (social) properties, our version of CPE studies the variation, selection and retention of semiosis and semiotic practices, their role in complexity reduction, and their articulation with technologies and agency (see below). It is far from the only variant and is compatible with several others, such as that proposed by Ray Hudson, an economic geographer, who suggested that our version of CPE as of 2007 should be supplemented by greater concern with the political economy of the circuits of capital and the materiality of production and consumption flows (including its environmental impact) (Hudson 2008). We return to these fruitful suggestions in Chapters 6 and 13. CPE as presented below is not exclusionary. Indeed, this would conflict with the meta-theoretical foundations for CPE that we set out below. Hereafter, the term CPE will usually refer to our approach rather than the wider set of cultural turns in political economy, which may often use other self-descriptions. The context should make it clear when CPE is used more broadly.

TOWARDS A POST-DISCIPLINARY CULTURAL POLITICAL ECONOMY

As the Preface indicated, one of our several convergent paths to CPE has been critical engagement with the regulation approach, materialist state and/or governance theories (including Foucault's work on governmentality) and critical discourse analysis. Among their positive features is many adherents' commitment to dialogue and interdisciplinarity. This risks eclecticism based on superficial similarities between middle-range theories. A genuine rapprochement requires, as Dorothy E. Smith (2000) notes, work on the underlying ontological, epistemological and methodological foundations of different theoretical approaches as a basis for their subsequent articulation. Not all studies that have something to 'say' on specific middle-range phenomena or processes are really commensurable; thus unreflexive attempts to combine them (especially when this is based on fad and fashion) risk serious inconsistency. Chapter 1, which considers institutionalism, identifies and criticizes this problem.

This said, our 2006 volume ended with a call for a creative synthesis of regulationist, state-theoretical and discourse-analytic concepts:

> All three approaches work with realist ontological and epistemological premises; they have each produced concepts to describe the principal underlying causal mechanisms, powers, liabilities, tendencies and counter-tendencies in

their respective fields; and they have also produced concepts on a middle range, institutional level to facilitate detailed conjunctural analyses. The regulation approach and state theory have also been concerned with stages and phases of capitalist development rather than with abstract laws of motion and tendencies operating at the level of capital in general and/or the general form of the state. But the three approaches differ in their emphases on different institutional clusters in the process of societalization. The regulation approach stresses the successful development and institutionalization of a mode of regulation whose principal features are defined in terms of their contribution to maintaining the capital relation. State theory is more concerned with the state's central role as a factor of social cohesion in class-divided societies more generally and is more inclined towards politicism. Discourse analysis, strongly influenced by Gramsci's work on hegemony, emphasizes political, intellectual, and moral leadership. In short, while all three approaches concern societalization, they tend to prioritize economic, political, and ideological factors respectively. (Jessop and Sum 2006: 376)

This project still has merit and is feasible because these approaches do not focus exclusively on separate economic, political and discursive fields but productively privilege different starting points, standpoints and concepts for addressing capital accumulation and bourgeois domination. This may facilitate development of commensurable sets of concepts for what are described, more conventionally, as economic, political and ideological analysis. CPE aims to overcome this compartmentalization of analysis into distinct fields of inquiry. Its two-track strategy to achieve this is to bring semiosis into the analysis of economics and politics (or, better, political economy) and to analyse semiosis in institutional and evolutionary terms. We suggest how to do this and indicate its potential in Parts II to IV.

One turn that has been useful in developing this trans-disciplinary synthesis is the 'complexity turn'. The intuition, hypothesis or discovery that 'complexity matters' leads to two conclusions: (1) a major task of science and other disciplines concerned with complexity systems is to develop theories or models of complex systems; and (2) complexity requires individuals and social agents to reduce it in order to be able to 'go on' in the world. We take the first conclusion as an important *theme* and heuristic *entry-point* in our work on how social agents understand complexity in seeking to govern complex systems (e.g. Jessop 1997b, 2002, 2007; and Jessop and Sum 2010). The second conclusion is a *foundational (or ontological)* premise of the entire CPE project. We develop this point in Part I and trace its implications in our case studies as part of the broader CPE agenda.

While an ontological complexity turn has played a catalytic role in developing CPE, CPE can also be seen as a response to the malign influence of certain types of cultural turn. We have sometimes described our approach as making a consistent cultural turn in critical political economy. On reflexion, this claim is misleading. For CPE is better understood as a *response* not only to a one-sided emphasis on the materiality of economic and political institutions but also to one-sided cultural turns in political economy. This explains why, referring to the mythic Greek challenge to steer a perilous path between two sea monsters on either side of a narrow strait, we describe CPE as attempting to navigate between a structuralist Scylla and a constructivist Charybdis (see Chapter 4). Thus, while we recognize the value of cultural turns in escaping the dangerous structuralist rocks of Scylla, it is equally important not to be sucked inescapably into the cultural whirlpool of Charybdis.

Our integration of semiosis into political economy does not mechanically add the study of 'culture' to studies of politics and economics to generate CPE through simple aggregation. It does not aim to produce an additive, three-dimensional analysis but stresses the role of semiosis in enabling social actors to 'go on' in a complex world in *all* spheres of social life. It does not accept that there is a separate field of culture (comprising semiotic practices and relations) that can be contrasted with other kinds of social relations. Indeed, the view that there is a distinctive 'cultural sphere' is itself the product of cultural (and other) imaginaries.

As we argued in *Beyond the Regulation Approach* (2006), Antonio Gramsci's work provides an important link between the critique of political economy and critical semiosis (see Chapters 2, 3 and 5). We draw on his anticipations of the regulation approach, his application of historical linguistics to the analysis of everyday life and the task of developing a new language to help build a new social order, and, most famously, his work on hegemony as political, intellectual and moral leadership. Thus, rather than constructing CPE through mechanical aggregation, we have been elaborating it stepwise through a recursive and reflexive synthesis of regulationist, state-theoretical and discourse-analytical concepts. Another important catalyst has been Michel Foucault's work. This provides a bridge between discourse analysis and critical political economy and, in particular, through the concept of dispositive, offers powerful conceptual tools to explore the intersection of different types of strategic selectivity along with the role of techniques of government. Thus we consider power/knowledge relations, governmental technologies, and the production of subjects and identities. Indeed, we argue in Chapter 5 that their work can be used to 'governmentalize' the critique of political economy in important ways. This demands sustained theoretical and empirical engagement between a materially grounded critical semiotic analysis and an evolutionary and institutional political economy informed by the cultural turn.

SIX FEATURES OF CULTURAL POLITICAL ECONOMY

The novelty of our approach can be seen in six features that *in their combination* distinguish it from others on similar terrain (see Box 0.2). Not all features are developed to the same extent (let alone in every chapter), but listing them helps locate the contributions of different parts of the book, our individual and joint interests, and how different arguments fit into the bigger CPE picture.

The first three features are the most distinctive. In this sense, even before we endeavour to show how competing economic, political and social imaginaries in capitalist social formations are related to the fundamental categories of the critique of political economy, we can show that it is essential to combine them because they are relatively concrete–complex instantiations of the need to reduce the complexity of the real world. CPE

BOX 0.2 SIX DISTINCTIVE FEATURES OF THE PRESENT CPE APPROACH

(1) The manner in which it grounds the cultural turn in political economy in the existential necessity of complexity reduction.

(2) Its emphasis on the role of evolutionary mechanisms in shaping the movement from social *construal* to social *construction* and their implications for the production of domination and hegemony.

(3) Its concern with the interdependence and co-evolution of the semiotic and extra-semiotic and the diverse ways in which this co-evolution is mediated.

(4) Its integration of individual, organizational and societal learning in response to 'problems' or 'crises' into the dialectic of semiosis and structuration and, by extension, of path-shaping and path-dependency.

(5) The significance of four modes of selectivity: structural, discursive, (Foucauldian) technological and agential in the consolidation and contestation of hegemony and domination in remaking social relations.

(6) Its denaturalization of economic and political imaginaries and, hence, its role in *Ideologiekritik* and the critique of specific forms of domination.

posits an existential need for complexity reduction as a condition for social agents to 'go on' in the world and distinguishes two basic forms of such reduction: semiosis (*Sinnmachung*) and structuration (*Strukturierung*).

Reference to semiosis has ontological and terminological functions: first, sense- and meaning-making is one of the two crucial bases of the ontological grounding of the CPE approach; and, second, given the great variety of cultural turns with their diverse theoretical and methodological assumptions, semiosis is a useful umbrella concept that subsumes them all. This reflects Umberto Eco's definition of semiotics as 'concerned with everything that can be *taken* as a sign. A sign is everything which can be taken as significantly substituting for something else' (Eco 1976: 7; cf. Eco 1984: 59–67). Note that the referent need not exist for the sign to be acted upon. Indeed, Eco adds that '*semiotics is in principle the discipline studying everything which can be used in order to lie*' (Eco 1976: 7, italics in original; cf. 1984: 58–9). This expansive description indicates the reciprocal but variable relation between the sign and meaning beyond the sign. Thus it rejects the 'fatal semiotic confusion between the *signified* and *referent*' (Eagleton 1991: 209) and explores the contingent relations among signifier, signified and referent. This confusion is the specific semiological expression of the more general 'epistemic fallacy', that is, the interpretation of statements about being as statements about knowledge. By analogy, the semiotic fallacy reduces statements about being to statements internal to discourse and regards ontological and ontic questions as unanswerable (Chapters 3 and 4). This must be rejected if we are to understand and explain experience and learning as well as evaluate the adequacy of crisis construals, crisis management and so on.

The other ontological basis of CPE is the need to reduce unstructured complexity in the 'relations among relations'. This involves setting limits (however achieved) on the articulation of different sets of social relations such that 'not everything that is *possible* is *compossible*'. In other words, in contrast to the immense variety of individual *elements* of a social formation that are possible when considered in isolation at a given point in space-time, there is a smaller set of elements that can be combined as articulated *moments* of a relatively coherent and reproducible structure. This limits the chaotic variation of social relations in a given spatio-temporal matrix but cannot eliminate all interstitial, residual, marginal, irrelevant, recalcitrant and plain contradictory elements. Indeed, these may provide redundancy and flexibility in the face of crises. In addition, a key part of securing order within a given spatio-temporal framework depends on the capacity to displace and defer problems elsewhere and into the future (see Chapter 6).

Cross-cutting these themes, we draw on the strategic-relational approach (SRA) to explore four modes of evolutionary selection. These are structural, semiotic, technological and agential. These involve different modalities of variation, selection and retention within and between the semiotic and extra-semiotic. Examining the interaction of these selectivities helps to provide explanations that are adequate at the level of meaning (semiosis) and material causality (through discursive, strategic, agential and technological selectivities). Their interaction also illuminates the nature and effects of dispositives, that is, contingent discursive–material fixes that emerge in response to specific (and specifically problematized) challenges to social order (see Chapters 3 and 5). Thus these four selectivities are crucial to the theoretical elaboration of features 3 to 5 and we illustrate their significance in Parts III and IV.

Although the study of crisis is not included in the six defining features of CPE, we argue that combining these features provides a powerful heuristic for this topic. Indeed, crisis is of great theoretical and practical interest for the CPE agenda. First, when linked to specific theories about the natural and social world, it provides the means to observe crises and investigate their real causes and their actualization in specific conjunctures. Second, because of their profound disorienting effects, crises are important revelatory moments about the improbability of sedimented discourse and structured complexity in any social formation. This may prompt efforts to repoliticize discourse and seek new ways to re-establish order, whether through restoration, reform or more radical transformation. And, third, it provides the means to observe how actors engage in retroduction to make sense of the phenomenal forms and underlying mechanisms that produce crisis. In other words, given its concern with meaning-making, structuration and evolutionary mechanisms, it offers a framework to understand why semiosis and extra-semiotic factors have varying weight across different stages of economic crisis and why only some of the many competing crisis construals get selected and why even fewer strategies are retained. In addition, crises are powerful stimuli to learning processes that shape discursive as well as structural, strategic and technological innovation (see Chapters 11 and 12).

OUTLINE OF THE BOOK

We build on these six features and elaborate them through case studies to redirect the cultural turn(s) in political economy and put them in their place by making and illustrating the case for a distinctive approach to 'cultural political economy'. We suggest that analogous approaches are possible for non-capitalist regimes and also that the CPE approach to semiosis and structuration is useful in other fields of inquiry in the humanities and social sciences.

Chapter 1 distinguishes four types of institutional turn, introduces different kinds of institutionalism, and assesses their limitations from a critical-realist, strategic-relational perspective. It reviews a wide range of institutionalist analyses in political economy and the social sciences more generally. In particular we critique the three conventionally identified institutionalisms (rational choice, historical and sociological) and address one recently suggested and actively promoted 'fourth institutionalism', that is, constructivist, discursive or ideational institutionalism. This variant marks a belated acknowledgement, by some in the field of new institutionalism, of the importance of ideas, discourse and argumentation in institutionalization, institutional dynamics and institutional change. We ask what needs to be recovered from classical political economy and classical social theory in order to 'put institutions in their place' and connect them with questions of agency and meaning-making. We examine recent social theory and heterodox political economy for critical concepts and insights that reveal the potential static bias of institutional analysis and its privileging of social order over potential sources of instability. And we indicate how institutions can be related to broader questions of sense- and meaning-making, social practice, power and knowledge.

Chapter 2 considers one possible supplement to institutionalism when we review the initiatives by some regulation schools and scholars to make a cultural, hermeneutic or, as we would say, semiotic, turn (Jessop and Sum 2006). This is often intended to break with rationalist accounts of economic agency (especially where the rationality is that of *homo economicus*) and/or to illuminate the socio-cultural embedding of economic calculation, conduct and institutions. We consider the value of cultural turns in ways analogous to our critique of institutional turns. This is where we introduce the concept of the 'imaginary'. Whereas 'institution' belongs to a family of terms that identify mechanisms implicated in regularizing expectations and conduct within and across different social spheres, despite tensions and crisis tendencies, the 'imaginary' is one of a family of terms that denote semiotic systems that shape lived experience in a complex world. In short, institutions and imaginaries can be studied as sets of mechanisms that contribute crucially to the always problematic, provisional, partial and unstable *reproduction–régulation* of the capital relation (and much else besides). Bringing them together productively requires that both institutions and imaginaries are 'put in their place', that is, located in wider sets of semiotic and structural relations and their articulation – with all due regard for the possibilities of contradiction, conflict and crisis.

Third, given the relative failure of the main regulation schools to realize the potential of the cultural turn (especially compared with their advances in institutional analysis and periodization), Chapter 3 introduces some basic concepts, assumptions and analytical tools for a more profound and critical analysis of semiosis. It does not aim to provide a complete review of critical discourse analysis (let alone of linguistics, semiology, semiotics or symbology more generally), but to highlight some useful theoretical resources that would facilitate an ontological and reflexive cultural turn in the critique of political economy without this becoming one-sided. Thus, whereas Chapters 1 and 2 address the limits of the institutional and cultural turns that have occurred in political economy, Chapter 3 reviews semiosis in general and semantic change in particular from institutional and/or evolutionary perspectives.

Recognizing the importance of semiosis and identifying the limited capacities of some contributions to political economy (including the regulation approach) to address this topic does not entail that semiosis is always the best entry-point into the critique of political economy, let alone that it is the only valid approach. It does imply that semiosis must be brought in sooner or later to provide explanations adequate at the level of meaning as well as other forms of causality. This requires attention to semiosis and structuration, their interpenetration and their disjointed co-evolution. Thus the chapters in Part II present the core conceptual and methodological features of the CPE research programme in its own terms, drawing on the results of the preceding analyses. Chapter 4 introduces our current synthesis of these two bodies of theoretical work and highlights the specificity of CPE and its foundational concepts. Chapter 5 presents several ways to operationalize the CPE research agenda in terms of the articulation of structural, discursive, technological and agential selectivities. These chapters aim to synthesize, within a critical-realist, strategic-relational framework, insights from the regulation approach, materialist state theory, semiology and relevant Foucauldian studies. Attentive readers will have noted the substitution of semiology for discourse analysis in this list, and the addition of Foucauldian studies compared with our 2006 book. This reflects subsequent work, especially in the field of semiosis and semantics, to discover the most appropriate and commensurable approaches for the grand theory that we aim to develop.

Parts III and IV reflect our individual and collective development of the CPE research programme with one or other of us as the principal author of specific chapters (as indicated in the list of sources in the Acknowledgements). Individual chapters develop specific aspects of the overall research agenda. For example, Chapters 6 and 11 focus mostly on the cultural political economy of social imaginaries and their role in shaping accumulation regimes and modes of regulation, paying particular attention to the role of semantics, and institutional and spatio-temporal fixes in facilitating 'zones of relative stability' within the contradictory flux of the world market. Chapters 7, 8 and 12 are more focused on economic imaginaries, the social practices (which always have discursive as well as structural, 'material', or 'extra-discursive' moments) that promote them, and the ways they are selected, recontextualized and retained to remake social relations. Chapters 9 and 10 explore in turn the changing, always uneven, interaction of four different modes of strategic selectivity (structural, discursive, technological, agential) to examine, interpret and explain recent developments in particular enterprise forms (Wal-Martization), economic strategies (leading to a 'new ethicalism'), and the hegemonic project of competitiveness–integration (dis)order. Part V summarizes the main points in the CPE research programme and explores their implications for future research.

CONCLUDING REMARKS

Critical-realist analyses do not call for an 'anything-goes' approach to scientific investigation but nor do they provide an automatic warrant for the set of disciplines that happen to prevail in a specific stretch of time-space. Indeed, through its interest in the distinctive properties of the intransitive and transitive worlds and their coupling in scientific inquiry, critical realism indicates the importance of studying the history of disciplines and resisting the fetishization of disciplines and disciplinary boundaries. While these certainly have instrumental value in the development of scientific inquiry, this benefit should not be emphasized at the expense of critical reflection on the histories of disciplines, their articulation and the epistemological selectivities involved in defining disciplines in one way or another. After all, scientific practice is another field amenable to strategic-relational analysis that also contains its own ideological elements and plays its own roles in maintaining different forms of domination. Our approach to CPE draws, *faute de mieux*, on concepts, theoretical arguments and empirical studies written from existing disciplines. It is just as impossible to start with a tabula rasa in the scientific field as it is in any other. But we describe our approach as pre-disciplinary in inspiration and post-disciplinary in aspiration. It addresses specific problems in the critique of political economy and many others have followed similar paths in their own fields. The contingency of the concepts, assumptions and methods developed in CPE precludes that it become another discipline. Like many other critical approaches, it is bound to exist in a limbo at the intersection of disciplinary, multi-disciplinary and trans-disciplinary practice.

In this light, let us bring a provisional end to this beginning by repeating that we are not so much concerned to 'bring culture back in' for the purposes of economic or political analysis as to make the cultural concerns of recent contributions to critical political economy more explicit and to highlight their compatibility (indeed, compossibility) with the more self-conscious concern with semiosis found in some versions of critical discourse analysis. We emphasize that the cultural and social construction of boundaries between the economic and political has major implications for the forms and effectiveness of the articulation of market forces and state intervention in the *'reproduction–régulation'* of capitalism. And, in offering an alternative interpretation of this insight, we combine arguments from the regulation approach, neo-Gramscian state theory, historical semantics, and some key theoretical and methodological insights from Foucauldian analysis to highlight the contingency of social imaginaries, the contingency of structuration, and the contingency of their translation into social practices and institutions.

NOTES

1. While semiosis initially refers to the inter-subjective production of sense and meaning, it is also an important element/moment of social practice (and hence 'the social') more generally. It also involves more than spoken or written language, including, for example, forms of 'visual imagery'.
2. Note that reality 'exists in the way that it does, only in so far as it is assigned meaning by people, who are themselves entangled into and constituted by discourses' (Jäger and Maier 2009: 44).
3. Meaning systems are shaped in various ways, with different theories identifying different mechanisms. Cognitive linguistics emphasizes neural and cognitive frames and includes conceptual metaphor theory, which argues that language is inherently, not contingently, metaphorical (Lakoff and Johnson 1980). Other approaches emphasize social interaction, meaning-making technologies and strategically selective opportunities for reflection and learning (e.g. Nord and Olsson 2013).
4. Core linguistics (Kress 2001) comprises the main subdisciplines (e.g. phonetics, phonology, morphology, syntax, semantics); to this can be added 'non-core' linguistics, such as psycholinguistics, sociolinguistics and discourse analysis.
5. 'In using the metaphor of construction it is vital to distinguish participants (constructors) from spectators (construers) and acknowledge that constructions succeed or fail according to how they use the properties of the materials – physical and ideational – involved in the construction process' (Sayer 2006: 468).
6. See, for example, Ferguson and Schularick (2007, 2011).
7. Affordance is an important concept in critical realism and the strategic-relational approach. For introductions, see Gibson (1979) and Grint and Woolgar (1997); Hutchby (2001) uses this concept in treating technologies as texts.
8. Post-structuralism is a broad intellectual and academic reaction to an equally ill-defined structuralist tradition. Its proponents reject the latter's claims about the feasibility of 'scientific objectivity' and universal truths. It denies that there are firm grounds for knowledge (hence its description as 'anti-foundationalist') and it highlights the plurality of meanings and difference. It also foregrounds the role of discourse and knowledge not only in construing but also in constructing reality.

9. This remark concerns the overall tendencies in the organization of scientific practices. It is not a comment on the scope for particular individuals or schools, through years of reskilling, to adopt the attitudes and practices of the pre-disciplinary age. But this would involve the reinvention of a pre-disciplinary tradition in specific circumstances – not a return to an age of pre-disciplinary 'innocence'.
10. For a good survey of seven turns (interpretive, performative, reflexive or literary, post-colonial, translational, spatial and iconic), see Bachmann-Medick (2006). For an accessible introduction to the tools of cultural studies, see Thwaites et al. (1994). And, for introductions to different kinds of critical discourse analysis, see Fairclough (2003); Lakoff and Johnson (1980); Hodge and Kress (1993); Kress (2001); van Dijk (1977); van Leeuwen (2008); Wodak and Mayer (2009); and Chapter 3.

PART I

The logos, logics and limits of institutional and cultural turns: challenges and responses

1. Institutional turns and beyond in political economy

This chapter addresses the logos, logic and limits of the institutional turn. It reviews the grounds for institutional turns (their logos), their explanatory value (their logic) and the blindspots of a monocular concern with institutions (their limits). We ask what needs to be recovered from classical political economy and social theory, and what lessons can be learnt from recent work, so that institutions can be 'put in their place'. We note that they rest on fragile institutionalized compromises, that agency (including potentials for bricolage, innovation and resistance) is primary, and that institutions are linked to broader structures of domination. We also ask what further turn(s) might be made to advance critical political economy. Of interest here is the 'fourth institutionalism': constructivist, discursive or ideational. Old institutionalists might well consider this a cultural *re*turn. Addressing the limits to the institutional turn(s) and calls for a fourth institutionalism are our bridge to Chapter 2, which considers the logos, logic and limits of cultural turns in heterodox political economy.

INSTITUTIONS AND INSTITUTIONALISM IN GENERAL

Institutionalism can be defined, broadly and loosely, as the more or less consistent elaboration of the intuition, hypothesis or discovery that 'institutions matter' in one or more theoretical, empirical or practical contexts. Just as institutions are not confined to economics (however defined), so institutionalism is not limited to economic analysis. It is significant across the social sciences, including anthropology, history, human geography, international political economy, international relations, policy sciences, political science, socio-legal studies and sociology. This suggests that core institutionalist themes may be useful for the trans- and/or post-disciplinary CPE project. Indeed, in its pre-disciplinary phase, economics explored the relations among economic and extra-economic institutions and behaviour; then, after its institutionalization as a distinct discipline, largely forgot about history and institutions in its dominant mainstream variants, moving towards mathematized ideology (for reviews and criticisms, see Hodgson 1989, 2001, 2004; Rutherford 1994; Schabas 2006). More recently there has been a rediscovery and recovery of institutions even in the mainstream (leading, in some cases, to 'Nobel prizes'). We return to these issues below but now consider the nature of institutions and why they matter.

There is wide variation in definitions of institutions within and across different social science traditions and schools and, *a fortiori*, about why they matter. This poses two complementary problems. The first is 'the inclination to opt for a discipline-based, theory-impregnated internalist-style definition of the term' that makes most sense for one discipline – but may be hard to transfer to others (Goodin 1996: 21). Such tendencies certainly exist (see below) but even within disciplines, let alone across them, we find, as a second problem, an array of vague, diffuse and mutually inconsistent definitions. For some, this is a 'productive fuzziness, permitting trans-disciplinary dialogue and collaboration, with institution serving as a "floating signifier" that can acquire different content in different contexts' (cf. Senge 2011: 82–3). This can be seen in the broad, but underspecified, mainstream consensus that institutions involve complexes of social practices that are: (1) regularly repeated; (2) linked to defined roles and social relations; (3) associated with particular forms of discourse, symbolic media or modes of communication; (4) sanctioned and maintained by social norms; and (5) have major significance for social order (Burns and Flam 1987; Eisenstadt 1968: 409; Goodin 1996: 19; March and Olsen 1984, 2006; Peters 1999: 18–19; Wallis 1985: 399–401).

Examples of institutions in this sense include the family, religion, property, markets, the state, education, sport and medicine. Structuralists and regulation theorists sometimes use the concept of 'structural forms' to describe such institutions – although, from a regulationist perspective, structural forms comprise *clusters* of institutions, organizations and forms of interaction structured around specific forms of the capital relation and/or particular problem constellations associated with different accumulation regimes and modes of regulation. Other theorists substitute apparatus for institutions, especially in the case of political and administrative apparatuses, and, in particular, where a nexus of institutions is involved (for a broader approach, in which apparatus is one dimension of an institution, see Dubet 2002). Instead of institutions or structural forms, some French post-structuralist theorists refer to *appareils* (apparatuses) or *dispositifs* (dispositives), and this usage has been adopted in some institutionalist and post-institutionalist circles. The two terms are not just alternative *descriptions* of institution, however, because they are deployed *critically* to disclose how heterogeneous sets of instituted social practices (including their discursive as well as material aspects) instantiate, reflect and refract power relations and contribute to domination and hegemony (see next section and Chapters 3 and 4). In this sense, compared with much mainstream institutionalism (especially in economics, political science and sociology), the focus is on how institutions aid the provisional stabilization (institutionalization) of specific systems of exploitation and domination. The emergence of a self-described 'critical institutionalism' is related to these more emancipatory rather than scientific or problem-solving knowledge interests.

Whatever the chosen nomenclature, institutions thus defined should not be mistaken for their actualization in particular exemplars or confused with organizations. Thus, taking the list above, individual families, church congregations, commodities, economic transactions, cabinets, schools, athletic competitions or hospitals would not count as institutions.[1] An important alternative view defines *as institutions* those organizations or social bodies that have major significance for the wider society and act in a quasi-corporate manner. Examples are the executive, legislative and judicial branches of government; transnational firms, banks or the peak organizations of capital and labour; established religious faiths; or organizations more generally. This latter approach owes much to the economics and/or sociology of organizations (e.g. Williamson 1994; Aranson 1998; Greenwood et al. 2008). There are also disagreements within and across new institutionalist approaches about the role of informal as well as formal rules, norms, procedures and so on; and about the significance of the cognitive as opposed to normative properties of institutions (for surveys, see North 1984b; Hall and Taylor 1996; DiMaggio 1998; Brinton and Nee 1998; Powell and DiMaggio 1991; Rhodes et al. 2006; and Morgan et al. 2010).

We are less convinced that such organizations should be called 'institutions', however, although they can be analysed in institutionalist terms. But we are interested in organizational ecologies (i.e. competition and symbiosis among organizations in organizationally dense environments) as well as 'organizational institutionalism' (i.e. the study of the institutional conditioning, regulation, governance and meta-governance of organizations and inter-organizational relations) (see, respectively, Aldrich 1999; and Powell and DiMaggio 1991).

More generally, institutions are closely linked to modes of calculation, sets of rules and norms of conduct, whether through explicit attempts at institutional design and/or unintended evolutionary stabilization. In short, institutions are always-already semiotic. Social scientists also disagree about the nature of the rationalities, rules and norms that are implicated in institutions and their causal significance in this regard. For example, orthodox economics offers robust accounts of causality based on a *thin* conception of rationality – the formal maximizing behaviour of rational calculating subjects; and this is reflected in the attempts of economists and their fellow travellers to expand economic inquiry into other fields in the form of rational-choice institutionalism (for a positive survey, see Shepsle 2006; critically, on economics imperialism, see Zafirovski 2000; Fine 2001; Milonakis and Fine 2008). In contrast, as Hall and Taylor (1996) note, sociological and historical neo-institutionalists are often rather imprecise about causal links between institutions and individual behaviour. They tend to work with a *thick* conception more suited to variable institutional contexts that involve quite varied cognitive frames, bounded rationalities, logics of appropriateness, conventions, modes of calculation and so on.

This said, institutionalists all agree that institutions matter. Indeed, without major social structural significance within a given research context, such practices would not count as institutions. This poses a whole complex of questions about differences in individual institutional forms, inter-institutional configurations, institutional histories, or other properties of institutions and the differences that they make, especially for any particular theoretical or practical problem. For most institutionalists, this leads to the treatment of institutional variations as independent or intervening variables in one or another causal chain. We sometimes follow this path below but, because institutions are not *the* ontological basis of CPE, we are also interested, as a pet phrase goes, in putting institutions in their place.

This exercise involves several steps. The first is to define, locate and thematize institutions so that they can be given form and content. The next is to address how institutions operate and are reproduced through routine actions that 'do' or perform institutions. This is illustrated in Bourdieu's arguments about the potential convergence of objective history and embodied history, habitat and habitus, position and disposition to enact history (Bourdieu 1981: 306).[2] We can add to Bourdieu's agent-centred list by including enactment in organizational routines and institutionalization. There is also a large literature on the agent-mediated, recursive reproduction of institutions. One might then look behind sedimented institutions to examine institutional emergence as a complex evolutionary phenomenon that involves institutional entrepreneurship and/or creative institutional bricolage and also depends on specific mechanisms of variation, selection and retention in specific spatio-temporal contexts (on institutional entrepreneurship, see Crouch 2005; Leca 2006; Garud et al. 2007; Levy and Scully 2009; and, on bricolage, see de Koning and Cleaver 2012; Arts et al. 2013).

Further steps in a 'para-institutionalist' or 'post-institutionalist' research agenda might include work on institutional embeddedness, that is, the embedding of institutions in specific institutional orders or functional systems, in the interface among institutional orders or functional subsystems, or in wider, macro-societal contexts. Interesting here are questions of institutional isomorphism, that is, the formal correspondence or equivalence among institutional forms in a given social formation; or, alternatively, of institutional complementarities, that is, the mutual support and reinforcement among institutions that may lack self-similar forms and, indeed, where differences may be crucial to this complementarity (on isomorphism versus complementarity, see Amable 2009; Crouch 2010). Issues of formal isomorphism and institutional complementarities are considered in relation to variegated capitalism (see Chapters 6, 7 and 11). Another theme is the governing of institutions and inter-institutional relations and their systemic environments (cf. Jessop 1997b). Moving on, one might also examine institutional design and implementation – issues that require attention to the variable reflexive skills and capacities of actors as well as to the inevitable disjunctions between intentions and institutional outcomes (e.g. Elster et al. 1998; Goodin 1996; Grafstein 1992; Mayntz 1997; Weimer 1995).

Finally, in moving from single institutions to institutional ensembles, institutional arrangements, institutional interfaces, institutional design, inter-systemic relations and so on, the focus will shift to the structural coupling and co-evolution of institutions and to issues of their strategic coordination or guidance. The dialectic of path-dependency and path-shaping is important here. Path-dependency implies that an institution's prior development limits current options in institutional innovation. However, while history matters, it does not require fatalistic acceptance of past legacies. Social forces could intervene in current conjunctures and actively re-articulate them so that new trajectories become possible – especially where sedimented, taken-for-granted institutional legacies reveal unexpected crisis tendencies and/or come, for whatever reason, to be reactivated or repoliticized. This is where capacities to read conjunctures and reflexivity come into play, and indicates the heuristic value of a systematic concern with structure–agency dialectics.

INSTITUTIONAL TURNS

Turns of various kinds are moments in the self-organization of scientific investigation and/or in the translation of scientific into policy paradigms. In the former regard, we can distinguish analytically among four forms of turn: thematic, methodological, ontological and reflexive. These are by no means confined to institutionalism but are generic and can be observed in

Table 1.1 A typology of institutional turns

Type	Character	Motto
Thematic	Institutions can provide a new theme of inquiry for an existing approach, as a simple incremental extension and/or a means to develop it further	Studying institutions can be interesting
Methodological	Institutions provide a useful entry-point for studying a research or policy problem – but move beyond institutions as the analysis develops	Studying institutions can generate new insights into the social world
Ontological	Institutions are crucial factors in social cohesion and/or system integration: without them, there can be no social order	Studying institutions is essential because they are foundational
Reflexive	One or more of the turns above can be fruitfully applied, or must be applied, to the development of institutionalism	Studying institutionalism in institutionalist terms is interesting, insightful or essential

various forms of cultural turn (see Chapter 2). A thematic turn involves the (re)discovery of a neglected theme for investigation; a methodological turn involves the (re)adoption of that theme as the entry-point for a broader research inquiry; an ontological turn claims that the real world is fundamentally constituted by the elements and relations in question; and a reflexive turn applies one or more of these turns to institutionalism itself (see Table 1.1).

An institutional turn can occur only when the existence and/or relevance of institutions have previously been overlooked, deliberately ignored, or denied. This does not take us far, however, because of wide variation in how institutions are defined, the respects in which they are held to matter, and the reasons for suggesting that they do. An institutional turn can also refer to personal intellectual trajectories; to general developments in a particular approach; and to shifts in the weight of approaches in a broader disciplinary field – or even in the social sciences more generally. Thus one can say that a scholar makes an institutional turn when she rejects her earlier, essentialist account of patriarchy and studies the institutional specificities and dynamics of gender regimes; that neoclassical economics made an institutional turn when it adopted a transaction costs approach to explain the problematic existence of the firm as an economic institution; and that the social sciences as a whole have shown renewed interest in institutions in the last 30 years.

How one evaluates institutional turns depends on the reference point. For example, whereas interest in institutions marks an advance on a methodological individualism that assumes a trans-historical *homo economicus*, it could mark a retreat *vis-à-vis* the critique of political economy if it leads to neglect of the competing logics of capital. Our concern is the intellectual use-value-added of institutional turns for critical political economy rather than for neoclassical economics or other forms of methodological individualism in whatever disciplinary or multi-disciplinary context they are found. We consider cultural turns in similar terms in Chapter 2. Others might want to judge the value-added relative to the German Historical School (including figures such as Werner Sombart, Max Weber, Joseph Schumpeter and Gustav Schmoller) or the old (or original) American institutionalism of the early twentieth century (Thorstein Veblen, John R. Commons, Wesley C. Mitchell, Walter Hamilton) with its links to classical political economy and critical legal scholarship (for brief comments on the German Historical School, see Djelic 2010; at greater length, Shionoya 2001; on Weber, see Swedberg 1996; for a comparison of the regulation school and German Historical School, see Labrousse and Weisz 2001; on the history of old and new institutionalisms and their battles with neoclassical economics, see Hodgson 2001, 2004; Rutherford 1994, 2011; and Yonay 1998).

There is no necessary sequence or overall relationship among the first three turns and they vary across schools or disciplines. This typology provides no information about definitions or why institutions are held to matter thematically, methodologically, ontologically or practically. No turn is good or bad in itself. Its significance depends on where its initiators are coming from, currently situated, and ultimately headed. The rest of this section discusses the first three types of turn.

Thematic Turns

The first, and simplest, turn is a *thematic* one. Sometimes this involves no more than a simple thematic extension of an established paradigm as a case of puzzle-solving in 'normal science' (Kuhn 1962; Lakatos and Musgrave 1970). Since institutions are taken seriously in most social sciences, the interesting question about *thematic institutional turns* is why they should be deemed necessary. Shifting intellectual fashion may, as Myrdal (1978) remarked, be part of the answer. Scholars in the humanities and social sciences may shift focus when topics become boring or when it becomes too hard for newcomers to master and influence an established field. Thematic turns may also be related to shifts in techniques of investigation, the organization or funding of scientific research, the education system, the demands of policy-makers or other users, or, indeed, external events that disturb received scientific wisdom. For example, Andersen (2003: ix) suggests that the 'constructivist turn' occurred because 'it has simply become too difficult not to be a constructivist' on account of the major changes and discontinuities occurring in so many areas of life that tend to disorient taken-for-granted values, categories and assumptions.

A key part of the answer may lie in the methodologies and ontologies adopted in the prior work of scholars, schools or disciplines that make turns. In economics, for example, these generally involve methodological and/or ontological individualism. This posits that the methodologically appropriate or ontologically irreducible micro-foundations of social life are located in the identities, interests, calculations, meaning systems and actions of individual actors. Thus, in making a *thematic* turn, they seek to explain institutions in terms of individualist micro-foundations and/or study how emergent institutions react back in turn on individual conduct. Other disciplines host holists. They assume the primacy of wider cultural or societal dynamics and seek to interpret and explain lower-order phenomena in terms of macro-level laws, logics, functional needs or other macro-properties. For holists, a thematic turn would direct attention to how macro-properties affect institutions. Others may take a thematic turn when institutional crisis, change or design becomes a major concern in the real world and stimulates awareness of earlier neglect of institutions.

A well-known example of a thematic turn is the attempt by neoclassical economics to explain institutions, such as the firm, in terms of transaction costs. This takes institutions seriously by problematizing their existence – but then argues that they can be fully explained within the neoclassical paradigm. This is the strategy of endogenization, which step by step includes more relevant factors within the logic of rational calculation (Eggertsson 1990). The firm is an economically rational institution because it serves in certain circumstances to lower transaction costs as compared to operating in and through markets (see, classically, Coase 1939; and, for a review, Williamson 1996). Analogous arguments have been made for networked industrial districts and agglomeration economies in cities. However, whilst this approach problematizes the existence of the firm, network or agglomeration, these entities are usually seen as dependent or, at best, intervening variables in rational conduct. Indeed, some rational-choice theorists suggest that the survival of institutions is explicable in terms of an equilibrium in transaction costs because it is rational for almost all individuals to adhere routinely to institutional prescriptions, given that nearly all others also do so (e.g. Calvert 1998: 60). In this sense, 'rational choice theory defines institutions as though they are subject to a continuing recall by their participants ... tantamount to contract renewal' (Grafstein 1992: 6, 7).

Methodological Turns

Here institutions are deemed to matter because they provide the best entry-point to understanding social life, even if the study later moves to micro-foundations or emergent macro-structural phenomena. This turn is often associated with the alleged mediating role of the institutional turn for well-established and troublesome ontological antinomies, epistemological dualisms and methodological dilemmas in the social sciences. Thus institutions have been endorsed as an entry-point for overcoming such ontological antinomies as

- Structural determination and social agency (e.g. the structuration approach sees institutions as recursively reproduced sets of rules and resources that constrain and enable social action).
- Holism and individualism (e.g. as emergent meso-level phenomena, institutions are said to connect macro- and micro-phenomena or macro-social logics and micro-social foundations).
- Necessity and contingency (e.g. because they need to be interpreted and can be renegotiated, institutions do not fully determine action but nor are they consistent with any and all actions whatsoever – they are sites of the necessarily contingent and the contingently necessary).

They are also proposed as entry-points in resolving epistemological issues such as

- Abstract–concrete (e.g. institutional analysis allows one to reveal the specificities of different varieties or stages of capitalism relative to its generic features before one analyses particular crises, conjunctures etc.).
- Simple–complex (e.g. analyses of the institutional embeddedness of economic activities can bridge simple economic and more complex societal analyses) (e.g. Beckert 2003).
- Empirical description or grand theory (e.g. the claim that a series of middle-range institutional theories could be developed to make sense of fine-grained empirical data and later be combined to generate a general theory or, conversely, that institutionalism provides

a 'middle way' between the search for generality of theory and the desire for relevance to specific applications).
- Idiographic versus nomothetic approaches (e.g. arguments for institutionally 'thick description' as a way to avoid simplistic empiricism and covering law models or, again, for middle-range analyses that transcend the choice between idiographic studies of particular places and an overly abstract spatial science).

And they have been proposed as resolutions for methodological dilemmas such as

- Bottom-up versus top-down approaches (e.g. institutions codify the strategies that connect the micro-physics of power to attempts to impose a more general strategic line on 'street-level' or 'grass-roots' politics).
- Global and local approaches to spatial or scalar phenomena (e.g. institutions serve as 'intermediaries between the specific everyday moments of human interaction (localized in time and space) and the general distribution of economic, political, cultural, communicational, symbolic and other resources (reaching across time and space)' [Philo and Parr 2000: 516]).

Such methodological turns are common in comparative and/or historical analyses, in studies of crises and crisis management, and in work on path-dependency and path-shaping. More generally, institutions are said to matter in so far as they provide the best entry-point to understanding social life, even if the search for understanding subsequently descends towards micro-foundations or ascends to emergent macro-structural phenomena. So it is no surprise that a methodological turn is often presented as one option among several entry-points that should be selected on pragmatic grounds. For example, James March and Johan Olsen present the 'exchange' and institutional perspectives as alternative methodologies without recommending one or other on ontological grounds (1984, 1996). They later added a third option, a cultural community that highlights shared values and world-views (March and Olsen 2006: 4). Pragmatism also marks the 1980s proposal to 'bring the state back in' (the *locus classicus* is Evans et al. 1985). And a much-cited survey of rational-choice, economic, sociological and historical 'new institutionalisms' suggests that, despite differences in how they treat institutions, their origins, the relationship of institutions to individual behaviour, and so forth, a productive synthesis is possible (Hall and Taylor 1996). This is echoed in Paul DiMaggio's recommendation that new institutionalists search for 'common ground around particular ideas and approaches to obdurate problems' (1998: 699).

Ontological Turns

The most radical type of turn asserts that institutions (and institutionalization) are the primary axis of collective life and social order. Indeed, institutions 'are typically conditions of choice, not objects of choice' (Grafstein 1992: 3). This approach often presupposes the existence of an instituted, encompassing social order (or, at least, the primacy of tendencies and efforts to develop and reproduce such an order) with little concern shown for the conditions of its emergence and survival (Wagner 1994). Thus institutions matter because they are seen, *inter alia*, as the points of crystallization of social forms, as defining the rules and resources of social action, as defining opportunity structures and constraints on behaviour, as shaping the way things are to be done if they are to be done, as path-dependent path-defining complexes of social relations, as the macro-structural matrices of societies and social formations, and so on.

Emile Durkheim, the French sociologist, provided an early and strong version of this position in his rules of sociological method. He identified the essence of social life in the externally constraining, collectively produced 'institutions' that every single individual must confront fully formed, unable to evade or change them (1938: lvi). Interestingly, at least in CPE terms, Durkheim included the *conscience collective* (collective consciousness) among such externally constraining social facts. As we shall see, this theoretical assumption was taken up in French work on *mentalités* (historical mentalities). 'Mental models' and 'ideology' also figure in the work of Douglass C. North, the 1983 co-winner of a 'Nobel prize' in economics, but he interprets these very differently from Durkheim (see below).

Likewise, in political science, albeit less radically, March and Olsen claim that:

> Intentional, calculative action is embedded in rules and institutions that are constituted, sustained, and interpreted in a political system . . . Political actors act and organize themselves in accordance with rules and practices which are socially constructed, publicly known, anticipated and accepted. Actions of individuals and collectivities occur within these shared meanings and practices, which can be called institutions and identities. (1996: 249; cf. idem, 1984, 2006)

Karl Polanyi, a polymath whose work influenced some early Parisian regulation theorists, takes an ontological institutionalist position (not a turn) in his studies of the substantive institutedness and social embeddedness of economies. He asks how the economy acquires unity and stability, that is, how the interdependence and recurrence of its parts is secured. This question shifts attention to different modes of 'material provisioning' in non-market and market economies and 'centers interest on values, motives and policy' (Polanyi 1982: 34). He then argues:

> The human economy . . . is embedded and enmeshed in institutions, economic and noneconomic. The inclusion of the noneconomic is vital. For religion or government may be as important for the structure and functioning of the economy as monetary institutions or the availability of tools and machines themselves that lighten the toil of labor. (Ibid.: 34)

In this context, Polanyi focused on the dominant principle of distribution of 'want-satisfying material means'. He identified three such principles: (1) reciprocity among similarly arranged or organized groupings (e.g. segmentary kinship groups); (2) redistribution through an allocative centre linked to a political regime; and (3) householding based on production to satisfy the needs of a largely self-sufficient unit such as a family, settlement or manor (1957: 47–53; 1977: 34–47; 1982: 35). These principles are contrasted with the anarchy of exchange as mediated through price-making markets in a disembedded and potentially self-regulating economy (1982: 35).[3]

A similar argument can be applied to the reification of other institutional orders that come to be disembedded from pre-capitalist social formations and then acquire their own distinctive logics (despite their material interdependence with other orders). This holds, for example, as Otto Brunner, one of the founders of German conceptual history, argued, for the state and its juridico-political order, leading to the forgetting of the pre-disciplinary study of political economy and the rise of economics and political science (Brunner 1992). Thus he argued that 'phenomena basic to the structure of the medieval world may be overlooked because the position allotted to them in the system of modern disciplines may conceal their significance for earlier periods' (ibid.: 101, cited in Melton 1996: 26).

Other institutional schools have also rediscovered or finally recognized that economic activities are irreducible to the actions of *homo economicus* but are mediated through institutions that socially embed and socially regularize behaviour. This is also the original stance of the regulation approach (RA), which can be interpreted in large part as a major current within historical institutionalism. Thus, rather than study economizing behaviour and formally rational calculation of opportunities for profit on the market, regulationists study the differential constitution of economic rationality; the role of family, education and so on in reproducing labour-power as a fictitious commodity; the historical emergence and generalization of specific norms of production and consumption; the embedding of structural forms and economic practices in specific and changing institutions in particular times and places; the coupling of these forms and practices to environing, embedding institutions; and the role of law and the state in reproducing money as a fictitious commodity (Boyer 1990; Boyer and Saillard 2002; Jessop and Sum 2006).

THE POLYMORPHISM AND POLYVALENCE OF INSTITUTIONAL TURNS

The four types of institutional turn can occur from diverse starting points and follow different paths. Since a turn is always relative to a prior position or path, it is unlikely that institutional turns will automatically promote convergence in and across relevant theoretical or disciplinary contexts. Indeed, they could produce divergence. This is evident from Peter Hall and Rosemary Taylor's review of differences among rational-choice, sociological and historical new institutionalisms in political science (1996). The next three paragraphs provide our gloss on these three approaches.

Rational-choice institutionalism shares many failings of neoclassical economics and, in so far as it yields interesting results, often does so in terms of the logic of situated action (cf. Shepsle 2006; Katznelson and Weingast 2010). This is seen, for example, in the firm-centred 'explanation' provided by Hall and Soskice (2001) for the lesser efficiency of hybrid varieties of capitalism compared to pure liberal *or* pure coordinated market economies. They claim that firms in hybrid regimes find it harder to work out optimizing strategies. For obvious reasons, we reject 'thick' versions of rational-choice institutionalism but believe that thin versions oriented to situated action can be useful in developing CPE. We offer a critique of the varieties-of-capitalism literature in Chapter 6.

Sociological institutionalism has several forms: they include cultural, normative, and organizational variants, and these in turn span scales from world society to the institutional environments of particular organizations (on world society, see Thomas et al. 1987; Krücken and Drori 2010; on organizational institutionalism, see Powell and DiMaggio 1991; and Greenwood et al. 2008). In economic analysis, attention focuses on the social embedding of economic action, the key role of extra-economic institutional supports to economic action and, recently, the effects of the neoliberal disembedding of market forces from their social integument. This approach is inspired in part by Polanyi's (1957) critique of liberalism in *The Great Transformation* – a work that continues to inspire critics of commodification (see also Chapter 6). Thus sociological institutionalism offers a useful counterfoil to studies that consider the market economy in isolation (or abstraction) from its wider social context (for a comprehensive survey, see Vidal and Peck 2012; see also Amable 2011). Sociological institutionalism also provides a useful supplement to Marxist approaches that start from the fundamental forms of the capital relation (such as the commodity, money, price and wage forms). These never exist in 'pure' form but only in specific structural or institutional guise. Whilst exploring these specificities, one should not forget that they cannot fully and permanently contain, let alone harmonize, the inherent contradictions of the basic forms (see Jessop 2013e; and Chapter 6).

Historical institutionalism links evolutionary and institutional concerns with interest in path-dependency and path-shaping. The RA belonged here from the outset and, more recently, has included this among its self-descriptions. Overall, noting that history and temporality matter, this approach examines institutional inertia, institutional transformation and institutional rupture (e.g. Pierson 2004; Streeck 2010). For this reason, it partly overlaps with 'middle-range' or more concrete–complex analyses that seek to respecify basic categories of analysis (e.g. structural forms) to study their instantiation in particular historical contexts. This has been important in advancing comparative and historical studies of capitalist formations. This approach can also clarify how institutional and spatio-temporal fixes help to stabilize specific regimes (see below).

Summarizing, Hall and Taylor (1996) note that, whereas rational-choice neo-institutionalists offer robust accounts of causality based on a thin conception of rationality, sociological and historical neo-institutionalists are often rather imprecise when identifying the causal links between institutions and individual behaviour. This imprecision could occur because the latter two institutionalisms have a strong negative, or diacritical, heuristic (avoid methodological individualism, avoid structural or functional determinism) but lack a robust, let alone consensual, positive heuristic. In short, they constitute a terrain for a continuing 'conversation' rather than a consolidated, imperious 'standard theory' akin to neoclassical economics.

Such typologies are an open invitation to reduce the set, extend it, or reorder it. Thus Hall and Taylor's threefold classification is often cited prior to, and as a pretext for, offering alternatives. For example, Guy Peters identifies, admittedly in an *ad hoc* fashion, seven forms of institutionalism in political science alone (1999).[4] There are similar divergences in institutional turns in other disciplines considered individually (e.g. Brinton and Nee 1998 on sociology; Powell and DiMaggio 1991 on organizational analysis; Ensminger 1998 on anthropology; or Djelic 2010 on the East and West Coast variants of historical institutionalism in the USA).

Conversely, Paul DiMaggio identifies three forms of new institutionalism within the social sciences as a whole – rational action, social constructionist, and an approach concerned with how institutions mediate conflict – but argues that each is rooted in a different discipline – economics, sociology and political science respectively (1998: 696–7).

Goodin suggests that institutionalisms can be distinguished in terms of the key variables that they 'own', the distinctive problems that institutions are said to resolve, and their ideas about how institutions shape social life (1996: 2). He argues that the old and new historical institutionalisms focus on the past (and how it shapes the present and the future) (see, especially, Pierson 2004), that sociological institutionalism is concerned with 'the collective' – the old institutionalism having focused on how collective entities subsume and subordinate individuals and the new one examining the impact of different forms of social embedding on individuals; that economic institutionalism deals with institutional constraints on individual choice; and, finally, that political science is concerned with organizational and institutional constraints on the exercise of power and its outcomes (Goodin 1996: 2–16). By analogy, one might claim that institutionalism in geography 'owns' space as its key variable, regards areal differentiation and uneven development as its key problems, and studies how institutions shape landscapes, regions, places and spaces. Likewise, organizational institutionalism owns organizations (see the contributions to Greenwood et al. 2008). Feminist institutionalism(s) would 'own' gender (Mackay et al. 2009)[5] and the 'queer new institutionalism' would not only 'own' heteronormativity but also efforts to destabilize any and all assumptions about the banality, normality and stability of institutions (e.g. Burgess 1999). A last example, discussed later, would be that institutionalism in interpretative policy analysis – or constructivist, discursive or ideational institutionalism more generally – 'owns' ideas or discourse as its key variable.

Depending on how starting points and turns are combined, institutional turns can lead to convergence or divergence. For example, a *thematic* economic turn within critical semiotic theory (which is *ex definitione* ontologically grounded in semiosis) could facilitate the development of cultural political economy. But CPE could also result from a *methodological* or *ontological* turn in political economy itself. This would occur as some political economists discovered the relevance of semiosis and semiotic practices for the investigation, interpretation and explanation of some traditional themes of economics and political economy. Likewise, 'network institutionalism' reflects an internal differentiation in institutionalism such that it takes networks as its *thematic* focus and uses new *methodological* (analytical) techniques to map networks (Ansell 2006). A different example is 'feminist institutionalism'. This involves attempts to ride the institutionalist bandwagon (witness the pragmatic exploration of the potential of different institutionalist approaches) and to remind mainstream institutionalists (male or female) that institutions are deeply implicated in reproducing gender hierarchies, patriarchy and so forth (see, e.g., Chappell 2006; a special issue of the journal *Politics & Gender* 2009; and a 2011 collection edited by Krook and Mackay).

Recognition of the limits of institutionalism is also seen in the rise of 'post-institutionalism' (Mehta et al. 2001). This moves beyond institutions to other themes – in other words, in our terminology, it involves, minimally, a thematic turn that somehow puts institutions in their place. Thus Mehta et al. (2001) bring in institutional frailties. But many other post-institutionalisms (with or without this self-designation) are feasible. Other trends adopt the label 'critical institutionalism'. In some cases this involves reinterpreting original economic institutionalism as compatible with critical realism (e.g. Tauheed 2013), in some cases a recognition of the centrality of institutional failure (e.g. de Koning and Cleaver 2012)[6] and, in others, a commitment to critiquing historical and sociological institutionalisms (e.g. May and Nölke 2013).

A STRATEGIC-RELATIONAL APPROACH TO INSTITUTIONS

A strategic-relational approach (SRA) provides one way to put institutions in their place. We first present it in general terms, then link it more directly to institutional analysis, and, in a final step, respecify it to illustrate how it can bring spatio-temporality into institutional analysis. Much work on structure and agency brackets structure or agency to focus on the effects of its counterpart. But bracketing tends thereby to relate structure and agency in a rather mechanical fashion. It treats structure at any given time in isolation from action and so implies that a given structure is equally constraining and/or enabling for all actors and all actions. Similarly, action at any given time is isolated from structure, since actors are seen to choose a course of action more or less freely and skilfully within these rules and resources.[7] Attempts to resolve the structure–agency problem in these terms are inherently unstable. A major reason for this, as Mitchell Dean notes, is that

> their conception of social agency is reductive. Social agency becomes identified with the human subject and its capacities and attributes. Other forms of social agency, including various forms of collective or corporate agency, are either written out of these accounts, or themselves conceived as composed of and reducible to human agents. Secondly, a further untenable conflation is made

between human agents and the actions of individuals or persons ... Attempts to grasp the properties of social relations and social systems from such categories of agency cannot be sustained. When such categories are combined in basic sociological concepts themselves, such as the famous 'duality of structure', they form an unstable amalgam sliding between a structure whose effectivity knows no limits and a form of agency that knows no determination. (Dean 1994: 9)

In addition to this fundamental weakness, Giddens's structuration approach is largely atemporal. The mutual theoretical isolation of these complementary moments *at any given time* (as expressed in the bracketing of one or other term) is resolved theoretically *over time* by claiming that specific structures are modified in and through the intended and unintended effects of action and inaction, thereby creating new sets of constraints and opportunities for action. However, even allowing for reflexive transformation of structure by agency, there is little, if any, recognition (let alone adequate explanation) of the differential capacities of actors and their actions to change different structures.

One way to go beyond this duality is to examine structure in relation to action, action in relation to structure, rather than bracketing one of them. Structures are thereby treated analytically as strategic in their form, content and operation; and actions are thereby treated analytically as structured, more or less context-sensitive, and structuring. Applying this approach involves examining how a given structure may privilege some actors, some identities, some strategies, some spatial and temporal horizons, some actions over others; and the ways, if any, in which actors (individual and/or collective) take account of this differential privileging through 'strategic-context' analysis when choosing a course of action. In other words it involves studying structures in terms of their structurally inscribed strategic selectivities and actions in terms of (differentially reflexive) structurally oriented strategic calculation.

Figure 1.1 depicts the logic of conceptual development and different degrees of theoretical sophistication in the analysis of structure and agency towards the SRA position. It does *not* present a necessary historical sequence of institutional development or a mandatory order of presentation for empirical arguments. Instead it illustrates the logic of concept development in efforts to overcome the fallacies of determinism and voluntarism or, again, materialism and idealism. A similar logic of concept formation can be applied to other dichotomies (see, e.g., the analysis of spatio-temporality presented in Figure 1.2 and of dialogism in Figure 3.1).

Thus row one of Figure 1.1 presents the inadmissible dichotomy between (absolute) external constraint and (unconditional) free-willed action – the two terms that serve as the initial thesis and antithesis of the theoretical movement leading to the SRA analysis. The second row presents the

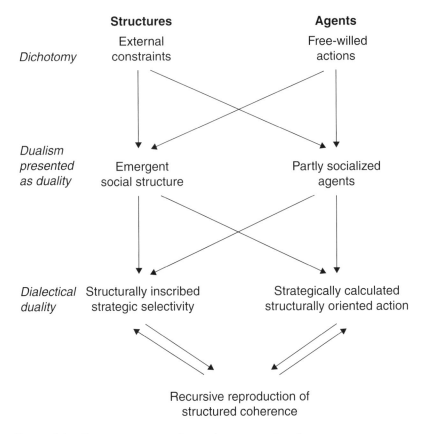

Figure 1.1 Structure–agency beyond structuration theory

so-called structure–agency duality developed by the British sociologist Anthony Giddens (1984), which sublates both thesis and antithesis by treating structure (defined in his terminology, however, as 'system') as an emergent effect of action and agency as a structurally constrained and enabled mode of skilful action. But this alleged solution retains a dualistic form because, at any given point in the analysis, it brackets one or other aspect of the resulting duality.

The concepts introduced in rows three and four preserve the admissible elements of the preceding row(s) and reveal the SRA's radical 'methodological relationalism', that is, its treatment of social phenomena in terms of social relations. Thus the concepts that appear under the agency column in row 3 indicate the possibility of reflection on the part of individual and collective actors about the strategic selectivities inscribed within structures so that they come to orient their strategies and tactics in the light of their understanding of the current conjuncture and their 'feel for the game'. This can (but need not) extend to self-reflection about the identities and interests that orient their strategies. Individuals and organizations can be reflexive, reformulate within limits their own identities, and engage in strategic calculation about the 'objective' interests that flow from these alternative identities in particular conjunctures. Likewise, the concepts in the structure column highlight the tendency for specific structures and structural configurations to selectively reinforce specific forms of action, tactics or strategies and to discourage others.

This implies that the scope for reflexive reorganization of structural configurations is subject to structurally inscribed strategic selectivity (and thus has path-dependent as well as path-shaping aspects); and that the recursive selection of strategies and tactics depends on individual, collective or organizational learning capacities, and on the 'experiences' that result from pursuing different strategies and tactics in different/successive conjunctures. This possibility is indicated in row 4 and reflects what Bourdieu, rather deterministically, refers to as individual agents' practical anticipation of the immanent necessity of their social world, with the result that they reproduce their subjection to conditions similar to those in which they are placed (1988: 783). Bourdieu's emphasis on habitus is problematic in SRA terms because it presents practices as largely pre-reflective, making it hard to explain social change and to consider differential capacities for reflective and strategic conduct.

Two recent attempts to resolve the over-emphasis in habituality on the internalization of structural constraints have been proposed from critical-realist and activity-theory perspectives respectively. Dave Elder-Vass insists that 'we, as reflexive beings, are sometimes able to critically evaluate and thus modify our dispositions in the light of our experience, our reasoning capacities, and our value commitments' (2007: 346; see also Chapter 11). In turn, Reijo Miettinen, Sami Paavola and Pasi Pohjola note that 'the classical practice theories, pragmatism and cultural-historical activity theory – an heir of the dialectical tradition – focused . . . on how people can influence [social] changes when emerging problems or contradictions in practices are faced' (2012: 346). They argue for activity theory, which studies how individual and social artefacts (signs and material objects) can be creatively remediated (that is, remade and redeployed) in response to new challenges (we return to this topic in Chapter 3).

The results of conceptual development in row 4 can also be connected to Michel Foucault's account of how *dispositifs* emerge from the double movement of strategic logics and apparatuses (see Chapter 4). He asks how discursive tactics and strategies are generalized to create a specific strategic logic (or strategic imperative as a condition of effective action in response to an urgent problem); and, conversely but reciprocally, how a heterogeneous ensemble of diverse (structural) elements are articulated to become functional moments in an apparatus that facilitates a specific strategic logic.[8] Foucault also emphasizes the spatial aspects of *dispositifs*. In short, his account of the double movement is equivalent to the dialectical duality depicted in Figure 1.1 and, for spatio-temporality, in Figure 1.2.

Finally, in so far as reflexively reorganized structural configurations and recursively selected strategies and tactics co-evolve to produce a relatively stable order out of a potentially unstructured complexity, we can talk of the structured coherence of this co-evolving, self-organizing order (row 5). This can be related to the interaction of the reflexive reorganization of strategic selectivities inscribed in an institution (or institutional ensemble) and the recursive selection and retention (or evolutionary stabilization) of specific strategies and tactics oriented to those selectivities. This involves a structurally inscribed strategic selectivity that rewards actions compatible with the recursive reproduction of the structure(s) in question. Structured coherence in an institutional complex can be ascribed to accumulation regimes, modes of regulation, innovative milieus, industrial districts, worlds of production and so forth. Antonio Gramsci (1971: 377; Q7, §21: 869)[9] describes one such form of structured coherence as a historical bloc, that is, a relatively stable, mutually constitutive, co-evolving relation between the economic base and ethico-political superstructure of social formations (see Chapter 5). In Chapters 4 and 5 we relate structured coherence to discursive and technological selectivities.

Adopting the SRA (or an equivalent) has several implications for how to make an institutional turn. First, institutions never exist outside of specific action contexts. They do not matter as such but in terms of their structurally inscribed strategic selectivity: that is, only in so far as institutions are reproduced (a crucial caveat), do they select behaviours. This framing role is now recognized, for example, in rational-choice theories; but it is also conceded that institutions do not fully and precisely determine actions (see March and Olsen 1996: 251–5). Actors have some freedom of manoeuvre more or less skilfully and reflexively to choose a path of action. Second, actors not only engage in action within a given institutional matrix but, in certain circumstances, can reflexively reconstitute institutions and their resulting matrix. Their capacity to do so depends both on the changing selectivities of given institutions and on their own changing opportunities to engage in strategic action.

Thus the spaces in Figure 1.1 could easily be renamed to take account of the different forms of institutional turn. For, apart from the crudest neoclassical or rational-choice institutionalists (for whom institutions are subject to a continuing voluntaristic 'contract renewal'), those who have made the institutional turn also reject the dichotomy of external constraints and universal modes of rational action. On the structural side of the dichotomy, for example, they argue at the least for analyses of emergent conventions or 'rules of the game', including laws, inherited organizational structures, and formal and informal norms and sanctions. Likewise, on its action side, they have noted at the least the role of bounded rationality, context-bound forms of rationality, cognitive habits, selective attention, the logic(s) of appropriateness, how atomized individuals are transformed into molecular groups through their embeddedness in an inherently social world with socially determined preferences and ideologies, and so forth.

Some institutionalists have moved to the third level by emphasizing, on the structural side, asset specificity, rigidities in transaction costs, the differential dynamics of organizational ecology, path-dependency, differentiated and competitive institutional environments, 'structural holes', and other forms of structural selectivity; and/or, regarding the agency side, noting the scope for deliberative rather than automatic cognition, the key role of strategic choices, agenda control, gatekeeping, sequencing, strategic interaction, coalition formation, or various forms of entrepreneurship. Some argue, for example, that these rules can be reflexively reorganized (March and Olsen 1984, 2006; Shepsle 2006: 25–6; Blyth in Boyer and Labrousse 2008).

Yet others have approached the fourth level by examining how institutions come to be reproduced and regularized via their co-evolution with distinctive forms of appropriate conduct so that temporary equilibria are achieved in an otherwise turbulent environment. In short, in advocating the SRA in this context, we are not denying the returns from institutional turns. Instead we are offering a more general, and essentially heuristic, model that may help to locate types of institutional turn as well as to highlight the limitations of approaches that are one-sided and/or fail to move from dualisms or dualities to genuine recursive–reflexive dialectical analyses.

The SRA is also relevant to power and language. Although they do not reference the SRA, the socio-linguists José Antonio Flores Farfán and Anna Holzscheiter make the following pertinent observation:

> In sociolinguistics . . . discourse has offered itself as an interface that allows us to understand the emergence and effects of power relations through a complex co-constitutive relationship between agents and structures. Discourse is, on the one hand, seen as the most important location for the production of asymmetric relationships of power and, on the other hand, seen as the place where individuals are in a position to renegotiate or even level out relationships of

power. Discourses in themselves act as powerful structures of social conventions (meaning-conventions) by limiting the potentially indefinite ways of talking about and perceiving social and material reality. Yet, it is also linguistic interaction which is seen as constantly transforming and challenging dominant perceptions of this social and material reality. Every speech-act, thus, at the same time represents **and** transforms patterns of meaning. (2011: 141; emphasis in original)

We return to this remark when we consider semantics for CPE and discuss power and ideology (see Chapter 4). For now, it provides a useful bridge to the discussion of the fourth institutionalism, albeit more in relation to large discursive shifts than more micro-level communicative interactions.

A FOURTH INSTITUTIONALISM?

Discussions of institutionalism (as opposed to applications of one or another variant) can be regarded as interventions in theoretical disputes, disciplinary turf wars, and, often, struggles for policy relevance. For example, in political science and, by extension, mainstream international political economy, a debate has continued from the mid-1990s about the strengths and weaknesses of three main forms of institutionalism: rational-choice, sociological and historical. One response has been to claim recognition for, and to identify and promote the potential of a 'fourth' institutionalism. This has been described variously as constructivist, discursive or ideational. This turn is most explicit in political science, which has laboured for many decades under the dire influence of American 'behaviouralist' and rational-choice approaches, with their antipathy to institutions and bias towards explanations grounded, respectively, in individual behaviour and the rational calculation of self-interested agents (cf. Blyth 1997; Rhodes et al. 2006). In contrast, interpretivism is more common in sociology and international relations (for reviews, see Béland and Cox 2010; Bevir and Rhodes 2006; Farrell 2002; Finnemore and Sikkink 2001).

The case for constructivist, discursive or ideational institutionalism could be understood in four ways. First, it could be dismissed as a late, somewhat opportunistic, intervention in the debate, staking a claim to a 'place in the sun' in an increasingly dominant and mainstream institutionalist 'conversation'. Second, conversely, it could be a revival of the early, and highly systematic, tradition of Saussurean linguistics. Ferdinand de Saussure, its founder, argued in the posthumously published *Course in General Linguistics*, that '[s]peech always implies both an established system and an evolution; at every moment it is an *existing institution* and a product of the past' (1915: 8; italics added). However, interesting as this is, the fourth institutionalism does not seek to bring linguistics as such into institutionalism, even if it does represent a linguistic turn. Nor does it treat language as an institution. Third, it has been presented as an effort by those interested in discourse and policy narratives to problematize institutions and to show 'the limits to explanations in terms of interest-based logics, historical path-dependencies or cultural framing' (Schmidt 2012: 86). At stake here is the claim that ideas, culture, epistemic communities, discourse coalitions and discursive policy communities matter as much as (if not more than) institutions as conventionally understood and, accordingly, that it is worthwhile to consider their role in and/or articulation with institutions alongside factors emphasized in the other institutionalisms. And, fourth, one could see the 'fourth' institutionalism as part of a thematic and/or methodological *cultural* turn. In other words, it could involve either the thematic extension of discourse analysis to institutional innovation and transformation and/or the methodological argument that institutions can be better interpreted and explained by taking culture (discourse, ideas etc.) as an initial analytical entry-point. In both cases this might simply subsume familiar interpretivist or ideational themes under the institutionalist canon or, more significantly, contribute to its transformation. These interpretations reinforce our claim about the relative, relational and historical nature of turns and indicate that there can be several routes and rationales for, in this case, a discursive turn.[10]

The constructivist turn marks an advance on the institutionalist–cognitive models developed by Douglass North. As noted, he modified his initial, pure neoclassical emphasis on individual self-interest to integrate ideas, myths, prejudices, dogmas and so on to explain why people obeyed rules even if they would gain from breaking them and, more generally, to account for secular change that does not satisfy the neoclassical constraint of individualistic, rational purposive activity (1981: 12, 58). He introduced a pair of thin ideational concepts to explain learning in conditions of uncertainty: (1) 'mental models' are cognitive maps that shape learning by guiding calculation about the expected payoffs from acquiring different kinds of knowledge in conditions of uncertainty; and (2) 'ideologies' are 'shared frameworks of mental models that groups of individuals possess that provide both an interpretation of the environment and a prescription as to how that environment should be ordered' (North 1983). Later he added that changing perceptions of the legitimacy of institutions, such as slavery, are also key drivers of change (North 1984a, 1986). Describing his approach as institutional–cognitive, he claimed that both institutions and belief systems must change for reforms to succeed – it is actors' mental models that shape choices (North 1983). Without a theory to explain ideational shifts in normative or consensus institutions, however, North's approach is incomplete according to its own programmatic statements because key institutional and ideational factors remain exogenous.[11] These include, importantly, norms and identities as well as political regimes. The question to ask of the fourth institutionalism is whether it has endogenized construals, discourse or ideas, or, at least, put them into a more robust and balanced dialectical relation.

Mark Blyth's constructivism is superior in this regard. He argues that 'the ideas people have about how the world works and the convergence in expectation and actions that this allows clearly matter all the time, but their valence and variance is a function of the observability and complexity of the [risk] generators agents face' (interview in Boyer and Labrousse 2008). Some parts of our world are directly observable and are governed by rational calculations. However, faced with uncertainty, agents cannot behave like classical rational agents with a risk model and rational calculus. Instead they become 'default constructivists' for very practical reasons. Indeed, he continues, 'the more one moves from situations of risk to situations of uncertainty, the more constructivist one becomes' (ibid.). This analysis begins to endogenize construals inside what remains an orthodox institutionalist position. We present an alternative account of crisis and crisis construals from a CPE perspective in Chapter 11.

The case for discursive institutionalism gets stronger when we note: (1) discursive frames privilege some interlocutors, some discursive identities/positionings, some discursive strategies and tactics and some discursive statements over others (e.g. Hay 1996; Jenson 1995); and (2) these selectivities depend on institutional supports and have institutional consequences. Such arguments can also be parlayed into a case for the fourth institutionalism. Indeed, Colin Hay, who has done much to popularize the SRA, uses the latter more or less openly in developing his own case for 'constructivist institutionalism' (2006).

More specifically, constructivist, discursive or ideational institutionalism claims that ideas mediate institutional effects; that institutions filter the role of discourses; and/or that they reflect, embody or reproduce particular social imaginaries, discursive practices and projects (e.g. Schmidt 2010; Walsh 2000). For example, in making the case for the 'newest "new institutionalism"', Vivien Schmidt argues that it

> lends insight into the role of ideas and discourse in politics while providing a more dynamic approach to institutional change than the older three new institutionalisms. Ideas are the substantive content of discourse. They exist at three levels – policies, programs, and philosophies – and can be categorized into two types, cognitive and normative. Discourse is the interactive process of conveying ideas. It comes in two forms: the coordinative discourse among

policy actors and the communicative discourse between political actors and the public ... The institutions of discursive institutionalism, moreover, are not external-rule-following structures but rather are simultaneously structures and constructs internal to agents whose 'background ideational abilities' within a given 'meaning context' explain how institutions are created and exist and whose 'foreground discursive abilities,' following a 'logic of communication,' explain how institutions change or persist. Interests are subjective ideas, which, though real, are neither objective nor material. Norms are dynamic, intersubjective constructs rather than static structures. (Schmidt 2008: 303; cf. Schmidt 2012: 85–8)

These broad claims mark an important advance on the vague notion of 'ideas' as the products of individual authors, on the ill-defined notion of 'tradition' as a system of thought and practice passed from generation to generation, and on the idea of *Zeitgeist* (spirit of the times), which identifies the unity of thought not as a diachronic legacy but as a synchronic structure (cf. in a different context, Cousins and Hussain 1984). In particular, in developing her case, Schmidt distinguishes the differing roles of 'ideas' in philosophies, programmes and policies respectively, and notes that they have different effects, depending on whether they are cognitive (subject to revision if disappointed) or normative (liable to provoke sanctions if infringed) (on the latter point, see Luhmann 1995). She identifies these alternatives mainly with comparative politics and political economy, on the one hand, and international relations, on the other (Schmidt 2010, 2012). Moreover, in a brief but wide-ranging survey she notes:

Among the scholars concerned most with the substantive content of ideas and discourse, differences abound with regard to the forms of ideas they identify, of which there are a vast array (see, e.g., Goodin and Tilly 2006: pt. 4). Such ideas may be cast as strategic weapons in the battle for 'hegemonic' control (Muller 1995; see also Blyth 2002); 'frames' that provide guideposts for knowledge, analysis, persuasion, and action through 'frame-reflective discourse' (Rein and Schon 1994); narratives or discourses that shape understandings of events (e.g., Roe 1994); 'frames of reference' that orient entire policy sectors (Jobert 1989; Muller 1995); 'storytelling' to clarify practical rationality (Forester 1993); 'collective memories' that frame action (Rothstein 2005); discursive 'practices' or fields of ideas that define the range of imaginable action (Bourdieu 1994; Howarth, Norval, and Stavrakakis 2000; Torfing 1999); 'argumentative practices' at the center of the policy process (Fischer and Forester 1993); or the results of 'discursive struggles' that set the criteria for social classification, establish problem definitions, frame problems, define ideas, and create shared meaning on which people act (Stone 1988). (Schmidt 2012: 88)

Other issues in a discursive institutionalist research agenda include: (1) the timing and speed of changes in ideas and discourses, theoretical and policy paradigms, political traditions and broad philosophical outlooks; (2) the 'background ideational abilities', or, in our terms, sense- and meaning-making abilities, and the 'foreground discursive abilities' of different actors – which together ground discursive institutionalism; (3) the relative importance of taking everyday experience or more abstract models of reality as the starting point for analysis; and (4) the relative importance of elite discourse coalitions and social movements in communicating and/or coordinating responses to discursively framed problems (Schmidt 2012: 88–108).

Schmidt's survey reveals the richness of the discursively demarcated 'discursive institutionalist' approach. Nonetheless it is worth recalling the remark of Bas Arts and Innocent Bahili that discursive institutionalism is often 'light' or 'thin' on *discourse theory* (2013: 118). Moreover, as Terry Threadgold, a prominent critical discourse theorist, has observed, it can also be thin on *discourse analysis*. For the fourth institutionalism often uses discourse theory as a meta-language that does not so much provide discourse-analytical tools as macro-categories that organize 'large chunks of often undeconstructed text'. Indeed, if these macro-categories are nominalized, that is, treated as abstract nouns endowed with causal powers rather than being grounded in agents' practices, they 'can be bandied about as names for things which apparently exist, but the work which would have to be done on the materiality of language to demonstrate that existence in recognisable and replicable linguistic terms is rarely done' (Threadgold 2003: 16).[12] Similar charges are found in socio-linguistics, where Wilson and Stapleton note that 'modern social theory highlights the role of language in social change/reproduction, yet rarely draws on actual linguistic resources or theory. Equally, sociolinguistics situates linguistic practices within the social domain, but only weakly makes links to social theory' (2007: 393).[13] Reinhart Koselleck, its doyen, notes that semantic conceptual history, too, has been criticized for lacking rigorous linguistic analytical methods (1992: vi).

Relatedly, some discourse analysts note the twin problems of under-specification and overgeneration of linguistic discourse analysis. The former occurs when its full heuristic and analytical potential is not realized, whether in terms of its available methods or the full range of relevant data; and the latter occurs when an analyst strives to learn more about discourse and discursive practices than can be achieved through linguistic analysis alone, requiring help from other disciplines. For example, under-specification is evidenced in an exclusive focus on digitalized mass media texts; and overgeneration in a neglect of non-textual modes of communication (such as iconography), socio-political processes, historical contexts and other discourse-relevant issues (see Spitzmüller and Warnke 2011: 79–81).

Such critiques should not be limited to discourse institutionalism. They pose a major challenge to CPE in general and individual CPE studies in particular. This makes it even more necessary to clarify at which level(s) a given critical semiotic and structural analysis is being conducted (see Table 4.1, 158). The closer the explanandum is to the discoursal aspects of discursive practices than it is to the overall features of social practices, the more necessary are detailed discourse-analytical methods in order to disclose their linguistic and extra-linguistic features and assess their effects. This applies most strongly when the focus is on intratextual semantic features of individual utterances, propositions, arguments or texts. However, it would be unfair to expect individual discourse institutionalists (or CPE scholars) to retrain as discourse analysts and grasp all relevant discourse-analytical tools, their demands and their limitations. But multi-disciplinary teams should include discourse linguists. Moreover, if discourse institutionalism is to realize its purported potential within the extended family of institutionalisms, its claims must be related to the diverse factors that shape the variation, selection, retention and recontextualization of 'ideas' in specific conjunctures. We return to this topic in Chapters 3–5 and 11. For now we draw five general lessons about institutionalism and institutional turns.

PUTTING INSTITUTIONS IN THEIR PLACE

Taking institutional turns seriously requires attention to the micro-foundations, meso-connections and macro-contexts of an institution. We identify five complementary ways to put institutions in their place. The order of presentation is intended to make the argument easier to follow; it does not indicate a mandatory chronological sequence in these responses.

Micro-foundations and Macro-contexts

Institutions are not only sustained and instantiated in individual, organizational and inter-organizational activities, but also embedded in more or less distinct institutional orders in a complex, decentred societal formation. This is where historical institutionalism is superior to rational-choice institutionalism (cf. Thelen 1999). However, as Colin Hay has observed, some leading historical institutionalists have resolved the rational calculus versus cultural norms conundrum in favour of the former. He writes that their attempt at bridge-building 'runs from historical institutionalism, by way of an acknowledgment of the need to incorporate microfoundations into institutionalist analysis, to rational choice institutionalism' (Hay

2006: 63). A similar point is made by Graça, writing on the new economic sociology, when noting that

> it dared to refute, if only in part, some of the assumptions and methods of academic economics. At the same time, however, it hastened to delimit the scope of the refutation, and again and again tended to retrace its steps and revert to the traditional, self-legitimizing allegation that there are a number of points of view or analytical angles and that its own view is just one among several, in juxtaposition with – rather than in opposition to – that of economics. (Graça 2005: 111, translated and cited in Cardoso Machado 2011: ¶18)

Thus to rescue sociological and historical institutionalism from their 'friends' is an important task in the battle against economics imperialism. More generally, analyses that focus on micro-foundations and fail to locate institutions in broader contexts find it hard to address the limitations of institutional design or institutional change. This problem has been addressed in the 'actor-centred institutional approach' of the Max Planck Institute for Social Research in Cologne and associated, above all, with its former co-directors, Renate Mayntz and Fritz Scharpf. This approach investigates strategic, goal-oriented political action *and* its limits, as rooted in various kinds of institutional constraint. From the mid-1980s, their work has focused on the limits to political steering (a form of goal-oriented, purposeful political action) that originate from the complexity and resulting opaqueness of modern societies. They combine two themes in various case studies: (1) problem-solving activities, strategies and policies, especially those pursued by organizations, collective actors (such as industrial associations), state agencies and policy networks; and (2) the limits of attempts to steer the development of large technical infrastructure systems, the evolution of particular functional systems, or societal development more generally. They address these limits in part through actors' bounded rationality and in part through the complexity of functional systems and functionally differentiated societies, which have their own special logics (*Eigendynamik*) that make them resistant to steering and produce unintended and unanticipated outcomes that are historically surprising, even to informed social scientists. This is related in turn to the non-linear dynamics of complex systems, with their proneness to sudden ruptures and transformations.

In dealing with actors, agent-centred institutional theorists focus on complex actors rather than individuals, on actors' interests, identities, action orientations and resources in specific actor constellations rather than in generic, context-free terms, and on different forms of interaction (e.g. negotiation, multi-level decision-making and hierarchical command). In dealing with institutions, they focus on the logics and particular dynamics of different institutional orders and functional subsystems. One link between the two is the analysis of the asymmetries involved in specific interaction arenas, including those that involve multi-level and/or multi-site interactions. Within this school, Mayntz has maintained a more sociological approach, whereas Scharpf has moved towards rational-choice and game-theoretical analyses. Actor-centred institutionalism is a research heuristic and makes no claims to become a general theory (for a representative selection of work of its founding figures, see Mayntz 1997; Mayntz and Scharpf 1995; Scharpf 2000).

This approach has theoretical and methodological advantages over Giddens's structuration theory (especially as regards operationalization) but it still has three major limitations. First, it does not ask, as a Foucauldian or discourse-institutionalist analysis would, why and how particular collective problems come to be 'problematized' and treated as potentially solvable in ways that serve some construal of the collective interest (see Chapter 3). Second, it does not provide the broader contextualization offered by the SRA, especially in relation to questions of domination (as Mayntz 2001 later conceded). And, third, it does not address, where relevant, the limits to collective problem-solving that are rooted in the contradictions of capitalism and/or of social formations in which profit-oriented, market-mediated accumulation is the dominant principle of societal organization. This would reveal more fundamental limits to institutional redesign, policy-making and problem-solving than can be derived from bounded rationality and system complexity alone.

In this regard, without seeking to engage in a capital- or class-reductionist analysis of all institutions (thereby contradicting its foundational principles), the SRA as developed here and elsewhere would – where appropriate – investigate institutions and institutional clusters as particular, overdetermined instantiations of the basic social forms of the capital relation, which, while they have their own dynamics, also reproduce, in different ways, these incompressible contradictions. Institutional analyses certainly permit distinctions among different forms or stages of capitalism and facilitate historical and comparative studies of capitalist societies. But they cannot explain the generic features of capitalism and they ignore the generic constraints imposed by the self-organizing dynamic of capitalism in favour of more middle-range analyses. This is also a potential weakness, for example, in more recent work in the RA in so far as it ignores the inherent limitations, contradictions and dilemmas of any and all accumulation regimes and their modes of regulation. This is reflected in problems with some recent regulationist analyses of the neoliberal forms of globalization and post-Fordism (see Jessop 1999, 2013e).

Similar points hold for critical institutionalist analyses of other forms of domination or discursively and structurally reproduced social exclusion. Commonly studied forms include: different modes of patriarchal domination and heteronormativity; 'ethnic' and 'racial' discrimination and oppression; and uneven spatial development that reinforces social exclusion. This is also a field where issues of the intersection of different forms of domination and exclusion can be posed (see Chapter 4).

Spatio-temporality

Institutions emerge in specific places and at specific times, operate on one or more scales and with specific temporal horizons, develop their own specific capacities to stretch social relations and/or to compress events in space and time; hence they have their own specific spatial and temporal rhythms. These spatio-temporal features are not accidental or secondary features of institutions but constitutive properties that help to distinguish one organization, institution or institutional order from another (cf. Pierson 2004). They also define the power geometries or 'envelopes of space-time' associated with different ways of organizing and institutionalizing social interaction (Massey 1994) and condition social forces' capacities to reproduce, transform or overturn institutions. Institutions provide a framework in which relevant actors can reach and consolidate agreements over (albeit possibly differential) spatial and temporal horizons of action *vis-à-vis* their environment. Thus institutional analyses should examine (1) the spatio-temporalities inscribed in (and reproduced through) specific institutional forms; and (2) the differential temporal and spatial horizons of various actors and their capacities to shift horizons, modify temporalities and spatialities, jump scales and so on. These inquiries must go beyond time and space as external parameters of institutions and/or action.

Institutions as Strategic Contexts

The social meaning of institutions involves the rules, modes of calculation, logics of appropriateness and so on associated with the 'doing' (the performative realization) of an institution. The incomplete specification of institutions makes their reproduction dependent on skilled, reflexive and adaptable actors who understand the purposes of the institution and can reproduce it. These actors should have the corporeal, social and intellectual dispositions, capacities and skills to produce specific types of institutional behaviour and thereby reproduce the institutions (cf. Foucault). From a more radical constructivist position, subjects not only 'do' institutions but, in performing them, also constitute themselves as subjects through their performance (e.g. from a radical feminist perspective, Butler 1990). In

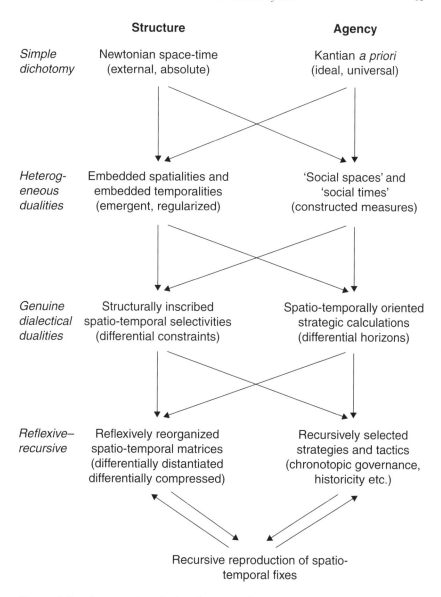

Figure 1.2 A strategic-relational approach to spatio-temporality

addition, we must consider the changing perceptions of institutions among those who reproduce them, seek to transform them, are affected by them, or observe them from a distance. Institutions can have different functions in different contexts, be accorded different material weights, semiotic values and meanings, and be re-evaluated. For example, the institution of taxation is perceived and operates differently in the economy, juridical system and polity; it becomes more legitimate during military crises; its role is regularly re-evaluated over economic cycles, structural crises and swings of the political pendulum; and it is contested by different interests.

Relatedly, we must study how, if at all, actors (individual and/or collective) take account of structurally inscribed strategic selectivities through 'strategic-context' analysis when adopting a course of action (Stones 1991, 2005). They may do so to reinforce, modify or undermine these selectivities. Of course, because actors (individual and/or collective) have different capacities, they will be more or less well equipped to interpret institutions as a set of rules and resources for action and to circumvent constraints and exploit opportunities. They will also vary in their capacity to reflect on their experiences and to learn lessons and, *a fortiori*, to engage in 'double-loop' learning – learning how to learn and enhancing their capacities to engage in such reflection (on learning, see also Chapter 11). For actors are more or less able to modify their identities, recalculate interests, modify spatial and temporal horizons of actions, formulate new strategies and tactics, and so on, to improve their opportunities and chances of effective action. A *reflexive turn* might explore actors' capacity to monitor their own actions; learn from experience; integrate social science knowledge into their activities; and programme their own development (producing evolution in modes of evolution). It is likely that less skilled actors who fail to realize their objectives will eventually exit the institutional field or survive in permanent subordination because there is no 'exit' option (cf. Archer 2012). This leads to the recursive selection of strategies and tactics through individual, collective or organizational learning about the results of pursuing different strategies and tactics in different conjunctures and through the structurally mediated selection and retention of some behaviours as habits (cf. Hodgson 2002). Such agential selectivities must be explored alongside the structural and discursive selectivities indicated above (later chapters will discuss technological selectivities). The scope for the reflexive reorganization of structural configurations is subject to structurally inscribed strategic selectivity (and thus has path-dependent as well as path-shaping aspects).

Institutions cannot be meaningfully or productively analysed without locating actors in a wider strategic-relational context. At any given instant, institutional analysis is prior to action – even if the latter subsequently transforms institutions and institutional contexts (cf. Grafstein 1992). Interrelated constraints matter because actors cannot change all the conditions of action at once. In this sense, 'explanation of the rules of the game and the focal points that attract [strategic] actors rests on the sort of institutional analysis provided by sociology' (Nee and Strang 1998: 713–14). Social science explanations must be formally adequate in the sense that they explain all the effects included within the explanandum (which will not, of course, exhaust its referent); and they must be socially adequate in so far as they explain the discursive (intentional, meaningful, subjective, interpretive etc.) features that mediate the chain of events producing the explanandum (cf. Weber 1949, 1977; Ringer 2000). Weak social constructionist forms of institutionalism can be useful here.

Institutional Emergence

Against the temptation to reify or naturalize institutions, we agree with those new institutionalists who analyse them as complex, path-dependent, emergent phenomena, reproduced through specific forms of action. But we stress that their reproduction is inevitably incomplete, provisional and unstable, and that they co-evolve with diverse other complex, emergent phenomena. Institutions must be deconstructed and located historically. Institutionalization involves not only the conduct of agents and their conditions of action, but also the very constitution of agents, identities, interests and strategies. Institutionalization co-constitutes institutions as action contexts and actors as their institutional supports. This co-constitution is problematic from both sides. Thus neo-institutionalists should examine the many and varied struggles over the constitution of institutions, competing strategies, tactics and techniques of institutionalization, and the contingently necessary incompleteness, provisional nature and instability of attempts to govern or guide them. Moreover, because institutions are never fully constituted, there is space for competing institutional projects and designs. Sensitivity to this surplus of possibilities is found in many versions of sociological and historical institutionalism.

We should look behind the naturalization of institutions to examine institutional emergence as a complex evolutionary phenomenon that depends on specific mechanisms of variation, selection and retention in specific spatio-temporal contexts. Some rational-choice theorists argue that institutional variations emerge, are selected and are retained because they are efficient in a given environment. This risks tautology, where efficiency is reduced to allocative efficiency and given a 'thin' interpretation analogous to rational-choice concepts of rationality. More complex accounts of efficiency (including recognition that actors' accounts of efficiency can vary, may be mistaken and may conflict with each other) could avoid this temptation. Moreover, as other institutionalists argue, selection and retention are not quick, precise, frictionless and reversible, but slow, haphazard and path-dependent (March and Olsen 1996: 255). The issue becomes yet more complex when one follows other institutionalists in claiming that institutions and their environments co-evolve as the latter are modified by institutions as well as vice versa. In so far as reflexively reorganized structural configurations and recursively selected strategies and tactics co-evolve over time to produce a relatively stable order out of a potentially unstructured complexity, we can talk of the structured coherence of this co-evolving, self-organizing order (see above).

The Limits to Institutional Coherence

From a strategic-relational perspective, the coherence of institutions and institutional complexes is always multiply tendential. Four reasons justify this conclusion:

1. Because the reproduction of institutions (like other structures) is only ever tendential, their strategic selectivities are tendential too.
2. Because institutions are strategically rather than structurally selective (Jessop 1990, 2001a, 2007b; Boyer and Saillard 2002; see also this chapter), there is always scope for actions to overflow or circumvent structural constraints through bricolage, innovation, resistance and so forth.
3. Because subjects are never unitary, never fully aware of the conditions of strategic action, never fully equipped to realize their preferred strategies, and always face possible opposition from actors pursuing other strategies or tactics, failure is an ever-present possibility.
4. Because institutions often embody structural contradictions and create strategic dilemmas, crisis tendencies and poor solutions to dilemmas can produce failure (see, in SRA terms, Jessop 1990; from an Anglo-Foucauldian perspective, Malpas and Wickham 1995; in discourse-analytical terms, Scherrer 1995; and, from an actor-network perspective, Dumez and Jeunemaître 2010).

All four of these disruptive and disorienting factors critique the common (but not universal) trend in the three main new institutionalisms to assume a tendency towards equilibrium in institutional orders. For example, economic institutions will be stable: (1) for rational-choice institutionalism when the conditions for efficient institutions exist and the 'rules of the game' enable dispassionate rational behaviour; (2) for historical institutionalism when chance discoveries and/or gradual or punctuated evolution select the right set of institutional complementarities or isomorphism and maintain them through path-dependent inertia; and (3) for sociological institutionalism when the market economy is embedded adequately in a market society. Likewise, for discursive or ideational institutionalism, stability would entail 'getting the ideation right'. In contrast to these approaches, which prioritize institutions and tend to take their reproduction for granted, a strategic-relational CPE approach emphasizes the possibility that social practices can overflow and disrupt institutions[14] (cf. Poulantzas 1973: 264–7; 1974: 63; 1978: 38; and Buci-Glucksmann 1980: 48–9).

CONCLUDING REMARKS

A strategic-relational institutionalist research agenda requires new concepts and methodologies to transcend disciplinary boundaries. This matters more for new institutionalisms, which, in contrast to their old predecessors, are often firmly rooted in distinct disciplinary traditions and epistemic communities. Thus it is worth noting the trend, observed by DiMaggio (1998), that different institutionalisms have already moved from 'mutual disengagement' through constructive criticism to mutual dialogue. This aims to build bridges between disciplines that have hitherto favoured different forms of institutionalism to enhance their overall influence in the social sciences (cf. Campbell and Pedersen 2001). However, this can lead some adherents to engage in disciplinary expansion or imperialism; to engage in eclectic forms of empirical analysis when they step outside the home domain; or to produce incommensurable conceptual schemes when they seek to endogenize previously exogenous factors. In addition to fruitful 'conversations', we find growing recognition that many key issues actually demand pluri-, trans- or post-disciplinary approaches that operate across established disciplinary boundaries. These include social capital, trust, knowledge, learning, uncertainty, risk, innovation and entrepreneurship, competitiveness, governance, network economies, organizational dynamics, varieties of capitalism and social exclusion. These have closely linked economic and extra-economic dimensions and also raise central issues of structure and agency.

Taking account of these concepts, we highlight the heuristic potential of the strategic-relational concepts of 'structurally inscribed strategic selectivity' and 'structurally oriented strategic calculation'. The SRA argues that institutional structures have important strategic biases inscribed in their form, content and operation; and that actors are more or less context-sensitive in evaluating this strategic selectivity and their ability to exploit, contest or transform it. The material, discursive and spatio-temporal selectivities of an organization, institution or institutional ensemble privilege some practices and strategies over others (see Chapter 5). This depends on how such practices and strategies 'match' the material possibilities, meanings, and temporal and spatial patterns inscribed in these structures. Some actors, some identities, some interests, some strategies, some spatial and temporal horizons, some actions will be better positioned than others to realize the possibilities or circumvent the constraints associated with a given institutional ensemble. However, because specific institutional constraints are tied to specific time horizons and spatial scales of action, a short-term constraint for an agent or set of agents could become a conjunctural opportunity over a longer time horizon if there is a shift in strategy. Constraints could be rendered inoperable through competent actors' choice of longer-term and/or spatially more appropriate strategies and tactics that are concerned to disrupt or reconfigure the existing hierarchies of structures (including institutions) and the selective patterns of constraint and opportunity with which they are associated. In addition, agents may be able to pursue different types of alliance strategy and so modify the selective impact upon themselves and others of institutional constraints and opportunities.

Five lessons can now be drawn from this review. First, there is no generic institutional turn that is made wherever and whenever a scholar, school or discipline adopts a new institutionalism or discovers an old one. There are only specific turns in particular contexts made for specific purposes. The actual meaning and import of a given turn depends on its nature (thematic, methodological or ontological), the point or path from which the turn began (micro–macro, idiographic–nomothetic, bottom-up versus top-down and so on), the particular theoretical or disciplinary framework within which it occurs, and the extent to which institutions are reified or, alternatively, analysed in relational terms. Thus the descriptive and explanatory returns, if any, of a given institutional turn depend on how it is integrated into a research programme – and on its protagonists' willingness and capacity to make further turns. In short, institutional turns are particular moments in scientific inquiries that unfold through successive shifts rather linearly.

Second, an institutional turn is justified in certain conditions as part of continuing scientific development. But institutional frameworks also change as world society changes. Yet mainstream economics and political science seem to be lagging in so far as they rest on the micro–macro division, with the macro-level being constituted by national economies and national states. This is one of three issues that Marie-Laure Djelic identifies in her agenda for institutional analysis. She writes:

Contemporary transnationalization implies processes of deinstitutionalization and reinstitutionalization that go across and beyond the level of the field, or of the industry, or of the nation-state. There is a need for more empirical work as well as more systematic theoretical reflection on this interplay ... A second challenge has to do with issues of power, interests, and hegemony. We need to go beyond benign and neutral depictions of processes of deinstitutionalization and reinstitutionalization as reflecting a combination of exogenous and endogenous mechanisms. We need to inject in our readings of those processes a healthy dose of preoccupation for associated power games ... [and] also explore patterns of hegemony building and hegemony contestation. Ultimately, we should probably be looking further into the complex interplay of hegemony logics and more classical and 'visible' resource- and interest-based power games. There lies, I suggest, an important dimension of contemporary institutional dynamics. A related third challenge, obviously, is our capacity to reintegrate notions of conflict and disorder into institutional perspectives. (Djelic 2010: 34–5)

We endorse the importance of a spatial turn (broadly interpreted) to take account of the complex spatialities of institutions, just as we note their temporalities. It is also important to consider how to integrate struggles over hegemony and hegemonic logics and/or the antagonisms inherent in particular institutional arrangements into institutionalism. In short, if institutions matter, what else matters? What other turns could – and perhaps should – be made?

Third, outside of the 'fourth institutionalism', institutionalists would benefit from a more consistent and elaborate cultural turn, whether thematic, methodological, ontological or reflexive (see Chapter 2). The narrative, rhetorical, hermeneutic and other turns could be useful where uncertainty, risk, social polarization or contradictions among institutions mean that the latter underdetermine behaviour and thus open a major space for argumentation, rhetoric and so on (see, weakly, North 1983; and, more robustly, Blyth in Boyer and Labrousse 2008; Walsh 2000). Rational-choice and normative sociological institutionalism could also benefit from practice or pragmatic turns. A pragmatic turn focuses on 'the *situation* in its temporality, the individual's *uncertainty* about the identification of the situation and the *interpretative effort* that is required to determine, together with others, the situation as a shared and common one' (Wagner 1994: 274; italics in original). Whether these turns occur will depend, of course, on the evolution of particular research agendas, paradigms or disciplines.

Fourth, institutionalists operate, deliberately or by default, at middle-range analytical levels. Given their rejection of functionalism and structuralism, they seldom ask whether institutions are instantiations of more basic social forms and/or result from attempts to solve or, at least, manage more basic structural contradictions or strategic dilemmas that are inherent in particular forms of societalization. This means in turn that institutional failures are explained in terms of bounded rationality or design flaws rather than in terms of the overall improbability of long-term institutional solutions to foundational problems of social order (Jessop 1997b; and Chapter 6).

Finally, a self-reflexive turn would be useful. Social theorists must be reflexive about the nature of their work and its implications, including its repercussions on what is studied. A common problem with the institutional turn is that its adherents do not reflect on its nature – and thus its possible limits. Applying the SRA to institutional turns suggests that they are path-dependent as well as path-shaping – generated by specific problems but shaped by theoretical selectivities. This could explain both the easy rapprochement between neoclassical and rational-choice paradigms and the resistance to the new institutionalism found in anthropology. In short, the institutional turn itself needs to be studied in institutional terms. The benefits of a self-reflexive turn more generally in political economy are explored in Chapter 13.

NOTES

1. Goffman (1961) applied the concept of 'total institution' to asylums, prisons and so on, but his analysis actually identified features of a distinctive class of organizations.
2. This quotation comes from Parker (2000).
3. These principles parallel the four main principles of governance: heterarchy or horizontal self-organization; imperative coordination through hierarchy; solidarity based on unconditional commitments; and the anarchy of market exchange.
4. The seven forms are: rational choice, historical (exploring the path-dependent impact of institutional innovation), empirical (pragmatic studies of how institutions matter), sociological (studying social embedding, population ecology etc.), interest representation (asking whether social movements are institutions like political parties), international (focusing on international regimes), and normative (how institutions define situational logics of appropriateness).
5. Vivien Lowndes describes this new institutionalism as examining 'how gender norms operate within institutions and how institutional processes construct and maintain gender power dynamics' (2010: 65).
6. De Koning and Cleaver (2012) emphasize the complexity and polyvalence of institutions when they are entwined with everyday life and the importance of creative institutional bricolage to escape institutional failure.
7. For the SRA, this 'freedom' exists only in relation to a given structure. It does not mean that actors have free will – their choices within the range of freedom permitted by a given structure are typically constrained by other factors, which we explore through other types of selectivity (see Chapter 3).
8. For an insightful commentary on apparatuses and dispositives, see Bussolini (2010); on dispositives in Foucault's analytical strategy, see Andersen (2003: 27–30); for a Deleuzian interpretation of *dispositif*, see Deleuze (1992); and for the Duisburg School's efforts to integrate dispositives into critical discourse analysis, see Jäger (2001, 2012: passim). See Chapters 4 and 5.

9. As is now conventional in Gramsci scholarship, in addition to citing an English translation, we also provide the Notebook number (Q for *Quaderno*), section number (§), and page numbers in the critical 1975 Italian edition issued by the *Istituto Gramsci* and edited by Valentino Gerratana.
10. See, for example, Colin Hay's case for 'constructivist institutionalism', which conflates its thematic and ontological distinctiveness (Hay 2006).
11. Rutherford (1994) locates North in new institutional economics more generally.
12. Threadgold refers here to work in cultural studies but her point also holds for discursive institutionalism.
13. We owe this quotation to Irwin (2011: 100).
14. 'If class powers are not reducible to the State and always outmeasure its apparatuses, this is because, being rooted in the social division of labour and in exploitation, these powers have primacy over the apparatuses that embody them, most notably the State' (Poulantzas 1978: 38; cf. 41–3).

2. Cultural turns and beyond in political economy

The cultural turn in political economy could well be interpreted as a cultural *re*turn. As noted in the Introduction, classical political economy, historical materialism, the German Historical School and 'old institutionalisms' included the cultural moment of political economy as a matter of course, and some, such as the German Historical School, privileged it in the guise of different 'spirits' of capitalism. As economics was reorganized as a specialized discipline, especially when linked to a commitment to formalization, semiotic topics were marginalized or abandoned. This chapter considers two examples of the survival of interest in 'culture' in political economy, in the work of Antonio Gramsci and the so-called Italian School in international political economy. We then examine some proposals, explicit or implicit, from different regulation schools and scholars on how to integrate discursive practices into the analysis of accumulation and its improbable regularization. This is worth considering because, as Robert Boyer and Agnès Labrousse note, 'in the 1990s, the French Regulation theory was led to integrate more and more the role of ideas, beliefs and legitimization. Lordon [1999] argued that this "hermeneutic turn" is compatible with the open structuralism of Regulation theory' (Boyer and Labrousse 2008). Similar trends are found elsewhere as regulationists have pondered the inherently semiotic nature of *régulation*-cum-governance (Table 2.1 presents a typology of cultural turns). After reviewing various cultural, hermeneutic, linguistic and semiotic turns that regulation schools and scholars have made since the approach emerged, we draw some conclusions about their limits and how CPE can take them further.

GRAMSCI AS A PIONEER OF CULTURAL POLITICAL ECONOMY

The potential of a critical engagement with semiosis for developing critical political economy can be seen in the rich and challenging work of Antonio Gramsci. He can be read as a proto-cultural political economist provided that one looks beyond his alleged contributions to cultural criticism or

Table 2.1 A typology of cultural turns

Type	Character	Motto
Thematic	Cultural practices and products can provide a new theme of inquiry for an existing approach, as a simple incremental extension and/or as a means to develop it further	Studying culture can be interesting
Methodological	Sense- and meaning-making provide a useful entry-point for studying a research or policy problem – but move beyond semiosis as the analysis develops	Studying culture can generate new insights into the social world
Ontological	Sense- and meaning-making are foundational to society: without semiosis, there is no society	Studying 'culture' is essential because semiosis is foundational
Reflexive	One or more of these turns can be fruitfully applied, or must be applied, to the development of cultural sciences (including CPE)	Studying 'cultural turns' in their own terms is interesting, insightful or essential

cultural studies (an invention of the 1970s) or his proto-regulationist notebook on Americanism and Fordism. Far more relevant are his comments on Ricardo's notion of *mercato determinato* (determinate market). Gramsci criticized classical economists and 'pure economics' for their abstract treatment of the market and its 'eternal', universal and 'natural' laws (cf. Chapter 1). In response, he redefined 'determinate market' to highlight the historical specificity of economic forms, institutions and dynamics. It was 'equivalent to [a] determined relation of social forces in a determined structure of the productive apparatus, this relationship being guaranteed (that is, rendered permanent) by a determined political, moral and juridical superstructure' (Gramsci 1971: 410; Q11, §52: 1477). To describe a determinate market is to describe 'the determinate social form, of the whole as opposed to the part, of the whole which determines – to a determinate extent – that automatism and ensemble of uniformities and regularities that economic science attempts to describe with the greatest exactness, precision and completeness' (1995: 171; Q10II, §30: 1269). In short, he proposed that critical political economy start from the historical character of the 'determinate market' and its social 'automatism' as expressed in the so-called invisible hand of the market.

Gramsci developed these arguments in his accounts of the historical specificity of the capitalist mode of production and his more concrete–complex analysis of the rise of Fordism and its subsequent diffusion from America to Europe and, indeed, beyond. He showed the importance of new economic imaginaries and organic intellectuals in promoting 'Americanism' as a mode of growth in response to the crisis of liberal capitalism and identified how new social and cultural practices helped to consolidate Fordism as a novel mode of regulation and societalization. He also predicted that Fordism would enter crisis once it was adopted widely and American mass producers lost the monopoly profits that enabled them to pay high wages (1971: 310–13; Q22, §13: 2171–5). Gramsci also noted that it would be even harder to implant Fordism in Europe and ensure its stable reproduction. This is because of the deadweight of tradition, the incrustations of the past that must be swept away, and the presence of parasitic classes and strata (ibid.: 281, 285, 317; Q22, §2: 214–47, §15: 2179). This argument explains why Gramsci was interested in the ambivalent status of corporativism (the organization of economic and political life around occupational groupings) in Italy as a form of 'passive revolution' (social transformation directed from above) promoted by an autonomous industrial productive bloc committed to modernizing Italian industry in opposition to semi-feudal and parasitic elements. In short, while he made the struggle for political, intellectual and moral leadership (hegemony) crucial to the more general struggle to establish, consolidate and reproduce the capitalist social relations, he also recognized the material foundations and future limits of the structured coherence and competitive advantage of Americanism and Fordism.

Thus Gramsci's analyses have more radical implications for CPE than the idea, so often misattributed to him, that economic transformation depends on the battle for hearts and minds (see Chapter 3). For, as Italian commentators have noted for several decades and Anglophone scholars began to argue more recently, Gramsci's whole approach was inspired by his university studies in philology under the direction of Matteo Bartoli, who initiated an approach that was first called neolinguistics[1] and later known as *linguistica spaziale* (spatial linguistics). This was rooted in the idealism of the philosopher and organic intellectual, Benedetto Croce, and in linguistic geography. It emphasized that language is an evolving human creation, that language innovation is normal, and, significantly, that it diffuses geographically and socially in regular ways mediated through relations of prestige and power (see Bartoli 1925; for comments on the school, see Albrecht 1996).

Gramsci followed this new approach (1985: 174; Q15, §43: 1082–3; on the influence of Bartoli and philology more generally on Gramsci, see

Carannante 1973; Lo Piparo 1979; Rosiello 2010 [1986]; cf. Boothman 2004; Brandist 1996a, 1996b; Carlucci 2013; Helsloot 1989; Ives 1998, 2004a, 2004b; Ives and Lacorte 2010). Gramsci argued that 'the whole of language is a continuous process of metaphor, and the history of semantics is an aspect of the history of culture; language is at the same time a living thing and a museum of fossils of life and civilisations' (1971: 450; Q11, §28: 1438–9). Reinforcing this point, with clear implications for CPE (among other semiotically influenced approaches), is Gramsci's argument that

> All men are philosophers. Their philosophy is contained in: 1. *language itself*, which is a totality of determined notions and concepts and not just words grammatically devoid of content; 2. 'common sense' and 'good sense'; 3. popular religion and, therefore, also in the entire system of belief, superstitions, opinions, ways of seeing things and of acting which are collectively bundled together under the name of 'folklore'. (1971: 323; Q11, §12: 1375)

These views are not confined to culture, as if this were separate from the economy, politics, law or other fields. Language permeates all social relations. Thus Gramsci argues that these can only be fully understood and explained through the 'determined notions and concepts' (Marx calls these 'categories') in and through which determinate social practices develop and are institutionalized. Ives glosses this by stating that 'Gramsci views language as a system whereby meaning is created through signs (to use the semiological terminology) by their reference not to non-signs, but to other signs' (Ives 2004a: 14). We challenge this restrictive reading of semiology in Chapter 3, when we compare Ives's interpretation of vernacular materialism with other approaches to political economy that make a cultural or semiotic turn. Notably, we argue that signs are often involved in a three-way relation that involves, admittedly in uneven ways, signifier, signified and referent. In short, the extra-semiotic also matters in the variation, selection and retention of meaning systems and social imaginaries (we explore this in terms of structural, technological and agential selectivities). Indeed, one cannot understand Gramsci's work on the determined market, Americanism and Fordism, the state and the varieties of political practice, hegemony as political, intellectual and moral leadership, sociospatiality and so on without adopting this more complicated, three-way approach (Jessop and Sum 2006; and, on the symptomatology of crisis, see also Chapter 9).

These comments on the determined market were largely overlooked by Gramsci scholars until recently and are still largely ignored by economists and, more surprisingly, sociologists, political scientists and cultural theorists.[2] This is probably because he is widely, but mistakenly, regarded as a theorist of the superstructures (especially politics and culture) rather than the material base (forces and social relations of production). Yet he explicitly rejected the validity of this distinction and sought to transcend it. Combined with his remarks on the state and state power, Gramsci's reinterpretation of Ricardo implies that the analytical object of critical political economy should be the economy in its inclusive sense. We can express this in regulationist terms as 'an accumulation regime + its mode of regulation' (cf. Jessop 1997a; Jessop and Sum 2006: 350–55). But this concept can also serve to highlight how the self-valorization of capital depends on a socially embedded, socially regularized ensemble of economic activities, organizations and institutions and their articulation with extra-economic factors and actors that interact to impart a distinctive dynamic to specific capitalisms in distinct times and places. This is where the concepts of social, institutional and spatio-temporal fix introduced in Chapter 1 are significant, and they were all anticipated in Gramsci's work.

ON THE 'ITALIAN SCHOOL' IN INTERNATIONAL POLITICAL ECONOMY

Gramsci's work on Americanism, Fordism and hegemony had a distinctive impact in international political economy (hereafter IPE) through the so-called Italian School. It was initiated by Robert W. Cox (1981, 1983 and 1987). Cox aimed to give equal analytical weight to production, institutions and ideas, to do so in relation to world developments rather than specific national economies, to develop rich historical analyses based on mixed methods, and to deploy his research for critique rather than problem-solving on behalf of existing power elites. This programme marks an attempt to integrate culture (ideas) into an institutionally sensitive political economy and, as such, engages much more directly with issues of culture and hegemony than all regulation schools apart from the first-generation Amsterdam scholarship, which was strongly influenced by Cox's work (e.g. van der Pijl 1984).

This said, as Randall Germain and Mike Kenny (1998) note, the Italian School contains no Italians and is not a School. The reference to Italy merely indicates that its aficionados are inspired by a distinctive reading of Gramsci and differ from the 'English School' of international relations (on the latter, see the useful summary by a leading representative, Barry Buzan, 2001). Besides Cox, other major 'Italian School' theorists, albeit with their own 'takes' on how to apply Gramsci, include Stephen Gill (1991a, 1991b), Mark Rupert (1995a, 2003) and William I. Robinson (1996). Thus, as Germain and Kenny suggest, these (and other associated) scholars share a broad, pluri-disciplinary research programme, but do not form a tight bloc.

The School builds on three features that Cox identified, rightly or wrongly, in Gramsci's anti-economistic philosophy of praxis: (1) the grounding of class hegemony in political, intellectual and moral leadership, albeit linked to a 'decisive economic nucleus' and the role of the hegemonic class or fraction in the economy, with coercion used as a last resort; (2) the interpretation of power blocs as long-term strategic alliances of economic and political forces; and (3) interest in the relation between the economic base and ethico-political superstructure of social formations in terms of a relatively stable, mutually constitutive historical bloc.[3]

Given these apparent commonalities, what distinguishes the 'Italian School' is its rescaling of these concepts from national class configurations and national states to the international field.[4] Thus its authors examine (1) the scope for a transnational class to emerge; and (2) the potential for one (or, at most, a few) national states to be dominant or hegemonic in regional or world orders. In other words, Cox's neo-Gramscian IPE views 'production' and 'social forces' in terms of 'states' and inter-state relations in a 'world order' dominated by the expanding logic of capitalism and relates the formation of power blocs and historical blocs in late capitalism to the rise of a trans-national bourgeoisie. As critics note, this implies that, although Coxian scholarship has a broader account of the state, it still shares the top-down, state-centric approach of the dominant realist and neo-realist tradition in international relations (Robinson 2004; Worth 2009). However, given that the Italian state did not become a modern nation-state (Gramsci 1985: 335; Q16, §13), Gramsci did not fetishize the national state as the basic unit of analysis. Instead he developed a sophisticated, multi-scalar analysis of the tangled hierarchies of state formation and state power that took into account 'the fact that international relations intertwine with these internal relations of nation-states, creating new, unique and historically concrete combinations' (Gramsci 1971: 406; Q11, §17: 1585). Indeed, he was strongly interested in international relations and studied geo-politics and demo-politics (which might now be called bio-politics) to better understand the political implications of the international balance of forces (for a critique of the Italian School account of internationalization based on a careful reading of Gramsci, see Ives and Short 2013; on Gramsci as a spatial theorist, see Jessop 2005b). On this basis, we can see that the Italian School fails to develop the full implications of Gramsci's concern with civil society and its role in constituting power and hegemony (see Chapter 4).

Early Coxian analyses adopted an additive approach to the economic, political and ideational spheres, and this led to neglect of the constitutive presence of discourse inside the economic and the political as well as the ideational sphere. This is reflected in Cox's initial focus on the first two terms of the production institution–ideas trilectic. Thus, within a world order, hegemony may exist when 'based on a coherent conjunction or fit between a configuration of material power, the prevalent collective image of world order (including certain norms) and a set of institutions which administer the order with a certain semblance of universality' (1981: 139). He likewise claimed that world hegemony can be described as 'a social structure, an economic structure, and a political structure; and it cannot be simply one of these things but must be all three' (1983: 171–2). He also emphasized that each historical structure was contradictory, contested and liable to eventual break down (1987). Thus 'world order' is equivalent in several respects to Gramsci's notion of historical bloc but, in contrast to the real Italian's analysis of the determined market, Cox had a more structuralist reading of production orders and a limited engagement, initially, with the general significance of language and signification (for further criticisms of the early studies, see Bieler and Morton 2004; and Schecter 2002).

Based on these concepts, Cox detailed the succession of relatively stable world orders under the hegemony (armoured by coercion) of particular national economies that dominate the most advanced production technologies and production regimes and that have also solved at least temporarily the problems facing the preceding world order. For example, in the 'great transformation' that produced the post-1945 world order, the leading US capital fractions consolidated their domestic rule by developing a new hegemonic vision and gradually reshaping key national institutions to create a cohesive culture rooted in production relations. They generalized their conception of social and political order to the international level to create an international system supportive of capital's profit and power interests. They created partners abroad, controlled interest formation by influencing domestic environments and socialized them into the hegemonic worldview. Nonetheless, such attempts to develop trans-national hegemony are limited by domestic modes of production and emerging social forces outside the dominant social formation (for an exemplary analysis of changes in Fordism, see Rupert 1995a). Recent trends reflect a fundamental shift from the previously nation(al)-state-oriented mode of production towards a global economy that also entails major redesigns of the institutional architecture of states and international relations (Cox 1996).

As such, despite its support for Gramsci's anti-economism and its emphasis on trans-national historical blocs, early Italian School work had a residual 'economism'. This can be seen in four problems. First, its analysis of power and institutions focused on class identities and interests. Yet, given Gramsci's account of hegemony as political, intellectual, and moral leadership grounded in a decisive economic nucleus, non-class identities (e.g. gender, race and ethnicity) also matter in the construction of hegemony on different scales. One should not jump directly to classes as actors but consider how identities, interests and social movements may acquire class relevance. Second, it tended to examine 'ideas' (even those central to economic hegemony and governance) in largely ideational terms rather than in terms of the specific discursive processes and mechanisms involved in securing the dominance of a given economic order and historical bloc. Third, it treated intellectuals as the prime producers of ideas and regarded ideas as relatively fixed rather than as polysemic and unstable. This marginalizes the articulation of folklore, popular common sense, specialized disciplines, science and philosophy. And, fourth, it largely ignored the co-constitutive relation among ideas, power and institutions in favour of an analysis that juxtaposes these factors and treats them in ideal-typical terms: Jessop and Sum 2001; de Goede 2003; Germain and Kenny 1998; Burnham 1991). All of this contrasts markedly with Gramsci's own concerns with the always-already ideological character of economic practices and agents – witness his classic analysis of how hegemony in American Fordism was deeply rooted in the factory, the labour market and the reordering of domestic life, as well as in a broader array of social practices and institutions (Gramsci 1971: 279–318; Q22; see also Chapter 5).

Apart from the obvious move to develop this approach through empirical extension (undertaking more case studies), second-generation neo-Gramscian IPE studies have sought to address some of these problems through conceptual deepening. This is reflected in four developments:

1. Taking the cultural turn more seriously to counteract the initial bias towards (economic) production and (political) institutions and thereby returning to Gramsci's more integral analyses. For example, Mark Rupert (1995b, 1997, 2003) has discussed how Americanism and Fordism were translated and embedded in common sense and thereby also shaped forms of resistance in the USA, North America, and more globally. Cox himself incorporated 'otherness' into his later work on civilizations (1995) and on 'civilization and intersubjective meanings' (Cox with Schechter 2002). Other important work in this regard includes Matt Davies on 'transnational hegemony' (1999), Daniel Egan on the movement against the Multilateral Agreement on Investment (2001), Manfred Steger on 'globalism' (2002), Owen Worth and Carmen Kuhling (2004) on globalization and counter-hegemony.

2. Integrating Foucault's work on disciplinary technologies and governmentality. For example, Stephen Gill (1995b, 1997) examined the 'global panopticon' and disciplinary neoliberalism, and asked whether global social movements might provide the basis for a counter-hegemonic 'post-Modern Prince' to challenge the power of trans-national capital. He has also extended his analyses to Europe and the European Union (Gill 1998, 2003a, 2003b). A similar 'disciplinary' move is seen in Timothy Sinclair's analysis of bonds and debt-rating agencies as producers of financial knowledge (Sinclair 2005).
3. Providing a more rigorous analysis of the institutional mediations involved in the organization, articulation and embedding of production and political domination. Thus Cox discussed the new world order in terms of the 'new medievalism' – 'a multi-level system of political authorities with micro- and macro-regionalisms and trans-border identities interacting in a more complex political process' (Cox 1992: 179).
4. Shifting, in later Amsterdam scholarship, whose first generation was strongly influenced by Cox, from a state- to a class-centric analysis of trans-national blocs and trans-national hegemony that explores the multi-faceted nature of class rule and resistance. Other studies in this vein include Alan Cafruny and Magnus Ryner's edited collection on embedded neoliberalism in 'Fortress Europe' (2003), which also includes a critique of realist, constructivist and institutionalist positions in studies of European integration (see below).

Our brief survey indicates that Coxians have re-evaluated Gramsci's arguments about 'ideas'/culture and made a more general 'cultural turn'. What is less clear is whether any 'Italian' scholars have taken a radical onto-logical turn that makes culture (semiosis) foundational to their work. This point is central to Owen Worth's criticisms of the Italian School, when he urges IPE scholars to turn to Raymond Williams's cultural materialism and Stuart Hall's cultural studies to enhance IPE understanding of the complexity of hegemony by integrating a 'bottom-up' approach into a rather top-down approach to hegemony in the new world order (Worth 2009; on cultural materialism and cultural studies, see also Chapter 3).

CULTURAL TURNS IN THREE REGULATION SCHOOLS

One aspect of the RA's *thematic* development is a halting engagement with discourse, semiosis and culture. A more ontologically sensitive 'hermeneutic' (Boyer and Labrousse 2008) turn is evident in three trends. First, several schools stress the contribution of new economic and political imaginaries to institutional transformation and innovation in the trial-and-error search process for a new accumulation regime, mode of regulation and societal paradigm. Second, regulation schools have investigated how accumulation regimes *en régulation* depend on the hegemony of particular techno-economic paradigms, norms of production, norms of consumption, state projects, and forms of institutionalized compromise that are expressed in specific 'comprehensive concepts of control' (to use an Amsterdam School term). And, third, some regulationists have explored the profoundly disorienting impact of crises *in* and/or *of* accumulation regimes and their effects on the hegemonic economic and political imaginaries that had become 'common sense' when these regimes seemed relatively stable. Crucial in all cases is the changing articulation and/or disarticulation of the economic and the political forms of modes of regulation (see Chapters 5, 6 and 8). Albeit in ways that vary by school, the RA argues that the institutional separation between the economic and political varies across stages of capitalism as well as accumulation regimes and, rather than emerging quasi-automatically from structural transformations, has to be constructed and, as such, is mediated in and through new economic and political imaginaries.

These are the themes that now occupy us. In exploring them, we identify the reasons, rationalities and restrictions of types of regulationist cultural turns and assess whether and, if so, how they have advanced the interpretation and explanation of accumulation regimes, modes of development, modes of regulation and societal paradigms. Like the institutional turns analysed above, cultural turns can be thematic, methodological, ontological and, perhaps, reflexive. The connotations of cultural turns nonetheless differ from those of institutional turns. For, whereas the latter are located *within* a broader ontological concern for structuration, an ontological cultural turn occurs at the same level of generality as an emphasis on structuration. So the content of Table 2.1 differs from its counterpart in Chapter 1.

The Parisian School

In this School, the cultural turn was, initially, largely thematic or methodological. For example, in examining how an accumulation regime acquires a certain dynamic regularity (in other words, comes to be *'en régulation'*), attention turned to various semiotic dimensions of accumulation, *régulation* and governance. Likewise, in insisting that institutions matter in these and other ways, the RA also accepts that 'institutions are unintelligible without reference to a social dynamics' (Favereau 1997; 2002a: 317).

During the 1980s some Parisian regulationists flirted with the 'economics of "conventions"', that is, the idea that agents must agree on rules and norms in order to interact and to provide normalizing micro-foundations for coordinated, regularized economic behaviour. This approach over-emphasizes consensus and, as the actor-network theorist Michel Callon notes, economic performation (or performativity) is something very different from agreed-upon rules (cf. Dumez and Jeunemaître 2010: 28). Others have emphasized the role of 'representations' (visions, projects etc.) in mediating institutional transformation (Lordon 1997, 1999, 2000a, 2000b, 2002). And, unsurprisingly, especially given the discovery of Gramsci as a 'western Marxist' (sic) in the 1970s and 1980s, there are often usually gestural but recurrent references in Parisian work from the first texts onwards to the *thematic* importance of Gramsci's analysis of the state and his concept of hegemony and their potential contributions as addenda or supplements to the main focus of the Parisian School. This began with the first major contribution (Aglietta 1979).

However, while many Parisian theorists have shown an occasional *thematic* interest in culture (especially in techno-economic paradigms, norms of production and consumption, societal paradigms and institutionalized compromise), they have rarely taken a *methodological* cultural turn, that is, taken semiosis or culture as their entry-point into the analysis of accumulation and regulation. Their primary entry-point remains economic categories and economic crisis tendencies and/or general ideas about institutions and their embedding. Some theorists do refer to notions such as Bourdieu's concept of *habitus* to indicate how the values, norms and routines that might sustain a mode of regulation could be internalized in individual conduct (e.g. Lipietz 1988, 1992, 1994; Goodwin and Painter 1997; Boyer 2004a, 2004b). However, not only are these references gestural; the concept of habitus is inconsistent with the RA's overall thrust (Demirović 1992). In addition, Bourdieu's concept of capital is said to reproduce the assumptions of neoclassical economics (Favereau 2002b). Moving beyond gestures, Parisian scholars make three moves that highlight the semiotic character of fundamental economic categories and could therefore facilitate moves towards CPE.

First, the leading regulationist, Robert Boyer, once argued that the explanation (as opposed to identification) of regularities in accumulation regimes and their modes of regulation is the 'central question', which the works of the Regulation School are only beginning to analyse (Boyer 1990: 27). He later argued that the symbolic (in our terms, semiotic) provides both the overarching framework for macro-social order and a meaningful reference point for actors and their strategic conduct in specific micro-social contexts, each with its localized institutions and rules of the game. This holds even for those market relations that are supposedly most dominated by market rationality, such as financial markets, where trust, belief and confidence are absolutely crucial (Boyer 2004a; cf. Lordon 1999, 2000a, 2000b).

In one attempt to advance this agenda, he tried to bring culture into the RA through his critical reflections on the work of Pierre Bourdieu. While Boyer had previously flirted with the economics of conventions, he later noted the usefulness of Bourdieu on two counts – first because his analysis of habitus offered an alternative to rational-choice theory in interpreting individual action as action situated in particular institutional contexts or, better, specific forms of institutionalized compromise. And, second, and later, Boyer appropriated his compatriot's account of the foundations of institutions and emphasis on the coupling and co-evolution of habitus and field, of strategies and institutional selectivities (2003, 2004a, 2004b). Boyer concludes that Bourdieu shows how important the symbolic is in securing social and institutional coherence across different fields and how severely such coherence is threatened when institutions (including those in the economic field) either lack symbolic legitimation or become disconnected therefrom. Yet, while there are certain commonalities across fields of social action, each with its own type of social capital, the economic field has its own logic, different from the political, educational, artistic or other fields. Thus, while the RA should integrate the symbolic into its analyses of accumulation at all levels from the macro to the micro, it must continue to recognize the specificities of the economic field rather than conflate it with other fields of social action (Boyer 2004a). We fully support this conclusion: it represents an early statement of our later, more elaborated critique of constructivist views that reduce the economic to discourses about the economy.

Another important exception is Frédéric Lordon, who has been seeking an anthropology and ontology suited to the RA and draws these from works of Baruch Spinoza, Pierre Bourdieu and structural Marxists such as Louis Althusser (e.g. Lordon 2010). He aims to overcome the separation between the subjective and objective, the social and the economic, by deploying the Spinozist concept of *conatus*, that is, the innate striving of every entity to survive and perfect itself in the face of any threat to its existence. He links this to the concept of desire and the differential capacities of one agent to enrol others in the realization of its desires. He suggests, for example, that the capitalist enterprise strives to enrol the desires of its workers in the service of capital's desire for endless accumulation. This is reflected in the institutional form of the wage relation. The striving to produce an alignment (*colinéarité*) between dominant and dominated individuals is most marked (reaching its most totalitarian form) in neoliberalism, in which individuals internalize and freely serve capital's desires. Lordon has applied this concept to the rise of finance-led accumulation and the survival of finance after the financial crisis and in the eurozone crisis (e.g. Lordon 2008, 2011). He also criticizes rational-choice models that assume that actors have high cognitive capacities: representations and social action are typically shaped by rather elementary schemes. He describes this as the 'strength of simple ideas' (Lordon 2000b).

Two other exceptions are Bruno Amable and Stefano Palombarini. Partly inspired by Gramsci, these scholars study institutionalized compromises and the formation of dominant social blocs and emphasize that both the dominated and dominated classes engage in ideological thinking (Palombarini 2001; Amable et al. 2012). For these reasons, they are strong critics of the heterogeneous 'economy of conventions'. Crudely put, this current posits economically disinterested actors who are morally disposed to seek solutions to social problems that serve the common good (e.g. Favereau 2002a). In contrast, Amable and Palombarini propose a 'neo-realist' theory of institutions, in which ethics is inseparable from politics and, consequently, actors, their interests, their perceptions and their normative expectations are moulded and mediated by ideologies. It follows that institutional change must be explained through the interaction of interests and ideas mobilized by social groups (Amable and Palombarini 2005). These three theorists (Amable, Guillard and Palombarini) go beyond empirical extension to engage in real theoretical deepening of Parisian work.

Even before considering other schools, such trends undermine the claim by Mark Blyth, a leading constructivist institutionalist, that the RA operates at a high level of abstraction (regimes of accumulation, modes of regulation) and thereby ignores their constructivist dynamics. Blyth suggests that agents' conduct is not simply a function of their institutional position but reflects real scope for adaptation and innovation, especially in moments of crisis and change, which are more random and underdetermining than most situations (2008). This point was already well known in the RA. Blyth's claim is further proof of Robert Boyer's remark that 'English language readers have had access to only a few texts, which were already outdated, on the basis of which they made their critiques, which were often apt, but which did not take into account subsequent developments in research' (2002a: 1).

The Amsterdam School

In the Amsterdam School, partly because of links to the 'Italian School' but mostly because of earlier Dutch scholarship on the rival outlooks of different fractions of capital, sense- and meaning-making figure significantly as a methodological entry-point. Above all, taking class fractions and class alliances as its starting point, it emphasizes the discursive and material construction (through social practices) that creates 'comprehensive concepts of control'. More recently, in the context of debates about institutionalism and constructivism, sense- and meaning-making have become, at least for some adherents, an ontological premise for research and an important point of difference with other approaches to European integration and global political economy (see, e.g., Cafruny and Ryner 2003).

Now described as trans-national historical materialism, this School was inspired by Robert W. Cox (see above) and Dutch work on capital fractions that built on Marx's account of the circuits of capital (Marx 1967b, 1967c). It seeks to historicize Gramsci's concept of hegemony and link the 'decisive economic nucleus' of hegemony to accumulation dynamics in specific periods and varieties of capitalism. Thus Amsterdam scholars study broad political responses to the challenges posed by social contradictions (between classes, between various segments of the bourgeoisie, between domestic and foreign bourgeoisies) and the claims articulated in these responses to represent the 'general interest' (formulated from a particular fractional vantage point) in specific periods and varieties of capitalism (Overbeek 2004: 118).

The reference point for these analyses were two proto-concepts of control, that is, ideal-typical depictions of the 'spontaneous' or self-evident interests of a given fraction of capital and how to secure them in different economic, political and social fields. One such proto-concept is the *liberal concept of control*, which prioritizes the maximum mobility of money as capital and is oriented to exchange-value; the other is the *productivist concept*, which is concerned with the material nature of production and use-values, and reflects the interests of industrial capital. Amsterdam scholars then consider more concrete, historically specific 'comprehensive concepts of control' that unify the ruling class and attract mass support and can become hegemonic in so far as they combine mutually compatible blueprints for handling relations among various fractions of capital and for conducting labour relations (van der Pijl 1984: 31; 1998: 3–8). These relations are hard to handle because they involve various social contradictions (see above) and stability depends on constructing a 'general interest' (formulated from a particular fractional vantage point) transcends narrowly defined fractional interests and, above all, 'combines mutually compatible strategies in the field of labour relations, socio-economic policy and foreign policy on the basis of a class compromise' (Overbeek 1990: 26; 2004: 118; van der Pijl 1998: 4–8; both authors cite Ries Bode (1979), a key Dutch text on class fractions in the interwar period in the Netherlands).

A leading second-generation Amsterdam scholar, Bastiaan van Apeldoorn, has recently restated the School's aims: to develop historical materialism as a 'theory of praxis', giving due weight to consciousness, ideology and culture in the reproduction, restoration and reordering of social formations and to the roles of collective (class) agency in this regard (2004a: 152). He continues:

> to constitute themselves as a class, capitalists somehow have to 'discover' their common interests and construct a shared outlook and identity that transcends the narrow view of their position as individual and competing capitalists. The moment of class agency – or the process of class formation – is thus always a political process in which capitalists transcend the logic of market competition and reach a temporary unity of strategic orientation and purpose, enabling them to articulate (vis-à-vis other social classes or groups, as well as vis-à-vis the state) a 'general capitalist interest'. (Ibid.: 155)

For example, the *corporate liberal concept*, which helped to organize Atlantic Fordism after the New Deal, involved a creative synthesis of liberal and state monopoly productivist concepts (van der Pijl 1984; Overbeek 1990). In contrast, *embedded neoliberalism* is a synthesis based on the money concept of control in a trans-national framework that seeks to limit the destabilizing effects of unregulated markets (e.g. Ryner 2002). In this connection, van Apeldoorn has studied the role of the European Roundtable of Industrialists as an organic intellectual actively engaged in reorganizing the interests of trans-national capital in a changing European Union and world market and, in particular, as an active promoter of embedded neoliberalism on a European scale (van Apeldoorn 2002, 2004b). It is worth noting that more recent Amsterdam work seems to have abandoned the idea of proto-concepts of control and often replaces 'comprehensive concepts of control' with the more common notion of hegemonic projects (e.g. van Apeldoorn 2009: 22). This brings it into line with more general neo-Gramscian scholarship.

The German Regulation Approach

The German RA attributes a key role to the state, hegemonic apparatuses (such as parties and labour unions) and hegemony in the regularization of capital accumulation (e.g. Hirsch 1998; Buckel and Fischer-Lescano 2007; Buckel et al. 2012). The School emerged from the heady but abstract debates in West Germany on the capitalist state. These were provoked by post-war reconstruction and the unexpected German economic miracle and, more generally, the apparent ability of post-war states in advanced capitalism to abolish economic cycles (cf. Shonfield 1965). The School has affiliates in Austria, Switzerland and the Netherlands. One development was a turn from a concern with the basic form and functions of the capitalist state in regulating Fordism and post-Fordism at a national level (notably in Germany) to a more neo-Gramscian and/or neo-Poulantzasian emphasis on accumulation strategies, state projects, hegemonic visions and, more recently, ecological imaginaries as crucial factors in shaping nature–capital relations, accumulation regimes, modes of regulation and societal organization (see the collection by Demirović et al. 1992; Brand and Görg 2008; Wissel 2007; Ziltener 2001).

FIVE MORE RADICAL CULTURAL TURNS

Far less often and mostly outside the main regulationist schools, there have been several *ruptural theoretical redefinitions* of older themes that undermine (or radically transform) hitherto unquestioned assumptions, concepts and arguments. This is where an ontological cultural turn could contribute significantly to fourth-generation regulationism as part of the more general movement towards CPE. However, as we show below, many of these attempts at ruptural redefinitions have not borne fruit – because scholars were always on the margins of the RA, ceased to work within or identify with it, or because their interest in the cultural turn was a simple thematic or methodological variation without long-term consequences for making an ontological breakthrough in the approach. Considering these different factors would be a fascinating reflexive exercise in the CPE of CPE but would, unfortunately, represent a diversion from our primary objective in exploring these issues.

We now present five examples of more or less radical cultural turns in regulationist work in the 1990s and 2000s to illustrate the growing interest in semiosis and culture. The examples are: (1) Alain Lipietz, originally a structural Marxist and one of the three main founders of the Parisian School; (2) the Canadian feminist scholar Jane Jenson, who worked for a time along regulationist lines before turning to the study of citizenship regimes; (3) Christoph Scherrer, a German scholar who advocated a discourse-analytical turn as a necessary supplement in the West German approach; (4) Alex Demirović, a German critical theorist who has undertaken detailed archival work to explore the role of organic intellectuals in securing hegemony; and (5) Mario Candeias, a transdisciplinary neo-Gramscian who uses Gramscian concepts to study the rise of neoliberalism and its implications for political, intellectual and moral hegemony. This is neither a representative nor a random selection of the many interesting individual contributions to the RA. Other cases are George Steinmetz's interest in specific forms of identity formation and subject formation, and correlative extension of the RA to include non-class movements and forces (1994), work on the overdetermination of the wage relation and other aspects of regulation by gender, race and ethnicity (e.g. Diettrech 1999; Kohlmorgen 2004; Naumann 2000, 2003); and the CPE of care work in post-Fordism written from the perspective of an intersectionalist variant of the RA that has extended the set of structural or institutional forms to include the form of the 'care economy' (Chorus 2012). Other scholars might have been included, but these illustrate a wide range of approaches.

Alain Lipietz

Lipietz located his early regulationist work in Marx's methods of research and presentation. He identified a 'double movement' in Marx's critique of political economy. He not only moved from the abstract to the concrete to analyse the natural necessities (laws, tendencies) that emerged from the internal articulation of objective social relations, but also moved from the 'esoteric' to the 'exoteric' to analyse the connections between these objective relations and the fetishized world of lived experience, and the impact that this enchanted world has on the overall movement of capital (Lipietz 1986: 11–12; cf. Marx 1967a: 46–59, 76–87; 1967b: 133; 1967c: 388–97, 823–6). According to Lipietz, this exoteric, enchanted world comprises all those representations created by economic agents regarding their own behaviour and the circumstances they face. Even though their conduct and circumstances are rooted in the esoteric world, which operated 'behind their backs', people live their lives through these representations. Ignoring these external forms and their social effects would prevent any significant understanding of a large part of reality (1986: 12–13). For Lipietz, the key category for deciphering the enchanted world of lived experience is 'fetishism', with particular forms of fetishism associated with each of the three main contradictory relations in capitalism – capital–labour, capital–capital, capital–nature – as well as a number of secondary forms (ibid.: 18–31, 45–52). He also argues that crisis is rooted as much in the exoteric as in the esoteric world and, *a fortiori*, cannot be explained purely in terms of capital's hidden laws of motion. For example, different connections between the esoteric world of values and the exoteric world of prices obtain in the competitive and monopoly modes of regulation, and this entails different forms of crisis. Stagflation is inconceivable in the former, but is a characteristic feature of the latter (ibid.: 102–3). And this shapes the forms of lived experience, the stakes in economic and political struggle, and the search for alternative economic strategies.

Jane Jenson

This influential Canadian scholar sought to extend regulationism to include discourse theory as well as structure–agency dialectics (1989; 1990a; 1990b; 1995). Her critical commentaries on the Parisian approach mark a move towards CPE proper (as opposed to a partial integration of some cultural concepts into an otherwise unchanged regulation approach). She calls for analyses of 'the historically developed sets of practices *and meanings* that provide the actual regulatory mechanisms for a specific mode of growth and broader "societal paradigms" that govern a wide range of social relations beyond the realm of production' (Jenson 1990a: 60). Emphasizing the scope for agents to make a difference, she presents accumulation regimes and modes of regulation in terms of scripts that individuals and social forces can interpret and modify. Using this theatrical metaphor, Jenson emphasizes that economic crises involve more than a final encounter with pre-given structural limits. They are actually manifested and resolved in an interdiscursive field in which social forces assert their identities and interests. Newly visible and active forces emerge in a crisis and participate in the expanding universe of political discourse; these forces offer alternative modes of regulation and societal paradigms, and engage in struggles to institutionalize a new compromise. If a new 'model of development' does become hegemonic, it establishes new rules for recognizing actors and defining interests (1990b: 666). Jenson's analysis highlighted how objects of regulation are in part discursively constituted by showing how the entry of new social subjects into the context of economic crisis can lead to the rise of new economic paradigms.

Christoph Scherrer

Strongly critical of the structuralist bias in West German regulationism, Scherrer argued that this could be overcome by introducing discourse analysis to deconstruct the ruling ideas of a given accumulation regime (1995). He alleges that the West German school takes the dominance and hegemony of the capital relation for granted and thereby focuses on their structural forms, structural contradictions and structurally grounded crisis tendencies. This limits the role of social agency to the short – overdetermined but open – periods of transition before a new accumulation regime and its mode of regulation are structurally consolidated. In other words, the West German School privileges periods of stability and considers the ruptures between them as parentheses between stable periods. This is a standard criticism of regulationism more generally. Scherrer's particular response was to argue, correctly in our opinion, that: (1) structures were never complete and closed totalities; (2) the contradictions between the social nature of the relations of production and private ownership could have no meaning (and hence provide no grounds for action) outside the prevailing 'politics of production'; and (3) crises in social relations had no meaning unless they undermined normative expectations about social fairness.

He then claimed that structural determinism could be overcome through an anti-essentialist discourse analysis that allows for contingency in social practices and analyses structural coherence as the product of hegemonic articulation (1995: 467–73). Drawing on the post-Marxist discourse analysis of Laclau and Mouffe (1985), which we critique in Chapters 3 and 4, Scherrer argued that hegemony rests on sedimented practices that have become taken for granted but are always liable to dislocation. In the latter case, subjects are forced to adopt new identities and translate them into new structures of action. In developing a new 'imaginary', these subjects can give new meanings to inherited structures and may seek to replace them. But this cannot occur where sedimented structures have not been dislocated and have thereby created opportunities for rearticulation – a claim that rules out a purely voluntarist account of economic restructuring (Scherrer 1995: 478f).

Scherrer drew five main conclusions from his discourse-analytical turn. First, the RA should abandon the idea of a self-reproducing capitalism and focus on how hegemonic articulatory practices secure the always-precarious dominance of the capitalist form of societalization. Second, '[a]ssuming that the essential capitalist societalization modes are fixed in relatively stable ways through hegemonic practices, form analysis can be adapted to understand certain functional connections and/or incompatibilities [within a given accumulation regime and its mode of regulation]' (1995: 479, our translation). Third, given the West German RA's special concern with the state's role in regularizing accumulation, it should examine how the state helps to establish a hegemonic structure that corresponds to the dominant accumulation regime (ibid.). Fourth, the RA should abandon the idea of a fixed succession of time-limited accumulation regimes mediated through the predetermined unfolding of contradictions that culminate in terminal crises. It should accept that accumulation regimes are not closed totalities but are always partial, incomplete and vulnerable to dislocation. Thus individuals have wide scope to act as the subjects of social reproduction and/or transformation such that '[t]he development of an accumulation regime is all the time implicitly open' (1995: 480, our translation). Nonetheless, fifth, in so far as individuals remain embedded in structures, crises can never be fully open situations. Thus both the reproduction of a given accumulation regime and the outcome of its crises depend on the reciprocal subversion of contingency and necessity as these are established in and through discursive practices (ibid.).

Alex Demirović

Drawing on the critical theory tradition of the Frankfurt School (with its interests in culture) and Gramsci's analyses of hegemony and organic intellectuals, Demirović argued that the concept of 'hegemony' is a central weakness in regulationist analyses of Fordism. He proposed that economic forms and their associated modes of life (*Lebensweise*) should be seen as collective practices that result from social compromises achieved in large part through the 'knowledge practices' (*Wissenspraktiken*) of intellectual groups (1992). Indeed, in so far as the concept of hegemony remains vague and underspecified, so will the theoretical connections that can be made among economic processes, social struggles, compromise-building, and their institutionalization. In contrast to the abstract logic of capitalist reproduction analysed at the level of general laws of motion, the historical specificity of accumulation regimes *en régulation* depends on the stability of social compromises that organize the regularities of social relations among social classes, groups and individuals in specific forms of institutionalized compromises. Drawing on Lipietz (1984, 1987), Demirović suggests that it is

> an embodiment of the system of accumulation in the form of norms, habits, laws, regulating networks, that ensures – by establishing routines in the behaviour of agents struggling against each other (in the economic struggles between capital and wage-labour and in the competition between capitals) – the cohesion of the process and an approximate conformity with the reproduction schema. (Demirović 1992: 137)

In other words, an emerging, socially constructed totality of norms and procedures attunes individuals' expectations and modes of conduct to the socially dominant production and consumption pattern. Concrete social relations among actors are appropriated and incorporated, and constituted as a society that is recognized, experienced and lived practically by individual actors. As one illustration of this project, we can cite Demirović's mammoth study (1999) of the first-generation Frankfurt School critical theorists in the quasi-public as well as public struggle to reconstruct the German university system as a potential home for non-conformist intellectuals. This is a small part of a much larger story about the challenges of post-war reconstruction in Western Germany and illustrates the importance of wars of position inside organizations and institutions as well as in the public sphere.

Mario Candeias

This scholar has developed an approach to regulation based on the motto '*mit Marx und Gramsci*' (with Marx and Gramsci). His analysis of neoliberalism starts from the argument that, if we treat hegemony as something accomplished, the hegemonic struggle over the nature and direction of change tends to get neglected (Candeias 2005; cf. Borg 2001: 69). He therefore recommends refocusing attention on hegemony as both 'the object of contestation and the medium of struggle' (Haug 1985: 174) in order to analyse the form in which a new capitalist societalization is actually realized. In this respect it is necessary to avoid essentialist or structuralist reductions of new elements to the practical imperatives of capital valorization, as well as the intentionalist or voluntarist short-circuiting of arguments that derive simply from the identification of political-economic actors and their strategies. Instead it is necessary to put the transformation of the political and broader societal balance of forces into a dialectical relation with the transformation of politico-economic structures (Candeias 2005: 10). Gramsci is important here because he does not aim at peaceful resolution of existing contradictions but seeks instead to develop the very theory of these contradictions, focusing on their changing forms and attempts to address them (ibid.: 12–14, citing Gramsci 1995; Q10II, §41xii: 1320; cf. 1995: 395). To do this requires moving beyond the opposition between base and superstructure, privileging one or other moment (as, he alleges, the Parisian Regulation School and Frankfurt critical theory do respectively), to explore how contradictions condition forms of action and limit resolution (Candeias 2005: 18–19).

In more recent work, Candeias has extended this analysis to include the organic crisis of neoliberalism. He seeks to explore this through the use of Gramsci's richly complex analyses of crisis dynamics and to relate this to the role of political parties and social movements, and the challenges that this poses for developing alternative economic strategies, political projects suited to a 'mosaic left', and a hegemonic project that can address environmental issues. Still drawing heavily on Gramsci's *Prison Notebooks*, he writes:

> The ruling power bloc has no productive solutions to offer in the face of rising manifestations of the crisis – solutions that could induce a boost of accumulation, while at the same time incorporating the interests of the subaltern segments, and thus succeed in once again creating an active consensus in favour of the neoliberal project. Neoliberalism is exhausted – yet, its institutions will continue to have a severe impact for a long time – similar to the end of Fordism, their position still dominant, but not hegemonic in the sense of organizing active consent (Gramsci, Q2: 354).[5] The 'molecular aggregation of elements'

may 'cause an "explosion"' (Q9: 2063), or lead to the disintegration of the hegemonic bloc and ultimately to the transformation of the mode of production and the mode of living. This would be a long and highly competitive process, full of struggle . . . The disintegration of the transnational historical bloc has begun. A lack of alternatives and a 'bizarre' everyday consciousness maintain a passive consensus. While the neoliberal ideology is discredited among major segments of the population, these subjects have inscribed this ideology deeply into their patterns of action and into their habits. Many openly support positions critical of capitalism, or even in favour of 'socialism'. At the same time, they consider them unrealistic, since they are not connected to any real perspective for political power, or even to any expansion of their own capacity to act (*Handlungsfähigkeit*). (Candeias 2011: 10)

Candeias elaborates these ideas to interpret and explain the surprising passivity of subaltern groups in the global financial crisis, indicating how hard it is to break with habits ingrained in the body as well as in the mind, and how the ruling bloc has lost its hegemonic capacities but continues to rule. Various crisis-management and exit strategies are being tried at the same time. What is important in such analyses is the careful interweaving of Gramscian concepts for the analysis of hegemony (and its limits) with structural and conjunctural economic and political analyses in which both aspects have an equal role. Different steps in the analysis then highlight one or other of these interdependent moments. Candeias also relates these analyses to questions of agency, subjectivity, despair and hope. These are key elements of a CPE analysis.

CONCLUDING REMARKS

There are many examples in regulationist schools and individual scholarship of thematic cultural turns (as part of the incremental extension of the approach) or, more radically, of one or another discursive turn as a methodological entry-point into the study of techno-economic paradigms, accumulation regimes, modes of regulation, modes of growth and societal paradigms. This step is fairly obvious because these (and several similar) key regulationist concepts have both a structural and a strategic moment. Indeed it is a core assumption of RA analyses that modes of regulation cannot be adequately interpreted and explained if they are understood as emerging teleologically in order to ensure regulation or, in a weaker version of functionalism, as *ex post* functional solutions to the problem of how to regulate a pre-given object of regulation (for an interesting discussion, see Lipietz 1987).

However, regulationists have not followed through consistently on the ontological cultural turn, which is an obvious route for conceptual deepening and radical, ruptural redefinition. This could be partly explained by the fact that the scholars who took the most radical ontological turns belong to one or more of three partly overlapping groups. They (1) were always on the margins of the regulation approach; (2) ceased to work within or identify with it; and/or (3) failed to consolidate proposals for a potential ontological turn. We could add that many regulation theorists are economists and prone to the economist's temptation to explain economic events and processes in economic terms. But this does not explain the failure of regulation theorists with backgrounds in political science, political economy or international political economy to make the break. This suggests more fundamental reasons. Three worth testing are: (1) some regulation scholars take a multi- or inter-disciplinary attitude towards RA research and consign work on semiosis to specialists and/or draw concepts from relevant fields in an *ad hoc*, eclectic fashion for particular purposes – making it hard to develop cumulative conceptual gains; (2) interest in semiosis is stronger during periods of crisis and transition – and the 1990s and early 2000s appear to have been years of great moderation in the heartlands of Atlantic Fordism; and (3) a serious engagement with semiosis requires a conceptual framework that is well developed, with depth and breadth, and has a clear understanding not only of the exoteric, surface features of the semiotic world but also of the underlying mechanisms that are involved in the variation, selection and retention of particular economic and political imaginaries. Whatever the merits of these speculations, it would certainly be worthwhile to explore the third explanation. However, this is not our task in this volume.

Of more interest is the regulationist argument that objects of regulation do not fully pre-exist their regulation but are partly constituted by the attempts to regulate them. More precisely, while important elements of a potential object of regulation pre-exist attempts to regularize and/or govern it, their articulation into a relatively stable object of regulation depends on how these elements are combined through trial-and-error to form specific moments of such an emergent, contingent object. Where this process of problematization leads to the selection and retention of these objects of *régulation*-cum-governance, they transform the circuits of capital and bring them into an always-partial, improvised, temporary and premature 'harmony' based on an unstable equilibrium of compromise (see Jessop and Sum 2006: 313–16). One cannot understand the mechanisms in and through which this improbable achievement is secured without including the semiotic aspects of strategy formulation and their relation to alternative and competing economic and political imaginaries. This involves examining more closely the resources that might be available in critical semiotic analysis for productive integration into critical political economy. This is the task of the next chapter.

NOTES

1. Bartoli developed neo-linguistics in response to the German neo-grammarian approach, which focused on idiolects, phonological surface phenomena (sounds) at the level of words, and focused on historical rather than contemporary languages.
2. Two important exceptions are the Gramsci scholar Derek Boothman (1991), and the political economist Michael Krätke (2011).
3. Some Italian School theorists equate power bloc, historical bloc and the social bases of stable orders of production and political power – we distinguish them to identify the three key themes that the 'School' derives from Gramsci.
4. Gramsci was no methodological nationalist – he was a pioneering theorist of scale and interscalar relations, and made many interesting comments on international political economy (Jessop 2005b, 2007b).
5. We follow the usual convention here of citing the Notebook (*Quaderno*) plus section and page numbers. The annotated English-language translation is not yet complete.

3. Semiotics for cultural political economy

This chapter switches entry-point to evaluate the potential of semiotic analysis in developing the CPE agenda. It addresses two questions. First, how can we ground the cultural turn in political economy ontologically in sense- and meaning-making? This matters because we criticized other work on cultural aspects of political economy for (1) being limited to a thematic cultural turn; (2) adopting discourse-analytical methods in an *ad hoc* way regardless of their consistency with other features of the theoretical approach or the substantive analysis in question; or (3) having an underdeveloped set of concepts to explore sense- and meaning-making and their effects. The last problem is especially challenging. For, where semiosis is undertheorized relative to structuration, analyses may be asymmetrical, unless the analysis of structuration is also diluted. This can lead to overemphasis on a few simple semiotic concepts, to the marginalization of semiotic factors because of descriptive and explanatory overkill from structural analysis – with semiotic factors sometimes being residual (and also) elements in an explanation – or to semiotic factors becoming exogenous variables that merely supplement the structural analysis.

The second question is how evolutionary approaches in semiotic analysis can help understand the variation, selection and retention of specific attempts at complexity reduction through semiosis (e.g. through social imaginaries). This matters because an evolutionary turn in semiotic analysis is one of CPE's six defining features and so it behoves us to suggest how these evolutionary mechanisms can be studied consistently with our overall approach. This will strengthen our account in so far as we can integrate historical semantics (broadly defined) not only with structural selectivities but also with the technological and agential selectivities that also bear on linguistic and/or semiotic evolution. These two other forms apply to semiosis and structuration (and to each other) just as the structural and discursive (or semiotic) selectivities operate in shaping technological and agential selectivity (see Chapter 5).

In seeking answers, we draw mostly on semiological and linguistic analyses of semantics and pragmatics. Semantics examines the relation of signs to what they denote; and pragmatics studies the relation of signs to their users and interpreters (Horn and Ward 2004).[1] We cannot review all relevant approaches and will focus on those that address textual material. We therefore ignore other sign systems as well as the production of inter-subjective meaning-making that occurs by mixing modes of representation (visual, musical, verbal, textual etc.). An extended review should consider other sign systems and multi-modal communication. Failure to integrate these topics is currently a source of 'underspecification' (Spitzmüller and Warnke 2011), that is, of failure to exploit the full heuristic and analytical potential of semiological analysis in terms of methods and data. This must be remedied sooner rather than later. Given the wide variation in vocabulary, we present these theories largely in their own terms rather than translating them (and losing something in translation) into the schema to be introduced in Chapter 4. We also focus on their distinctive ontological, epistemological and methodological assumptions, concepts and analytical strategies rather than illustrating how they are applied.

SOME CONCEPTS FOR CRITICAL SEMIOTIC ANALYSIS

Consistent with our opening remarks, we work with three main levels of analysis: semantics, social practices and discourse. In the present context, and consistent with the general definition, semantics denotes historically specific macro-discursive vocabularies that frame social practices across significant periods of time and many sites of social practice. These operate at a similar level to the social forms explored in the analysis of structuration. Social practices are meaningful practices that have both discursive aspects (which can be analysed as discursive practices) and specific, substantive practical ('material') aspects that differentiate, say, the legal field from the religious or scientific field. Where the focus is on the substantive rather than discursive aspect (even though the latter is always present), these can be referred to as, say, legal, religious or scientific practice respectively. Discourse refers to practices of sense- and meaning-making at the level of linguistic as well as semantic meaning. This is the field *par excellence* for core linguistic methods but its comprehension also demands socio-linguistic and contextual analysis.

In short, while recognizing the risks of linguistic reductionism, we focus on the semantics and pragmatics of textual practices. Of interest here would be texts, their paratextual (surrounding) features, supra-texts, intertext, and context (agential, conjunctural, and socio-historical). This said, our case studies address intertextuality and supratextual units rather than texts. Intertextuality refers to the relation among texts (especially through reference to and reception of past texts) and supratextual units are bigger analytical units that have been variously described/defined as genres, discourses, forms of discourse, forms of thought (*Denkformen*), semantic fields, imaginaries and ideologies. A related concept is interdiscursivity, which refers to the interweaving and articulation of different themes, genres or fields of discourse (e.g. economics, law, politics and religion). Lastly, CPE is also concerned with non-text, that is, with different kinds of context. These range from immediate interaction contexts to broad societal contexts and always have specific spatio-temporal as well as socio-cultural and material features (see Chapter 1). Subject to these qualifications, we now comment on some wide-ranging attempts to integrate semiosis and/or culture into social analysis, including different approaches to historical semantics (broadly defined) and critical discourse analysis.[2]

In selecting approaches to language, discourse or semiosis we check whether they are commensurable with critical realism, the SRA approach and an evolutionary perspective. These criteria are important if CPE is to avoid a chaotic bricolage of methods without regard to their overall consistency with its basic premises. Thus we exclude forms of semiotic analysis that are:

1. universalist and/or trans-historical in character, seeking to develop universal laws of language and language use;
2. structuralist in their denial of authorship, agency or subjectivity;
3. methodologically individualist in their explanation of language development; and
4. reductionist in seeking to reduce the world to language or semiosis.

While these criteria provide grounds for *excluding* some approaches from the purview of CPE, we aim to *include* work that explores how selection, retention, recontextualization and restabilization of 'texts', 'intertexts', 'supratexts' and interdiscursivity operate in broader contexts. Moreover, because diachrony is more important than synchrony for our concerns, we are more interested in schools and currents that privilege the former without neglecting the latter.

GENERAL THEORY VERSUS GRAND THEORIES OF SEMIOSIS

These themes are addressed in several 'grand theories'. This term does not denote here the kind of abstract systematic general theory that seeks to integrate and explain everything about humankind and society in a universal, trans-historical manner via the logical unfolding of concepts – the sense in which C. Wright Mills (1959) criticized the structural-functionalism that dominated American sociology in the 1950s. Efforts to construct such a general theory do not fit CPE's meta-theoretical premises (see Introduction). Nor do we fully endorse, to quote W.G. Runciman, that, '[i]f not frankly pejorative, the term [grand theory] is at best ironic, implying a loftiness of tone, an inflation of aim, and a pretentiousness of content which no serious academic author could possibly want to be charged with' (1985: 18). In exploring some grand theories and proposing our own approach, we aim to avoid giving such an impression.

Rather, we use the notion of grand theories diacritically, that is, to establish both a negative and a positive heuristic. On the one hand, our usage rejects aspirations to develop a unified, trans-historical 'natural-science' model of explanation and also disavows the fetishism of fact-gathering as the royal road to cumulative scientific development. On the other hand, our usage is associated with a positive heuristic. For us, grand theories aim to develop:

1. a preliminary set of basic and sensitizing concepts and positive guidelines (that is, not a closed system) that are
2. relevant to historical description, hermeneutic interpretation and causal explanation;
3. scalable, that is, applicable to different scales of analysis without seeking to unify the micro-, meso- and macro-levels (however defined) within a single system, whether this attempt is made through upward or downward reduction that ignores emergent properties or through a simple conflation that denies the specificity of different 'levels'; and
4. recognize the importance of evolutionary mechanisms and contingent effects without assuming they are always progressive and/or irreversible.

Our meta-theoretical approach affirms the legitimacy of competing grand theories and, indeed, encourages combining at least some of them in a playful spirit during research discovery phases and more systematically and consistently when presenting results. This is an important part of the spiral process of research. This is possible because such grand theories (1) typically offer alternative entry-points into describing, making sense of and seeking to explain the dynamics of social order; but (2) do not seek to explain social order as a closed totality but simply provide the tools for understanding past and present attempts at totalization and their limits.

The political theorist Quentin Skinner introduced an essay collection on *The Return of Grand Theory in the Human Sciences* (in the 1970s and

1980s) by noting that grand theorists refuse to treat the human sciences like natural sciences. They favour a hermeneutic approach that 'will do justice to the claim that the explanation of human action must always include – and perhaps even take the form of – an attempt to recover and interpret the meanings of social actions from the point of view of the agents performing them' (1985: 6). The theorists considered in the collection shared

> a willingness to emphasise the importance of the local and the contingent, a desire to underline the extent to which our own concepts and attitudes have been shaped by particular historical circumstance, and a correspondingly strong dislike – amounting almost to hatred in the case of Wittgenstein – of all overarching theories and singular schemes of explanation. (Ibid.: 12)

Yet these iconoclasts, almost in spite of themselves, have made major contributions on a grand scale across many disciplines. This is why they are similar to the grand theories of the past. They also operate in a pre-disciplinary spirit, destabilize disciplinary boundaries and have major implications for the conduct of trans-disciplinary work. Furthermore, provided that they operate with critical-realist, strategic-relational assumptions, they can also be combined, following appropriate conceptual labours, to produce more comprehensive analyses – especially when they are sensitive, as our CPE approach requires, to both semiosis and structuration.

Several grand theories are relevant to the overall CPE project. Three that we find useful for the study of semiosis and structuration are: vernacular materialism, historical semantics, and Foucauldian archaeology and genealogy.

- Vernacular materialism is adumbrated in Ives's account of Antonio Gramsci's distinctive version of historical materialism, based on his studies in historical linguistics and its relevance to understanding everyday life, hegemony and patterns of social domination. Moreover, in contrast to historical semantics (see below), it also emphasizes structural contradictions, social antagonisms and unstable equilibria of compromise (Ives 2004a).
- Historical semantics is interpreted broadly here to refer to a 'grand theory' developed by the German semantic conceptual history school and, even more significantly, by Niklas Luhmann and his followers, in order to study the co-evolution of semantics and social structure (see Koselleck 1981; Luhmann 1980, 2008; Richter 1990). It also finds parallels and echoes in other work in historical linguistics and historical genre analysis, which includes the evolution of scientific, professional, commercial and corporate genres.

- Foucault's archaeology of discourse and discursive formations, covering the 'general system of the formation and transformation of statements' (1972: 130), has implications for construal and construction, veridiction and truth regimes, power–knowledge relations, and the writing of 'critical and effective histories' (1970, 1972, 1977, 1979, 1980). It becomes even more powerful when combined with his work on dispositives (1977, 1979, 2008a, 2008b).

These approaches are interesting because they focus, respectively, on the linguistically mediated meaningfulness of everyday life and its implications for the critique of ideology and domination; on the evolutionary mechanisms that lead to the co-constitution of basic concepts and semantics, and the transformation of social structures from the viewpoint of the *longue durée* and periods of transition; and on the history of discursive formations and their role in constituting objects and subjects of governmentality and shaping discursive selectivities and semantic fields, and their link to dispositives. Albeit rather differently, then, they treat language/semantics/discourse as historically instituted, relational phenomena that change (but not in a symmetrical, one-to-one manner) with structural changes and, more importantly, they treat them as phenomena that interact with and may co-determine structural change.

We introduce these approaches below and identify their strengths and weaknesses for the CPE project. They do not exist in neatly pre-packaged, clearly bounded, mutually exclusive theoretical and methodological bundles, however; therefore we also comment on other accounts that overlap them, are often confused with them, or can be used to supplement them. This explains the order of presentation below.

In addition to these 'grand theories', which can help to shape broad-brush analyses with wide-ranging spatio-temporal implications, we will also draw on more tightly focused approaches and their associated analytical methods. The most important of these is critical discourse analysis (hereafter CDA) and similar analytical heuristics. These paradigms not only offer a set of methodological guidelines and useful techniques to explore text–intertext–context relations but also, to quote van Dijk (2013), reflect a critical 'attitude of mind'. Indeed, given our interest in the critique of ideology and domination, this makes CDA especially attractive. Scholars in this relatively new tradition have developed their analytical toolkit with a view to critique rather than simple technical-cum-instrumental analysis. This does not obviate the need for rigorous application of discourse-analytical methods, but we take cautious comfort from the honing of this toolkit by scholars who want to link texts to context and to consider their social reception and societal effects.

THREE GRAND THEORETICAL APPROACHES

This section introduces the three 'grand theoretical' approaches that we believe, on the basis of a selective acquaintance with the field, offer useful *ontological* foundations for the study of semiosis and, on this basis, provide useful analytics (heuristics, methodologies and methods) to investigate sense- and meaning-making. Flirting for the moment with Foucauldian and Luhmannian language, we might describe these approaches as 'objectivated' or 'marked' fields.[3] We have constituted them as 'objects' for discussion here by drawing a distinction within a more complex field of semiotic and/or discursive inquiries, and this does rough justice to many other schools, scholars and texts. We selected these approaches because they are relevant to the CPE agenda. This section presents the three to facilitate an understanding of their importance and interrelations. In the next section we present some other approaches relevant to this aspect of our CPE project.

Vernacular Materialism

This term was introduced by Peter Ives (2004a) to denote the approach developed by Gramsci to overcome the errors of idealist and positivist approaches to language. It combines 'the tenets of a historical materialist approach to language and a linguistically concerned theory of politics and society' (Ives 2004a: 3). This term is a deliberate play on words with four aims: (1) to oppose vernacular to vulgar materialism; (2) to establish the dialectical character of Gramsci's work, with its emphasis on the organic relation between language and social structures; (3) to identify Gramsci's concern to develop a political programme that would 'popularize' culture rather than impose the culture of the dominant class from above or force the development of a national – or international – culture through the teaching of an artificial language, such as Esperanto; and (4) to contribute to the historical materialist analysis of society (Ives 2004a: 4; Ives in de B'Béri 2008: 328–9).

Vernacular materialism introduces power relations into language use and also posits that language is central to social life and domination. It distinguishes the linguistic and extra-linguistic[4] but treats them as interdependent and co-evolving. Indeed, they co-participate in meaning-making. Building on a seminal study of *Language, Intellectuals, and Hegemony in Gramsci* (Lo Piparo 1979), Ives demonstrates how Gramsci's account of hegemony is rooted, at least intellectually, in his understanding of the relations between spontaneous grammars learnt as part of natural language use and the normative grammar used to regulate speech in more formal ways and associated with official domination and social exclusion. A hegemonic cultural formation emerges through the molecular translation of diverse, immanent communicative practices into a coherent and (relatively) unified grammatical structure. Gramsci sees language as 'culture and philosophy [that] is very much a substantial part of social reality' (Ives 2004a: 13).

Gramsci's linguistics professor, Matteo Bartoli, developed a 'spatial' analysis of language that sought to trace 'how a dominant speech community exerted prestige over contiguous, subordinate communities: the city over the surrounding countryside, the "standard" language over the dialect, the dominant socio-cultural group over the subordinate one' (Forgacs and Nowell-Smith 1985: 164). He also charted the continuing flow of *innovations* from the prestigious *langue* to the receiving one, such that 'earlier linguistic forms would be found in a peripheral rather than central area, an isolated rather than an accessible area, a larger rather than a smaller area' (Brandist 1996a: 94–5; see also Albrecht 1996). Gramsci inflected Bartoli's analysis in a materialist direction and explored its practical implications. He saw the problem of revolution as tied to the unification of the people – something that had to pass through the medium of language if a coherent 'collective will' is to emerge that could unify different classes, strata and groups (cf. Helsloot 1989: 561). The resulting complexities are evident from Gramsci's analyses of how language use is stratified (e.g. how country folk ape urban manners, how subaltern groups imitate the upper classes, how peasants speak when they move to the cities etc.) (Gramsci 1985: 180–81; Q29, §2: 2342–3). In short, there is a strong sense of spatiality in Gramsci's work on language as a medium of hegemony (Lo Piparo 1979) – an issue we explored in relation to the 'Italian School' in critical international political economy in Chapter 2.

Using the historical linguistic approach that he developed at Turin University, Gramsci showed that the main error of every mechanical materialism/realism/positivism was to contend that reality can exist apart from human beings (Selenu 2009: 350). In the *Appunti di glottologia*[5] ['Notes on Historical Linguistics'] (1912–13, vol. 1: 9), co-authored with Bartoli, Gramsci praised the German-language historical linguistics movement that published a series on *Wörter und Sachen* [Words and Things] for paying attention to the co-development across time and space of words and artefacts (what nowadays would be called material culture). He nonetheless rejected this approach for its tendency to focus on things at the expense of their relation to linguistic forms and, in addition, the co-evolution of words and things (Selenu 2008). Peter Ives elaborates on these points as follows:

Gramsci displaces the debate about whether language belongs to the base or the superstructure, whether it is purely determined by material conditions or in fact determines those conditions. For Gramsci, language is material, albeit historically material . . . [L]anguage is rooted in the materiality of the production of words. And the structures within which words are produced are not based on an extra-historical (or 'human') essence, and the same is true of the production of words themselves. (Ives 2004a: 34)

Like Gramsci's cultural and political writings, especially the *Prison Notebooks*, the work of Mikhail M. Bakhtin (1895–1975), a Russian philosopher, literary critic and semiotician, was rediscovered in the 1960s. It also has interesting parallels with Gramsci's studies. Indeed, Bakhtin's work in his middle period (on its phases, see Gardiner 1992) and the work of the Bakhtin Circle provides a different, but complementary, approach to vernacular materialism. The Circle aimed to develop a materialist account of language and symbolic forms that can be juxtaposed to 'abstract subjectivism' (e.g. Saussurean structural linguistics) and 'individualistic subjectivism' (e.g. idealistic hermeneutics oriented to individual creativity) (cf. Vološinov 1973: 48–54). Focusing on language as a symbolic medium through which social relations are constituted, Bakhtin regarded language as a 'material' (i.e. potentially transformative causal force) rather than as a purely epiphenomenal effect of the economic base. Indeed, as another member of the Circle, Valentin N. Vološinov, noted in 1929: 'the very foundations of a Marxist theory of ideologies – the bases for the studies of scientific knowledge, literature, religion, ethics, and so forth – are closely bound up with the problem of the philosophy of language' (1973: 9).

Rather than interpreting ideology as a form of 'false consciousness', a distorted representation of the real, or a coherent 'belief system', Bakhtin studies ideology in linguistic and semiotic terms as a signifying practice that is produced in particular contexts, shaped by broader societal contexts and antagonisms, and sufficiently open-textured to allow for interference, dialogue and contestation (Gardiner 1992: 7). Among other issues, Bakhtin studied speech genres, that is, relatively stable types of utterance (with respect to content, linguistic style and compositional structure) that correspond to particular kinds of social activity (Bakhtin 1986; Gardiner 1992: 81). These speech genres exist in everyday life but can assume more specialized forms in distinct fields such as art, law, science, politics or religion (e.g. a sonnet, formal contract, scientific paper, party manifesto or liturgy). They mediate everyday life and language and, over time, connect the history of society and the history of language (Bakhtin 1986: 65). (Other scholars refer to speech genres as 'forms of discourse'.) Bakhtin emphasized heteroglossia (i.e. the coexistence of different genres, styles of discourse or diversity of voices in a text, intertext or supratext) and stratification as inevitable features of language. This highlights the importance of intertextuality, that is, the appropriation, interweaving and recontextualization of utterances or, more broadly, texts as social actors interact. This approach gives a more emphatic social and material dimension to the more philologically oriented programmatic statements in Vološinov's *Marxism and the Philosophy of Language* (1973). Thus, as Michael Gardiner notes,

> it could be said that his life-long ambition was the development of an interdisciplinary approach to the study of socio-cultural life as it is constituted in and through forms of symbolic interaction – what has been generally referred to as 'metalinguistics' or 'translinguistics'. . . Bakhtin was motivated by a discernible (if largely implicit) political and moral stance. Bakhtin's politics of culture can be characterized as the desire to understand and indeed encourage what I will call the 'popular deconstruction' of official discourses and ideologies. (1992: 2)

The Bakhtin Circle sometimes adopts a weak constructivist position, sometimes a stronger Marxist emphasis on the centrality of class conflict (Roberts 2004). This occurs because ideology *qua* social practice reflects and refracts social antagonism. Overall, despite some ambiguities about whether language is always-already ideological or just provides the raw materials for ideologies and ideological domination (e.g. Vološinov 1973: 10–15), ideology is generally seen as a second-order or meta-linguistic object of criticism. Thus critics of ideology must not restrict their gaze to surface phenomena. They should study the tacit understandings and deep structure of language and linguistic practice in their social context.

This approach constitutes language as a polysemic, heteroglossic, multi-accentual field of struggle and resistance that refracts the natural and social world in specific ways that reflect its material and socio-political features. Figure 3.1 represents one possible logic informing this approach. Like Figures 1.1 and 1.2, it is a thought-experiment. On this occasion the experiment is intended to show the dialectical connections between different aspects of the Bakhtin Circle's analysis, with the top row depicting the target of its criticisms and the bottom three rows showing the interconnections of different aspects of its analysis of dialogical heteroglossia.

The ideological content-value of the heteroglossic field is reflected in a hierarchical ordering of speech genres that reproduce social asymmetries (e.g. 'received pronunciation' versus dialects, argot, patois or creole). Speech genres also privilege some themes over others and they vary in their moral, affectual and emotive as well as neutral, cognitive and descriptive aspects. This opens the space for variation, rearticulation and recontextualization. The dominant class(es) seek to fix (or sediment) meaning and neutralize semantic flux, to colonize and fix cultural

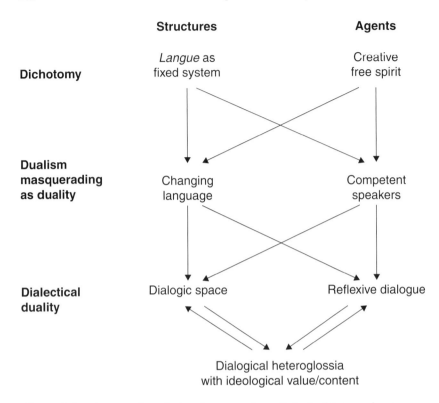

Figure 3.1 A strategic-relational approach to dialogical heteroglossia

forms and institutional arrangements, so that they are taken for granted and acquire a fixed, uncontested (monological) meaning. Maintaining this sedimented framing is improbable, however, because language is inherently 'dialogic'.

> at any given moment of its historical existence, language is heteroglot from top to bottom: it represents the co-existence of socio-ideological contradictions between the present and the past, between differing epochs of the past, between different socio-ideological groups in the present, between tendencies, schools, circles and so forth, all given a bodily form. These 'languages' of heteroglossia intersect each other in a variety of ways, forming new socially typifying 'languages'. (Bakhtin 1981: 291)

It is heteroglossic and multi-accentual, leading to struggle over the sign (Bakhtin 1981). Thus subaltern classes and marginal social categories seek to disrupt this to express their own resistance (see Chapters 4, 7 and 10).

Language is the path-dependent condensation of past ideological struggles and socio-ideological contradictions (Gardiner 1992: 7; Roberts 2004). Similar principles apply to the analysis of identity, the sense of self, and subjectivity. This is why Bakhtin saw the self as fragmented, dialogical and constructed through shifting self–other relations.

Begriffsgeschichte (Semantic Conceptual History)

This approach to historical semantics is associated above all with the mammoth project, published in seven main volumes over 20 years and dealing with some 120 concepts, on *Basic Concepts in History: A Dictionary on Historical Principles of Political and Social Language in Germany* (1972–92).[6] It takes language as the elementary organizing matrix of experience in so far as historical facts are expressed in concepts. Indeed, Reinhart Koselleck, the leading figure in this tradition, argues that without concepts there can be no society and no political fields of action (Koselleck 1982: 414).[7] Thus semantic conceptual history traces the mutual conditioning of language and social structure from the viewpoint of the *longue durée* and transitions. It develops a social history of concepts in terms of both their discursive and social (historical) contexts. In this respect, the reception of texts and their long-term effects are more important than authorial intention. Some concepts are more important than others in guiding the development of social life and societal organization, and in shaping collective experience, collective memory and collective utopias. These concepts are called *Grundbegriffe* (basic concepts), which are complex, contested, organize experience, and shape expectations. An interesting example, especially relevant to later chapters, is Koselleck's analysis of the concept of *Krise* (crisis) (translated in Koselleck 2006); other pertinent examples are Burkhardt (1992) on *Wirtschaft* (economy), Dierse (1982) on *Ideologie* (ideology), Günther (1982) on *Herrschaft* (domination), Hölscher (1982) on *Kapital*, *Kapitalismus* and *Kapitalist*, and Ruedel (1975) on *bürgerliche Gesellschaft* (civil society).

Basic concepts are associated with *Nebenbegriffe* (neighbouring, linked or sister concepts) and, in many cases, to *Gegenbegriffe* (adversary or counter-concepts). Together these constitute semantic fields. For, as another German conceptual historian, aligned with French[8] historical semantics, observes: '[h]istorical concepts do not develop . . . in isolation, but rather with [other] concepts – both complementary and antithetical – with which they form common semantic fields' (Reichardt 1998: 225, cited by Ifversen 2003. These concepts and semantic fields provide the research object of this School (Koselleck 1992; 1996).

This School explores 'the ways in which language both shaped and registered the processes of change that transformed every area of German political and social life, from approximately the middle of the eighteenth century to the middle of the nineteenth' (Richter 1996: 10). These changes in language that are identified in this period both conceptualized rapid transformations in the structures of government, society and the economy and helped to shape reactions to them. As Koselleck, its main driving force over many years, notes:

> all concepts have two aspects. On the one hand, they point to something external to them, to the context in which they are used. On the other hand, this reality is perceived in terms of categories provided by language. Therefore, concepts are both indicators of and factors in political and social life. Put metaphorically, concepts are like joints linking language and the extralinguistic world. (Koselleck 1996: 61)

Interestingly, this argument is reminiscent of Ferdinand de Saussure's original (but never realized and, after his death, largely forgotten) project for semiology as a science of the linguistic *and its extra-linguistic context*. Thus he noted that the development of language (*langue*) is interwoven with the history of a race or civilization, political history (especially great historical events like the Roman conquest or colonization), the history of institutions (such as the Church or the school), language politics (e.g. regarding a unified national language, the use of dialectics), and the geographical spread of languages (de Saussure 1915: 20–21). He regarded these factors both as extra-linguistic (because they are irrelevant to a synchronic analysis of the internal structure of a *langue*) and as essential factors to be included in a future diachronic as well as synchronic discipline of semiology. This discipline, he declared, was unrealized in his lifetime (1857–1913). While we do not suggest that semantic conceptual history has realized Saussure's vision, we do wish to stress its interest in the uneven and combined development of the semantic and extra-semantic in a synthesizing diachronic–synchronic analysis.

Begriffsgeschichte seeks a path between (1) an epiphenomenalist reading of language and concept formation according to which semantic and linguistic shifts merely reflect and register underlying shifts in structures and/or the shifting interests of the real drivers of social change (such as pre-given classes with fixed identities); and (2) an idealist account according to which political and social language is autonomous, unaffected by extra-linguistic factors, and capable of driving change by promoting new concepts, language and ideas. This is one version of the Scylla and Charybdis dualism that we will encounter several times in this book.

This approach is also oriented to critique in three senses: it reveals the asymmetries in semantics and their character as a terrain of struggle; it shows how changes in society and means of communication change the ways in which concepts become politicized, shift temporal horizons (e.g. from past legacies to possible futures), are more or less available for partisan or ideological recontextualization and open up or close down democratic debate; and it sensitizes actors in the current conjuncture to the uses and abuses of political and social language.

The overall aim of German conceptual history is to put words and concepts in their place historically and to show why some concepts become foundational. In a manner reminiscent of the *Wörter* und *Sachen* tradition that interested Gramsci, Koselleck (1972) employs a triad of concepts: word (designation), meaning (concept) and object (fact). This triad acquires its historical force because a concept is a discursively mediated condensation of a shifting balance of forces engaged in struggle on a semantic battlefield over the past, present and future meaning of concepts, linked concepts, and counter-concepts and their interrelations. There is a certain discursive or semantic selectivity at work here because of the historical–political semantics of asymmetric counter-concepts (Koselleck 1982: 420). In these semantic struggles, positions must be won linguistically before they can be occupied by specific social forces – with different forces attempting to identify themselves with the privileged side of asymmetric concepts or to reverse the asymmetries (ibid.: 413–14). The semantic fields that exist in a particular period (synchrony) are the path-dependent product of past struggles over concepts. In this regard there are some obvious similarities – seen in strategic-relational terms – with Gramsci's ideas about wars of position as well as with Poulantzas's argument that state power is the institutionally mediated condensation of a changing balance of forces (Poulantzas 1978).

It is impossible to distinguish fundamental concepts from concepts in purely linguistic terms, whether lexical or semantic. What marks them is their central role in organizing social, especially political, discourse. They provide the minimum shared lexicon to facilitate consensus and to order conflict. As Koselleck puts it in the Foreword to volume 7 of the *Geschichtliche Grundbegriffe*:

> Historically, one can speak of a basic concept, when all conflicting strata and parties share it to communicate their different experiences, their stratum-specific interests, and party-political programmes. Basic concepts ... comprise those minimal commonalities that frame experiences and without which conflict cannot occur or consensus be reached. (1992: vii, our translation)

The *Grundbegriffsgeschichte* (history of basic concepts) project maps how the rapid societal changes occurring in the transition between hierarchically stratified feudal or absolutist society and 'modern' societies that spanned the Enlightenment, the French Revolution and the Industrial Revolution were perceived, conceptualized and incorporated into political and social language. It studies

> key constitutional concepts; the keywords of political, economic and societal organization; the self-descriptions of corresponding disciplines; the guiding concepts of political movements and their slogans; designations of dominant occupational groups and social stratification; theoretically challenging core concepts and ideologies that classify fields of action and divide the world of work. (Koselleck 1972: xiv, our translation)

An important general point is Koselleck's observation that 'our concepts are founded in politico-social systems that are far more complex than would be indicated by treating them simply as linguistic communities organized around specific key concepts' (1985: 74). This has a dual significance: first, the forced selection in conceptual development that opens the space for disjunction between what can be thought and said and the extra-discursive realities of societal development. And, second, it indicates that society is not reducible to the concepts in play in a given period or conjuncture and that society cannot be modelled, or explained, purely in conceptual terms. As Nicolas Rescher notes in another context,

> It is the very limitation of our knowledge of things – our recognition that reality extends beyond the horizons of what we can possibly know or even conjecture about – that most effectively betokens the mind-independence of the real. A world that is inexhaustible by our minds cannot easily be seen to be a product of their operations. (1998: 52)

Koselleck's claim implies that *Begriffsgeschichte* must be combined with *Sozialgeschichte* (social history or, better, we suggest, societal history) and that societal evolution (with all its continuities and discontinuities) occurs through the uneven, mutual constitution of conceptual and institutional development (see Koselleck 1985; Koselleck 2011 is a translation of the 1972 'Introduction' to the *Geschichtliche Grundbegriffe* and also includes the 1992 preface noting and responding to criticisms of the approach). This approach has also been applied by Scandinavian scholars (see, e.g., Palonen 2004, 2006; Stråth 2000; Ifversen 2003, 2011) and by Melvin Richter in the USA (e.g. Richter 1995). There are parallel traditions in France and Italy. For a good overview, see Ifversen (2011). Another variant, linked to Cambridge University, is sufficiently different to be considered in a separate subsection later in this chapter.

Foucault's Discourse (and Dispositive) Analysis

Foucault's *oeuvre* cannot be reduced to discourse analysis. If one were to look for a single phrase to summarize his approach (and Foucault abhorred such efforts), he is better seen as a 'formation analyst' who sometimes prioritizes discursive formations and sometimes institutional formations (cf. Andersen 2003: 1). As Mitchell Dean, who has analysed the successive displacements in Foucault's 'critical and effective histories', notes, he shifted 'first toward an analysis of the regularities of the formation of discourses, then toward the embeddedness of that discourse in institutional practices and power relations, and finally toward the relation of such practices to ones concerning the self and forms of ethical conduct' (Dean 1994: 2). In each phase, Foucault is concerned with transformation processes, with continuity and discontinuity, rather than an inertial synchrony. His work is always concerned with specific problems and struggles rather than with building a systematic general theory. He conforms nonetheless to our definition of a grand theorist. His concepts of discursive economy and dispositive are especially useful (Foucault 1970; see below and Chapter 4; also Bührmann and Schneider 2008). Foucault is also reflexive, interested in the historical, discursive and institutional conditions in which his work is possible – witness the rationalization and systematization of his previous work in *The Archaeology of Knowledge* (1972):

> The longer I continue, the more it seems to me that the formation of discourses and the genealogy of knowledge need to be analyzed, not in terms of types of consciousness, modes of perception and forms of ideology, but in terms of tactics and strategies of power. Tactics and strategies deployed through implantations, distributions, demarcations, control of territories and organizations of domains which could well make up a sort of geopolitics where my preoccupations would link up with your methods. (Foucault 1980: 77)

In short, Foucault's approach to discourse does not pursue the kind of analysis offered by core linguistics or socio-linguistics. Nor does it consider the role of language in positioning subjects (e.g. the work of Emil Benveniste), its role in shaping lived experience (subjects' imagined relation to reality, on which see Althusser, Pêcheux and Chapter 11), intellectual history or the history of ideas, or settling disputes about the true nature of the real world. Instead what Foucault offers us in his archaeological study of archives or epistemes is a study of how meanings are produced and circulated in a discursive economy. Rather than meaning residing in a given text (let alone in authorial intention) or deriving from socio-political change, Foucault's analysis of discourse insists on its materiality and its specific spatio-temporal location. He poses four sets of question.

1. How do 'objects' in the natural and social world get demarcated and delimited as appropriate entities of discursive practice? This process of 'objectivation' entails drawing a distinction and then elaborating it through discourse and discursive practices. 'Objectivation' occurs in various ways and these can be related to different technologies of power/knowledge. This line of questioning denaturalizes objects, especially those that appear long-lasting and unchanging because the same word is used to designate them, such as the economy, the state, madness or knowledge.
2. What is the 'conceptual architecture' of a discourse, that is, the permissible combinations, series and networks that can be formed with the available concepts and discourses, and who is authorized to utter them?
3. What are the semantic macro-areas, that is, the themes/thematics/theories to which different concepts might be related? In some other approaches to discourse, these are also called semantic fields. These comprise networks of (strategically motivated) statements and, by virtue of strategic decisions, limit what can (and cannot) be said within a discourse.
4. What positions can be occupied in this discourse considered as a set of 'enunciative modalities'? This is another way of asking about the differential positioning of subjects in relation to discourse, about who is empowered to speak, or, again, about 'subjectivation' as a complement to 'objectivation'. Subjectivation involves not only the creation of subject positions but also of 'willing' subjects, that is, subjects who are willing and able to play their allotted roles. This is later linked to interest in technologies of the self, that is, with the diverse practices involved in self-subjectivation and self-responsibilization. This is the field *par excellence* for pragmatics, that is, the branch of semiotic analysis that deals with language use. Foucault is especially interested in how discursive formations (sets of statements) create objects, concepts, semantic fields and subjects.

Combining these four sets of question permits analysis of different kinds of discourse and their effects at both the textual and intertextual level, of construals and construction, of the uneven capacities to shape the institutionalization of discourses, and of their interaction in a 'discursive economy' (which might be better phrased as an ecology of discourses in which discourses coexist and interact, producing patterns of subordination, segmentation, fracture, hierarchy and so on).

Foucault's research on discursive formations moved from a more archaeological to a more genealogical focus, that is, from how 'archives' (sets of statements) were structured to the contingent emergence of discourses and discursive formations. This was linked to an interest in 'dispositives'. This term indicates the strategic alignment between the semantic and material features of an apparatus. It is a 'thoroughly heterogeneous ensemble consisting of discourses, institutions, architectural forms, regulatory decisions, laws, administrative measures, scientific statements, philosophical, moral and philanthropic proposition' (1980: 194). As often with Foucault, however, no definitive treatment exists and the concept must be reconstructed from dispersed statements in books, lectures, articles and interviews that deal explicitly or implicitly with dispositives and their relation to other topics (see Bührmann and Schneider 2008; Coté 2004; Jäger 2012; Link 2007; Peltonen 2004).[9]

In these terms, the dispositive is more of a place-holding concept that suggests the need to extend and deepen the analysis of linkages between the discursive and the extra-discursive. As Peltonen expresses it, the term denotes 'historically specific totalities of discourses and practices' (2004: 206). Summarizing some diffuse and diffused comments, a dispositive emerges in response to a discursively constituted problem (with a referent in the 'real world') and involves the co-evolution of strategies and apparatuses and, eventually, their strategic alignment and codification. The result is a configuration embodying a general strategic line that no one willed but that emerges from the clash of different strategies and tactics and that is, even at best, incomplete and provisional and, of course, subject to resistance that threatens to undermine routinization and confinement within the dispositive (see Foucault 1977, 1979).

Andersen summarizes the concept as follows:

> Whereas archaeology divides the world into the regulation and dispersion of statements, genealogy into continuity and discontinuity, and self-technology analysis into subjection and subjectivation, dispositive analysis divides the world into *apparatus* on one hand and *strategic logic* on the other hand. The distinction between apparatus and strategic logic is the 'eye' of dispositive analysis. The apparatus is the 'heterogeneous ensemble'; it is a system of elements between which there exists a functional connection. The strategic imperative or logic is a generalised schematic that brings about a particular logic. These are always relative in relation to one another. There is no apparatus without the apparatus acting as an apparatisation and, thus, a function of a strategic logic. In turn, there is no strategic logic except through the effects it defines through an apparatus. (Andersen 2003: 27; see also the work of the Duisburg School, discussed below)

The development of a dispositive is complex. On the one hand, the emerging general strategic line depends on the path-dependent contexts in which a dispositive is assembled; and, on the other hand, a dispositive emerges from the intersection of different, potentially path-shaping strategic lines. It develops in response to urgent problems and, hence, involves not only discursive practices but also wider social practices that are developed to resolve the problem as interpreted and reinterpreted over time. So we must ask about the adequacy of the construal of the problem (its definition, its objectivation, thematization, relation to power/knowledge relations etc.), the adequacy of the discursive–material response assembled in the dispositive (the regime of practices, including diverse power/knowledge technologies, apparatuses, inclusions, exclusions etc.) for resolving the 'strategic imperative' in a situation where both problematization and social practices are contingent, and, finally, the scope to recontextualize (generalize or respecify) this dispositive to new problems, modifying the heterogeneous elements that are combined to produce its effects. On this basis, we suggest that 'dispositivization' is interpretable as the recursive interaction of structurally inscribed strategic selectivity and strategically calculated, structurally oriented action aimed at the definition and resolution of an *urgence*. In short, the emergence, retention and consolidation of a dispositive involves a strategic-relational 'dialectical duality' (Figures 1.1 and 1.2).

This brief summary must serve to introduce Foucault's analytical model and, even if presented at greater length, ambiguities and aporias would remain. For Foucault, this would pose no problem because he continually reworked his toolkit and welcomed its creative use by others.

An example of the latter is the work of scholars such as Jürgen Link, from Dortmund and Bochum Universities and co-founder of the journal *KultuRRevolution*, and Siegfried and Margarete Jäger, the key figures in the Duisburg School, which is based at the Duisburger Institut für Sprach- und Sozialforschung (DISS).[10] They examine the relations between the discursive and non-discursive, between discourse and dispositive, and between knowledge and power, in the context of domination in bourgeois-capitalist societies, often focusing on neo-fascist and racist discourse. Link defines discourse as 'an institutionalized way of talking that regulates and reinforces action and thereby exerts power' (Link 1983: 60, cited in Jäger and Maier 2009: 35). In turn, Link regards dispositives as 'the synthesis of discursive practices (i.e. speaking and thinking on the basis of knowledge), non-discursive practices (i.e. acting on the basis of knowledge) and materialization (i.e. the material products of acting on the basis of knowledge)' (ibid.). Power/knowledge relations figure significantly in both definitions: this indicates a recursive relation in which discourses exert power by transporting knowledge through discursive and non-discursive activities that shape reality. Link investigates (1) synchronic *systems of collective symbols* (cultural stereotypes or topoi with their associated repertoires of images), which act like a net overlaying discourse; and (2) *interdiscourse*, which interweaves specialized or macro-thematic discourses into more encompassing forms of speech that shape common sense (Link 1982, 1986; Jäger 1993: 152–63). On this basis, he explores discourse in a series of steps from discourse fragments via discourse strands to discourse nodes (*discursive Knoten*), which connect different discourses and link conventional collective symbols into social discourse.

The Duisburg School puts discourse in its place in two ways: it refers it back to human thinking and consciousness (and, hence, to their historicity) and, via the activities of individual and collective subjects, forward to the (re)making of reality. Subjects have a key role in connecting discourse and material reality (Jäger and Maier 2009: 45; Jäger 2012). But subjects are not posited as rational, centred individuals but, rather, understood as being formed through subjectivation, with plural identities, and occupying several subjects. Regarding both objects and subjects, then, discourses create their own reality, which feeds back into discursive formations.

Link is particularly interested in the historical development of different regimes of 'normalism' (the norming and naturalization of particular forms of thought, speech and action), their correlation with (and contribution to) different modes of growth and societalization, and their implications for particular kinds of ideologies and patterns of domination (e.g. 'racial' discrimination) (Link 1997, 2013). He also notes that crises can trigger denormalization (2013: 199–232). Link combines this with an interest in how subaltern groups resort to 'tricks' that enable them to express resistance without sanctions (Jäger 2001: 35). There are similarities here with Foucault's analysis of power/resistance but also with Bakhtinian carnival, Michel de Certeau's tactics of resistance in the face of the strategies of power, and James Scott's discussion of subaltern resistance (de Certeau 1984; Scott 1985, 1990). However, individual texts and individual acts of resistance are less influential than the cumulative impact of the dull force of repetition that solidifies knowledge through discourse.

Overall, for the Duisburg School, text analysis contributes to critiques of dominant discourses by revealing their contradictions, silences, exclusions and temporary truths (regimes). It also reveals how these effects are reinforced institutionally (Jäger 2001: 34; Jäger and Maier 2009: 35–39). Jäger has distinguished his approach (critical discourse and dispositive analysis) from the Anglo-Saxon and Austrian traditions of CDA in terms of the former's strong interest in dispositives and commitment to systematic *Ideologiekritik* as opposed to criticism based on assumed knowledge of the truth (Jäger and Diaz-Bone 2006; cf. Angermüller 2011).

A different example of the linguistic recontextualization and development of Foucault's work is the *Diskurslinguistik* (discourse linguistics) approach, which uses (corpus) linguistics to provide a more descriptive, historical semantic analysis of cognitive frames and social epistemologies rather than a critique of power/knowledge relations. This historical–linguistic epistemology is oriented to 'how the historically and culturally rooted knowledge (epistemes) can be described with linguistic means and how such knowledge shapes social communication and meaning' (Spitzmüller and Warnke 2011: 76). The initiator of the approach, Dietrich Busse (1987), reports that it

> is not so much interested in discursive practice and in social actors (and hence neither in issues such as power and inequality) as in the question as to what people (in a given era and social setting) need to know in order to understand each other (and consequently, what historians need to know in order to understand historical texts). In recent papers, Busse stresses that it is the 'knowledge relevant to understanding' . . . which he actually attempts to reveal. (Spitzmüller and Warnke 2011: 76)

In more recent work, however, Busse has begun to consider discourse linguistics after Foucault, which reflects the latter's more general influence in Germany (e.g. 2000, 2013).

COMPETING, COMPLEMENTARY, SUPPLEMENTARY APPROACHES

This section reviews some competing approaches to these grand theories, some complementary approaches, and some that might usefully supplement them. Those in haste or with a less burning interest in these matters can move to the next section, where we synthesize all the approaches under review. The order of presentation is the same. Thus we first address cultural materialism, an influential theme in literary criticism and cultural studies, which is relevant to vernacular materialism; and then we deal with two other approaches to historical semantics, namely, the Cambridge School of conceptual history and the *Annaliste* approach to *mentalités* (which, loosely translated, denotes epochal mental mind-sets).

Cultural Materialism

This approach is associated above all with Raymond Williams, a Welsh literary critic, novelist and left-wing intellectual. Two other leading cultural materialist scholars are Richard Hoggart (1957) and Edward P. Thompson (1963). Here we concentrate on Williams. Cultural materialism should not be confused with the study of material culture (the embodiment of culture in objects or the cultural significance of material objects) or with cultural materialism in anthropology (e.g. Harris 1980), which relies on a base–superstructure distinction[11] rejected by Williams. His own cultural materialism focuses on the place of culture in historical materialism, that is, culture as a social and material productive process. Williams used the term to denote his own break from vulgar materialism (which consigns culture to the superstructure) and from the then influential, idealist approach of literary humanism (Milner 2002: 18, 55). Cultural materialism sought to transcend these alternatives and, in its later developments, used Gramsci to recast the base–superstructure couplet by revaluing the two terms and the meaning of determination. Thus base now denoted the primary production of society itself and of people themselves, rather than the merely 'economic'; superstructure now referred to the whole range of cultural practices, rather than a merely secondary and dependent 'content'; and determination became the 'setting of limits and exertion of pressures', rather than predetermined causation (Williams 1973; see also Jones 2004).

This placed culture 'inside' the economic base and, indeed, whether Williams recognized it or not, marked a return to the Marx and Engels of *The German Ideology*. These founding fathers of historical materialism argued that production is the production of a mode of life – not just the satisfaction of immediate physical needs. It has day-to-day, life-cycle and intergenerational aspects, and involves both immediate production and the production of the material and social conditions that enable production to occur. A crucial moment of this is language, which, as practical consciousness of nature, of other humans and of social relations, exists also for others (and hence for the speaker too). It arises and develops from the necessity of social intercourse and is part of the mode of life (Marx and Engels 1976a: 31–93).

This said, three themes investigated by Williams are especially relevant to CPE. First, he studied the development of 'keywords', that is, words that played a key role in the semantics of modern, bourgeois society. This analysis is similar to the German semantic conceptual history approach (Williams 1993). As Williams explained,

> I called these words *Keywords* in two connected senses: they are significant, binding words in certain activities and their interpretation; they are significant, indicative words in certain forms of thought ... The kind of semantics to which these notes and essays belong is one of the tendencies within *historical semantics*: a tendency that can be more precisely defined when it is added that the emphasis is not only on historical origins and developments but also on the present – present meanings, implications and relationships – as history. This recognizes, as any study of language must, that there is indeed community between past and present, but also that *community* – that difficult word – is

not the only possible description of these relations between past and present; that there are also radical change, discontinuity and conflict, and that all these are still at issue and are indeed still occurring... In a social history in which many crucial meanings have been shaped by a dominant class, and by particular professions operating to a large extent within its terms, the sense of edge is accurate. This is not a neutral review of meanings. It is an exploration of the vocabulary of a crucial area of social and cultural discussion, which has been inherited within precise historical and social conditions and which has to be made at once conscious and critical – subject to change as well as to continuity – if the millions of people in whom it is active are to see it as active: not a *tradition* to be learned, nor a *consensus* to be accepted, nor a set of meanings which, because it is 'our language', has a natural authority; but as a shaping and reshaping, in real circumstances and from profoundly different and important points of view. (Williams 1993: 15, 23)

Second, he explored material culture and literary production and the changing means of cultural production and communication (e.g. the novel, radio, television). This work complements the unique analysis of modes of communication and their inherent biases, considered over several millennia, in the work of the Canadian political economist Harold Innis (e.g. 1950, 1951),[12] which influenced his student, Marshal McLuhan, author of the famous aphorism, 'the medium is the message',[13] and Régis Debray's work on mediology, which is an innovative interdisciplinary approach to the socio-logistics of communication[14] (Debray 1991, 1996, 2000). Regarding Innis, Babe comments:

Innis related shifts in media technologies to changes in the distribution of political and economic power, both domestically and internationally. He invented the term 'monopolies of knowledge' to represent not only concentration of media ownership and control, but also of the knowledges circulating in society as they affect people's perceptions and understandings. He coined the term 'information industries' to highlight the economic-industrial dimensions of cultural production. He related industrial processes generally, such as the quest for economies of scale and mass marketing, to the production and distribution of culture through such constructs as 'the mechanization of knowledge'. Moreover, Innis' analysis of the political-economic dimensions of media and changes in media technologies and patterns of media control were fully integrated to such cultural categories as conceptions of time, conceptions of space, education, literacy, the news and mass entertainment, and the mass production of culture. (Babe 2009: 21)

All these approaches to the effects of communication media or socio-logistics bear on the question of reception, to which we return in our 'grand synthesis'.

Third, Williams's work opened the field of cultural studies in Britain, influencing especially the Birmingham School of Cultural Studies under its first two directors, Richard Hoggart and Stuart Hall (see Babe 2009; Grossberg 1993, 2010). And, fourth, it also resonates with studies of material culture and the political economy of everyday life. In these respects, among others, it is clearly relevant to the development of CPE without, however, anticipating to any great extent the six features that make this approach distinctive.

Given the similarities between vernacular materialism and cultural materialism, Table 3.1 compares some of their key respective features with our version of CPE. This table shows important affinities but also significant differences across the approaches, reflecting not only some common influences but also the different theoretical purposes for which each approach was developed. We will continue this compare-and-contrast perspective as we explore alternative approaches to critical semiotic analysis.

Pragmatic Conceptual History (Cambridge School)

Based on analytical philosophy and logical positivism, the Cambridge School does not focus on a few grand texts in terms of their authors' intentions, even though intentions certainly matter. Instead its members explore the intertextuality of political texts in their changing intellectual and societal context. In short, praxis matters. Thus adherents aim to reconstruct political language through the study of *parole* (language use) within the constraints of changing political lexicons. Its founding spirits are John Pocock and Quentin Skinner. The former regards a language as a complex structure comprising a vocabulary, grammar, rhetoric, and a set of usages, assumptions and implications. It is available to a community of language-users to articulate a (political) worldview (Pocock 1996: 47; also Pocock 1973). Thus he does not focus on *langage* as studied in Saussurean structural linguistics or on individual texts but on how language is used to create a shared philosophy of life.

Pocock explores the plurality of, and contestation among, political languages, discourses or 'paradigms' that shape the production and reception of a set of ideas. He explores both the structure of a particular text as it exists 'here-now' and how it intervenes in a continuum or flow of discourse through time (1985: 28). This requires attention to how texts are received and recontextualized. For example, Pocock's seminal analysis of Machiavellian political theory, that is, Florentine republican discourse, explores how it was adopted, adjusted and altered in dialogue with a broader range of political languages found in contexts ranging from the Italian city-states to the Anglo-American world (Pocock 1975).

Skinner's approach is more philosophical, posing questions of intentionality and the rules and conventions that govern discourse. He draws

Table 3.1 Three approaches to culture in radical social theory

	Vernacular materialism	Cultural materialism	CPE
Key author(s)	Antonio Gramsci	Raymond Williams	Jessop and Sum
Key question	Place of language in historical materialism	Place of culture in historical materialism	Place of semiosis in political economy
Basic answer	Language is not in base or superstructure as it is present throughout a social formation Involves historical production of meaning by defining semiotic relations in language	Culture as social and material productive process, focusing on material culture and literary production Involves production of people themselves as well as cultural objects	Semiosis is one way to reduce complexity. Like language (one form of semiosis), it is everywhere in a social formation but does not exhaust it
Supplementary answer(s)	No language-in-general: specific living languages develop historically and spatially and are linked hierarchically and through core–periphery relations	Literature must be related to the whole way of life, not just to the 'economic base' We need to revalue base, superstructure and the nature of social determination	Semiosis is subject to variation, selection, retention and recontextualization There are four types of selectivity: semiotic, structural, technological and agential
Gramsci's role	Critical philology shows key roles of language and intellectuals in winning hegemony. It gives metaphors for war of position, passive revolution etc.	Provides insights into how to explain that 'structures of feeling' are common to different classes, yet represent interests of a particular class	Gramsci as theorist of hegemony, integral economy, integral state, and role of language in securing hegemony. Includes Gramsci's analyses of coercion
Key text(s)	*Prison Notebooks.* Also Peter Ives, *Gramsci's Politics of Language*; and *Language and Hegemony in Gramsci*	*The Long Revolution*; *Keywords*; *Marxism and Literature*; *Culture*; essay on 'Base and Superstructure in Marxist Theory'	*Beyond Regulation Approach*; essays in *New Political Economy, Critical Discourse Studies, Critical Policy Studies*

on J.L. Austin's speech-act theory (Austin 1975), according to which language has illocutionary force, that is, performative effects, by virtue of the act of speaking or producing a text (e.g. to make a promise). In short, he asks what the speaker/writer was doing when producing a text (on meaning and understanding in historical interpretation, see Skinner 1969). Like Pocock, Skinner focuses on historical traditions and linguistic contexts, earlier writings and inherited assumptions, and the present ideological context (Skinner 1978). Skinner believes that the character of political language is best discovered by studying as many texts as possible to render authorial intentions intelligible and meaningful. A good example of this genre is the 'mirror-of-princes' literature (advice books for rulers) in Italian city-states, into which Machiavelli's *The Prince* (1532) was a major intervention. For example, Machiavelli's *The Prince* is best understood by putting it into its argumentative context and asking what he hoped to achieve by writing and producing it (for a different reading, see Althusser 1999). Given his interest in pragmatics in the Anglo-American sense of the performative force of language in use, Skinner pays particular attention to questions of rhetoric and argumentation (for background and a summary of criticisms, see Melve 2006).

The *Annales* School and *l'Histoire des Mentalités*

The *Annales* School is a distinctive French School with several interrelated foci. It derives its name from its house journal, *Annales d'Histoire Economique et Sociale*,[15] which was co-founded in 1929 by Lucien Febvre and Marc Bloch.[16] It is hostile to Marxist class analysis and economic reductionism (being said by some to invert Marxism by focusing on ideas and superstructures), and also criticized top-down political and diplomatic histories written from the viewpoint of metropolitan elites. It has developed over at least four generations and the main research foci have changed accordingly. Here we focus on a thematic approach that crystallized in the 1960s, namely, *l'histoire des mentalités* (history of mentalities), an expression that a fourth-generation *Annaliste*, Roger Chartier, describes as 'all the more encompassing for the fuzziness of its conceptual content' (1988: 27).

Four themes are important for present purposes:

- Different time frames of analysis: (a) the *longue durée* of economic, political and social structures, the long span of an apparently motionless history that can escape social cognizance but exercises powerful constraints on thought and action; (b) the conjuncture – recognizable

and recognized periods in which strategic action occurs; and (c) the short time span of individual actions and specific 'events', which are the ephemera of history.
- Everyday life in all its rich and mundane variety, especially, in the present context, how 'ordinary' people or groups appropriate and recontextualize systems of belief, values and representations, and how, if at all, this is shaped by social affiliations.
- The history of *mentalités*, that is, historically specific unconscious mental processes or habits of thought and their role in shaping everyday life (on *mentalités*, see Greimas 1958; Barthes 1967; Febvre 1979).
- The *outillage mental* (mental equipment) that each 'civilization' or era has to hand and develops. This equipment comprises *matériaux d'idées* (ideas materials, such as words, symbols, images, myths, sentiments, sensibilities, feeling and affect) and *mental tools* (techniques), including both material and conceptual instruments (techniques and knowledges). For some scholars this includes a history of modes of individuation and corresponding types of personality, that is, a psychological history oriented to typical personalities or even collective psychology rather than to specific persons.

This approach shifted the questions asked by historians of ideas from 'the audacities of thought' to 'the limits of the thinkable'; from 'an intellectual history based on unbridled minds and unsupported ideas' to 'a history of collective representations, of mental equipment and intellectual categories available and shared at a given epoch'; or, again, from a history of ideas as 'the conscious construction of an individualized mind' to that of '[t]he always collective mentality that regulates the representation and judgments of social agents without their knowledge' (Chartier 1988: 27, 28). This shift is reminiscent of Emile Durkheim's *conscience collective* as a social fact (see Chapter 1) and of the notion of the French anthropologist, Lucien Lévy-Bruhl (1923), of the 'primitive mentality' as a particular mode of thought coherent with its time. This account of mentalities can also be presented in terms of an investigation into *idées-forces* (idea-forces or, loosely, structures of thought as material forces).

In the 1960s, Mandrou and Duby (1964) connected the history of *mentalités* to Fernand Braudel's threefold division of the structures of historical time to explore the relation between *mentalités* and changing social conditions. Many studies of *mentalités* were published during the 1970s and 1980s but interest waned in favour of a cultural and linguistic turn in the 1990s on the grounds that *mentalités* had been analysed in excessively psychological, habitual and structuralist terms. This shift brings the French School closer, in some respects, to work on historical semantics.

Linking these three topics produces, *inter alia*, a concern with history and language that goes well beyond an internal signifier/signified relation to include the study of words in relation to their referents and, hence, their role in shaping institutions and material culture. However, in addition to its structuralist reading of mentalities, this approach is also reductionist and functionalist. Individuals are seen as the unconscious bearers of mentalities (leading to the disappearance of the subject), their conduct is reduced to these habitual frames, and, lastly, they are interpreted as functional to power (for reviews see Burke 1992; Hunt 1986; Megill 2007). On this point, a little Bakhtinian resistance would not go amiss!

Some commentators note analogies between the *Annales* School and Foucault's work on the archaeology of knowledge (epistemes), his use of historical oddities to denaturalize taken-for-granted modern practices,[17] and his opposition to humanistic accounts of the subject. Indeed, Foucault uses *Annaliste* terminology in examining history in the *Archaeology of Knowledge* (1972: 3–11) and Braudelian ideas on the materiality of civilization. He also suggested (in an interview) that the *Annalistes* and English historians had freed history from its subjugation to philosophy and the imposition of narrative as a historiographic mode on past events – themes that he pursued in his own work (Foucault 1996). But he condemned functionalist analyses of power relations, which would disqualify the *Annaliste* account of mentalities (on Foucault and the *Annalistes*, see Dean 1994: 37–41).

FROM GRAND THEORIES TO GROUNDED ANALYTICS

The approaches so far are grand theories with major implications for understanding the relation between semiosis and structuration. Just as we distinguish grand theory from general theory (and prefer the former), so we distinguish grounded theory from grounded analytics (and prefer the latter). Grounded theory is a theoretically agnostic, empiricist research method that begins with data collection, codes the data based on distinctions that 'emerge' from observation thereof, and then, via iteration, produces a series of generalizations to 'reverse-engineer' theoretical hypotheses. It claims to avoid preconceived hypotheses that are imposed on the data and aims instead to ground its theory in a naïve observation of 'raw' data gathered without prior theoretical contamination. The approach is most often used in the study of personal interactions in specific organizational and institutional contexts (for the pioneer text, see Glaser and Strauss 1967; and, for further information, Bryan and Charmaz 2007).

In contrast, grounded analytics, as we use the term, refers to various strategies that are used to analyse the articulation of discoursal and non-discoursal practices and that develop robust methodologies and techniques of analysis grounded in linguistic or semiotic theory. We can relate this to Bob Hodge's remark that an important strength of CDA from the outset is its 'practice of generating theory out of analytic practice. This has allowed the theory to grow by accumulation, becoming something richer than individual analysts could have hoped for, more contradictory than most would want to admit' (2012: 8). This approach is not linked, however, to grander theories about the character of the interaction contexts, organizational arrangements or ecologies, institutional settings, structural forms or general principles of societalization in which the texts, intertexts and supratexts are embedded. Indeed, it is the tendential dissociation of such analytical strategies from broader sets of theoretical commitments that is both a source of strength (they are easily transferred) and a source of weakness (in so far as they play an underlabouring role in more general social science inquiry). These analytical strategies are therefore more useful in providing answers to 'how' questions and must be related to other theories to provide adequate answers to 'why' questions.

This section introduces theoretically informed, empirically grounded analytics, that is, approaches that meet our four selection criteria for work relevant to CPE. To remind readers, relevant work must (1) eschew universal laws of language and language use; (2) show interest in authorial intention, agency and subjectivity; (3) adopt a relational account of text–intertext–context; and (4) allow for analysis of the discursive and extra-discursive. We begin with CDA, consider the discourse-historical approach, and end with some comments on Laclau and Mouffe, who use CDA to develop a general theory of the social and to emphasize the essential 'political' (contestable) nature of all social relations.

Critical Discourse Analysis

CDA emerged as a distinct school through a cooperation established in 1991 among Norman Fairclough, Gunther Kress, Teun van Dijk, Leo van Leeuwen and Ruth Wodak.[18] Applying CDA methods reflexively to CDA as an acronym, Bob Hodge notes that it does a great deal of work.

> It homogenises the practices that give the group its identity. The claimed homogeneity can then become a cover for heterogeneous practices. It allows individuals to belong to the group without having to say what the group does or stands for . . . [But] CDA cannot do the job it sets itself unless it can explore complex meanings that emerge in social interaction, and the complex processes which produce them, no less social for being located in minds. (2012: 2, 3–4)

CDA aimed to break with the type of 'core linguistic' analysis that focused on micro-textual units, text and intertext and also to bring context into its analytical purview. Thus critical discourse analysts investigate texts in both their semiotic and broader social contexts. Texts are useful as well as important research objects because, as Ehlich (1983)[19] noted, they objectify linguistic actions. They provide ready-made data but could also introduce biases into the research in so far as CDA ignores other modes of semiosis that rely less on written text and, hence, the significance of multi-modal semiosis (on which, see especially the works of van Leeuwen and van Dijk). This said, as the many recent handbooks and guidebooks demonstrate, both theoretically and methodologically, CDA is as diverse as linguistic analysis in general. Perusing these resources reveals that, as trained linguists and socio-linguists, CDA scholars, howsoever they gather their research material, tend to analyse discourse in linguistic terms. Thus 'CDA studies may [use] grammatical (phonological, morphological, syntactic), semantic, pragmatic, interactional, rhetorical, stylistic, narrative or genre analyses, among others, on the one hand, and . . . experiments, ethnography, interviewing, life stories, focus groups, participant observation, and so on, on the other' (van Dijk 2013). Not all available techniques are used equally and the choice of topics is also uneven, with some important topics relevant to CPE seriously underexplored.

Overall, using this wide range of methods, CDA aims to go beyond description to offer explanation and critique and, in particular, to show how language is linked to ideology and power. Indeed, the focus of this approach could be summarized in the triplet: *language, ideology, power* (Fairclough 1989; Hodge and Kress 1993; van Dijk 1998; van Leeuwen 2008; Wodak 1989; see also Bartlett 2013). This indicates why CDA can be described as 'an attitude of mind'. Its practitioners oppose, albeit for different reasons and on rather different grounds, the abuse of power through discourse, especially by the symbolic power elites that dominate public discourse, above all in politics, the media and education (van Dijk 2013). Relevant research topics include the epistemic structures of discourse, seen in terms of both selective access and authority in a conversation or the epistemic organization of distinctive genres. The key issue is how attitudes and ideologies are expressed in discourse. This is problematic because ideology does not necessarily reside in the content of a discourse but can also be contextual by virtue of its ideological effects (e.g. through the diversion of blame in a crisis; see Chapter 11).

Reflecting different research objects and entry-points, CDA develops a wide range of methods and analytical tools. But there is no consensus on how to analyse ideology, power and domination in substantive terms. This is unsurprising because this will depend on specific forms of domination (e.g. class, gender, 'race' or region). Accordingly, CDA largely provides a methodological supplement to critical political economy, revealing the specific mechanisms through which semiotically mediated practices and social relations are reproduced. In this sense, it presupposes substantive theoretical work on what critical realists would call the real mechanisms of linguistic effects, examining the horizontal and vertical relations in a given period and/or over time among text, paratext (the surroundings of a text), intertext, supratexts and context. This can tell us how discursive effects are produced but it does not explain why, that is, how discourse is related to (or motivated by) relations of power and domination (cf. Fairclough 1989: 7–8). Of current approaches to CDA that exist, the three that are closest to our approach to CPE are the Duisburg School (see above), Fairclough's approach, which, as Wodak and Meyer (2009: 29) note, has a 'rather grand-theory-oriented position' with links to historical materialism, and the Essex School, which has deepened Laclau and Mouffe's post-Marxist analysis through attention to different logics of social explanation that brings it close, on occasion, to the regulation approach (Glynos and Howarth 2007; Howarth 2013).

Thus Teun van Dijk is a little disingenuous when he claims that CDA is not so much an explicit analytical method as an attitude of mind and that its practitioners belong to a social and political movement critical of linguistic abuses by those with power. For, while the attitude of mind distinguishes it from discourse analysis *tout court* and may explain the choice of research topics, van Dijk's remark underplays the significance of the interpretive and explanatory power of linguistic analysis in particular and semiotic analysis more generally. But this also means that CDA is an inherently multi- or trans-disciplinary exercise concerned with the articulation between discoursal and non-discoursal change (cf. Fairclough 2006b; Reisigl and Wodak 2009). In short, discourse analysts should aim for 'the productive integration of textual analysis into multi-disciplinary research on change' (Fairclough 2005: 76).

Fairclough's approach emphasizes the imbrication between language, social practices and wider political and social structures (1989, 2001). Social practices are partly defined by the structures of society and partly by social events that shape everyday life. Language matters here because it is the medium of ideology, which is the primary mechanism of social control and power in modern society (1989: 2–3). Indeed, 'language has grown dramatically in terms of the uses it is required to serve, in terms of the range of language varieties, and in terms of the complexity of the language capacities expected of the modern citizen' (ibid.: 3). Social change is not random but influenced by events and texts. A key concept here is the order of discourse (derived from Foucault), which 'is a social order looked at from a specifically discoursal perspective – in terms of those types of practice into which a social space is structured, which happen to be discourse types' (ibid.: 29). It comprises networked social practices formed through the articulation of discourses, genres, and styles (2006a: 24–5) that provide relatively durable and stable resources for meaning-making and set limits to what is semiotically possible.

Although Fairclough emphasizes the centrality of language to social order, he cannot be charged with the exorbitation of discourse because he emphasizes that 'whereas all linguistic phenomena are social, not all social phenomena are linguistic – though even those that are not just linguistic (economic production, for instance) typically have a substantial, and often underestimated, language element' (1989: 23). Change can be studied through the interaction of genre, discourse and style, and the space thereby opened for linguistic innovation that can break through sedimented layers of meaning. For example, genre chains can selectively filter out and exclude possibilities as well as recontextualize the discourse to new sites and scales to reaffirm existing social relations. We also endorse Fairclough's move from synthesizing text-analytical techniques (Luke 2002) to greater engagement with social theories on contemporary economic, political and social change (e.g. Chouliaraki and Fairclough 1999). Two good examples are *New Labour, New Language* (Fairclough 2000) on Third Way discourse and a critical dissection of discourses of globalization (Fairclough 2006). Thus we regard his approach as straddling (or bridging) the divide between grand theory and grounded analytics because its adherents regularly link their analyses to the changing character of capitalism.

The Discourse Historical Approach (DHA)

This approach (also known as the Vienna School) should not be confused with historical discourse analysis. The latter term covers the study of lexical, semantic and linguistic change; on semantic change, see Allan and Robinson (2011) and, for a general survey of historical discourse analysis, see Landwehr (2008) and historical socio-linguistics; see Nevalainen and Raumolin-Brunberg (2012). Some versions of historical discourse analysis can be read as arguing, with Derrida, that there is nothing behind the text: the text constructs social reality through performative praxis. These versions apply the more general 'constructivist' approach in the humanities and social sciences that we criticize in Chapter 4 for failing to distinguish construal from construction. In contrast, the DHA aims to combine critical discourse analysis with a more developed account of its historical contextualization than most CDA work provides. The key figure in the

School is Ruth Wodak. It emerged from a multi-disciplinary project in Vienna (hence the name) on anti-Semitism and has since developed an explicit programme to advance its broader objectives. At the same time, however, '[a]though DHA is aligned to critical theory, "grand theories" play a minor role compared with the discourse model and the emphasis on historical analysis: context is understood mainly as historical' (Wodak and Meyer 2009: 26). It eschews 'inoperationalizable grand theories' in favour of developing 'conceptual tools adequate for specific social problems' (ibid.). This is why we describe it here as a grounded analytics. DHA investigates *intertextual* and *interdiscursive relationships* among utterances, texts and co-texts, genres and discourses, and connects these to extra-linguistic social/societal variables, the history of relevant organizations and/or institutions, and specific conjunctures or situations. While focusing on intertextual and interdiscursive relations between utterances, texts, genres and discourses, it also investigates how changes in texts, genres and discourses are related to extra-linguistic social variables and institutional frames of specific situational contexts as well as to socio-political change(s) and broader historical contexts (Reisigl and Wodak 2009: 93).

The DHA presents itself as critical, claiming, contestably, an affiliation to the second-generation Frankfurt School (notably Jürgen Habermas), and, in this regard, proposes three modes of critique. These comprise, successively: (1) an immanent critique of arguments; (2) a socio-diagnostic critique based on normative commitments that differ from those articulated, or discoverable, in the texts in question; and (3) a retrospective/prognostic critique connecting the past (including its representations in memory) and the future (proposing scenarios to improve conditions for the victims of discrimination, exclusion or oppression). In connecting these three lines of critique, the DHA moves across internal co-text, intertextual and interdiscursive relations (e.g. genres and fields of discourse) via extra-linguistic social variables and institutional frames to the broader socio-political and historical context in which discursive practices are embedded and to which discoursal topics are related (Reisigl and Wodak 2009).

Although Vienna School adherents claim affinities to the German conceptual history school (for a heroic attempt to demonstrate this, see Krzyżanowski 2010), DHA lacks the depth and breadth of the latter approach to the co-evolution of semantics and social history. Indeed, on our reading, there are stronger, if unstated, affinities to pragmatic conceptual history. But DHA differs from both by taking socio-linguistics, critical discourse analysis, rhetoric (especially the use of specific topoi, i.e. lines of argument) and argumentation theory (the critical reconstruction of the grounds, warrants, and conclusions of specific arguments) as its principal entry-points into the rhetoric and pragmatics of political language (see, e.g., the list of typical questions and the tabulation of discursive strategies provided in Reisigl and Wodak 2009: 93–4).[20] Furthermore, DHA seems to have no explicit or coherent programme to develop a particular line of institutional or structural analysis and no consistent approach to historical periodization (on this topic, see Jessop and Sum 2006: 323–33). This leads to rather *ad hoc* and eclectic contextualization, depending in part on the choice of co-investigators from other disciplines. Hence its theoretical and methodological centre of gravity remains firmly anchored in critical discourse analysis. In contrast, CPE has a more eclectic approach to the methods and techniques to be used in critical semiotic analysis and a more elaborated account of structuration, periodization and the mechanisms involved in the co-evolution of semiosis and structuration.

Given these comments, we now present a table that compares CPE with the three 'grand theories', two supplementary or complementary approaches in the field of conceptual history, and the discourse historical approach. In different ways, each of these is concerned with the variation, selection and retention of discourse (see Table 3.2). Nonetheless, as the table indicates, they differ in their discursive focus, the key sources of inspiration, their temporal focus, their key themes and the role of history. In its 'cultural' aspects, CPE looks to several grand theories and Cambridge conceptual history and also acknowledges, for some purposes, the *Annaliste*–Braudelian emphasis on different temporalities and history from below. It also has strong affinities with the grounded analytics of different approaches to CDA, especially Fairclough's approach, which draws fairly systematically on substantive concepts and arguments from critical political economy and media studies. Without this kind of supplementation, CDA would involve analytical strategies rooted in linguistic mechanisms (and in this sense, consistent with critical realism) but lack a coherent and consistent articulation to substantive theories about the non-discursive aspects of social practices and the historical and social contexts in which these mechanisms may reproduce the social order and/or transform it. In both cases, it behoves advocates of CDA (including DHA) to clarify the often unstated but clearly present substantive theories that enable them to analyse social practices rather than restrict their analyses to discursive practices (see Chapter 4).

Laclau and Mouffe's Discourse Analysis

We now review the self-proclaimed 'post-Marxist' approach of Ernesto Laclau and Chantal Mouffe because, if valid, it represents a fundamental challenge to the CPE project. Individually and together they have developed a coherent set of linguistic and discourse-analytical tools to analyse

Table 3.2 Approaches to semantic histories and historical semantics

Approach	Vernacular materialism	*Begriffs-geschichte*	Foucault: archaeology	Conceptual history	*Histoire des mentalités*	DHA	CPE
Discursive focus	Spatial historical linguistics	Key concepts (*Grundbegriffe*) Counter-concepts	Episteme Discursive formation	Political languages, vocabulary	Everyday collective mental models	Discourse, genre, text, ideologies	Multiple imaginaries (complexity reduction)
Key figures	Marx, Croce, Bartoli, Russian linguistics	Heidegger, Gadamer, Carl Schmitt	Kant, Marx, Nietzsche, Husserl	Wittgenstein, J.L. Austin, T. Kuhn	Marc Bloch, Lucien Febvre, Fernand Braudel	Husserl, Habermas, [Foucault]	Gramsci, Fairclough, Foucault
Temporal focus	Modernity Revolution Passive revolution	Epochal shifts, historical time, layering of time, temporalization	Epochal shifts, events, the present	Specific events, conjunctures (e.g. crises) Paradigm shifts	*Longue durée* cycles, events and 'total history'	Periods, 'episodes', conjunctures, 'crisis'	Multi-temporal (incl. crises) spatio-temporal fixes, constitutive outsides
Key themes	Hegemony Translation Intellectuals	Semantic fields (concepts and counter-concepts)	Episteme Dispositive Governmentality Ethics	Rhetoric Convention Co-textuality	History from below (thick description of everyday life)	Argumentation, identity politics, politics of memory	Hegemony, sub- and counter-hegemonies
Role of History	Historicism	Historical semantics (focus on [dis-]continuity of key concepts)	Origins Archaeology Genealogy *Urgences*	Historical pragmatics (focus on use of language and intentions)	Changing *mentalités collectives* (world views)	Historical contexts (incl. organizations, institutions), and shifting situational frames	These plus variation, selection, retention, de- and recontextualization

130

politics and hegemony and to provide a theoretical rationale for a radical pluralist democracy that breaks decisively with economism and class reductionism (Laclau 1977; Mouffe 1979). The key to this approach is the following statement:

> By 'the discursive' I understand nothing which in a narrow sense relates to texts but the ensemble of phenomena of the societal production of meaning on which a society as such is based. It is not a question of regarding the discursive as a plane or dimension of the social but as having the same meaning as the social ... the non-discursive is not opposite to the discursive as if one were dealing with two different planes because there is nothing societal that is determined outside the discursive. History and society are therefore an unfinished text. (Laclau 1980: 87)

This 'unfinished text' is produced through 'articulatory practices'. The notion of articulation implies that discursivity (in other words, the social) is always constituted relationally, always under construction, and liable to disarticulation. Articulation is also the basis of hegemony. The 'raw materials' of this social-cum-societal construction are polysemic discursive units that exist as unfixed *elements* before being articulated as specific *moments* within particular discourses. The social is located uneasily between attempts at fixing meaning and the ultimate infeasibility of these attempts. To the extent that these attempts succeed it is because certain nodal points (*points de capiton*) emerge within discourse as privileged signifiers, or key principles, that limit the 'play of meaning' and around which discursive forms crystallize. However, because these nodal points are internal to discourse, not grounded outside it, they are inherently unstable. Key principles always have what Derrida (1988) calls a 'constitutive outside', that is, they exclude some elements in order to establish and stabilize a boundary but, in doing so, reveal the contingency of a hegemonic or dominant discourse.

It follows that meaning is only ever partially fixed and, given an ever-present surplus of possible meanings, any fix is contingent (it could have been fixed differently).[21] Discourse therefore continually overflows the limits of any possible stabilization by nodal points (Laclau and Mouffe 1985: 113). Paradoxically, this lack of fixity is the precondition of hegemony. Contingency is the ground, the space, in which struggles for hegemony move. Thus the greater is the contingency, the greater is the scope for hegemonic contestation. At stake here is the relation between signifiers and signified, which, on Laclau and Mouffe's account, occurs entirely within discourse and has no outside referent. Indeed, having claimed that all social practices are discursive practices, they then ignore their extra-discoursal aspects. They conclude that an adequate social explanation must refer to signifying relations rather to any type of physical or material causality. Above all, they reject the base–superstructure metaphor.[22] In emphasizing the purely contingent discursive articulation of the social world, they deny lawful links among events and qualities in the social world (Laclau and Mouffe 1985). In short, they embrace an 'anti-determinist acausalism' (cf. Bunge 1961: 29). Such claims ignore the need, long ago noted by Max Weber (1949), for explanations that are adequate at the level of causality as well as meaning.[23]

Although this equation of the social and discourse is a foundational ontological claim, it is presented as anti-foundational and anti-essentialist. This is certainly useful in critiquing 'hard political economy', that is, the naturalization and fetishization of economic and political relations as objective facts of social life (see below). It also vastly expands historical contingency and hence the scope for agents and strategies to make a difference. Yet this ignores the emergent, path-dependent specificities of various institutional orders and their forms of articulation in favour of a pan-politicist ontology that insists on the permanent possibility of reactivation of sedimented structures. This introduces another form of essentialism. It reduces the social to politics such that every social space is either actually politically contested or, although 'sedimented' (i.e. stabilized, naturalized), can be repoliticized (Laclau 2005: 154). This goes beyond a claim about the primacy of the political (which depends on the existence of extra-political regions or spheres) to dissolve any ontological distinction between the political and other fields on the grounds that such differences are constituted semantically and their boundaries are inherently unstable. Presumably this also holds for any emergent, extra-discursive structuring effects of such semantic distinctions. This ontological and epistemological anti-foundationalism leads Laclau and Mouffe to abandon any critical and effective account of the relations between semiosis and structuration in a social world beyond discourse.

The impact of their work depended on a specific theoretical and political conjuncture when classical Marxism was in yet another crisis and provided a convenient foil for their post-Marxist linguistic (discursive) turn. In terms of our previous distinctions, this turn was more of a thematic extension of post-structuralist linguistics into a terrain where Marxist and liberal democratic theoretical and political discourses previously dominated. This is evidenced by the fact that most of the concepts deployed by Laclau and Mouffe are borrowed from other theoretical currents. 'Discourse', 'discourse analysis', 'moment', 'genealogy', 'articulation' and 'regulated dispersion' all derive from Foucault. 'Floating signifier', 'empty signifier', 'overdetermination', 'suture' and 'nodal point' are taken from Freudian and Lacanian psychoanalysis and the work of the Slovenian psychoanalyst and political enfant terrible Slavoj Žižek. Paradigm and syntagm come from Saussure; sedimentation from phenomenology; and Derrida delivers 'undecidability', 'deconstruction', 'logic of supplementation' and 'never fully closed structures' (cf. Andersen 2003: 48–9). There is no parallel systematic appropriation, rearticulation and recontextualization of concepts from political economy or critical social science more generally. Instead, where reference is made to phenomena in these domains, they are introduced from ordinary language or lay social-scientific observations and employed in an *ad hoc* manner. Lest these remarks be misunderstood, we do not oppose the appropriation and recontextualization of concepts from other disciplines or currents of thought – this is part of the normal process of scientific development. Our criticism has two targets: first, these concepts are deprived of their external referents; and, second, the borrowings are asymmetrical – focusing exclusively on the semiotic rather than structural moment of social practices and their emergent effects.

Because these concepts are borrowed, it is easier to disembed them from their discourse-centred deployment and recontextualize them in CPE (we considered one example in the work of Christoph Scherrer in Chapter 2). Three especially useful concepts are sedimentation, sutures and nodal points.

- Sedimentation refers, in this context,[24] to the naturalization and institutionalization of social relations so that they are reproduced through dull repetition rather than deliberate articulation (Laclau 2005: 154; cf. Torfing 1999: 69–71; Glynos and Howarth 2007: 116). This can be reversed through a new hegemonic articulation that deconstructs and repoliticizes and rearticulates sedimented relations.
- The concept of suture (Miller 1966) refers to the inevitably temporary nature of attempts to bind different elements and relations together, despite their differences and distinctions. Consistent with its metaphorical connotations, a suture is a short-term fix that is bound to dissolve. This metaphor can be applied in other ways to social, semantic, institutional and spatio-temporal fixes (see Chapter 6).
- 'Nodal points' are provisional and unstable centres that emerge from the primordial flux of social relations to provide temporary points of reference for the contingent articulation of social relations and attempts to suture them into relatively stable, sedimented ensembles.

Given their pan-politicism, Laclau and Mouffe insist that power cannot be localized in the state or some other power centre but occurs across the whole field of discursivity. This argument is, of course, familiar from Foucault's critique of state-centred theorizing and his emphasis on the micro-politics of power. For Laclau and Mouffe, it follows that hegemony is 'free-floating' and must be articulated everywhere and in all directions (1985: 139). Moreover, because there is always a plurality of power centres, any one of them will be limited in its effectiveness by the others (ibid.: 139, 142–3; on decentred interpretive analysis in political science, see Bevir and Rhodes 2006). This argument is important but can be extended beyond discourse to nodal apparatuses, *dispositifs* or points of crystallization where dominant principles of societalization and domination are anchored (see Chapter 6).

TOWARDS A GRAND AND GROUNDED SYNTHESIS

One of the key features of CPE is its concern with the co-evolution of the semiotic and extra-semiotic. Preceding sections sampled some well-known approaches to this topic in work on historical semantics, broadly defined. We then offered a second set of comparisons, this time concerned with the mechanisms of variation, selection and retention of semantics. We now briefly inquire whether and, if so, how these approaches can be combined in a CPE approach. Here we use the four selectivities identified in earlier chapters (and elaborated in Chapter 4) to map some key issues in historical semantics (still broadly defined) and show how different schools with their different thematic foci and methodological preferences might be applied to variation, selection and retention (restabilization, recontextualization) within the broad remit of CPE.

To develop these proposals we draw two theoretical rabbits out of the CPE hat that are consistent with the six features of this approach and its concern with the interaction of the four modes of selectivity. The first rabbit is another approach to historical semantics, which has been proposed by Niklas Luhmann, one of the key influences on our overall theoretical approach. The second is the work of a Norwegian historian, Leidulf Melve, who has suggested that reception theory offers an important means to supplement and round out the history of ideas. We will develop this suggestion far beyond its author's original intentions – but this is, of course, one of the ironies involved in the reception of a text!

Historical Semantics

Niklas Luhmann, whose analyses influenced our 'complexity turn', developed an approach to historical semantics that differs in key respects from the German semantic conceptual history school.²⁵ He focused on the contingently necessary, mutually constitutive, unevenly developing relation between semantics and social structure (2008: 59). Luhmann distinguishes semantics from semiosis. The latter is a feature of all communication from trivial everyday chance encounters to the system codes and programmes that characterize specific functional systems, such as law, economics, politics, religion and art. Semantics refers to the socially available 'sense' (or meaning systems) that is (are) generalized on a higher level (beyond everyday life) and so becomes relatively independent of specific situations in everyday personal and organizational life (Luhmann 1980: 19). There is both an everyday, common semantics (or common sense) that provides the basic medium and substratum of social communication and more 'cultivated' semantics that correspond to specific codes and programmes in specific functional systems (Møller 2006: 51); for a critique of this distinction, see Andersen (2011). Semantics condenses multiple meanings and forms of difference (concepts, ideas, images and symbols) that permit a wide range of communicative possibilities in many different contexts. Thus semantics provides the general understanding of 'things' or the 'world' – including the social world – that a society has and uses in communication. The similarities with Koselleck's *Begriffsgeschichte* should be evident – the difference lies in his concern to combine conceptual and social history and Luhmann's concern to explore the co-evolution of semantics and structure (in addition, for a useful comparison of Foucault and Luhmann on discourse and semantics respectively, among other topics, see Kabobel 2011).

For Luhmann, semantics evolves through the selection mechanisms of meaning-making (including intertextuality) and structuration evolves through material causality. There are limits to plausible arguments in semiosis and to possible structural combinations. Nonetheless he identifies greater scope for variation in semantics than in structures.²⁶ Semantics and structures also co-evolve in a spiral relation. Thus, while ideational changes facilitate changes in structure, structural changes likewise open possibilities for new ideas. There is no one-to-one correlation between semantics and social structure: indeed, too tight a connection would block innovation in both. They develop unevenly. As it is, there is scope for play in meanings without immediate structural repercussions; and structural change can occur without being immediately reflected or refracted in ideational change. Yet, over time, they are related. Lexical change leads to semantic change (e.g. the turn from Negroes to African Americans also changes communication). *Sinnmachung* unfolds within the limits of combinability of structural and semantic evolution (Luhmann 2008: 60). As societal complexity increases, greater variety is required in both semantics and in structures – more specialized codes and programmes on one side, more specialized functional systems and institutional orders on the other. Luhmann notes that structures of modernity are often described with a pre-modern semantics. Accordingly, he regards post-modernism as a new self-description of modern society that seeks to catch up semantically with well-established structural changes.

Reception Theory

A concern with the reception of discourse and communication is an obvious extension of discourse analysis and occurs in all variants of semiotic analysis reviewed above. There are also more specialized bodies of theory that focus specifically on reception, beginning in literary theory but rapidly spreading beyond. This is 'reception theory', which goes under several names and involves several different traditions and foci. It studies the reception rather than the production of ideas and is, of course, a key aspect of any sociological analysis of meaning-making and communication. It is also crucial to any analysis of variation, selection and retention. It has found its strongest reception as a branch of literary studies, which focuses on how (literary) work is 'received' by readers. It is also influential in hermeneutic interpretation more generally. In both cases, reception involves more than a passive, one-off reading. It includes rereading, the active anticipation of sense and meaning, the testing of understandings, and the capacity to supplement the text to apprehend and recontextualize it from the viewpoint of a given reader. This downplays the role of authorial intention in literary production and reception, and emphasizes the intertextual, supratextual and contextual aspects of (literary) communication. It has obvious broader significance for discourse as well as textual analysis and, hence, for the variation, selection and retention of sense- and meaning-making more generally. The question of reception is also raised in cultural criticism and was a key theme in Williams's cultural materialism, the work of the Birmingham School of Cultural Studies, and many other currents in cultural studies.

Considering the initial production of a text as well as its reception, we can distinguish three moments. The first is the production of the text in its intertextual and historical context. Authorial intention is relevant here but is not a freely chosen, unconstrained act of creativity. It is shaped by historical legacies, the constraints of language, genre, styles and so forth, authorial competence, and the available means of production and transmission. Next is the short-term *reception* of the text. As Gareth Stedman Jones, a leading social historian, notes, any good historian of ideas must go beyond the analysis of authorial intention to 'give equal or greater attention to questions of intended constituency, to the different forms of appropriation of particular texts – what meanings were actually conveyed, how they were understood and interpreted' (1996: 29). The third moment is the long-term impact of the text in its broader context. Drawing on German work in the history of ideas, these moments can be studied in terms of *Entstehungsgeschichte, Rezeptionsgeschichte* and *Wirkungsgeschichte*. These refer respectively to the history of a text's development in its broader social context, the history of its reception, and the response that it triggers and/or the effects that it produces in the long run.[27] These can be linked to the themes of variation, selection and retention that comprise the key general mechanisms of evolution provided that each moment is also seen as involving these mechanisms too. The same argument holds, of course, for discourse more generally (cf. Link 1997).

Leidulf Melve's synthesis of approaches to the history of ideas is useful here. After a detailed survey of the history of political thought from the mid-1970s to the mid-2000s, he proposed to combine approaches that, he claims, are usually considered antithetic and incommensurable. These are linguistic contextualism, German *Begriffsgeschichte* and the Cambridge School of conceptual history. The key to such a synthesis is a fourth theoretical and methodological approach with its two divisions into short-term resonance and medium- to long-term impact (see Melve 2006 for further discussion). He then suggests:

> By combining the insights of linguistic contextualism in dealing with the synchronic dimension with *Rezeptionsgeschichte* and *Wirkungsgeschichte* in relation to the diachronic dimension, the end result is an approach that is able to grasp the innovative ideas at the moment they appear as well as to trace their eventual further destiny through subsequent receptions. *Begriffsgeschichte* is introduced because of its focus on the institutional and diachronic side of the mediation of political concepts. The stress which the so-called 'critical conceptual history' lays on 'contradictions' as a means to explain political-theoretical as well as political change has been used in order to introduce *a pragmatic dimension* to the synthesis. (Melve 2006: 406; final italics added)

This proposal is not novel in general terms. What is original and important is Melve's identification of the relevant theoretical tools. We can build on this to explore the relationship among mechanisms involved in the variation, selection and retention of discursive practices. Indeed, as the attentive reader might now expect, all four of the selectivities that we have identified in earlier chapters have a bearing on reception. This is not just a question of discursive selection and retention of discourse. Structural asymmetries, technological biases and agential capacities also matter for the critical or uncritical rejection, appropriation and recontextualization. In this sense, reception is a mediated (and increasingly mediatized) everyday practice.[28]

Table 3.3 *Approaches to historical semantics in the light of the four selectivities as they operate in and through semiosis*

Mode of selectivity	Field of selection	Evolutionary mechanisms		
		Variation (*Entstehung*)	Selection (*Rezeption*)	Retention (*Wirkung*)
Structural	*Langue*	*Parole*	Context	Language change
Discursive	Textuality	Text	Intertextuality	Semantics
Technical	Semio-logistics	Inscription	Medial selectivities	Dispositive
Agential	Situated practice	Authorial intention	Reception	Effects

Based on Melve's suggestion and other work in intellectual history and cultural studies reviewed above, Table 3.3 presents a first attempt to outline a research programme and methodological tools for studying historical semantics and social structure in the spirit of CPE. It crosstabulates the three mechanisms of evolution that, we argue, apply as much to semiosis as to structure, with the four types of selectivity that we have identified above and explore in more detail in Chapter 4.

In interpreting this table it is important to remember that it concerns the four modes of selectivity *in relation to semiosis*. Thus: (1) structural factors bear on the structure of semiosis, for example, *langue*, semantics, orders of discourse, and not on the features of social structuration; (2) discursive factors deal with the selection, retention and variation of textual features linked to text, paratext, intertext and supratext; (3) technical factors deal with the medium and materiality of discourse – the themes explored in what Debray calls sociologistics; and (4) agential factors deal with subjectivation and authorial intention from the viewpoint of situated enunciation. Chapters 4 and 5 present a more elaborate account of all four selectivities.

An earlier version of this table named one or two relevant discourse-analytical approaches in each cell, but we decided against reproducing it here on three grounds. First, few analytical approaches, let alone grand theories, relate to just one cell. Second, naming a limited set might suggest, mistakenly, that these are the only relevant theoretical and/or analytical strategies. Third, it could also imply that these are already fully commensurable without the need for further theoretical work.

PUTTING SEMIOSIS IN ITS PLACE

We have reviewed diverse approaches to semiosis and semantics. Our review was organized on the basis of a distinction between grand theories (not to be confused with general theory) and grounded analytics (not to be confused with grounded theory). We chose this strategy because most efforts to integrate semiosis into political economy use grounded analytics rather than grand theory. Yet CPE requires grand theories of semiosis to match those theories that it draws on and develops to analyse structuration. Thus we propose a two-stage meta-theoretical strategy for 'putting semiosis in its place' in CPE:

- First, select one or more *grand theories* from the variety that exist on the grounds that they meet certain criteria needed to facilitate the development of CPE. Above all, these theories should take semiosis seriously without absolutizing a semiotic perspective; this is crucial for locating semiosis within a more general account of social order. The set of grand theories that can do this remains to be defined and we surveyed only those within our admittedly limited purview that seem most compatible with our overall approach to the critique of political economy.
- Second, select one or more approaches to *grounded analytics* that are consistent with the preferred grand theories of semiosis. The choice of grounded analytics depends on their operating with assumptions that are consistent (or eventually commensurable) with the grand theories. Which of these grounded analytics and, especially, which particular methods and analytical tools are deployed will depend on pragmatic considerations.

In other words, concern with grand theories should come before grounded analytics. One problem that critics identified in discourse institutionalism, for example, is that it is light on discourse theory and weak on analytics (see Chapter 1). It tends to focus on the genesis of 'ideas' (narratives, policy paradigms, projects etc.) or their effects. It has not elaborated a broader account of semiosis and its place within the semiotic–structure relation and it lacks the theoretical and analytical tools for a coherent account of variation, selection and retention. Some other approaches in the field (such as the post-Marxist discourse analysis of hegemony or political discourse analysis more generally) seem to be located at the other extreme – they engage in the 'exorbitation of language' to such an extent that they provide an epistemology to study the social. This results in their being light on non-discursive accounts of structuration and weak on structural analytics. Overall, this implies that, in line with the above stipulations, critical discourse analysis and similar methods belong in the realm of grounded analytics. It is the grand theories that have the bigger role to play in developing CPE. This helps to explain why our approach to discourse analysis is closer to the Foucauldian and German traditions identified by Angermüller (2011), with their interest in dispositive as well as discourse analysis, than to the Anglophone tradition, and it is also why we incline to 'grand-theory'-oriented CDA rather than more empiricist, positivistic analytical methods that focus on textual analysis.

On the basis of this distinction, we now suggest five steps to put semiosis in its place. These comprise: (1) elaborating the ontological significance of semiosis in complexity reduction; (2) presenting some foundational concepts for the analysis of sense- and meaning-making; (3) exploring semiosis through the same evolutionary approach that is applied in the study of structures, that is, explore the variation, selection and retention of different efforts at sense- and meaning-making; (4) considering not only how textual factors (broadly interpreted) influence this evolutionary process but also how it is shaped by three other selectivities that are crucial for CPE; and (5) considering the uneven structural coupling and co-evolution of semiosis and structuration in the *longue durée*, more immediate socio-cultural contexts and conjunctures, and the more immediate responses to events. We have already indicated many of the concepts that would be useful to develop this agenda. Chapter 4 combines them with those needed to analyse structuration, and explores these issues further in the context of the relations among Marx, Gramsci and Foucault, and their relevance to the analysis of structural, discursive, technological and agential selectivities.

CONCLUDING REMARKS

CPE joins concepts and tools from critical semiotic analysis with those from critical political economy. It explores the interpenetration and co-evolution of semiosis (an umbrella term for diverse forms of intersubjective meaning-making) and structuration in regard to the emergence, consolidation and transformation of the instituted features of an improbable political economic order. Different forms of the cultural turn all assume that semiosis is causally efficacious as well as meaningful, and that actual events and processes and their emergent effects can not only be *interpreted* but also *explained*, at least in part, in terms of semiosis. In this chapter we have shown how grand semiotic theories and grounded discourse analytics can be combined to provide organizing concepts, identify underlying mechanisms, and generate plausible hypotheses about the role of semiosis in societalization and societal evolution. One implication of this analysis is that semiosis cannot be explained in purely semiotic terms. Other factors are also involved in the contingent emergence, provisional consolidation and ongoing realization of competing imaginaries. It is the continuing interaction of the semiotic and extra-semiotic in a complex co-evolutionary process of variation, selection and retention that gives relatively successful economic and political imaginaries their performative, constitutive force in the material world.

Returning to more programmatic questions and including the results of the Introduction and chapters one and two, our reflections invite two sets of questions. These were addressed initially from the viewpoint of institutions and their embedding in broader structural configurations; and then from the viewpoint of semiosis and its embedding in specific semantic fields. They provide the bridge to Chapter 4.

First, given the structural contradictions, strategic dilemmas, indeterminacy and overall improbability of capitalist reproduction, especially during its recurrent crises, which make any stable institutional fix improbable, what role does semiosis play in construing, constructing and temporarily stabilizing capitalist social formations at least within specific spatio-temporal fixes and their zones of relative stability even as it displaces and defers conflicts, contradictions and crisis tendencies elsewhere and/or into the future? Translated into a CPE research agenda, and by way of illustration, one could ask: in the face of economic and political crises, what contribution do established or new economic and political imaginaries make, if any, to crisis management and resolution?

Second, given the infinity of possible meaningful communications and potential (mis)understandings enabled by semiosis, how do extra-semiotic as well as semiotic factors affect the variation, selection and retention of semiosis and its associated practices in ordering, reproducing and transforming capitalist social formations and their various spatio-temporal features? In other words, one might ask why, given the meaning-making and path-shaping potential of competing economic and political imaginaries, only some of these get selected and institutionalized and thereby come to co-constitute and embed economic subjectivities, interests, activities, organizations, institutions, structural ensembles, emergent economic orders and their social embedding, and the dynamics of economic performance. In short, how do such imaginaries come to provide not only a semiotic frame for *construing* the world but also for contributing to its *construction*? Similar arguments hold for political and other imaginaries. Together these sets of questions pose the problem of how to navigate one's way between the structuralist Scylla and constructivist Charybdis. This is the problem that we now consider.

NOTES

1. We therefore ignore syntax, that is, the formal relation of one sign to another.
2. As no entry-point is innocent, a different starting point (e.g. in rhetoric, argumentation theory or authorial intention) would lead to a different kind of CPE.
3. For Luhmann (1995), actors and observers reduce complexity 'by drawing a distinction' that distinguishes a 'marked' field from its environment and it is the 'properties' of the marked field that form the basis for action.
4. Ives (2004a) sometimes suggests, wrongly but understandably, that Gramsci does not separate the linguistic and extra-linguistic.
5. Glottologia studies the structure of language, including etymology and grammar, from a historical viewpoint. It is now known as *linguistica storica* or *diacronica* (historical or diachronic linguistics).
6. In German, *Geschichtliche Grundbegriffe: Historisches Lexikon zur politisch-sozialen Sprache in Deutschland*.
7. Vološinov (1973): 'Everything ideological possesses *meaning:* it represents, depicts or stands for something lying outside itself. In other words, it is a *sign. Without signs there is no ideology*' (1973: 9; italics in original).
8. The French project has published its results in the *Handbuch politisch-sozialer Grundbegriffe in Frankreich, 1680–1820* (*Handbook of Political and Social Basic Concepts in France, 1680–1820*). It examines the period up to and beyond the French Revolution. Its contributors focus on political struggles, popular mentalities and popular, even ephemeral, texts like political catechisms rather than on social history, economic struggles and the canonical texts of 'grand theorists'.
9. This is complicated by the several words or phrases used to translate or express '*dispositif*' in English: alignment, apparatus, complex edifices, construct, deployment, device, grid of intelligibility, mechanism, patterns of correlation, positivities, regime of practices, system, topologies of power, and so forth (Collier 2009; Coté 2007; Crampton and Elden 2007; and, especially, Peltonen 2004).
10. The Duisburg Institute for Language and Social Research.
11. We reject Marvin Harris's commitment to the base–superstructure distinction but accept his distinction between emic and etic: emic refers to descriptions and explanations deemed right and meaningful by a participant; etic denotes descriptions and explanations used by scientific observers to generate and strengthen theoretical explanations (Harris 1988: 131–2). With different phrasing, this distinction is also found in Niklas Luhmann.
12. Harold Innis was a trans-disciplinary holist who emphasized the radical contingency of historical development based on the interaction of, *inter alia*, environmental, technological, logistical, political and ideational factors. He studied epochal shifts in the *longue durée*. Regarding communication technologies, for example, he analysed 5000 years of discontinuous development, showing their spatio-temporal selectivities and how they conditioned political and religious organization, the fate of civilizations and empires, and societalization more generally (for a clear introduction, see Diebert 1999).
13. Compare Marshall McLuhan (1964) on 'the medium is the message'.
14. For example, Debray writes: '[t]he dominant medium is the one that has a larger reach, that is faster, that is cheaper for the sender and requires less effort from the receiver (and is thus synonymous with greater comfort). In this sense, television dominates the radio, which dominates the newspaper, which dominates the brochure, which dominates the book, which dominates the manuscript, etc.' (1991: 301). There is a clear connection here with historical materialist and geographical concepts of time-space compression and time-space distantiation.
15. This translates as *Annals of Economic and Social History*. The current name is *Annales. Histoire, Sciences Sociales*.
16. Other key figures are Fernand Braudel, Michel de Certeau, Robert Mandrou, Georges Buby and Roger Chartier.

17. The work of one founding father (Marc Bloch 1973) on collective illusions, such as the healing power of the 'royal touch', can be cited here. Foucault adopted a similar technique of using past oddities to challenge current 'normalities'.
18. Hodge (2012: 1) claims that he and Gunther Kress first identified the need for CDA in a co-authored article in 1974 (Hodge and Kress 1974).
19. We draw this quotation from Reisigl and Wodak (2001).
20. Thus the DHA approach poses such questions as: (1) how are persons, objects, phenomena/events, processes and actions named and referred to linguistically? (2) What characteristics, qualities and features are attributed to social actors, objects, phenomena/events and processes? (3) What arguments are employed in the discourse in question? (4) From what perspective are these nominations, attributions and arguments expressed? And (5) are the respective utterances articulated overtly; are they intensified or mitigated? (see Reisigl and Wodak 2011: 93).
21. Cf. Luhmann (2000) on the contingency and paradoxical nature of decisions.
22. Laclau and Mouffe totally reject the base–superstructure distinction. They take this allusive and elusive metaphor literally and conclude that it posits total determination of the superstructure by an economic base that is a wholly self-sufficient *sui causa* (Laclau and Mouffe 1985: 120–21, 142; Laclau 1990: 6–14, 55; Laclau 2005: 250). They ignore alternative meanings and never consider whether it could be reinscribed into post-Marxist analysis.
23. While Luhmann is also suspicious of causal explanation, his operative constructionism allows a regulative role for the real world beyond communication. Laclau concedes this in his analysis of populism, in which external reality expresses itself via negation, that is, by providing a 'reality check' that limits the resonance of alternative political projects, making some more plausible and appealing than others (2005: 89, 91–6, 190–91, 201ff.).
24. In Husserl's phenomenology, sedimentation refers to the gradual accretion of past experiences in the memory, with a steady forgetting of their origins, so that they become taken for granted. He also refers to the 'retending' or retention of past experiences and memories, so that they form part of a subject's current world. This produces the *Lebenswelt* (lifeworld), in which we live our everyday lives in a 'present present' shaped by the legacies of 'past presents' (see, *inter alia*, Husserl 1936/1970). Husserl also sees social and cultural traditions in terms of sedimentation – leading to the idea of shared, or communalized, lifeworlds. These also shape horizons of action, that is, the variable perception of future possibilities. Discourse analysts extend this to the sedimentation of intersubjective meaning (e.g. Laclau and Mouffe 1985; Torfing 1999; Howarth 2013). Social constructivists have highlighted the dialectical nature of lifeworld – shaped as it is also by the nature of the world (e.g. Kraus 2006). We suggest that sedimentation also works in the naturalization of codes, programmes, modes of calculation and so on in the system world, that is, in specific institutional orders with their specialist 'truth regimes'.
25. Koselleck, the key figure in this School, was a colleague of Luhmann at Bielefeld.
26. For Luhmann, whereas semantics is a subset of semiosis, structures refer here to basic patterns of societal organization. If this claim referred to semiosis in general and variation at the level of individual practice, it would be harder to maintain.
27. As Robert Holub comments, *Rezeption* and *Wirkung* both concern the impact of a work *on someone* but are hard to distinguish. In a literary context, he suggests hesitantly, *Rezeption* relates to the reader and *Wirkung* to textual aspects (1984: xi–xii and passim). We distinguish them in terms of an immediate reception by 'readers' and longer-term social transformation as mediated through the text and its reception – which is closer to Melve's usage. It is also important to note that *Wirkung* involves unevenness, non-simultaneity, and various types of feedback.
28. A fourth-generation *Annaliste*, Roger Chartier, explores this through the inscription and reception of texts in the early modern period in terms of reading, note-taking, copying, translating and composing. He also considers the relations among 'writing surfaces (including stone, wax, parchment, paper, walls, textiles, the body, and the

heart), writing implements (including styluses, pens, pencils, needles, and brushes), and material forms (including scrolls, erasable tables, codices, broadsides and printed forms and books)' http://en.wikipedia.org/wiki/Annales_School, accessed 7 April 2013). This work complements Innis's more macro-historical analyses of technologies of communication (1950, 1951); see note 12.

PART II

Towards a post-disciplinary cultural political economy

4. Between Scylla and Charybdis: locating cultural political economy

This chapter synthesizes arguments from earlier chapters to provide the theoretical foundations for the first three of the six features of CPE listed in the Introduction. The full set is: (1) the grounding of the cultural turn in political economy in the existential necessity of complexity reduction; (2) an emphasis on the role of evolutionary mechanisms in shaping the movement from social construal to social construction and their implications for the production of hegemony; (3) its concern with the interdependence and co-evolution of the semiotic and the extra-semiotic; (4) the integration of individual, organizational and societal learning into the dialectic of semiosis and structuration; (5) the significance of technologies, in a broadly Foucauldian sense, in the consolidation of hegemony and its contestation in remaking social relations; and (6) its de-naturalization of economic and political imaginaries and contribution to the critique of ideology and domination.

We approach the first three features in 12 main steps. First, we discuss the two modes of complexity reduction that provide our entry-points into the field of CPE. These are semiosis and structuration. Both are necessary for social agents to 'go on' in the world, and each involves specific forms of enforced selection. Second, we introduce the terms to describe the discursive and extra-discursive aspects of social practices, distinguishing analytical levels or thematic foci ranging from the generic features of semiosis and structuration through to specific statements (or other communicative practices) and social interactions. We focus here on different aspects of social practices at a given temporal moment – diachronic relations are introduced later, especially in the section on the co-evolution of semiosis and structuration (see also Chapter 11). Third, we return to the crucial distinction between construal and construction, focusing on how and why only some construals come to be selected and retained as the basis for sedimented meaning. Fourth, building on this analysis, we examine how social imaginaries contribute to social structuration. Because semiosis is the novel element in CPE, we illustrate this analysis from economic imaginaries and economic order. Fifth, we relate sense- and meaning-making to different systems, institutional orders and the lifeworld, and indicate how to link semiosis to ideology.

Having established these points, we address this chapter's main focus: the challenge of navigating between Scylla and Charybdis. Thus, sixth, we discuss the consequences of a one-sided emphasis on structuration (the structuralist Scylla); and, seventh, we then turn to the consequences of a one-sided focus on semiosis (the constructivist Charybdis). Eighth, based on this even-handed critique, we indicate the magnitude of the challenge. More specifically, ninth, we present a diachronic account of the interdependence of the semiotic and extra-semiotic moments of social order and explore how their co-evolution operates. Tenth, in this context, we indicate how the CPE approach tackles one of the major challenges in the social sciences: subjectivation, subjects, their identities and their interests. Eleventh, we seek to refute misunderstandings that the co-evolution of sedimented meaning and structured complexity is unproblematic and results in durable, tension-free consensus and synchronous, friction-free stable structures. Such an impression would be quite contrary to CPE's principal arguments. Thus section eleven explores the inevitable, ever-present counter-tendencies to sedimented meaning and structural coherence. These counter-tendencies are grounded in the first instance in the lack of closure of any discourse and in the contradictions and crisis tendencies inherent in structures. Finally, twelfth, we draw some conclusions about the interconnections of the first three features and indicate how the other features can be brought into the analysis.

For the sake of completeness, we note here the chapters that discuss CPE's three remaining features: learning is explored in Chapter 11; technological and agential selectivities and the notion of dispositive are explored in Chapter 5; and the critique of ideology and domination is present throughout Chapters 5 to 12. All six features in their interconnection are discussed in the concluding chapter, Chapter 13.

ON TWO MODES OF COMPLEXITY REDUCTION

Semiosis and structuration are both necessary for social agents to 'go on' in the world, and each involves specific forms of enforced selection and selectivities. Semiosis is a dynamic source of sense and meaning. Structuration sets limits to compossible combinations of social relations and thereby contributes, as far as CPE research interests are concerned, to the institution of specific political economies. Together these two modes of complexity reduction tend through time to transform relatively meaningless and unstructured complexity into relatively meaningful and structured complexity. They succeed, *in so far as they do*, when the world becomes meaningful to actors and social interactions undergo structuration. In other words, the social and natural world becomes relatively meaningful and orderly for actors (and observers), and social interactions acquire a certain structural coherence in so far as limits are imposed on compossible social relations in a given spatio-temporal matrix. Many other meanings are thereby excluded, as are many other possible social worlds. This does not exclude competing imaginaries concerning different scales and fields of social action or, indeed, rival principles of societalization (*Vergesellschaftung*) more generally. For, in a world characterized by exploitation, oppression and exclusion, there are many possible standpoints for construing them as well as many possible sources of social disruption. Thus CPE aims to explain how such an order, in so far as it occurs, is enabled by semantic fixes (e.g. hegemonic meaning systems), social fixes rooted, for example, in institutionalized compromise, and spatio-temporal fixes that displace social problems elsewhere and/or defer them into the future (see Chapter 6).

Sense-making reduces complexity for actors (and observers) by directing attention to, and focusing action on, some aspects of the world out of countless possibilities. While the real world pre-exists complexity reduction (and is transformed in some respects through it), actors/observers lack direct access to it apart from the sheer facticity[1] (factuality) of the concrete historical situations into which they are 'thrown'. They do not encounter the world as pre-interpreted once-and-for-all, but must engage with and reflect on it in order to make some sense of it. The 'aspects' of interest are not objectively pre-given, nor subjectively pre-scripted, by hard-wired cognitive capacities. They depend for their selective apperception (recognition and misrecognition) mainly on the prevailing meaning systems of relevant actors and observers as these change over time.[2] In addition to reducing complexity for actors (and observers), sense-making also gives meaning to the world (Luhmann 1990: 81–2; Kress 2001: 74; for some implications in organizational studies, see Weick 1995; and, on public policy, Morçöl 2005). Such reductions are never wholly 'innocent': in construing the world, sense- and meaning-making frame lived experience, limit perceived courses of action, and shape forms of social contestation, alliance-building and domination. Furthermore, construals may help to constitute the natural and social world in so far as they guide a critical mass of self-confirming actions premised on their validity. This is the rational (ideational?) kernel to the weak constructivist position that we elaborate below.

The other mode of complexity reduction central to CPE is structuration. This concerns the emergent pattern of social interactions, including direct or indirect human interactions with the natural world. If these interactions are not to be random, unpredictable and chaotic, possible connections and sequences of action must be limited – but not so tightly constrained that adaptation in the face of changing circumstances is impossible. While structuration refers to a complex, contingent, tendential process that is mediated through action but produces results that no actors can be said to have willed, structure refers to the contingent outcome of diverse structuration efforts. (For an influential sociological account of structuration, see Giddens 1984; for German regulationist analyses of the structuring role of institutions, see Esser et al. 1994; for a Foucauldian critique of structuration that substitutes process-change analysis for structure and agency, see Caldwell 2007; for a communications-theoretical perspective that emphasizes the limits on understanding and social action imposed by the demands of compossibility, see Rustemeyer 2006; for a useful temporality-sensitive, systems-theoretical approach, see Tang 2007.)

Structuration, with its mix of constrained opportunities, recursivity, redundancy and flexibility, facilitates social reproduction somewhere between an impossible stasis and the edge of chaos. Reproduction is not automatic but is mediated through situated social action that occurs in more or less structured contexts. Hence structuration creates a complex assemblage of asymmetrical opportunities for social action, privileging some actors over others, some identities over others, some ideal and material interests over others, some spatio-temporal horizons of action over others, some coalition possibilities over others, some strategies over others and so on (Chapter 1). Revealing these biases and the variable scope for strategic action in different periods and conjuncture is the key to *Herrschaftskritik*.

Chapter 1 discussed structuration in strategic-relational terms but focused largely on institutionalization and its limits. It highlighted the importance of institutional complementarities (the goodness of fit across institutions and institutional clusters) and of institutional innovation (whether due to institutional entrepreneurs, incremental change or continuing bricolage). Anticipating arguments developed below and in Chapters 6, 7 and 11, Chapter 1 also noted the challenges to structured coherence that are rooted in the contradictions inherent in specific social forms, the crisis tendencies linked to particular accumulation regimes, and diverse social conflicts and antagonisms. These challenges lead to 'problematizations' and strategic and/or tactical efforts to manage them. In previous work we have discussed these in terms of improbable, partial and temporary social fixes, institutional fixes and spatio-temporal fixes (Jessop 2002; Jessop and Sum 2006). To this we would now add semantic (or discursive) fixes grounded in the sedimentation of particular imaginaries and their role in building and consolidating, at least temporarily, taken-for-granted interpretations of the social world. This chapter suggests ways in which these different fixes are related and may co-evolve, and Chapter 5 takes these arguments further by connecting them to dispositives and governmentality.

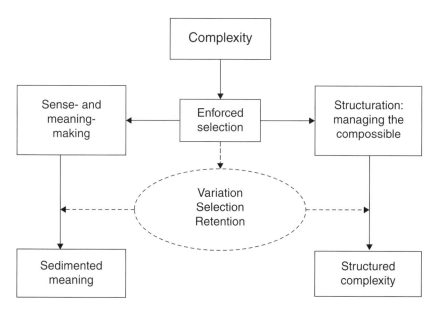

Figure 4.1   Complexity reduction through enforced selection

Figure 4.1 presents a highly simplified model of what complexity reduction through semiosis and structuration involves; this model will be elaborated in successive sections of this chapter. Its first iteration presents only the basic features of complexity reduction in its crudest form and does not indicate how this approach can be applied in the critique of ideology and domination. This is the purpose of Figure 4.2, which introduces additional elements to highlight the improbability of sedimented meaning and structured coherence. This iteration is nonetheless still static. A more dynamic version, highlighting the differential contribution of semiotic and 'material' factors to variation, selection and retention of crisis construals, which can be applied to other examples, is presented in Figure 11.1. Missing from all three figures are technological and agential selectivities – these are introduced in the context of dispositive analysis in Chapter 5.

SOCIAL PRACTICES AT THE INTERFACE OF SEMIOSIS AND STRUCTURATION

This section clarifies key terms that we will use to discuss semiosis. 'Discourse' is a conceptual minefield and has provoked many misunderstandings and controversies. It can refer to *language* (whether spoken or written) and/or to *semiosis* (sense- and/or meaning-making) more generally. Further, in either case, discourse can refer to *linguistic or semiotic features* alone and/or to their articulation with *social practices*. Viewed from a CPE perspective, adopting a social-practice perspective is preferable because it opens more connections to the social world.

Semiosis

This is the most general term for sense- and meaning-making. Scholars of pansemiosis or biosemiosis, such as Barbieri (2008, 2012), insist that semiosis occurs in the natural as well as the social world.[3] If one accepts this, social semiosis is distinctive for the intersubjective quality of sense and meaning. Semiosis exists in 'the space between expression and understanding' created by the separation of subjects (cf. Hirschkop 2000: 3–4). In other words, sense- and meaning-making in the social world are not individual acts: they involve communication. Thus semiosis is dialogical rather than monological but may also be hierarchical and contested. It can involve conversation, negotiation, contestation and, indeed, open conflict (extending well beyond dialogue) about the sense and meaning of communications. This is another area where the SRA is relevant (see below). Indeed, just as institutions are typically conditions, not objects, of choice, so semiosis (here, the available semantics, rules and modalities that govern or shape communication) cannot be chosen but can be deployed creatively within these limits. They are also liable to change over time, including through deliberate interventions.

Semiosis involves more than language, verbal or written. Sociolinguistics reveals that sense- and meaning-making (or, for some authors, *representation*) 'happens at all levels and engages very many aspects of linguistic behaviour well beyond those encompassed in "core linguistics" ... blurring the boundaries between that which is linguistic, that which is social, and that which lies in other semiotic modes' (Kress 2001: 67). Historically, the forms and mediation of communication also shift – which affects in turn the content of communication. Thus language must now be analysed as 'just one of a number of modes of communication, all of which are culturally and socially shaped. Verbal language is being displaced as a communicational mode by image, in many sites of public communication' (ibid.).

These remarks by Gunther Kress, a co-founder of CDA (see Chapter 3), are important for CPE work on four counts. First, they indicate that critical linguistic analysis cannot be confined to the core linguistic features of language but must examine both text and context. Second, language should not provide the primary model for studying semiosis, let alone social practices and their effects more generally. Yet this discourse-imperialist exorbitation of language uses the latter as a model to understand the world beyond language (examples include Lévi-Strauss 1972; Kristeva 1969, 1975; Coward and Ellis 1977; Laclau and Mouffe 1985; for critiques of exorbitation, see Anderson 1983; Boucher 2008; Eagleton 1991; and, more generally, Pêcheux 1982: 47, 55–7; Jones 1996). Such one-sided interpretations neglect structuration as the other side of complexity reduction. This has its own distinctive features, which cannot be adequately modelled on language.

Third, CPE would benefit from a multi-modal analysis of semiosis that considers not only the various modes of sense- and meaning-making but also their relative importance in different historical periods and different social contexts. Quoting Kress again, this raises the issue of specialization: 'if other modes take some of the communicational load, then the question of what load language takes arises; and following from that, if there is a functional specialization between the modes – writing doing one kind of job, image another – what effect will that have on language itself?' (2001: 67). And, fourth, communication occurs through different modes with different materialities and different affordances regarding what can be communicated and with what effects, involving different types of asymmetry in social relations, and opening space for (constrained, reflexive) choice about meaning-making. These are also topics for which a strategic-relational approach is suited, including the technological selectivities associated with particular modes of semiosis.

Discourse

Discourse can be usefully deployed to designate and differentiate particular sets of semiotic practices that produce and communicate sense and meaning. In other words, whereas semiosis can be regarded as a broad but thin concept (or, as Fairclough notes, an abstract noun) that characterizes the generic features of semiosis, regardless of form or modality, discourse is a 'count noun' that denotes particular types of semiosis (e.g. forms of discourse, codes, genres, styles, and representations of self-identities and alterity). These share the generic features of semiosis but have their own particularities as discourses, distinctive preconditions and specific effects. Discourses can be studied in terms of their semiotic form and content (i.e. the communication of sense and meaning) or, more broadly, in terms of how these features are linked to other aspects of communicative practices. These semiotic practices, when viewed in the round (integrally), can be called discursive. It is nonetheless important to distinguish between their discoursal (semiotic) and non-discoursal (non-semiotic) aspects and to consider their interplay (cf. Fairclough 2003). 'Basically, everybody agrees that discourse entails linguistic practices, and hence that linguistic investigation is an important part of discourse analysis. Nevertheless, nobody denies that discourse is more than language, and hence linguistic investigation can only cover a part of discourse analysis' (Spitzmüller and Warnke 2011: 79). Thus to describe only its discoursal features is insufficient for interpreting and explaining the effects of a discursive practice.

Social Practice

All social practices have sense and meaning for their agents: without this, they could not be designated as social. But no social practice is reducible to its semiotic moments. It also has what, for now, we will call 'substantive' aspects, including social forms, institutional contexts, social embedding and social effects. Hence CPE considers not only how texts produce meaning and thereby help to generate social structure, but also how this is constrained by emergent, non-semiotic features of social structure as well as by inherently semiotic factors.

For example, considered as a discursive practice, economic activity is defined by its use of a semantics (codes, programmes, vocabulary etc.) that refers in some way to the 'economy'. This is already problematic, of course, because some discursive practices are situated at the intersection of several semantic systems (e.g. a contract negotiation over the appropriate legal form of intellectual property rights in a scientific discovery with a view to determining the future division of revenues in a public–private partnership). Discourses in everyday life have their own complexities and rely far more on ordinary language than specialized semantics, jargons, expertise and so on. Considered as a social practice, economic activity also involves the appropriation and transformation of nature for the purposes of material provisioning (cf. Polanyi 1957). Or, in more historically specific terms, such activity could be defined by its role in, for example, profit-oriented, market-mediated capital accumulation or, alternatively, in the operations of a workers' cooperative that challenges the dominance of the capitalist order. These substantive economic aspects must obviously be associated with particular discursive practices, but their conditions, logic, dynamic and effects cannot be fully interpreted and explained by an analysis that focuses only on the discoursal and non-discoursal features of these more encompassing social practices.

It is tempting to describe those aspects not included under the rubric of discursive practice as 'material'. This would be doubly misleading. First, discourse has material aspects and material effects. And, second, while a social practice has important extra-discursive features, these are connected to its meaning and motives. This is why social explanations must be adequate at the level of meaning and material causation. This argument can be extended to the social world more generally. Because complexity reduction has both semiotic and structural aspects, we should treat the 'semiotic' and the 'social' as dialectically related moments of the social world. Its semiotic moment refers to meaning-making and the emergent properties of discursive formations (such as distinct discourses, genres, genre chains, styles or intertextuality) regardless of their condensation, or otherwise, in social structures. And its social moment concerns the extra-semiotic features of social practices and their role as objective conditions and results of action (such as social cohesion and institutional integration, dilemmas and contradictions, and institutional logics) that operate 'behind the backs' of agents and may not correspond to their meaning-making efforts. In other words, in so far as they have different emergent properties, the semiotic (cultural) and social (material) are ontologically as well as analytically distinct. Conversely, in so far as the social is grounded in discursively constituted and meaningful action, it is also semiotic; and, in so far as semiosis is realized in/through social relations with distinctive emergent properties, it is social. The scope for disjunction and non-correspondence between the cultural and social moments makes it necessary to study both in their articulation.

This is why CPE insists on the ontological specificities of at least some *emergent* aspects of the form, content and logics of social relations. Without analysing such specificities, the social world is reduced to its semiotic moments. To escape this trap, it is essential to develop categories for analysing the substantive aspects of social practices and their role in structuration. In the field of political economy, for example, these categories define the specific logic of profit-oriented, market-mediated accumulation in the context of an evolving world market. On this basis one could investigate, for example, the disorienting impact of crises on taken-for-granted (sedimented) economic imaginaries; or, again, examine how changing economic imaginaries may reconfigure economic practices, institutions, accumulation regimes and modes of regulation.

PUTTING DISCURSIVE AND SOCIAL PRACTICES IN THEIR PLACE

The distinctions introduced above undermine the common distinction (at least common in the 1980s and 1990s) between the 'discursive' and 'non-discursive' in which the latter is somehow unmediated and pre-discursive – whether this is understood (!) at the level of experience or of practice (cf. Jones 1996: 27). This is especially troubling where it implies that the social world comprises separate discursive and non-discursive fields of action. Gareth Stedman Jones's comments on the limits of the linguistic turn in history are pertinent here:

> activities generate meaning – or to be more accurate – a myriad of meanings – which reside in, and can be deciphered through their juxtaposition to other meanings within a vast and practically infinite semiological field. Complex phenomena like 'institutions', 'political events' or 'economic practices' are not non-discursive in the sense that they lack, or have not acquired, meaning or particular sets of meanings. On the contrary, they represent concentrates of meaning, arenas within which large numbers of often heterogeneous discursive practices of different weight, different temporality and different provenance, overlap and intersect. Such phenomena are never prior to meaning; rather from the beginning they are prone to be overloaded with different and often incompatible meanings – hence the difficulty, perhaps impossibility – of unambiguous signification. (Jones 1996: 26–7)

We use the terms 'discursive' and 'non-discursive' *within* the broader concept of social practice to distinguish between its semiotic moment and its (potentially) transformative moment. In this context, it might sometimes be useful to arrange social practices along a continuum ranging from, say, improvised tool-making in response to an immediate need to, say, metaphysical reflections on the historiography of philosophies of other-worldly religions. This said, CPE cannot rest content with an analysis of discursive practices, of their articulation to social practices, and of social practices as sites where discursive and non-discursive practices intersect. Exploring what more is required provides the space for thinking about other connotations of the 'non-discursive'.

There are three ways to interpret this term: (1) the pre-discursive as the set of conditions of discursive practices, (2) the post-discursive as those emergent, unintended effects of these practices that are unacknowledged by first-order, unreflexive agents; and (3) the extra-discursive as the diverse emergent, unintended and unacknowledged effects and aspects of structuration. We discuss the first two now and the extra-discursive in regard to structuration.

The *pre-discursive* concerns the conditions that facilitate a given practice question, whether or not these conditions are acknowledged by some or all of its practitioners. Semiosis is never a purely intra-semiotic matter without external reference. It cannot be understood or explained without identifying and exploring the extra-semiotic conditions that enable semiosis and make it more or less effective – including its embedding in material practices and their relation to natural and social constraints and affordances. When we discuss discursive practices, these conditions can be described as pre-discursive (or pre-textual), discursively relevant or discourse-conditioning. For language, these include features of the kind studied in structural linguistics (in other words, its synchronic aspects) in so far as these constrain language use and/or provide affordances for statements within these limits or, indeed, facilitate or prompt linguistic innovation. Other modes of sense- and meaning-making also have such structural features that are conditions of choice rather than objects of choice. CPE is concerned not only with how texts produce meaning and thereby help to generate social structure, but also how such production is constrained by emergent, non-semiotic features of social structure as well as by inherently semiotic factors. This said, the present approach emphasizes the diachronic aspects of language and semiosis (we explore the implications of this in the next section). Similar arguments obtain for the pre-discursive conditions that make for effective social practices. These include the 'raw materials' and practical means through which the practice is actualized, instituted and sedimented. We discussed this for communication above, and similar points hold for other social practices. This is the home domain of 'practice theory' and the basis for a 'practical turn' in the social sciences (e.g. Turner 1994; Knorr-Cetina et al. 2000).

The *post-discursive* is the domain of the effects of discursive and/or social practices. In addition to intended and/or anticipated effects (over diverse horizons of action), these include unintended and unanticipated effects. Some or all of these effects may not be describable within the semantic or discursive frames associated with the relevant discursive practices – apart from recognition that they 'do not make sense' within these frames. This holds both for incomprehension of communications and unexpected substantive effects relative to the 'material' moment of a social practice, that is, failure to achieve intended results or the actualization of unanticipated effects. The relative success or failure of construals of the world depends on how both they and any attempts at construction match the properties of the materials (including social phenomena such as actors and institutions) used to construct social reality. We explore these aspects of practice in Chapters 10 and 11.

To conclude this section, Table 4.1 identifies five meanings of discourse depending on its non-semiotic 'other'. Lack of clarity on this point is a major source of confusion in discourse analysis, constructivism, interpretivism and other discourse-centred analytical strategies. Our approach aims to avoid these confusions in order the better to put semiosis in its appropriate place in critical political economy. This is also why we have defined the pre-discursive, post-discursive and extra-discursive as three further 'others' of discourse.

Table 4.1 *Disambiguating the discursive and non-discursive*

CPE analytical foci	Semiotic moment	Non-semiotic moment
Mode of complexity reduction	Semiosis	Structuration
Form analysis	Orders of discourse	Social forms
Social practice	Discursive	Structural ('material')
Aspects of social practices	Discoursal + Non-discoursal	Content (object) + Form (structure)
Social event	Utterance	Encounter
Mode of explanation	Hermeneutic interpretation, reasons as causes, semiotic effects	Material causation, social emergence, structural effects

Level one indicates that semiosis (and, *a fortiori*, discourse) and structuration both serve to reduce complexity and enable actors to go on in the world. Level two presents orders of discourse as the semiotic equivalent to social (or structural) forms. Turning to social practice, the third row indicates that these are not reducible to discursive practices (the temptation to which discourse analysts sometimes succumb) but have other moments that are also constitutive of social practice. This is emphasized in the 'practice turn', which, in contrast to the discursive turn, considers all moments of practice. Likewise, row four indicates that discursive practices have non-discoursal as well as discoursal features, and that both must be included in an integral analysis of these practices (see, e.g., Fairclough 2003). Fifth, at the most micro-level of analysis (a semiotic or social event), we identify the units of analysis as an utterance (or its equivalent in other forms of signification) and a social encounter. The final row switches perspective to identify interpretation and explanation as the appropriate modes of explanation for the two moments of complexity reduction (and their more concrete manifestations).

Table 4.1 and the preceding discussion suggest that, as we move from semiosis to discursive practice to social practice, even a comprehensive discourse-analytical account will prove incomplete in its own terms. Linguistic or semiotic analysis cannot generate from its own (disciplinary) resources the concepts needed to analyse the emergent effects of language use and/or semiotic practices on social structures and the specific features and emergent properties of structuration. Of course, few linguists argue that their discipline is self-sufficient in these respects. Even the founder of linguistics, de Saussure, proposed that semiology would combine internal linguistics (the study of linguistic signification) and external linguistics (the study of the historical, geographical and national factors that shape language development and use). But even more is at stake: the integral analysis of social practices in terms of the interdependence and co-evolution of semiosis and structuration, each of which has its own 'grammar' and 'logic' that interact to shape their path-dependent, path-shaping co-evolution. This requires a conceptual vocabulary for structural analysis. Even when one is introduced there is a risk of quasi-reductionism in so far as the structural analysis is underdeveloped. This is likely when the tools for linguistic or semiotic analysis are far more elaborate and coherent, include well-specified causal mechanisms, and have been fine-tuned for years and, conversely, when the tools for structural analysis are *ad hoc* and eclectic, introduced for specific purposes, and not well integrated into the overall analysis. This is why semiotic analysis needs to be supplemented by a consistent and commensurable set of structural concepts. We introduced some concepts for putting institutions in their place in Chapter 1 and add some fundamental concepts for analysis of capitalist social formations in Chapter 6.

The opposite risk exists where scholars of structuration have well-developed concepts and theories for dealing with aspects of structure and resort in *ad hoc*, eclectic fashion to discourse-analytical tools for specific purposes. This criticism has been levelled against the 'fourth institutionalism', which is said to be light on discourse theory (see Chapter 1). Avoiding this danger is even more important because social structuration and, *a fortiori*, the structuring of capitalist social formations have three general semiotic aspects that require careful analysis. First, semiotic conditions affect the differential reproduction and transformation of social groups, organizations, institutions and other social phenomena. Second, they also affect the variation, selection and retention of the semiotic features of social phenomena. And, third, semiotic innovation and emergence is a source of variation that feeds into social transformation. In short, semiosis can generate variation, have selective effects, and contribute to the differential retention and/or institutionalization of social phenomena. The present book is particularly concerned, as its subtitle indicates, with addressing this set of challenges and this explains why Chapters 3 to 5 focus more on semiosis as the weaker beacon guiding the effort of CPE to navigate between the structuralist Scylla and the constructivist Charybdis. In other words, semiosis was the weak link in the CPE project. We indicate some ways to overcome this in the next but one section of this chapter.

Figure 4.2 illustrates some of these points. While it may appear similar in form to the figures on structure/agency in Chapter 1, we do not regard

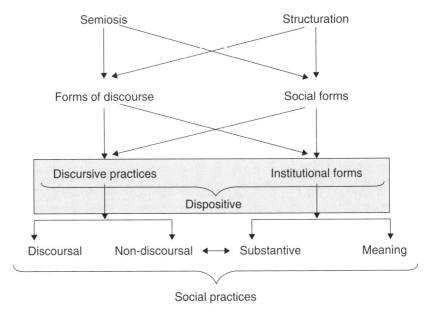

Figure 4.2 Dialectical relations among the basic concepts

its starting point as an unacceptable dichotomy. This figure serves to emphasize that semiosis has its own forms of structuration (appropriate to sense- and meaning-making rather than social structuration) and, conversely, that there are semiotic moments to social forms and the setting of limits on compossible social relations. Dispositives can be located at level three, in the potentially complementary interaction between discursive practices and institutional forms. Like the figures in Chapter 1, however, this figure results from a thought-experiment: it does not depict the historical unfolding of relations between semiosis and structuration. The arrows do not represent causal processes but lines of dialectical reasoning. This important distinction will become clear as we proceed.

CRUCIAL ASPECTS OF SENSE- AND MEANING-MAKING

What distinguishes sense- meaning-making from semiosis elsewhere in the living world is its mediation in the first instance through *language* as a means of social communication. While the biological foundation of language is the unity of hand, larynx and brain, this is overdetermined and driven forward socially by the unity of labour, language and practical consciousness (Höppe 1982: 28; Møller 2003: 17–20, 38; Lieberman 2006).[4] The key to the development of language and semiosis is the capacity for learning and for reflexivity through meaning-making about meaning-making (with scope for nth-order reflections at various removes from first-order meaning-making). CPE accepts the common claim that language is *the* quintessential cultural phenomenon and that it is an important reference point in all subsequent semiosis (cf. Benveniste 1966: 28; Jakobson 1971: 658). But it does not share the common *non sequitur* that all semiosis can be interpreted and explained as if it were language or no more than language.

Language provides the primary horizon of sense-making for actors/observers and thereby shapes lived experience of being in the world, focusing on just some meanings from the infinitude of possible meanings. When making sense of the world, even nonsense is sense – it is not non-sense. Making sense of the world is making sense of ourselves too, our place within it, and our identities. Language enables humankind to construe the natural and social world, use language tactically or strategically, and, indeed, make a reflexive cultural turn. Further, for language to be intelligible, linguistic rules must limit compossible combinations of signs without overly constraining productive lexical, semantic, pragmatic and conversational innovations. These are subject to the evolutionary processes of variation, selection and retention. Thus, even if linguistic innovation is initially little more than arbitrary variation, natural languages are not socially and historically arbitrary *a posteriori* because selection and retention also have effects (on historical semantics, see Chapter 3). This poses problems at the interface of diachrony and synchrony in linguistic analysis. Rather than privileging the synchronic structure of *langue*, as often occurs in structural linguistics *à la* Saussure, therefore, a CPE approach would examine how linguistic variation comes, through processes of selection and retention, to be integrated into *langue* and semantics, producing more or less radical changes as it does so. This also provides the basis for thinking about semiosis in terms of variation, selection and retention – since there is far greater scope for random variation in one-off construals than there is in construals that may facilitate enduring constructions. Although individual words or phrases have no one-to-one relation to the objects to which they refer, the world still constrains language and ways of thinking. This occurs over time, if not at every point in time.

The evolutionary moment of CPE is relevant here. There is continuing *variation* in discourses as actors intentionally or unintentionally redefine the sites, subjects and stakes of action and articulate innovative strategies, projects and visions. While most of this variation is arbitrary and short-lived, lacking long-term consequences for overall social dynamics, some semiotic innovations are *selected*. This occurs because they resonate discursively with other actors and social forces and/or because they are reinforced through various structural mechanisms. So we must explore the discursive and extra-discursive mechanisms that select some discourses for further elaboration and articulation with other discourses. This is not just a question of coherence, rhetoric, resonance and so on; it also depends on capacities to translate discourses into effective strategies and policies. Relevant factors include differential location in key organizations, networks and institutional configurations of inclusion, exclusion and domination; relative control over specific strategic resources, technical capabilities, communication media, disciplinary instruments and means of coordination; and the qualities of particular individual and collective agents in relation to particular conjunctures. These factors are especially important during crises, which often prompt profound strategic disorientation and trigger many alternative construals and proposals to solve them (see Chapters 11 and 12).

Construal and Construction

While any construal may be as good as any other in terms of purely internal sense-making, matters change when we consider the capacity to translate construals into social practice. There is a crucial difference between *construal* and *construction* that is not always adequately drawn, if at all, in more interpretivist approaches in the social sciences. Whereas construal views sense-making from the actor's apprehension of the natural and social world, construction denotes the socially transformative effects, in so far as they occur in the natural and social world that follow from action premised on that apprehension (for a critical-realist perspective on this distinction, see Sayer 2000; for a cognitive linguistic perspective, see Harder 2011). Construal views meaning-making from the actor's perspective; construction refers to the external effects of construals. Although every social practice is semiotic (in so far as social practices entail meaning), no social practice is reducible to its semiotic moments. The 'play of difference' among signifiers could not be sustained without extensive embedding of semiosis in material practice, in the constraints and affordances of the material world.

There is a key distinction here between first-order social relations (seen from the viewpoint of their social agents and their construal of these relations) and second-order (or nth-order) observation of these relations by external observers, where the focus is on the structural features and overall dynamic (logic) of these relations. It is the latter that make it possible to see what others (or oneself as a first-order, non-reflexive agent) cannot see. This does not escape meaning-making but it introduces a distinction that is important in order to avoid a simplistic constructivism in which all construals are equal and all participate equally in making the world. We also argue that the distinction among the four selectivities provides further means to discuss the discursive and non-discursive in fruitful ways (see Chapter 5).

A useful concept here is 'sedimentation' (see Chapter 3). This covers all forms of routinization that lead, *inter alia*, to forgetting the contested origins of discourses, practices, processes and structures. This gives them the form of objective facts of life, especially in the social world. In turn, 'politicization' covers challenges to such objectivation that aim to denaturalize the semiotic and material (extra-semiotic) features of what has become sedimented. Sedimentation and (re)politicization are not confined to a specific 'political' domain (separate from others); they are contingent aspects of all forms of social life (Glynos and Howarth 2007). Indeed, the role of extra-semiotic mechanisms seems to grow with the passage from the disruption of sedimented discourses and relatively structured complexity through the (re)politicization of discourse and the rise of relatively unstructured complexity and thence to new forms of sedimentation and structuration. Sedimentation is not purely discursive. It is also related to the other selectivities and, in this sense, can be seen to be part of dispositive formation as discussed above. Nonetheless, the four selectivities are not so tightly articulated in a dispositive that disorientation and repoliticization cannot occur without immediately disrupting its overall functioning. Indeed, the structurally inscribed selectivities and technological selectivities associated with an apparatus/dispositive may hinder the translation of repoliticization into durable social transformation (for examples, see Chapters 11 and 12).

To paraphrase George Orwell (1945), while all social *construals* are equal in the face of complexity, some are more equal than others in their impact on social *construction*. In other words, some are more fundamental to structuring interaction and to limiting possible combinations of social relations. These hegemonic (or at least dominant) construals provide fundamental *Denkformen* (forms of thought or, for Foucault, epistemes) and *Existenzweisen* (modes of existence, forms of life) – notably the necessary illusions for specific patterns of exploitation and domination (for discussion, see, respectively, Sohn-Rethel 1978; Foucault 1984; Maihofer 1995; Hanfling 2002). They are often more powerful because adopted and promoted by dominant social forces, apparatuses and institutions that use various social and material technologies to promote semiosis and structuration. They are also the focus for struggles to sediment language and worldviews and to embody power relations in language (Bakhtin

1986; Lecercle 2006; Ives 2004a; Wainwright 2010). This reinforces our earlier arguments about the dialectic of discursivity and 'materiality', and their joint importance to an adequate account of the reproduction of political economies. Not all possible discursive construals can be durably constructed materially, and attempts to do so may have unintended effects (Sayer 2000).[5]

Semiosis and Ideology

In analysing semiosis, it is important to consider it initially as sense- and meaning-making and not to equate it with ideology. Not all semiosis is ideological even if all semiosis is selective. Semiosis provides the raw materials of meaning-making, its affordances, so to speak, but does not predetermine specific propositions, statements, arguments, imaginaries, frames and so on. *Ideologiekritik* enters later in the analysis of semiotic practices and their content. It may reveal the immanent contradictions and inconsistencies in relatively coherent meaning systems (immanent critique of texts and discourses); uncover the ideal and material interests behind specific meaning systems and ideologies more generally (socio-diagnostic critique, based in part on contextual knowledge); explore the semiotic and extra-semiotic mechanisms involved in selecting and consolidating the dominance and/or hegemony of some meaning systems and ideologies over others (which links to the critique of domination); and contribute to the repoliticization and rearticulation of sedimented, naturalized discourses and practices (prospective critique, oriented to emancipation). It examines struggles to shape the identities, subjectivities and interests of the forces engaged in social struggle, as well as to transform patterns of domination. This offers more solid foundations to develop a critique of domination.

HOW IMAGINARIES CONTRIBUTE TO STRUCTURATION

In developing its approach to complexity reduction through meaning-making, CPE deploys the notion of the 'imaginary'. This can be considered as equivalent to the notion of the semantic as a 'master' set of signs (signifier, signified, signatum). Our adoption of this term is inspired by French use of *l'imaginaire* to designate an imaginary relation to the real world or, alternatively, *lived experience*; but we also pay more attention than much French work to the material dimensions of this imaginary relation and its implications for lived experience.

Semiosis and the imaginary are closely related but not identical, and this is reflected in their place within CPE. First, whereas semiosis is a generic term for the social production of intersubjective meaning and can be studied productively with the tools of semiotic analysis (especially, for CPE, those of critical discourse analysis), the 'imaginary' not only refers to semiosis but also to its *material supports*, and this requires a broader toolkit. Imaginaries are semiotic systems that frame individual subjects' lived experience of an inordinately complex world and/or inform collective calculation about that world. Second, whereas semiosis can be studied without asking how some *construals* come to *construct* the real world, a key issue concerning imaginaries is their differential performance in durably shaping that world. This is why CPE explores selection and retention not only in terms of discursive selectivity (semiotic mechanisms) but also in terms of structural, technological and agential selectivities. This broader set of questions also bears on the CPE commitment to the critique of domination and *Ideologiekritik*.

An imaginary is a semiotic ensemble (or meaning system) without tightly defined boundaries that frames individual subjects' lived experience of an inordinately complex world and/or guides collective calculation about that world. Without imaginaries, individuals cannot 'go on' in the world and collective actors (such as organizations) could not relate to their environments, make decisions, or engage in strategic action. In this sense, imaginaries are an important semiotic moment of the network of social practices in a given social field, institutional order, or wider social formation (Fairclough 2003). Imaginaries are not pre-given mental categories but creative products of semiotic and material practices with more or less performative power. This is why they have a central role in the struggle not only for 'hearts and minds' but also for the reproduction or transformation of the prevailing structures of exploitation and domination. An imaginary provides one entry-point (among many others) into a super-complex reality and can be associated with different standpoints, which frame *and contain* debates, policy discussions and conflicts over particular ideal and material interests. There are many kinds of imaginaries and most are loosely bounded and have links to other imaginaries within the broad field of semiotic practices. Indeed, social forces typically operate in different contexts with different imaginaries reflecting different logics of appropriateness.

Imaginaries exist at different sites and scales of action – from individual agents to world society (Althusser 1971; Taylor 2004). Social forces will therefore seek to establish one or another imaginary as the hegemonic or dominant 'frame' in particular contexts and/or to develop complementary sub-hegemonic imaginaries or, again, counter-hegemonic imaginaries that motivate and mobilize resistance. Hegemonic and dominant imaginaries are generally socially instituted and socially embedded, and get reproduced through various mechanisms that help to maintain their cognitive and normative hold on the social agents involved in the field(s) that they map. Such 'mental maps' or 'mental models' matter most where the sum of activities in relevant field(s) is so unstructured and complex that it cannot be an object of effective calculation, management, governance or guidance. However, while a shared imaginary assists agents to 'go on' in that supercomplex world, the necessary simplifications can prove counter-productive.

We now illustrate and elaborate some of these points from the case of economic imaginaries. This reflects our interest in the critique of political economy rather than an assumption that economic imaginaries are somehow inherently more important than other kinds. As our previous discussion notes, there are as many imaginaries as there are entry-points and standpoints for sense- and meaning-making. In other contexts political imaginaries, state projects, spatial imaginaries, hegemonic visions, and so on might be more appropriate starting points.

In terms of what orthodox economics misleadingly describes as the macro-level, CPE distinguishes the 'actually existing economy' as the chaotic sum of all economic activities (broadly defined as concerned with the social appropriation and transformation of nature for the purposes of material provisioning)[6] from the 'economy' (or, better, 'economies' in the plural) as an imaginatively narrated, more or less coherent subset of these activities occurring within specific spatio-temporal frameworks. The totality of economic activities is so unstructured and complex that it cannot be an object of effective calculation, management, governance or guidance. Instead such practices are always oriented to subsets of economic relations (economic systems, subsystems or ensembles) that have been semiotically and, perhaps organizationally and institutionally, fixed as appropriate objects of intervention. Economic imaginaries have a crucial constitutive role in this regard. They identify, privilege and seek to stabilize some economic activities from the totality of economic relations and transform them into objects of observation, calculation and governance. Technologies of economic governance, operating sometimes more semiotically, sometimes more materially,[7] constitute their own objects of governance rather than emerging in order to, or operating with the effect that, they govern already pre-constituted objects (Jessop 1990, 1997b). Nonetheless, because they are always selectively defined, what is excluded limits the efficacy of economic forecasting, management, planning, guidance, governance and so on because such practices do not (indeed, cannot) take account of excluded elements and their impact.

Economic imaginaries also exist at the so-called meso- or micro-level. Here they develop as economic, political and intellectual forces seek to (re)define specific subsets of economic activities as subjects, sites and stakes of competition and/or as objects of regulation and to articulate strategies, projects and visions oriented to them. The forces involved in such efforts include parties, think tanks, bodies such as the OECD and the World Bank, organized interests like business associations and trade unions, and social movements; the mass media are also crucial intermediaries in mobilizing elite and/or popular support behind competing imaginaries.[8] These forces tend to manipulate power and knowledge to secure recognition of the boundaries, geometries, temporalities, typical economic agents, tendencies and counter-tendencies, distinctive overall dynamic and reproduction requirements of different imagined economies. They also seek to develop new structural and organizational forms that will help to institutionalize these boundaries, geometries and temporalities in an appropriate spatio-temporal fix that can displace and/or defer capital's inherent contradictions and crisis tendencies. However, due to competing economic imaginaries, competing efforts to institute them materially, and an inevitable incompleteness in specifying their respective economic and extra-economic preconditions, each 'imagined economy' is only ever partially constituted. There are always interstitial, residual, marginal, irrelevant, recalcitrant and plain contradictory elements that escape any attempt to identify, govern and stabilize a given 'economic arrangement' or broader 'economic order'. These provide major sources of resistance and help preserve a reservoir of semiotic and material resources that enables dominant systems (through the agency of associated social forces) to adapt to new challenges through their rearticulation and recombination in the service of power.

Relatively successful economic imaginaries presuppose a substratum of substantive economic relations and instrumentalities as their elements. Conversely, where an imaginary gets operationalized and institutionalized, it transforms and naturalizes these elements and instrumentalities into the moments of a specific economy with specific emergent properties. This is depicted in Figure 11.1 as the movement from (re)politicized discourse and unstructured complexity to sedimented discourse and structured complexity. This process is mediated by the interaction among specific economic imaginaries, appropriately supportive economic agents – individual or collective – with appropriate modes of calculation and behavioural or operational dispositions, specific technologies that sustain and confirm these imaginaries (e.g. statistics, indexes, benchmarks, records), and structural constellations that limit the pursuit of contrary or antagonistic imaginaries, activities or technologies.

When an imaginary has been operationalized and institutionalized, it transforms and naturalizes these elements into the moments of a specific, instituted economy with specific emergent properties. An instituted economy comprises subsets of economic relations that have been organizationally and institutionally fixed as appropriate objects of observation, calculation, management, governance or guidance. This process of institution (or structuration) sets limits to compossible combinations of social relations and thereby renders them more predictable and manageable as objects of social action.

IMAGINARIES AND IDEOLOGY

We now relate the arguments in the preceding section to the question of *Ideologiekritik*. A useful starting point is the critical appropriation and reinterpretation of *The German Ideology*, a *locus classicus* of this practice, proposed by the feminist sociologist and proponent of standpoint theory (to include class, race and gender), Dorothy E. Smith. She writes:

> Marx's use of the concept of ideology in *The German Ideology* is incidental to a sustained critique of how those he described as the German ideologists think and reason about society and history. This critique is not simply of an idealist theory that represents society and history as determined by consciousness but of methods of reasoning that treat concepts, even of those of political economy, as determinants. His view of how consciousness is determined historically by our social being does not envisage some kind of mechanical transfer from 'economic structure' or 'material situation' to consciousness. Rather, he works with an epistemology that takes the concepts foundational to political economy as expressions or reflections of the social relations of a mode of production. The difference between ideology and science is the difference between treating those concepts as the primitives of theory and treating them as sites for exploring the social relations that are expressed in them. Thus the historical, rather than further undermining claims to knowledge, provides both the conditions under which knowledge is possible and its limitations. (Smith 2004: 446)

In short, Marx's critique of ideology is not a critique of popular false consciousness or of ideological manipulation by the ruling class. Joe McCarney (1980) offers a useful overview of explicit uses of the stem 'ideol*' in Marx's work during his writing career. He records that, in line with its etymology (ideology = science of ideas, their formation and effects), Marx essentially connects 'ideological' to products of consciousness: conceptions, ideas, theories, postulates, systems, and their linguistic expressions (e.g. formulas, names, phrases, manifestoes). McCarney reports that:

- Marx rarely uses the bare substantive 'ideology' on its own, it is more common to find it with a qualifier, e.g., republican, Hegelian, political, German; or, ideology of the bourgeoisie, of the political economist.
- Also common are adjectival uses in which something has an ideological character, for example, expressions, forms, phrases, conceptions, contempt, theory, standpoint, reflex, echo, nonsense, distortion, method, etc.
- Marx also refers to ideologists, ideological representatives, ideological cretins, ideological classes (e.g., government officials, priests, lawyers, soldiers, etc.). (McCarney 1980: 3–4)

This analysis suggests a distinction between (1) sense and meaning systems as a way of going on in the world and (2) their ideological effects. This does not make the former 'neutral' (they always contain biases), but nor does it entail that such biases are always and everywhere 'ideological', that is, inevitably related to power and domination. Indeed, McCarney notes that Marx typically uses the term in the context of motivated practices and not in general discussions of language, forms of thought, consciousness and so forth (ibid.: 10–11). While this holds for explicit references to the ideological, we should note that the most powerful ideological effects may not stem from immediate conscious action: this is because they have been inscribed and sedimented in signification (e.g. in the form of fetishism, the taken-for-grantedness of the foundational categories of the capitalist mode of production and so forth).

Consistent with the second and third of McCarney's findings, Smith (2004) notes that *The German Ideology* critiques German philosophers rather than the illusions of everyday lived experience. Marx and Engels dissected the manner in which named intellectuals take the organizing categories of the capitalist mode of production and bourgeois society as the primitive terms of theories about these social relations and thereby naturalize features that are actually historically specific moments of specific social forms and practices. In short, regarding these categories, ideologists 'treat them as given and build theory on the categories, ignoring the social relations in which they arise' (Smith 2004: 455). In contrast, for Smith, science 'explores the actual social relations expressed in the concepts and categories on which ideology builds' (ibid.: 454). Such a sharp distinction between ideology and science is problematic from a CPE perspective, especially as scientific (and not just ideological) practices are socially embedded. But scientific practices do produce knowledge in different ways and the overall point is valuable.

Needless to say, this critique is also relevant to many contemporary economic theories, state theories and work in international relations. For example, Mark Rupert, who works within the neo-Gramscian 'Italian School' tradition, notes:

Table 4.2 Imaginary versus ideology

Imaginary	Ideology
Not 'true' or 'false' but may be more or less adequate basis for 'going on' in the world	Ideology is linked to 'truth regimes' related to specific ideal and material interests
Can lead to learning based on actors successive experiences (*Erlebnis* ◄─► *Erfahrung*)	Ideology frames and limits *Erlebnis* (lived experience) and scope for *Erfahrung* (learning)
Alternative imaginaries are based on different entry-points and standpoints	Alternative ideologies privilege some entry-points and standpoints
This opens space for varying degrees of self-reflexion	Ideologies may be promoted intentionally and become part of common sense

> Both the system of sovereign states and the global division of labour – taken as ontologically primitive units by neorealism and world-system theory, respectively, – may instead be understood as aspects of the historically specific social organisation of productive activity under capitalism, as embodying relations of alienation, and as potentially transcendable. (Rupert 1993: 83)

Generalizing these remarks, a CPE approach interprets orders of discourse and discursive practices (the second and third semiotic categories in Table 4.1) as aspects of specific institutional orders and more or less instituted social practices respectively. At stake in ideological critique in these contexts are the sources and mechanisms that 'bias' lived experience and imaginaries towards specific identities and their changing ideal and/or material interests in specific conjunctures. Some indications of the analytical differences between imaginaries and ideologies are presented in Table 4.2. The first column presents imaginaries in terms of relatively simple variation; the second suggests how some of this variation may have ideological significance.

The 'raw material' of ideology is found in meaning systems, social imaginaries and lived experience. Thus a CPE-based critique of ideology would involve four main steps: (1) recognize the role of semiosis as a meaning pool in complexity reduction; (2) identify social imaginaries, that is, specific clusters of meaning (or semiotic) systems, and describe their form and content; (3) analyse their contingent articulation and functioning in securing the conditions for domination serving particular interests; and (4) distinguish between cases where these effects are motivated and/ or where they are effects of sedimented meaning. Meaning systems and social imaginaries have a central role in struggles over exploitation and domination. This goes beyond deliberate strategies to capture 'hearts and minds' – a common way of describing struggles for hegemony. It is also a matter of the ideological assumptions inscribed in language and other forms of signification even before such a strategy is pursued.

Thus we must ask how basic categories and general social imaginaries come to more or less durably shape, dominate or hegemonize the world. One aspect is the extent and manner of links to 'lived experience', that is, how actors experience and understand their world(s) as real and meaningful seen from one or more subject positions and standpoints, and also how they empathize with others. Lived experience never reflects directly an extra-semiotic reality but involves meaning-making based on the meaningful *pre*-interpretation of the natural-cum-social world. Lived experience may be sedimented but its form is not pre-given and this creates space for learning. Lived experience is open to dislocation, contestation, repoliticization and struggle to restore, alter or overturn meaning systems, including those involved in diverse social imaginaries (on lived experience and learning, see Chapter 11).

Social imaginaries are not as unified as Charles Taylor (2004) and Cornelius Castoriadis (1987), among others, have suggested. This is, of course, a key point for Gramsci and the Bakhtin Circle, with their emphasis on the polyvocal, multi-accentual, dialogic nature of language and signification (see Chapter 3). Any unity is contingent and unstable, and this holds, *a fortiori*, for the ensemble of social imaginaries. Social forces try to make one or another imaginary the hegemonic or dominant 'frame' in particular contexts and/or to promote complementary or opposed imaginaries. Success may lead to a historical bloc, in which, to paraphrase Gramsci, '*material forces* are the content and *imaginaries* are the form'. Such struggles occur through semiosis, structuration, particular technologies and specific agents.

Where a meaning system or social imaginary encompasses a wide range of social activities, institutional orders and the lifeworld, it can become sedimented and have correspondingly wide-ranging effects. Charles Taylor defined a social imaginary as follows: 'the ways people imagine their social existence, how they fit together with others, how things go on between them and their fellows, the expectations that are normally met, and the deeper normative notions and images that underlie these expectations' (2004: 23). He expresses the notion of sedimentation (which he does not use) in terms of becoming 'so self-evident to us that we have trouble seeing it as one possible conception among others': it is 'the only . . . one that makes sense' (ibid.: 2). Of course, it is not only at the level of social formations that this sedimentation occurs. It occurs at all levels, from everyday lived experience through specific organizational 'ideologies' and institutional outlooks to the codes and programmes of systems and dominant principles of societalization. The multitude of sites where this occurs creates a heteroglossic field in which ideological effects can be contested.

Only when the analysis reaches steps three and four could one demonstrate that specific sense- and meaning-making systems operate to legitimize the orders of discourse, social forms and social practices associated with particular hegemonic and/or dominant power relations. As such, the ideological process refers to the contribution of discourses to the contingent reproduction of power relations, especially where this involves hegemony (political, intellectual, moral and self-leadership). Whether a particular cultural ensemble has an 'ideological' moment depends on the form of (hegemonic) domination at stake: this could be capitalist, patriarchal, heteronormative, 'racial', national, regional and so forth. In this sense, a discourse could be ideological in regard to capitalism but non-ideological in relation to patriarchy (or, of course, vice versa). In short, *Ideologiekritik* requires an entry-point and a standpoint and must also be related to specific conjunctures rather than conducted *in abstracto*. In this sense, ideology is a *contingent* feature of culture and discourse that gets naturalized articulated, selected and sedimented in the (re)making of social relations.

FOUR MOMENTS OF SEMIOSIS AND STRUCTURATION

Semiotic and structuring practices can be classified in relation to: (1) their system relevance; (2) their relation to spheres of life transversal to system logics; (3) their spatio-temporal location, horizons of action and role in securing spatio-temporal fixes; and (4) their associated types of social agency.

First, the two forms of complexity reduction may be more or less implicated in creating and stabilizing the always-tendential, provisional and partial structured coherence of institutional orders and functional systems. We will illustrate this from economic imaginaries and their relation to imagined economies. From a CPE perspective, the economy has both semiotic (discursive) and extra-semiotic (material) aspects, which coexist and influence each other. Considered as the sum of all economic activities, the economy is too complex to be fully grasped in real time by economic actors or external observers. This forces them to engage in simplification as a condition of 'going on' in the economic world. Thus economic imaginaries are always selectively defined – due to limited cognitive capacities and to the discursive and material biases of specific epistemes and economic paradigms. They typically exclude elements – usually unintentionally – that are vital to the overall performance of the subset of economic (and extra-economic) relations that have been identified. Different entry-points and standpoints lead to different economic imaginaries that identify different subsets of economic actions and relations as objects of observation, calculation, regulation, governance or transformation (Jessop 2004a, 2008a). Each imaginary depicts the economic world in its own way (albeit with scope for overlap, articulation and hybridization) and those that become hegemonic or sub-hegemonic help to shape economic orders and embed them in wider ensembles of social relations. Marginal and counter-hegemonic imaginaries also affect economic conduct in their own ways and, in some circumstances, may become more influential, shaping accumulation regimes, modes of regulation and modes of material provisioning.

There is necessarily wide variation in economic imaginaries. If they are to prove more than 'arbitrary, rationalistic and willed', they must have some significant, albeit necessarily partial, correspondence to real material interdependencies in the actually existing economy and/or in the relations between economic and extra-economic activities. Alternatively, especially in periods of crisis, they should have some correspondence to feasible alternative economic arrangements. This poses the question of the performative force of economic imaginaries in shaping the economic realm. It also highlights the need to explore the discursive and material factors and forces that shape the selection and retention of hegemonic, sub-hegemonic, counter-hegemonic or marginal accounts of the economy, its dynamic and its conditions of existence (Sum 2005).

Second, while many social activities are appropriately observed in terms of instituted systems and, indeed, some, such as the payment of taxes, could be ascribed to several systems, other social activities lack direct system relevance. This holds especially for activities that are not anchored in particular system logics but relate to other identities and interests that are transversal to these logics. Examples include the national and/or regional identity of an imagined community (Anderson 1993), gender and sexual orientation, socially constructed 'racial' identities, or the formation of political generations rooted in shared experiences. By virtue of this lack of direct system relevance, these could be referred to various spheres of life, the 'lifeworld' (broadly interpreted) or, again, to 'civil society' (as long as this is not equated with 'bourgeois' society). They may nonetheless acquire system relevance through their integration into the operation of system logics (e.g. the use of gender to segment the labour force, the mobilization of 'racial' identities to justify educational exclusion). System-relevant and lifeworld imaginaries provide the basis for agential identities and interests, whether individual, group, movement or organizational. Agents normally have multiple identities, privileging one or more over others in different contexts. This is the basis for social scientific interest in 'intersectionalism', that is, the analysis of the effects of different combinations of system-relevant and 'lifeworld' identities.

Third, imagined economies (or their equivalents for other systems) are discursively constituted and materially reproduced on many sites and scales, in different spatio-temporal contexts, and over various spatio-temporal horizons. They extend from one-off transactions through stable economic organizations, networks and clusters to 'macro-economic' regimes. While massive scope for variation typically exists at an individual transactional level, the medium- to long-term semiotic and material reproduction requirements of meso-complexes and macro-economic regimes narrow this scope considerably. The recursive selection of semiotic practices and extra-semiotic processes at these scales tends to reduce inappropriate variation and to secure thereby the 'requisite variety' (constrained heterogeneity rather than simple uniformity) that supports the structural coherence of economic activities. Stable semiotic orders, discursive selectivities, social learning, path-dependencies, power relations, patterned complementarities and material selectivities all become more significant, the more that material interdependencies and/or issues of spatial and intertemporal articulation increase within and across diverse functional systems and the lifeworld. Yet this growing set of constraints also reveals the fragility and, indeed, improbability of the smooth reproduction of complex social orders.

Fourth, the relation between semiotic and structuring practices can be classified in terms of their associated types of social agency. Everyone is involved in semiosis because meaning-making is the basis of lived experience. However, just as Gramsci observed that, while everyone is an intellectual, not everyone performs the function of an intellectual, we suggest that there is no equality in individual contributions to meaning-making. Each system and the different spheres of the 'lifeworld' have their own semiotic divisions of labour that overlie, differentially draw on, and feed into lived experience. There are individuals and/or collective intellectuals (such as political parties and old and new social movements) who are particularly active in bridging these different systems and spheres of life and attempting to create hegemonic meaning systems or develop sub- or counter-hegemonic meaning systems. And, of course, increasingly, semiosis is heavily 'mediatized', that is, shaped by mass and social media (e.g. Cardoso 2008; Innis 1951; Hjarvard 2008; Martin-Barbero 1973; Williams

1971). Given the diversity of systems and the plurality of identities in the 'lifeworld', one should not privilege *a priori* one type of social actor as the leading force in semiosis in general or in the making of hegemonies in particular. Likewise, there are competing societalization principles and no *a priori* guarantee that one principle will be dominant. Nonetheless, as a working hypothesis at the level of world society, the profit-oriented, market-mediated logic of differential capital accumulation seems to be becoming more dominant as the world market has been increasingly integrated under the logic of neoliberalism and, in particular, of finance-dominated accumulation (see Chapter 6).

THE STRUCTURALIST SCYLLA

Now that we have provided some essential tools for addressing questions of semiosis and structuration and their articulation, we can suggest how CPE can navigate between the Scylla of hard political economy and the Charybdis of constructivism. This section identifies risks associated with a one-sided emphasis on structuration and structured complexity. In its home domain, CPE aims to avoid two specific expressions of the general temptations towards structuralism (especially economism) and voluntarism (ideationalism).

Corresponding to the former temptation is the hard, fetishized economics of classical political economy and some versions of orthodox political economy that tend to establish a rigid demarcation between the economic and the cultural. This sort of fetishized approach thereby reifies the separation of the economic and political in capitalist social formations, naturalizes the formal, market-rational, calculative activities of *homo economicus* and the *Realpolitik* of state power without regard to their discursively mediated, socially constructed character, and suggests the inevitability of rigid economic laws and the constraints associated with globalization. At its most extreme, this leads to claims allegedly valid for all forms of what Polanyi (1982) terms 'material provisioning'; in other cases, it tends to separate economizing activities from their extra-economic context and supports, to regard the economy as a self-reproducing, self-expanding system with its own laws, and to provide the theoretical underpinnings for economic reductionism. Moreover, as many theorists have noted, the reproduction of the basic forms of the capital relation and their particular instantiation in different social formations cannot be secured purely through the objective logic of the market or a form of domination that operates 'behind the backs of the producers' and/or political subjects. Capital's laws of motion are doubly tendential, that is, their tendencies depend on tendential reproduction of the social relations that depend in turn on contingent social practices that extend well beyond what is from *time to time* and from *site to site* construed and/or constructed as economic. This means that capital accumulation cannot be explained in terms of a self-correcting, self-expanding logic. Outside a purely imaginary 'pure capitalist economy', capitalism is 'structurally coupled' to other systems with their own operational logics or instrumental rationalities and to the 'lifeworld' formed by various social relations, identities, interests and values not otherwise anchored in specific systems.

Orthodox Economics as a Structuralist Scylla

Hard political economy fetishizes economic categories, naturalizes economic actions, institutions and 'laws', and neglects their ties to the wider social formation. Orthodox economics illustrates this *par excellence*. It regards *homo economicus* as a universal, trans-historical species, treats labour as a factor of production, and proposes rigid economic laws. It offers impoverished accounts, at most, of how subjects and subjectivities are formed, and how different modes of calculation emerge, come to be institutionalized, and get modified. It takes formal, market-rational, calculative activities for granted and analyses them apart from their discursive significance and broader extra-economic context and supports. It tends to naturalize or reify its basic categories (such as land, machines, the division of labour, money, commodities, the information economy). It suggests the inevitability of rigid economic laws. And, last, in so far as material transformation is studied apart from its semiotic dimensions and mediations, explanations of stability and change risk oscillating between objective necessity and the sheer contingency of 'exogenous shocks'.

This asymmetrical theoretical development involves two risks. The first is that it favours one-sided structural explanations because they tend to be more specific and elaborate – especially as the RA can deploy a rich set of 'middle-range' institutional concepts, whether developed within one or another school or borrowed from other institutional and evolutionary approaches. There is a far more limited set of concepts for addressing the semiotic moment of the critique of political economy. This has reinforced the permanent temptation of economistic explanations when economists (even institutional and evolutionary economists) investigate economic matters (Boyer 1990: 14–15; Jessop and Sum 2006: 377–8). Conversely, in rejecting structuralism and economism, the risk arises of a turn to constructivism at best and voluntarism at worst in so far as ideational or agential factors are invoked in an *ad hoc* or eclectic manner to explain the success or failure of *régulation*, concepts of control, societal paradigms, institutionalized compromise, crisis responses and so on. As we have emphasized, semiosis matters: indeed, it is foundational to social relations.

Similar points hold for the categories of mainstream political science and/or (neo-)realist international relations theory. Political science tends to take the institutional separation of the economic and political in capitalist social formations for granted and to focus on how governmental institutions are deployed to pursue interests that are objectively grounded in their respective social positions. It also tends to naturalize national states and national interests in explaining the necessary logic of state action in terms of the realpolitik of state power. A parallel debate has developed and remains unresolved in the field of international relations. On the 'hard' side we find realists and neo-realists, who posit the state as a subject agent with real material (geo-political and geo-economic) interests that it pursues in the international arena; and, on the 'soft' side, the new constructivists who regard not only states but other social forces in the international arena as discursively constituted agents that discursively frame their interests and seek to construct international order on the basis of specific construals of the overall situation and their interests within it. The 'Italian School' of international political economy is more inclined to the latter position but has a robust notion of material interests grounded in the historical materialist approach to the world order.

CONSTRUCTIVIST CHARYBDIS

The other temptation – and a more recent one in the wake of cultural turns – is 'soft cultural economics' or 'soft economic sociology'. This subsumes economic and political categories and activities under broad generalizations about social and cultural life, especially their inevitably semiotic character. While such currents correctly reject a sharp division between the cultural and material and stress the cultural (we prefer semiotic) dimensions of material life, they tend to lose sight of the specificity of economic and political forms, including their distinctive logics, contradictions, dilemmas and crisis tendencies. This is common in economic sociology and in claims about the 'culturalization' of economic life in the new economy (e.g. Lash and Urry 1994); it also occurs in more discourse-theoretical work, such as cultural materialism (Williams 1980; Milner 2002), the linguistic mediation of economic activities (Gal 1989) and/or economic antagonisms (Laclau and Mouffe 1985), and in the 'new economic sociology'. In so far as semiosis is studied apart from its extra-semiotic context, however, the accounts will prove inadequate. Indeed, reliance on hermeneutic interpretation alone can lead to semiotic reductionism and/or semiotic imperialism so that extra-semiotic factors are ignored (see below).

Excursus on Laclau and Mouffe as Charybdians

Ernesto Laclau and Chantal Mouffe provide an important but unwitting example of the risks of soft economic (and political) sociology – albeit from a discourse-analytical rather than sociological perspective. Their argument that the discursive and the social are coextensive entails that the economy has no extra-discursive 'material' base but is also constituted discursively (see Chapter 3). The unity between the economy – now seen as a discursively demarcated sphere within a social whole – and the rest of society therefore derives from the contingent articulation among discursive practices rather than from some necessary correspondence between an extra-discursive base and a discursive superstructure. This also implies that the subjects through whom social relations are mediated and reproduced are also constituted in and through discourse. All subject positions derive from the particular discursive identification (or 'interpellation') of subjects. This excludes the privileging – on what would be spurious extra-discursive, material grounds – of class subjects and class antagonisms. The relation between class and non-class forces, if any, also depends on discursive articulation.

All of this implies that the causal primacy of the economy, which Laclau and Mouffe regard as foundational to Marxism (and its errors), must be replaced with a 'primacy of the political' (1981: 22). This is not a claim for political rather than economic determinism because both are equally discursive parts of the social whole. As such, hegemonic (i.e. political) articulations also operate inside the 'economy' (Laclau and Mouffe 1985: 77ff., 120–21, 140, 180). Thus they provide no account of the specificity of the political or the economy. They argue that 'all struggles are, by definition, political . . . There is no room for a distinction between economic and political struggles' (Laclau 2005: 154). This ontologization of the political, that is, the claim that all of social being or existence is political, means that they feel no need to introduce specific concepts for analysing state structures, state capacities, or state power or the historically specific features of the capitalist mode of production.

Thus the market economy is just as much a field of struggle as the political and ideological regions; and, further, its so-called laws of motion are not governed by an extra-discursive capital logic (or its equivalent in other modes of production) but are grounded in the prevailing hegemonic (discursive) articulations in a given society. By seeking to remove all traces of essentialism (and, one might add, all traces of contingent historical specificity that derive from specific structural and institutional forms and the emergent effects of discursive practices), Laclau and Mouffe evacuate the economy of any determinate theoretical content (see Jessop 1982, 1990 and 2008b).

In this light, Jonathan Diskin and Blair Sandler argue that Laclau and Mouffe are forced to examine hegemony in an institutional vacuum because of their *ontologization* of the political; they turn the economy into an *ontic* void. Referring to these authors' *Hegemony and Socialist Strategy* (1985) as *HSS*, Diskin and Sandler note that they then

> fill [this void] in an *ad hoc* fashion with unexamined economic concepts and relationships which, ironically, retain their essentialist underpinnings. In the latter half of *HSS*, the economy is a blank space, with a marker ('the economy') and sign posts ('commodification'), inscribed upon its surface ... There are economic concepts in *HSS* but no concept of the economy. (1993: 30)

The same point holds for their class analysis, which effectively reduces Marx's critique of political economy to a variant of Ricardo's classical political economy. They accuse Marx of three fatal theoretical errors: (1) he defines labour as a commodity like any other; (2) ignores the role of power in shaping the forces and relations of production; and (3) identifies a necessary contradiction between capital and labour in their encounter as commodity-owners *in the labour market*.[9] They refute all three errors – just as Marx had done (with better reasons) over a century earlier. They then argue that the capital relation is a purely contingent political one and add, correctly but misleadingly, that anti-capitalist resistance does not (and cannot) derive exclusively from the relations between capitalist and worker in the labour market. Such claims eliminate any understanding of the historical specificity of the capital relation, the distinctive form of capitalist exploitation (which is based on the peculiar combination of formally free and equal exchange in the labour market and 'factory despotism' in the labour process), and the material grounding of class identities in the relations of production rather than the relations of exchange.

In short, the discourse-analytical approach of Laclau and Mouffe, for all its post-Marxist swagger, cannot provide the conceptual tools or identify the mechanisms needed to critique political economy or 'modern' societies more generally. At best, this approach can contribute to the analysis of identity formation and subjectivation, which are discursively constituted, and social practices that are mediated primarily through mental labour. Even in these cases it tends to overlook issues of embodiment and the inscription and mediation of the products of mental labour (see Chapter 3). In conflating discourses and material practices under the rubric of discursive practices and treating the discursive as coextensive with the social whole, Laclau and Mouffe cannot distinguish *in material terms* between capitalist and non-capitalist economic practices, institutions and formations – they are all equally discursive and can be differentiated only through their respective semiotic practices, meanings and contexts, and their performative impact. Accordingly, when discussing economics or politics, they use conventional terminology drawn from ordinary language, policy debates and mainstream paradigms. This lends an air of plausibility to their empirical examples but does not generate rigorous analyses adequate at the level of meaning and causality.

NAVIGATING BETWEEN SCYLLA AND CHARYBDIS

In stressing the interdependence and co-evolution of these semiotic and material moments in complexity reduction and their consequences for meaning-making and social structuration, the version of CPE presented below aims to avoid two complementary theoretical temptations. The first is seen in different forms of structuralism and social determinism, which reduce agents and actions to passive bearers of self-reproducing, self-transforming social structures. There is currently little support for this position. The second temptation is radical social constructivism, according to which social reality is reducible to participants' meanings and understandings of their social world. This generates an arbitrary account of the social world that ignores the unacknowledged conditions of action as well as the many and varied emergent properties of action that go un- or misrecognized by relevant actors. It ignores struggles to transform the conditions of action, alter actors' meanings and understandings, and modify emergent properties (and their feedback effects on the social world). And it leads to the voluntarist vacuity of certain lines of discourse analysis, which seem to imply that agents can will almost anything into existence in and through an appropriately articulated discourse (see Table 4.3).

CPE offers a 'third way' between a structuralist Scylla and a constructivist Charybdis. It rejects the conflation of discourses and material practices and the more general 'discourse imperialism' that has influenced social theory for two decades (see above). And it aims to explore the dialectic of the emergent extra-semiotic features of social relations and the constitutive role of semiosis.

More generally, if all social phenomena (including the economic) are discursively constituted and never achieve a self-reproducing closure, isolated from other social phenomena, then any natural necessities (emergent properties) entailed in the internal relations of a given object must be tendential. Such properties would be fully realized only if that object

Table 4.3 CPE between the constructivist Charybdis and structuralist Scylla

Constructivist Charybdis	Structuralist Scylla
Grasps the semiotic-material construction of social relations, reveals their social embedding, and notes the performative impact of semiosis	Grasps the *distinctiveness* of specific economic categories and their structured/structuring nature in wider social formations
But finds it hard to define the specificity of economic relations *vis-à-vis* other relations – because they are all equally discursive in character	But reifies such categories, regards economic structures as natural, and views agents as mere *Träger* (passive bearers) of economic logics
Strong risk of idealism, defining economic relations in terms of their manifest *semiotic content*	Strong risk of economic determinism, explaining economic processes in terms of *'iron laws'*
'Soft economic sociology'	*'Hard political economy'*

were fully constituted and continually reproduced through appropriate discursive and social practices. This holds as much for the 'laws of motion' of capital considered as a social relation as it does for other social phenomena. Such closure is inherently improbable with respect to both key moments of complexity reduction. Thus discursive relations are polysemic, heteroglossic and multi-accentual; subjectivities are plural and changeable; and extra-semiotic properties are liable to material disturbances as well as discursive deconstruction. Likewise, capitalist relations are, at most, only relatively dominant in the economic order and their operation is always vulnerable to disruption through internal contradictions, the intrusion of relations anchored in other institutional orders and the lifeworld (civil society), and resistance rooted in conflicting interests, competing identities and rival modes of calculation.

A further consequence of this approach is that the economy cannot be adequately conceived (let alone managed) as a 'pure' economic sphere that reproduces itself in total isolation from the non-economic and that can therefore determine non-economic spheres in a unilateral manner. At least some of these extra-economic conditions and forces must be integrated into accumulation strategies to make them feasible. The operations of the economy are co-constituted by other systems and co-evolve with them: these include technologies, science, education, politics, law, art, religion and so on. They are also articulated more generally to the lifeworld. The latter comprises all those identities, interests, values and conventions that are not directly anchored in the logic of any particular system and that provide the substratum and background to social interaction in everyday life.

Moreover, in so far as these extra-economic mechanisms also reproduce the contradictions and dilemmas inherent in the economic mechanisms of the capital relation, they further expand the scope for agency, strategies and tactics to shape the course of accumulation and the manner in which these contradictions and dilemmas are expressed. This is why the more successful accumulation strategies are often connected to hegemonic projects that link economic success to the national/popular (or some equivalent) interest that aims to mobilize a broader social constituency behind the growth strategy. This extends in turn the influence of accumulation via its modes of regulation to the overall character of social formations.

Thus, overall, there is no single and unambiguous 'logic of capital' but, rather, several such logics with a family resemblance. Given the open nature of capitalism's overall dynamic, each accumulation regime and/or mode of regulation imparts its own distinctive structure and dynamic to the circuit of capital – including distinctive forms of crisis and breakdown. This in turn requires any analysis of the improbable nature of capital accumulation to take agency seriously. Thus it is essential to combine critical semiotic analysis with the critique of political economy.

On the other hand, although CPE emphasizes that all social phenomena are discursively constituted and cannot achieve a self-reproducing closure (see above), it also insists on the contradictory, dilemmatic and antagonistic nature of the capital relation. This makes soft cultural economics inadequate. To neglect these structural contradictions, strategic dilemmas and potential antagonisms would be to subsume the economic under the general rubric of the socio-cultural and thereby lose sight of the distinctive materiality and overall logic of the capital relation. The economy should not be dissolved back into society (or culture) as a whole. It has its own specificities that derive from the distinctive extra-discursive properties of its various forms (cf. Slater 2002 on the key role of the commodity and property forms in differentiating the economy from other social relations). Thus successful economic governance depends on the co-presence of extra-economic as well as economic forms and on extra-economic as well as economic regularization.

A materialist CPE provides a powerful means both to critique and to contextualize recent claims about the 'culturalization' of economic life and/or the 'economization of culture'. It sees these claims as elements within a new economic imaginary with a potentially performative impact as well as a belated (mis)recognition of the semiotic dimensions of all economic activities (for sometimes contrasting views, see Du Gay and

Pryke 2002; Lash and Urry 1994; Ray and Sayer 1999). In particular, CPE emphasizes: (1) the constitutive material role of the extra-economic supports of market forces; and (2) the role of economic imaginaries in demarcating economic from extra-economic activities, institutions and orders and, hence, how semiosis is also constitutive in securing the conditions for accumulation.

Taking the cultural turn risks the temptation of soft cultural economics (see above). To minimize this risk we can return to first-generation RA work, which owed more to Marx and Marxism than later generations. It is the contradictory, dilemmatic and antagonistic nature of the capital relation that makes soft cultural economics inadequate. For the historically specific economic forms entailed in the capital relation (the commodity form, money, wages, prices, property etc.) have their own effects that must be analysed as such and that therefore shape the selection and retention of competing economic imaginaries. At best, different modes of regulation will modify the relative weight of these inevitable and incompressible contradictions and displace and/or defer some of their crisis tendencies and externalities through specific spatio-temporal fixes (Chapter 6). Note, too, that 'the reproduction of these contradictions with their contradictory effects and their impact on the historical tendency of capitalist development depends on the *class struggle*' (Poulantzas 1975: 40–41; italics in original). If we ignore these contradictions in developing CPE, it becomes too easy to conduct a relatively harmonious meso-level institutional analysis in and for which discourse provides only the ideological legitimation of the prevailing institutions (cf. Röttger 2003: 18–27). This would be to subsume the economic under the general rubric of the socio-cultural and thereby lose sight of the distinctive materiality and overall logic of the capital relation (see above).

CPE can adopt both bottom-up and top-down perspectives and, ideally, should combine them. In the first case, it considers how particular economic objects are produced, distributed and consumed in specific contexts by specific economic and extra-economic agents; traces their effects in the wider economy and beyond; and explores how different subjects, subjectivities and modes of calculation come to be naturalized and materially implicated in everyday life.[10] Conversely, when adopting a macro-level viewpoint, CPE would focus on the tendential emergence of macro-structural properties and their role in selectively reinforcing certain micro-level behaviours from among the inevitable flux of economic activities – thereby contributing to the reproduction of a more or less coherent economic (and extra-economic) order. Moreover, in this context, it seeks to identify the tendential laws, dynamics or regularities of economic conduct and performance that are reproduced only in so far as this structured coherence is itself reproduced. Any such coherence is always spatially and temporally delimited, however, being realized through particular discursive–material spatio-temporal fixes. Finally, from the viewpoint of agency, a macro-level CPE would also explore how the inherently improbable reproduction of these relatively stable and coherent economic (as well as extra-economic) orders is secured through the complex strategic coordination and governance of their various heterogeneous elements.

ON THE CO-EVOLUTION OF SEMIOSIS AND STRUCTURATION

Given its interest in structuration as well as meaning-making, CPE also explores the articulation of cultural (semiotic) and structural, agential and technological (extra-semiotic) factors that, starting from *variation* in construals, seeks to identify the factors that shape their differential *selection* and eventual *retention*. These three evolutionary mechanisms shape the movement from *construal* of the world to the *construction* of social facts as external and constraining, and hence from politicized meaning and unstructured complexity to sedimented meaning and structured complexity (Glynos and Howarth 2007). In other words, the evolution of social order involves the coupling and co-evolution of meaning-making and structuration with neither form of complexity reduction being reducible to the other. This co-evolution also shapes the scope for lesson-drawing (see below).

There is constant variation, witting or unwitting, in apparently routine social practices. This poses questions about the regularization of practices in normal conditions and about possible sources of radical transformation, especially in periods of crisis. The latter typically lead to profound cognitive and strategic disorientation of social forces and a corresponding proliferation in discursive interpretations and proposed material solutions (on learning in, through and from crisis, see Chapter 10). Nonetheless the same basic mechanisms serve to select and consolidate radically new practices and to stabilize routine practices. Simplifying the analysis in Fairclough et al. (2004) and extending it to include material as well as semiotic factors, the following factors shape the co-evolution of semiosis and structuration:

1. Continuing *variation* in discourses and practices, whether due to their incomplete mastery, their skilful adaptation in specific circumstances, new challenges or crises, or other semiotic or material causes.

2. *Selection* of particular discourses (the privileging of just some available, including emergent, discourses) for interpreting events, legitimizing actions, and (perhaps self-reflexively) representing social phenomena. Semiotic factors act here by influencing the resonance of discourses in personal, organizational and institutional, and broader meta-narrative terms and by limiting possible combinations of semiosis and semiotic practices in a given semiotic order. Material factors also operate here through conjunctural or entrenched power relations, path-dependency and structural selectivities.
3. *Retention* of some resonant discourses (e.g. inclusion in an actor's habitus, hexis and personal identity, enactment in organizational routines, integration into institutional rules, objectification in the built environment,[11] material and intellectual technologies, and articulation into widely accepted accumulation strategies, state projects or hegemonic visions). The greater the range of sites (horizontally and vertically)[12] in which resonant discourses are retained, the greater is the potential for effective institutionalization and integration into patterns of structured coherence and durable compromise. The constraining influences of complex, reciprocal interdependences will also recursively affect the scope for retaining resonant discourses.
4. *Reinforcement* in so far as certain procedural devices favour these discourses and their associated practices and also filter out contrary discourses and practices. This can involve both discursive selectivity (e.g. genre chains, styles, identities) and material selectivity (e.g. the privileging of certain dominant sites of discourse through structural biases in specific organizational and institutional orders). Such discursive and material mechanisms recursively strengthen appropriate genres, styles and strategies, and selectively eliminate inappropriate alternatives; they are most powerful where they operate across many sites to promote complementary discourses within the wider social ensemble.
5. *Selective recruitment, inculcation, and retention* by relevant social groups, organizations, institutions and so on of social agents whose predispositions fit as far as is possible with the preceding requirements.

This list emphasizes the role of semiosis and its material supports in securing social reproduction through the selection and retention of mutually supportive discourses. Conversely, the absence or relative weakness of one or more of these semiotic and/or extra-semiotic conditions may undermine previously dominant discourses and/or block the selection and retention of appropriate innovative discourses. This poses questions about how practices are regularized in normal conditions and about possible sources of radical transformation, especially in periods of crisis. Rapid social changes and/or crises are often moments of profound disorientation that trigger major semiotic and material innovations in the social world. It should be noted in this regard that the semiotic and extra-semiotic space for variation, selection and retention is contingent, not pre-given. This also holds for the various *and varying* semiotic and material elements whose selection and retention occur in this 'ecological' space. In a complex world there are many sites and scales on which such evolutionary processes operate and, for present purposes, what matters is how local sites and scales come to be articulated to form more global (general) sites and scales, and how the latter in turn frame, constrain and enable local possibilities (Wickham 1987). These interrelations are themselves shaped by the ongoing interaction between semiotic and extra-semiotic processes.

Discourses are most powerful where they operate across many sites and scales, and can establish and connect local hegemonies into a more encompassing hegemonic project. These discourses will be *retained* (discursively reproduced, incorporated into individual routines and institutionally embedded) when they are able to reorganize the balance of forces and guide supportive structural transformation. Although any given economic or political imaginary is only ever partially realized, those that succeed, at least in part, have their own performative, constitutive force in the material world – especially when they correspond to (or successfully shape) underlying material transformations, can mobilize different elites to form a new power bloc, can organize popular support, disorganize opposition and marginalize resistance. They will be most successful when they establish a new spatio-temporal fix that can displace and/or defer capital's inherent contradictions and crisis tendencies in the international political economy. In short, discourses and their related discursive chains can generate variation, have selective effects – reinforcing some discourses, filtering others out – and contribute to the differential retention and/or institutionalization of social relations through the recursive selection of certain genres, performances and strategies (Jessop 2004a).

Two provisional hypotheses grounded in these general considerations suggest themselves at this point, though neither has been fully tested in CPE work. First, the relative importance of semiosis declines from the stage of variation in imaginaries through the stage when they are selectively translated into specific material practices and institutional dynamics to the stage when they are embodied in a structurally coherent set of social relations with a corresponding spatio-temporal fix. Second, the relative weight of semiotic and extra-semiotic mechanisms varies across social fields. No great leap of imagination is needed to suggest that extra-semiotic mechanisms matter less in theology and philosophy than in natural science and technology, and that, conversely, semiosis matters more in the former than in the latter. However, as every field is always-already semiotic and also socially structured, each has its own mix of semiotic and extra-semiotic mechanisms (see Chapter 4).

SEMIOSIS AND MATERIALITY OF SOCIAL AGENCY

To illustrate how CPE can navigate between Scylla and Charybdis we comment on how it addresses the constitution of subjects and subjectivity. Marxism has always had problems in this regard because of its prioritization of class (most egregiously so in the unacceptable reductionist claim – not elaborated in Marx – that there is a natural movement from objective 'class in itself' to subjective 'class for itself'). But rational-choice theories, which have become increasingly dominant in contemporary political economy, are no better: they simply naturalize one version of rationality and show no interest in the formation of different subjects and modes of calculation. These problems are especially relevant, of course, to the emergence of new subjects and social forces in political economy – an issue related closely (but not exclusively) to periods of crisis and struggles over how to respond thereto (e.g. Jenson 1990b). More generally, CPE implies that interests do not exist independently of the discursive constitution of particular subject positions and the modes of calculation from which their interests are calculated in specific material–discursive conjunctures.

In avoiding hard political economy, we draw on the tools of semiosis, including their application to identity formation and *assujetissement* (or subjectivation). This suggests that class struggle is first of all a struggle about the constitution of class subjects before it is a struggle between class subjects (cf. Przeworski 1977: 371–3). Thus the field of political intervention is extremely broad. For the class struggle is no longer confined to the articulation of pre-given classes to popular-democratic or national-popular forces but extends to include the very constitution of class forces themselves. A key theme here is strategic essentialism. Instead it suggests how to combine semiotic and material concepts in political economy to understand and explain typical forms of social contestation based on particular forms of societalization and their interconnections in particular social formations. While a CPE analysis could start *either* with identities and interests *or* with contradictions and antagonisms, the interconnections among these alternative starting points mean that, sooner or later, these interconnections must come to the analytical foreground. It is in this context that the notion of 'strategic essentialism' is theoretically as well as practically productive.

The cultural turn in CPE is grounded in part in the existential necessity for actors to reduce complexity through semiosis as a condition for 'going on' in the world. This implies that all identities ('class' and non-class alike) are arbitrary *in the first instance* because they are semiotically mediated forms of complexity reduction that orient the observations, self-descriptions and self-observations of individual agents, organizations or social forces, and also guide the analyses and analytical self-reflection of third parties (including social scientists) who observe these actors. In short, identities serve as reference points for meaning-making. The key question becomes how just some of many competing identities come to be selected, retained through embodiment and intellectual and behavioural dispositions, and institutionalized at different scales from interpersonal relations to macro-structures. This is where the CPE focus on the contingent interaction among discursive, structural, technological and agential selectivities is especially relevant and provides a way to round out the notion of 'strategic essentialism'.

This notion was introduced by Gayatri Chakravorty Spivak (1987), who uses it to describe the discursive construction of an 'essential unity' among heterogeneous groups as a basis for strategic political action. While she discussed strategic essentialism in relation to nationalities, ethnic groups, gender politics and other movements, a CPE perspective implies that it can (and should) be applied also to class politics. It denies that economic, political and ideological positions are epiphenomena of objective economic class location and that there are coherent, hermetically sealed and mutually exclusive ideologies produced by each class in isolation or that all ideological elements have a clear class belonging. Instead, CPE highlights the role of discourses and practices in establishing a contingent equivalence among members of different social classes and/or categories that privileges one identity and its associated interests over other identities (cf. Marx and Engels 1976b). There are some affinities in this regard with post-Marxist discourse analysis (e.g. Laclau and Mouffe 1985), but CPE combines these arguments with consistent accounts of structural selectivities, the effectivity of technologies of power and knowledge, and the difference that agency can make. What matters for the moment, however, is that 'strategic essentialism' highlights the role of political and ideological as well as organizational practices in forming and shaping identities that bear on class (or, better, class-relevant) struggles as well as identities that directly concern, or are relevant to, other fields of contestation.

When it is integrated into CPE, strategic essentialism has the following implications:

- It is anti-essentialist because it denies any automatic movement from some objective location in social relations to a corresponding subjective identity.
- It emphasizes the role of discursive practices in establishing equivalences among different locations as the basis for shared subject positions.
- It highlights the scope for deconstructing and denaturalizing essentialized identities when they have become sedimented and taken-for-granted.
- The ideal and material interests associated with subject positions depend on particular conceptions of strategy and tactics in particular conjunctures.
- In focusing on class relevance rather than explicit class struggle, it opens space for 'intersectional' analysis and different kinds of alliance politics.

Intersectionalist analyses emphasize the semiotic and material interdependence of different forms of exploitation, oppression or disadvantage, and tend to reject (or at least be agnostic about) the primacy of any given identity, set of interests or type of domination (on intersectionalism, see, e.g., Ferguson 1990; Collins 1998; and, critically, Nash 2008). Whilst acknowledging the *prima facie* appeal of this position, CPE offers a toolkit for analysing and explaining why certain principles of societal organization (*Vergesellschaftung*) may become hegemonic or dominant in certain periods, places and conjunctures without rejecting the solid theoretical and empirical arguments indicating that these principles are always overdetermined by other sites and modes of exploitation, domination or asymmetrical differentiation. It considers not only the articulation of particular subject positions or identities around specific imaginaries, but also their embedding in specific structures, their connection to particular technologies of power and knowledge, and the scope for certain agents to make a difference in certain circumstances. This implies, among other things, that the influence of semiosis can no more be explained purely in semiotic terms than the influence of structuration can be explained solely in terms of its direct effects on possible combinations and sequences of action.

A strategic essentialist CPE does not assume pre-given, structurally inscribed 'class identities' associated with particular class interests – let alone pre-given forms of class organization. Instead it examines efforts to construct explicit class identities and associated interests (which may be more or less arbitrary fantasies or, conversely, more or less adequate reflections of underlying class locations in general terms or in regard to specific conjunctures) and to align them in class terms. Thus CPE does not assume that class identities, in so far as they are ever explicitly articulated, actually correspond to objective class location or objective interests in a given spatio-temporal horizon. What matters for capital accumulation or political class domination is the '*class relevance*' of social identities, imaginaries and projects in specific conjunctures and their medium- to long-term effects on the balance of forces. In this context, mobilization in the name of non-class rather than class identities could well have greater relevance to capital accumulation and/or to political class domination.

Moreover, once specific subjective identities emerge, a CPE approach would aim to identify objective interests (ideal and/or material) that are linked to these identities. Such interests are always relative (involving questions of more or less) and can be calculated only for specific fields of struggle and particular conjunctures rather than on a permanent and comprehensive basis. This relates to the more general strategic-relational claim that interests can be assessed only in relation to particular conceptions of strategy. This does not make the interests any less objective since there are still specific material conditions of existence for the realization of specific strategic objectives. But adopting such an approach does mean that class interests can no longer be seen as permanently and exclusively inscribed in the relations of production and thus as absolute and unconditional (cf. Jessop 1982: 242–3).

SEDIMENTATION AND STRUCTURATION IN CRISIS

After the financial crisis broke out in the USA, the following exchange occurred at the House Committee on Oversight and Government Reform:

> REP. WAXMAN: Do you feel that your ideology pushed you to make decisions that you wish you had not made?
> MR. GREENSPAN: Remember what an ideology is: a conceptual framework for people to deal with reality. Everyone has one. You have to – to exist, you need an ideology. The question is whether it is accurate or not . . . I've found a flaw. I don't know how significant or permanent it is. But I've been very distressed by that fact . . . A flaw in the model that I perceived as the critical functioning structure that defines how the world works. (Greenspan 2008)

From a CPE perspective, what Representative Henry Waxman and Alan Greenspan, the US Federal Reserve Chair, call 'ideologies' are better seen as personal interpretative and calculative frameworks derived from social imaginaries that shape 'lived experience'. As Greenspan implies, 'everyone' must simplify the real (natural and social world) to be able to 'go on' within it. We would add that Greenspan's belief that 'everyone' must have an ideology to deal with reality is itself a simplification that rests on a naturalized reading of agency tied to individuals as whole persons. We have already shown that many critical theories challenge the idea of personhood and emphasize instead modes of individuation, subjectivation and the possibility of decentred personhood. In addition, as other analyses reviewed above make clear, not just every individual but any 'calculative agent' (e.g. movements, organizations or smart machines) must simplify reality to be able to 'go on' in the world.

However, as Greenspan concedes, ideologies (or imaginaries) may be 'flawed'. As *enforced selection and hence simplification*, imaginaries may ignore key features of the actually existing natural and social world. There can be no one-to-one mapping of imaginaries to that world, which will always have structural features and phenomenal forms that are perforce neglected in any given imaginary. This is why CPE must examine both semiosis and structuration, and the ways in which certain semiotic and structural 'solutions' are privileged over others thanks to the operation of structural, discursive, technological and agential selectivities. In capitalist economies, for example, these structural features include: contradictions, dilemmas, crisis tendencies and counter-tendencies; important extra-economic conditions of existence and effects of economic practices and institutions; and the uneven links across different scales of economic action and their embedding in broader spatio-temporal frameworks. These features operate even when they are unacknowledged by first-order social agents (and/or are denied by observers) and, because of their interaction in specific contexts and conjunctures, may generate crisis tendencies or otherwise disorient agents and observers, leading to distress about the 'flaws' in their 'ideologies' and prompting the occasion for learning more about the facticity of the natural and social worlds. The 'unmarked' and 'unobserved' take their revenge on those who ignore them, and this leads to crisis or other system failures.

The exchange between Representative Henry Waxman and Alan Greenspan provides a useful introduction to a necessary development in the account presented so far in this chapter. Given our insistence on CPE's commitment to the critique of ideology and domination, it could seem that we have forgotten this commitment. So we now indicate how the analysis is modified in the light of the limits of the institutionalist and cultural turns in political economy. Figure 4.3 thematizes, in the same terms as Figure 4.1, the *inherent improbability* of sedimented meaning and structured complexity. Sedimentation is improbable because, as

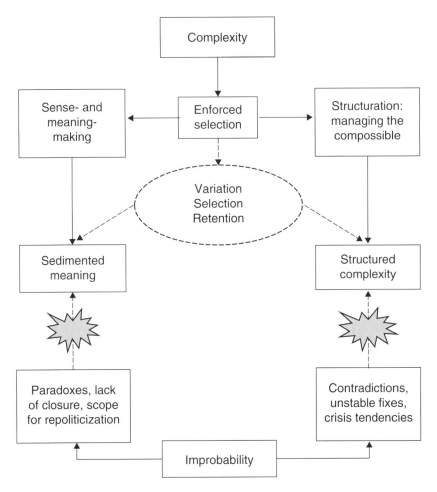

Figure 4.3   The improbability of complexity reduction via enforced selection

various approaches to semiotic analysis indicate, the closure of a *langue*, semantics, discourse and so on is implausible (see Chapter 3). Indeed, the flexibility inscribed in semiosis, the provisional nature of sutures, the paradoxes and contradictions in discourse, and so on make discourse permanently vulnerable to repoliticization, critique, recontextualization and so forth. Likewise, given the basic features of capitalism as a mode of production and an object of regulation/governance, with its contradictory, crisis-prone and conflictual dynamic, we highlight the inherent improbability of capital accumulation based solely on market forces. Indeed, there is a permanent (if abstract) possibility of crises in accumulation and domination that is likely to be profoundly disorienting (see Chapter 11). The same holds for many other social forms. In this sense both sedimented meaning and structured complexity are vulnerable to dissolution. This creates space for efforts to promote new hegemonic semantics and new institutional forms and complexes. We return to these issues in Chapters 5 and 6.

CONCLUDING REMARKS

The evolutionary and institutional approach to semiosis advocated here recognizes the semiotic dimensions of political economy but also suggests how and why only some economic imaginaries get selected and institutionalized. This approach enables us to identify the contradictions and conflicts that make capital accumulation inherently improbable and crisis-prone, creating the space for economic imaginaries to play a role in stabilizing accumulation in specific spatio-temporal fixes and/or in identifying an exit strategy from recurrent crises.

It offers a 'third way' between two equally problematic approaches. Against hard political economy, it insists that the economy in its broadest sense includes both economic and extra-economic factors. Capitalism involves a series of specific economic forms (the commodity form, money form, wage form, price form, property form etc.) associated with generalized commodity production. These have their own effects, including their role in shaping the selection and retention of competing economic imaginaries. These effects must be analysed in their own terms.

CPE recognizes the constitutive role of semiosis, the other moments of social practice (which must be explored in their own terms), and the emergent extra-semiotic features of the discursive and non-discursive moments of social practices and their emergent effects. It posits that semiosis and structuration conjointly shape capacities for action and transformation. This chapter focused on identifying some basic concepts and methods for analysing semiosis along lines consistent with our complexity-reductive, critical-realist, strategic-relational approach. At the level of research investigations (as opposed to grand-theory-building), the results from this chapter can be translated into at least five interrelated injunctions regarding the first three features of the CPE research programme: (1) take semiotic turns (such as the argumentative, narrative, rhetorical and linguistic turns) seriously in the analysis of political economy, either as the entry-point for analysis or as essential adjuncts to other methodological entry-points; (2) examine the role of discursive practices in the making and remaking of social relations and their contribution to their emergent extra-discursive properties; (3) investigate discourses and discursive formations as a system of meanings and practices that have semiotic structuring effects that differ from those of emergent political and economic structures and, *a fortiori*, study how these different principles or logics interact and with what effects; (4) focus on the (in)stability and the interplay of objects–subjects in the remaking of social relations – and hence the importance of remaking subjectivities as part of the structural transformation and actualization of objects; and (5) examine the relationship between the politics of identity/difference and political economy – especially the complex articulations between class and non-class identities over different times and spaces.

There are three other features of the overall approach that require attention. Individual, collective and organizational learning occur in regard to both semiosis and structuration. They can be explored at all five levels represented in Table 4.1 and, like semiosis and structuration, are subject to the mechanisms of variation, selection and retention (see Chapter 11). Technological and agential selectivities characterize both moments of complexity reduction too. We explored the former in relation to the general biases of communication (Innis 1950, 1951; Williams 1971, 1974) and socio-logistics in Chapter 3 and introduce a more Foucauldian account of technologies in Chapter 5. We touched on agential selectivity in discussing the strategic-relational approach in Chapter 1 as well as subjectivation and intersectionality above; we return to this theme in relation to specific conjunctures in Chapter 5 and the case studies. Finally, once one recognizes the incompleteness of discourse, its lack of closure, and the fragility of efforts at the deparadoxification of semantic fixes and the contradictory and crisis-prone character of some of the most significant social forms, institutions and social practices, it becomes important to ask how specific social practices serve to disguise these phenomena and, in doing so, maintain their ideological effects and contribute to the reproduction of domination. We return to these issues in the concluding chapter (Chapter 13), when we revisit all six features and explore their interconnections.

Pursuing the themes elaborated in this chapter should enable political economy to become more self-reflexive epistemologically and methodologically, and to broaden its traditional, structuralist research agenda. Indeed, a self-consistent CPE would also involve calls for reflexivity on the part of social scientists about the conditions of their own practices and a concern with the conditions in which a cultural turn in political economy has been recommended, sometimes gets selected and, less commonly, gets institutionalized within the scientific system.

NOTES

1. Facticity is a term originating in European philosophy; its meaning varies with the philosophical tradition into which it is integrated. Three relevant meanings here are: (1) those aspects of the real world that resist explanation and interpretation; (2) the character of the world into which we are 'thrown' and within which we must 'go on'; and (3) the totality of the concrete details (circumstances) that shape social forces' capacity to make their own history. The second meaning is primary in the sentence to which this note refers.
2. These meaning systems are shaped by neural, cognitive and semiotic frames (Lakoff and Johnson 1980; Nord and Olsson 2013), as well as, of course, social interaction, meaning-making technologies and strategically selective opportunities for reflection and learning.
3. For Barbieri, life is essentially about: (1) manufacturing objects; (2) organizing objects into functioning structures; and (3) interpreting the world. These are all semiotic processes – not just the last. He concludes that we must 'come to terms with the existence of manufacturing semiosis and associative semiosis in all forms of life, and realize that they actually are the preconditions for the origin of interpretive semiosis in animal life' (Barbieri 2012: 47).
4. While Höppe (1982) summarizes the position from a historical materialist perspective, which emphasizes the role of labour and its divisions in the development of language, Møller (2006) summarizes it from a systems-theoretical perspective, which relates growing societal complexity to the growing complexity of language as the basis for communicating about a complex world. Møller also notes that the body (including the brain), consciousness and communication are structurally coupled and that the mind is the filter between body and communication. From an evolutionary-biology perspective on language, Lieberman shows that language capacity is closely related to motor abilities, which confirms, without citing him, Engels's views on the role of labour in the transition from ape to man (1876 [1987]).
5. On the pre-linguistic and material bases of logic, see Archer (2000).
6. Polanyi (1982) distinguished *substantive* economic activities involved in material 'provisioning' from *formal* (profit-oriented, market-mediated) economic activities. The main economic imaginaries in capitalist societies ignore the full range of substantive economic activities in favour of a focus on formal economic activities.
7. Although all social practices are semiotic *and* material, the relative causal efficacy of these two moments varies.
8. We are not suggesting that mass media can be disentangled from the wider networks of social relations in which they operate, but seeking to highlight the diminished role of an autonomous public sphere in shaping semiosis.
9. Marx argues that capital and labour encounter each other as equals in the labour market; exploitation and antagonism begin when workers pass through the factory gates and enter the hidden abode of production.
10. Here we adopt Wickham's view that the distinction between micro and macro (or particular and global) is always relative to an object of analysis rather than inscribed in a given set of social relations (Wickham 1987).
11. For a narrative account of the meaning of buildings, see Yanow (1995).
12. Horizontal denotes sites on a similar scale (e.g. personal, organizational, institutional, functional systems); vertical denotes different scales (e.g. micro–macro, local–regional–national–supranational–global).

5. Elaborating the cultural political economy research agenda: selectivities, dispositives and the production of (counter-)hegemonies

This chapter has two main tasks. One is to answer a common question: how can one turn some of CPE's abstract macro-theoretical claims about semiosis and structuration into a middle-range research agenda? The other is to address the fifth feature of CPE, namely, technological selectivities. The first task involves a more detailed account of the semiotic and structural aspects of social forms and social practices. In previous work we called this meso-level agenda a 'discursive–material' approach (Sum 2004, 2009), distinguished the modes of effectiveness and emergent properties of the discursive and material, and emphasized the material aspects of discourse and the discursive aspects of the material (Jessop 2004a, 2009). Chapter 4 clarified these aspects as a basis for navigating between a constructivist Charybdis and a structuralist Scylla in order to provide an integral analysis. We now show how discursive and 'material' moments are articulated (while respecting their differences) and explore their joint impact on, in and through specific (sets of) social practices. The second task requires more attention to the significance of technologies, in a broadly Foucauldian sense, to the consolidation and/or contestation of domination and hegemony. We also comment briefly on the sixth feature, that is, the denaturalization of economic and political imaginaries and the critique of ideology and domination. This is a challenging agenda theoretically and empirically. We address the theoretical challenges here and provide empirical illustrations in Parts III and IV of this book.

This chapter has five sections. First, we suggest both how to transcend the structuralist bias of institutional turns and how to avoid discourse-centric accounts of social practices. Thus we summarize six key themes regarding the substantive as well as discursive moments of social practices. Second, we consider one aspect of Gramsci's analyses of historical bloc and hegemony in terms of a distinction between 'hegemonies in production' and 'production of hegemonies'. Third, we propose a trans-disciplinary approach to the 'production of (counter-)hegemonies' that builds on the SRA and critical discourse analysis (CDA). This explores the theoretical and heuristic potential of combining key insights in Foucault and Gramsci. On this basis we identify parallels, explicit and implicit borrowings, and potential linkages in the work of Marx, Gramsci and Foucault. This involves a double movement that could be summarized, provisionally but inelegantly, as the governmentalization of Gramsci and the Marxianization of Foucault. These moves indicate the uneven and asymmetrical relations among hegemony, intellectuals, discourses, objectivation, subjectivation and power/knowledge relations in different contexts. We also elaborate four previously identified modes of strategic selectivity: structural, discursive, technological and agential, and, in this context, offer a strategic-relational definition of Foucault's concept of dispositive. Fourth, as the weight of these selectivities varies conjuncturally, we suggest one way to study their interaction in terms of seven 'discursive–material moments' in the production of hegemony, sub-hegemony and counter-hegemony. Fifth, we summarize the key points, indicate their relevance to the critique of ideology and domination, and re-emphasize the many routes to delivering the CPE agenda.

CHARTING A ROUTE BETWEEN SCYLLA AND CHARYBDIS

We now chart a route between our two monsters that is ontologically as well as epistemologically consistent with the complexity turn, critical realism and the SRA. It takes its bearings from six major themes from earlier chapters: (1) the two modes of complexity reduction, namely, semiosis and structuration; (2) the different levels at which semiosis and structuration and their interaction can be studied and, relatedly, the need, whether one begins with semiosis or structuration, to introduce the other side sooner or later and integrate it into the analysis; (3) the coupling of the discursive and 'material' moments of social practices, highlighting their respective modes of variation, selection and retention at this level of analysis; (4) as an important conclusion from these three themes, the recognition that, in addition to the semiotic and structural moments, each with its own selectivities, there are two further modes of selectivity that cross-cut them – namely, technological and agential; and (5) the argument that the differential articulation of these four modes of strategic selectivity, when condensed into dispositives, shapes both the semiotic and 'material' moments of the dynamic of social relations. A sixth point is that the weight of these selectivities varies at different stages in the variation, selection and retention of actions to resist, restore, reform or radically transform social relations. In sum, CPE explores the uneven interaction of the discursive and the material as mediated through four forms of selectivity – with agential selectivities as the efficient force in social transformation.

These six themes are elaborated in relation to the semiotic and substantive aspects of social practices. Thus CPE considers not only how texts produce meaning and thereby help to generate social structure, but also how this is constrained by emergent, non-semiotic features of social structure as well as inherently semiotic factors. To illustrate this, we draw again on Gramsci, who can be seen both as a proto-regulationist and as a pioneer in CPE (see Chapters 2, 3 and 4). Thus we first introduce the concepts of historical bloc and hegemony; and, on this basis, distinguish different sites and scales of hegemony in capitalist social formations. We link these to the four modes of selectivity to reveal its structurally inscribed, socio-discursive nature.

HEGEMONIES IN PRODUCTION AND PRODUCTION OF HEGEMONIES

Gramsci's prefigurative role as a cultural political economist arises in part from his attempts to renew Marxism. Rejecting, *inter alia*, the base–superstructure distinction, he criticized the Second International and Bolshevik theorists for their neglect of civil society as a key site and stake in economic, political and ideological struggles. This mattered whether the state was everything, and civil society was gelatinous, as in the East; or, as in the West, which was the focus of his analyses and political practices, civil society was a key factor in class power. In the latter case, while class power had a 'decisive economic nucleus', it also rested on hegemony protected by the armour of coercion (Gramsci 1971: 263; Q6, §88: 763–5). A useful distinction here is between 'hegemonies in production' and 'production of hegemonies'. Although this might seem to involve no more than a play on words, there are, as we shall see, important theoretical and practical issues at stake.

Hegemonies in Production

Regarding the historical bloc, Gramsci's notes on Americanism and Fordism explored the potential for grounding hegemony in production. He reflected on the ascendancy and dominance of Americanism (the American system of manufacturing, including the fragmentation of the division of labour through Taylorism and the Fordist moving assembly line) and its associated Fordist mode of regulation; and he discussed the problems of transferring this model to Europe after the Great War. He suggested that Fordism represented potentially a new industrial–productive historical bloc that rationalized mass production and *temporarily* resolved the crisis tendencies and dilemmas of capitalism (particularly the tendency of the rate of profit to fall) within the constraints of that system (see Chapter 2). Rationalizing production in this way enabled products to be sold more cheaply, and workers to be paid a 'high' wage to buy the products that they made. The development of the American system of manufacturing anchored hegemony in production by socializing workers into accepting new norms of production and consumption and thereby providing the basis for a historical bloc. The latter reorganized economic, political and societal relations on the basis of economic growth and widening prosperity based on a virtuous circle of mass production and mass consumption.

Gramsci employs the concept of historical bloc to resolve the otherwise problematic relationship between the economic 'base' and its politico-ideological 'superstructure'. He asks how 'the complex, contradictory and discordant ensemble of the superstructures is the reflection of the ensemble of the social relations of production'. He answers in terms of how the historical bloc reflects 'the necessary reciprocity between structure and superstructure' (1971: 366; Q8, §182: 1051–2). This reciprocity is realized through specific intellectual, moral and political practices. These translate narrow sectoral, professional or local (in his terms, 'economic–corporate') interests into broader 'ethico-political' ones. Thus the ethico-political not only helps to co-constitute economic structures but also provides them with their rationale and legitimacy. Analysing the historical bloc in this way can also show how 'material forces are the content and ideologies are the form, though this distinction between form and content has purely didactic value' (1971: 377; Q7, §21: 869).

In this regard, Fordism provided the social integument of the new social order through a complementary set of social relations inside and outside the factory. This is reflected in new social forms in the family, corporatism, new forms of trade union and party organization, government interventions in welfare provisions (e.g. through New Deal reforms) and so forth. Thus, in Fordist sectors, while the 'hidden abode of production' (Marx 1976a: 280) remained the site of capital's domination over labour power oriented to the intensification of work and securing economies of scale, this was tempered by the emerging mode of regulation. The structural coherence between new forms of production and new social forms explains the survival of this hegemonic order for some 50 years in the USA (backed, as Gramsci would have been the first to note, by coercion, e.g., through private police forces such as Pinkerton agents, the blacklisting of militants, 'red scares' and mobster influence in trade unions). It also explains some of the difficulties of transplanting Fordism along with Americanism to Europe, which had entrenched and resistant traditions in the fields of production, political life and the wider civil society. When similar institutional complementarities were eventually established (especially through postwar reconstruction in Europe), Atlantic Fordism proved relatively stable, albeit for a shorter period, until its crisis in the 1970s (see also Chapter 6).

The crisis of Atlantic Fordism led regulationist and like-minded scholars to explore the prospects for a new accumulation regime and mode of regulation. If established, this would engender a new historical bloc with a new set of complementary social forms and a decisive economic nucleus in new techno-economic paradigms and new relations of production. Other scholars studied the intensification of Fordism (neo-Fordism) and/or the revival of flexible specialization (Piore and Sabel 1984). Yet others identified a shift to finance-led accumulation (Aglietta 2002; Boyer 2000) and, more recently, to Waltonism as a retail-led model (Vidal 2012) (see Chapter 9).

We explored many of these theoretical and historical issues in Jessop and Sum (2006) and address retail-led Waltonism and finance-dominated accumulation in Chapters 9 and 11 respectively. In addition, based on new theoretical developments, Chapters 6, 7 and 11 elaborate a new approach to the historical bloc by introducing the concepts of discursive, social, institutional and spatio-temporal fixes, and applying them to Atlantic Fordism and its crisis, the knowledge-based economy and finance-dominated accumulation. Other scholars, influenced by trans-national historical materialism, have examined *trans-national* historical blocs in North Atlantic economic and political space and, more recently, on a global scale (Carroll and Carson 2003; Robinson 2004). In particular, 'Italian School' analysts (Chapter 2) have not only explored the trans-national dimensions of economic restructuring in more detail (e.g. Cox 1987) and the rise of a US-centred international historical bloc (Gill 1991a), but have also examined the emergence of 'market civilization' anchored in disciplinary neoliberalism and a new constitutionalism (Gill 1995a) (see Chapter 9).

Production of (Counter-)Hegemonies

Gramsci also offered original analyses of the production of (counter-) hegemonies. He investigated the processes through which hegemonies are constituted in and across different institutional orders and civil society (including in particular everyday life). Of special interest is his account of organic intellectuals (alongside other social agents) as the crucial intermediaries in these respects. Building on these analyses, CPE highlights their various discursive aspects.

Hegemony

Hegemony refers to the modalities of securing domination through social practices oriented to the winning of overt or tacit consent. This definition derives from Gramsci, who related hegemony to the capacity of dominant groups to establish and maintain political, intellectual and moral leadership, and secure the 'broad-based consent' of allied and subordinate groups to prevailing relations of economic and political domination. Hegemony was secured through operations within civil society (i.e. the 'ensemble of organisms commonly called "private"' (Gramsci 1971: 12; Q8, §182: 1518) as well as within the state in its narrow, juridico-political sense (i.e. statal and parastatal apparatuses and personnel). Indeed, his analyses of the role of forces based in civil society to contribute to consent (and, in some cases, such as paramilitary groups, coercion) are an important contribution to a critical understanding of hegemony. Effective hegemony depends on the capacity of dominant groups to suture the identities, interests, emotions and values of key sectors of subordinate classes and other subaltern groups into a hegemonic vision and embed this in institutions and policies – leading in turn to their translation into common sense.

At the same time, reflecting the 'material' as well as discursive moment of social practice, hegemony was said to depend on material concessions to subaltern groups. This analysis also informed his account of counter-hegemonic practices and strategies. Gramsci's interest in the 'discursive face of power' (Fraser and Bartky 1992) is reflected in his studies of intellectuals (very broadly defined) as the creators and mediators of hegemony, as crucial bridges between economic, political and ideological domination, and as active agents in linking culture (especially knowledge) and subjectivity in the production of hegemony. A Gramscian approach can be combined with insights and arguments from Foucault on the normalization of subjects through disciplinary power and governmentality (1977, 1991). Indeed, introducing Foucauldian arguments into a neo-Gramscian analysis of hegemony, discourse, subjectivity and subjectivation is a productive step in developing CPE (see later on governmentalizing Gramsci). Indeed, in this regard, it emphasizes the multi-faceted nature of hegemonies and extends its scope from intellectual and moral leadership to include self-leadership (i.e. responsibility of the self as a moral agent to guide the self) (see below).

Hegemonies, intellectuals and discourses

'Italian School' studies stressed the processual and agential nature of hegemony. For example, Cox has consistently emphasized the importance of ideas and the mutual influence of ideational and material forces (1996: 132; cf. 1981; for a critique, see Chapter 2). In addition, in contrast to Machiavelli's call for a prince to unify Italy's many city-states to found an authentic Italian national state, Gramsci indicated the need for a 'modern prince' that would comprise a strategic centre (or party) and mobilize leading and subaltern forces behind a new democratic state project (this idea has since been reframed in terms of the rise of a post-modern prince; see Gill 2003a and 2011). The modern prince would articulate a hegemonic vision that integrated the identities, interests, passions, hopes and fears of subaltern groups as well as leading forces. This strategic centre mobilizes classes/groups and articulates their fears and offers visions, imaginations, hopes and passions that are shot through with affective energies/forces to reorganize capitalism or to offer active resistance (Chaput 2010 and 2011; Haynes and Sharpe 2009; Roelvink 2010).

This approach clearly relates to Gramsci's 'vernacular materialism' (see Chapter 3) and poses questions about the relation of historical bloc formation to the semiotic moment of hegemony, the role of intellectuals, and the elaboration of new truth regimes and forms of common sense. This is where the theoretical tools introduced in earlier chapters can be applied to the production of hegemonies, sub-hegemonies and counter-hegemonies in specific societal contexts and particular conjunctures. This requires exploring social practices in their discursive and structural (material) aspects and social agents' role in the remaking of (counter-) hegemonic social relations. Of interest here is how organic intellectuals may emerge through the variation, selection and retention of hegemonic visions, acquiring a clearer identity and role as the visions with which they are associated acquire form and effectiveness through their selection and retention, thereby consolidating their position as the bearers and interpreters of these visions and worldviews (see Box 5.1). In other words, rather than presupposing that organic intellectuals are always present, the present CPE approach explores how discourses make organic intellectuals and organic intellectuals make discourses in a contingent, co-evolutionary process without guarantees (see the case studies in Chapters 8 and 12). As Foucault suggests, this occurs through 'problematization', that is, the identification of certain problems, often in response to *urgences*, around which intellectuals (among others) elaborate a problem, its solution, truth regimes and social practices. In the case of the modern prince, then, Gramsci's problem was how to create a democratic socialist order in the face of a weak Italian state, the crisis tendencies of capitalism and the rise of fascism. Different sets of problems lead to different sets of intellectuals and different problematizations. We illustrate this in Chapters 7, 8 and 12 for the rise of intellectuals who problematize competitiveness and/or economic crisis and, on this basis, develop new knowledge brands, crisis construals and patent remedies for these problems (see Parts III and IV).

Thus viewed, there can be many types of organic intellectual. Which individuals or social forces come to play this role emerges from different problems and problematizations in a process marked by variation, selection and retention. After the Second World War, for example, this role has been performed on behalf of different fractions of capital through a wide range of institutions and organizations that identify, recalibrate and promote new accumulation strategies, state policies and projects, and hegemonic visions. These include think tanks, research institutes, business schools, management consultancies, business media, discourse coalitions, advocacy groups and epistemic communities, as well as political parties and the more traditional kind of 'grand intellectual'. To these we can add the equivalent economic, political and intellectual forces plus old and new social movements that promote sub- and counter-hegemonic strategies, policies, projects and visions. These agencies selectively construct/reinvent imaginaries, produce bodies of knowledge, steer discussions, balance different forces in the historical bloc and so forth. Focusing more on the social practices of these semiotic moments, the production of (counter-)hegemonies explores their roles in constructing, producing and circulating bodies of (moral, intellectual) knowledge that normalize (or resist) particular object fields, subject positions and relations of rule inscribed terrains.

A TRANS-DISCIPLINARY APPROACH TO THE PRODUCTION OF (COUNTER-)HEGEMONIES

This agenda requires a stepwise trans-disciplinary approach that examines issues of structure/agency, strategic selectivities, discourse/materiality and power/knowledge. Drawing on theoretical resources presented in Part I, we now consider the production of hegemonies and sub- and counter-hegemonies.

The Strategic-relational Approach and Critical Discourse Analysis

A useful starting point is the SRA with its dialectical heuristics for studying structural selectivity and agential selectivity in their interaction and, especially, for addressing path-dependency and path-shaping. As a first step, *structural selectivity* refers to structurally inscribed strategic selectivity; and *agential selectivity* refers to the differential capacity of agents to engage in structurally oriented strategic calculation. A second step in analysing structural selectivity is to explore forms, institutions, organizational structures and, eventually, conjunctures in terms of their strategic selectivities. In turn, a second step in analysing agential selectivity is to distinguish different social forces, their subjectivation as bearers of specific identities and ideal and material interests, their capacities for strategic calculation and their capacities for action. This is always overdetermined by discursive and technological selectivities. Ultimately, agential selectivity depends on the difference that specific actors (or social forces) make in particular conjunctures and/or in transforming conjunctures. Agents can make a difference thanks to their different capacities to persuade, read particular conjunctures, displace opponents, and rearticulate discourses and imaginaries in timely fashion. Nodal actors in this regard may include charismatic individuals, philosophical visionaries, organic intellectuals (in the usual sense), guru academics, consultants, technocrats, political parties, social movements, and so on.

Overall, this suggests that forces seeking to promote and realize hegemonic projects should analyse the relevant strategic contexts, engage in a stepwise transformation of the structural selectivities that may obstruct and/or facilitate the realization of the project, and promote individual and collective learning on the part of potential hegemonic subjects and subaltern forces so that they will share its values and objectives. This is, of course, what Gramsci calls a 'war of position' (1971: 243; Q13, §7: 1566) and it bears on the basic structural and agential mediations of competing hegemonic projects.

An obvious extension of the SRA, which initially focused on structural and agential selectivity, is to include discursive selectivity. This requires engaging with different modes of critical semiotic analysis to explore more fully the articulation and co-evolution of the discursive and extra-discursive moments of social processes and practices and their conjoint impact in specific contexts and conjunctures (see Chapter 3). Building on the three basic evolutionary mechanisms of variation, selection and retention, this step examines imaginaries and their associated objects/subjects as socially constructed, historically specific, and more or less socially (dis)embedded in broader networks of social relations and institutional ensembles. Although a 'cultural turn' is one way to escape the structuralist temptations involved in structural analysis, it should not neglect the materiality of social relations and, hence, the constraints of processes that operate 'behind the backs' of the relevant agents.

Semiosis (sense- and meaning-making) sets limits to what can be imagined by individual and social agents, and provides CPE's methodological entry-point into the analysis of imaginaries and, as appropriate, ideologies and their broader implications for social practice, social forms and social orders. Another aspect of selectivity is that the 'semiotic resources' in a given semantic regime, order of discourse, genre chain and so on are more or less accessible and reworkable depending on the rules of discursive formation and the linkages across different orders of discourse. Critical linguistic and discourse analysts have developed various ways to examine the constraints and opportunities, the rules and resources, available within particular types of discourse and, of course, the scope for their articulation in particular contexts and conjunctures. This was a key contribution of the Bakhtin Circle and has also been developed in different ways in CDA (see Chapter 3).

More specifically, genre chains (Fairclough 2003) comprise activities and documents, and, in the field of policy formation, these include consultancy reports, forum meetings, speeches, policy proposals and the like. A variety of potentially conflicting discourses may figure in a policy arena and be associated with different discourse coalitions and advocacy networks. In so far as specific genre chains are legitimized and able to connect many different discursive fields, however, this privileges discourses that can be expressed in these terms (see Jessop 2009; Sum 2010a; and Chapters 8 and 10 on genre chains in competitiveness discourses). Genre chains may also be used to recontextualize information and knowledge. Following Bernstein, recontextualization involves the selective relocation, refocusing and recombination of discourses in and across different discursive fields in ways that both fit and reaffirm existing social relations (1996: 47). The scope for this depends on general regulative principles and specific rules about what statements will count as valid in different contexts (ibid.: 116–17).[1]

Staging an Encounter between Gramsci, Marx and Foucault

We now remedy our relative neglect in previous chapters of technological (Foucauldian) selectivities by showing its importance for the overall CPE project. We argue that it is both valuable and feasible to integrate Foucault's work on disciplinary, normalizing and governmental technologies into the CPE agenda. The key to this is the distinction between 'how' and 'why' questions and how answers to both can be articulated into a coherent theoretical framework. Anglophone neo-Foucauldian studies (e.g. Miller and Rose 1990; Dean 1999; Rose and Miller 2008) have privileged Foucault's answers to the question of 'how' governance occurs and they have neglected the 'why' questions related to dynamics of socio-economic transformation (see later). These are obviously two different kinds of inquiry with different sets of tools but, from a CPE perspective, both are necessary and one should not in principle be privileged over the other. Thus the CPE agenda considers how discourses and discursive practices condition subjectivities and what role they play in consolidating domination and hegemony.

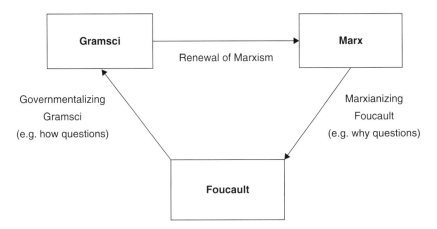

Figure 5.1   An encounter between Gramsci, Marx and Foucault

Given this wider agenda, this subsection stages a 'brief encounter', against the background of Marx's critique of political economy, between Gramsci's analyses of hegemony and the differential articulation of coercion–consent (and the associated role of traditional and organic intellectuals in these regards) and Foucault's analyses of objectivation, discursive formations, thematization, subjectivation, dispositives, and their relation to governmental technologies and issues of power/knowledge. This encounter is enabled by parallels, complementarities and potential synergies, including Gramsci's conceptions of the world and Foucault's regime of truth. We propose a double movement that could be termed the governmentalization of Gramsci (based on Foucault's insights into disciplinary normalization and governmentalization) and the Marxianization of Foucault (based on a return to the critique of political economy) (see Figure 5.1).

We have already indicated how Gramsci's analyses of the *mercato determinato* and the state in its integral sense contributed to a renewal of Marxism (Chapter 2). Class domination, expressed through state power, involves a variable mix of hegemony and coercion and, while it has a decisive economic nucleus, hegemony depends on the creation and diffusion of an appropriate common sense. This indicates the analytical value of distinguishing 'hegemonies in production' from 'production of hegemonies'. For a comprehensive CPE analysis should study the intermeshing, structural coupling and co-evolution of these moments of class domination. The work of Marx and Foucault can contribute much to clarifying these linkages. Commenting on Marx's explanation of the logic of profit-oriented and market-mediated accumulation (its 'laws of motion') and Foucault's discussion of disciplinary and normalizing power (its mechanics), Marsden once suggested that, whereas Marx explains 'why' but does not explain 'how', Foucault explains 'how' but does not explain 'why' (Marsden 1999: 135; cf. 24, 129, 131–2; on Foucault's avoidance of why questions in favour of how questions, see also Andersen 2003: 10–11). Marsden adds that, 'to marry "why" and "how" it is necessary to explicate "what": to synthesize Marx's description of relations of production and Foucault's description of the mechanisms of disciplinary power' (1999: 135). Gramsci provides several concepts that could facilitate this encounter/synthesis, notably in his account of the historical bloc, organic intellectuals, common sense, and everyday subjectivities and practices.

Governmentalizing Gramsci: hegemony, discourse, subjectivity and subjectivation

Although Gramsci and Foucault wrote and struggled in radically different conjunctures and were committed to quite different views on the feasibility of revolution in Western capitalism, their work displays interesting, important and illuminating parallels as well as tensions (Smart 1985; Kenway 1990; Stoddart 2005; Olssen 2006; Ekers and Loftus 2008; Springer 2010). Four issues worth exploring are: (1) the productive nature of Gramsci's 'conceptions of the world' and Foucault's truth regimes in objectifying, reifying and sedimenting social relations; (2) the diffuse and contingent nature of power relations in general terms and in specific conjunctures, including power–resistance dynamics; (3) the relationships among discourse (as semiosis and as specific discursive practices), subjectivity and hegemony; and (4) the selective nature of hegemony and knowledge production.

First, Gramsci rejects reified and fetishized treatments of institutional separations in favour of an integral analysis of specific fields of social practice and their articulation to form ensembles of social relations. His analysis of hegemony–consent–persuasion and intellectuals is not restricted to civil society but extends into what are conventionally termed the economic and political spheres. In particular, he observed that, while everyone is an intellectual, not everyone in society has the function of an intellectual (Gramsci 1971: 9; Q12, §1: 1516). This informs his account of the role of organic intellectuals in promoting and consolidating a conception of the world that gives homogeneity and awareness to a fundamental class in the economic, political and social fields; this, in turn, becomes the basis for efforts to create hegemony within the wider society (Gramsci 1971: 5; Q12, §1: 1513).

This has affinities with Foucault's analysis of discourse, knowledging technologies, dispositives and truth regimes. He focuses on how regimes of truth are produced through socially construed 'problematization' at the level of discourse and corresponding social practices through what one might call knowledging technologies. These produce object fields, subject positions and forms of power/knowledge that contribute towards the assembling of dispositives. They emerge in response to '*urgences*', that is, emergencies, challenges, ruptures that destabilize past solutions, disorient received understandings, and pose social problems. They reflect and refract a 'strategic-functional imperative' (see Chapter 3). This always has its own structural, discursive, technological and agential selectivities that are grounded in the complex topological ensemble that comprises the dispositive. Summarizing and seeking to inject some coherence into Foucault's unsystematic but broadly consistent reflections, we might venture the following extended (re)definition of a dispositive: it comprises a problem-oriented, strategically selective ensemble or assemblage of (1) a distributed apparatus, comprising institutions, organizations and networks; (2) an order of discourse, with corresponding thematizations and objectivations; (3) diverse devices and technologies involved in producing power/knowledge; and (4) subject positions and subjectivation.[2] Foucault also includes the effects of a dispositive on the material and built environment, which, of course, also have semiotic as well as extra-semiotic aspects (see, e.g., Elden 2001:120–50; Pløger 2008).

As such, dispositives should be studied in terms of how they are assembled, selected, and consolidated in response to specific 'problematizations' in specific structural contexts. This poses issues of variation, selection and retention. We should also note that Foucault also emphasized the mobile character of truth regimes and their associated technologies, such that, for example, disciplinary or governmental technologies developed in one context can be applied in other spheres (e.g., Foucault 1977). His detailed analyses of these processes are especially relevant to practices of self-governance.

Second, Gramsci and Foucault both stress the diffuse and contingent nature of power. For Gramsci, bourgeois hegemony rests on the permeation throughout a social formation (or significant parts thereof) of a system of values, attitudes, beliefs and morality that supports existing power relations. It is an 'organizing principle' (in our terms, a principle of societalization) that diffuses into daily life and becomes part of 'common sense'. For Foucault, too, power operates at many scales. He is especially well known for his middle-period studies of micro-power and micro-technologies, which he elaborated in opposition to state or juridico-political-centred analyses. One such micro-technology, explored initially for the prison, was the Panopticon. But even in *Discipline and Punish* (1977) he presented this as a diagram of power that can be adopted elsewhere and for other purposes, leading, through its generalization, to panopticism in the wider social formation. In this context he examines disciplinary power as a means to the panoptic organization of society, where all aspects of lives are visible and open for inspection by those in power.

Foucault later argued that the state played a key role in the strategic codification of power relations (1979: 96) and also noted that it was a matter of methodological choice rather than ontological primacy that his studies of governmentality initially focused on micro-power relations. He declared 'the analysis of micro-powers is not a question of scale, and it is not a question of sector, it is a question of a point of view' (Foucault 2008b: 186). Thus he went on to apply governmentality to the state, statecraft, state–civil society or state–economy relations just as fruitfully as to the 'conduct of conduct' at the level of anatomo-politics, interpersonal interactions, organizations or individual institutions. For example, in *The Birth of Biopolitics* (2008b), he traces the development of state projects and the general economic agendas of government over four centuries and notes how the rationales and mechanisms of state power (and their limits) change in different periods. Commenting on this shift in perspective, Michel Senellart argues that 'the shift from "power" to "government" carried out in the 1978 lectures does not result from the methodological framework being called into question, but from its extension to a new object, the state, which did not have a place in the analysis of the disciplines' (2008: 382). This is why this is a useful concept for exploring the multiple sites of hegemony.

Marsden's aphorism about Marx and Foucault on the how and why of the capital relation is less applicable to the Gramsci–Foucault relation because both were interested in how, why and what questions about the dispersion and codification of social power. Yet Gramsci has a richer set of concepts for exploring 'why' and Foucault for explaining 'how'. In particular, while Gramsci examined the micro-level in terms of everyday life and common sense, Foucault studied it in terms of micro-level disciplinary, normalizing, control and knowledging technologies and practices. Conversely, whereas Foucault refers to the strategic codification of power relations at the meso- and macro-levels in pursuit of specific strategies of governmentalization, Gramsci highlights the importance of what we term accumulation strategies, state projects and hegemonic visions, and links these to unstable equilibria of class compromise.

This suggests fruitful links between Foucault and Gramsci across certain scales of social analysis. This can be seen, for Foucault, in his studies of: (1) *capillary power* – power that stretches into the smallest and most private aspects of life; (2) *anatomopolitics* – the disciplining of individuals at the corporeal and personal level; (3) *biopolitics* – power that controls lives through hygiene, public health, education and so on, and that takes 'population' as its object of governance; and (4) *governmentality* – the multi-scalar ensemble of governing rationalities and technologies that facilitate the governance of social relations at a distance. Together these create the modern subject and subjectivities. Instead of weakening power regimes, they contribute towards their strengthening.

Third, for Gramsci, just as the moment of force is institutionalized in a system of coercive apparatuses (which may not coincide with the formal juridico-political apparatuses of the state), hegemony is crystallized and mediated through a complex system of ideological (or hegemonic) apparatuses located throughout the social formation. But the practice of hegemony is nonetheless concentrated in the sphere of civil society or so-called 'private' organizations, such as the Church, trade unions, schools, the mass media or political parties (Gramsci 1971: 10–14, 155, 210, 243, 261, 267; Q12, §1: 1518–24; Q13, §23: 1602–3; Q13, §27: 1619–20; Q26, §6: 2302–3; Q17, §51: 1947–8). The apparatuses are also anchored in the activities of intellectuals whose function is to elaborate ideologies, educate the people, organize and unify social forces, and secure the hegemony of the dominant group (Gramsci 1971: 5–23; Q12, §1–3: 1511–52). Thus apparatuses have a key role in organizing personal and social identity, common sense, collective memory and conceptions of the world, as well as organizing material concessions, administrative routines and coercive practices. There are some affinities with the concept of dispositive here that would be worth exploring and developing, especially to avoid the erroneous inference that the production of hegemony is reducible to discursive practices and/or the activities of intellectuals alone.

Foucault and his followers study similar topics in terms of the diagram of power, governmentality, dispositive and so on, and their various roles in the strategic codification of power relations in and across different sites and scales. Major aspects of these social forms and practices, this time presented less systematically (but reflecting Foucault's own intellectual habits), include:

1. the role of discursive formations (including, but not limited to, language) in constructing objects, in defining discursive selectivities (e.g. through rules of conceptualization), in establishing semantic fields, in constructing subject positions, in coagulating subjectivation, and in vitalizing affective energy;
2. the apparatus logic and strategic logic inscribed in dispositives (or similar mechanisms), including their associated governmental and knowledging technologies, that lead to a general strategic line without this having been willed by a particular subject, that is, that lead to the actualization of a 'strategy without a subject'; and

3. technologies of the self, through which individuals self-transform their identities, develop 'appropriate' competencies and modes of calculation, and reshape their modes of existence.

These assemblages (to use a broad term) organize the patterned dispersion of power relations across different sites and scales. They are unstable but relatively robust. They are unstable because they are everywhere and consist of 'unbalanced and tense force of relations'. They are also robust because they are 'repetitious, inert and self-producing' (Foucault 1980: 92). In this regard, these (un-)stable formations of power relations in dispositives concentrate certain power effects and form the bases of Gramsci's 'common sense' and the (re-)making of hegemonies (see Box 5.1).

Our proposal to governmentalize Gramsci by including dispositives and governmental technologies reinforces our critique of approaches that give ontological primacy to discourses and discursive practices at the expense of structuration. Nonetheless, the concept of dispositive helps to explain *how* questions but it cannot answer (nor is it intended to do so) the *why* questions that also concern CPE (in part because of Foucault's ontological agnosticism or empty ontologies; see Chapter 1). In short, why do some accumulation strategies, state projects, hegemonic visions and modes of societalization become hegemonic (or, at least, dominant), and what interests do they serve? Unless one reduces this to a simple question of utility, namely, that some dispositives are more effective than others, further questions need to be answered. Indeed, as Foucault notes, dispositives can be judged only in terms of their relation to strategic objectives.

Fourth, both thinkers highlight the selective nature of hegemony and knowledge production as reflected in inclusive worldviews and universal truth regimes respectively. To the extent that this occurs in the sedimentation of systems of rules and norms, their 'grammar' limits (K. Smith 2010) the scope for developing alternatives and mobilizing opposition to the dominant order (for the case of competitiveness discourses, see Chapter 8). At best it allows for proposals to reform the existing order rather than to radically transform, let alone overthrow, its foundational principles. Foucault and neo-Foucauldian scholarship complement such arguments with their work on the *technological selectivities* of knowledge production, that is, the asymmetries inscribed in particular disciplinary and governmental technologies as well as interwoven dispositives (see Table 5.1). These selectivities merit a broader reading than Foucault provided in order to cover the full range of the social technologies for constituting subjectivity, organizing power relations, and regularizing social relations in the face of the improbability of the smooth reproduction of social order (see also Box 5.1).

Marxianizing Foucault: capitalist formations and contradictions

This encounter between Gramsci and Foucault should also lead, sooner or later, to recognition of the limits of governmentality and dispositive analytics. While Foucault and neo-Foucauldians shy away from explicit mention of Marx in their analyses (and, in many cases, are oblivious to the richness of his work), the analyses of objectivation, problematizations, sites of intervention and modes of governance cannot be disentangled from the processes and practices involved in the rebuilding of social relations in response to '*urgences*', such as lost competitiveness, a financial crisis or an epidemic. Strategic interventions cannot be reconfigured at will or completed according to plan; indeed, they routinely produce contradictory and uneven effects as they interact with other forces and vectors on structurally inscribed terrains. As Foucault emphasizes, this is a strategy without a (master) subject. At stake is an emerging strategic line (see, e.g., Foucault 1979). Where the objects of governance are economic (broadly conceived), these limits can be interpreted and explained by drawing on the Marxist critique of political economy. This is not such an outrageous suggestion as many Foucauldian scholars might believe. Foucault argued (incorrectly, in our opinion) that Marx's analysis of value stayed within the classic episteme of Smith and Ricardo; but he still praised Marx's epistemic break in the fields of history and politics. This is reflected in increasingly sympathetic but often covert references to some core themes in Marx's critique of political economy and, even more importantly, his historical analyses, some of these references being deliberately and provocatively undeclared (Balibar 1992; Kalyvas 2002; Macdonald 2002; Lemke 2003; Elden 2007). Indeed, Foucault argued that capitalism has penetrated deeply into our existence, especially as it required diverse techniques of power to enable capital to exploit people's bodies and their time, transforming them into labour power and labour time respectively to create surplus profit (1977: 163, 174–5; 1979: 37, 120–24, 140–41; and 2003: 32–7; see also Marsden 1999). This prompted Balibar to suggest that Foucault moved from a break to a tactical alliance with Marxism,

> [with] the first involving a global critique of Marxism as a 'theory'; the second a partial usage of Marxist tenets or affirmations compatible with Marxism . . . Thus, in contradictory fashion, the opposition to Marxist 'theory' grows deeper and deeper whilst the convergence of the analyses and concepts taken from Marx becomes more and more significant. (Balibar 1992: 53)

Macdonald went further and argued that Foucault's work 'never intended to articulate a position free from a certain Marx, but rather one that was free from a specifically restrictive Marxism' (2002: 261). He argued that 'a certain Marx' is embedded within Foucault's work and cited Marsden's investigation (see above) as one illustration. Thus it is not entirely inappropriate to propose a Marxianization of Foucault to link his work on governmentality with the forms, institutional fixes and *régulation*-cum-governance of the capital relation. This is consistent with Foucault's claim that contradiction is only one particular configuration of a power relation because Marxist theory itself posits the inherent fragility of any social, semantic, institutional or spatio-temporal fix.

Thus, drawing on Foucauldian concepts helps to produce a better understanding of the mechanisms of capitalist societalization and its relative stabilization, the inevitable fragility and provisional nature of these fixes and, hence, the limits and eventual breakdown of classical, social and advanced liberalism and other approaches to governance. These are not just a question of the inevitability of power/resistance dynamics because the forms of failure, the character of resistance and the scope for recuperation are all conditioned by the capital relation (for an extended discussion of Foucault's concept of governmentality and its relation to statecraft, particularly viewed from an evolutionary perspective, see Jessop 2010a).

Bringing Marx back helps to identify the tensions in governmentality that arise from the contradictions and crisis tendencies present in the 'objects' of governance and the capacities of resistance on the part of its 'subjects'. While the Anglo-Foucauldian tradition follows Foucault in identifying the productive role of disciplinary and governmentalizing technologies in constituting the objects and subjects of social control, it tends to ignore the limits to control that lie less in plebeian instincts of rebellion than in the material resistances to control that are rooted in the social relations being controlled. These include, above all, those features of the social world that are not envisaged, let alone encompassed, in any given project (the Anglo-Foucauldian account of the 'Foucault effect' is criticized in Jessop 2010a).

This is another illustration of the limits of complexity reduction – this time through specific mixes of governmental rationality. This indicates the limits to the power of organic intellectuals and technical experts in creating political, intellectual and moral hegemony on the one hand (Gramsci) or durable truth regimes on the other (Foucault). We present studies of the knowledge-based economy, 'growth' and 'competitiveness' in Chapters 6 to 10. In addition, interventions to secure the conditions for growth also shape, whether knowingly or unintentionally, the conditions for some groups to be dispossessed or otherwise lose out (Li 2007: 19–22). Winners and losers do not emerge naturally through the magic of the market; they are included/excluded through the interaction of the four modes of selectivity (see Table 5.1). By combining Foucauldian interest in governmental technologies (with their implicit Marxian engagements) with a more explicit account of the contradictions and crisis tendencies of capital accumulation, we will obtain a more nuanced version of the semiotic–material moments of social development.

A HEURISTIC SCHEMA: FOUR SELECTIVITIES AND SEVEN MOMENTS

Based on these reflections, we now offer a heuristic schema for CPE based on the four modes of selectivity: structural, discursive, technological and agential. These interact across different conjunctures and settings to condition the variation, selection and retention of hegemonic, sub-hegemonic and counter-hegemonic projects and their societal repercussions and contradictions. These interactions in space-time imply that there are more than four modes in which selectivities operate. Even in a two-dimensional space one could identify 12 different combinations, and this would certainly be too restrictive given the complexities involved. Here we identify seven 'discursive–material moments' that by no means exhaust all possibilities but are those most relevant to illustrate the issues of hegemony posed in our case studies. Different sets of research problems or other particular explananda will require attention to different combinations. This is perfectly consistent with the CPE approach, which emphasizes the importance of different entry-points, different standpoints and spiral movements in which more and more of the full CPE conceptual instrumentarium and analytical toolkits are deployed.

Four Modes of Selectivity in Social Relations

This section elaborates the four selectivities introduced above and considers their articulation in dispositives. It draws on the notion of complexity reduction, the insights of critical realism and the strategic-relational approach (SRA). Initially developed to address structure–agency dialectics, the SRA is easily extended from structural selectivity to discursive selectivity. It is also relevant, we claim, to technological selectivities and dispositives.

Structural selectivity is a short-hand term for structurally inscribed strategic selectivity and denotes the asymmetrical configuration of constraints and opportunities on social forces as they pursue particular projects. This configuration exists only in so far as it is reproduced in and through social practices and can be transformed through time, through cumulative molecular changes and/or more deliberate attempts to transform the pattern of constraints and opportunities. Whether these attempts succeed or not, they are likely to have path-dependent legacies (see Table 5.1). Gramsci's insights into molecular transformation, passive revolution, wars of manoeuvre and wars of position are all relevant here.

Discursive selectivity is also asymmetrical. Like structural selectivity, it has several dimensions. The primary aspect and principal stake in this regard are the asymmetrical constraints and opportunities inscribed in particular genres, styles and discourses (or, more generally, particular forms of discourse or broader semantic orders), in terms of what can be enunciated, who is authorized to enunciate, and how enunciations enter intertextual, interdiscursive and contextual fields. Semiotic resources set limits to what can be imagined, whether in terms of 'objects', possible statements within a discursive formation, themes that can be articulated within a given semantic field, or subject positions that can be adopted. In other words, discursive selectivity concerns the manner in which different discourses (whether everyday or specialized) enable some rather than other enunciations to be made within the limits of particular languages and the forms of discourse that exist within them (cf. de Saussure on *parole* and *langue*, or Gramsci on the different hierarchies and asymmetries involved in the use of Latin, national languages, minority languages and subaltern dialects).[3] A further aspect concerns how different forms of discourse and/or genres position subjects in specific situations: this is the field, *par excellence*, of socio-linguistics. A related set of selectivities concerns the extent and grounds that make some discursive forms more or less accessible to some agents rather than others either because of their sense- and meaning-making competence (Schmidt's 'background ideational abilities') and their discursive competence (Schmidt's 'foreground discursive abilities') in relation to everyday interactions, or because of the demands of socialization into specialized discourses (e.g. law, medicine and engineering). Regarding spatio-temporal selectivities, different languages have different ways of expressing temporality and spatiality, privileging some spatio-temporal horizons over others and allowing for greater or less anticipation of as-yet-unrealized possibilities (the 'irrealis' as opposed to 'realis' aspects of communication, on which see the Introduction). In combination, these aspects of discursive selectivity make it more or less easy to develop specific appeals, arguments, recontextualizations, claims, legitimations and so on than others by virtue of their filtering effects (see Table 5.1).

Discursive selectivity is not purely discursive – to claim otherwise would entail linguistic reductionism. It derives from the differential articulation and co-evolution of the discursive and extra-discursive moments of social processes and practices, and their conjoint impact in specific contexts and conjunctures (see Chapter 3). The primary aspect of discursive selectivity (i.e. the asymmetries inscribed in language as a repertoire of discursive possibilities) is overdetermined by the media of communication used in enunciations (its technological mediation and the biases these contain) and by the linguistic and communicative competences of particular agents (its agential mediation). In short, by including the discursive and extra-discursive, we are better placed to understand and explain discursive selectivities. Semiotic constructions are neither independent nor neutral; they derive meanings as a part of a network of statements and social practices in the interdiscursive fields. Foucauldian discourse analysis has much to offer here in terms of conceptual architectures and semantic fields; and CDA has much to offer in clarifying how discursive selectivity operates in terms of its lexical, semantic and pragmatic features, and their relation to modes of expression, forms of discourse, genre chains, framing and so forth (see especially Fairclough 2003).[4]

Technological selectivities are considered here, paradoxically, both in broader and narrower terms than Foucault was wont to investigate them. In the broader sense, they typically include the full range of forces of production and technical and social relations of production involved in the social division of labour. Nonetheless these are often studied in narrowly technological terms. Foucault is less concerned to develop an all-encompassing account of technologies in this sense and more concerned to examine the social technologies involved in constituting objects, creating subject positions and recruiting subjects, and, in particular, in this context, creating relations of power/knowledge and the possibilities of governmentalization (see also Box 5.1). These technological selectivities can be studied in strategic-relational terms along the lines of Foucault and neo-Foucauldian scholarship – indeed, as we have shown elsewhere, there are strong strategic-relational affinities in Foucault's work on the strategic codification of power relations and the emergence of a general strategic line of action associated with specific technologies of governmentalization and the articulation with dispositives (see Table 5.1). At stake, then, are the asymmetries inscribed in the use of technologies (and their affordances) in producing object and subject positions that contribute towards the making of dispositives and truth regimes. For example, in the case of object/subject formations, rules for conceptualization selectively define what and how objects are created, ordered and classified, as well as what subject positions open/limit observations. As for dispositives and regimes of truth, their apparatuses and strategic logics may selectively limit choice and regulate bodies, thoughts and conduct. These limit the scope for developing alternatives and opposition to possibilities that are inscribed in, or imaginable within, the logic (on competitiveness, see Chapter 8). At best this allows for proposals to reform the existing order rather than to radically transform it, let alone to challenge the basic principles on which it is founded.

Much work in actor-network theory (especially that of Callon) also addresses technological selectivities. Three affinities are worth noting: (1) they embrace a relational ontology based on the mutual constitution and interpenetration of the material and social linked to their determined rejection of rigid object–subject and material–cultural distinctions; (2) they deny any fixed ontological distinction between the 'macro' and the 'micro' or the 'global' and the 'local' in favour of their mutual conditioning and continued interaction; and (3) they examine the interaction between mechanisms and strategies that gives some semblance of unity to economic and political agencies, the conditions and points at which these unities can break down, and the mechanisms and strategies that may restore these unities. Nonetheless, although Callon was influenced by Foucault, he seems to have abandoned (at least partially) one key element in the latter's analysis of dispositives. This is the transition from the emergence of devices or dispositives in response to an 'urgent need' for the acquisition of 'new, unanticipated functions, strategies, and processes [that] emerge and contribute to stabilize and entrench the device (if it does not rapidly disappear)' (Dumez and Jeunemaître 2010: 31). In examining both the appearance of the device and its stabilization, which is clearly related to mechanisms of variation, selection and retention, Foucault is better able than Callon to explore continuities and discontinuities. Despite these differences, however,[5] each, in his own way, highlights the importance of the asymmetrical impact of social technologies.

Agential selectivity is the theoretically necessary (but empirically contingent) complement to structural and, by analogy, discursive selectivities. Specifically, agential selectivity refers to the differential capacity of agents to engage in structurally oriented strategic calculation – whether in regard to structurally or discursively inscribed strategic selectivities – not only in abstract terms but also in relation to specific conjunctures. A second step would be to distinguish different social forces, their subjectivation as bearers of specific identities and ideal and material interests, their capacities for strategic calculation, and their capacities for action. Agents can make a difference thanks to their different capacities to persuade, read particular conjunctures, displace opponents and rearticulate in timely fashion discourses and imaginaries (see Table 5.1). This is always overdetermined by discursive and technological selectivities. Ultimately, agential selectivity depends on the difference that specific actors (or social forces) make in particular conjunctures.

The four selectivities in Table 5.1 are presented in general terms on two grounds. First, they derive from a synthesis of approaches that

Table 5.1 *Four modes of strategic selectivity in CPE*

Modes of strategic selectivity	Grounded in	Effects
Structural	Contested reproduction of basic social forms (e.g. capital relation, nature–society relations, racism, patriarchy), their specific instantiations in institutional orders, organizational forms, and interaction contexts.	Structures favour certain interests, identities, agents, spatio-temporal horizons, strategies and tactics over others. Path-dependency limits scope for path-shaping. Selectivities are always relative and relational: structure is not an absolute constraint that applies equally to all actors but is necessarily asymmetrical.
Discursive	Semiosis is rooted in enforced selection of sense and meaning in the face of complexity. It operates at all scales from the micropores of everyday life to the self-descriptions of world society.	Discursively-inscribed selectivity frames and limits possible imaginaries, discourses, genre chains, arguments, subjectivities, social and personal identities, and feelings. It also shapes scope for hegemony, sub-hegemonies and counter-hegemonies.
Technological	Technologies regarded as assemblages of knowledge, disciplinary and governmental rationalities, specific affordances, sites and mechanisms of calculated intervention, and social relations for transforming nature and/or governing social relations	These involve specific objectivation, subjectivation, knowledging technologies, interwoven dispositives and social coordination. In addition to their differential capacities to transform nature, technologies also shape social relations through (1) horizontal and vertical divisions of labour and knowledge, (2) their material effects (e.g. the built environment or anatomo- and biopolitics), and (3) their epistemological effects ('truth regimes').

Table 5.1 (continued)

Modes of strategic selectivity	Grounded in	Effects
Technological		Technologies shape choices, capacities to act, distribute resources and harms, convey legitimacy through technical rationality and effectivity.
Agential	Capacities of specific social agents (or sets of agents) to 'make a difference' in particular conjunctures thanks to idiosyncratic abilities to exploit structural, discursive and technological selectivities	'Agents make their own history but not in circumstances of their own choosing'. Making a difference depends on abilities to (1) read conjunctures and identify potentials for action; (2) repoliticize sedimented discourses and rearticulate them; (3) recombine extant technologies or invent new ones; and (4) shift the balance of forces in space-time.

employ sometimes radically different vocabularies (e.g. Gramsci, Marx, Foucault, various old and new institutionalisms, critical discourse analysis, actor-network theory and conjunctural analysis). Second, they must be reinterpreted and respecified as the analysis moves from abstract or general reflections to more concrete and particular cases. Thus later chapters translate these general reflections into concepts that are more germane to the individual cases being explored. The next section illustrates some meso-level ways in which this might occur by developing a heuristic schema that has been developed for the study of the production (and contestation) of hegemony.

Seven Discursive–Material Moments in Producing (Counter-)Hegemonies

This subsection illustrates the variable interaction of the four selectivities by identifying seven 'discursive–material moments' in the production of hegemonies and the associated scope for elaborating counter-hegemonic imaginaries and projects (see Box 5.1). These processes have three important discursive–material aspects: the micro-construction of hegemonic projects, co-constitutive ties between organic intellectual and discourses,

BOX 5.1   THE SEVEN DISCURSIVE–MATERIAL MOMENTS IN THE PRODUCTION OF HEGEMONIES

A. Discursive–strategic moment of socio-economic restructuring (from variation through selection to retention)

- Faced with the profound disorienting effects of political and economic crises and challenges to act in the face of *urgences*, actors at different scales and sites with varying degrees of embeddedness in institutions, organizations and social relations may rethink their opportunities for economic and political actions, leading initially to a proliferation of a variety of responses
- This often involves struggles/cooperation over renewal of imaginaries where diverse social, economic and spatio-temporal imaginaries emerge to re-evaluate past meaning systems and to interpret the conjuncture
- Issues are problematized and new objects of governance proposed to provide new entry points and ways of framing from one or more standpoints
- These discursive frames are more influential when promoted by nodal actors (see moment B)
- These frames are often linked and recontextualized to different sites and scales
- The knitting together of discourses and practices mediates the emergence of (inter)discursive spaces (see also moments C and D)

B. Agential selective moment rooted in the wider social formations (the role of agency in variation, selection and retention)

- The differential embedding of actors in social relations affects their capacities to deploy (inter)discursive networks to build new objects of governance
- Some agents, by virtue of their nodal position in social networks, have better capacities to read particular conjunctures, refocus arguments, displace opponents, structure responses, introduce timely imaginaries and worldviews

- Their discursive framings and subsequent retentions consolidate these agents as intellectual forces
- They inspire other agents, individual and collective, to share their conception (hegemony integrates subaltern concerns) and forge a particular worldview. This mode of knowing and sensing is not based on 'false consciousness' or ideological manipulation but involves the construction of object fields and subject positions (see also Moments D and E)

C. (Inter)discursive selective moment in the order of discourses (the role of discourse in selection and retention)

- The knitting together of genres in particular social practices gives rise to the (inter)discursive space
- This space comprises activities and documents of different genres (e.g. conferences, reports, speeches and workshops)
- In these chains, combination of genres can selectively restrict or transfer meanings
- The transfer and combination of genre(s) also entails the recontextualization of ideas and information to new sites, scales and conjunctures
- This allows for the selective reconfiguration of knowledge to new contexts and create image of (dis)continuity as well as density/fragility

D. Technological–selective moment in constituting social/economic reality (the role of technologies in selection)

- Discursive technologies involve a set of knowledge, expertise, techniques, technologies and apparatuses that construct authority and marginalize others as well as guide actions and modify processes
- These knowledging technologies could include:
  - economic, social, managerial and norm-based knowledge of market competitiveness, globalization, development, poverty reduction, sustainability etc.
  - modalities of expertise of significant agents (e.g. top academic economists, management gurus, IMF/WTO/

WB officials, standard-setting agencies, politicians, opinion makers etc.)
  ○ knowledging techniques/technologies and their epistemic grammar (logics of inevitability, linearity, classification, performance, metaphors etc.) that constitute and speak about the object
  ○ apparatuses (e.g. consultancy reports, plans, programmes, blueprints, guidelines, standards, codes of conduct, best practices, numbers, indexes, targets, scorecards etc.)
- This ensemble of micro-technologies and interwoven dispositives selectively map sites of intervention, regulate behaviour of people, and guide practices
- Through sedimented bodies of knowledge they discipline behaviours, normalize judgements, and mediate self-governing and self-leadership

E. Moment in the constituting/consolidating of subjects and sedimenting of common sense (the role of technologies in retention)

- Under the actual or imagined gaze of an authority or interwoven dispositive and truth regime, objects are identified and subjects positions are bought to life
- These processes of objectivation and subjectivation involve the intermeshing of top-down and bottom-up (re)production of object fields and subject positions in multiple sites (e.g. databases, guidelines, codes, indexes) and settings (e.g. offices, families, schools)
- These dispositives frame sense perceptions of the social and help to form the bases of Gramsci's 'common sense'
- These forms of governing common sense are heteroglossic, i.e., multi-faceted, composite and even contradictory
- This 'contradictory consciousness' means that agencies view the world from a perspective that contains both hegemonic modes of thinking *and* forms of critical insights. This mix varies across individuals, with some more energized affectively to maintain hegemonic modes of thinking while others are more ambivalent

F. Moment in re-regularizing and sedimenting social relations (the discursive–material dimensions of selection and retention)

- These subjectivities and identities are performed, repeated and stabilize over time
- As forms of strategic logic, they become regularized and sedimented through various strategies, institutions and governance (this is a further stage in dispositivization)
- They institute certain forms of (capitalist) life and preclude others in uneven and contradictory ways
- The greater the range of (sub-)hegemonic sites in which these resonant logics are selected and strategies promoted, the greater the potential for coalition-building around hegemonic project(s)
- Efforts to conserve or rebuild social relations involve 'unstable equilibrium of compromise' between groups and class fractions
- These 'moving but unstable equilibria' may result in temporary strategic fixes that may accommodate some contradictions whilst others may fuel crisis
- This unevenness invites continuous challenges from the marginal/subaltern groups

G. Counter-hegemonic resistance and negotiations (discursive–material contestation, repoliticization, and further variation)

- The variety of sites, scales and social networks on which these processes unfold and the existence of 'contradictory consciousness' inevitably generate a surplus of meanings and unevenness with regard to class, gender, ethnicity, nature, place, etc. that cannot easily be contained by strategic essentialisms that privilege just one identity
- Hegemony is not a cohesive, unilateral, monovalent relationship of leaders and led; it is riddled with tensions, contradictions, and depends on the 'suturing' of difference that is always vulnerable to pulling apart and ruptures
- This opens up the possibility of counter-hegemonic struggles and the building of solidarity networks (e.g., movement-oriented NGOs, World Social Forum etc.), alternative knowledge and leadership

- These networks may disrupt/subvert dominant cultural symbols and practices in the forms of:
  - 'branding from below' (e.g. *'Another World is Possible'*)
  - use of strategies by unions and social movements (e.g. strikes, walk-outs, political demonstration, name and shame etc.)
  - use of tactics by the weak/subalterns (e.g. political theatre, insurrectionary art, resort to lies/secrets/fictions; refusal to speak etc.)
- Hegemonic forces have to enter into dialogues (or confined discussions in a monologue context) with other groups
- Hegemonic forces negotiate and constantly shift ground in order to accommodate these challenges through a mix of depoliticization, remoralization, coercion, and domination
- This may prompt further variation and further selection and retention in the material–discursive terrains

and the scope for resistance. First, even when hegemonic projects are macro-political, they are always underpinned by micro-political practices that involve elements of intellectual and self-leadership (see Moments C, D and E). Even if successful, the results of the production of hegemonies are always partial, provisional and unstable. Second, nodal actors demarcate 'object fields' (sites of calculation, control, governance, etc.) that also require the reproduction of corresponding (willing) subjects. Where there is a dense web of object-subject linkages, these actors may become 'organic intellectuals' who organize, promote and stabilize particular worldviews (see Moments A, B, D, E and F in Box 5.1). This is more an interactive process than one in which organic intellectuals pre-exist specific conjunctures and simply lead and persuade as circumstances change. Third, hegemony, which results from a multi-faceted assemblage of practices, is vulnerable to destabilization at the personal, institutional and macro-structural levels. On the personal level, the multiple subjectivities of individuals and the gap between discursive justifications and actual practices open a space for alternative conceptions of society and counter-hegemonic subjectivities. Similarly, on the institutional and macro-structural levels, because hegemonic projects exclude, marginalize or suppress some identities and interests in creating an 'illusory community', space opens for subaltern forces to engage in tactics of resistance, demands for reform, and counter-hegemony (see moment G in Box 5.1).

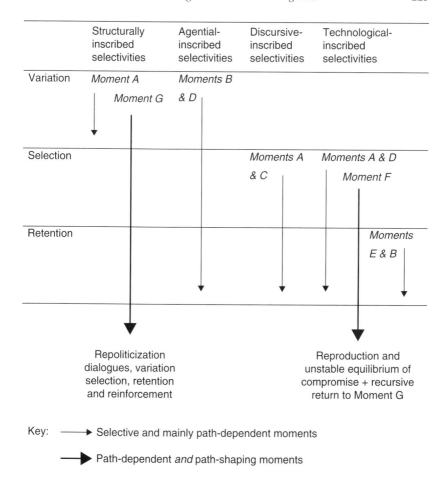

Figure 5.2 A preliminary mapping of the seven material–discursive moments in the selectivity space

These seven moments can help to map the case studies. Although the limits of visual and written presentation require that they be introduced sequentially (another enforced selection!), this does not imply that they unfold sequentially in time-space. The seven moments are just analytically distinct but interrelated discursive and structural aspects of the variation, selection and retention of different kinds of hegemonic projects and their contestations (see Figure 5.2). The selectivities in moments A to E involve different mixes of variation, selection and retention, and this means that they vary in the extent of their path-dependent selective power. Moments

F and G combine path-dependent and path-shaping dynamics through which subjectivities and everyday practices contribute to the reproduction of 'unstable equilibria of compromise' as well as the ever-renewed variation of imaginaries oriented to reproducing and/or challenging hegemonies.

Table 5.2 shows how the four modes of selectivity presented in Table 5.1 are deployed heuristically in some case studies in Parts III and IV. Chapter 8 addresses the structural selectivity of Fordism and the agential, discursive and technological selectivities involved in mapping competitiveness as an accumulation strategy. Chapter 9 examines the rise of industrial clusters and their link with global retail chains. Wal-Martization is analysed as a new accumulation strategy that is consolidated through various agential, discursive and technological selectivities, and is challenged in turn by subaltern groups and others, which triggers the demand for, and reinvention of, corporate social responsibilities. Chapter 10 explores the recontextualization of the competitiveness regime of truth to Hong Kong in two successive periods of economic and social restructuring. It illustrates the heuristic value of deploying agential, discursive and technological selectivities in examining these periods and highlights the production of a regime of hope in period two, which is infected by tensions, contradictions and ruptures of everyday life. Chapter 12 investigates the emergence of BRIC (Brazil, Russia, India, China) as an object of 'crisis recovery' in response to the North Atlantic financial crisis. It reveals the agential selectivity of an investment bank research team in churning out BRIC discourses and the ways in which they are developed subsequently into investment, consumer and lender stories partly via discursive and technological selectivities. Addressing such selectivities is only part of the CPE research agenda; ultimately, the analyses must highlight the contradictions and the discursive–material dialectics of who gains and who loses from the restructuring of global, national and local political economies.

Ultimately, a CPE approach differs from a neo-Foucauldian or a constructivist one in terms of the overall set of questions asked. A neo-Foucauldian approach mainly asks 'what' and 'how' questions such as: (1) what governmental knowledging technologies are involved in constituting subjectivities and identities; and (2) how do these imaginaries, subjectivities and identities become normalized in everyday practices? A CPE agenda also asks 'when', 'who' and 'why' questions, including: (1) when does a particular economic imaginary and its related discursive networks begin to gain credence; (2) what contradictions are they addressing; (3) who gets involved in the discursive networks that construct and promote different objects of governance; (4) what (additional) ideas and practices are selected and drawn upon to recontextualize and hybridize the

Table 5.2 Four modes of selectivity as applied in the various case studies

Chapter	Structurally inscribed selectivity	Agential-inscribed selectivity	Discursively inscribed selectivity	Technologically-inscribed selectivity
Ch. 8	Crises in/of Fordism Neoliberal institutional set-up reoriented from 'getting the market right' to 'getting the competitiveness right'	Nodal actors at different scales and sites (e.g. HBS, WEF, consultancy firms and international organizations) offer simple and easily portable policy toolkits	Genre chain of competitiveness and cluster models and their recontextualization across different sites and scales	Competitiveness and other benchmarks as disciplinary mechanism Catch-up and chain metaphors Training and cluster-building practices
Ch. 9	Challenges of Fordist crises Selectivity of neoliberal accumulation and the rise of Wal-Martization	Nodal actors of strategy firms and international organizations (e.g. UNIDO)	Genre chain of clusters, global markets and commodity chains and the articulation between consultancy reports, policy papers and activities such as consultancy, business intelligence research and data provision	Knowledging technologies such as map and database to render clusters and their products visible Disciplinary mechanisms related to category management, scorecards and factory ratings Governmental technologies of training, scholarships and empowering women

Table 5.2 (continued)

Chapter	Structurally inscribed selectivity	Agential-inscribed selectivity	Discursively inscribed selectivity	Technologically-inscribed selectivity
Ch. 10	Colonial legacy, rise of service sector, and path-dependent scope for reshaping its governance	Nodal actors at the interface of political and civil societies in Hong Kong and across border	Genre chains of service competitiveness and the articulation between reports, policy speeches, conferences, forums and public debates	Knowledging technologies of service competitiveness (e.g., chaining, closure etc.) and 'big gift' (e.g. combinability, partnership etc.) Knowledging technologies related to rule by baseline and norms
Ch. 11	North Atlantic financial crisis and the search for exit from crisis BRIC as investment, consumption and lender objects	Nodal actors from investment banks, fund managers and business press in the construction of BRIC	Genre chain of BRIC and the articulation between reports, books, webtours, newspaper articles, publication interviews and official summits	Knowledging technologies of identification, investability etc.

referents of these objects; (5) how far and in what ways do these changes have uneven impacts across different sites and scales (e.g. the lives of subaltern groups); (6) why are there unevennesses and contradictions; and (7) how are they being negotiated and/or resisted in the rebuilding of social relations?

These questions are not exhaustive. A fuller CPE analysis would examine the interaction of discourses, governmentalities and structure in the production of hegemonic discourses and practices. For example, the novel concept of 'knowledge brand' (see Chapter 8) is useful in understanding how power/knowledge acquires the force of a dispositive that modifies trans-national knowledge–consultancy–policy circuits. It indicates how knowledge is at the same time diffused and condensed along specific nodal points, the location of which is extradiscursively as well as discursively conditioned. While this chapter has focused on the production and the recontextualization of hegemonies, a fuller CPE account would analyse its intertwining relations with the 'hegemonies in production' (and other modes of accumulation) and 'production of hegemonies' with contradictions and unevennesses that cut across class, gender, race, place and nature as being the major concern of CPE.

CONCLUDING REMARKS

This chapter has taken a further step from the critique of other positions to the development of the CPE research agenda, specifically concerning more middle-range analytical strategies and research questions. Its entry-point was to chart a route between structuralist Scylla and constructivist Charybdis using the fifth and sixth features of CPE as navigational reference points. These features direct attention to the distinction between 'hegemonies in production' and 'production of hegemonies', and emphasize that each has its own material and discursive moments. To limit an otherwise huge agenda, we concentrated on developing a transdisciplinary approach to the 'production of hegemonies' and indicated how discursive practices are articulated with 'material' practices in specific sets of social practices. Such analyses bring us closer to the world of social agents and, drawing on the concept of problematization, objectification and subjectification, indicate how to tackle the interactive relations between organic intellectuals and discourses. Instead of assuming that there are organic intellectuals, a CPE approach explores how discourses make organic intellectuals and organic intellectuals make discourses. By staging an encounter among Marx, Gramsci and Foucault, we proposed a dual strategy based on governmentalizing Gramsci and Marxianizing

Foucault. We suggest that this provides an interesting and heuristically useful way to examine the production of hegemonies with their four modes of selectivities and seven discursive–material moments.

Of interest has been how the four selectivities identified earlier are condensed to form specific dispositives (for case studies, see Chapters 8, 9, 10 and 12) and/or evolve unevenly in different contexts. The articulation of these modes of selectivity condenses particular dispositives and strategic logics that help to secure hegemonies and dominations. Thus this approach also indicates how to conduct an ideological critique that exposes the socially constructed nature of hegemonies and dominations in which discourses and social practices produce strategic logics that legitimize the sectional interests of particular groups at the expense of others.

Finally, we repeat that this chapter provides only one way to translate (which is also always modification) the macro-theoretical discussions to middle-range arguments by focusing on a particular set of questions about the production of hegemonies. Other researchers can adapt these meta-theoretical and theoretical resources to their own trans- and post-disciplinary projects, choosing their theoretical and/or empirical entry-point(s) to suit the specific explananda in their research. The key to deploying CPE, at least in the medium term, is to ensure that, whatever the particular entry-point, attention turns sooner or later to its semiotic and structural aspects in their co-evolutionary articulation. Parts III and IV apply these arguments to selected cases that appeal to us for testing the approach and indicate how to deliver the CPE commitment to critique of ideology and domination.

NOTES

1. For an extended discussion on Bernstein and recontextualization of management thinking, see Thomas (2003).
2. This paraphrase attempts to make sense of Foucault's clearly incomplete list of heterogeneous elements. It also reflects Jürgen Link's definition of dispositive (Chapter 3, p. 114).
3. This is clearly relevant to a major concern of critical linguists, namely, official-language policy.
4. For Fairclough, genre chains link different genres of discourse together and involve systematic transformations from genre to genre (2003: 31–2).
5. For example, actor-network theory is stronger on the social construction of the material and immaterial features of marketized and/or marketizable use-values than it is on the logic of surplus-value and exchange-value (Slater 2002). For a more detailed comparison of CPE and actor-network theory, see Jessop (2005a).

PART III

Reimagining and institutionalizing competitive governance: narratives, strategies and struggles

6. A cultural political economy of variegated capitalism

The essential role of semiosis in social practices underpins the CPE critique of 'hard political economy'. CPE is not intended to replace critical political economy, however, but to interpret and explain the logic of capital accumulation even more powerfully. Indeed, as indicated in our comments on the siren call of the constructivist Charybdis, making a cultural turn risks losing sight of the specificity of the 'economic' by subsuming the 'economic' under a general analysis of semiosis, meaning-making, identity formation and performativity. This would imply that there is no difference between the emergent logic of a profit-oriented, market-mediated economy and, say, law, education, politics or science. They would all be equally constructed and reproduced through discursive practices (see Chapters 3 and 4). Against this erroneous conclusion, we argue, following Weber, for explanations adequate at the level of material causation as well as meaning; and, following Marx, for recognition of the contradictions and crisis tendencies of an economic order organized under the dominance of the capital relation. Thus we now develop the critique of 'soft economic sociology' by exploring the commonalities of capitalism and the bases for its variegation in the world market. This analysis is consistent with, and, indeed, draws on arguments in, *Beyond the Regulation Approach* (Jessop and Sum 2006), but has been elaborated and refined on the basis of Parts I and II of the present work.

This chapter illustrates how CPE addresses both the generic features of capitalism and their specific, structurally coupled and co-evolving instantiations in a variegated capitalist order. As early regulationist work recognized, both aspects are important for a critical analysis of capitalism. A one-sided emphasis on its commonalities risks subsuming all forms of capitalism under a generic logic, losing sight of its specific forms and mistaking the abstract possibilities of crisis for an explanation of specific forms of crisis and particular crisis conjunctures. But a one-sided emphasis on varieties of capitalism can lead to an emphasis on differences to the neglect of the generic features of capitalism (for a recent recognition of this problem, see Streeck 2010). This is even more problematic when it leads to neglect of the incompressible contradictions and crisis tendencies of the capital relation, which can lead in turn to the belief that any market failures are accidental or remediable provided that the appropriate market and framework conditions are in place and sound economic policies are pursued.

WORLD MARKET, VARIETIES OF CAPITALISM AND VARIEGATED CAPITALISM

The world market is both the presupposition and the posit (result) of the development of the capitalist mode of production. It must be seen as 'doubly tendential' on the grounds that, first, the formation of the world market is itself tendential, subject to leads, lags and reversals;[1] and, second, the world market, in so far as it is formed, provides the global context in which all the laws of capital accumulation and their overdetermination come to operate. These observations do not commit us to the proposition that there is a single, generic, unified and global mode of production or that the world market has its own unique logic that somehow governs the overall development of capitalism (for an argument tending in this direction, see Wallerstein 1975, 1980). As Marx notes in the 1857 Introduction, there is 'no production in general' or 'general production', only a 'particular branch of production' and the 'totality of production' (1973: 85–6). Moreover, particular production is always associated with 'a certain social body, a social subject' (ibid.). This argument can be respecified to capitalism: there is no such thing as capitalist production in general or general capitalist production, only particular branches of capitalist production and the totality of capitalist production. This also informs our rejection of the view that the logic of capitalist competition on a world scale tends to drive all capitals and their associated 'space economies'[2] to converge on a single model of capitalism.

Adopting contemporary terminology, this might seem to justify distinguishing analytically among varieties of capitalism (VoC), each with its own logic, that coexist in a heterogeneous global economy (the contemporary 'classic' is Hall and Soskice, 2001), that interact as so many monads in the framework of the world division of labour. While this second approach is superficially attractive, it has fundamental limitations. We note these in Table 6.1 (for further discussion see Jessop 2011, 2013e). Its first column presents four features of the VoC approach in which the 'monadic' character of different varieties is noted along with the emphasis on internal coherence, the internal character of its cycles and rhythms, and the manner in which they are treated as typologically equal. The second column presents the alternative assumptions of the variegated capitalism

Table 6.1 *Varieties of capitalism versus variegated capitalism*

Varieties of capitalism	Variegated capitalism
Distinct (families of) local, regional, national models, seen as rivals on the same scale or terrain for the same stakes	Possible complementarities (or not) in a wider division of labour in a tendentially singular, global but variegated capitalism
Describe the forms of *internal* coherence of distinct VoC on the false assumption that they can and do exist in relative isolation from each other	Zones of relative stability linked to instability in or beyond given national spaces in a complex ecology of accumulation regimes, modes of regulation, and spatio-temporal fixes
Study temporal rhythms and horizons of VoC as internal, specific, short or medium term, unrelated to long-term global dynamic of capital	Analyse costs imposed on other spaces and/or future generations by uneven capacities to displace or defer contradictions, conflicts, and crisis tendencies
All varieties are equal and, if one is more 'productive', 'efficient' or 'progressive', it could and should be copied, exported or even imposed elsewhere	Some varieties are more equal than others, with neoliberalism tending to ecological dominance. Not all economic formations can adopt the dominant model

approach. The table is relatively self-explanatory and the arguments about variegated capitalism are developed at length here and later (see especially Chapters 7 and 11). In critiquing the VoC approach we draw in part on two important structural principles that were introduced in *Beyond the Regulation Approach* (Jessop and Sum 2006): the principle of structural coupling and co-evolution (which we now relate to compossibility) and the notion of ecological dominance.

Compossibility means no more (but no less) than 'not everything that is possible is compossible' (cf. Rescher 1975).[3] In the present context, compossibility involves more than fleeting coexistence due to chance variation: it depends on the actual scope for co-selection, then co-retention and, later, co-institutionalization based on the structural coupling of compossible processes and their social supports. We illustrated this in the Introduction from the case of the growing tensions between different models of capitalism when constrained within the Economic and Monetary Union and the eurozone regime. Analysing compossibility requires a shift from individual events to identifying the features of emergent ensembles that have a relative coherence that can be reproduced for significant periods; the actualization of specific socio-spatial possibilities depends on interaction among different elements of co-evolving socio-spatial configurations.

Ecological dominance refers in general to how far and how, in a self-organizing ecology of self-organizing systems or institutional orders, one system or order is a problem-*maker* for the others rather than a problem-*taker*. This can be examined in terms of the relative weights of different 'varieties of capitalism' and/or the uneven impact of different circuits of capital. These weightings are not an automatic, mechanical outcome of market forces but depend on specific economic and political strategies, which may include the use of violence as well as rigging market rules. Thus one could investigate the conditions making for uneven development and structural coupling of capitalist regimes in a regional or global division of labour (e.g. the Rhenish, Nordic and liberal market models in Europe or the global dominance of the liberal market model); or, again, examine the weight of commercial, industrial or financial capital in capitalist circuits at different scales.

On these grounds, we draw two conclusions. First, it is useful for some purposes (and sooner or later it becomes essential) to employ the general notion of the world market and the more middle-range (or more concrete–complex) notion of variegated capitalism to enable those concerned to put varieties of capitalism in their place alongside *and in their articulation with* all those marginal, interstitial, residual, irrelevant, recalcitrant and plain contradictory forms of economic activity that are not so easily classifiable in terms of accumulation regimes, modes of regulation, varieties of capitalism, business models and so on. Second, in doing so, it is also important to consider the critical hierarchical orderings, centre–periphery relations, and patterns of adhesion and exclusion that emerge from the contingent process of world market integration. If variegated capitalism is a useful notion for the first exercise, the second can benefit from critical deployment of the notion of ecological dominance. Together they suggest that an interesting and powerful account of the global economy can be generated by exploring the claim that it involves variegated capitalism in a world market organized in the shadow of neoliberalism.

COMMONALITIES OF CAPITALISM

We now identify a series of specific economic forms (the commodity form, money, wages, capital, prices, property etc.) associated with generalized commodity production. We argue that these have distinctive effects that must be analysed as such and that they also influence the selection and

BOX 6.1   SOME COMMONALITIES OF CAPITALISM

- *Wealth* appears as an immense accumulation of *commodities*
- The *commodity form* is generalized to *labour-power*, which is treated *as if* it were a commodity, although, like land, money and knowledge, it is in fact a fictitious commodity
- The duality of labour-power as *concrete labour* and *abstract labour time*
- A specific political economy of *time* that continually rebases abstract time, creating a treadmill of different forms of competition, which tend to subsume more and more forms of social relations
- The commodity and other forms of the capital relation involve specific expressions of the core *contradiction* – and their associated dilemmas – between their use-value and value (or exchange-value) aspects
- These contradictions are *incompressible*: at best their effects can be obscured through semantic fixes and displaced or deferred through spatio-temporal fixes that are also social and institutional
- *Money* as a social relation has a key role in mediating the profit-oriented, market-mediated accumulation process (but can get disconnected for a time from the 'real economy', creating possibilities for monetary crisis)
- *Competition* (and, hence, in part, *entrepreneurship*) is central to capital's dynamic: its foci and stakes include (but are not limited to) innovation to reduce socially necessary labour time, socially necessary turnover time and naturally necessary reproduction time
- *Market forces* alone cannot secure all the conditions for the expanded capitalist reproduction (even ignoring the dual nature of the labour process as concrete labour and a process of valorization)
- Capital accumulation has major *extra-economic* conditions of existence in other social forms, institutions, organizations and social practices, which must be included as crucial *factors of power and domination* in its analysis

retention of competing economic imaginaries. However, while it is useful to explore these in relatively abstract terms, this would not enable comparative historical analysis of accumulation regimes, modes of regulation or varieties of capitalism. Because some of the foundational arguments about the capitalist mode of production, its *régulation*-cum-governance, and capitalist social formations are retained from the earlier work, we do not develop them at length but present ten key themes in Box 6.1. Some of these themes are pursued in more detail below; others are developed in Chapters 7 and 11.

Capital as a Social Relation

Given the basic features of capitalism as a mode of production and object of *régulation*-cum-governance, stable capital accumulation is inherently improbable, even within a specific geo-economic space, let alone at a world scale. Its preconditions are opaque, indeterminate and changeable, and, even without these problems, could not be secured from one central point, place or node. It is here that, as Marsden notes, Foucault and Marx offer complementary perspectives on capital accumulation. This process continually throws up 'urgent problems' at different sites and scales to which competing social forces respond in a trial-and-error search to develop and consolidate appropriate dispositives, with spatio-temporal parameters and horizons of action. This is where Foucauldian perspectives have much to offer. Those dispositives that are retained may co-evolve to produce more or less coherent clusters organized around basic structural forms, specific accumulation regimes and modes of *régulation*-cum-governance. This is where Marx, the regulation approach, and other heterodox analyses are relevant. The challenges of accumulation also highlight the importance of variation, selection and retention in both the semiotic and extra-semiotic aspects of capital accumulation. This requires close attention to its co-constitution through the interaction of market-mediated and non-market social relations and, in turn, to their impact on the wider social formation.

Marx begins *Capital I* with the observation that the 'wealth of those societies in which the capitalist mode of production prevails, presents itself as "an immense accumulation of commodities"' (Marx 1967a: 43; cf. Marx 1970: 27). He then takes the commodity form as the starting point of his analysis of the capitalist mode of production, describing the 'commodity form of the product of labour', in the Preface to the first German edition, as the economic cell form of bourgeois society (Marx 1967a: 19). Had he lived to see the revolution in genetics, he might well have described the commodity form as the *stem-cell form* of the capital relation. As is now known, stem cells in a developing embryo are pluripotent: they can both differentiate with appropriate triggers into any of the many specialized cells (e.g. brain, kidney, muscle or bone cells) and also maintain the normal turnover of regenerative organs, such as blood, skin or intestinal tissues. By analogy, we suggest, first, that the commodity form differentiates into specialized forms (e.g. money, price, wage, credit, state etc.) to generate a social formation and, second, that the reproduction of the capital relation as a whole depends on the continuing circulation of commodities through the metamorphosis of capital.

In his critique of political economy, Marx used a dialectical mode of presentation to unfold these differentiations conceptually, starting with the commodity and moving to such complex forms as interest-bearing capital. However, historically, different forms have their own genealogies. They may not emerge in the logical sequence presented in *Capital*; nor do they immediately acquire their final role in the circuits of capital and/ or wider social formation. He also demonstrated the improbable renewal of the capital relation by exploring the 'turnover' of different forms of capital, the problematic coordination of these different, and potentially disjointed, turnover times, and the competitive pressures to reduce them. These processes may appear 'natural' (*naturwüchsig*) but they are necessarily mediated through social practices, which have, as we have seen, both discursive and extra-discursive moments. They are also subject to reflexive reorganization to produce new forms (e.g. fictitious commodities, credit and capital) and to differentiate or combine existing forms and thereby modify the process of differential accumulation. We end these observations by emphasizing that these remarks involve analogical reasoning and should not be taken literally.

The commodity form is not co-eval with the capitalist mode of production based on the rational organization of production and free trade in markets: it precedes it by millennia. What most distinguishes capitalism from other forms of producing goods and services for sale is the generalization of the commodity form to labour power, that is, its treatment *as if* it were a commodity. It is this that permits the organization of the economy on the basis of generalized commodity production and leads to wealth taking the form of a massive accumulation of commodities. This entails the historical development and subsequent reproduction and expansion of a labour market in which workers offer their labour power for sale to capitalists in a formally free and equal commercial transaction. In this regard, the wage serves as a cost of production (for all capitals), a means of self-reproduction (for labour) and a source of demand (in the first instance for capitals that produce consumer goods and, indirectly, for those capitals that produce capital goods). Further, with the fictitious commodification of labour power, the appropriation of surplus labour gains its distinctive capitalist mediation in and through market forces. In short, exploitation[4] takes the form of exchange.

Although capital appropriates and transforms natural resources and also draws on the productive powers of nature (so that these resources and powers contribute to the production of use-values and any resulting increase in wealth), the socially necessary labour power that is consumed in producing commodities is the sole source of real added value (and hence profit) for capital taken as a whole. This point holds in the aggregate regardless of how the resulting surplus may later be divided. Moreover, far from excluding superprofits from innovation, other temporary advantages, or monopoly positions at the expense of below average profits for other capitals, competition to secure such superprofits is a basic source of capital's overall dynamic.[5] In addition to the search for ways to reduce the socially necessary labour time – whether manual or mental – embodied in commodities (and other fictitious commodities), there are two other major sites of capitalist competition. These are competition to reduce the *socially necessary turnover time of capital* through cost-cutting and innovation outside the sphere of production, and, increasingly, competition to lower *naturally necessary reproduction time* by speeding up rhythms of nature as a major (natural) source of wealth (e.g. through bio-technology and the life sciences) (see Chapter 7).

While the generalization of the commodity form to labour power is a historically specific feature of the capitalist mode of production, there are three other key categories of fictitious commodity: land (or nature), money, knowledge. Each is often treated as a simple factor of production, obscuring the conditions under which it enters the market economy, gets transformed therein, and so contributes to the production of goods and services for sale. But this tendency to naturalize fictitious commodities as objectively given factors of production leads to the fallacious belief, strongly criticized by Marx, that economic value arises from the immanent, eternal qualities of things rather than from contingent, historically specific social relations. This is an important area for *Ideologiekritik* and the critique of domination. The relative weight of these fictitious commodities is one way (among others) to distinguish different stages of capitalism, different regimes of accumulation and different modes of competition within the overall framework of the world market, which is the ultimate horizon of differential accumulation. Thus, in these terms, one might compare rentier extractive economies, regimes based mainly on absolute surplus-value, finance-led and knowledge-based economies.

Commodification turns both the labour market and labour process into sites of class struggle between capital and workers[6] and also shapes the competition among capitals to secure the most effective valorization of labour power and the appropriation of the resulting surplus-value. The basic economic forms of this struggle are shaped by the wage form, the technical and social division of labour and the organization of capitalist production as an economy of time. The semiotic dimensions of this field are crucial in shaping its dynamics (for a comparative historical case study, see Biernacki 1995). But the dynamic of economic class struggle also has many other economic and extra-economic determinants and, in addition, class struggles typically spread beyond the economy in its narrow sense to other areas of social organization. This economic class struggle is overdetermined, of course, by juridico-political and ideological structures and struggles, the complexity of class relations in actually existing social formations, and the intersection of class with other social categories. Class struggle and competition are significant sources (but by no means alone) of capitalism's open-ended dynamic and underpin the differential accumulation that reflects the ability of some capitals to grow through market *and non-market* means faster than others (or at least to suffer less in cyclical downturns and/or in periods of crisis). Lastly, when capital accumulation becomes the dominant principle of organization in the economy in its narrow sense, it also gains a major influence on societies more broadly and, in certain circumstances, may become the dominant principle of societal organization (on ecological dominance, see below).

CAPITAL AS AN OBJECT OF REGULATION

The capital relation cannot be reproduced entirely through market exchange and is therefore prone to 'market failure' (an interesting semiotic construct in its own right). The most important general law in capitalism is the law of value. This describes the *tendency* of capitalists to allocate resources to different fields of production according to expectations of profit (Box 6.2). Although this law is mediated through market forces and the price mechanism, the operation of which may or may not socially validate these private decisions, it is ultimately grounded in the sphere of production. For it is only here that new value is created through the application of socially necessary labour time and so becomes available for any subsequent validation, redistribution or even destruction.[7] Anticipating the approach that would be codified by critical realism, Marx also described other laws and tendencies of capitalist economies[8] but treated none of them as iron necessities. Instead he emphasized their mediation through capitalist competition and class struggles.

> **BOX 6.2   THE 'LAW OF VALUE' IN CAPITALISM**
>
> In general terms, the law of value suggests that more time will be spent on producing commodities whose market price is above their price of production as measured by the socially necessary labour time involved in their creation. Conversely, less time will be spent on producing commodities whose market price is lower than their price of production. In capitalist economies this mechanism is complicated as competition tends to equalize rates of profit even though individual capitals may employ different ratios of physical capital and wage labour – although the latter is the only source of 'added value'. Accordingly it is fluctuations in *profits* (market price less cost price) that mediate the law of value in capitalism. In response to these fluctuations and in anticipation of how they might develop in future, individual capitals decide how to allocate not only labour power but also physical capital to production, distribution and circulation. Whether or not these calculations prove correct and they can sell the resulting commodities at a profit depends on the subsequent operation of market forces and is therefore inherently uncertain. Total production in capitalist economies depends on the uncoordinated decisions of competing capitals about opportunities for profit from different patterns of investment and production. Profit depends not only on the demand for different commodities (reflecting their prevailing use-value) but also on the rate of economic exploitation in different branches of production. It is therefore crucially related to the course and outcome of struggles between capital and labour at many different points in the circuit of capital and in the wider social formation.

The mechanisms through which, despite capital's contradictions, accumulation may get regularized (dispositivized) and reproduced actually extend well beyond the capitalist economy in its narrow sense (profit-oriented production, market-mediated exchange) to include various direct and indirect extra-economic mechanisms. Moreover, in so far as these extra-economic mechanisms also reproduce the contradictions and dilemmas inherent in the economic mechanisms of the capital relation, they further expand the scope for agency, strategies and tactics to shape the course of accumulation and the manner in which these contradictions and dilemmas are expressed. This in turn calls for analysis of the improbable nature of accumulation to take semiosis, agency and technologies of regulation/ governance seriously.

We can understand what this involves by asking why capitalism needs regulating. The answer lies in three key aspects of the capital relation:

- the incompleteness of capital as a purely economic (or market-mediated) relation such that its continued reproduction depends, in an unstable and contradictory way, on changing extra-economic conditions;
- its various inherent structural contradictions and strategic dilemmas and their changing structural articulation and forms of appearance in different accumulation regimes, modes of regulation and conjunctures; and
- conflicts over the regularization and/or governance of these contradictions and dilemmas as expressed in the circuit of capital and the wider social formation.

We have addressed the first aspect in previous chapters and now focus on the second and third. Marx (1967a) identified an essential contradiction in the commodity form between its exchange- and use-value aspects. Exchange-value refers to a commodity's market-mediated monetary value for the seller; use-value refers to its material and/or symbolic usefulness to the purchaser. Without exchange-value, commodities would not be produced for sale; without use-value, they would not be purchased.[9] On this basis he dialectically unfolded the complex dynamic of the capitalist mode of production – including the necessity of periodic crises and their role in reintegrating the circuit of capital as a basis for renewed expansion.

We suggest that all forms of the capital relation embody different but interconnected versions of this basic contradiction and that these impact differentially on (different fractions of) capital and on (different categories and strata of) labour at different times and places. (See Table 6.2 for some contradictions in the capital relation.) Thus productive capital is both abstract value in motion (notably in the form of realized profits available for reinvestment) and a concrete stock of already invested time- and place-specific assets in the course of being valorized; the worker is both an abstract unit of labour power substitutable by other such units (or, indeed, other factors of production) and a concrete individual (or, indeed, a member of a concrete collective workforce) with specific skills, knowledge and creativity; the wage is both a cost of production and a source of demand; money functions both as an international currency exchangeable

Table 6.2 Some contradictions in the capital relation

Form	Exchange-value moment	Use-value moment
Commodity	Exchange-value	Use-value
Labour-Power	(1) abstract labour as substitutable factor of production (2) sole source of surplus-value	(1) generic and concrete skills, different forms of knowledge (2) source of craft pride
Wage	(1) monetary cost of production (2) means of securing supply of useful labour for given time	(1) source of effective demand (2) means to satisfy wants in a cash-based society
Money	(1) interest-bearing capital, private credit, international currency (2) ultimate expression of capital in general	(1) measure of value, store of value, means of exchange, national money, legal tender (2) general form of power in the wider society
Productive capital	(1) abstract value in motion (or money capital) for investment in future time/place (2) source of profits of enterprise	(1) stock of specific assets to be valorized in specific time and place in specific conditions (2) concrete entrepreneurial and managerial skills
Land	(1) alienated and alienable property, source of rents (2) securitized absolute and differential rents from 'land'	(1) 'free gift of nature' that is (currently) inalienable (2) transformed natural resources
Knowledge	(1) intellectual property (2) monetized risk	(1) intellectual commons (2) uncertainty

against other currencies (ideally in stateless space) and as national money circulating within national societies[10] and subject to some measure of state control; land functions both as a form of property (based on the private appropriation of nature) deployed in terms of expected revenues in the form of rent and as a natural resource (modified by past actions) that is more or less renewable and recyclable; knowledge is both the basis of intellectual property rights and a collective resource (the intellectual commons). Likewise, the state is not only charged with securing key conditions for the profitability of capital in general and with the reproduction of labour power as a fictitious commodity, but also has overall political responsibility for maintaining social cohesion in a socially divided, pluralistic society.[11] In turn, taxation is both an unproductive deduction from private revenues (profits of enterprise, wages, interest and rents) and a means to finance collective investment and consumption to compensate for 'market failures'. And so on (see in part Table 6.1; and, for further discussion, Jessop 2002).

These contradictions also affect the wider social formation and are reproduced as capitalism itself is reproduced. This helps to explain why accumulation involves an ever-changing balance among repeated cycles of self-valorization, continuous self-transformation, bouts of crisis-induced restructuring and other modalities of change. Nonetheless, differences in the relative weight of these contradictions (and their different aspects) provide one way to distinguish different stages and/or varieties of capitalism – especially as they are often linked to new patterns of time-space distantiation and compression as well as to shifts in the dominant spatio-temporal horizons and the leading places and spaces for accumulation. The complexity of these aspects vitiates any unilinear account of the stages of capitalism because they permit different trajectories in different sets of circumstances.

The tension between the coexisting poles, each of which is a naturally necessary or inherent feature of a given contradiction and, indeed, which together define it in their opposition, generates strategic dilemmas on how to handle the contradiction. For example, does – or should – the state treat the (social) wage mainly as a source of demand or a cost of production, or does it attempt to reconcile these aspects? The first case is illustrated in the Keynesian welfare national state (or KWNS), the second in neoliberal austerity politics or export-led growth, and the third in welfare regimes based on 'flexicurity'. Analogous arguments hold for other contradictions and dilemmas. The plurality of contradictions and their interconnections, the possibilities of handling them at different sites, scales and time horizons and so on creates significant scope for agency, strategies and tactics to affect economic trajectories. How they are handled also shapes the form of subsequent crises but does *not* determine the nature of subsequent regimes, which also depend on the formal and material adequacy outcome of path-shaping initiatives.

An important caveat is needed here. To paraphrase Marx in the 1857 'Introduction' (1973: 24), 'there is no contradiction in general, there is also no general contradiction'. Each contradiction has its own aspects and is actualized in its own ways in particular institutional and spatio-temporal contexts, generating a complex, overdetermined, contradictory and multiply dilemmatic ensemble of social relations that is associated with clusters of dispositives that regularize the capital relation. In strategic-relational terms, institutions and dispositives have their own distinctive discursive and structural selectivities, favouring some actors, alliances, identities, interests, projects, spatio-temporal horizons and so forth. They are linked to specific technologies of governance; and articulated into specific institutional orders and ensembles of dispositives that create specific forms of domination. While many institutions and/or dispositives are related to fundamental categories of the capital relation, their specific forms and logics are irreducible to these basic categories. They are not just simple forms of appearance of underlying essences. Institutions matter. They have their own distinctive discursive–material selectivities, are associated with specific technologies of governance, and are articulated into specific institutional orders and ensembles (see Chapter 1).

This approach to institutions and dispositives is essential to understanding accumulation regimes, their modes of *régulation*-cum-governance, and their integration into broader societal configurations. Some first-generation Parisian regulation theorists sometimes combined institutional analysis with a form-analytical account of the contradictions inherent in the capital relation (e.g. Aglietta 1979; Lipietz 1985). We follow them in defining an accumulation regime as a complementary pattern of production and consumption that is reproducible over a long period; and a mode of growth as a coherent combination of accumulation regime and mode of regulation. However, we modify their definition of mode of regulation as follows: an ensemble of norms, institutions, organizational forms, social networks and patterns of conduct (in Foucauldian terms, a dispositive) that can temporarily stabilize an accumulation regime through its *régulation*-cum-governance of specific structural forms despite the conflictual and antagonistic nature of the capitalist social relation. This reflects our view that, whereas Atlantic Fordism was easier to *regularize* because of the coherence of its structural forms, the relative primacy of the national economy governed by a national state, and the apparent success of crisis-management routines, post-Fordist regimes are less coherent and more turbulent, requiring more active *governance*. In contrast with some later Parisian work, which tends to be more one-sidedly institutionalist, we still start from the fundamental features of the capital relation. In addition, like the Grenoble School and the Amsterdam School, we emphasize the world market as the ultimate horizon of capital accumulation (on the Grenoble School, see Jessop and Sum 2006).

Contradictions and dilemmas can be resolved through social fixes (where social is understood in terms of social practices with discursive and extra-discursive moments). Social fixes can be analysed in semantic, social (especially institutional) and spatio-temporal terms. Fixes emerge, in so far as they do, in a contested, trial-and-error process, involving different economic, political and social forces and diverse strategies and projects; and they typically rest on an institutionalized, unstable equilibrium of compromise. By analogy with the Foucauldian concept of dispositive, they can be explored through the pursuit of a strategic line within specific semantic, structural and technological selectivities. Semantic selectivities limit what can be seen, imagined, communicated and understood, and, through specific discursive fields (orders of discourse) they provide the categories that connect to particular fields of social relations. A social fix can be explored in terms of formal isomorphism and/or complementarities among forms in a social formation. However, since a fully structured social formation is improbable (but useful to explore at the level of a thought-experiment), it is more productive to explore social fixes at the level of an institutional fix (or, in some cases, a series of organizational fixes). An institutional fix comprises a complementary set of institutions that, via institutional design, imitation, imposition or chance evolution, helps to provide a temporary, partial and relatively stable solution to the *régulation*-cum-governance problems involved in constituting and securing a social order. It can also be examined as a spatio-temporal fix (or STF), and vice versa. STFs establish spatial and temporal boundaries within which the always-relative, incomplete, provisional and institutionally mediated structural coherence of a given order (here, a mode of growth) is secured – in so far as this occurs. Issues of institutional design apart, this also involves building support in and across many conflictual and contested fields for the respective accumulation strategies, associated state projects and, where relevant, hegemonic visions. STFs help to displace and defer the material (*stofflich*) and social costs of securing such coherence beyond the spatial, temporal and social boundaries of the institutional fix. Hence they only *appear* to harmonize contradictions, which persist in one or another form (see Box 6.3).

Fixes are nonetheless improbable, whether in the guise of sedimented meaning (semantic fixes) or in the guise of structured coherence (social fixes), institutional 'constitutive outside' or, more broadly still, the unacknowledged, unanticipated natural and social world that are not included in a given form of complexity reduction, whether semiotic or structural. In each case, what lies beyond the purview of a discourse or the structuring effects of a social fix in its extra-discursive moments has the potential to disorient, disturb or fracture the fix. For example, given the inherent improbability of a comprehensive STF instituted at the level of the world market, certain factors and processes necessary to the success of a given accumulation regime will lie beyond the reach of its mode of regulation

BOX 6.3 SPATIO-TEMPORAL FIXES

- A spatio-temporal fix (STF) (which is necessarily social and typically also institutional and/or organizational) emerges when an accumulation regime and its mode of regulation co-evolve to create a certain structural coherence among the elements of that political-economic order *within a given spatio-temporal framework* (or time-space envelope).
- Structurally an STF is typically linked to a distinctive hierarchy of structural forms that affects interactions in the institutional architecture as a whole and so shapes the overall logic of the STF. This hierarchy gives greater priority to regularizing some structural forms (and gives greater priority, perhaps, to one or other aspect of their associated contradictions and dilemmas) than others. These priorities vary across accumulation regimes, modes of growth, and governance capacities.
- Strategically, because capitalism's contradictions and dilemmas cannot be solved *in abstracto*, they are resolved – partially and provisionally, if at all – via the formulation–realization of specific accumulation strategies at various economic and political scales in specific spatio-temporal contexts.
- The significance here of accumulation strategies (and their associated state projects and, where relevant, hegemonic visions) illustrates again the importance of discourse, agency and governmental technologies. Such fixes delimit the main spatial and temporal boundaries within which semantic and structural coherence is secured, and externalize certain costs of securing this coherence beyond these boundaries.
- Even within these boundaries some classes, class fractions, social categories or other social forces are marginalized, excluded or oppressed.
- STFs also facilitate the institutionalized compromises on which accumulation regimes and modes of regulation depend, and subsequently come to embody these compromises. This can involve super-exploitation of internal or external spaces outside the compromise, super-exploitation of nature or inherited social resources, deferral of problems into an indefinite future and, of course, the exploitation and/or oppression of specific classes, strata or other social categories.

or sets of dispositives. This is the other face of the capacity of an STF to displace and defer contradictions and crisis tendencies. But, where one such strategy becomes dominant or hegemonic and is institutionalized in a specific STF, it may help to consolidate an accumulation regime in its corresponding economic space.

Nonetheless, because the underlying contradictions and dilemmas still exist, all such regimes are partial, provisional and unstable. The circuit of capital may still break at many points within and beyond the STF. Economic crises will then provoke restructuring through market forces and/or more deliberate attempts to restore the conditions for accumulation. If such attempts are compatible with the prevailing accumulation regime, growth will be renewed within its parameters. If not, a crisis *of* – and not just *in* – the accumulation regime will develop, provoking a search for new strategies, new institutionalized compromises and new spatio-temporal fixes (cf. Boyer 1990; Lipietz 1988).

These arguments imply that no regime has just one (fundamental) contradiction that must be regulated and/or governed appropriately to ensure continuing accumulation. The relation among contradictions and dilemmas is not mechanically additive but reciprocally, albeit asymmetrically, overdetermined: they are not simply aggregated as 'so many potatoes in a sack' but modify each other in distinctive ways. Their significance varies, posing differently configured sets of *régulation*-cum-governance problems at different sites and scales (cf. Gough 1991, 2004). The asymmetries can be analysed by deploying three key concepts elaborated by Louis Althusser on the basis of Mao Zhe-Dong's insightful, ill-specified and politically too malleable essay on contradiction: (1) the distinction between the *principal contradiction* and other, *secondary contradictions* in a given social order – with their articulation being complex and overdetermined rather than simple and set exclusively by the principal contradiction; (2) the distinction between the *primary* aspect and the *secondary* aspect of a given contradiction in a given conjuncture, that is, which of its poles is more problematic for expanded reproduction; and (3) the *uneven development* of contradictions, that is, changes in the principal and secondary contradictions and their primary and secondary aspects (Althusser 1965; Mao 1967).

These distinctions are useful in exploring how institutional and spatio-temporal fixes contribute to the overall *régulation*-cum-governance of the capital relation. Specifically, contradictions and their associated dilemmas may be handled through:

- *hierarchization* (treating some contradictions as more important than others);

- *prioritization* of one aspect of a contradiction or dilemma over the other aspect;
- *spatialization* (relying on different scales and sites of action to address one or another contradiction or aspect, or displacing the problems associated with the neglected aspect to a marginal or liminal space, place or scale); and
- *temporalization* (alternating regularly between treatment of different aspects or focusing one-sidedly on a subset of contradictions, dilemmas or aspects until it becomes urgent to address what has hitherto been neglected).

On this basis, a given type of capitalism would differ in terms of the weights attributed to different contradictions and dilemmas (hierarchization), the importance accorded to their different aspects (prioritization), the role of different spaces, places and scales in these regards (spatialization), and the temporal patterns of their treatment (temporalization). The same criteria can be used to analyse the *régulation*-cum-governance of modes of growth. In all cases, because the capital relation is reproduced – when it is – through social agency and entails specific forms, stakes and sites of conflict and struggle, the weight of contradictions and dilemmas is not structurally inscribed or strategically pre-scripted. Fixes are not purely technical but reflect the institutionally mediated balance of forces in a given situation.

The prevailing strategies modify each contradiction, with the result that they are mutually presupposed, interiorizing and reproducing in different ways the overall configuration of contradictions. Different configurations can be stabilized based on the weights attached to (1) different contradictions and dilemmas and their dual aspects; (2) the counter-balancing or offsetting of different solutions to different contradictions and dilemmas; (3) different patterns of social conflict and institutionalized compromise; (4) differences in the leading places and spaces for accumulation; and (5) the changing prospects of displacing and/or deferring problems and crisis tendencies. The complex structural configuration of a given accumulation regime depends on institutional and spatio-temporal fixes that *establish* the primacy of one or more contradictions and assign a primacy for governance to one rather than another of its aspects. Other contradictions are regularized/governed according to how they complement the current dominant contradiction(s). Nonetheless, these fixes are not 'magic bullets': they cannot eliminate contradictions and dilemmas and, whatever their capacity to temporarily 'harmonize' or reconcile them, they create the conditions for the next crisis.

RENEWING THE PARISIAN REGULATION APPROACH

We now draw on these arguments to reinvigorate the early Parisian work that explored how the inherent contradictions of the capital relation were regulated through specific structural forms and institutionalized compromises in different stages of capitalism. Early studies decomposed the capital relation into a series of structural forms, each of which has its own characteristic contradictions and dilemmas, requiring specific forms of regulation. These are conventionally described as the wage relation (individual and social wage, wage form, lifestyle); the enterprise form and competition (internal organization, source of profits, forms of competition, ties among enterprises and/or banks); money and credit (form and emission, banking and credit systems, allocation of capital to production, national currencies and world monies, and monetary regimes); the state (institutionalized compromise between capital and labour, forms of state intervention); and international regimes (trade, investment, monetary and political arrangements that link national economies, national states and the world system). The choice of these forms probably reflects the institutional configuration of Atlantic Fordism in a specific world-historical context rather than a generic set of forms applicable to all accumulation regimes (Röttger 2003). This is why it is better to premise comparative analysis on the inherent contradictions of the capital relation rather than take for granted the features of a particular growth regime. This makes it easier to distinguish the specific institutional configurations corresponding to other growth regimes, especially where they involve strong elements of political capitalism (Weber 1965). And, compared with the presumption that there are always five basic structural forms, it provides a less restrictive grid of intelligibility for exploring social forms, orders of discourse, and discursive and social practices and their configuration into what Foucault would term dispositives.

Pascal Petit suggests that one structural form will predominate in each period or accumulation regime and shape its institutional dynamics (1999). Translating this proposal into our terminology, we could say that the *dominant structural form* is the one linked to the principal contradiction in a given period or regime. We propose that one way to distinguish modes of growth is in terms of how they handle contradictions and dilemmas in terms of the four above-mentioned methods. Thus one can study their principal contradictions and their primary and secondary aspects when they are *en régulation*, how this configuration displaces and/or defers for a while the inherent contradictions of the capital relation and, indeed, contributes to the typical crisis tendencies of a given mode of growth, and how the primary and secondary aspects of contradictions and the overall hierarchy of contradictions change when a mode of growth is in crisis. A useful insight in this regard is Boyer's distinction between stable and transitional periods. He suggests that, in periods *en régulation*, the dominant institutional form is the one that constrains the covariation of other institutional forms and thereby secures their complementarity or coherence. For Fordism, he claims, this was the wage–labour nexus. In transition periods, however, the dominant structural form is the one that imposes its logic on the others – without this ensuring coherence among all five institutional forms, at least in the short term (2000: 291). He suggests that, 'in the 1990s, finance appeared to govern the dynamics of other institutional forms' (Boyer 2002b: 320) and, indeed, that a deregulated, internationalized and hyper-innovative financial system had destabilizing effects on other structural forms (Boyer 2002b, 2004, 2011).

Drawing on these arguments, we further suggest that, whereas the economic dynamic of periods of stability rests on complementary institutional hierarchies and institutionalized compromise, periods of instability involve disruptive institutional hierarchies and struggles to roll back past compromises and establish new ones. In both cases, thanks to the presence of multiple contradictions and dilemmas, agents are forced, *nolens volens*, to prioritize some over others. This is not a neutral technical matter but is essentially political and typically contested. This is especially evident in periods of economic crisis, which provoke restructuring through the normal working of market forces as well as through more deliberate, typically conflictual, attempts to restore the conditions for differential accumulation, often through institutional innovation and efforts to modify the balance of forces. This may include changes in the priority of opposing aspects of a contradiction as the previously secondary aspect becomes more urgent and/or in the sites and scales on which contradictions are handled and dilemmas are juggled. These issues become even clearer when there is a crisis of crisis management, that is, when conventional ways of dealing with crisis no longer work well, if at all. And this holds particularly when it is the dominant contradiction that generates the most severe challenges and destabilizing, disorienting effects. This will vary with the accumulation regime and its mode of regulation, and with the shifting conjunctures of a variegated world market.

Louis Althusser claimed, rather dramatically, that contradictions have three forms of existence: '*non-antagonism*', '*antagonism*' and '*explosion*' (Althusser 1965). Utilizing the strategic-relational approach, we reinterpret this claim as follows. Non-antagonism exists when there is a relatively stable institutional and spatio-temporal fix associated with a hegemonic economic imaginary and institutionalized compromise within a given time-space envelope. Antagonism occurs when contradictions and crisis tendencies can no longer be managed, displaced or deferred, with the result that growth cannot be renewed within the usual parameters, producing a crisis of crisis management that provokes struggles over how best to reconfigure the contradictions and dilemmas and secure a new, but inherently unstable, equilibrium of compromise. This is especially likely where one of the structural forms operates to destabilize the inherited growth regime. An explosion is an overdetermined ruptural moment that opens the possibilities of radical restructuring on a qualitatively new basis. Whether or not the search for solutions to economic crisis restores the prevailing accumulation regime and its mode of regulation does not depend solely on the objective features of the crisis and the feasibility of resolving it within this framework; it also depends on the institutional, organizational and learning capacities of the social forces seeking to resolve the crisis and on the outcome of the contest to define the nature of the crisis, to explain its various objective causes, to attribute blame for its development and to identify the most appropriate solutions.

Atlantic Fordism

We now illustrate these arguments for Atlantic Fordism. Its fixes can be analysed in terms of the hierarchization, prioritization, spatialization and temporalization of its basic contradictions, thereby securing the conditions for its dominance in Fordist social formations and giving the appearance that contradictions had been harmonized, social conflict moderated, and the conditions for permanent prosperity established. Crucial here was a spatio-territorial matrix based on the socially constructed congruence between national economy, national state, national citizenship, embracing social as well as civic and political rights, and national society; and the consolidation of institutions relatively well adapted to the twin challenges of securing full employment and economic growth and managing national electoral cycles. The dominant (or principal) structural forms (with their associated contradictions and dilemmas) around which this specific resolution was organized in and through the KWNS were the wage and money forms. Whereas Petit (1999) and Boyer (2000) focused on the wage–labour nexus, Aglietta also regarded the money constraint as important (see Aglietta 1979, 1986).

In our account, whether Fordism was *en régulation* or *in crisis*, the social wage relation and money form were joint sites of dominant contradictions. On this assumption, Table 6.3 presents an ideal-typical configuration of this growth regime *en régulation*, which also provides a reference point for studying its crisis tendencies. It focuses on four structural forms and deals

Table 6.3   Atlantic Fordism en régulation

Basic form	Primary aspect	Secondary aspect	Institutional fixes	Spatio-temporal fixes
(Social) wage	Source of domestic demand	Cost of production	Keynesian welfare + rising productivity	Creation of national economies
Money	National money	International currency	Keynesianism + capital controls + Bretton Woods and role of US dollar	Managing uneven development and international relations
State	Social cohesion in national societies	Economic intervention	Welfare state + spatial planning	National state and local relays
Capital	Stock of assets that must be used profitably in given time-place	Mobile money capital in search of most profitable investment sites	Reinvested Fordist profits + financing of consumption	Atlantic Fordist circuits in embedded liberalism

K
E   Principal (or dominant) structural form   Secondary structural form
Y
     Primary aspect of principal form   Primary aspect of secondary form

     Secondary aspect of principal form   Secondary aspect of secondary form

with the issue of international regimes in terms of the spatio-temporal aspects of how other forms are embedded at different scales. This reflects our view that international regimes are closely tied to the other four forms and should be studied in these terms rather than presented as a separate structural form. Similar tables are presented for Atlantic Fordism in crisis (Table 6.4), the knowledge-based economy (Table 7.1), and finance-dominated accumulation *en régulation* and in crisis (Tables 11.1 and 11.2).

The primary aspect of the wage form was its role as a source of domestic demand rather than as a cost of international production. This reflected a context where full employment levels of demand served the interests of industrial capital as well as the Fordist labour force (especially semi-skilled male wage-earners). Although Keynesian fine-tuning contributed

Table 6.4 Atlantic Fordist crisis

Basic form	Primary aspect	Secondary aspect	Institutional fixes	Spatio-temporal fixes
(Social) wage	Cost of international production	Source of domestic demand	Internationalization inverts role of (social) wage	Crisis of national crisis management
Money	International currency	National money	Breakdown of Bretton Woods, change in US dollar's role	Crisis in international regimes
State	Social exclusion, rise of new social movements	Rise in economic intervention to manage crises	Fiscal, rationality, legitimacy and hegemonic crises	Declining power of national states
Capital	Mobile money capital in search of most profitable site of investment	Productive capital integrated into changing global division of labour	Disruption of Fordist circuits due to neo-liberal globalization	Crisis of Atlantic Fordism, rise of East Asia, then of 'BRIC' powers

at best modestly – and often counter-productively – to achieving this goal, the principal foundation was the virtuous circle of mass production and mass consumption reinforced by the KWNS. Wages as a cost of international production were secondary because of the relative closure of national economies, the capacity to live economically and politically with modest inflation, and resort to modest devaluations to protect full employment levels of demand. The state was permissive towards wage costs as long as they rose in line with productivity and prices. This was relatively easy to achieve in the 1950s and early 1960s, as Fordist firms and branches expanded thanks to their economies of scale and as collective bargaining operated within the Fordist class compromise. Labour market pressures were also alleviated in this period by processes such as the transfer of workers from low-productivity agriculture, the mobilization of women into the labour force and, later, the state support for responsible trade unionism, collective bargaining, industrial modernization, the consolidation of big business, and forms of corporatism.

The primary aspect of the money form in most Fordist regimes was its character as national credit money. The development of adequate national, macro-economic statistics and the steady expansion of the peacetime state budget gave the KWNS considerable leverage in fiscal and monetary terms to steer the economy. Private debt also played a major role in the post-war boom by financing fixed investment and working capital as well as by funding the growth of mass consumption. In turn, lubricated by public and private credit, growth helped to legitimate Keynesian welfare policies, and to generate the tax revenues for collective consumption, welfare rights and social redistribution, as well as for infrastructure provision. It also helped to consolidate a social basis for the Fordist accumulation regime based on a class compromise between industrial capital and organized labour.

Thus, in the expansion phase of Atlantic Fordism, the role of money as an international currency was secondary. This aspect was managed through the embedding of Atlantic Fordism in the Bretton Woods monetary and GATT (General Agreement on Tariffs and Trade) regimes. Most national economies were more closed on their capital accounts than on their trade accounts, with national states enjoying effective capital controls, fixed but adjustable exchange rates and significant and legitimate trade controls in place or to hand. Thus economic policy adjustment and intervention were more oriented to economic growth and full employment than to defence of a fixed exchange rate. This was gradually undermined, however, as increasing flows of stateless money and near-money instruments induced national governments, reluctantly or willingly, to abandon capital controls and adopt a floating exchange rate system. The USA was a partial exception because its national money was the hegemonic international currency. Initially beneficial during its expansion phase, this later became another source of instability and crisis for Atlantic Fordism.

Finally, we should note that some costs of the Fordist compromise and the KWNS were borne inside Fordist societies by the relative decline of agriculture, the traditional petite bourgeoisie, small and medium firms; by the decline of cities, regions and sectors that could find no competitive role in the Fordist circuits; by workers in the disadvantaged parts of segmented labour markets; and, especially in liberal welfare regimes, by women subject to the dual burden of paid and domestic labour. One of the mechanisms for deferring the contradictions of Atlantic Fordism and the KWNS and redistributing their costs was inflation. Based on the capacity of banks and the state to expand credit, inflation served to (pseudo-) validate otherwise unprofitable production and to maintain high levels of capacity utilization and employment (Lipietz 1986). Provided that all the relevant economies had similar mild rates of inflation or that higher-inflation economies could engage in occasional modest devaluations, this did not hinder integration of the Atlantic Fordist circuits (Aglietta 1982). It did produce problems later in the form of stagflation and, throughout this period, it had significant redistributive effects in class, sectoral and regional terms, favouring big capital in particular (Galbraith 1967). Other costs were borne by economic and political spaces tied to international regimes (such as those for cheap oil or migrant labour) necessary to Atlantic Fordism's continued growth but not included in the Fordist compromise. This regime gained from a Janus-faced temporal fix. For, while it depended on accelerated (and unsustainable) exploitation of nature (especially raw materials and non-renewable resources laid down over millennia, such as fossil fuels), it also produced environmental pollution and social problems that remained largely unaddressed. Increasing difficulties in maintaining this institutional and spatio-temporal fix prompted attempts to challenge the institutionalized compromises on which it rested.

The crisis of the Atlantic Fordist growth regime emerged when internationalization and other spatio-temporal changes inverted the primary and secondary aspects of the dominant contradictions, undermining the corresponding institutional and spatio-temporal fixes. This disorganized the typical configuration of Atlantic Fordism and triggered struggles to introduce a new growth regime (or regimes). Table 6.4 on Atlantic Fordism in crisis uses the same grid as that for this regime when it is *en régulation*; but the content of every cell has been changed to reflect the inversion of the primary and secondary aspects of the dominant contradictions, the factors that contributed to the crisis, and the repercussions of the growing unsustainability of the institutional and spatio-temporal fixes that supported Atlantic Fordism in its heyday. Considerations of space prevent a full discussion of all these features, but they are taken up in the ensuing discussion of two major alternatives proposed as successor regimes to the Fordist growth regime (for more detail on the crisis itself and initial responses thereto, see de Vroey 1984; Jessop 2002).

CONCLUDING REMARKS

This chapter has had two main sets of objectives. The first set was to introduce the commonalities of capitalism, to provide some conceptual tools for distinguishing different stages and forms of capitalism, and to suggest that these different stages and forms could be related to the concept of variegated capitalism. The second set of objectives was to return to the insights of some early Parisian regulationist work on the unstable relationship between the basic contradictions of the capital relation and the institutional forms through which they are contingently resolved, always provisionally and partially, for a significant period of time. It extended this pioneering analysis by identifying some additional contradictions inherent in the capital relation, linking them to corresponding dilemmas, and indicating how accumulation regimes and their modes of growth can be studied in terms of the semantic, social, institutional and spatio-temporal fixes (in sum, dispositives) that contribute to their *régulation*-cum-governance. In particular, four interrelated strategies for handling contradictions were discussed and we indicated how specific configurations of these strategies could be used to characterize different modes of growth. On this basis, we showed how this approach could be applied to Atlantic Fordism *en régulation* and in crisis, relying in part on a tabular form of summarizing the institutional and spatio-temporal fixes associated with this regime in both periods.

Two issues are worth noting here before we proceed to the next chapter. First, assuming that the world market is both the presupposition and the posit (result) of capital accumulation and that the integration of the world market generalizes and intensifies its contradictions (Jessop 2010b, 2011), it is especially important to look beyond national–territorial boundaries in examining the institutional and spatio-temporal fixes that contribute to the provisional, partial and temporary stabilization of the capital relation. If the world market is the ultimate horizon of capital accumulation and of capitalist strategies, then our analyses must take account of this too, without falling back on some abstract, trans-historical logic of a capitalist world system.

Second, a systematic concern with multiple, overdetermined contradictions need not lead to structuralist analyses that marginalize social agency. For, as Christoph Scherrer, among others, has noted (see Chapter 2), contradictions entail dilemmas that open space, practically as well as theoretically, for agents, their strategic choices and the changing balance of forces to make a difference to the course of accumulation. This invites a far more detailed analysis of economic (and ecological) imaginaries, accumulation strategies, state projects and hegemonic visions, and their role in the *régulation*-cum-governance of the contradictions, dilemmas and antagonisms of the capital relation.

NOTES

1. The doubly tendential nature of tendencies is already implied in *The German Ideology* (drafted in 1845), where Marx and Engels noted: '[t]he movement of capital, although considerably accelerated, still remained, however, relatively slow. The splitting up

of the world market into separate parts, each of which was exploited by a particular nation, the exclusion of competition among themselves on the part of the nations, the clumsiness of production itself and the fact that finance was only evolving from its early stages, greatly impeded circulation' (1976a: 56n). Marx also studied uneven and combined development grounded in the national intensity and productivity of labour, the relative international values and prices of commodities produced in different national contexts, the relative international value of wages and money in social formations with varying degrees of labour intensity and productivity, the incidence of surplus profits and unequal exchange, and so on (e.g. Marx 1967a: 390–94).
2. The notion of 'space economy' is compatible with local, metropolitan, regional, national, supranational or cross-border economies. Its use here avoids the implication that an economy is always national in scope.
3. Research on compossibility goes beyond what is *possible* by virtue of *real* causal mechanisms and tendencies considered individually to explore what is *compossible* at the level of the *actual* as diverse causal mechanisms and tendencies interact in a given socio-spatial field. It invites questions about what is *incompossible* due to such causal interaction. In complex fields marked by multi-causality and equifinality, the number and range of incompossible combinations typically far exceed those that are compossible. Most interesting are those due to real opposition, antagonism or contradiction among events that are possible in isolation but incompossible together.
4. The term 'exploitation' is used here in a morally neutral manner.
5. Innovations that enable a given enterprise to produce commodities below the socially necessary labour time typical for such commodities and/or to keep realization costs below average will produce surplus profits until these innovations become generalized and thereby redefine 'social necessity'. In this sense, capitalist competition revolves around the average rate of profit.
6. Class relations are never defined purely at the level of economic relations but are overdetermined by the intervention of juridico-political and ideological structures and the articulation of class with other social categories. Moreover, from strategic and/or tactical viewpoints, workers, capitalists and other social forces may seek to organize labour markets and the labour process in terms of other interests and categories, leading to segmented labour markets and skewed divisions of labour.
7. Innovations that enable a given enterprise to produce commodities below the socially necessary labour time typical for such commodities and/or to keep realization costs below average will produce surplus profits until these innovations become generalized and thereby redefine 'social necessity'. In this sense, capitalist competition revolves around the average rate of profit.
8. These laws and tendencies include: (1) the growing concentration of capital, that is, the accumulation of capitalist assets by single firms through reinvestment of past profits; (2) the increased importance of productivity gains as opposed to longer working hours and greater effort in the creation of surplus; (3) the increasing urgency of overcoming the obstacles to capitalist expansion rooted in the tendency of the rate of profit to fall – which emerges in so far as all enterprises seek a competitive edge by substituting labour-saving machinery for the (social) wage relation even though the latter is, for Marx, the sole source of profit on the total capital advanced to buy capital goods and materials as well as labour-power; (4) the growing centralization of capital, that is, the management of assets owned by different individuals or firms by one enterprise (e.g. joint-stock companies or banks); (5) the growing separation of legal ownership and effective control of the means of production thanks to joint-stock companies and related forms of business organization; (6) the growing importance of credit in the functioning of the capitalist system; and so forth (on Marx's laws, see Duménil 1978).
9. Labour power as a fictitious commodity is not produced as an exchange-value; in addition, its use-value in capitalism is its capacity to produce exchange-value.
10. The same principle applies where money circulates within plurinational spaces, such as formal or informal empires, dominated by one state.

11. As we have argued elsewhere, it is impossible for the state to function as if it were an ideal collective capitalist because of the institutional separation of the economic and the political, the opacity of the interests of capital in general, the efforts of particular capitals to instrumentalize the state in their own (perceived) interests, and the fact that state power is overdetermined by the shifting balance of class (and other) forces (see Jessop 1982, 1990, 2002, 2007; and Jessop and Sum 2006).

7. A cultural political economy of competitiveness and the knowledge-based economy

The previous chapter focused on the economic and political imaginaries and the institutional and spatio-temporal fixes characteristic of Atlantic Fordism *en régulation* and how these were undermined by their 'constitutive outsides'. In other words, it focused on some imaginaries and structures that happened to have been selected and retained. It did not examine the initial variation in imaginaries oriented to post-war reconstruction nor, again, the transition period with its structural crises. This chapter switches perspective to consider the search for a plausible economic imaginary during the crisis in/of Atlantic Fordism and identifies the knowledge-based economy (KBE) as the imaginary that was eventually selected and translated into policies. However, illustrating the importance of retention too, it suggests that the KBE was not always retained and institutionalized as the basis for a stable post-Fordist accumulation regime. Instead, for economies undertaking a neoliberal regime shift, it was finance-dominated accumulation that came to prevail – even though no widely accepted economic imaginary explicitly advocated this. Thus, in contrast to our presentation of the institutional and spatio-temporal fixes associated with Atlantic Fordism in Chapter 6, here we engage in a more speculative thought-experiment to divine what a KBE *en régulation* might be like. While this does not exist at a national, let alone quasi-continental (e.g. European) level, it is partially instantiated at a local or regional level and in certain forms of cross-regional economic spaces. After exploring the rise of the KBE imaginary in general terms, we consider intellectual property rights as one of its new (or newly valorized) social forms. This will demonstrate the structural coupling and co-evolution of semiosis and structuration at the level of orders of discourse and social forms.

What is especially interesting here is the 'disconnect' between the emergent hegemony of the KBE imaginary and the steady development of finance-dominated accumulation. We address the latter regime in comparable terms in Chapter 11. Thus a key challenge to CPE is to explain (or else deparadoxify) the contrast between (1) the selection of the KBE imaginary over other available post-Fordist scenarios in the 1990s as the basis of meso- and macro-economic and political strategies, actively promoted by the OECD (and equivalent bodies), and adopted at many sites and scales around the world; and (2) the increasing weight of finance-dominated accumulation in differential accumulation on a global scale such that crises in this mode of growth have destabilized and disrupted the KBE strategy.

It is precisely here that the always-problematic articulation between semiosis and structuration can be illuminated from a CPE perspective thanks not only to the available tools for critical semiotic analysis but also to the availability of a rich set of concepts for exploring the capital relation and its contradictions. Thus, in developing our analysis, we draw heavily on the *semiotic* arguments of CPE in discussing hegemonic economic imaginaries and their role in orienting economic, political and socio-cultural strategies, especially since the mid-1970s. We also refer to the changing dynamic of competition and competitiveness, and the changing articulation of the economic and extra-economic conditions that sustain competitiveness in the world market. For it is in this context that the KBE imaginary was especially resonant. Finally, we use key concepts from historical materialism, including proto-concepts versus comprehensive concepts of control, the distinction between profit-producing and interest-bearing capital, the contradictions in the capital relation (notably in this regard in the money form, including the distinction between money as money and money as capital, and in knowledge as intellectual commons and intellectual property), the sedimentation of a neoliberal economic, political and social imaginary (which creates a space in which finance-dominated accumulation can expand, even without being associated with a hegemonic imaginary), and the ecological dominance in the world market of neoliberalism.

The chapter is structured as follows. First, we introduce the topic of competition, competitiveness and the world market. It might have been more appropriate to discuss this earlier but one cannot present everything at once or hyperlink arguments in a printed text. In addition, the competitiveness imaginary is particularly relevant to the envisioning of the KBE considered in this chapter. Competition and competitiveness are foundational features of the capitalist mode of production and its expansion (see Chapter 6) and, importantly from a CPE perspective, are associated with different visions on the nature and mechanisms of competition and on strategies to win competitive advantage. Second, we consider some of the meta-narratives that circulated during the crisis of Fordism to explain that crisis, highlighting especially the appeal of the narratives of globalization, competitiveness and the KBE. In this context, we explore how the KBE narrative was translated into three successive economic imaginaries – national systems of innovation, the learning economy, and the KBE – and why the last of these was selected as a leading theoretical paradigm and as the basis of an economic policy paradigm. Indeed, whether or not the KBE provides the most adequate description of current trends in contemporary economic development, the 'KBE discourse' became a powerful economic imaginary in the 1990s and early 2000s and, as such, has been influential in shaping policy paradigms, strategies and policies in and across many different fields of social practice. We also ask about the KBE vision: its origins, selection and gradual hegemonic stabilization; and about its translation into and/or articulation with other discourses. Third, we present an account of the KBE *en régulation* and explore its implications for two representative issues: the expansion of intellectual property rights as a contradictory social form closely articulated to the KBE accumulation regime and mode of growth; and, in the same context, the restructuring of education, vocational training and higher education. We end with general comments on the variation, selection, retention and institutionalization of economic imaginaries. A full account of the paradox that we noted above must await Chapter 11, when we consider finance-dominated accumulation.

COMPETITION, COMPETITIVENESS AND THE WORLD MARKET

Competition is a general feature of social life – but it is not its most important feature, it has many different forms connected with different principles of societalization, and it should certainly not be esteemed above all other features of the social world. It acquires several distinct forms in the capitalist mode of production, which is based on the generalization of the commodity form to labour power, making labour power into a 'fictitious commodity' (like land, money and, more recently, knowledge) (cf. Marx 1967a; Polanyi 1957; Jessop 2007a; see also Chapters 1 and 6). The resulting extension of property rights, contracts and markets to include the sale and purchase of labour power leads to distinct laws (in the descriptive–sociological sense rather than the normative–legal sense) of competition that distinguish capitalism from other modes of production. In this regard, to pre-empt misunderstanding, we do not adhere to the 'labour theory of value' (which assumes that labour power is a commodity like any other and that its value is determined by the value of the commodities that are 'required' to reproduce it). But we do subscribe to the 'value theory of labour', that is, the view that the specific dynamic of capital accumulation derives from the treatment of labour power as if it were a commodity (cf. Elson 1979; see also Chapter 6).

Competition is the external expression of the internal drive of capital *as capital* to expand, to produce surplus value, and realize it in the form of profit. Competition realizes the contingent necessities of the differential accumulation of particular enterprises, clusters or sectors and the differential growth of particular economic spaces. Competition takes many forms and plays out in many ways. It is not confined to any particular type of economic activities although, in today's neoliberal, financialized world, financial innovation and competition are especially significant.

The ultimate horizon of competition and differential accumulation is the world market, but the world market is not a constant. It changes not only through the anarchic effects of market-mediated competition (and the crises that this periodically produces), but also through competing hierarchical or heterarchic efforts to redesign its rules and institutional architecture, and to govern the conduct of the economic (and extra-economic) forces with stakes in the competitive game. As Marx often noted, world market integration tends to universalize competition and, in so doing, to generalize and intensify the contradictions of capital accumulation on a world scale. Globalization is a recent catchphrase for this process, with important ideological effects. It is an obfuscating description for a new form of imperialism that depends less on territorial conquest and enclosure within military, commercial or other barriers than on the capacity to dominate the division of labour, commodity chains and financial flows on a world scale. The key stake here is competition among transnational companies to achieve the most profitable organization of the global division of labour across different scales and sites. This continually rebases the modalities of competition and reinforces its treadmill effects for all market actors.

Competition occurs on a stratified terrain rather than a level playing field. As the modes of this stratification alter, so do the patterns and dynamics of competition. Changes can occur in the weight of different markets (mainly financial, industrial, commercial and intellectual) in setting the parameters of competition, in the relative super- and subordination of different forms of competition, and in the corporate forms assumed by competition-setters in different markets (Jessop 2002). The dominant competitive forces are those that set the terms of competition in the most important market. We consider the implications of this for finance-dominated accumulation in Chapter 11. Recall here that economic competition includes 'extra-economic' factors, forces and capacities, and this is increasingly seen in the KBE. Lastly, the state's capacity to promote competitiveness depends on its ability to adapt relevant strategies to the role of its local, regional, cross-border, national or multi-national economic spaces and their key economic actors in the changing hierarchies of competition in the world market.

From a CPE perspective, of course, the economy has both semiotic (discursive) and extra-semiotic (material) aspects, which coexist and influence each other. Considered as the sum of all economic activities, the economy is too complex to be fully grasped in real time by economic actors or external observers (see Chapters 2, 4 and 6). This is implied in the very notion of an 'invisible hand'. Different entry-points and standpoints lead to different economic imaginaries that identify different subsets of economic actions and relations as objects of observation, calculation, regulation, governance or transformation. While all social agents (individuals, groups, organizations, movements etc.) are forced to engage in such simplifications as a condition of 'going on', not all simplifications are created equal. There is wide variation in economic imaginaries. This poses the question of the performative force of economic imaginaries in shaping economic orders and the manner of their embedding in wider ensembles of social relations (or social formations), that is, that they may involve not only construal but also construction. It also highlights the need to explore the discursive and material factors and forces that shape the selection and retention of hegemonic, sub-hegemonic, counter-hegemonic, or marginal accounts of the economy, its dynamic and its conditions of existence. Each imaginary depicts the economic world in its own way (albeit with scope for overlap, articulation and hybridization), and those that become hegemonic or sub-hegemonic help to shape economic orders and embed them in wider ensembles of social relations. Marginal and counter-hegemonic imaginaries also affect economic conduct and, in some circumstances, may shape accumulation regimes, modes of regulation and modes of material provisioning.

Viewed in these terms, competition is both a real process that 'works behind the backs of the producers' (and other economic actors) through the metaphorical 'invisible hand of the market' (and other processes that bear on the outcome of competition) and a simplifying reference point for orienting economic action that can never fully grasp all the factors that shape the competitive process and its outcomes. This distinction is one way to make sense of the simultaneity of the 'invisible hand' metaphor and the recurrent efforts of social actors to shape the ways in which markets operate and to enhance their chances of success in competition. The factors, actors and forces relevant to economic competition and economic competitiveness are essentially contested, inherently relational, and often politically controversial notions. There are many ways to define competition, many modalities and many sites of competition. We illustrate these claims below for both theoretical and policy paradigms.

Definitions and discourses of competition and competitiveness date back centuries and are linked to different economic imaginaries at different times and in different contexts. They are also liable to change. Thus mercantilist notions from the seventeenth century tied to state policies to control trade and increase financial reserves can be contrasted with 1890s imperialism oriented to state enclosure of territory for military–political as well as geo-economic goals (see Reinert 1995; ten Brink 2007). During the mercantilist period, for example, economics was regarded strongly as a matter of political calculation because it concerned state policies to control trade in order to increase financial reserves and because the economy was not yet seen (rightly or wrongly) as a distinct system with its own economic logic (Magnusson 1994). Following the transition from classical imperialism to a more liberal post-war order (in the shadow of US hegemony), competition focused more on domestic growth and multi-national foreign investment, leading to conflicts between techno-nationalism and techno-globalism (Ostry and Nelson 1995; Ruggie 1982). And, with the rise of the neoliberal trans-national financial order and the theoretical and policy interest in the globalizing KBE, competition has refocused on innovation (including in finance and securitization) and how best to link extra-economic factors to the 'demands' of economic competition (Cho and Moon 2000).These shifts are reflected in part in a well-known periodization proposed by Michael Porter (1990), who initially distinguished four stages in the development of competition among nations, and then generalized this to competition among cities, regions, inner cities and regional blocs. These stages are factor-driven competition (based on static comparative advantage); investment-driven competition (based on dynamic allocative advantage); innovation-led competition (based on Schumpeterian entrepreneurship leading to creative destruction); and wealth-driven competition (based on the legacies and prestige of past success, e.g. in luxury goods, art markets, consultancy) (Porter 1990; and Chapter 8).

Given these complexities, it is hardly surprising that economists disagree about the relevant units of competition. Some argue that only owners of economic resources (such as firms, banks, workers and households) compete and that it is mistaken to treat cities, regions, nations or supranational blocs (such as the European Union) as units of competition (e.g. Krugman 1994a). Others argue that these entities can, indeed, compete and that the outcomes of such competition can be measured (e.g. Porter 1990). Yet it is unclear whether this is literally true, metaphorically plausible or merely rhetorically useful – each interpretation having different implications for how to define competition, understand competitive strategies and evaluate success. Overall, while the critics are right that 'economies' (as imaginatively construed subsets of all economic activities) are not real subjects capable of more or less strategic economic action, they err in so far as real agents do identify 'economies' (construed at different scales and in different ways) as engaged in competition, consider that their material and/or ideal interests may be affected as a result, and act on this perception in a more or less concerted manner. This can occur for political or military as well as economic reasons, and is reflected in the rise of 'competition states' at different scales of political organization. A competition state seeks to secure economic growth within its borders and/or to secure competitive advantages for capitals based in its borders, even where these capitals operate abroad, by promoting the economic and extra-economic conditions that are currently deemed vital for success in economic competition with economic actors and spaces located in other states (cf. Cerny 1990; Jessop 2002; Hirsch 1995).

The idea of 'competitiveness' is conceptually ambiguous, politically controversial and ideologically charged. Essentially it comprises the key set of resources and abilities that underpin competition. It refers to the capacity to engage in competition and prevail in the struggle over differential accumulation – whether or not this capacity is fully realized is, as critical realism suggests, another, contingent matter. As such, competitiveness varies with the forms and modalities of competition. There are many ways to define and measure it, and past and current legal and policy debates over its nature indicate the political issues that are at stake. Key indicators in the post-war period include factor endowments; unit labour costs; productivity increases; relative prices, costs and exchange rates; labour market flexibility; shares in world exports or ratios of foreign penetration of home markets; ready access to cheap capital; and ease of setting up new businesses. Given these concerns, real subjects may try to enhance macro-economic competitiveness either because of its perceived impact on the overall competitiveness of individual firms operating in a given national economic space or because of how it affects other objectives – economic (e.g. trade balance, employment, inflation) or non-economic (e.g. electoral consequences or military capacities). When this occurs, it indicates the transition from the study of competition and competitiveness from the viewpoint of rival theoretical paradigms to the design of policies and strategies to promote competition (because of faith in the benefits and virtues of market forces) and/or to enhance the competitiveness of specific economic agents, related stakeholders and sites of such competition. This marks the shift from theoretical paradigm to policy paradigm for economic imaginaries and discourses concerned with competition and competitiveness. A further stage occurs with the transformation of these paradigms into knowledge brands (see Chapters 8 and 10).

Once deemed relevant, macro-economic competitiveness can be targeted for action. But the definition of competitiveness, the target variables and the strategies adopted are all discursively constituted and will vary from case to case. In so far as that competition is mediated through market forces, it will depend on the struggle to increase efficiency. But in other cases, extra-economic factors – such as tariff and non-tariff barriers to trade, or access to state subsidies – can prove crucial. This extends economic competition to a virtual competition among entire societal regimes mediated through the audit of the world market and increases pressures to (develop the capacity to) valorize a wide range of extra-economic institutions and relations. Examples include social capital, trust, collective learning capacities, institutional thickness, untraded interdependencies, and local amenities and culture. Likewise, discourses and strategies of structural or systemic competitiveness now emphasize not only firm-level and sectoral-level factors, but also the role of an extended range of the social and extra-economic institutional contexts and socio-cultural conditions in which economic actors also 'compete' (cf. Deyo 2013). Overall, this involves redrawing the boundaries between the economic and the extra-economic such that more of the latter are drawn directly into the process of the valorization of capital.

Thus, rather than living in an increasingly 'flat world' (Friedman 2005; Augustine 2007) in which all factors of production for goods and services are mobile and respond readily and quickly to changing market conditions, the competitive 'playing field' is better described as striated and even 'spiky' (on the latter, see Florida 2005). It involves an uneven terrain with uneven flows, differential frictions and unevenly distributed capacities to enhance local, regional or national competitive advantages. New forms of 'stickiness' are thereby created in the competition for skilled labour, investment and innovation. In these conditions territorial planning, place-building (or at least place-marketing), developing institutionally thick local or regional networks, and connecting different scales of economic, political and social organization are important factors in taking the 'high road' to competitiveness rather than engaging in a 'race to the bottom'. Education institutions often become important factors in these strategies (for a recent study of problems of competitiveness in the USA and the need to build coherent ecosystems of innovation, see Augustine 2007).

INTERLUDE: NARRATIVES

Three powerful economic narratives during the past 30–40 years have been 'globalization', 'competitiveness' and the rise of the KBE. Their appeal has persisted despite obvious problems with each. These include the material, political and cultural limits to economic globalization, especially in its dominant neoliberal form, as revealed most recently in global contagion; the dismissal of competitiveness as a 'dangerous obsession' and the treadmill compulsion to run ever faster to stay in the same place; and the turn in liberal market economies towards finance-dominated accumulation and the latter's role in the North Atlantic financial crisis and the subsequent Great Recession.

The first two narratives are closely linked. Thus the emerging geo-economic meta-narrative concerning 'globalization' is being translated into pressures to prioritize policies to boost 'competitiveness' on various territorial scales. This meta-narrative has been linked to other narratives that were persuasively (but not necessarily intentionally) combined to consolidate a limited but widely accepted set of diagnoses and prescriptions for the economic and political difficulties confronting nations, regions and cities and their various economic branches in the 1980s and 1990s. Significant discourses included the enterprise culture, enterprise society, innovative milieux, networks, strategic alliances, partnerships, governance and so forth. A second major set of meta-narratives was more geo-political in character and concerned the end of the cold war, the collapse of communism and the economic threats to national survival from East Asia.

These and other stories combined to reinforce the claim that the national state's borders had been undermined, thereby rendering it anachronistic, and that all national economies had become subject to greatly intensified global competition that is hard to evade, thereby exerting downward pressure on 'unproductive' public expenditure and prompting either a 'race to the bottom' and/or efforts to climb the hierarchy of competitive nations by investing in the KBE. The prime goals of post-war economic policy (full employment, stable prices, economic growth and a sustainable balance of payments) could no longer be delivered in and through the national state. This in turn undermines the national state's capacity to deliver redistributive social welfare and limit the degree of social exclusion. In this sense, the post-war economic and political regime has failed and, if economic forces are to escape the consequences, it is essential to modify economic strategies, economic institutions, modes of governance and the form of state. These must be redesigned to prioritize 'wealth creation' in the face of international, interregional and intraregional competition since this is the prior condition of continued social redistribution and welfare. Such narratives lead, *inter alia*, to the discovery of triad regions, the 'region state', the 'trans-national territory', 'entrepreneurial cities' and so forth, as new phenomena and their naturalization on practical, if not normative, grounds.

Another master narrative, which shapes economic strategies, state projects and societal visions, is the KBE. It is closely linked to other notions or visions, like the information economy, learning economy, creative economy and information society. Indeed, official economic strategies – from towns, cities and regions through national states and supranational bodies like the European Union to more encompassing international agencies and global regimes – have increasingly posited the rise of the KBE on a global scale, its centrality to future growth at all scales, and its critical role in long-term competitive advantage and sustained prosperity for new and old industries and services. This has been emphasized even more in the wake of the North Atlantic financial crisis and the Great Recession, with the promotion of knowledge-based, design-intensive or otherwise creative industries and services as the route to growth and full employment (see Chapter 11).

In significant respects, of course, every economy is a knowledge economy, but not all economies have been so described and governed, let alone find themselves so labelled by their most prominent spokespersons as one of their most significant contemporary self-descriptions (on the polyvocal nature of self-descriptions of society, see Luhmann 1987, 1995). Many prominent and competent observers have nonetheless adopted this term during the period of restructuring following the crisis of the Atlantic Fordist accumulation regime from the mid-1990s onwards; in addition, policy-makers around the world used it to guide economic and social strategies (a foundational document is OECD 1996). It has gained influence in part because it is promoted by three powerful international organizations: the OECD, the World Bank and the European Union. Respectively, these bodies have led the way in articulating the concept of the KBE and constructing databases to compare and rank progress towards the KBE nirvana; advocated policies of 'Knowledge for Development' as the best route to economic progress in 'developing economies'; and committed the EU to becoming the most competitive KBE in the world by 2010 without, however, being able to deliver on this ambition. States at local, regional, national and other levels have been accorded a key role in each of these three cases in implementing the structural changes and wide-ranging policies needed to promote an innovative, entrepreneurial and competitive KBE. Many other international organizations as well as regional blocs in the semi-periphery and periphery have jumped on the KBE bandwagon. These include the Arab League, ASEAN (Association of South East Asian Nations), Asia Pacific Economic Cooperation (especially through its Economic Committee), the Asian Development Bank, the IMF (International Monetary Fund), NAFTA (North American Free Trade Agreement), the United Nations in its various organizational guises

(UNCTAD, UNESCO, UNECE, CEPAL etc.), the Viségrad Four, the WTO (World Trade Organization) and the World Intellectual Property Organization.

THEORETICAL AND POLICY PARADIGMS

To address these interrelated issues we draw on the concept of economic imaginaries. Nonetheless, discussion of the KBE as an economic imaginary and/or economic reality is complicated by two theoretical and practical issues. First, different disciplines draw on different theoretical paradigms to discuss it. This is reflected, for example, in the contrasting concepts of knowledge economy and knowledge society, which draw respectively on economics and sociology. Each of these two concepts is associated with a broader set of cognate concepts that produce distinctive types of imaginary, each with its own semantics. The former considers knowledge in terms of factors of production, intellectual property, the skills-based economy, national systems of innovation, the knowledge base, the knowledge-driven economy, knowledge management, knowledge transfer, the learning economy, the learning organization, the learning region and so on. The latter sees knowledge as a collective social resource, the intellectual commons, the division of manual and mental labour, technical and organic intellectuals, the information society, post-industrial society, life-long learning, the learning society and so on (cf. Jessop 2002, 2007a; and, for a general survey that contains 57 definitions of knowledge economy, knowledge-based economy, knowledge society and cognate terms, see Carlaw et al. 2006). This distinction is, of course, a reflection at the level of the economic imaginary of the contradictory unity, in capitalist social formations, of knowledge as a fictitious commodity, such that is both an intellectual commons and, as intellectual property, a source of rents (see Jessop 2007a; Chapter 6 and below).

Second, cross-cutting the distinction between knowledge economy and knowledge society is that between theoretical and policy paradigms. Dollery and Wallis differentiate them as follows:

> [p]olicy paradigms derive from theoretical paradigms but possess much less sophisticated and rigorous evaluations of the intellectual underpinnings of their conceptual frameworks. In essence, policy advisers differentiate policy paradigms from theoretical paradigms by screening out the ambiguities and blurring the fine distinctions characteristic of theoretical paradigms. In a Lakatosian sense, policy paradigms can be likened to the positive heuristics surrounding theoretical paradigms. Accordingly, shifts between policy paradigms will be discontinuous, follow theoretical paradigm shifts, but occur more

frequently than theoretical paradigms since they do not require fundamental changes in a negative heuristic.[1] (1999: 5)

That this distinction is recognized by people situated at the interface of the academic and policy worlds is evident from the complaint of a key independent scholar and OECD policy adviser, Bengt-Åke Lundvall, lamenting, in relation to his concept of 'national innovation system, 'how it has "degenerated", how it has been "abused" and "distorted" while travelling from the academic to the policy world, compared with the connotations he originally intended for it' (2006: 2, 10, 14; as cited by Eklund 2007: 17).

This distinction (and its conflation) helps us to situate and understand the then-explosive interest in the KBE. For this theme is not just a matter of theoretical and empirical curiosity for disinterested observers, but is being actively translated into a wide range of policies and this, in turn, affects the ways in which the contemporary economy is described, examined and explained. Indeed, as Godin (2006) shows, the concept of the KBE, as developed above all by the OECD, has suggested that

> [t]he concept of a knowledge-based economy is simply [one] that serves to direct the attention of policy-makers to science and technology issues and to their role in the economy and, to this end, a concept that allows one to talk about any issue of science and technology and generate a large set of statistics under one roof. This kind of concept I will call an umbrella concept. A related, but less controversial, thesis . . . is that the (resurgence of the) concept of a knowledge-based economy in the 1990s owes a large debt to the OECD – and to the consultants it supported . . . [Indeed,] viewing the OECD as a think-tank is the key to understanding the popularity of the concept among member countries. (2006: 17–18)

Reijo Miettinen (2002) and Magnus Eklund (2007) offer similar remarks on how ideas and arguments transfer between theoretical and policy paradigms. This reinforces the need to distinguish them in order to avoid misunderstandings about the nature and role of discourses about the KBE. Indeed, in the absence of this distinction, two complementary fallacies can arise. The first is that the theoretical status of the concept of the KBE, when viewed largely from the perspective of the ideas that inform the policy paradigm, will be dismissed on the grounds that it is merely a political concept or, worse still, an essentially incoherent buzzword (cf. Godin 2006). The second is that, when assessed with the analytical rigour appropriate to a scientific concept, the policies proposed to promote the KBE will be dismissed as inconsistent efforts at 'muddling through' and as bound to fail on these grounds alone. What gets missed here is the constitutive or performative force of the policy paradigm in helping to shape the emergence, provisional stabilization and eventual consolidation (if any) of the KBE as an actually existing phenomenon. This confirms the overall importance of the potential disjunction, mutual influence and, indeed, interpenetration of theoretical and policy paradigms – a topic that is particularly suited to a CPE analysis.

The significance of this distinction is noted by Michael Peters, a critical education scholar, who, remarking that concepts have histories and family resemblances, argues that this also applies to the 'knowledge society' and 'knowledge economy':

> These twin concepts while displaying similar characteristics – among them the attempt to describe society or economy in terms of a dominant axial principle from which other societal or economic trends can be inferred – belong to different disciplines and discourses. To all intents and purposes these are separate and parallel discourses that are not cross-threading – in each case the trajectories of the disciplines seem to be powered by their own problematics, by the set of problems thrown up by the discipline rather than any external pressures, and they seem particularly impervious to radical cross-disciplinary borrowing or analysis. Where they do come together is in the area of policy, in policy studies, in actual policies or policy discourse, where the master concepts borrowed from the sociology and economics of knowledge have come to help shape and define policy templates for economic and social development and wellbeing. At the level of policy the same demands for theoretical consistency or disciplinary rigor or internal consistency do not seem to operate; rather the easy dualism of the knowledge society and the knowledge economy is embraced without difficulty or contradiction. While there is, of course, some analysis of trends and even the collection of relevant data, these twin concepts are empirically underdetermined. They operate more like performative ideologies with constitutive effects at the level of public policy. And there are a whole series of self-legitimating sibling concepts spawned by policy analysts and think-tanks that now roll off the tongue of any sociology undergraduate: 'information society', 'learning society', 'information economy', and, more recently, 'learning economy'. (Peters 2007: 17)

Three interrelated conclusions follow from this discussion. First, having accepted the *prima facie* usefulness of the distinction between the two types of paradigm, one should not conflate them or reduce one to the other but explore their changing articulation in different contexts. Second, one must resist the temptation to derive immediate policy lessons from theoretical paradigms and/or to subject policy paradigms to a purely theoretical critique. Third, from a CPE perspective, the distinction poses interesting questions about (1) the relative hegemony or dominance of different paradigms (or, as we call them here, imaginaries); (2) the discursive and material factors and forces that introduce variation, shape the selection, and consolidate the retention of hegemonic, sub-hegemonic, counter-hegemonic or marginal accounts of the economy, its dynamic and its conditions of existence; and (3) the performative force of economic imaginaries in shaping the actually existing economic realm. These issues affect the changing discursive and material boundaries of the economic and extra-economic, and their implications for economic performance. This could be reflected in changes in the scope, scale and relative primacy of different policy fields. This is significant, as we will see, for the role of education, knowledge creation and knowledge transfer to competitiveness.

A fourth conclusion could be added if we consider how knowledge can circulate as a knowledge brand in the academy, policy networks and consultancy circles. Knowledge brands play a key role in fast policy transfer at multiple sites and scales in the world market, and in the world education system and world society more generally (cf. Peck 2010). We explore their recontextualization and circulation in Chapters 8 and 10. We now present four brief cases studies drawn from East Asian and Western experience to illustrate the points about theoretical and policy paradigms and their changing articulation.

FOUR EXAMPLES

Our first case is the idea of the information economy in Japan in the 1960s–1970s as a scientific paradigm and tool for scenario planning related to neo-mercantilist catch-up competitiveness. The second is the growing sensitivity of US policy-makers and stakeholders to innovation and knowledge as strategic assets. Third is the 'national system of innovation', which was the precursor of the KBE as the dominant economic imaginary in the OECD, and was transferred as a theoretical and policy paradigm to member states and other economies. Its significance here is that, although 'the OECD always looked for conceptual frameworks to catch the attention of policy-makers' (Godin 2006: 18), the national system of innovation failed on this score. Case four is the knowledge(-based) economy, which had more hegemonic potential and has seen a revival in the wake of the North Atlantic financial crisis, in part through its articulation to another economic imaginary, the Green New Deal.

The Information Economy

The idea of the 'information economy' as a distinct stage in economic development may have emerged first in Japan. The term was introduced there by Tadeo Umesao in the 1960s but did not really take off until the late 1970s, by which time 'information economy' and analogous ideas had also been firmly established elsewhere in East Asia and in many advanced

Western capitalist societies (cf. Dordick and Wang 1993; Masuda 1981; May 2002). The use of such terms was based largely on the *speculative extrapolation* of contemporary trends into the future, focusing on trends in the most advanced national economies as if other economies would simply follow their path with a greater or lesser time lag. So we find references to the information economy, post-industrial economy, knowledge economy and so forth (for a comprehensive list of 75 such terms, which were introduced at various times from 1950 to 1984, see Beniger 1986; cf. Carlaw et al. 2006). In turn the first wave of information economy strategies was mainly focused on investment in information and communication technologies (ICTs) rather than the move to a knowledge-driven or knowledge-based economy. Typical of these was the American National Information Infrastructure programme launched in 1991, which was rapidly followed by many Western European economies and the European Union.

A broader notion of information economy developed in Japan and other East Asian economies. This was linked to the exhaustion of export-led growth based on catch-up dynamics, which prompted various intellectuals, think tanks, business leaders and policy-makers[2] to search for new bases for competition. The solution was not only to invest in ICTs but also to upgrade to an innovative, information-based economy; in later discourses and strategies, this idea was expanded to the more encompassing notion of the knowledge economy. The first explicit information economy and/or KBE strategies in East Asia were the 'Intelligent Island' strategy (1991) in Singapore, and Malaysia's '2020 Vision' (1991). Other East Asian countries followed, including Japan's High Performance National Information Infrastructure (NII) Plan (1994), Taiwan's NII 2005 (1994), South Korea's NII 2003 (1994), Vietnam's IT 2000 plan (1995), and Smart Philippines (2000). Despite the similar timing in East and West, Asian models and strategies tended to be more comprehensive, going beyond ICTs to broader economic and, even more importantly, extra-economic dimensions of innovation-led growth (for an outline of information economy strategies in the 1990s, see Ducatel et al. 2000). The overriding conclusion to be drawn from this period, however, is the key role of economic narratives and linked imaginaries in identifying turning points and/or crises and reorienting technology, industrial and wider-ranging economic policies.

From Industrial Competitiveness to Knowledge-based Economy

From almost as soon as it became the undisputed hegemonic power in the capitalist world following the Second World War, the USA has experienced agitated and ongoing debates about its alleged lack of economic competitiveness. These have coexisted with equally angst-ridden concerns about threats to its national military security, whether from the Soviet bloc, China or, most recently, asymmetric warfare waged by terrorist networks (on the role of these twin myths in legitimating government support for industry in a regime officially opposed to 'socialistic' or 'communistic' state intervention in the market economy, see Belabes 1999). Worries about competitiveness prompted Congress to establish in 1978 the Office of Technology Assessment to monitor the competitiveness of American industries. Its remit covered industry and market structures, the nature of workforces, availability of materials and components, supporting infrastructures, the environment for innovation and technology diffusion, business and economic conditions, government policies and interactions with the private sector, and international trade relations. In 1983, in response to the perceived threat of 'Japan as Number One' and other indicators of technological, industrial and financial decline, President Reagan set up the President's Commission on Industrial Competitiveness. Two key outcomes were the Young Report (President's Commission 1986; see also Young 1988) and a 'Council on Competitiveness' to act as a national 'forum for elevating national competitiveness to the forefront of national consciousness' (Council on Competitiveness 2007). Commissions have continued to report regularly since 1983, with recent documents including the Palmisano Report 2005 and Council on Competitiveness 2007, 2009, 2012. The Council is also very active, focusing on national innovation and identifying the importance of action to promote this in three main fields: talent, investment and infrastructure.

Regarding talent, the focus is on education and training to enable 'talented people' to acquire 'cutting-edge skills' so that they can create 'new ideas and innovative technologies' and 'keep the economy strong and growing stronger'. A particular concern has been lack of competitiveness in 'such critical fields as science, engineering, math and technical skills' and hence on measures to build 'a world-class workforce by initiating programs to encourage diversity in the S&E [i.e. science and engineering] pipelines and excellence in math and science education in America's schools at all levels' (Council on Competitiveness 2001). This in turn is reflected in a whole series of policy recommendations concerning the reorganization of grade-school education, further and higher education, and lifelong learning (see below). In addition, at all levels from NAFTA down through the federal state, regional blocs of states, states, metropolitan regions, and cities to towns and neighbourhoods, we find concerted efforts to promote competitiveness in these and other areas.

National System of Innovation

'National system of innovation' (sometimes known as the 'national innovation system' and also referred to below as NSI) is a paradigm that is actively promoted internationally by, even if it did not originate in, the OECD (cf. Albert and Laberge 2007; Eklund 2007; Freeman 1995). Established as part of the post-war international regime of embedded liberalism, the OECD identified problems in the late 1960s and early 1970s around the declining economic performance of advanced capitalist economies and the best ways to insert emerging economies into the world market. Its initial response to the unfolding economic crisis was to call for greater flexibility compared to the rigidities of an Atlantic Fordism based on mass production and mass consumption, big business, powerful unions and big government; it then called for greater structural and/or systemic competitiveness[3] in terms of extra-economic as well as economic institutional arrangements (although this was framed primarily within the old economic imaginary); it shifted again, this time to recommendations about how to improve national systems of innovation (the start of a shift towards the KBE), to subsequent calls for a learning economy (an even stronger shift in this direction), and, finally, to measures to effect the transition to the KBE as the next stage in capitalist development. The NSI refers to the flow of technology and information among people, enterprises and institutions that is held to be central to continuing innovation on the national level. The concept emphasizes the contribution of a complex web of relations among private, public and third-sector actors in the NSI, including enterprises, universities and government research institutes at national, regional and local level that contribute to the production and, even more importantly, diffusion of new technologies and the wider knowledge base that supports their adoption in economically useful ways (cf. Freeman 1995; Lundvall 1992; Nelson 1992; OECD 1997). It has been closely linked in the work of the OECD with the concepts of learning economy and learning region (Foray and Lundvall 1996; Lundvall 1992; Lundvall and Johnson 1994; Maillat and Kebir 1999).

In a study of Finland in the OECD context but with broader implications, Reijo Miettinen (2002) has explored NSI as a metaphor performing several rhetorical functions. He argues that it simplifies, persuades and reorients thinking about the interrelationships of science and society; it incorporates tacit value schemes and promotes a vision; helps forge consensus; mobilizes various actors in particular ways; and it contributes to the shaping of events prescribed by the NSI model. He adds that these functions can be performed in part because the NSI is so loosely defined, allowing different actors to impute different meanings to it. Further, the associated vision of boosting national economic competitiveness often resonates with broader political trends in society.

After presenting the Finnish case, Miettinen develops an 'epistemology of transdiscursive terms', that is, terms with significant rhetorical functions that flourish at the interface of science, public discourse and politics, and thereby provide the basis for textual interlacing and circulation of self-referentiality. In the language deployed above, these are terms that have a key bridging role in linking theoretical and policy paradigms, facilitating the translation between them but also disguising important differences in their form and function. In particular, he identifies six key functions that they perform (see Box 7.1).

Miettinen argues that trans-discursive terms must be loose to provide the interpretative flexibility needed to accommodate different interests expressed by actors across different domains, such as government,

---

BOX 7.1 SIX SOCIAL–EPISTEMIC FUNCTIONS OF TRANS-DISCURSIVE TERMS

- They must have a minimal traditional epistemic function in the sense of providing a representation or empirically anchored account of aspects of reality.
- They serve as epistemic organizers, synthesizing earlier accounts and providing a new angle on things. Suitable terms and metaphors are used in organizing one's perspective, integrating various themes that formerly were separated. They provide a sense of interconnection or holism.
- They supply a worldview or a diagnosis of an era, a function that is also central to the integrative power of the conceptual framework.
- They serve as boundary-crossers by engaging various social groups and institutions in shared discussion. That is why they are called trans-discursive (they cross between and link different discourses).
- They serve ideological and consensus-creating (or vision-carrying) functions.
- They help mobilize and empower a multiplicity of actors under what the participants themselves come to perceive as a common banner.

Source: Adapted and expanded from Miettinen (2002: 137).

university and industry. The credibility of a term will in part depend on linkages with scientific communities because political viability derives from the semblance of scientific credibility. It follows that the tension between the epistemic reality-representing function of the term and its future-oriented rhetorical and discursive organizing functions has to be contained to prevent the puncturing and consequent collapse of the metaphor. This risk is illustrated by the OECD's admission in a review paper that 'there are still concerns in the policy making community that the NIS [sic] approach has too little operational value and is difficult to implement' (OECD 2002: 11, cited in Godin 2006: 19). This failure is one factor behind the rise of the KBE as an alternative concept. Thus Dominique Foray, one of the OECD consultants behind the new term, criticized the concept of NSI for being 'neither strikingly original, nor rhetorically stirring' (David and Foray 1995: 14) and for placing too much stress on national institutions and economic growth and not enough on the distribution of knowledge.

Knowledge-based Economy

The prominence of the knowledge economy or its cognates has become a most contemporary self-description of the economy and, indeed, society. In many cases, especially early on, more weight was put on information than on knowledge. More recent uses of the terms 'knowledge economy' and 'knowledge-based economy' (plus related abbreviations and acronyms such as the K-economy and KBE) are less concerned with forecasting the future than with the *empirical description* and *quasi-prescriptive benchmarking* of central features of actually existing economies. Related theoretical paradigms seek to establish the novelty of the KBE by identifying its distinguishing features in terms of some combination of the reflexive application of knowledge to the production of knowledge, the key role of innovation, learning and knowledge transfer in economic performance, and the increasing importance of the intellectual commons and/or intellectual property rights in contemporary competition. In turn, the hegemonic policy paradigm is especially concerned to establish the reality of the KBE through the compilation and repetition of statistical indicators, through the development of benchmarks and league tables, and through the elaboration of an interwoven set of useful concepts, slogans and buzzwords. These can then be applied to generate a relatively simple set of policy prescriptions and legitimations to be applied to many sectors, many scales and many countries.

The key document was published by the OECD in 1996 under the title *The Knowledge-Based Economy*. This was followed in 1997 by guidelines for competitiveness in the form of *National Innovation Systems*. This prompted institution-building within and across the public and private sectors at many scales and in regard to many spheres bearing more or less directly on competitiveness in a KBE. Within larger firms, knowledge management became a key discipline and knowledge audits were conducted regularly to identify strategic knowledge assets (Malhotra 2000); governments established knowledge ministries, departments and agencies; national states began to map their NIS and take measures to strengthen them; standardized vocabularies were promoted to guide public and private sector debate (cf. American National Standards Institute and Global Competitiveness Council 2001). This was taken further with the production of competitiveness indexes, such as the *Global Competitiveness Report* (World Economic Forum) from 1979 onwards and the *World Competitiveness Yearbook* (published by the Institute for Management Development in Geneva from 1989 onwards.[4] This highlighted 'the softer side of competition' in a KBE, that is, the role of value-adding through the creation, management and transfer of information. There is now a global growth industry that produces multiple competitiveness rankings for countries, regions, cities and so on, each of which employs different statistical and other sources, directed at economic actors and policy-makers around the world (for discussion, see Lall 2001; Bristow 2005; Oxley et al. 2007; see also Chapter 8).

Godin has identified the leading role of the OECD in promoting the KBE as the key site of competition and key focus of competitive strategies. He explains this in terms of the OECD's efforts to respond to the inadequate rhetorical appeal of NSI and 'learning economy' by reviving and consolidating the idea of the KBE and, on this basis, identifying the importance of knowledge management and knowledge transfer. He notes above all the OECD's enrolment of the promoters of the KBE concept (e.g. Lundvall and Foray) as consultants and, even more importantly, the production of statistics to give the concept some empirical content and plausibility (Godin 2006: 19). This new approach was needed so that the OECD could influence the policy process, and Godin notes that the rhetorical appeal of the KBE concept depends on its 'easy translation of readily available academic fads into keywords (or buzzwords), then into slogans in order to catch the attention of policy-makers' (ibid.). In addition, the OECD and policy-makers in its member states are under continuing pressure to publish reports on the measures they have taken to promote, and their progress towards, a KBE.

> The OECD publishes biannual, yearly and biennial reports, among them those for ministers' conferences, where timeframes are very tight. Umbrella concepts

are very fertile for producing documents. They synthesise what is already available, what comes from day-to-day work conducted in other contexts and, above all, what is fashionable, often at the price of original work. (Godin 2006: 19, 24)

A key factor in reinforcing the ability of memorable buzzwords and slogans to sell ideas is their association with 'a plethora of figures and graphs' (Godin 2004: 684). These have a spurious scientific authority as well as intuitive persuasive force even though the OECD itself occasionally concedes that its indicators did not adequately capture the complex, dynamic nature of knowledge development and acquisition (e.g. OECD 1996). For, as Godin notes, this presentational strategy appeals to the typical OECD readership: ministers, policy-makers, journalists and the like. Thus, writing on the OECD's promotion of the idea of the 'New Economy', Godin argues that

> [t]he strategy developed at the DSTI [i.e. Directorate for Science, Technology, and Industry] to integrate productivity into its statistics and reports was threefold. First, digest all available academic work in order to imitate their methodology. Second, internationalise the (academic and national) statistics to make a convincing case for its member countries. Third, organise the discourse into a policy-oriented framework, using buzzwords. In the present case, it was new growth theories and the New Economy that were the buzzwords. But over the OECD history the latter also shared their popularity with others: high technology, national system of innovation, globalisation, knowledge-based economy, and information economy. (Godin 2004: 688)

The KBE has been promoted, selected and retained as an important economic imaginary in many economies and at many scales. It has resonated in economic spaces formerly associated with Atlantic Fordism, East Asian exportism, Latin American import substitution industrialization and, albeit less obviously, state socialism in the Soviet bloc and Mainland China. An integral part of the rise of the KBE imaginary are three shifts in the construal of the 'economy', each of which is associated with significant performative effects on economic restructuring:

- A shift from imaginaries that treat the macro-economic mainly in national terms to imaginaries oriented to multiple, interpenetrating scales of economic organization up to and including the world market.
- The expansion of the 'economic' to include an increasing array of factors and forces that were previously considered 'economically irrelevant'.
- The widening of 'extra-economic' factors and forces that are now considered 'economically relevant'.

The OECD played a key role in linking and promoting all three sets of changes so that they tend to be mutually reinforcing within the limits of a world market that is organized mainly through sovereign national states but in the shadow of neoliberalism. This organization is primarily concerned with securing an appropriate balance between competition and cooperation between developed capitalist economies in regard to the economic strategies of enterprises as well as the economic and economically relevant policies pursued by governments at different scales. At each step, the nature, scope and significance of the extra-economic as well as economic factors making for competitiveness has tended to expand. This holds not only for firms as they seek to identify an ever-widening range of sources of dynamic competitive advantage (and disadvantage) and to capitalize upon the former and eliminate the latter; but also for the economic and extra-economic policies to be pursued by policy-makers and associated stakeholders on all scales from industrial or central business districts through cities and regions to nations and supranational blocs. A key element in all areas is the promotion of entrepreneurialism and an entrepreneurial culture supported, in more recent policy paradigms, by calls for investment in social capital and for the promotion of good governance. The wide range of indicators of competitiveness that are now included in benchmarks for technological, structural, systemic and future-oriented growth competitiveness is a good index of this transformation in theoretical and policy paradigms.

Interim Conclusions

These four examples, illustrative of many other economic imaginaries, indicate that crisis construals are subject to both semiotic and material *selection*, in terms of the initial resonance among personal, organizational and meta-narratives' as well as social forces' differential capacity to access and control the key sites and media in and through which competing discourses are communicated. Resonant discourses that are also widely disseminated to key social forces and get translated into effective strategies and policies will eventually be *retained*. This involves even more important material mediation in so far as these strategies and policies must be (seen to be) effective within the spatio-temporal horizons of the social forces that matter in a given social formation. Where economic imaginaries satisfy these semiotic and material tests, they are likely to be retained in three key areas: (1) incorporation in habitus, hexis, personal identity, organizational routines, institutional rules; (2) objectification in built environment, material and intellectual technologies; and (3) continuing expression in economic strategies, state projects and hegemonic visions (see Chapters 4, 6 and 11). In general, the wider the range of sites (horizontal and vertical) where resonant discourses are retained, the greater the potential for effective institutionalization. This in turn should lead to relative structured coherence across institutional orders and modes of thought, and in relatively durable patterns of social compromise among key actors.

These examples suggest four further conclusions on the power of economic imaginaries in the emergence, selection and retention of theoretical and policy paradigms. First, in any period of economic discontinuity, many alternative economic imaginaries may be proposed, each based on a specific ensemble of economic categories linked in turn to wider vocabularies. Second, some of these economic imaginaries may be more resonant than others in a given conjuncture. This will depend in part on the ease of any interchange of theoretical and policy paradigms – reflecting the need both for scientific authority and for easy communicability to lay decision-makers – and in part on the centrality of the organizations and institutions that mediate these worlds and undertake the necessary translation. Only when the theoretical and policy paradigms promoted by central organizations and institutions lack resonance and/or are held to have manifestly failed when pursued for significant periods does it become possible for marginal or counter-hegemonic forces to provide alternative economic imaginaries. Even here, if the central organizations and institutions are sufficiently powerful, they may persist in their error(s) and seek to repress or, at least, marginalize alternative imaginaries and policy proposals (cf. Deutsch 1963: 111).

Third, where, as in the case of the KBE, theoretical and policy paradigms tend to reinforce each other because theoretically justified policy paradigms are widely adopted and, more importantly, acquire a performative and constitutive character, then the relevant economic imaginary will be retained through normalization and institutionalization. But this will depend on its capacity to envisage potentialities in a relatively fluid conjuncture, to orient the actions of critical social forces towards their realization, and to provide means to consolidate this movement once it is initiated.

And, fourth, from a critical CPE perspective, this depends in turn on the capacity of the economic imaginary, once translated into economic strategies and appropriate economic and extra-economic policies, to regularize and stabilize the course of capital accumulation within specific spatio-temporal fixes, including their facilitation of the displacement and/or deferral of associated contradictions, conflicts and crisis tendencies elsewhere and/or into the future (cf. Jessop 2002, 2004a).

'FIXING' THE KNOWLEDGE-BASED ECONOMY

In contrast to the Atlantic Fordist accumulation regime analysed in Chapter 6 (see also Jessop and Sum 2006), the two principal (or dominant) structural forms in the KBE are capital and competition. The primary aspect of capital is the valorization of the general intellect in the form of knowledge- and design-intensive commodities (real or fictitious). This involves the production, management, distribution and use of knowledge as a key driver of economic growth, wealth generation and job creation across the private, public and 'third' sectors. In a true KBE, it is suggested, knowledge is applied reflexively to the production of knowledge and most sectors tend to become more knowledge-intensive. As such it could help to reduce socially necessary labour time, socially necessary turnover time and, through bio-technology, naturally necessary reproduction times. KBE discourse can be translated into many visions and strategies (e.g. smart machines, expert systems, knowledge transfer, creative industries, intellectual property rights, lifelong learning, e-government, smart weapons, the information society and cybercommunity). It can also be pursued at many scales (firms, organizations, cities, regions, nations, supranational regions, transnational institutions etc.). While it tends to favour productive over money capital, it has sometimes been inflected in a neoliberal manner that highlights the role of market forces as the driving force behind innovation.

Table 7.1 depicts the institutional–spatio-temporal fix of an ideal-typical KBE mode of growth with its principal structural forms and complementary forms on the assumption that it is *en régulation*. However, because knowledge is a fictitious commodity that depends for its valorization on a broad range of extra-economic supports, there are limits to its commodification and this indicates that an effective fix depends on embedding the KBE in a multi-scalar knowledge *society* (Jessop 2007a; cf. Polanyi 1957 on market economy and market society). A suitable state form for this accumulation regime is the Schumpeterian workfare post-national regime in so far as this fits an innovation-led, flexicurity-oriented, multi-scalar and governance-based mode of growth (for details, see Jessop 2002). Note that this table rests on a thought-experiment because most examples of the KBE are local, regional or based on specific global networks rather than being truly national, supranational or global.

This said, we can observe multiple efforts on many scales to create the conditions for a transition to the KBE. In the following sections we explore two of these: (1) the massive extension of intellectual property rights to increase the returns to investment in 'creativity', design, inventions and knowledge; and (2) the transformation of education at all levels

Table 7.1 Knowledge-based economy

Basic form	Primary aspect	Secondary aspect	Institutional fixes	Spatio-temporal fixes
Capital	Valorize design- and knowledge-intensive capital	Capital as intellectual property	Competition state plus moderate IPR regimes	Knowledge-intensive clusters, cities, regions
Com-petition	Innovation-led, Schumpeterian competition	'Race to the bottom' + effects of creative destruction	Wider and deeper global investment, trade, IPR regimes	Complex + multi-spatial with local and regional forms
(Social) wage	Production cost (for mental as well as manual labour)	Source of local or regional demand (hence flexible)	Flexicurity aids demand and global competitiveness	Controlled labour mobility, globalized division of labour
State	Competition state for innovation-led growth	'Third Way' policies to cope with new social exclusion(s)	Schumpeterian workfare post-national regime	Multi-scalar meta-governance (e.g. EU type 'OMC')

from kindergarten to post-compulsory secondary education up to and including the new mantra of 'lifelong learning'. These two cases correspond, respectively, to the primary structural forms (capital, competition) and the reorganization of labour power and the social wage relation in the KBE.

Intellectual Property Rights

Knowledge is a collectively produced resource that can (and does) circulate in the form of an 'intellectual commons' (in orthodox economic terms, it is a 'non-rival' good). It acquires a *commodity form* in so far as it is made artificially scarce through technological, organizational, legal or political means so that access thereto comes to depend on the payment of some form of rent. This said, even if knowledge were freely available as part of the intellectual commons, not everyone would have effective and costless access. First, access may require certain linguistic, cognitive, experiential, professional or other capacities on the part of the subject; and, second, effective access may require specific technological or logistical capabilities as well as monetary resources beyond the reach of many potential users. Not all aspects of inequalities in the division of knowledge within the intellectual commons can be attributed to the capital relation (cf. Sayer and Walker 1992).

Intellectual property rights (IPRs) have a long history as *legal* categories. The distinction between industrial property rights and the copyrights complex originated in the Middle Ages and was easier to draw before and during the age of machinofacture than in the current period of 'post-industrialism' (Bell 1973) and a globalizing neoliberal, KBE. 'Intellectual property' is a generic term that refers to several distinct legal forms that confer rights of ownership over 'ideal, immaterial, or intangible objects'. They became important *economically* with the consolidation of industrial capitalism, grew in scope and significance in the late nineteenth century with the expansion of large industry and/or science-based industries, and have become a crucial economic category in the KBE. Some of these forms are centuries old, others quite new. They have been regularly reinterpreted judicially and redefined legislatively to enhance capital's economic, political and ideological power with each major transition in capitalism. Such transitions are always contested and conflictual, involving intra-class, cross-class and popular struggles.

In high-tech, design-intensive and 'creative' capitalism, the appropriation of knowledge and creativity through IPRs has become central to accumulation. While they are justified in the name of protecting the 'creativity' of intellectual labour (especially in the KBE), and, as such, appear to be pre-eminently cultural rights, their primary role today is as an economic category. For example, the legal doctrine of 'work for hire' plays a role in promoting the formal subsumption of mental labour under capitalist control because it transfers the results of authorship to the employer. More generally, IPRs secure the *chance* of (but do not guarantee) an *average rate of profit* to enterprises that specialize in intellectual outputs that are crucial inputs to the division of labour but that cannot obtain this profit rate through more traditional avenues. In this sense, IPRs serve to protect the capital invested in mental labour and innovative products from rapid devalorization due to the ease of reproduction of immaterial products once they are marketed. Another positive function *for capital* is to facilitate the tendential realization of the average rate of profit across capitals with different technical and organic compositions. This is an important aspect of competition in capitalist economic formations. In offering prospects of a normal rate of return, however, IPRs may also enable producers to sell their intellectual products *above* their value (or price of production) and thereby secure *super-profits* that would otherwise be competed away. This is because they grant a monopoly that limits legal free-riding on development costs and provides sanctions against illegal free-riding (on this and other points in this subsection, see Jessop 2004b).

A shadowy side of the KBE is the primitive accumulation of capital (in the form of intellectual property) through private expropriation (or enclosure) of the collectively produced knowledge of past generations. Essentially this involves the formal transformation of knowledge from a collective resource into intellectual property (e.g. patent, copyright) as a basis for revenue generation. Its forms include: (1) the appropriation of indigenous, tribal or peasant 'culture' in the form of undocumented, informal and collective knowledge, expertise and other intellectual resources, and its transformation without recompense into commodified knowledge (documented, formal, private) by commercial enterprises – biopiracy is the most notorious example (Shiva 1997); (2) colonization of new domains of scientific inquiry, especially in the life sciences, so that life forms are enclosed and commodified (Görg and Brand 2002); (3) divorcing intellectual labour from control over the means of production that it deploys – this is achieved through its formalization and codification in smart machines and expert systems – and thereby appropriating the knowledge of the collective labourer; (4) new forms of 'knowledge management' in individual enterprises, the economy and other systems in order to enclose more and more areas of activity (e.g. university research) under intellectual property regimes (Bollier 2002); and (5) a creeping extension of the limited nature of copyright into broader forms of property right with a consequent erosion of any residual public interest. Each of these forms is hotly contested by different forces, for example indigenous peoples, scientists, consumers, workers, teachers and students.

The acceleration in scientific activities and scientific knowledge, the incorporation of scientific research into enterprise activities, and the reflexive use of knowledge in the production of knowledge make industrial and intellectual property rights increasingly important means of competition. Unsurprisingly, then, as the products of intellectual labour are increasingly commodified and increasingly important in valorization, IPRs must be extended *pari passu* to ensure their profitability. Much effort has been invested to establish the concept of 'intellectual capital' or 'knowledge capital' as the principal basis for capital accumulation in the KBE, to give it strong positive connotations, and to transform the identification and management of intellectual capital into an important specialist managerial discipline. For bourgeois management science and business strategy, such efforts are essentially exercises in economic and legal mystification and/ or the marketing of management science consultancies. They offer no real insight into the dynamics of contemporary capitalism or its continuities with previous stages of capitalist development. As such, then, they count as ideological categories in the sense discussed in Chapter 4. Moreover, with ideological support from the neoliberal theory of property rights (North 1981), IPRs are used to massively extend the commodity form into the natural and social worlds. Capital is appropriating indigenous peoples' age-old knowledge about plants and seeds; parts of the human genome are being patented; and university research is subordinated to the profit motive.

Intellectual property comprises a disparate set of legal forms. IPRs differ significantly from property rights in material objects. Without effective material possession of knowledge-based advantages, IPRs cannot be treated as the juridical expression of real property rights but serve as means to create such rights artificially. Neoliberalism reproduces the Ricardian idea that knowledge is one factor of production among others and should be bought and sold in order to maximize allocative efficiency and ensure that factor returns correspond to their relative scarcity and productivity. In contrast, from a Marxian perspective, intellectual property should be considered not as a thing but as a social relation. To paraphrase Marx, it is 'a relation between persons, established by the instrumentality of *immaterial* things' (cf. Marx 1967a: 717). Indeed, as Drahos notes, '[e]ach time the law constitutes new abstract objects by, for instance, increasing the scope of patentable subject-matter or legislatively creating new forms of abstract objects such as plant variety rights, the law in effect creates capital' (1996: 158). It is their political character that explains the enormous ideological effort required to legitimate the creation and defence of IPRs against those who argue that 'knowledge should be free'. It also explains why state sanctions (trade, financial, investment, juridical, police, military etc.) are needed to reinforce respect for intellectual property and its associated rights against unthinking 'home copying' as well as commercial 'pirates'. The state thereby reinforces the objectivity of law as a mechanism of appropriation and exploitation of the intellectual commons, intellectual labour and intellectual production.

In addition, the diverse sets of rights associated with different forms of intellectual property can be unbundled and distributed in different ways and across different rights-holders. What unifies these forms is their relation in the first instance to ideal, immaterial, intangible objects; what differentiates them is the material objects with which they are – or may be – linked. For example, whereas patents, trademarks, copyright, plant breeders' rights and authors' moral rights all involve ideal, immaterial or intangible objects, they are linked to inventions, brands, artistic works, plants and moral personality respectively.

The relation between these intangible and tangible aspects matters for four reasons. First, the nature of the connected material objects affects the relative significance of different legal forms and the allocation of specific intellectual property rights. Second, intellectual property rights, their specific features and their implications for expected profits shape corporate strategies, production, distribution and consumption. Third, although IPRs are legally distinct from the material objects in which they may be instantiated (e.g. copyright in a literary work as opposed to a printed copy of that work), the owners of these rights in immaterial objects nonetheless typically also have certain derivative rights against the owners or users of the related material property (e.g. in the case of unfair use of the book). Indeed, once property rights in intangible objects (in ideas as assets) are recognized, they enable their owners to reach deep into the material world.[5] And, fourth, the formation of a world market in which monopoly profits and well-paid employment in the advanced capitalist economies now depend increasingly on legal forms to create, prolong and protect competitive advantages. These are promoted in the hope that they will enable the advanced economies to control the forms and direction of technology transfer, catch-up development and export-led growth in underdeveloped (or underdeveloping) economies. That this is not happening can be seen in the rise of the BRIC economies (see Chapter 12) and is related, in part, to the deformations introduced into some advanced capitalist economies by the rise of finance-dominated accumulation (see Chapter 11).

The growing importance of these economic contradictions and their repercussions within the KBE and/or 'information' or 'knowledge society' explains the resistance that these rights provoke and the proliferation of alternative imaginaries and practices that characterize the production and circulation of knowledge in contemporary capitalism. Some forces contest the very concept of IPRs in favour of free access to the intellectual commons; others call for alternative IPR regimes with radically different forms of organization of production and distribution. For capital, the struggle to define IPRs is also a struggle for hegemony in so far as private firms' commercial appropriation and monopolization of social knowledge is represented as a just reward for intellectual labour that must be defended against parasitic, free-riding capital and generalized consumer theft. In contrast, many opponents of this trend demand IPR regimes that guarantee indigenous peoples' control over their traditional knowledge, protect open-source software producers against the blocking tactics and appropriation attempts of software monopolies and so on. Conflicts over IPR crystallize on the global level in negotiations over the TRIPS (Trade Related Intellectual Property Rights) agreement as an 'instrument to adapt civil society to the economic structure' (Morera 1990: 163, citing Gramsci 1971: Q12, §1: 1524).

One final observation, which we will pick up again in discussing finance-dominated accumulation, concerns the implications of the fictitious commodification of knowledge for social inequality and polarization within and across national societies. If firms in the information economy are to maintain profit rates despite the tendency for technological rents to be competed away, less technologically advanced sectors must secure below-average profits. This is one of the driving forces behind globalization and the tendencies towards unequal exchange and uneven development with which it is associated. In the longer term, however, this poses problems of demand for the products of the information economy on a global scale

Education

Many commentators have noted the significant shifts in the theoretical and policy paradigms for the institutional design and strategic reorientation of education, skill formation and higher education in response to certain diagnoses of the initial crisis in/of Atlantic Fordism. In the initial phase, education was criticized for failing to meet the needs of a changing economy and a more flexible labour market. This was associated with an increased emphasis on inculcating flexibility and adaptability as a short-term response to the vagaries of the business cycle and greater volatility in the labour market (Robins and Webster 1989). Flexibility and flexible learning were also linked to organizational change, especially with the rise of open and distance learning enabled by new ICTs and new methods of context-situated and problem-oriented teaching and learning. Later, there was a broader emphasis on the role of education in promoting the globalizing KBE through the development of human capital. This was linked to growing concern with the certification of transferable as well as specific skills in schools, post-compulsory education and on-the-job training. Training and lifelong learning became a central component of economic as well as social policy in all advanced capitalist economies and they were tied to the growing consensus that successful competition depends on building the knowledge base and human capital.

These trends are evident at all levels of education from schools through further and higher education to on-the-job training and career-linked lifelong learning and thence to 'universities of the third age' for older people. For example, schools are increasingly expected to enable children to become enterprising subjects and develop their personal skills and capacity for team-working. They are also expected to provide the basis for the transition to work and to forge closer links with future employers. This is related to active labour market policies and reflected in a proliferation of programmes to integrate education and work through vocational training, partnerships, work experience, training credits and so on. In neoliberal regimes this is also linked to the extension of the new managerialism and audit culture into schools (as well as universities) with its emphasis on quasi-markets, internal cost centres, performativity, targets, benchmarking, staff appraisal and the like (Clarke and Newman 1997; Fairclough 1993; Mautner 2005; Power 1997).

The tightened connection between schooling, employment, productivity and trade is reflected in a cross-national reorientation of the notion of skill, with increasing emphasis on key skills, lifelong learning and employability, as technology, corporate restructuring and volatile markets are believed to have ended the Fordist fantasy of jobs for life (Lauder et al. 2001). Education was integrated into the workfarist project that downgrades the Keynesian state's commitment to full employment and substitutes the state's role in creating conditions for full employability. This devolves responsibility for becoming employable to individual members of the labour force, who should acquire the individual skills, competencies, flexibility, adaptability and personal dispositions to enable them to compete for jobs in national and global labour markets. They may exercise this responsibility as enterprising individuals investing in their own human capital and/or as equal citizens entitled to support from the state and social partners to improve their skills (see Chapters 8 and 10). As part of these shifts, employers and practitioners are involved in curriculum development, managers are drawn into educational governance and agenda-setting, mobility between the academy and non-academic worlds was encouraged, and colleges and universities were expected to deliver lifelong learning through advanced professional programmes, continuing professional development, part-time, evening and distance teaching, remedial and second-chance courses, and so on (Teichler 1998: 85).

Notwithstanding this cross-national policy discourse convergence, marked differences in take-up and implementation remained. Brown et al. (2001) report, for example, that, where economies were dominated by a belief that the future lay in a post-industrial service economy, there was a polarization between education and training for high-skilled elites and for a flexible, low-skilled service sector. The latter sector also had relatively low investment and generated output more through long working hours than through increasing productivity. Conversely, where manufacturing was still accorded a key role in accumulation strategies, the state emphasized intermediate skills and the need for education and training to link industry and services. This was coupled with high capital investment to harness skills for a high-productivity economy. The USA and UK exemplify the first model; the second is illustrated by Germany. In Chapter 10 we consider how different models of Hong Kong's future economy were also reflected in contrasting economic strategies.

Turning more directly to further and higher education, there has been a great emphasis on shifting university teaching and research from its ivory-towered intellectual isolation back into closer and more continuous contact with the economy, the state and the community as vital co-producers and consumers of useful knowledge. This is especially clear in technology, the sciences and medicine, and has also penetrated the social sciences so that it is not merely graduates but faculty members themselves who are expected to develop extensive links with users in industry, business, the professions, government and local communities. There is growing emphasis on external fundraising, patenting, technology transfer, research parks, commercial spin-offs, science and technology parks, incubators, consultancy services – amounting to the emergence of a veritable 'academic capitalism' in liberal economies that encourages entrepreneurial universities and transforms faculty members into enterprising bearers of intellectual capital (Slaughter and Leslie 1997). This change was encouraged in the USA (the principal cheerleader for the KBE in the 1990s as a response to the perception of declining industrial competitiveness) through changes in federal funding for research, enabling universities to keep the intellectual property in their discoveries, as well as through the more general extension of the scope and duration of IPRs. Universities are also encouraged to commercialize their research. This was intended to encourage academic entrepreneurialism, to subsidize corporate R&D, and to facilitate regional economic development. Similar patterns can be found in other university systems.

Overall, in the words of Henry Etzkowitz, a leading researcher on the 'triple-helix' interface between university, business and the state, writing at an early stage in this transformation:

> Virtually every country that has a university, whether it was founded for reasons of education or prestige, is now attempting to organise knowledge-based economic development ... As the university becomes more dependent upon industry and government, so have industry and government become more dependent upon the university. In the course of the 'second academic revolution' a new social contract is being drawn up between the university and the wider society, in which public funding for the university is made contingent upon a more direct contribution to the economy. (Etzkowitz 1994: 149, 151)

Two apparently contrary but actually complementary strategies are identified here. On the one hand, the state is asserting the importance of education in the realization of national economic interests, the realization of which is not always best left to the selfish interests of private economic agents, especially where the world market rather than national economic space is the ultimate horizon of profit-oriented, market-mediated economic strategies.[6] And, on the other hand, it is conceding greater autonomy to educational institutions in how they serve these interests on the assumption that they share the same broad vision as the dominant economic and political forces regarding future trends in economic development and competition. Key issues here are the hegemony of the knowledge-based accumulation strategy, the increasing participation of the bearers of this strategy in the shaping of education mission statements, the increasing financial dependence of further and higher education on third-party revenues deriving neither from the state nor from the students, and the growing dependence of university revenues on student fees, business research contracts, third-mission activities and university branding strategies relative to the share of income as block grants from government agencies. In this context, then, the first strategy 'involves a reaffirmation of the state functions of education as a "public good", while the second subjects education to the disciplines of the market and the methods and values of business and redefines it as a competitive private good' (Marginson 1999: 122). Together, these strategies serve to reinforce the primacy of accumulation within the organization of education and to promote differentiation in the higher education sector between top research universities at the cutting edge of the KBE that engage in world-class international research cooperation and others that tend to specialize in cost-effective mass credentialization and opportunities for lifelong learning at a more local or regional scale. At both ends of this increasingly stretched-out spectrum, however, there is emphasis on close links to the users of research and education to ensure, as far as possible, that economic needs are being served.

CONCLUDING REMARKS

This chapter has pursued five main objectives. First, we explored the contested concepts of competition and competitiveness from both structural and semiotic perspectives, noting how the increasing integration of the world market generalizes competitive pressures and leads to an increasing range of economic and extra-economic factors being subsumed into the logic of competition. Second, we applied the CPE approach to the emergence of the KBE as the hegemonic economic imaginary in the 1990s and early 2000s – relating this to the crisis of the main forms of economic growth in the post-war period, not only within the advanced capitalist economies but also in Latin America, East Asia, the Soviet bloc and Mainland China, as well as in relation to the role of organizations and institutions charged with developing theoretical and policy paradigms that draw on and contribute to new economic imaginaries. Third, we presented as a thought-experiment an account of the KBE *en régulation* – noting at the same time that there are few examples of *national* economies dominated by a KBE accumulation regime. Fourth, we turned the CPE stick in the other direction by examining the significance of property rights in immaterial, intangible, intellectual property as a key social form in the KBE, into which enormous efforts have been invested to protect, widen and deepen IPRs as part of attempts to select and retain the KBE imaginary as the basis of a viable accumulation regime. We also illustrated some of the contradictions that this entails, which provide important bases of new problems, new *urgences* and new forms of resistance. And, fifth, we briefly reviewed some work on the transformation of education in the first decade of the KBE project to illustrate how labour power as creative labour and abstract labour was the target of new disciplinary and governmental interventions. In short, we have sought in this chapter to illustrate how the semiotic and structural dimensions of the KBE can be explored at the levels of orders of discourse and social forms and, more concretely, in terms of genre chains and institutional innovation. We return to these themes in later chapters.

NOTES

1. For Imre Lakatos (1978), a research programme provided rules about which paths of inquiry to pursue (positive heuristic) and which to avoid (negative heuristic). The clarification at the end of the quotation is ours.
2. Key figures here, in addition to East Asian intellectuals, think tanks, business strategists and officials, were two Western thinkers, Alvin Toffler (1980) and Daniel Bell (1973, 1989).
3. On structural competitiveness, see Chesnais (1986); on systemic competitiveness, Messner (1996); Esser et al. (1996). See also *STI Review* (published by the OECD).
4. The World Economic Forum and the Institute for Management Development (IMD) published a joint report for a time but moved to separate reports because of measurement differences.
5. 'Artists, authors and inventors have to turn their intangible assets into material ones in order to survive economically in the world. Once the law recognized property in abstract objects, the significance of the materiality that governed property relations in the physical world grew stronger and not weaker. It grew stronger because through abstract objects many more material objects, both in number and in kind, could be reached by individual property owners. The abstract object became a way of gaining control over the material objects. One patent could relate to an indefinite number of physical objects. The corporeality of intellectual property is, legally speaking, never very far away and

manifests itself in various requirements which impose a condition of materiality on the abstract object' (Drahos 1996: 21).
6. There are many well-known market failures in the provision of goods and services with strong positive externalities (such as public sanitation, control of contagious diseases, literacy or knowledge as a public good).

8. The production of a hegemonic knowledge brand: competitiveness discourses and neoliberal developmentalism

The crisis of Atlantic Fordism in developed economies and of import substitution industrialization in some developing countries prompted many economic and political imaginaries proposing more or less radical alternatives to these crisis-hit paradigms. These new imaginaries include neoliberal narratives such as flexibility, privatization, deregulation, globalization, export orientation, innovation, competitiveness, and so on. There has been increasing focus upon the supply side and getting 'competitiveness right' as the neoliberal policy prescription since the end of the 1990s (Reinert 2007). This chapter has four parts. First, it examines the production of 'competitiveness' discourses over three overlapping stages from theoretical through policy paradigm to knowledge brand. Focusing on the latter two, it discusses an influential account offered by Michael E. Porter and his Harvard Business School associates. It examines how these academic-cum-consultant figures and their narratives gradually became a 'knowledge brand' and, with time, condensed discursive and institutional power in the knowledge–consultancy–policy circuit. Within this circuit, different actors promote diverse elements and negotiate particular meanings of 'competitiveness', with some being more academic-policy in orientation whilst others are more technical–managerial. The discursively selective nature of this genre chain is discernible from academic books, consultancy reports, official documents/plans, (inter)national outlooks, forums, global reports, policy speeches, development manuals and best practices. Second, this knowledge brand is recontextualized to new sites and frames new situations. Discursive apparatuses such as competitiveness indexes and growth metaphors (e.g. catch-up competitiveness, cluster, chains and entrepreneurship) are constructed, relayed and streamlined for implementation in workshops and training courses. This discourse/discipline set shapes new subjectivities that are selected and regularized as growth strategies and hegemonic visions at different sites and scales.

Third, it argues that such hegemonic visions are not only discursively unstable with their own surpluses of meanings; their related growth strategies are materially uneven with impacts upon class, gender, nature and place. Fourth, the chapter ends by consolidating the value added of a CPE approach in examining the production and recontextualization of a hegemonic knowledge brand at different sites and scales (see also Chapter 9).

RISE OF NEOLIBERAL COMPETITIVENESS AND ITS PRODUCTION AS A HEGEMONIC KNOWLEDGE BRAND

The production of policy discourses has a long history. Examples from the modern period include the promotion of Adam Smith's *laissez-faire* policies to colonial regimes (Crowder 1978); and of modernization theories to Cold War policy establishments (Latham 2000). Market discourses, which are promoted by numerous think tanks (e.g. Cato Institute, Heritage Foundation and Institute for Economic Affairs) are increasingly being challenged because of persisting problems of unemployment, unequal distribution of income and largely unregulated financialization. Since the late 1990s, these challenges towards the free market paradigm have prompted the reorientation of the mantra of 'getting prices right' to one of 'getting competitiveness right'. This new priority involves a complex translation of theoretical and policy paradigms into 'knowledge brands' to meet the demand for express consultancy knowledge and fast policy in a globalized era of space-time compression and acceleration. There are many complementary, competing and hybridized 'knowledge brands' (e.g. Porter's competitiveness advantage in organization strategy, Lundvall's national systems of innovation in innovation and learning, Florida's 'creative class' in urban regeneration and Gereffi's 'global commodity chain' in globalization of production) in the current policy market. This chapter focuses on the rise of one among many 'competitiveness' discourses and its development as a knowledge brand in three overlapping stages.

Discourses on 'competitiveness' date back centuries and have been linked to very different economic imaginaries at different times and in different contexts (cf. Reinert 1995; Lodge and Vogel 1987; Hämäläinen 2003). This chapter tracks the development of 'competitiveness' discourses from the 1960s through three overlapping stages from theoretical through policy paradigms and then knowledge brand (see Table 8.1). Stage one saw the development of the theoretical paradigm that underpins the neoliberal competitiveness imaginary. This paradigm draws in part on a Schumpeterian body of knowledge that emphasizes the creatively

Table 8.1 Three overlapping stages in the development of 'competitiveness' discourses and practices since the 1960s

Overlapping stages in the development of the 'cultures of competitiveness'	Articulation of major discourses and practices	Major authors/institutions
Stage 1 Theoretical paradigm	Technology, innovation and national competitiveness research monographs and papers	Schumpeter, Posner, Vernon, Freeman etc.
Stage 2 Policy paradigm	Competitiveness policy, competitiveness commissions, White Papers and technology policy	Commission on Industrial Competitiveness, Council on Competitiveness, OECD, EU etc.
Stage 3 Management/ consultancy knowledge and knowledge brand	Diamond model, clusters, cluster charts, indices, pilot projects, methodology, observatory, workshops and training courses	Porter, Harvard Business School, Monitor Group, World Economic Forum etc. (see also Table 8.2)

destructive nature of innovation and the virtues of entrepreneurial competition as well as the neoliberal emphasis on the role of market forces as the key driver in competition (Schumpeter 1934). With the end of the post-war boom and the emergence of major new technologies (especially ICTs), Schumpeter's analyses were used to highlight technological change and innovation as central to long-run economic dynamics. In this stage competitiveness is framed largely in terms of academic accounts of technological and organizational innovation, R&D in enterprises, the role of patents, competitiveness and trade policy (e.g. Posner 1961; Vernon 1966; Freeman 1982).

These theoretical accounts were translated into policy discourses around questions of national geo-economic competitiveness at this second stage. Policies were narrated in terms of innovation- and technology-driven growth corresponding to a competitiveness framework (for two overviews of this development, see Dosi and Soete 1988; Fagerberg 1996). This occurred in the 1980s, a conjuncture when the USA and UK were experiencing low growth, rising unemployment, high inflation and techno-economic decline *vis-à-vis* Japan and East Asia (d'Andrea Tyson 1988; Krugman 1994b). These economic changes were seen in terms of a 'loss of competitiveness' compared to faster-growing economies in Europe and the East. The Reagan Administration responded in 1983 by establishing the Commission on Industrial Competitiveness, followed in 1988 by the Council on Competitiveness. Both bodies comprised industrial, labour and academic leaders, and placed national competitiveness at the centre of national policy discourses and public consciousness. A parallel trend marked the Organisation for Economic Co-operation and Development (OECD), which is a service-oriented think tank for member states on the importance of science and technology. This theme was first raised as early as 1962 (OECD 1962) but the OECD intensified its engagement therewith in the 1980s and 1990s, producing detailed policy data and analyses on technology, productivity and economic growth (e.g. OECD 1991). Narrated more in the language of 'technology policy' and 'national system of innovation' (Miettinen 2002), this gradual move from theoretical to policy paradigm was reinforced by the reorientation of the EU on similar lines with the publication of the European Commission's *White Paper on Growth, Competitiveness and Employment* (1993), *Green Paper on Innovation* (1995), *Lisbon Strategy for Competitiveness* (2000), *European Competitiveness Report* (2012) and so on.

Porter's Diamond Model and Cluster Concept as Intellectual Technologies

The rise of Schumpeterian accounts of competitiveness as a major policy paradigm was reinforced and supported by parallel developments in management and business studies. This signals stage three, when the new policy paradigm was translated into management/consultancy knowledge about how to 'get the competitiveness right'. This knowledge was articulated by business school professors and consultants. An important example is Michael E. Porter, a Harvard Business School (hereafter HBS) professor initially celebrated for his analyses of the competitiveness of firms and industries (1980, 1985). It had long been known that firms compete and Porter advised firms on how to establish and maintain monopoly positions to ensure superprofits. Mainstream economics (in contrast, e.g., to mercantilism) did not regard territorial states as involved in economic competition. Yet this issue was increasingly placed on the agenda by the crisis of Atlantic Fordism. Problematizing it as related to pressures from globalization, challenges from East Asian economies, and the inability of traditional macro-economic policies to increase outputs and prosperity, Porter's firm-level analysis was seen as a new entry-point to revive national competitiveness (see Chapter 7). On this basis he was recruited in 1988 to President Ronald Reagan's Council on Competitiveness.

Seeking to extend his approach from firm-level competition to nation-states, Porter coordinated ten national case studies[1] and published his

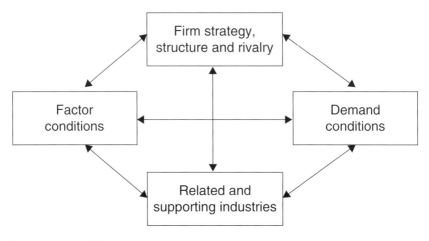

Source: Porter (1990: 127).

Figure 8.1 Porter's diamond model of national advantage

results in a best-selling book, *The Competitive Advantage of Nations* (1990). This sought to justify the notion that nations competed with each other and, in this context, to explain both why a nation might succeed in some industries but not in others and why some industries were more competitive in some nations than in others. On this basis, he constructed the interactive 'diamond model' (see Figure 8.1) based on four factors conducive to the development of competitiveness: demand conditions, factor conditions, firm strategy, structure and rivalry, and related and supporting industries, which were reinforced by 'chance' and the 'government' as additional considerations. For Porter, the co-evolution of these supply-side factors creates the 'micro-economic foundations of prosperity' that enable national firms to gain and sustain competitive advantages. He added that these micro-foundations would be strongest when they formed a 'cluster', a concept that depicts 'a geographic concentration of competing and cooperating companies, suppliers, service providers, and associated institutions' (Porter 1990).[2] Concentration enhances interaction among the four factors in the diamond to boost productivity, growth, employment and, hence, competitiveness. The invention of the diamond model and cluster concept allowed Porter to argue for enhancing competitiveness *vis-à-vis* competitors by shaping the business environment so that firms could increase their productivity and profits and nations could increase national well-being.

From a CPE viewpoint, the 'diamond model' and the 'cluster concept' are the two major intellectual technologies that distinguish Porter's analysis. In a period with demands for new imaginaries and fast and ready-made policy advice, these technologies are simple, user-friendly, problem-oriented, and permit recontextualization to diverse interpretations, applications and policy solutions (Thomas 2003). Porter's solutions include the provision of infrastructure, enhancement of human capital and innovation for firms/clusters so that nations (or other economic spaces) can move from factor-driven to innovation-driven economies (Porter 2005). This strategy-oriented toolkit is readily useable, saleable and transferable. It can be easily leveraged and transferred to the consultancy-policy world. To this end, the Institute for Strategy and Competitiveness was established in 2001 at HBS. This Institute is headed by Porter and focuses its research on the strategic implications of competitive forces for firms as well as for nations, regions and cities (Snowdon and Stonehouse 2006: 163). Its website at http://www.isc.hbs.edu/ declares that this international research institute 'is dedicated to extending the research pioneered by Professor Porter and disseminating it to scholars and practitioners on a global basis'. Accordingly, a number of HBS-associated institutions (e.g. the Institute for Competitiveness in Barcelona and the Asia Competitiveness Institute in Singapore) and consultancy-strategy firms (e.g. Monitor Group and ontheFRONTIER Group)[3] were set up. Through their joint claims to expertise and efforts, Porter's cluster-based strategy is flexibly applied to quite different countries (e.g. Canada, Denmark, New Zealand, Portugal, Sweden and Switzerland) and regions/cities (e.g. Atlanta, Rhône-Alpes, Baltic Sea, Singapore and Hong Kong/Pearl River Delta). Strategy firms such as ontheFRONTIER Group have also adapted it to so-called 'emerging markets' (e.g. Mexico, Peru, Bolivia and Rwanda).[4]

Apart from the Harvard-associated organizations, these intellectual technologies – albeit not always purely Porterian – have also been adopted/adapted on different scales by international authorities (e.g. World Economic Forum and United Nations Industrial Development Organization), regional banks (e.g. Asian Development Bank), national agencies (e.g. United States Agency for International Development and Asia Competitiveness Institute) and city governments/strategy firms (for Enright, Scott and Associates, Ltd; see Table 8.2 and Chapters 9 and 10). Complementary sites in these knowledge networks include other business schools, consultancy firms, chambers of commerce, think tanks, research institutes, government departments, consultancy firms, business and mass media, town hall meetings, luncheon gatherings and public performances (e.g. conferences and speeches) organized by speaker agencies (e.g. NOPAC Talent).

Table 8.2 Examples of institutions and discourses related to competitiveness at different scales

Scales/spatial foci	Examples of institutions involved	Examples of competitiveness discourses/instruments
Global/international	World Economic Forum Institute for Management Development The Competitiveness Institute (Barcelona) United Nations Industrial Development Organization (UNIDO)	• *Global Competitiveness Report* and *Global Competitiveness Index* • *World Competitiveness Yearbook* and *World Competitiveness Scoreboard* • *The Cluster Initiative Database* • *The Cluster Initiative Greenbook 2003* • *Clusters and Networks Development Programme 2005* • *Tanzania: Sustainable Industrial Development and Competitiveness 2001*
Regional	World Bank Asian Development Bank Asia Competitiveness Institute (Singapore) African Union Inter-American Development Bank	• *Cluster of Competitiveness 2009* • *Asian Development Outlook 2003: III Competitiveness in Developing Countries* • *ASEAN Competitiveness Report 2010* • *Pan African Competitiveness Forum 2008* • *Competitiveness of Small Enterprises: Cluster and Local Development 2007*

National	United States Agency for International Development (USAID) Japan International Cooperation Agency (JICA) Foundation of MSMEs Clusters (India) Enright, Scott and Associates, Ltd	• African Global Competitiveness Initiative 2009 • Strategic Investment Action Plan (Competitiveness/SME) 2005 • Cluster Observatory • *Australia's Competitiveness Survey 2012*
Local/city	Economic Intelligence Unit (*The Economist*) Asia Competitiveness Institute (Singapore) (see also Table 8.6) Enright, Scott and Associates Ltd (Hong Kong) (see also Table 8.6 and Figure 9.1)	• Global City Competitiveness Index 2012 • *Remaking Singapore 2008* • *The Hong Kong Advantage 1997*

Source: Authors' own compilation based on website information of these institutions, accessed 29 December 2012.

This body of intellectual technologies and management knowledge circulates widely and resonates strongly in policy-consultancy networks in developed and developing countries, gaining credibility from its promotion by idea entrepreneurs, strategists, opinion-forming journalists, leading policy-makers and executives who recontextualize, streamline and disseminate the genre to different sites and scales. This genre chain gives an impression of continuity via key documents such as economic outlooks, consultancy reports, indices, scoreboards, databases, development outlooks, surveys, strategic cluster plans, best practices, training courses and the like (see Tables 8.2 and 8.4).

Competitiveness as a Knowledge Brand

Porter's diamond model and cluster concept have generated support and provoked debates and criticisms. Some business and management scholars (e.g. Gray 1991; Stopford and Strange 1991) criticized the diamond model for lack of formal modelling, while others (e.g. Thurow 1990; Rugman 1991; Dunning 1992) challenged its originality. Several scholars recommend extending it to interlinked double or multiple diamonds (Rugman and D'Cruz 1993; O'Malley and van Egeraat 2000), especially regarding the insertion of small open-economy diamonds into more encompassing sets of regional or world market factors. Porter's 'cluster' concept has also been criticized in regional studies as chaotic, loose and imprecise, making it hard to use for concrete public intervention (Martin and Sunley 2003). Nonetheless the cluster approach is often discussed as a major strand in the 'spatial agglomeration' and 'industrial district' literature (e.g. MacKinnon et al. 2002) and has often been circulated, repeated and recontextualized in policy circuits as a leading idea that frames regional development and proposals for local and national development. For some, it has even acquired a certain status. For example, the UK government's Improvement and Development Agency for local government (IDeA) has a special website page on Porter's ideas, noting that 'despite [the] plethora of competing but similar ideas, Porter's theory became, for some time, the established "industry standard"'.[5]

Its status as an 'industry standard' can partly be explained by the specific capacities of some well-placed intellectuals (and related civil-society organizations) to acquire and consolidate leadership in the face of demands for fast policy (see agential-inscribed selectivity in Chapter 5). These include: (1) the cliché and 'industrial quality' guarantee that comes with Harvard University and the HBS; (2) the generality, simplicity and flexibility of Porter's intellectual technologies; (3) the communication skills of these guru-consultants (e.g. Porter) and related speaker agencies that organize and promote their lectures in person and online; (4) the accumulation of credibility of these guru-consultants and support from high-profile conferences, business media and journals;[6] (5) Harvard-trained practitioners and related trainers in the consultancy industry that 'cluster' around the brand (see Huczynski 1996; Collins 2000; Jackson 2001; Clark and Fincham 2002); (6) abilities of these actors to offer ready-made policy advice (e.g. cluster-based strategies) as re-engineering solutions; and (7) the promotion and circulation of this body of knowledge by diverse institutions across the global, regional, national and local scales (see Table 8.2).

Given its status as an industry standard and the capacities of these academic-cum-consultant figures and practitioners to organize knowledge, this knowledge brand can be used to persuade policy-makers and offer ready-made solutions. Porter-inspired ideas about competitiveness gradually acquired distinctive and brand status. The mantra of 'getting competitiveness right', with its ready-made supply-side toolkits (e.g., 'factor conditions', 'firm strategies', 'support for industries' and 'cluster building'), fits easily into a neoliberal worldview. These techniques add allure to its brandized status and, in turn, branding adds strength to the mantra. Like commercial brands (Lury 2004; Schroeder and Morling 2005), knowledge brands address the rational and irrational aspects of human nature. *Cognitively*, a brand like Porter's competitiveness 'diamond'/'cluster' model is commodified, rationalized and legitimated by its association with HBS, its circulation among policy elites, its distinctive policy advice, re-engineering solutions and individual career benefits. *Emotionally*, it addresses pride, anxieties, threats and social tensions linked to growth or decline, development and the intense pressures of economic restructuring in a globalized information age. These rational and irrational affects shape struggles to make a brand hegemonic. Summarizing, a knowledge brand can be defined as a resonant hegemonic meaning-making device advanced in various ways by 'world-class' gurus–academics–consultants who claim unique knowledge of a relevant strategic or policy field and pragmatically translate this into (trans-)national policy symbols, recipes and toolkits that address policy problems and dilemmas and also appeal to pride, threats and anxieties about socio-economic restructuring and changes. In this regard, a knowledge brand is a trans-national manifestation and condensation of institutional, organizational and discursive power in the knowledge–consultancy–policy circuit. After all, not all forms of knowledge are equal; some are more prominent and 'brandized' than others. Thus knowledge is at the same time diffused and condensed along specific nodal points, the location of which is extra-discursively as well as discursively conditioned.

DEVELOPING AND RECONTEXTUALIZING THE KNOWLEDGE BRAND: REPORTS, INDICES, CLUSTERS AND CHAINS

In circulating trans-nationally, such brands offer simple but flexible templates that can be developed and recontextualized to changing global, regional, national and local conditions. Basil Bernstein's concept of recontextualization suggests that agents selectively appropriate, relocate, refocus and recombine pedagogic discourses in applying them to other discursive fields in ways that both fit and reaffirm existing social relations (1996: 47) (see Chapter 5). Drawing on Bernstein, this section now examines the recontextualization of the 'competitiveness' brand in two sites and scales. The first is the construction of benchmarking reports and indices by the World Economic Forum for global application. The second is the use of metaphors such as 'catch-up', 'poverty reduction', 'clusters' and 'chains' in economic outlooks/ commissioned reports in the Asian region and local levels. Each of these knowledge apparatuses has its own technologically inscribed evaluative rules and managing techniques that discipline and governmentalize individuals, countries and their population (see Tables 8.3 and 8.7 and Chapter 5).

Table 8.3 Two knowledge apparatuses and knowledging technologies in the construction of 'competitiveness'

Knowledge apparatuses/ instruments	Knowledging technologies in meaning-making	Major institutional sites/actors
Benchmarking reports and indices constructed in:		
Global Competitiveness Report	Technologies of performance, judgement and gaps	World Economic Forum
Growth and Business Competitiveness Indices and Global Competitiveness Index		
Cluster-and-chain metaphors constructed in:		
Asian Development Outlook 2003: III Competitiveness in Developing Countries	Technologies of agency (see Table 8.8)	*Asian Development Bank*
Cluster Development Workshops 2006 (see also Table 8.7)		*UNIDO*

On a Global Scale: Construction of Benchmarking Reports and Indices

In line with and as part of the rise of global managerialism (Murphy 2008) and global benchmarking (Larner and Le Heron 2004: 212–32), 'competitiveness' narratives are linked to the development of knowledging apparatuses such as benchmarking reports and indices. The two best-known series of reports, which have been published since the 1990s, come from international private authorities (Cutler et al. 1999). The *Global Competitiveness Report* is issued by the World Economic Forum (WEF) in Geneva and the *World Competitiveness Yearbook* is published by the Institute for Management Development (IMD) in Lausanne. The *Global Competitiveness Report* is based on the Global Competitiveness Index, which is connected to Porter (and associates); the *World Competitiveness Yearbook* relies on the World Competitiveness Scoreboard. After cooperating to produce the *World Competitiveness Report* in 1989, these bodies have published separate reports after 1995. This chapter concentrates on the WEF not only because of its connection with HBS but also because of its wide influence. From a CPE viewpoint, this report functions as a discursive apparatus that frames the understandings of 'competitiveness'. Its 2004–05 version presented the report as a 'unique benchmarking tool in identifying obstacles to economic growth and assist [sic] in the design of better economic policies'.[7] It achieves this partly through its use of knowledging instruments such as 'indices' and 'best practices' that construct countries as competing market actors. These instruments combine disciplinary and governmental power in one set of evaluative–performance discourses.

More specifically, instruments such as indices are dominated by the principles and language of competition. In 2000, the WEF constructed the Business Competitiveness Index (BCI)[8] and the Growth Competitiveness Index based on the work of Porter, Jeffrey Sachs, and others. The former index is premised on Porter's micro-economic factors of competitiveness and the latter derives from the Sachs–McArthur theory of sustainable economic growth processes (see Table 8.4). In 2004 and again in 2008, the WEF model was twice updated to integrate the latest thinking on the drivers of competitiveness (see Table 8.5). In 2004, Xavier Sala-i-Martin and Elsa V. Artadi were asked to add macro-factors to the micro-elements to form a new Global Competitiveness Index (GCI); this replaced the Business and Growth Competitiveness Indices. In 2008, the GCI was revised in turn by a team assembled by Porter to produce a single measure called the New Global Competitiveness Index, which aggregates four broad sets of drivers, that is, productivity, endowments, macro-economic competitiveness and micro-competitiveness (for details, see *Global Competitiveness Report* 2008–09: 43–64). In 2011, Xavier Sala-i-Martin led a team and outlined

Table 8.4 World Economic Forum and the development of its Competitiveness Indices 2000–2012

Year	Major developers	Name of index	Framing of index
2000–2004	Michael Porter from Harvard Business School	Business Competitiveness Index (BCI)*	Micro-drivers of prosperity based on the 'diamond' model
2000–2004	Jeffrey Sachs and John McArthur from Harvard University	Growth Competitiveness Index	Sustainable economic growth theory based on productivity (e.g. technological change)
2005–2008	Michael Porter assisted by Xavier Sala-i-Martin of Columbia University	Global Competitiveness Index (GCI)	Broaden to include micro- and macro-factors of competitiveness (e.g. institutions, macro-stability, technological readiness, security etc.)
2008–2009	Michael Porter assembling a team including Mercedes Delgado, Christian Ketels and Scott Stern	New Global Competitiveness Index	Replace the GCI. Broadened to include productivity, endowments, macro- and micro-factors of competitiveness
2011–2012	Under the leadership of Xavier Sala-i-Martin	Global Competitiveness Index	Introduce 12 pillars of competitiveness. Examine sustainable competitiveness by taking into account environmental and other vulnerabilities

Note: * The Business Competitiveness Index was called the Microeconomic Competitiveness Index until 2002 and was called the Current Competitiveness Index even earlier.

Source: Authors' compilation based on various issues of World Economic Forum's *Global Competitiveness Report 2000–2012*.

the 12 pillars of competitiveness (e.g. infrastructure, health, education and training, technological readiness etc.) and also studied the idea of sustainable competitiveness by taking into account environmental and other vulnerabilities (for details, see *Global Competitiveness Report* 2012: 3–74).

Table 8.5 *The World Economic Forum and its global competitiveness rankings of the USA and selected Asian countries, 2004–12*

Country	Index 2011–12	Rank 2011–12	Rank 2004–05
USA	5.47	7	2
Singapore	5.67	2	7
Japan	5.40	9	9
Hong Kong SAR	5.36	11	29
South Korea	5.12	24	21
Taiwan, China	5.28	13	4
Malaysia	5.06	21	31
China	4.83	26	46
India	4.32	56	55
Indonesia	4.40	46	69

Source: World Economic Forum, *Global Competitiveness Reports 2007–12*.

Despite the increasing sophistication in index construction, this knowledge apparatus still relies on assigning numbers to countries. It ranks and scores countries in terms of evaluative rules scoring the presence/absence of certain factors of competitiveness (see Tables 8.4 and 8.5). Notwithstanding their relatively short history, these indices are becoming part of a global statistical instrumentarium produced by international private authorities. This does not mean that they are not questioned (Krugman 1994a; Lall 2001; Kaplan 2003) but their circulation and recognition in the policy-consultancy world reinforce their hegemonic potential in and across many economic and political spaces. As a largely exogenous and constraining body of economic discourse, it is dominated by the language of competition in and through which indices serve to bench*mark* countries by visibilizing their competitive strengths and weaknesses (cf. Chapter 7). Countries are located in a number order which then functions as a disciplinary tool (or paper panopticon) with surveillance capacities over them. Its draws (more and more) countries into its number order, and countries are compared in terms of economic performance to each other and/or over time (see Table 8.5). It deploys numbers and tables to rank them. Annual revisions create a cyclical disciplinary art of country surveillance that institutionalizes a continuous gaze through numbers that depicts countries' performance via changing rank and score orders. Its power operates through the hierarchization of countries and their division into high/rising and low/falling economies in the competitive race.

As Table 8.3 showed, such performance, judgement and gap technologies are used to subject countries to the treadmill of competitiveness. Emphasizing gaps opens them to pressures to change economic and social policies in line with specific recommendations and 'best practices'. Places with a low or slipping position in the rank order are visibilized and targeted to become more competitive. Such ranking discourses are often used by government officials, think tanks and journalists to convey pride, needs, desires, gaps and even panics over economic restructuring. For example, actors may narrate a fall in this index order as threatening and/or a sign of 'hollowing out'/being marginalized. Performance- and gap-related questions often include 'who has it right', 'who has something to learn' and 'what direction to take for innovative activities'. They induce governments, firms and communities to embrace the competitiveness buzz. Indeed, some individuals, via workshops and training, even refashion themselves to become competitive subjects and economic categories (e.g. entrepreneurs and catch-up economies) in the race to gain a world-class ranking or, at least, surpass their immediate comparators.

There is more to this discourse, however, than its disciplinary power. Cox et al. (1997: 290–91) distinguish bench*marking* (as competition) from *bench*marking (as collaboration) and argue that, whereas the former is more externally imposed and top-down, the latter is more joint and responsive. But the notion of benchmarking in the *Global Competitiveness Report* is ambivalent in so far as it combines both aspects. On the one hand, the bench*marking* elements of the discourse on indices discipline countries in terms of an annual number order; on the other, its *bench*marking qualities see countries as sharing some 'bench' space with others, and each country acts upon its own conditions of competitiveness in the hope of enhancing them and acquiring greater capacities for self-guidance. Thus, in terms of technologies of power, the WEF's benchmarking report combines disciplinary and governmental power in so far as countries are externally regulated by the coercive force of indices and also expected to rework the managerial climate and public/private common sense so that it becomes more conducive to catch up, build clusters, enhance FDI and develop entrepreneurship and so on (see Tables 8.6 and 8.7).

On Regional–Local Scales: Framed by Catch-up, Poverty-reduction, Cluster-chain and Entrepreneurial Metaphors

On the regional scale, efforts to combine 'competitiveness' and 'development' discourses have increased since the early 2000s. Notable examples include the USAID's African Global Competitiveness Initiative, the Inter-American Development Bank (IADB)'s Multilateral Investment Fund for SME competitiveness, and the Asian Development Bank (ADB)'s Asian Development Outlook 2003. This chapter focuses on Asia and discusses briefly two ways in which the competitiveness discourses have been recontextualized by regional actors such as the ADB, the Asia Competitiveness Institute (ACI) in Singapore and strategy firms such as Enright, Scott and Associates Ltd with different foci (see Tables 8.2 and 8.6). The first focuses on the ideas of 'catch-up competitiveness' and 'poverty reduction', whereas the latter two are offshoots of the HBS and emphasize Porter's brand of cluster-building and competitiveness advice. Chapter 10 will focus on the recontextualization of this brand in Hong Kong by strategy firms.

The ADB, which is a regional counterpart of the World Bank, recontextualized 'competitiveness' in 'developmental' terms. Section 3 of its *Asian Development Outlook* (2003) narrates Porter-inspired ideas in terms of successive stages of technological and innovation development. Accordingly, Asian newly industrializing economies (NIEs) are seen as engaging in original equipment manufacturing (OEM), which produces standard and simple goods for export to developed countries. The recommended path is to imitate and 'catch up' with the developed countries via the development of own-design manufacturing (ODM) and own-brand manufacturing (OBM). With the electronics sector as its shining example, the term 'catch-up competitiveness' was coined by the ADB (2003) thus:

> The nature of catch-up competitiveness in the NIEs contrasts sharply with the traditional definition of technological innovation, namely the production of new (or improved) products, based on R&D . . . Furthermore, the stages model captures the fact that innovation occurs, not just in technological terms but also, and very importantly, in institutional terms. The technological change which took place in East Asia in electronics probably could not have occurred with such rapidity without the OEM and, later, ODM systems.

'Catch-up competitiveness' deploys 'path and journey' metaphors to frame goals and visions for the future. The 'path' metaphor structures movements of the East Asian NIEs and normalizes them as 'laggards' (with their own internal hierarchy) moving forward. Accordingly, their future trajectory is seen in terms of development through the promotion of technological innovation and market-friendly institutions. Taking Singapore as a paradigm of the export-oriented, MNC-led and FDI-driven growth model, Porterian industrial clusters are identified as the objects of competitiveness governance. They can be normalized and themed for other parts of Asia (e.g. the 'computer disk-drive' cluster in Thailand) by the ADB (2003) as follows:

The exploitation of MNC investment began in Singapore (Goh 1996) and was imitated by other countries wishing to export to OECD countries. Although FDI occurred prior to 1960s, the electronics industry brought with it a huge expansion of FDI in Southeast Asia, leading to the development of several industrial clusters. For example, the computer disk-drive cluster in Thailand is the largest of its kind in the world. Similarly, in Penang, Malaysia, the semiconductor assembly and testing cluster is the largest exporter of semiconductors worldwide.

The same section of the *Outlook* connects these themed clusters to the global market via the conceptual bridge of 'global value chains' (GVCs). This is a common term in the study of global capitalism (Gereffi and Korzeniewicz 1994). No mention is made of the uneven power relations between subcontractors/suppliers and global buyers and the term is invoked to indicate how the resulting market opportunities create the following advantages for Asian firms and 'clusters' by the ADB (2003):

> GVCs can enable firms to enter global production networks more easily, allowing them to benefit from globalization, climb the technology ladder, and gain wider access to international markets. GVCs provide firms with a wide spectrum of options to operate in global markets with a view to staying competitive... Entry into GVCs is easiest when an agglomeration of local buyers and manufacturers already exists, so that newcomers can learn from the established players. Sometimes, new entrants emerge as spin-offs from existing local firms or from MNC subsidiaries with which they establish a new GVC linkage. For countries and groups of firms outside successful clusters, accessing GVCs can be difficult.

Framed as 'beneficial' and offering 'opportunities', participation in GVCs is said to offer firms and 'clusters' access to global markets and chances to 'climb the technology ladder'. This way of reimagining how Asia might compete within the world market deploys a 'nodes and links' metaphor to frame the relationship between 'clusters' and the 'global chains'. More specifically, 'clusters' are presented as 'nodes' that can become drivers of development when 'linked' into GVCs. This combination of the 'path-journey' and 'node-link' metaphors in the 2003 *Outlook* constructs a regional identity and trajectory based on 'catch-up competitiveness'. This catch-up imaginary and its associated vision are also articulated with the World Bank's agenda of 'poverty reduction' and, thus, the 'catch-up competitiveness' discourses are also mixed with 'poverty-reduction', 'resilience-building' and 'cluster-based capacity-building' narratives.

This has implications not only for national policy but also for local policy and everyday life. Implicit in 'catch-up competitiveness' and/or 'poverty reduction' is the 'path' metaphor. It signifies a movement towards

The production of a hegemonic knowledge brand 313

a goal (goal attainment) and this in turn implies that clusters are objects of intervention. The development of 'intervention tools' to guide cluster growth becomes part of the agenda of the ADB and related institutions. In line with the World Bank's self-description as a 'knowledge bank', the ADB 'shares' development knowledge and builds capacity in the region via technical assistance, advice, training and grants. 'Capacity-building' discourses and practices of this kind are not simply a rational-adjustment process of socio-economic changes; they constitute a technology of power that involves a body of assistance-training knowledge that targets specific objects and locations (cf. Eade 1997; Cornwall 2007). The Asian Development Bank Institute (ADBI), in conjunction with other policy institutes, local governments, strategy firms and service-oriented NGOs, co-constructs this body of knowledge that managerialized and streamlined cluster-building via specific cluster programmes, strategic plans, pilot projects, toolkits, technical assistance schemes, policy workshops and training courses. More specifically, Table 8.6 illustrates some of these institutions and related discourses, practices and spatial foci on cluster-building (see Table 8.6).

In the case of Vietnam, the ADBI entered into partnership in 2006 with local development agencies (e.g. Institute for Industrial Policy and Strategy). With financial support from the Italian government and academic input from the Institute of Development Studies (IDS) of Sussex University, technical assistance and managerial techniques were formulated by UNIDO to promote clustering as part of Vietnam's industrial policy to enhance pro-poor growth. Here, the 'poor' were problematized as facing 'entry barriers' to employment, which restricted overall industrial development. This interpretation facilitated the use of 'supply-side capabilities' as entry-points to reflect on policies as well as to set up particular policy practices (e.g. cluster promotion) as the way forward. To this end, the National Programme Officer in Charge of the UNIDO Country Office, Le Thi Thanh Thao (United Nations Office Vietnam 2011) noted the following:

> Clusters and cluster promotion policies have become keywords in the policy debate in industrialized and developing countries. Under the framework of the Project SME Cluster Development, UNIDO wants to support the development of SME clusters in Vietnam through the UNIDO cluster methodology combined with tailored technical assistance and the promotion of business partnerships with Italian industries and clusters.

Funded by sponsors, UNIDO provided seminars/training courses for senior officials and practitioners. These practices subjectivized the 'poor' into the art of building clusters and related capacities. These included:

Table 8.6 Institutions and practices in building capacities and organizing themed clusters in Asia

Institutions	Spatial focus	Practices	Examples of workshop, report and themed clusters
Asian Development Bank Institute, Institute for Industrial Policy and Strategy in Vietnam and UNIDO	Transitional economies in Asia (e.g. Vietnam)	Policy seminars, workshops, courses, pilot projects, technical assistance etc.	Cluster-Based Industrial Development Workshop (2006) • Vietnam: software/ICT, fruit, ceramics, and agricultural products (rice, coffee, pepper, rubber etc.)
Asia Competitiveness Institute (Singapore)	ASEAN countries	Reports, information repository, training courses (for postgraduates and executives) etc.	Country report on *Remaking Singapore* (2008) • Petrochemicals, transport and logistics, finance, information technology and biopharmaceuticals *ASEAN Competitiveness Report 2010*
Enright, Scott and Associates Ltd (Hong Kong)	Hong Kong and Pearl River Delta	Consultancy reports, conferences, seminars, new briefings, luncheon meetings etc.	City report on *The Hong Kong Advantage* (1997) • Business and financial services, transport and logistics, light manufacturing and trading, property and construction, and tourism Report on *Hong Kong and the PRD: the Economic Interaction* (2003) • Pearl River Delta: electrical/electronic goods, software, toys, furniture, telecommunication products, plastics, clothing, port services, ceramics etc.

Source: Authors' own compilation based on Asian Development Bank, Asia Competitiveness Institute and Enright, Scott and Associates Ltd.

Table 8.7   UNIDO's managerial–technical discourses and practices related to cluster development

Training areas	Details
Methodology of a Cluster Development Programme	• Selection of clusters: based on cluster's importance, promotability, viability and sustainability • Diagnostic study: a participatory study to identify gap areas and to draw up strategic response • Trust-building: through pilot activities among stakeholders • Action plan: participatory activities to exploit opportunities and overcome problems • Implementation: initiated by cluster development agents, by local institutions and business service development providers • Monitoring and evaluation: for quantifying the outputs, feeding into new plans and disseminating best practices
Cluster maps	A pictorial description of a cluster system with: • important stakeholders groups and their numbers • their number and type of business distribution • business linkages among various cluster actors
Cluster development	• Foster entrepreneurship • Promote investments • Link to mature clusters (in Italy, China and elsewhere)

Source: Summary of information obtained from Asian Development Bank Institute, http://www.adbi.org/event/1641.clusterbased.industrial.development/events.resources.php?TypeID=21, accessed 20 December 2012.

(a) learning the methodology of a cluster development programme, (b) mapping potential industrial clusters in pictorial forms, and (c) enhancing cluster development and so on (see Table 8.7).

These UNIDO practices were further recontextualized in India under the stewardship of the Foundation of Micro, Small and Medium Enterprises (MSMEs) (Gulati 1988). It is beyond the scope of this chapter to examine the details of their cluster-based programmes and related best practices such as diagnostic studies, cluster observatory, study tours, writing of project reports, building common facilities centres, risk assessment of clusters and so forth (see Chapter 9). However, these managerial–technical discourses and practices related to clustering, capacity-building, training,

Table 8.8   Technology of agency that (re)organizes regional spaces, policies and populations

Sites of organizing agency	Ways of controlling/mapping agency
Regional space	• Market and foreign direct investment promotion • Themed clusters that link local SMEs with value chains and global market (see also Chapter 9) • Export-oriented and trade-based
Policies	• Governments playing catalytic or micro-economic supply-side roles • Improvement of access through knowledge, technology, innovation, skills, education, training, infrastructure and micro-finance • Improvement of FDI incentive packages (e.g. low tax, cheap land, establishment of 'one-stop shop') • Relaxation of foreign exchange controls • Provision of growth, development and poverty reduction
Types of agency	• Competitive, entrepreneurial and self-responsibilized individuals for 'catch-up competitiveness' and/or 'poverty reduction'

Source: Authors' own compilation based on Asian Development Bank and UNIDO documents.

risk assessment recall what neo-Foucauldians term the technology of agency (Cruikshank 1999), which combines participation and capacity-building in the processes of governing as well as controlling the exercise of agency. This array of discourses and practices on regional development produces 'participatory' actors equipped to perform their constructed but eventually self-guided role in promoting catch-up competitiveness, enhancing entrepreneurship and meeting neoliberal market challenges. Despite their capacitating aspects, they also control the organization of regional space, the policy for exercising agency and types of agency (see Tables 8.3 and 8.8).

Through this knowledging technology, actors were encouraged to treat regional spaces as (potential) clusters in which SMEs, suppliers, service providers and associated institutions interact to form export-led production- and/or service-oriented nodes (e.g. fruit, transport and logistics, apparel, electrical/electronic products, software etc.) that were opened to foreign direct investment and the sourcing of global retail chains (e.g. Wal-Mart) (see Chapter 9). It also self-responsibilized public and private agencies to meet market challenges by becoming competitive, entrepreneurial and world-market-oriented in their journey towards 'catch-up competitiveness' and/or 'poverty reduction'. In other words, it decomposed spaces, policies and population into objectivated factors of competitiveness that were governed through themed clusters, value chains, FDI, MNCs, entrepreneurship, technical assistance and competitive intelligence to improve access to global production and trade. Nisipeanu aptly described these practices as the 'regulation of the government in order to deregulate to support Porter's diamond' (2013: 2)

Such reinventions of the knowledge brand at regional level involve the articulation of discourses, technologies, institutions and practices that contribute towards the naturalization of the mantra of 'getting competitiveness right' in developing countries. Discursive apparatuses comprise ready-made, heterogeneous conceptual and practical tools (e.g. benchmarking reports, indexes, cluster programmes, manuals, methodology, observatory, best practices, technical assistance etc.). These apparatuses are also tied to forms of intellectual expertise (e.g. business school professors, world forum, knowledge bank, consultants, government officials and trainers/practitioners from development agencies). This assemblage of expert knowledge condenses and sediments 'competitiveness' as a dispositive of 'managerial truth' that disciplines and governmentalizes at a distance. Institutional and individual actors contingently articulate, subjectivate, guide and (re-)organize themselves to produce new practices and institutions through planning, training and affective–pragmatic identification with the competitiveness project across different sites and scales. Depending on their locations and related interests, individual subjects may reorganize themselves through training and affective–pragmatic identification with the competitiveness project, whilst others are ambivalent and even resistant in the institutional and everyday life of neoliberal developmentalism.

Nonetheless, these forms of governing common sense at a distance resonate and are reworked at different sites and scales with unintended consequences. They are recontextualized for different purposes and strategic actors selectively appropriate them to narrate diverse conjunctures. Specific event(s) can become switching point(s) for this narration to cement a particular coalition of interests. More specifically, this may allow them to: (a) declare previous policies as a failure; (b) justify new policy settings, institutions and governance regimes; and (c) work towards new accumulation strategies based on an 'unstable equilibrium of compromise' between groups/factions. However, these strategies and governance regimes are far from being neutral and they tend to privilege groups/factions that are tied to product markets, export sectors, value chains, government authorities, policy-consultancy domains and so forth.

NEOLIBERAL DEVELOPMENTALISM, CLUSTER POLICY AND RELATED STRUGGLES

As an integral part of these catch-up developmental regimes are their neoliberal complements. More specifically, cluster policy in developing countries involves micro-economic policies such as FDI promotion, enhancement of entrepreneurship, human capital building, land grants and tax reliefs (see Table 8.8) as well as relaxation of foreign exchange controls, lax labour and environmental laws, marketized finance and so on (see Chapter 9). This policy cocktail can be seen as a form of neoliberal developmentalism based on the confluence of regulation, deregulation and self-regulation bundled in a selective manner. The regulation involves the government's catalytic roles in providing micro-economic supply-side interventions; the deregulation comprises the relaxation of foreign exchange controls and other resource entitlements (e.g. land) for development; and self-regulation rests on the subjectivation and self-responsibilization of individuals to be entrepreneurial and competitive in the world market.

This mode of rule is not neutral, especially when its elements are mixed in ways that may lead to poor labour and environment conditions, shape land-use changes, and generate marketized finance that displace particular groups (e.g. farmers) from their plots and thus livelihoods; environmental degradation that destroys land and harms health; micro-financing that creates debt-related discontents and so on. Others use competitiveness as a pretext to appropriate land for real-estate development and speculation (Sen 2008: 92; Ramachandariah and Srinivasan 2011: 60; Sum 2011: 205). Critics have called these 'race-to-the-bottom' strategies and noted their asymmetrical impacts upon class, gender, place and nature (Chapter 9). Depending on how regional and local governments take steps to provide social cushions to alleviate these 'pressures in lived spaces' (Vijsysbaskar 2011: 43–4), households also develop their own coping strategies and/or demand greater equality and protection. Labour organizations, social movements, NGOs and place-based communal groups may engage in counter-hegemonic resistance to improve their environment, land/labour rights, local livelihood, as well as respect for the body politics of workers and their families. In this regard, personal and social struggles are an integral part of making and remaking cluster life. Recognizing these tensions and contradictions between global production and the vulnerabilities of local labour and local environment, movement-oriented NGOs, political and alternative media, etc., press multi-national corporations to improve labour and environmental conditions. The discourses of 'competitiveness' are being reinvented through processes of variation, selection, and retention. New themes include 'corporate social responsibility' (hereafter CSR), 'resilience', 'environmental sustainability' (see Chapter 9) and responsible competitiveness.

NEGOTIATING THE MEANINGS OF COMPETITIVENESS: 'GREEN', 'RESPONSIBLE' AND 'RESILIENT'

Faced with consumer activism, NGOs' tactics to name and shame global firms, and negative reporting from the media, there is increasing concern about reputational loss by multi-national corporations and their subcontractors. With intellectual–practitioner support from business schools, think tanks and consultancies, these firms seek to address these global–local tensions by moving from a defensive to a pro-active position within the same genre. In Bakhtin's term, this can be seen as a dialogue in a monologue context (1984: 185) to reinvent the hegemony of competitiveness discourses. The meanings of 'competitiveness' are recoded to be 'green', 'responsible', 'environmentally sustainable' and 'resilient'.

The discourse of 'green' competitiveness was first promoted by Porter and van der Linde (1995). They argued that a reduction in pollution and the use of green innovation can be a driver for improved productivity and competitiveness. This greening of competitiveness did not gain much resonance until the late 1990s. This is when NGOs highlighted the contradictions of the capital–nature–labour relation. The challenges of the 2008 financial crisis, with the impact of recession and doubts raised about continuing growth, gave further impetus to policy actors in (inter)national/regional organizations and think tanks to recontextualize competitiveness discourses. In particular, they began to develop new 'green' imaginaries. These include the 'Green New Deal', 'green competitiveness' and 'green competitiveness and resilience'. For example, in the European Union, the concern for the prolonged effects of the recession and continued financial market uncertainty have led to a call for green stimulus packages that would promote energy efficiency and green exports. Such a strategy was said to be able to avoid 'a race to the bottom' (C. Fischer 2011). In the World Economic Forum meeting in 2013, 'competitiveness' was stretched to connect the 'resilience dynamism' of countries and regions with 'social entrepreneurs' playing important roles in times of global financial, environmental and social crisis. These social entrepreneurs were labelled as 'architects of social dynamism' who could help to negotiate 'scalable solutions' to issues such as severe income disparity, chronic fiscal imbalances, rising greenhouse gas emissions and water supply crises.

Indeed, this 'social' agenda can be seen in other think-tank narratives that combine sustainability with responsibility in competitiveness. AccountAbility, which is a London-based think tank directed until 2009 by Simon Zadek, is one example. Zadek, whose background includes the Center of Government and Business in Harvard's Kennedy School of Government and experiences in the Copenhagen Centre and John Ruggie's UN Global Compact project, co-authored many reports with AccountAbility staff on corporate responsibility, climate change and collaborative governance. Noting the new discursive tools (e.g. Responsible Competitiveness Index in 2003 and Climate Competitiveness Index in 2010) that they have constructed, this chapter concentrates on their narratives on 'corporate responsible clusters' since 2003.

Building on Porter's work on 'industrial clusters' and thus extending the reach of the discursive chain, AccountAbility constructed the concept of 'corporate responsibility clusters' that could 'create competitive advantage within one or several sectors arising through interactions between the business community, labour organisations and wider civil society, and the public sector focused on the enhancement of corporate responsibility (Zadek et al. 2003: 2). This conception injects an element of stakeholder partnership into cluster thinking. Supported by national and regional governments oriented to bilateral foreign aid and development, such as the UK Department of International Development (DFID) and the Swiss Agency for Development and Cooperation (SDC), this CSR-cluster concept was recontextualized to SMEs in developing countries. In 2006 AccountAbility, which teamed up with UNIDO's SME Branch, operationalized its expertise in cluster-building in these countries. They co-produced a study on *SME Clusters and Responsible Competitiveness in Developing Countries*. Cluster was identified, yet again, as the site of intervention but, this time, in the direction of 'race to the top' based on being 'responsible' and adopting CSR and higher standards of environmental performance (AccountAbility 2006: 4–11). These challenges were seen as 'responsible business opportunities' that SME clusters could seize with the co-development of 'collaborative governance' and 'local capacity' (ibid.: 33–6). Such adoption of responsible business practices could then be seen as a strategy for cluster upgrading in which businesses, governments, civil-society organizations, and academic and professional institutions cooperated to improve the business environment.

This reimagination of cluster-based 'collaborative' governance still leaves the links between CSR and global chains unclear. Many scholars and practitioners discussed this link (e.g. Lund-Thomsen and Nadvi 2010; Spence et al. 2011: 58) and focused on how to facilitate 'compliance' with CSR standards via new local work models, audit system, certification, partnership and so on. However, this kind of competitiveness-driven CSR does not question the unequal power relations along the supply chains, the fear and struggles of subcontractors and workers, as well as the subordination of the social to the economic processes (see Chapter 9). Nevertheless, this round of the thickening and broadening of the competitiveness knowledge brand and related governance mechanisms resonates in a denser academic–policy–consultancy circuit with the rise of the CSR codes and accumulation via the 'Green New Deal'. It is beyond the scope of this chapter to examine these in detail; but Chapter 9 will addresses some of these issues by focusing on a global retail chain – Wal-Mart – especially how it sources from clusters in southern China, how it controls its supply chains, and the struggles and challenges of its CSR practices.

CONCLUDING REMARKS

This chapter has analysed the reinvention of 'competitiveness' from a theoretical paradigm through a policy paradigm to a hegemonic knowledge brand. The final step in this transition occurred in a conjuncture when the neoliberal strategy for 'getting the market right' was widely seen to be failing. This prompted the search for a new rhetoric, new strategies and new institutional fixes. The discourse of 'getting competitiveness right' became the new mantra because it could be fitted easily into the neoliberal worldview and because, more specifically, the conjuncture favoured this over other solutions to neoliberal market failure. This can be seen in the distinctive mix of agential, technological and discursive selectivities that helped to select and consolidate the competitiveness mantra. Although Porter was not alone in filling this cognitive and policy gap, his influence and career are exemplary in this regard.

First, he and his consultancy relays were well placed to provide proven and flexible policy technologies to map present and future sources of growth and, indeed, were sought out to do so. They then skilfully exploited these opportunities and filled the policy gap with flexible and simple supply-side intellectual technologies and micro-economic toolkits to build clusters in an increasingly integrated and competitive world market. Second, to consolidate and enhance this new policy frame, Porter and his associated consultancy machine replicated and modified their intellectual technologies in books, reports and case studies as well as speeches, conferences and service on high-profile councils, commissions and expert groups. These activities helped to sediment the Porterian approach to competitiveness as a knowledge brand in the consultancy–policy world. In this regard, it can be said that discourses help to make organic intellectuals and organic intellectuals make discourses (see Chapter 5). Third, the semantics of competitiveness policy, as a genre chain, links many discourses, themes and styles. This regime of competitive truth was recontextualized at different scales and sites by diverse individual and institutional actors. Multi-scalar constructions ranging from the *Global Competitiveness Report*/Global Competitiveness Index of the WEF to localized cluster development programmes were promoted by the Asian Development Bank, research institutes, think tanks, strategy firms and local business media. They also deployed knowledge apparatuses (e.g. benchmarking reports, indices, numbers, charts, best practices, outlooks, pilot projects, policy seminars, training) and related technologies of power (performance, judgement and agency). They selectively discipline the (re)organization of space, policies and populations as well as the framing of everyday rationalities and worldviews on pro-poor growth.

In the making of pro-poor cluster policy in developing countries, spaces, policies and people are decomposed and reassembled as factors of competitiveness that are governed through export promotion, FDI, MNCs, development aids, SME clusters, global chains and the world market. From a CPE perspective, these are not purely narratives; they involve a mix of regulation, deregulation and self-regulation practices that are being sedimented as part of neoliberal developmentalism. These modes of neoliberal rule are not neutral and they marginalize some groups and benefit others. Unsurprisingly, they provoke resistance from labour organizations, social movements, place-based communal groups and consumer activism that demand greater equality and protection for local communities and the environment, and respect for the well-being of workers and their families. These challenges have led to the reinvention of competitiveness discourses and practices by incorporating 'corporate social responsibility', 'environmental sustainability' and 'resilience as social innovation'. These new discourses are articulated with the Porterian knowledge brand to create 'responsible' and 'green' competitiveness. These recontextualizations have thickened and broadened the meanings and practices of 'competitiveness'. These negotiations and struggles over meanings and social practices will continue as neoliberal developmentalism re-embeds itself through a socially responsible and environmentally friendly agenda (see Chapter 9).

NOTES

1. The ten countries are Denmark, Germany, Italy, Japan, Sweden, Switzerland, the UK, the USA, South Korea and Singapore.
2. Clusters are made visible via the technique of 'cluster charts', which identify local industries based on export statistics and use the diamond model to test selected cases to establish a pool of unique clusters.
3. Monitor Group filed for bankruptcy on 7 November 2012 and was bought by Deloitte for USD116 million. *The Economist* (2012b) attributes this in part to the 2008 recession as few firms were willing to pay for pure strategy consulting; Denning (2012) argues that customers had realized the advice added no value.
4. On the objectives, projects and cluster initiatives, see The Competitiveness Institute website (http://www.competitiveness.org/article/archive/1/), the Asia Competitiveness Institute (http://www.spp.nus.edu.sg/ACI/home.aspx), the Monitor Group (http://www.monitorgroup.com.cn/en/) and ontheFRONTIER Group (http://www.otfgroup.com/home.html). All websites were checked on 29 July 2009. On the fate of Monitor, see note 3; the ontheFRONTIER Group was active in 2012 but its website was inaccessible in July 2013.
5. On the implications of Porter's model for regional development, see http://www.local.gov.uk/web/guest/economy/-/journal_content/56/10171/3510371/ARTICLE-TEMPLATE, accessed 25 July 2013.
6. Hindle, who compiled the *Economist Guide to Management Ideas and Gurus* (2008), described Porter as the guru on the idea of cluster-building.
7. Palgrave-Macmillan published the *Global Competitiveness Report 2004–5*. In its website material, the report was described as a 'unique benchmarking tool'; see http://www.palgrave.com/products/title.aspx?PID=270902, accessed 6 August 2009.
8. The Business Competitiveness Index was called the Microeconomic Competitiveness Index until 2002 and, earlier, the Current Competitiveness Index.

9. Competitiveness clusters, Wal-Martization and the (re)making of corporate social responsibilities

Competitiveness discourses and practices on cluster-building are a pervasive part of the neoliberal accumulation strategy, especially in developing countries (see Chapter 8). Some strategy firms and international organizations are engaged in recontextualizing the Harvard–Porterian brand with a view to linking clusters with the global markets. This chapter illustrates how cluster-building and the liberalization of trade in services in the global political economy mediate the rise of global retail chains such as Wal-Mart, and how Wal-Mart negotiates its corporate social responsibilities when challenged by consumer activism. This chapter has five sections. Section one elaborates the roles of strategy firms (e.g. Enright, Scott and Associates Ltd) and (inter)national institutions in visibilizing regional clusters as production, agricultural or service spaces that are (or should be) opened for global sourcing. This development on the cluster front was conjuncturally articulated to the liberalization of services (e.g. retail and banking) under the GATS agreement and to advances in information technology and logistical infrastructure. Exploiting these global changes as well as the demand for cheap consumer goods at home and abroad (Vidal 2012), retail chains (e.g. Wal-Mart, Tesco, Carrefour, IKEA) began to source globally, thereby shaping industrial clusters in developing countries. These global chains source either via global trading firms (e.g. Li and Fung Ltd) or procure via their own regional sourcing offices with the support of local commercial intelligence services. Using Wal-Mart as a case study, this chapter focuses on the rise of these global retailers and the ways in which they organize their supply chains to uphold their slogans such as 'Always Low Prices'. This kind of price competitiveness strategy marked the development of global retail capitalism. The Wal-Mart case indicates the coupling between low-cost supply chain clusters with its strategies of 'getting clusters right' by entering into glocal (global–local) partnerships; and uses micro-management techniques such as 'category management' and 'scorecards' to facilitate its strategies of control. The resulting asymmetries of power between global retailers and suppliers/

labour can be captured by the concept of 'Wal-Martization'. Such asymmetries are being challenged by labour unions, environmental groups and movement-oriented NGOs as a 'race to the bottom'. This challenge encouraged corporations to adopt self-regulatory codes of conduct to enhance investor and consumer confidence. The second section examines Wal-Mart's corporate social responsibility (hereafter CSR) regime and the challenges and limits of corporate codes, especially in regard to its reliance on auditing. The third section investigates Wal-Mart's recent attempt to remake CSR via its so-called 'beyond audit' approach. The fourth draws from Gill's idea of 'new constitutionalism' but supplements it by introducing the notion of 'new ethicalism' to highlight the logic of some emerging features of global capitalism. The fifth section concludes on how these changes have mediated the development of enhanced neoliberalism and highlights the value of a CPE approach to understanding the global retail chain, Wal-Martization and the reinvention of CSR.

COMPETITIVENESS CLUSTERS, WAL-MART AND WAL-MARTIZATION

Some strategy firms and international organizations specialize in recontextualizing the Harvard–Porterian brand and cognate approaches to developing countries (see Table 8.7). There are many of these attempts to provide consultancy reports, research papers, diagnostic studies and training manuals to render production clusters visible through their representation in map, tabular or diagram form (e.g. see Figure 9.1).

Competitiveness Clusters and Global Chains

One prominent strategy consulting firm is Enright, Scott and Associates Ltd. This firm was led by Michael Enright, who was a professor in Harvard Business School (HBS). Among other work, he co-wrote with Michael Porter (and Graham Crocombe) *Upgrading New Zealand's Competitive Advantage* (Crocombe et al. 1991) (see Chapter 10). On his transfer from HBS to the School of Business in Hong Kong University in 1996, the strategy firm produced many consultancy reports on Hong Kong and the Pearl River Delta sponsored by policy think tanks (e.g. The Foundation 2022) and/or government quangos (e.g. InvestHK). Chapter 10 deals with Hong Kong; this one focuses on the Pearl River Delta, which is a region to the north of Hong Kong. Their first report on this region was *Pearl River Delta: The Economic Interaction* (Enright et al. 2003). It was sponsored by The Foundation 2022, which is a policy think tank supported by a group of business leaders. This think tank was then chaired by Victor Fung, who was an HSB professor and met Enright while they were both there. On return to Hong Kong, Fung, a well-known public figure, took up the family's large sourcing and trading firm (Li and Fung Ltd). Under his chairmanship of The Foundation 2022, the Enright-led strategy firm co-wrote with Li and Fung Research Centre's managing director Ka-mun Chang the 2003 report on the Pearl River Delta. Material from this report, apart from being turned into a book, *Regional Powerhouse* (2005), was also the basis for six *Greater Pearl River Delta* reports commissioned by InvestHK between 2003 and 2010.

This genre chain of reports, books, meetings and consultancy activities privileged the Harvard competitiveness paradigm. The 2003 report especially stressed the specialized product clusters on manufacturing and marketing that gave the Pearl River Delta its competitive advantage. Using map(s) as a way to represent the region, it constructs and visibilizes the delta as a production space of consumer goods and some services so that global firms can plan (see Figure 9.1). By the time this body of knowledge was transformed into reports commissioned by InvestHK, it was described as a way of providing 'hard facts' for multi-national firms. Thus Enright and Scott and Associates argued that '[m]ultinational firms need hard facts and examples of how the "Hong Kong-Pearl River Delta Combination" translates into market opportunities, cost savings, and other business advantages' (2007: 2).

This discursive strategy is a way of gaining power in the consultancy world. Business intelligence reports of this kind claim to fill the knowledge gap and build capacities of multi-national and related sourcing firms. The effects of this are to govern and manage risk by making global production and sourcing more calculable and by making more visible the location of production sites (including sweatshops)(see Figure 9.1). This provision of 'hard facts' on 'supply chain clusters' (Wang and Mei 2009: 5) was rolled out on a larger scale by the Ministry of MSME (Micro, Small and Medium Enterprises) in India. Influenced by the UNIDO style of cluster mapping and diagnosing (see Table 8.8), the MSME posted the results of its cluster-making strategy on its Cluster Observatory website (http://clusterobservatory.in/clustermap.php). This website has detailed information of 1158 cluster initiatives in India. It offers searchable information by sector, state, district and product. Table 9.1 illustrates and highlights some of the major clusters and products.

The MSME narrated cluster-building as part of industrial policies that could enhance both competitiveness and poverty reduction as part of the general story about industrial policies, and used 'inclusive growth' to designate this imaginary. In India, once these clusters are envisioned and supported, they can be linked to global markets via cluster-building

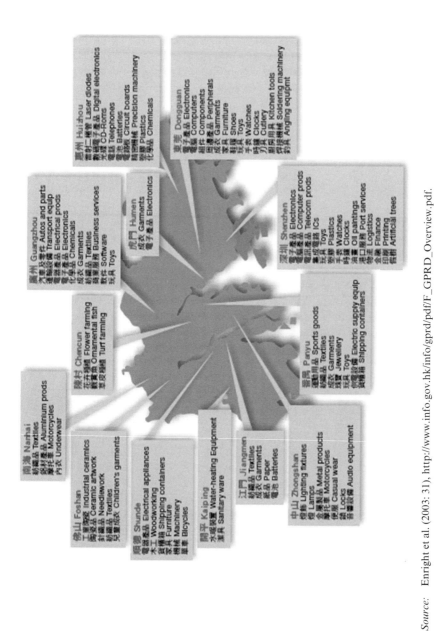

Source: Enright et al. (2003: 31), http://www.info.gov.hk/info/gprd/pdf/F_GPRD_Overview.pdf.

Figure 9.1   Mapping and making visible clusters in the Pearl River Delta

Table 9.1 Examples of products manufactured in major clusters in India

Sectors/products	Total no. of clusters	Examples of cluster and cluster name	State
Rice Mills	90	Sitapur Rice Mills Madurai Rice Mills Amritsar Rice Mills Ganjam Rice Mills	Uttar Pradesh Tamil Nadu Punjab Orissa
Textiles	88	Faizulre Powerloom Textiles Varanasi Powerloom Textiles Almedabad Yarn Jaipur Powerloom Textiles	Kerala Uttar Pradesh Gujarat Rajasthan
Garments	48	Noida Ready Made Garments Mumbai Ready Made Garments Kasaragod Garments Bangalore Ready Made Garments	Uttar Pradesh Maharashtra Kerala Karnataka
Plastic products	37	Jaipur Rope Noida Toys Agra Plastics Anand Egg Trays	Rajasthan Uttar Pradesh Uttar Pradesh Gujarat
Leather	19	Mumbai Leather Chennai Leather Wazirpur Leather Kanpur	Maharashtra Tamil Nadu Delhi Uttar Pradesh
Wood products	12	Nigina Wood Crafts Mathura Wood Drums Gonda Wood Products Churu Wood	Uttar Pradesh Uttar Pradesh Uttar Pradesh Rajasthan
Knitwear	6	Tirupur Knitwear Agartala Hosiery Ludhiana Knitwear Mumbai Knitwear	Tamil Nadu Tripura Punjab Maharashtra

Source: Authors' own compilation from the Cluster Observatory, MSME India.

facilitators and industry managers. These practitioners encourage cluster participants to: (1) exploit trade shows/import and export summits; (2) organize appointments with industry and trade contacts; (3) get listed on export databases; and (4) arrange site visits for buyers. Such trade facilitation enables these clusters to attract supply chains and the supply chains to shape the clusters around particular tasks demanded by global firms.

New Constitutionalism, Global Supply Chains and Wal-Mart

This development of export-oriented cluster strategies is coupled with the global neoliberalization of distribution and financial services under the WTO's General Agreement on Trade in Services (GATS) and Trade Related Investment Measures (TRIMS). These are multilateral trade agreements[1] that promote the gradual liberalization of international trade in services (e.g. finance, education, accounting and retailing) and investment. In the case of retail and wholesale services, the GATS rules mean that global supermarket chains that establish shops can challenge any local rules (e.g. opening hours and land-use laws) as barriers to trade. TRIMS is an attempt to prevent national governments placing conditions on foreign investors (e.g. the use of local produce or labour). From a neo-Gramscian perspective, the WTO–GATS–TRIMS strategy helps to tilt the global economic order towards neoliberal accumulation by creating a political–legal trade and investment framework that reconfigures power relations in favour of (trans-)national capital and against domestic government and citizens. On this particular scale of action, it fits into a political strategy designated by Gill (1995a) as 'new constitutionalism'. This involves 'the politico-juridical locking in of commitments to a disciplinary neoliberal framework of accumulation on the world scale' (Gill 2002: 2). In contrast with the old constitutionalism, which provides citizens with rights and freedom by limiting the power of the government, 'new constitutionalism': (1) locks in (or confers) privileged rights of (trans-)national capital by anchoring them in a cross-cutting web of (trans-)national laws and regulations; and (2) locks out (or insulates) market practices and issues from democratic scrutiny. In the retail trade arena, GATS operates as a form of new (global) constitutionalism to lock in the rights of 'big box' stores like Wal-Mart to set up stores in local sites by easing the local rules on number of stores, their locations and size limitations.[2] As for TRIMS, 'big box' stores are required to stock a certain percentage of local goods but this could be done via the self-certification of companies, making it hard to check for compliance. This 'softening' of the local allows global retail chains such as Wal-Mart to buy and sell in developed and developing countries alike.

These global structural changes help global retail chains (e.g. Wal-Mart, Tesco, and IKEA) to trade. Among these retail chains, Wal-Mart stands out as the world's second-largest firm according to Fortune 500 in 2012. It operates discount stores, supercenters, Neighborhood Markets and Sam's Club in the USA. Since 1991, it has run similar stores in Argentina, Brazil, Canada, China, Costa Rica, El Salvador, Guatemala,

Honduras, Japan, Mexico, Nicaragua, Puerto Rico and the UK, and through a partnership in India. It also sets up partnerships with global trading firms (e.g. Li and Fung) and has its own global procurement centres. Since 2002, Wal-Mart procurement has been headquartered in Shenzhen (southern China) with branches in Shanghai, Dongguan and Taiwan. Due to the rising value of the yuan (Chinese currency) and rising wages in China, it is increasingly sourcing from Bangladesh and India. In India, this is done through its partner (Bharti Walmart) and its own Procurement Centre in Bangalore, sourcing different products from export clusters (see Table 9.2).

Table 9.2   Wal-Mart's global procurement in India

Procurement centres/ partner	Product categories
Global Procurement Centre in Bangalore	Sourcing from India and Sri Lanka to Wal-Mart stores and Sam's Clubs globally
	Major product categories sourced from Indian clusters (e.g. Tirupur in Tamil Nadu, Mumbai in Maharashtra, Chennai in Tamil Nadu, Jaipur in Rajasthan etc.) (see Table 9.1) • Home textiles (including towels, shower curtains, bath mats, accessories, bedding sheets and kitchen linens) • Apparel (including woven, knitwear and leather footwear) • Leather accessories • Fine jewellery and housewares (including fine dining ware, home décor and table tops)
Bharti Walmart	Running seven farm procurement centres Purchasing directly from farmers from areas such as Narayangaon (near Pune)
	Product categories include cabbages, tomatoes, onions, grapes, cauliflowers and pomegranates
	Pilot scheme Sourcing grapes from farmers in Maharashtra for supplying to ASDA Wal-Mart in the UK Exploring opportunities to export other products such as musk melon, pomegranate and rice

Source: Adapted from *Economic Times* (India), 1 April 2012, and Domain-b.com, 24 May 2011.

Wal-Mart and Wal-Martization

Global procurement from developing countries, especially via SMEs in 'supply chain clusters', underpins Wal-Mart's price competitiveness. The latter is popularized under its slogan of 'Always Low Prices', which was replaced by 'Save Money. Live Better' in 2008. This discourse and related imagination of Sam Walton has its American origin in free-enterprise consumerism, 'servant leadership' combined with fundamental Christianity (Moreton 2007, 2009). It epitomized an amalgam of the cultures of business and Pentecostalist bible schools that drew on these discourses. Moreton (2007: 777) adds that this allied 'southwestern entrepreneurs, service providers, middle managers, students, missionaries, and even waged employees in the ethos of Christian free enterprise'. The resulting Christianization and 'southernization' of US corporate societal culture expressed itself in the service economy as *'how-may-I-help-you'?* Wal-Mart founded upon the imagined charisma of Sam Walton. The latter promoted the slogan of *'Everyday Low Prices'* and the beliefs in 'respect for the individual', 'respect for the customers' *and* 'striving for excellence' (Boje and Rosile 2008: 178).

Drawing on Sam Walton's special role in the American corporate landscape, Vidal (2012: 545–55) employed a regulationist perspective and named this accumulation regime 'Waltonism'. This suggested that the Wal-Mart model is replacing Fordism in the USA. For him, this regime, which is not limited to Wal-Mart, 'externalizes employment' (via outsourcing, downsizing, and anti-unionism) and 'internationalizes the economy' (leading to the reemergence of low-wage competition). Concentrating on the former (especially employment relations and modes of competition, Vidal 2012: 555), he attributed the latter to Wal-Mart's development as a buyer-driven supply chain (Gereffi and Korzeniewicz 1994) in global capitalism (Lichtenstein 2006). This chapter supplements Vidal's analysis with details on how low-cost accumulation is articulated to two supply-chain-related practices: (1) forming glocal (global–local) partnerships that connect to (and exacerbate) local forms of exploitation; and (2) developing micro-panoptic techniques to control the supplier system.

Forming glocal partnerships

During the crisis of Fordism and the search for viable post-Fordist models, leading intellectual forces were hard at work promoting and making cluster strategies in developing countries (see above and Chapter 8). In addition, the liberalization of services under the GATS agreement provided global contexts conducive to global production and cheap sourcing. Wal-Mart advisers, senior managers and consultants 'correctly' read this conjuncture as offering new possibilities and intervened strategically to extend its low-wage mode of accumulation globally via glocal partnerships. For example, it enters partnerships with local sourcing firms, wholesalers and supermarket chains. Wal-Mart took over or entered partnerships with local corporations (e.g. ASDA in the UK, Walmex in Mexico, Massmart in South Africa, Seiyu in Japan and Bharti Walmart in India). In China, it formed partnerships with the state-owned Shenzhen International Trust and Investment Company (SZITIC). The first of these glocal partnerships was the Wal-Mart SZITIC Department Store Co., Ltd, in which SZITIC holds a 35 per cent stake. SZITIC widened its Wal-Mart partnership by entering shopping mall development during the recent property boom. It set up the SZITIC Commercial Property Development Co., Ltd (SZITIC-CP) in 2003 and provides shopping centre spaces for Wal-Mart. This is achieved by entering joint ventures with regional–global financial capital coming variously from CapitaLand Group (Singapore property development consortium), Morgan Stanley (US corporate finance firm), Simon Property (US real-estate group), TimeWarner (US film and media corporation), and Prologis (US distribution facility provider) (see Figure 9.2). Such

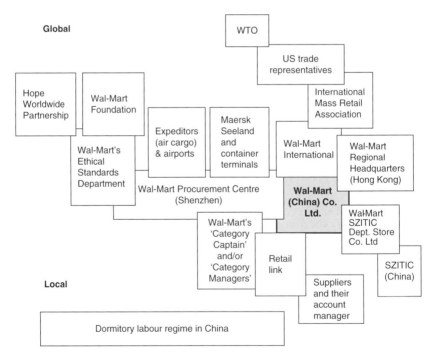

Figure 9.2 The glocal partnership of Wal-Mart in China

joint ventures between SZITIC-CP and trans-national capitals have facilitated Wal-Mart's expansion in China. Until the start of 2013, Wal-Mart operated 390 units in China.

Wal-Mart does not just retail in China; it famously sources from different parts of China. The rest of this chapter will focus on the sourcing side of the supply chain. Around 70 per cent of goods sold by Wal-Mart worldwide had a China component (Gereffi and Ong 2007: 48). It was estimated that Chinese exports to Wal-Mart were approximately US$25 billion for 2006 (ibid.). With rising wages, increasing exchange rate and product safety concerns, procurement from China is holding steady and Wal-Mart is stepping up its sourcing from India from 2007. Whether from China, India or elsewhere, Wal-Mart sources goods (directly or indirectly) from industrial clusters in massive volume with a tight turnover time. Local suppliers sustain Wal-Mart's price competitiveness via the intensification of pre-existing local forms of exploitation either from or beyond the production clusters (see above). There are ready global trading firms (e.g. Li and Fung), local wholesalers, commercial consultancy, economic intelligent firms, procurement centres that supply data, contacts and logistics links to major clusters. This array of supply-chain actors operates in clusters (and beyond) to link low-cost and labour-intensive SME suppliers with sourcing firms. These clusters are sites of cheap labour agglomerations or 'supply-chain cities/towns' with a plentiful supply of migrant workers from the hinterland (see Figure 9.1 and Table 9.1). In southern China, they use migrant workers who work long hours and live in nearby dormitories (Pun 2005) with rather lax labour regulations. They practise export-oriented flexible Taylorism (Jessop and Sum 2006: 167) by imposing overtime and long working hours under high seasonal work intensity (Chan and Unger 2011). Similar forms of local exploitation are found in India (with special reference to the knitwear cluster in Tirupur). It involves the use of migrant labour and youth, low salary packages compared with local workers, casualization of workers, weak unions, intense seasonal work schedules, subsidies from the state-run ration system, resilience of communities and families and so on (Vijsysbaskar 2011; Arnold 2010) (see Chapter 8).

Wal-Mart's panoptic control: database, categories and scorecards
Apart from employing cheap labour in its 'supply-chain clusters', suppliers in these clusters are subjected to tight production schedules as well as a managerial programme of control to reinforce Wal-Mart's lean retailing strategy. This squeezes costs based on economies of scale, turnover and low margins. This strategy is partly managed through a software programme called *Retail Link*, which was introduced in 1991, and connects

all Wal-Mart stores, distribution centres and suppliers. This system has made Wal-Mart the largest private satellite communication operator in the world. It operates a four-petabyte[3] data warehouse that collects and analyses point-of-sale (POS) data (e.g. store number, item number, quantity sold, selling cost etc.) as well as tracking inventory down to an individual item level. These capacities have allowed Wal-Mart and its suppliers to examine and forecast consumer demand patterns and to coordinate product sales and inventory data through the *Retail Link* system since 1996.

Mainstream economic and management studies argue that this technological prowess enables Wal-Mart to 'share information' with its suppliers and gain cost advantages based on automation, joint demand forecasting and the 'just-in-time' supply system (e.g. bar-code-triggered replenishment, vendor-managed inventory and faster inventory turnover time) (Holmes 2001; Basker 2007). However, the use of such 'data-gathering' and 'information-sharing' in lean retailing (Bonacich and Wilson 2006: 234–5) is not neutral (Free 2008: 637–40). From a Foucauldian perspective, the vast database on products and suppliers is an instrument of panoptic supervision that helps to reduce Wal-Mart's costs. This ordering machine of the mega-retailer is based on particular micro-calculations that transform products and suppliers into objects whose costs/margins are to be disciplined via procurement practices such as 'category management' and scorecards. We examine them in turn.

'Category management', which is a procurement practice that began in the supermarket business, allows giant retailers to improve sales and profits by managing product categories (e.g. apparel, toys and housewares) as separate business units. For Spector (2005: 77), this practice allows supermarkets 'to oversee the store not as an aggregation of products, but rather as an amalgam of categories, with each category unique in how it is priced and how it is expected to perform over time'. Wal-Mart began its own 'category management' in the food sector and extended it to other products. This practice allows the retailer to work with its suppliers to 'improve performance in a product through coordinating buying, merchandizing and pricing' (Pradhan 2010: 154). Category captains (formerly called 'buyers') and category managers are appointed to facilitate these retailer–supplier contacts and, in the case of Wal-Mart, via the Retail Link system. Underlying 'category management' is a range of calculating practices related to 'category planning' that requires, *inter alia*, the monitoring of the profitability of each product category (Christopher 2005: 111). In the name of improving profitability and efficiency, suppliers must open their accounts to retailers (called 'open-book accounting') with the aim of coordinating activities to reduce costs and/or maximize inevitably low

Table 9.3 Examples of knowledge produced in Wal-Mart Category Scorecards

Measurement criteria	Elements of measure
Sales measurements	• Overall % increase • Comparable same store sales • Average sales/store • Sales at full price vs markdown
Markdown measurements	• Markups and markdowns (dollars, units and %) • Previous and current retail price
Margin measurements	• Initial margin • Average retail price • Average cost • Gross profit at item level • Gross profit/item/store • Margin mix
Inventory measurements	• Replenishable store inventory • Non-replenishable store delivery • Warehouse inventory • Lost sales from out-of-stocks • Excess inventory • Past date code • Total owned inventory
Return measurements	• Customer defective returns • Store claims

Source: American Logistics Association, Exchange Roundtable 2005.

margins. For example, suppliers to Wal-Mart are trained through a help desk and classes (organized in house or outsourced) to submit reports to its Retail Link on matters such as inventory, pricing, performance, sales and promotion.

To assemble and manage this mass of information, suppliers are obliged to complete category scorecards. As a form of technically based selective knowing, these cards capture the financial details of the demand-driven supply chains (Christopher 2005). Scorecards allow Wal-Mart category managers (and their assistants) keyhole views into the suppliers' 'sales', 'markdown', 'margins', 'inventory' and 'return' (see Table 9.3). Further measurements concern changes in the environment (e.g. the demand for sustainability). In general, this technical apparatus produces a new knowledge space that renders suppliers' financial conditions visible in order to identify cause-and-effect relations bearing on the chain's efficiency and profitability (Edenius and Hasselbladh 2002: 249–57; Norreklit 2003: 601).

Under constant pressure to review product categories, the identification of cause-and-effect relations provides the everyday bases of calculation, intervention, hard-nosed negotiation and control. These control mechanisms enable category managers to perform the following routine activities: (1) evaluate the change of each supplier's costs and margins and require it to match its lowest price or even cut it; (2) compare each supplier's costs and margins with the average; (3) introduce a form of coordinated competition among suppliers (e.g. ask a specific supplier to match the lower prices of competing suppliers); (4) ask for alternatives based on a panoramic view of the suppliers' costs and margins; and (5) claw back funds (or in Wal-Mart's term 'payment from suppliers') in the form of 'volume incentives, warehouse allowances, and reimbursements for specific programs such as markdowns, margin protection and advertising' (Wal-Mart 2007: 44).

As illustrated by the micro-accounting practice of category scorecards, 'information-sharing' in the supply chain is technologically selective in that it privileges and sustains organizational control based on 'super-vision'. This term refers to control through superior information (cf. Willke 1997), based on its databases. The visibility and benchmarking of suppliers enable Wal-Mart's category managers to demand lower prices, benchmark the average, squeeze margins and demand refunds from suppliers. Such disciplining of suppliers can be seen, in neo-Foucauldian terms, as a cost-squeezing Panopticon constructed in virtual space.[4] Computerized corporate 'wardens' conduct organizational and data surveillance of suppliers who are also engaged in a self-disciplinary gaze. This does not mean that suppliers are 'docile bodies'; they conform (or act to conform) and avoid being struck off the Wal-Mart list, reduce their dependence on Wal-Mart, and sell elsewhere by claiming that they were Wal-Mart suppliers. In short, the capacity of this category management and scorecard-ordering machine enables Wal-Mart to squeeze margins from suppliers (see below on the factory-rating system as another example of organizational surveillance). This seemingly 'managerial–logistical–information fix' is micro-political as well as techno-economic in its surveillance of costs and margins. Thus it exhibits asymmetrical power relations that transform capital-to-capital social relations, in particular by tilting the balance in favour of the retailers over the suppliers–manufacturers in the buyer-driven commodity chains (French 2006).

With this informational 'super-vision', Wal-Mart's procurement staff are constantly making deals with thousands of suppliers to produce goods tailored to Wal-Mart's own stringent specifications, including pricing, quality assurance, sales, efficiency, delivery and, more recently, sustainability requirements. For many Wal-Mart suppliers entering the negotiations centre, the experience is tough. If their goods do not match Wal-Mart's specified sales/price level, suppliers are immediately shown the door. In the negotiation centre, supply deals are made, or terminated, 'in a heartbeat' (Bonacich and Wilson 2006: 239). This firm grip over suppliers–manufacturers and the unrelenting push for cost and price-value competitiveness means that manufacturers, in turn, must pass on their costs and production insecurity (e.g. penalty payments for missing deadlines or termination of orders) to their own workers and related ones (e.g. labourers in the logistics sector).

Suppliers are not only subjected to tight production schedules but also squeezed through the 'scorecard' calculating practices reviewed above. These top-down multiple pressures are passed on to Wal-Mart suppliers and related subcontractors and their workers further down the production chain. The lower the workers are in this chain, the lower their wages (Xue 2011: 40). The International Labour Rights Fund (ILRF) describes 'Wal-Mart Sweatshops' where wages are cut and safety and welfare measures ignored. This was disclosed in a report from Students and Scholars Against Corporate Misbehaviour (SACOM 2007), a Hong-Kong-based NGO that monitors Wal-Mart activities. The report identified extensive labour abuses (e.g. wage and hour violations, unsafe working conditions, deprivation of labour contract protection) in five factories in China that manufactured toys for Wal-Mart. Similar problems were identified by the Clean Clothes Campaign in its *Cashing In* report (2009). The latter focused on the garment supply chains of the five big retailers (Wal-Mart, Tesco, Carrefour, Aldi and Lidl), and highlighted the poor conditions of their workers in Thailand, India, Bangladesh and Sri Lanka.

It is not just labour issues in subcontracted factories that matter in the long buyer chains. Raw materials and finished goods must be (un)loaded in container ports, and these supplies are integrated into chains. Delays in the logistic flows mean missed deadlines and penalties for the suppliers. These cost- and time-based pressures of global sourcing/production place contractors and workers in container ports (e.g. crane controllers, workers responsible for fastening containers and trailer crew) under pressure to shift consignments quickly and cheaply. There is rising dissatisfaction with working conditions in container terminals (e.g. long working hours, irregular lunchtimes, injuries, long queuing time, lack of toilet facilities etc.). There were several strikes at container terminals at the beginning of 2013, notably in Vallarpadam in India, Ain al-Sokhna Terminal in Egypt, and Kwai Chung in Hong Kong, indicating further sites of tension along the stretched supply chains.

These unequal relations between retailers, suppliers and workers along the supply chains are better summarized as Wal-Martization than internationalization of the economy under Waltonism. Building on the definition provided by SACOM (2007), and concentrating on the production and production services side, this chapter has demonstrated how Wal-Martization promotes changes in the technical and social relations of production with the result that power shifts from suppliers–manufacturers to giant retailers, with the former trickling insecurity and hardship downwards to flexible workforces in the organization of disciplinary low-cost strategy. This process is mediated by changes in technological–logistical and managerial–calculative practices that enable the giant retailers to more effectively conduct organizational surveillance of suppliers and allow the latter, in turn, to engage in self-monitoring, as well as, to some extent, tactical manoeuvres in the buyer–supplier game.

CORPORATE WATCH, ETHICAL STANDARDS AND THEIR LIMITS

The process of Wal-Martization, with its associated contradictions along the long supply chain and its accumulation strategy based on profit via disciplinary cost-reduction practices, has prompted growing (trans-) national and local criticism and resistance. There are challenges coming from unions, NGOs and community groups such as AFL-CIO's Eye on WalMart, CorpWatch, Wal-Mart Watch, Wake-Up Wal-Mart, Sprawl-Busters, Frontline, Wal-Mart Class Website, Clean Clothes Campaign, SACOM and India FDI Watch targeting the activities of the corporation (Sum 2010b: 60). In general, groups within and beyond the USA are challenging Wal-Mart's non-union strategy, sexual discrimination, poor health care, unpaid overtime, threats to local small retailers, aggressive land-use policies, destruction of US jobs, low labour standards, use of child labour, long working hours and poor dormitory conditions in its suppliers' factories. This all started in 1992, when the National Broadcasting Company (NBC)'s *Dateline* news programme reported on the use of child labour in Bangladesh to produce clothing for Wal-Mart. These challenges led to consumer boycotts and (temporary) falls in Wal-Mart's share price. In order to maintain the fine balance between political demand and corporate interests, Wal-Mart began to adopt two pro-corporate strategies: (1) to improve its image as 'good corporate citizenship' by playing to its strengths; and (2) to adopt a corporate social responsibility strategy compatible with its business strategy.

First, it set up a 'war room' in 2005 to pre-empt criticisms and professionally manage discourses about the company. Its CEO, Lee Scott, was seen as the public relations voice of Wal-Mart and frequently advanced arguments that played to its strengths, For example, Scott emphasized that the low prices that Wal-Mart offered 'are a lifeline for millions of middle and lower-income families who live from payday to payday' (2005: 2). The company also conducts campaigns and provides press releases and website information on personal stories of how employees benefit from its health care plan and how Wal-Mart's schemes benefit the economy. This Wal-Mart genre chain, which is constructed to publicize the company's positive contributions to the community and economy, is often contested by anti-Wal-Mart groups, creating a public dialogue. The latter use cyber tools to organize local campaigns, provide 'alternative facts', host viewing of Greenwald's film *Wal-Mart: The High Cost of Low Price*, sign petitions, and send letters to politicians on Wal-Mart's excesses (Davies 2007: 51–3).

Second, Wal-Mart began to adopt a version of CSR that blends in with its business strategy. In the development of CSR, there are two schools of thinking, with one being more pro-economic as a business strategy and the other more pro-social to guarantee a living wage for workers (den Hond et al. 2007: 2). To protect its reputational and brand capital, Wal-Mart adopted a more pro-business version of CSR. It adopted self-regulatory codes/standards to boost investor and consumer confidence. Its CSR regime involves the setting up of an Ethical Standard Programme with elaborate factory certification protocols. This programme included standards for suppliers, certification of labour standards and training components, and, since 2006, audits have also verified environmental standards (see Table 9.4). Up to 2008, audits were performed by Wal-Mart-trained global procurement auditors and/or Wal-Mart associates. They have been carried out by third-party service providers since 2009 (Wal-Mart 2003).

Wal-Mart, in pursuance of reputational risk management, produces an ethical sourcing report that includes comments on its ability to monitor, train and enforce these standards. This has attracted much hostile comment. In 2007, Wal-Mart Watch criticized its 2006 report for glossing over the serious problems with its supply chain (Roner 2007). Some of these problems were highlighted by a SACOM report (2007), which described Wal-Mart's auditing process as 'self-policing'. According to this report, which was entitled *Wal-Mart's Sweatshop Monitoring Fails to Catch Violations: The Story of Toys Made in China for Wal-Mart*, factory inspections were announced in advance and managers coached workers to give the 'correct answers'. Workers were encouraged to become 'voluntary liars' through a material incentive of RMB 50 yuan (approximately US$8 at the prevailing exchange rate) and were also told the little capitalist tale

Table 9.4   Wal-Mart Ethical Standards Programmes 1992–2011

Year	Wal-Mart Ethical Standards Programmes
1992	• Wal-Mart's Factory Certification programme • Include Standards for Suppliers according to local employment and labour laws • Focus on Bangladesh and China
1993–96	• First Factory Certificate programme manual • Pacific Resources Exports Ltd auditing factories directly producing for Wal-Mart • PricewaterhouseCoopers was involved in auditing at a later stage
1997–2001	• Factories in Egypt, Pakistan, India and Nicaragua were added
2002	• Assumed its own global procurement and directly managing its Factory Certificate programme
2003	• Wal-Mart Ethical Standards associates train buyers, suppliers and factory managers on Wal-Mart Supplier Standard • A product quality assurance programme (including reviews and internal audit)
2006–11	• Expand to include environmental elements in the audit process (e.g. packaging scorecard and Sustainability Product Index) • Founding of the Sustainability Consortium • 'Beyond audits' and Supplier Development Programme • Third-party auditing • Global Women's Economic Empowerment Initiative

Source: Adapted and updated from Mutuc (2006).

that a factory's loss of orders would translate directly into workers' loss of future employment opportunities. In addition, factory owners manufactured 'wage documents' and 'time cards' that indicated that workers were sufficiently paid in terms of base and overtime wages without exceeding the maximum working hours. In reality, workers' monthly wages shrank significantly and overtime was not recorded (ibid.: 15).

All these criticisms indicate the pro-corporate and pro-management nature of the auditing practices in the implementation of a CSR programme (see also O'Rourke 2002 and 2003; Sum and Pun 2005; Clean Clothes Campaign 2005). Its 'self-policing' practices also allowed for 'self-serving' calculations in which the corporation and its suppliers appropriated CSR as part of their business strategies – to secure reputation and

Table 9.5 Wal-Mart's system of factory ratings and results

Factory ratings	Degree of violations/risk	Conditions of order	Audit validity	Audit results (in %)		
				2006	2005	2004
Green	No/minor violations	Orders can be placed	Re-audit after two years	5.4	9.6	19.1
Yellow	Medium-risk violations	Orders can be placed	Re-audit after 120 days	51.6	37.0	38.8
Orange	High-risk violations	Orders can be placed	Re-audit after 120 days	40.7	52.3	32.5
Orange-age	One or two under-aged workers found		Re-audit after 30 days	0.4	0.8	8.8
(Grey)			Four orange ratings in a two-year period result in a factory being disapproved	2.10	0.1	8.8
Red/failed	Most serious	Existing orders are cancelled No future orders	Permanently barred	0.2	0.2	0.8

Source: Wal-Mart (2006).

stock market value for the former and certificates and future orders for the latter. As part of its overall business strategy, Wal-Mart needs to secure its reputation and thereby its stock market value in the financial markets via its ability to manage its 'reputational risk'. Given that investors tend to be reactive rather than pro-active, the control of CSR information in company reports is critical. One particular knowledge apparatus deployed to demonstrate 'ethical sourcing' is the factory-rating system which benchmarks factories in the supply chains.

As a discursive micro-technique, its role is to assess suppliers in four colours (green, yellow, orange and red). Drawing loosely on a traffic-light metaphor, it selectively classifies, categorizes and excludes/includes suppliers according to their compliance with labour standards (see Table 9.5). As a discursive tool, it helps to showcase Wal-Mart's 'ethical sourcing' performance (see Table 9.4 on audit results), and indicate its efficiency and competence to the consumer and investor publics via its reports and the business media. This way of constructing suppliers as objects of Wal-Mart's ethicalism also allows the factories to become objects of intervention. By rating some of them as problems, Wal-Mart created a 'three-strikes' approach in its 2003 Factory Certification Report.[5] Thus: (1) if a factory owned and/or utilized by a supplier is deemed 'failed', it will not accept any merchandise from that particular factory and the supplier receives a 'first strike'; (2) if another factory owned and/or utilized by that supplier fails, it will not accept merchandise from that second factory and the supplier receives a 'second strike'; and (3) if a third factory owned and/or utilized by the same supplier fails, or if it concludes at any time that the supplier has a pattern of non-compliance, the supplier receives a 'third strike' and Wal-Mart will cease doing business permanently with the supplier (Wal-Mart 2003: 10–11).

Such discipline-and-punish mechanisms displace the costs of purging 'sweatshops' on to its suppliers; those found to be in serious non-compliance with its codes are struck off the Wal-Mart supply chain permanently (SACOM 2007: 15). This panoptic system of factory-rating, which categorizes and places suppliers in green, yellow, orange and red categories, is part of this vast database. In short, this panoptic system of scorecards and ratings produces calculating practices, constant surveillance and even fear that discipline, control and judge suppliers–manufacturers to: (1) visibilize their costs and margins; (2) review delivery dates, costs and prices of their products under constant gaze; (3) enter into hard-nosed negotiations with Wal-Mart's category managers; (4) routinize cost surveillance in everyday business life; (5) prevent their factories from being struck off the certification system and losing orders. This micro-politics of control trickles down to the workers in terms of job insecurities, longer working hours, welfare cuts and the spread of market logics. In this regard, the institutionalization of CSR procedures and systems produces the paradoxical result that more effort goes into preparing reports, auditing factories, obtaining certificates, ensuring orders and keeping jobs than actual advancement of labour rights protection. This tendency to managerialization and commodification of CSR has led to CSR-ization in which auditing and managerial practices of securing certificates/orders take priority over the social–moral elements in corporate responsibility. In this regard, the 'S' in CSR is taken over by 'A' as in corporate 'audit' responsibility.

In theoretical terms and drawing from Foucault (1977), CSR-ization can be seen as a technology of control in which the audit and certification discourses, practices and procedures are used to ward off dangers and gain mastery over social activism. More specifically, this technology of control involves a 'procedure of rarefaction', based on a selective thinning of the moral elements in corporate responsibility and its accompanying thickening of managerial practices (e.g. standards, audits, time cards, reports and certificates) in the name of CSR. These processes are mediated by ethical standard departments of big corporations, audit firms, consultancy firms, lawyers, service-oriented NGOs and so on. Apparatuses such as mission statements, programmes, standards, sourcing reports, audit reports and certificates are used. These are supported by managerial logics of inspection, auditing, form-filling, filing, ratings, certifications and indexes. This programme of power serves to control and discipline suppliers via hierarchical observation and categorization. Data are gathered under the managerial-surveillance gaze of CSR experts and their 'report and certification order'. They act as a kind of paper panopticon[6] that monitors and punishes suppliers by striking them off the Wal-Mart list. These control programmes normalize and discipline through principles of observability, monitoring, reporting, categorizing, benchmarking and rating. The dominance of the managerial-audit gaze by such rational instrumentalities as 'scorecards', 'costs', 'inventory', 'codes of conduct', 'certificates', 'reports', 'factory-rating' and the like are largely disciplinary in nature.

REINVENTING CSR: WAL-MART'S 'BEYOND AUDITS' AND TECHNOLOGIES OF SELF-GOVERNING

These criticisms of its self-regulatory codes as audit-centric and unlikely to lower 'reputational risk' have recently prompted the reinvention of Wal-Mart's CSR identity and practices. Acting on advice from various academics/consultants and stakeholders, Wal-Mart is attempting to manage its risk via selective appropriation of environmental and social discourses and practices (e.g. sustainability, community involvement and empowerment of women) (see Table 9.4). Its long supply chain has been criticized not only on account of labour conditions but also for being environmentally destructive and fossil-fuel-intensive. Using Hurricane Katrina as the pretext to address environmental and social issues in 2005, Lee Scott, the then CEO, partially reinvented Wal-Mart's image by introducing some environmental cost-saving measures such as waste reduction and use of renewable energy. The corporation also founded The Sustainability Consortium, a multi-stakeholder group that involves university research centres,[7] retailers, suppliers, NGOs and government, to develop a global database on product sustainability through their life cycles. Meanwhile, Wal-Mart itself created its own Sustainability Index and Sustainable

Product Index. These are managerial tools that enable Wal-Mart to claim environmental responsibility by imposing government rules on suppliers. However, advocacy groups such as Food and Water Watch pointed out that '[n]o amount of greenwash can conceal the fact that Walmart [sic] perpetuates an industrialized food system that diminishes our natural resources, causes excessive pollution, and forces smaller farmers and companies to get big or get out of business' (CorpWatch 2012).

For space reasons, this chapter now focuses more on the social-audit dimensions of Wal-Mart. In a global sourcing report, Wal-Mart acknowledged the rise of 'audit fatigue' as some suppliers can be audited up to ten times a month by different parties (Walmart Canada 2007). Drawing on the current round of (risk) management discourses (e.g. best practices, capacity-building, learning organization etc.), its 2009 CSR Report (Walmart Canada 2009) constructed new ethical labels (e.g. 'responsible sourcing') that reinvent CSR in at least three ways: (1) coordinating global retailers to work together to establish common audit standards and reference codes; (2) going 'beyond audits' via a supplier development programme; and (3) the provision of local support for workers (see Table 9.6).

First, Wal-Mart, Tesco, Carrefour and Metro jointly announced the establishment of the Global Social Compliance Programme (GSCP) in 2008 (see Table 9.6). This is a retailer-led scheme that advocates the aggregation of 'best practices' from existing social compliance activities to provide a universal, shared set of reference codes for buyers and suppliers. For Wal-Mart, the GSCP seeks to: (1) consolidate 'best practices' into a single toolbox; (2) enable existing supplier databases to share the cost and incidence of audit duplication; (3) reduce costs for the retailers and their suppliers; and (4) free resources to focus on building capacities of factory management. It has produced a reference code for labour practices based largely on international conventions and guidelines. The code specifically addresses forced, bonded, indentured and prison labour; child labour; freedom of association and recognition of the right to collective bargaining; discrimination, harassment and abuse; health and safety; wages and benefits; and working hours. The GSCP Secretariat asked several NGOs to join but it was rejected by the Clean Clothes Campaign.[8]

In 2009, GSCP pushed ahead with the development of more management instruments (e.g. 'methodology' and 'six-step plans'). Second, this managerially charged construction of 'best practices' and the building of capacities are also prominent in Wal-Mart's other new schemes tied to 'responsible sourcing'. One example of the 'beyond audit' scheme is the Factory Five Programme. It involved Wal-Mart choosing five suppliers/factories from each region, which then met the local Wal-Mart Ethical Standards team monthly to learn and identify 'best practices' in ethical

Table 9.6 Wal-Mart's reinvention of CSR, 2006–12

Nature of the scheme	Name of major programme	Characteristics/examples
Raising the standard	Global Social Compliance Programme (Reference Codes) 2008	• Recognizing 'audit fatigue' • Establishing common reference codes and databases among members (e.g., Wal-Mart, Carrefour, Tesco Metro etc.) • Aggregation of best practices

Beyond audits	Supplier Development Programme	• Improving factory performance
		• Building capacities and best practices
		• For example: Factory Five Programme 2006
		  ➢ Choosing five factories from each region
		  ➢ Meetings between five factories/ suppliers and local Wal-Mart Ethical Standards teams
		  ➢ Facilitating mutual learning, cumulating best practices

Local support for workers and women entrepreneurs	International Development Programme	Asia Foundation, China 2006 • Providing migrant women workers with scholarships • Recipients will go on to support other students Hope Worldwide, Training Programme, India 2007 • Setting up 'Industrial Centres of Hope' in industrial clusters • Empowering vocational training for factory workers and their families • Tailoring to the needs of local businesses Global Women's Economic Empowerment Initiative 2011 • Increase sourcing from women-owned businesses • Empower women on farms and in factories through training, market access and career opportunities • Increase gender diversity among major suppliers

Source: Adapted from Wal-Mart Canada (2008, 2009) and http://news.walmart.com/news-archive/2011/09/14/walmart-launches-global-womens-economic-empowerment-initiative.

sourcing. This knowledge would then be shared with other Wal-Mart suppliers and other retailers. Third, the 'local support for workers' scheme encompasses the provision of worker scholarships and training in industrial clusters through projects such as the Asia Foundation China (see Table 9.6).

These recent attempts to 'upgrade' Wal-Mart's CSR practices via management tools such as creating/dissemination of best practices, joint working by learning, and capacity-building via education and training can be seen as technologies of self-governing (Miller and Rose 1990). These governmental technologies aim to govern the conduct of dispersed actors and exercise indirect control via visibilizing suppliers, factories, workers and female entrepreneurs as sites of change.

Unlike the sole use of auditing, which operates mainly as a measurement–disciplinary mechanism, these 'beyond-audit' apparatuses and institutions condense a dispositive that operates through governing at a distance. In this regard, CSR responsibility has shifted on to these groups. They are (self-)responsibilized and work on themselves to adopt 'best practices' and develop their own capacities/aspirations to take advantage of learning, training, career opportunities and empowerment. Such technologies reframe corporate CSR in two new ways: (1) the sites of self-governing have increased; and (2) corporations, together with their suppliers, factories, workers and female entrepreneurs, become part of this self-governing and self-enterprising game. Put differently, this mode of self-governing has become multi-site and multi-actor with the result that more parties govern themselves by performing actions to become more productive and/or entrepreneurial along the global supply chains (see Chapter 8 on technology of agency). It operates through the governing of the self, and individuals refashion their subjectivities so that these distant parties concerned become part of a division of (self-)governing labour in the elongated supply chains.

ARTICULATION BETWEEN 'NEW CONSTITUTIONALISM' AND 'NEW ETHICALISM': ENHANCED NEOLIBERALISM

Wal-Martization and its associated CSR agenda illustrate the emergence of practices of global retail governance that are based on the articulation of institutional symbols and practices such as WTO's service liberalization, cost-cutting, codes of conduct, reporting, (beyond) audits, resilient supply chain, sustainability index and community involvement. This raises the question why such competitive–ethical discourses and practices are being combined and circulated trans-nationally. Inspired by the neo-Gramscian approach (Cox 1987; Gill 1995a), this chapter has argued that, by emphasizing and adopting CSR programmes, corporations are able not only to avoid legal regulation but also respond to civic activism in self-interested ways through 'risk management', building 'reputational capital' and enhancing 'responsible competitiveness' and sustainability (Zadek 2005) (see Chapter 8). These efforts represent, in part, a 'passive revolution'[9] in so far as corporate–consultancy–NGO actors adjust their discourses and practices in the process of adapting and reproducing neoliberal hegemony.

The present case reveals the enhancement of neoliberalism where new CSR coalitions are formed and critics are co-opted in a typical case of passive revolution. Such flanking mechanisms may offer temporary moral leadership under the rubric of CSR/sustainability-responsible sourcing and, more generally, by engaging private business in the 'social' dimension of globalization. This marketing of moral–social claims (albeit narrowly defined) and its related managerial practices are being institutionalized and serve to rebalance the unstable equilibrium of forces in favour of the coalition of retail, trade, professional and some third-sector actors. They also result from resistance and cannot suspend struggles. They reproduce the deep tensions between capital, labour and the environment in transnational production.

This new development in neoliberalism suggests that Gill's 'new constitutionalism' needs to be complemented by recognition of the emerging role of the 'new ethicalism'. 'New constitutionalism' involves international juridico-political strategies and mechanisms (e.g. WTO/GATS) that emphasize the locking in of the right of (trans-)national capital and locking out of domestic scrutiny of marketized policies/practices. To secure the unstable equilibrium of compromise to sustain economic expansion, dominant social forces such as trans-national corporations, service-oriented NGOs, audit firms, academics/consultants, research institutes and some international organizations (e.g. the UN's Global Compact) try to develop and support flanking mechanisms that can reshape hegemony via new CSR tools such as sustainability index, 'beyond audit', 'responsible sourcing', 'scholarships for workers' and the like. This development reveals the need to add to Gill's juridico-political focus by introducing the role of the socio-ethico-managerial dimensions.

The concept of 'new ethicalism' does this by capturing these strategies that seek to reconnect economic policies with (new) social–moral norms that are dominated by technicalized, managerialized and self-responsibilized practices (e.g. audits, databases, best practices, training etc.). While 'new constitutionalism' highlights the disconnection/

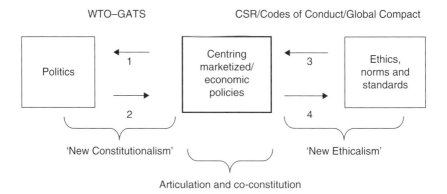

Key: 1: Locking out of domestic political scrunity of global marketized policies ('New Constitutionalism')

2: Repoliticization from consumer and civic activism

3: Reconnection of economic strategies with socio-ethical elements (e.g. CSR, 'beyond audits')

4: Managerialization and augumented self-regulation of the socio-ethical elements ('New Ethicalism')

Source: Sum (2010b: 68).

Figure 9.3 Articulation of 'new constitutionalism' and 'new ethicalism'

locking out of marketized policies from domestic political scrutiny, 'new ethicalism' highlights the reconnection of economic strategies with socio-ethico-managerial elements in corporate responsibility. However, this reconnection involves a procedure of rarefaction whereby social–ethical elements are thinned out selectively and there is thickening of managerial and self-responsibilization practices (see Figure 9.3). In this regard, 'new ethicalism' can be defined as an ethicalized managerial regime that seeks to stabilize/enhance neoliberalism through 'managerialization', 'technification' and augmented self-governing of the CSR subjects (e.g. women).

This articulation between 'new constitutionalism' and 'new ethicalism' promotes a passive revolution in global capitalism and facilitates a further, albeit more complex, round of enhanced neoliberalism. 'New ethicalism' not only helps to co-constitute 'new constitutionalism', but also provides the latter with a body of knowledge and regulatory instruments that can strengthen its micro-governing capacities (e.g. on factory and community levels). This helps to re-engineer temporary leadership by providing neoliberal common sense with a soft moral spin; but this is not so moral or so binding that it overwhelms neoliberalism's economic imperatives. Ethical–managerial practices in CSR (e.g. responsible sourcing, international development programmes), rather than exclusively moral projects, are selectively interpreted in neoliberal and neo-utilitarian terms in which actions are judged by their outcomes (e.g. reputational risks, performance and profit) and not social justice or the greatest good of the greatest number. These ways of 'managerializing' and 'self-responsibilizing' the ethical are uniquely suited to modern management techniques and the well-established grammars and languages of corporate auditing, performance, empowerment and self-governing. Alongside the rise of 'new ethicalism', we find the attempts of 'progressive' workers' and glocal movement-oriented NGOs to resist CSR-ization through various forms of action, negotiation and resistance. This is reflected in a wave of transnational initiatives that focus on corporate accountability (Bendell 2004) and wage issues (e.g. Asia Floor Wage Campaign). Yet, as part of the to-and-fro of power, resistance and counter-resistance, we find that Porter from Harvard Business School and Kramer from Harvard Kennedy School of Government are promoting the idea of 'creating shared value' (2011). This may spark another round of debate on the reinvention of CSR in the global–local political economy.

CONCLUDING REMARKS

This chapter has examined the connection between (1) 'supply-chain clusters' and the rise of giant retailers such as Wal-Mart and (2) the impact of Wal-Martization upon the politics of global supply chains; (3) the reinvention of Wal-Mart via a pro-business version of corporate social responsibility; and (4) the remaking of global capitalism with the inclusion of 'new ethicalism'. The CPE approach captures the modes of selectivity and material–discursive moments that are involved in cluster-building, and Wal-Martization as a cost-reduction accumulation strategy. The agential and discursive selectivities of strategy consultants and their practices at various levels mediate the rise of cluster strategies in developing countries that govern regions, policies and population as factors of competitiveness and FDI sites (see Chapter 8). The use of maps and databases as knowledging technologies visibilize them as 'supply-chain clusters' that link with the global market. With Wal-Mart's capabilities to capture global trade opened up through the WTO–GATS agreement and to build local partnerships, it can buy and sell from these clusters on a global basis by building glocal partnerships.

Focusing on the sourcing side, Wal-Mart thrives on the technological selectivity of its management tools (e.g. category management and scorecards) that discipline suppliers and thereby workers along the chains. It is a micro-political form of ordering and control that we termed Wal-Martization. This involves power shifts from suppliers–manufacturers to giant retailers with the former trickling insecurity and hardship downwards to flexible workforces in the organization of a disciplinary low-cost strategy.

This strategy of accumulation is challenged by labour unions and movement-oriented NGOs on labour and environmental excesses as well as Wal-Mart's own overstretched cost-reduction strategy. In response to social resistance, the giant retailer adopted versions of CSR that selectively favour its pro-business orientation and condense a dispositive that is disciplining and operates through self-governing. This is mediated by an assemblage of company codes, factory-ratings, 'beyond audit' practices and education training that are often managerialized, technicalized and shift burdens on to individuals. In sum, the emergence of the CSR dispositive shows that Gill's concept of 'new constitutionalism' needs to be complemented by the role of 'new ethicalism' in the understanding of changes in the global political economy that is marked by their co-constitution in which a body of CSR knowledge can help to re-engineer temporary leadership by providing neoliberal common sense with a soft moral spin; but this is not so moral or so binding that it overwhelms neoliberalism's economic imperatives.

NOTES

1. GATS is one of 17 major WTO 'Uruguay Round' agreements.
2. This easing of the local is evident in a letter from Wal-Mart Executive Vice President Michael Duke to US Trade Representative Robert Zoellick on 1 May 2002. Wal-Mart stated its policy preference as 'Countries also should be encouraged to remove any size limitations on individual stores, numeric limits on the number of stores in country and geographic limitations on store locations in the country' (http://www.citizen.org/documents/WalMart_GATS_comments.pdf, accessed 4 April 2013).
3. A petabyte is a quadrillion bytes of information.
4. The Panopticon was first proposed by Jeremy Bentham as a prison design. He planned a central observation tower housing wardens with prisoners' cells surrounding it. This 'all-seeing-place' was intended to enclose and discipline any group deemed to require supervision. Foucault (1977) applied this metaphor of a controlling space to the oppressive use of information and knowledge in modern disciplinary society. This chapter examines two kinds of panopticism as microtechnologies of control. The first is a 'virtual panopticon' that rests on the disciplinary use of database information such as Wal-Mart's Retail

Link and calculating practices in the scorecards. The second is a paper panopticon (see note 6).
5. This report is no longer available on the worldwide web.
6. A 'paper panopticon' uses words and numbers as disciplinary mechanisms. This can be found in mission statements, programmes, standards, audit reports and certificates that are used to discipline factory managers and workers to be more in line with the CSR regime.
7. These research centres are the Global Institute of Sustainability in Arizona State University and the Applied Sustainability Center in the University of Arkansas. Their European office is based in Wageningen University, the Netherlands.
8. The Clean Clothes Campaign rejected the invitation on the following grounds: (a) the code is completely voluntary for suppliers; (b) it excludes retail workers; (c) it prioritizes the sharing of social audits and distracts attention from other activities (e.g. changes in purchasing practices); (d) it lacks a complaints mechanism for workers; and (e) it is managerially focused with a growing number of self-assigned 'experts' jumping on the CSR bandwagon to give advice on what constitute best practices and so on (Clean Clothes Campaign 2009).
9. 'Passive revolution' is a term used by Gramsci (1971: 104–20; Q15, §11, 15, 17, 25, 59; Q10I, §9; Q10II §61*) to examine the ways in which a social class maintains its hegemony through gradual, molecular changes that operate through passive consent, the decapitation of resistance movements, and absorption of opposition through compromise and concession.

10. Competitiveness knowledge brands and service governance: the making of Hong Kong's competitiveness–integration (dis)order

As discussed in Chapter 8, discourses of 'competitiveness' have gone through three stages, from theoretical paradigm, through policy paradigm to knowledge brand. The last is speedily brought to policy markets by academics/consultants, prominent businessmen, ideas entrepreneurs, think tanks, strategy firms and international organizations. Given the multi-layered, multi-scalar, multi-site nature of these processes (Chapter 8), this chapter explores one particular site – Hong Kong's road to the (re)making of competitiveness and the politics of economic restructuring and integration. The purpose is to illustrate the recontextualization of Porter's knowledge brand to Hong Kong via strategy firm and sponsors, and to disclose the complexities and struggles that have been involved in the (re)making of service governance in the city between 1979 and 2013. We identify two overlapping periods with their own specific strategic–discursive moments. This chapter has three sections. First, it examines period one (1979–2004), starting when China opened its doors and saw the creation of a 'special economic zone' in the Pearl River Delta in southern China. Some strategic local–industrial actors sought new ways to connect with the zone. Using pre-existing social networks, they moved their industries to benefit from cheap labour, land, and tax benefits in the zone. This prompted the 'hollowing-out' debate and the imminent return of Hong Kong to the Mainland, and thus marked the first strategic–discursive moment in imagining its future mode of growth. This debate revolved around local attempts to promote and recontextualize two economic narratives about the way forward, inspired respectively by the Harvard–Porterian (backed by service capital) and Massachusetts Institute of Technology (MIT) knowledge brands (backed by industrial capital). In the ensuing contest for hegemony, the balance shifted towards the service–business–policy groups. Specifically, service-competitiveness discourses and practices were constructed through consultancy reports/papers, forums, luncheon meetings, policy documents, media coverage and the like. They were normalized as a regime of truth, circulated as part of policy common sense, and operated as a hegemonic project subject to challenge.

Second, period two (2003–12) involves the second strategic–discursive moment as a new structural conjuncture emerged. Hong Kong's competitiveness was, once again, called into question with China's entry into the WTO in 2001, the 2003 SARS crisis, and mounting public criticisms of the Hong Kong Special Administration Region (hereafter HKSAR) government. Different strategic actors responded to these challenges by developing several economic imaginaries (e.g. Mainland and Hong Kong Closer Economic Partnership, Individual Visit Scheme, Renminbi Business, Pan Pearl River Delta, China's 11th Five Year Plan etc.) to rebuild Hong Kong's competitiveness and, this time, integrate with the Mainland. Partly to boost the image of integrative partnership, some of these imaginaries were repackaged as 'big gifts' by cross-border actors. These gifts mediate the emergence of a regime of hope that frames the future and constructs 'possibility spaces'. These hope/gifts discourses and practices guided the remaking of Hong Kong's competitiveness–integration (dis)order. As these 'possibility spaces' increased and interactions deepened, they also swelled unease and even fears. Such unease was expressed in terms of the 'marginalization of Hong Kong'. With the push to remake Hong Kong's competitiveness–integration order intensified, cross-border tensions and contradictions also increased in a number of sites. This section examines the increased inflow of Mainland visitors to Hong Kong and how it challenges Hong Kong's shopscape and the struggles for everyday-life necessities. The chapter ends with an assessment of how CPE can help to understand the remaking of (counter-)hegemonies in Hong Kong's post-1997 transition in two periods.

PERIOD ONE: THE MAKING OF HONG KONG'S COMPETITIVENESS AND SERVICE GOVERNANCE, 1979–2004

The opening of China in 1979 and the creation of a special economic zone in southern China enabled some strategic actors in Hong Kong to link local development to global markets. For patriotic and/or pragmatic reasons, Hong Kong business and industrial capitals drew on their linguistic affinities and kinship ties to build factories and employ cheap migrant workers to produce for the export markets (Sum 1999). These arrangements attracted 80 per cent of Hong Kong's manufacturing firms into the Pearl River Delta. By the mid-1990s, 25 000 Hong Kong firms/factories were employing 3 million workers; and, in 2004, there were 80 000 firms with 11 million employees.

This northward march of Hong Kong's industry posed serious challenges to different groups. While Hong Kong's pro-industry groups (e.g. Federation of Hong Kong Industries) worried about industrial decline and the limited availability of high-tech support for restructuring, business-service groups (e.g. Hong Kong General Chamber of Commerce and its newly formed advocacy think tank, the Hong Kong Coalition of Service Industries) voiced concern about Hong Kong's increasing office and domestic rental costs and Shanghai's rise as a service centre. In the mid-1990s this prompted the 'hollowing-out' debate between industry and service interests (led by prominent entrepreneurs, think tanks and key policy-makers). This struggle for hegemony was reinforced by Hong Kong's impending return to China in 1997 and, later, by the Asian financial crisis with its high unemployment and falling property prices. Actors on both sides of the debate sought to reposition themselves by recontextualizing globally circulated policy ideas/brands to advance their interests in the restructuring processes.

Some of these ideas are global knowledge brands constructed and circulated by academic entrepreneurs, consultancy firms and policy think tanks that packaged knowledge into strategic and policy recommendations. They are constructed by intellectuals/practitioners who claim unique understanding of the economic world and translate this into policy recipes and methodologies to address social tensions, contradictions and dilemmas, and appeal to the pride and anxieties of the subjects experiencing socio-economic change (see also Chapter 8). During Hong Kong's debate on economic 'hollowing out', two competing knowledge brands were deployed.

Two Competing Knowledge Brands in Mapping Hong Kong

Facing the challenges of restructuring, industrial and service interests that cut through the government–civil society interface entered into a hegemonic struggle. Nodal actors such as policy-makers, executives from chambers/think tanks and the business press drew from a variety of knowledge brands to remap Hong Kong's new paths. Through the overseas alumni networks, they each commissioned consultancy reports that drew on different trans-national knowledge brands. These were, respectively, MIT–Berger–Lester's 'industrial performance' models (Berger and Lester 1997) and Harvard–Porter's 'competitive advantage' model (Porter 1985). These brands have influenced the meaning-making about possible economic futures for Hong Kong with important implications for a CPE understanding of the structural, agential, discursive and technological selectivities of changing power relations and the (re)making of everyday life (see Chapter 5). This chapter draws on many data sources (e.g. government newsletters/bulletins, policy remarks/speeches, consultancy reports/papers, minutes of meetings, newspaper reports, websites, blogs etc.) to uncover the dialectic of material–discursive forces as particular regimes of truth are constructed, selected, articulated and contested.

The MIT brand and Hong Kong's high-tech interlude

This MIT brand informed a consultancy report entitled *Made by Hong Kong* (Berger and Lester 1997). It was written by Susanne Berger and Richard Lester with the support of the MIT Made by Hong Kong Study Team. It offered an industrial and technological vision of Hong Kong's economic future. This report was sponsored by a network of strategic actors from the manufacturing/industrial capital (e.g. Chinese Manufacturers' Association of Hong Kong, Federation of Hong Kong Industries, Better Hong Kong Foundation etc.) and supported by parts of the bureaucracy (Hong Kong Productivity Council and possibly Department of Industry). It portrayed Hong Kong as locked into a 'Made by Hong Kong' manufacturing trajectory, that is, as organizing the low-cost manufacture of 'Hong Kong' goods in offshore locations such as the special economic zones in southern China. This path was considered 'unsustainable' due to rising labour and land costs in Guangdong Province, the 'craze for property' in the region and so on.

MIT's problematization of Hong Kong's restructuring rested on a development-gap metaphor that posited the need to 'climb the technology ladder' in order to achieve a higher-value-added and brand-based pathway. The upgrading metaphor was presented in the report through the contrasting use of 'Made by Hong Kong' and 'Made in Hong Kong' categories. The former referred to products made by Hong Kong firms 'through long production chains that may start in Hong Kong but use manufacturing sites in the Pearl River Delta, further inland in China, and beyond'; whereas the latter meant products that were produced 'within the territory of Hong Kong proper' (Berger and Lester 1997: xii–xiii). Discounting the former as dependent on inputs from the latter, this construction served to flag the 'Made in Hong Kong' path as the high and sustainable road for developing Hong Kong into a 'world-class industrial power'. This high-tech route involves: (1) acquiring technical knowledge from the People's Republic of China (PRC), diasporic Chinese, international experts and multi-national corporations; (2) promoting R&D agglomeration economies based on universities, technology-based enterprises, education institutes, a (virtual) science park and private firms;

(3) replacing original equipment manufacturing (OEM) with original design manufacturing (ODM) and original brand-name manufacturing (OBM); (4) acquiring new inputs such as government funding, human resources, information technology; and (5) strengthening government technological capabilities by injecting more technical expertise and raising the profile of technology-related policies.

This 'hollowing-out' debate developed in the conjuncture of the 1997 Asian crisis and global dotcom boom. Hong Kong suffered a currency attack, fall in real-estate prices, and general fear about the sustainability of finance as a growth path. Backed by two industrial-oriented executive councillors (Raymond Chien and Henry Tang),[1] and supported by Chinese officials (Goodstadt 2005: 133), the first HKSAR chief executive (Tung Chee-Hwa) was prepared to try the 'high-tech' route. He established the Commission on Innovation and Strategy in March 1998. It was chaired by Tien Chang-Lin, who was a world-class overseas Chinese scholar but little known to the Hong Kong public. Techno-economic words such as 'innovation' and 'technology' began to enter the policy lexicon and the Commission was tasked with exploring the chances of Hong Kong becoming a 'technology-intensive economy in the 21st century'. The Commission published two reports, one in September 1998, the second in June 1999.

Largely consistent with the MIT's upgrading imagination of Hong Kong, the Commission recommended the following: (1) strengthen technological infrastructure and promote technological entrepreneurship; (2) build human capital to meet the needs of a knowledge-based economy; (3) enhance technological collaboration with the Mainland; (4) foster university–industry partnership; and (e) reduce information, financing and regulatory barriers. This high-tech imagination was to be implemented by setting up the Innovation and Technology Fund of HK$5 billion and an Applied Science and Technology Institute Research Institute (Hong Kong SAR 1998: vi–vii).

However, some of these recommendations were too long-term for a chief executive who was under pressure from the Asian crisis to introduce some policy quick fixes. Influenced by the success of Silicon Valley and his visit to high-tech Israel with Richard Li (son of the property tycoon Li Ka-Shing), the CE selected the 'Cyberport' as his 'winner'. The latter was young Li's brainchild and was supposed to attract, nurture and retain innovative talent necessary to build a cyber-culture critical mass in Hong Kong. This Tung/Li choice of the Cyberport as Hong Kong's IT object won support from some local academics and leading IT supporters as a job-creating measure (Taylor 1999a; Shi 1999). The government then formed a partnership with the young Li and the project received a HK$6 million land grant (according to the Financial Secretary's 1999 Budget

Speech); and a lease that allowed one-third of the land to be used for residential construction.

Despite its iconic status, there was no open bidding process to build the hub. The CE's culpability was suspected, especially for the possible privileging of a particular individual (Richard Li) and even of the Li 'property empire'. Instead of a 'Silicon Valley' in Hong Kong that nurtured IT talent, it was criticized as comprising 'Cyber villas by sea', that is, as a real-estate rather than a high-tech project (Webb 1999). Ten real-estate developers excluded from this strategic project jointly denounced the CE's decision-making process as closed and accused him of using residential land to subsidize the Cyberport. The Democratic Party, for different reasons, challenged the government for lack of transparency, creating 'favouritism/cronyism' and departing from its 'positive non-intervention' policy.

Notwithstanding public scepticism over the 'Cyberport–IT' issue, the CE and other industry-related organizations (e.g. Hong Kong Productivity Council) continually supported a 'high-technology' strategy but profiled it in more general terms related to the 'knowledge-based economy'. On 1 July 2000, the Commission for Innovation and Technology was formally established within the SAR government's Commerce and Industry Bureau to 'spearhead Hong Kong's drive to become a world-class, knowledge-based economy'. Specific programmes included a 22-hectare Hong Kong Science and Technology Park at Pak Shek Kok in the New Territories and the Hong Kong Applied Science and Technology Research Institute to work in partnership with the private sector.

This technological push was soon hit by the bursting of the global dotcom bubble in April 2001 and the CE's declining popularity (see below). By 2003, the technology strategy was more an interlude in Hong Kong's restructuring. It survived but failed to hegemonize as an accumulation strategy for the following reasons. Structurally, Hong Kong's colonial legacies as a commercial entrepôt lacked a strong social basis of support for industrial–technological development. Although there was a manufacturing faction that supported this high-tech rhetoric, it lacked strategic capability to shift Hong Kong's then policy common sense from *laissez-faire*/'positive non-intervention' to 'pro-active economic management'. Strategically, the selection of the Cyberport project as the CE's flagship task without an open bidding process was clearly biased. Thus this project not only split the coalition of property interests; it also laid bare the cronyist nature of strategy-making, provoking criticisms from the wider civil society. There were articles such as 'IT does not matter' and other murmurs in civil society that 'high-tech' really meant '*hi tech*' ('*hi*' in colloquial Cantonese means 'get one's fingers burnt' and in this case 'burnt by technology'). As for the agential selectivity, although Tien was a world-class scholar, he was little known to the Hong Kong public. This handicapped a new strategy that required trust, local anchorage and public money. In addition, while the CE/Li Cyberport was a timely icon backed by a fashionable narrative, it was widely criticized for cronyism and did not fit well within the larger high-tech scheme.

As a result, the CE's own popularity began to decline. His reputation suffered two further blows when his pledge to build 85 000 social housing units was undermined by the collapse of the property market; and when he was seen to have mishandled the SARS crisis in 2003. In short, the structural and agential selectivities of the Hong Kong high-tech project were unfavourable and failed to condense into a major accumulation strategy. This is why it can be seen as an interlude. This does not mean that pro-technology groups are not active, however, or that they are excluded from the policy arena. Their interests continued to be represented by industrial constituencies in the Executive and Legislative Councils, manufacturing organizations, academic-consultancy supporters and so on. The MIT discourse had definitely provided them with the policy vocabulary (e.g. 'technology', 'innovation', 'upgrading') that can be (re)deployed at every stage of Hong Kong's development. At the second stage, it re-entered the dialogue on the upgrading of Guangdong, and supporters were advocating the return of industries to Hong Kong and entering Hong Kong–Mainland partnerships.

The Harvard brand and the hegemonies of Hong Kong's service governance
Concurrent with this interlude, but with longer-term consequences, was the rolling out of the Harvard–Porter version of competitive advantage (see Chapter 8). This was sponsored by commercial–financial interests. These groups, who were beneficiaries of the structural legacies and selectivities of Hong Kong's historical role as a colonial entrepôt, thrived on their business, trade and commercial set-ups. Compared with the industrial–technological faction, they had stronger social and political bases of support in articulating and condensing a hegemonic project tied to the Harvard knowledge brand. These included institutional networks of top government officials, chambers of commerce, business think tanks, prominent local business leaders, on-site academics/consultants, and economic quangos and business media. At the conjuncture of Hong Kong's 'hollowing-out' debate, concerted efforts were made by actors at the interface of political and civil societies to transfer the Harvard brand to Hong Kong. In terms of agential selectivity, there were three major strategic agents in the policy–academic/consultancy circuit who had (1) linkages with Harvard; (2) the ability to build a trilateral alliance; and (3) an interest in deploying the versatile and 'brandized' narratives of competitiveness.

We focus for the moment on the links to Harvard, which shape the second and third factors. The three figures concerned were: (1) the then financial secretary (Donald Tsang), who took his Masters of Public Administration at Harvard's Kennedy School of Government; (2) a prominent businessman (Victor Fung) who took his PhD from Harvard Business School and taught there for a few years before returning to Hong Kong to take over a large family global trading group called Li and Fung Ltd;[2] and (3) an academic/consultant (Michael Enright) who transferred from Harvard Business School to the School of Business at Hong Kong University as the Sun Hung Kai Properties Professor of Business Administration (see also Chapter 9). These three figures coordinated and repeatedly pushed for 'service promotion' under the Harvard brand.

The then financial secretary (FS) – Donald Tsang – worked closely with the service groups. Anticipating the need for more policy advocacy, in 1990 the Hong Kong General Chamber of Commerce set up a policy think tank. It was called the Hong Kong Coalition of Service Industry (HKCSI) and represented over 50 service sectors. At the time of the 'hollowing-out' debate, the FS coordinated with the HKCSI, especially its secretary-general, Chan Wai-Kwan.[3] For different reasons, they both selected 'service' as the key object of future economic governance and 'service promotion' was seen as important within the government and beyond. In August 1995, the FS formed a government task force on service promotion that required departments to report progress on 'service promotion'. In 1997, he set up a business service promotion unit in his office. The HKCSI not only backed his strategy but also pushed it further by advocating a 'tripartite effort' (business, government and academics) to promote the service industries with itself as 'lead organizer' of this partnership arrangement. This partnership was subsequently expanded to include more actors – councillors and media editors who were at the interface of political and civil societies.

This agential alliance-building competency could not consolidate intellectual leadership without a strong narrative grounded in gravitas. A key role was played by Victor Fung, keen to reinvent Hong Kong's service governance via the Porterian brand. With his support and sponsorship from the Vision 2047 Foundation, which is a think tank and lobby group for the interests of commercial, financial capital and related professionals, a report was commissioned in the mid-1990s. Michael Enright from Harvard Business School was invited as the team leader responsible for the recontextualization of the brand. He was regarded as suitable because he was a Harvard man and had co-written, with Michael Porter and Graham Crocombe, a previous report on *Upgrading New Zealand's Competitive Advantage* (1991). Instead of just accepting the commission to write a report, he transferred to Hong Kong University's School of Business in

1996. With expert input from two other strategists (Edith Scott and David Dodwell), the report was published in 1997. Highlighting its lineage and riding on Harvard–Porterian cachet, the report was called *The Hong Kong Advantage* (1997).

Discursively, the report highlighted the challenge of manufacturing decline as Hong Kong moved from a 'manual'/'enclave' to a 'knowledge'/'metropolitan economy' (Enright et al. 1997: 13). This narrative portrayed Hong Kong as an object of urban-service calculation that performed hub-like roles, such as 'packagers and integrators of activities for the global economy, a leading source of foreign investment, a centre for overseas firms, the capital for the overseas firms, and driver of the Mainland economy' (ibid.: 80). This 'hub' metaphor recontextualized Porter's 'diamond model' by identifying five linked 'clusters' contributing to Hong Kong's advantage as a service economy: (1) property, construction and infrastructure; (2) business and financial services; (3) transport and logistics; (4) light manufacturing and trading; and (5) tourism (see Table 10.1).

The 'cluster' concept is central to Porter's account of competitive advantage, depicting the organizational dynamism of geographically proximate companies, suppliers and associated institutions. Selectively translating this discourse to Hong Kong, it was linked positively to other local 'drivers of competitiveness' rooted in 'government as referee', the 'hustle and commitment strategies' of Hong Kong's merchant manufacturers and the societal ethos of 'hard-working people' (see especially Enright et al. 1997: 34–40, 45–6 and 85). Replicating these folklore elements helped to generate familiarity and local resonance with the imported brand.

This Harvard-branded metropolitan imaginary was interdiscursively articulated through commissioned reports, policy pamphlets and conference and forum activities. As a genre chain, its combination of documents and activities prioritized Hong Kong's service competitiveness and allowed for the construction of a service-based regime of truth via the articulation of knowledging apparatuses and related knowledging technologies (*à la* Foucault) (see Table 10.2). To illustrate how this was constructed, this section briefly examines the interdiscursive space mediated by policy forums, commissioned reports and newspapers and their use of knowledging technologies to frame economic thinking and of other procedures to establish 'truth'. Many discursive technologies are involved (Sum 2010a provides more details) and here we consider three that were important in period one.

Following publication of *The Hong Kong Advantage*, the government's Central Policy Unit (CPU) disseminated this body of knowledge on 22 April 1998 via a conference entitled 'Hong Kong Competitiveness'.

Table 10.1   Hong Kong's five clusters and their dynamics

Clusters	Dynamic linkages between major firms
Property, construction and infrastructure	• Property development and construction groups of engineers, architects, surveyors and interior designers • Engineering and technical services in real-estate surveying, valuation and consultancy
Business and financial services	• Private banking, fund management, corporate finance, currency trading, insurance, venture capital finance and stockbroking • Stock exchange and brokerage services; legal, and financial and accounting services
Transport and logistics	• Air cargo, sea cargo, freight forwarders and logistics-related services • Banks, maritime lawyers, adjusters, shipbrokers, shipbuilders, insurers and surveyors, and port management
Light manufacturing and trading	• Clothing, electronics, jewellery, plastics, toys and footwear • Subcontracting networks, trade finance, and export trading and management services
Tourism	• Hotels, restaurants, retail shopping centres, conference centres, trade fairs and entertainment

Source: Adapted from Enright et al. (1997: 95–107).

Deploying its resources as the official think tank, the CPU introduced the Harvard–Porter brand by positioning it prominently in the overall organization of the conference, reinforcing it through repetition and self-reference, and linking its promotion to Hong Kong's economic future. All three crucial agents were involved. Fung, who chaired the think tank that originally sponsored the Enright report, was a keynote speaker and, unsurprisingly, repeated the report's 'competitiveness' catch-phrases, marketed 'metropolitan economy' as a 'new paradigm', and claimed that Hong Kong's 'business service clusters' were the best-developed in Asia. Thus Fung stated:

> I would like to suggest a new paradigm, through which we can get a more accurate picture of our situation. I would suggest that we view Hong Kong as a 'metropolitan economy . . . (and) metropolitan economies tend to feature clustering

Table 10.2 *Examples of knowledge apparatuses and knowledging technologies for 'service competitiveness', 1998–2004*

Major actors	Practices	Knowledging technologies in meaning-making	Examples of discursive apparatuses and (re) invented symbols
Financial secretary, economic leaders, Hong Kong Coalition of Service Industries, think tanks, academics/ consultants, Trade Development Council	Conference speeches, commissioned reports, policy papers, blueprints, newspaper columns	Technology of performance and judgement Technology of boundary protection Technology of positive chaining/ linking	WEF and IMD rankings 'Technology as means' 'Technology to follow (not lead) business' 'Management consultancy' sector 'Asia's World City' 'Creative Industries'

of various business services such as finance, which facilitate not only local trade and manufacturing; but global business activities too . . . Hong Kong's financial and business services cluster is, on its own, the best-developed in Asia.

Hong Kong's cluster-based 'metropolitan economy' was immediately assessed in the same speech in terms of its ranking in major competitiveness indexes prepared by international institutions like the World Economic Forum (WEF) and the International Institute for Management Development (IMD). Conceding authority to these ranking devices, Fung argued that Hong Kong was 'in the middle of the pack' and needed 'to aim for the very top' (1998: 6). This is because '[a]ccording to the IMD, Hong Kong ranked 15th among the world's leading economies . . . This shows that we still have some way to go.'

From a Foucauldian perspective, invoking such ranking devices can be seen as a technology of performance/judgement (see Table 10.2 and Chapter 8) that encloses Hong Kong into an index-number order that ranks and judges its economic performance in and over time. This form of micro-power operates through the hierarchization of countries/cities and their division into highly ranked or rising countries and those with low or declining scores in the competitive race. This technology serves to benchmark performance and judge the city as 'middle ranking'. This panoptic judgement subjected Hong Kong to the treadmill of competitiveness and thereby shaped its 'will to improve'.

Competitiveness knowledge brands and service governance 363

Given the fluidity of discourses, steps were also taken to protect the 'service' boundaries, especially *vis-à-vis* the pro-technology MIT report promoted by the industrial groups. Addressing the challenges as coming from the 'technological revolution', Enright, a commentator at the same conference, defended the 'service-metropolitan' frame by subordinating 'technological revolution' to 'business' in the following way:

> I was a research scientist with GT Laboratories, a major communication company in the US. I know what technology has done and what it can do. Quite frankly, in many parts of the world, including Hong Kong, technology itself and the importance of technology has been overstated and overweighed. Because technology is often spoken of as an end rather than the means. Technology only makes sense as a means and not an end. The next revolution in Hong Kong business is not going to be a technological revolution. It is going to be a managerial revolution. It is only when managers here in Hong Kong understand that they could potentially, dramatically extend their business that they will leave money on the table to set up efficient operations, incorporate better systems and technology that will dramatically improve their bottom line. Technology is going to follow that. It is not going to lead that.

This guarding of the service boundary was reinforced by another discursive technique, that of chaining, which helped to strengthen the competitiveness genre and to identify and build possible alliances (see Table 10.2). The service-competitiveness frame was stretched and extended to include new clusters in the post-Asian crisis period. Thus, in January 1998, the FS revitalized the HKCSI's earlier suggestion to establish the Tripartite Forum between the government (e.g., the Business and Service Promotion Unit of the Department of Commerce and Industry), business (e.g., HKCCSI), and academics (e.g., the School of Business of the University of Hong Kong). This Tripartite Forum was later extended to Quad and Penta versions in 1999–2000 and 2002–04 through co-option of legislators and media editors respectively. Among many issues that the Tripartite Forum discussed and negotiated,[4] an interesting example is the selective chaining/linking of the service-competitiveness theme to other emerging service clusters. Thus the panel on 'Raising Competitiveness: Quality of Life Sectors' included the 'quality-of-life' sector (e.g. leisure and entertainment, education and health care) as a new spectrum of objects to be drawn into the competitiveness embrace. The later Quad and Penta Forums went on to include logistics, community services and health-care services in the Pearl River Delta, culture and entertainment within the service-competitiveness imaginary. Other subsequent reports commissioned by HKCSI and the Trade Development Council also deployed the competitiveness theme and chained it to Hong Kong's image as 'Asia's world city' (HKCER Letters 1999) and the clusters mapped by 'creative and cultural industry' (HKSAR, Central Policy Unit 2003) especially after the 1997 Asian financial crisis. This fastening of disparate elements into a service-competitiveness discourse had a key role in the technologies of chaining that continuously extended and renewed the imaginary and helped to consolidate and widen the social basis of support.

This ensemble of discursive apparatuses, knowledging techniques and institutions contributed to the extending/thickening/condensing of a service-competitiveness dispositive and brand of truth.[5] This brand was created through the interaction between discourses and nodal actors as the selection and retention of the former enable the latter to consolidate their leadership position. In this regard, discourses make organic intellectuals and organic intellectuals make potentially hegemonic discourses (see Chapter 5). This hegemonic way of seeing/speaking/acting was also entering major policy speeches and documents. A search of the chief executives' annual policy addresses revealed that the term 'competitiveness' was used on average 6.75 times in every speech between 1997 and 2004. It is impossible to examine here the contextual uses of the term in these speeches; but we can show that it became part of Hong Kong's policy lexicon in mapping policies and major projects. For example, the financial secretary's office profiled the building of a cultural cluster (West Kowloon Cultural District) as a way to transform Hong Kong's competitiveness as a city into a 'knowledge-based economy'.

These activities to produce competitiveness imaginations and projects were not only coming from the organic intellectuals located at the interface of political and civil societies; they were also emerging from diffused civil-society sites (e.g. newspapers, business press, advertisements, personal career planning etc.) related to everyday life. For illustrative purposes, this section now considers one major English newspaper in Hong Kong – the *South China Morning Post* (*SCMP*) – to show the production and dissemination of this mode of knowing. More specifically, the *Post* then hosted various related conferences (http://conferences.scmp.com/past.asp) and ran on its website a special report section up to 2006 called 'ADVANTAGEhk'. *Inter alia*, this: (1) relayed competitiveness-related news; (2) reported opinion surveys on Hong Kong's competitiveness organized by consultancy firms (e.g. TNS); (3) transmitted these results to business leaders through invited meetings; and (4) maintained an e-mail address (hkcompetitiveness@scmp.com.hk) for the public to submit their opinions.[6] Apart from its special themed section, the *SCMP* business pages regularly reported on Hong Kong's competitiveness as judged according to global indexes. For example, Michael Taylor (1999b), a business correspondent, reported its post-Asian-crisis loss of competitiveness as follows:

> Hong Kong – once considered the world's most competitive economy – has dropped to third place. According to the World Economic Forum, the SAR's strong currency, inflexible wages and weakening government finances are to blame for the slip. Every year the forum, which is in Geneva, Switzerland, announces a ranking of the most competitive economies. The ranking is the result of data from public sources and surveys of about 4000 executives in 59 countries. Singapore topped the list again this year. The United States moved into second place, displacing Hong Kong. According to the report, Singapore's competitiveness can be attributed to the island nation's 'high rates of saving and investment, an efficient Government ... and flexible labour markets'. Hong Kong was 'clearly suffering from the Asian Crisis and particularly from its currency policy' the report said, referring to local dollar's peg to the US greenback.

Such reporting helped to normalize the disciplinary treadmill of competitiveness (see Chapter 8) in the wider civil society. Competitiveness imperatives were internalized in everyday mind-sets and, for some, became part of personal identities. Such subjectivation was evident in the following letter from a student to the *SCMP* in response to Hong Kong's loss of competitiveness:

> Hong Kong is an international business and financial centre. In an era of hi-tech developments and globalization, we face keen competition from countries around the world ... According to the recent global competitiveness report from the World Economic Forum, Hong Kong has fallen to eighth place. The younger generation can help make Hong Kong more competitive ... It is important to have computer knowledge, as the Internet is playing an increasingly significant role in our life. We write e-mail instead of letters, chat with friends on ICQ instead of on the telephone and get our news from Web sites instead of newspapers. We use computers to do paperwork, keep our accounts and even order goods ... In the past, employers wanted graduates who were industrious and responsible whereas now they are looking for candidates who are creative and innovative.

This statement illustrates how 'competitiveness' discourses and practices shape the spaces in which one speaks and observes. It condones a rule of the common truth that links loss of competitiveness to the need for innovation and growth. While some assumed personal responsibility to become more competitive, others mimicked the need for competitiveness with more ambivalent responses.

The Emergence of a Global–Local Service Bloc in Hong Kong and its Challenges

These constellations (or dispositives in a Foucauldian sense) of subject positions, management knowledge, institutions, discursive apparatuses

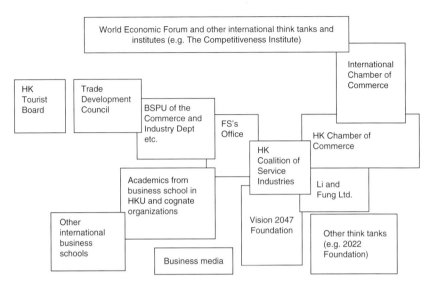

Figure 10.1 The emergence of a service bloc in Hong Kong between 1997 and 2004

and knowledging technologies operate at different sites to naturalize, subjectify and (self-)regulate service–competitiveness. These forms of governing common sense at a distance are multi-layered and multi-faceted. They interact to create service–competitiveness as a hegemonic project that gets consolidated in official policy and the mundane practices of everyday life. They become regularized through service-oriented strategy and governance. These 'commitments' and institutionalization narrowed the gap between top-ranking bureaucrats, think tanks, academics/intellectuals, business leaders/entrepreneurs and hopes (and fears) of the masses (cf. Gramsci 1971). This helps to form popular alliances with psychological–emotive as well as cognitive–rational elements behind a relatively coherent but shifting service bloc and its accumulation strategy (see Figure 10.1). We argue that, during period one, this service–competitiveness common sense was quite well articulated thanks to its structural, agential and discursive–technological selectivities of colonial legacies, agential competency, discursive technologies of ranking, chaining and closure, respectively.

This strategic alliance is by no means unitary, all-inclusive or fully functional. It was heterogeneous and marked by tensions and contradictions. The pro-industrial groups frequently came with pro-technology suggestions (e.g. the return of industries and neo-industrialization of Hong

Kong). New growth icons entered into arena and sparked off challenges from the local constituencies. For example, the West Kowloon Cultural District, which was a competitiveness project to build a cultural and creative cluster, prompted criticisms and resistance from local artists who complained about lack of consultation, and the project was conceived more as a commercial entity targeting the global market and not local residents (People's Panel on West Kowloon 2007). In addition, there was also public scepticism on the grounds that it was more a 'property' than a 'cultural' project (Webb 2004). Thus the bloc rested on an unstable equilibrium of compromise between existing and new challenging forces. These are accentuated with changing structural conditions in period two when the Mainland's national-integration project plays a more salient role in the hegemonic context of Hong Kong's continuous drive towards renewal of its competitiveness on a capitalist basis. At this juncture, competitiveness and integration provide both hope and unease/fear for Hong Kong's service governance. There were growing signs of ruptures, tactical (re)negotiations and deep-rooted contradictions related to the making of the competitiveness–integration (dis)order across the border in period two.

PERIOD TWO: THE MAKING OF COMPETITIVENESS–INTEGRATION (DIS)ORDER IN HONG KONG, 2003–13

Hong Kong's service governance was challenged by China's entry into WTO in 2000, the fears about competition from Shanghai and the rising costs of production in southern China. These were accentuated in 2003 by the Severe Acute Respiratory Syndrome (SARS) crisis in which tourism declined sharply and retail sales fell 15 per cent compared with 2002. Unemployment was rising and criticisms were mounting of the HKSAR government, especially its CE, for mishandling this crisis and other key political issues. The latter included the proposal to implement Article 23 of the Basic Law by legislating against acts such as treason, subversion, secession and sedition. Pan-democratic groups worried that this would infringe human rights in the name of the Mainland's 'national security'. On 1 July 2003 half a million participants demonstrated against the HKSAR government and the pro-Beijing groups. This was followed by the 'Striving for Universal Suffrage' march on 1 July 2004 and, thereafter, '1 July' becomes a symbol and an annual platform to express general grievances and the continuous demand for universal suffrage.

This iconic march on 1 July 2003 emphasized for HKSAR the need for a new leader. After carefully scrutiny by the Chinese central government,

Donald Tsang – the then FS – was accepted and elected as the new CE in 2005. A policy think tank called the Bauhinia Foundation (after the city's flower emblem, which also appears on the HKSAR flag) was established in 2006. It had close ties with him, and the competitiveness knowledge brand continued its framing of Hong Kong's economic imaginaries. Concurrent with Tsang's reign as CE, the Chinese central government was rethinking how best to integrate Hong Kong. The central Chinese government then set up a coordinating leading group on Hong Kong affairs (Lam 2004) and adopted a more pro-active approach towards HKSAR (Wang 2003). Problematizing the rising 'demand for democracy' and 'grievances' as challenges to Chinese nationalism, sovereignty, unity and even security (He 2003: 78–9), this way of thinking shaped later cross-border policies. With inputs from Tsang-led business factions and pro-China groups in HKSAR, new relations of cross-border rule are emerging.

New Relations of Cross-border Rule: Hope, Gifts and Fear

These new relations continue the service–competitiveness hegemonic project but are increasingly linked to national integration and the boosting of the economy. The churning out of competitiveness and integration icons mediates the rise of a regime of hope. In general terms, a regime of hope selectively frames the future and constructs 'possibility spaces' in policies that shape expectations and set limits (on the hope regime related to body and illness; see Brown 2006). It naturalizes and objectifies hope through discursive apparatuses such as policy statements, schemes, plans and programmes. In cross-border terms, these include cross-border economic schemes, national/patriotic education programmes and national/regional development plans that establish new relations of rule (see Table 10.3). This ensemble of programmes, schemes and related institutions can be seen as a Foucauldian dispositive that anticipates economic and national benefits but, at the same time, selectively sets parameters/limits that guide and discipline Hong Kong's integration with the Mainland with unintended consequences. Because this chapter cannot describe all the programmes and schemes in these new relations of rule, it now focuses on the key economic projects that frame and guide the building of the competitiveness–integration (dis)order.

The construction of 'hope' objects and their repackaging as 'big gifts'
Changes on the structural level such as the China's WTO entry and the SARS crisis led the HKSAR government and several service groups (notably the Hong Kong General Chamber of Commerce) to rethink their accumulation strategies, especially those that could revive Hong Kong's

Table 10.3 Major hope objects deployed to govern China–Hong Kong integration, 2003–13

Possibility spaces/ hope objects	Major discursive apparatuses	Shaping expectations and setting limits
National education	• *Moral and National Education Curriculum Guide* 2012 • *China Model National Conditions Teaching Manual* 2012	• Hope of the Mainland to build national unity and fulfil the 'China dream' • Shaping HK citizen to become Chinese patriotic subject
Economic schemes	• Mainland and Hong Kong Closer Economic Partnership Agreement (CEPA) 2003 • Other related schemes such as Individual Visit Scheme and Renminbi Business	• China–Hong Kong economic integration projects • Hope to revive Hong Kong's competitiveness • Shift the centre of economic gravity from Hong Kong to the Mainland
National plans	Mainland's 11th Five Year Plan (2006–10) and 12th Five Year Plan (2011–15)	• Hope to intensify China–Hong Kong integration and cooperation • Limiting Hong Kong's visions within the grammar of Mainland's national planning
Regional plans	Pan-Pearl River Delta Regional Cooperation and Development 2008 Outline of the Plan for Reform and Development of the Pearl River Delta 2008–09	• Hong Kong, Macau and nine provinces (9+2) in China* • Limiting Hong Kong's visions within the grammar of the regional plan • Hope to intensify China–Hong Kong integration and cooperation • Limiting Hong Kong's visions within the grammar of the regional plan of the Pearl River Delta

Note: * The Pan-Pearl River Delta includes '9 + 2' provinces/regions. They are the provinces of Sichuan, Yunnan, Guizhou, Guangxi, Guangdong, Hainan, Fujian, Hunan, Jiangxi and the cities of Hong Kong and Macao. This regional imaginary is promoted in terms of its economic benefits derived from a region with one-third of the country's population and gross domestic product, representing a huge potential market.

Source: Sum's compilation based on resources from various *Hong Kong Yearbooks*.

metropolitan clusters (e.g. finance and tourism). Service actors such as the HKCSI rose to the challenge and formulated the Mainland and Hong Kong Closer Economic Partnership Agreement (hereafter CEPA) as a new possibility space and lobbied for its adoption. With inputs from China supporters, the two governments co-launched CEPA in mid-2003; but it was polyvalent and hence interpreted differently. For Hong Kong service actors, this was a way to 'revitalize' Hong Kong's competitiveness; and for the central Chinese government, it was a way to accelerate Hong Kong's integration with the Mainland and to promote national unity and regional competitiveness. This coincidence of competitiveness–integration interests facilitate the launching of CEPA, which is a free trade policy arrangement between the Mainland and HKSAR (and Macau) whereby firms from Hong Kong (and Macau) were able to access the Mainland market in 18 sectors two years ahead of the time scheduled for China's opening under the WTO. To expand this hope space, nine supplements were added and new schemes to revive the tourism and finance clusters were subsumed under its rubric. In July 2003, the Individual Visit Scheme (hereafter IVS) was introduced under the CEPA to allow Mainland visitors/tourists to come to Hong Kong in their own capacity rather than as members of a group (for details, see below). In turn, Renminbi Business allowed Hong Kong banks with Mainland branches to conduct transactions (e.g. Renminbi deposit, dim-sum bonds etc.). These CEPA-related measures constructed 'hope', prefigured the revival of Hong Kong's competitiveness framed within Mainland-led schemes and were sold to the Hong Kong population as serving their economic interests.

Discursive constructions (e.g. CEPA and IVS) are never simple and monolithic. They are always polyvalent and heteroglossic and, where they bear on key power relations, are articulated to meaning systems tied to the strategic calculations of cross-border leading forces. In the present case, the officials from Chinese central government together with some Hong Kong counterparts (especially the mass media) co-packaged the CEPA proposals and sold them to the population on both sides of the border as 'the central government bearing big gifts'. Framed in national/emotive/economic language, these hopes/gifts are seen as gestures of goodwill that would: (1) demonstrate the care of the 'central'/'motherland' for Hong Kong's well-being; (2) accelerate cross-border integration by prefiguring 'win–win' benefits, 'mutual cooperation' and 'partnership' across borders; and (3) build a coalition with pro-business and pro-China groups that, for different reasons, are supportive of competitiveness and/or integration.[7] With the construction of the 'big gifts' rhetoric, other subsequent initiatives such as IVS, Renminbi Business and Offshore Yuan Centre were similarly packaged between 2003 and 2011 by the cross-border network of policy actors (see Table 10.3). Apart from these strategic actors, the mass media also helped to communicate these objects as gifts. Often, newspapers used the images of a 'gift box decorated with ribbon' and a 'gift list' to convey and reinforce the messages of 'the centre bearing big gifts' across borders.

These 'big gift' discourses can be seen, from a neo-Foucauldian perspective, as a discursive technology of cross-border integration that seeks to inspire hope and calm grievances. It enabled the stakeholders from both sides of the border to redefine central–HKSAR relations by promoting a positive image for the 'motherland' and, through their associated governmental practices, to accelerate integration as well as Hong Kong's economic reliance upon the Mainland (see also Table 10.4). These 'policy gifts' are not simple affective solutions to economic and political problems. They have been developed in specific contexts and are intended to have wider effects. In particular, they are planned and coordinated to coincide with special visits of top-ranking leaders (e.g. premier and president) to Hong Kong. For example, the gift of CEPA was announced during Premier Wen's visit on the 6th anniversary of Hong Kong's return to China in 2003. Likewise, another gift, the Offshore Yuan Centre, was publicized when the then Vice-Premier Li visited HKSAR on the 100th anniversary of Hong Kong University. The production of these events as 'spectacles' helped to deliver these 'gifts' as hope for HKSAR and implicit indebtedness to the 'motherland' (and, by extension, to its ruling regime).

In CPE terms, these 'big gifts' are more than just discursive/symbolic objects. They are soft labels for strategically motivated policy that has both discursive and material dimensions, especially at the local level. Discursively, these 'big gifts' are part of a mechanism of cross-border rule that enables integrative 'governance at a distance'. Drawing from a neo-Foucauldian perspective, they can be seen as a technology of cross-border integration that is used to govern collective life by inspiring (and manipulating) hope and promoting a positive image of the Mainland/'motherland'. This light-touch rule can cultivate positive cross-border sensibilities and subjectivities via governmental technologies such as domestication, combinability and agency (see Table 10.3). Let us examine their technological selectivities in turn.

First, the 'gift' discourse constructs a kind of giver–receiver relationship between China and the HKSAR population. Mauss's pioneering work (2000) on 'gift' relations can shed light on this relationship. For him, a 'gifting' relationship encodes implicit assumptions about the status and character of givers and receivers. 'Gifting' is an exchange that creates an obligation to return. It establishes a bond between givers and receivers and the latter are burdened with a sense of indebtedness. In this way,

Table 10.4 Major 'big gift' objects and governmental technologies of cross-border integration, 2003–11

Year	Major hope/gift objects	Cross-border actors	Discourses deployed	Governmental micro-technologies
2003	CEPA (and 8 supplementary agreements) Individual Visit Scheme (IVS) announced by Premier Wen's visit on 6th anniversary of HK's return to China (23 June 2003)	Either proposed by Hong Kong service actors and/or initiated by the central government 'Gift' trope repeated by Chinese author ties, pro-China groups/ individuals, media, trade bodies, policy makers etc.	Presented as 'big gifts' that provide 'opportunities' for 'integration' with 'win–win' outcomes This 'gift' object provides hope and (re)defines cross-border power relationships by: • creating a giver/receiver relation • positioning China as a generous sovereign power and Hong Kong as an obligated receiver	*Technology of domestication* that: • increases the scope of positive affective thinking about the giver (motherland) – enhances moral debts and emotive bonds (Mauss 2000) • creates obligation and obligates individuals who need to reciprocate Extends 'one-country' governance mechanism and its mode of 'control at a distance' in HK *Technology of combinability* • 'Win–win' rhetoric is created so that Hong Kong and the Mainland gifts can be co-processed via schemes, frameworks, agreements etc. • Little effort to identify losers and may even deflect attention from incongruities and conflicts *Technology of agency* Mix of participation, cooperation and control • Participate as part of 'win–win' opportunity • Control by advancing particular modes of self-conduct (1) Self-control to comply with integration/ cooperation imperatives (2) Self-blame for missing 'opportunities' (3) Self-criticism for being marginalized by not integrating
2004–	Renminbi Business			
2011–	Offshore Yuan Centre announced by then Vice-Premier Li Keqiang on his visit for the 100th anniversary of Hong Kong University (17 August 2011)			

'gifting' is more than just generosity; it is selectively staged and motivated by self-interest and calculation. As a technology of domestication, it creates obligation and requires individuals, groups, communities and so on to reciprocate in a 'gift' relation. In this case, the 'big gifts' discourse obligates the HKSAR population to be thankful to the 'motherland' for her generosity in 'saving' Hong Kong's competitiveness. This creation of a moral debt is a way of (self-)controlling the population by increasing the scope and warmth of affective thinking towards the giver (the motherland). This technology of domestication combines high-profile visits, policy announcements and media/policy-maker hype to (self-)shape Hong Kong's affective orientation towards the central government, and, of course, to sell newspapers and package public speeches and private conversations.

Second, these 'big gifts' are presented to the HKSAR population as contributing to the revival of Hong Kong's competitiveness and prosperity. They (self-)shape hope via the creation of 'win–win' expectation and possibility of 'mutual cooperation'. For example, the CEPA was signed in June 2003. Nine supplemental agreements have also been signed, from 2004 to 2012, providing 'preferential arrangements' for Hong Kong in two main fields: trade in goods and services; and trade and investment facilitation. These have gradually abolished tariffs on products manufactured in Hong Kong, expanded market access for Hong Kong services trade to the Mainland, and improved trade and investment facilities between the two areas. The signing ceremonies of these arrangements were major events with newspaper headlines such as 'CEPA creates a win–win situation between Mainland and Hong Kong' appearing in media on both sides of the border. This 'win–win' is often narrated as bringing hope for new business opportunities (e.g. tourism, financial services, insurance etc.) to the HKSAR; and improving the investment environment in the Mainland (e.g. in the retail and wholesale trades).

From a neo-Foucauldian viewpoint, this 'win–win' rhetoric can be seen as a technology of combinability in which the HKSAR and the Mainland can be selectively co-processed and acted upon as an entity via joint schemes, agreements, frameworks and so on. For example, the IVS was initially introduced for four Guangdong cities and then extended to 49 cities in total and, more recently, extended again to permanent residents of the border region of Shenzhen. It allows 'Mainland visitors' from these places to enter Hong Kong for seven days at a time and supposedly offers a 'win–win' opportunity for Mainlanders and locals. It would boost Hong Kong's tourist/retail trade, facilitate closer economic integration with the Mainland, and lessen the logistical and accommodation pressures resulting from China's National Day Golden Week holiday.[8] As far as Hong

Kong is concerned, this 'win–win' rhetoric is frequently presented as providing economic benefits for the economy, at least in quantitative terms (e.g. visitor arrivals and tourist spending). Such a market-oriented and quantitative calculus is depicted in positive terms via graphs and charts from official and commercial statistics to show that both sides gain from continuous cooperation to promote tourism growth. Whether this is really a 'win–win' situation for all, or whether this rhetoric disguises losses and diverts attention from incongruities, tensions and conflicts, is examined in greater detail below.

Third, the gift rhetoric also refers to building 'cross-border partnership' and integration. In this narrative, the 'P' in CEPA invokes a 'partnership' that covers areas such as banking and securities, tourism, legal, accounting, construction, medical services, computer and related services, placement and supply services of personnel, printing, telecommunications, audio-visual and distribution. These financial and commercial activities demarcate a partnership relation in which actors are to cooperate to bring about 'win–win' outcomes. However, 'win–win' or not, partnering is a technology of agency that involves participation and selective control of the self. Partnership discourse carefully shapes participants to become more self-responsible to make the partnership work. Relevant conduct-controlling activities here include: (1) self-disciplining in conformity with the partnership agenda (e.g. integration and/or competitiveness); (2) self-blame for missing 'opportunities' offered in the partnership (e.g. CEPA); and (3) self-criticism for becoming marginalized when partnership initiatives fail. These self-shaping behaviours mediate and underpin a subtle shift towards embracing the rationality of cross-border integration; they also limit Hong Kong's competitiveness imagination within Mainland-led partnership schemes and render it more dependent on income from Mainland tourists, renminbi business and so forth. Thus the partnership discourse is one way to create the competitiveness–integration subjectivities and render them as inseparable and co-joined.

In short, the co-construction of the 'big gift' discourse to repackage the hope spaces has positioned Mainland China and Mainland-led 'economic opportunities' in a good light. These discourses and selected governmental technologies of domestication and combinability have helped to depoliticize cross-border integration in affective and 'win–win' terms. A host of cross-border actors frame and communicate such discourses to (re)make cross-border partnerships as well as to construct hope in the complex conjuncture of change and uncertainties that developed from 2003 onwards. These shared cross-border norms and intersubjective hope of the 'big gifts' connect the material interests of the financial, tourist and business communities with the emotive–integrative support of the pro-China groups.

These ensembles of discursive and material practices have also controlled the development of Hong Kong's competitiveness strategy by making it more dependent on schemes related to the Mainland. In this regard, Hong Kong's competitiveness is increasingly defined (and even limiting the discussion) within Mainland's integration–hope regime.

Construction of fear: 'marginalization of Hong Kong' and the politics of gaps
Apart from the 'big gifts' regime, the HKSAR's 'possibility spaces' were quickly expanded to include, for the first time, HKSAR (and Macau) into China's 11th Five-Year Plan (2006–10). This move was narrated by the then CE, Donald Tsang (formerly FS), as opportunities to further develop Hong Kong's advantage in financial services, logistics, tourism and information services. Whilst some continued to convey hope, others expressed unease, especially in the changing regional contexts of Shanghai's and Guangdong's upgrading responses to this same national plan. Shanghai planned to climb the service ladder by improving its environment to become an international financial centre. Guangdong's provincial-level plan would speed up its financial-system reform and develop modern business services and logistics industry. These ambitions (at least rhetorically and strategically) might mean an impending loss of Hong Kong's advantage on the service front. This triggered fresh unease and was first communicated publicly on 20 March 2006 by Hong Kong's Chief Secretary for Administration, Rafael Hui, in a seminar on China's 11th Five-Year Plan. He expressed this unease in terms of the 'marginalization of Hong Kong'. This marginalization discourse was subsequently appropriated by some policy-makers, pro-technology and pro-China groups as they constructed Hong Kong's marginalities in terms of its gaps/deficits. Premier Wen Jiabao was quoted on 6 April 2006 as denying that it would happen as there were irreplaceable Hong Kong advantages such as the legal system and business environment. However, the unease of marginalization lingered and even circulated. For example, responding to Hui's comment, legislative councillors debated a motion on 3 May 2006 about 'Maintaining the Competitiveness Edge of Hong Kong'. While some saw marginalization as a 'threat', others suggested that it was already occurring as part of Hong Kong's declining competitiveness.

This discussion also took place in the wider society. Pro-technology and pro-China groups mapped Hong Kong's deficits and marginalities in their own ways. An example of the former is a Hong-Kong-based think tank, Savantas, set up by Regina Ip, a former secretary for security who left Hong Kong under a cloud to take a master's degree in Asian Studies at Stanford University. On her return, Savantas actively supported 'high-tech' and the need for 'national champions' in August 2006.[9] The pro-China media, such as Ta Kung Pao, mapped Hong Kong's gaps quite differently. In a column on 'Guiding Hong Kong' in *Ta Kung Pao* on 22 August 2006, a member of the PRC Consultative Committee, Lung Chi-Ming (2006), used the marginalization discourse to reframe Hong Kong's position from a firm-oriented view:

> The marginalization of Hong Kong firms in the Pearl River Delta has long-lasting influence not only by leading to the possible breakdown of the 'global value chains'; it may also affect Hong Kong's position in these same chains. In this regard, the marginalization of Hong Kong firms in the Pearl River Delta is one of the factors hastening Hong Kong's own marginalization ... At present, most businesses that are run by Hong Kong firms in the PRD are in decline. Even worse, they have fallen out of Guangdong's and the national list of targeted industries. Some of them are even listed as 'restricted type of industries' and will be forced out of the Pearl River Delta' ... Such restructuring in Guangdong and the Pearl River Delta is certain to occur but Hong Kong investments account for 60 percent of Guangdong's foreign direct investment, they are small in size, labour-intensive, low-tech and resource-absorbing, they are the ones most exposed to restructuring pressure. With the restructuring of Guangdong, labour shortage, land and resource scarcities and environment protection policy, etc., the marginalization of Hong Kong firms is most urgent. Guangdong province is calling for environmentally sub-standard Hong Kong firms to move away and this is estimated to involve 50,000 firms. If the SAR government pursues a long-term management and development policy in monitoring and assisting the northward march of Hong Kong firms to improve their competitiveness, the marginalization of Hong Kong firms will not occur.

This contrastive framing of Hong Kong firms in the Delta region as 'sub-standard' and of Guangdong as the 'restructuring' leader reinforced the deficit/gap thesis. It also encouraged Guangdong policy-makers to set upgrading targets with a view to: (1) distinguishing and judging Hong Kong firms as 'sub-standard'; (2) visibilizing Hong Kong's marginality with regard to its firms in the PRD; (3) privileging Guangdong's targeted list of industries; and (4) redefining Guangdong–Hong Kong relations with the former at the centre and the latter more marginal.

This construction of Guangdong's centrality and Hong Kong's marginality gained a more sensational twist when pro-China opinion leaders and scholars from Chinese think tanks added their voices in more emotive terms. For example, reporting in the *Singtao* newspaper on 11 September 2006, Zheng Tian-xiang, a professorial researcher from the Centre for Pearl River Delta Research, an official Pearl River Delta think tank located at Zhongshan University (Guangzhou), stated:[10]

> As Hong Kong became a world city, it saw China as depending on Hong Kong. However, the time for this has passed. China was closed to the world in the past

and thus 95 percent of the goods had to go through Hong Kong. Now China is completely opened and goods can be sent from Shanghai and Tianjian ... Guangdong suffered from lack of investment and international contact in the 1980s and thus Hong Kong was central to Guangdong's development. On approaching the 1990s, Guangdong's economic take-off meant that there was increased interaction between them in trade, logistics and infrastructural development. In addition, Hong Kong's colonial historical background and its 'borrowed time and borrowed place' mentality have engendered a lack of long-term vision. This applies to Hong Kong officials and Hong Kong people. They possess a superiority complex towards the Mainland and thus the Hong Kong-Guangzhou interaction is unequal. (Zheng 2006)

These marginality/centrality constructions use the discursive 'technology of differentiation'. China supporters have moved from depicting Hong Kong's firms as 'sub-standard' to more general attempts to depict Hong Kong as an arrogant other rooted in a colonial past and bureaucratic short-sightedness. This technology seeks to selectively discipline the Hong Kong population through normalizing the Mainland as the standard-setter. It thus sets Hong Kong firms/historical background apart from the Mainland; visibilizes Hong Kong's gaps; and centres Guangdong/national upgrading targets and plans. In this way, the Mainland's upgrading plans and national integrity operate as a minimal respectable threshold towards which Hong Kong firms, bureaucracy and people must move. This discursive privileging of the Mainland as the new nodal and dominant site in a changing spatial hierarchy means that Hong Kong's past and present have to be subjected to Mainland standards of normality. This technology of differentiation serves to transmit fear/hope and to shift the centre of economic gravity from Hong Kong to the Mainland with integration as the (only) hope to revive its competitiveness.

The disciplinary nature of these marginalization discourses and practices was inter-articulated with the continual supply of more hope objects, especially with the onset of the 2007 financial crisis. For example, Guangdong continued with the upgrading path in 2008 in line with the *Outline of the Plan for the Reform and Development of the Pearl River Delta 2008–2020* (National Development and Reform Commission 2008). This time, it was presented to Hong Kong as 'opportunity' in face of marginalization and new policy space such as the creation of 'cooperation zones' (e.g. Qianhai in Shenzhen) to enhance financial services, and high-tech industries were introduced (ibid.: 112). Not surprisingly, the discourses of 'competitiveness', 'integration' and 'win–win' were redeployed to state the case. This has, no doubt, added another layer to the ensemble of discourses, technologies and practices that were related to the competitiveness–integration order.

However, these attempts to produce new hope standards and integration rationalities do not eliminate challenges and fears as cross-border activities intensify. This is partly because they are associated with mixed motives on the part of the protagonists and partly because they produce unintended and potentially counter-productive effects. With the intensification of the competitiveness–integration (dis)order, more people, money and capital flow across the border. These flows and related practices have created a more compressed economic and social life, and disjunctures and tensions occurred in everyday social interactions. There are growing signs of ruptures and deep-rooted contradictions emerging in a number of sites (e.g. pregnant mothers from the Mainland giving birth in Hong Kong; Shenzhen's Qianhai as the financial cooperation zone that may rival Hong Kong's Central District; Mainland visitors becoming parallel traders; the continual demand for universal suffrage; house price inflation; pressure on school places from migrant children; and so forth. Indeed, these official 'gifts' coexist with everyday rifts. The next section will use the Individual Visit Scheme (IVS) as an illustration to shed more light on such (dis)order and the emergent gift/rift paradox.

The Individual Visit Scheme and Hong Kong's changing shopscape: gift/rift paradox

The SARS crisis disrupted the dynamism of Hong Kong's tourism cluster and competitiveness. Under CEPA, the IVS was a new hope object by which the 'Mainland visitor' could help to revive Hong Kong's economy. This object (packaged as 'big gift') was announced by the Chinese government in 2003 and initially allowed 'Mainland tourists' from four Guangdong cities (Dongguan, Zhongshan, Jiangmen and Foshan) to visit Hong Kong in an individual capacity rather than as members of approved tour groups. The scheme was later broadened and, by 2007, such tourists could come from 49 cities and enter Hong Kong for up to a week per visit. By 2009, the scheme was further extended and permanent residents of Shenzhen, which is located across the border, were allowed to apply for multi-entry permits (m permits) to visit Hong Kong.

Tourists who come under the IVS are often labelled as 'big spenders' (Hang Seng Economic Focus 2011) and 'cash cows' (*Global Times* 2012). Their contributions to the Hong Kong economy are judged primarily in quantitative and hard cash terms in newsletters, policy reports and research papers by major government departments, local university schools of hotel and tourism management, and, of course, the business media (e.g. Choi et al. 2007; Lee and Ho 2008). A report by the Financial Secretary's Office (2010) singled out IVS visitors as an economic category and their contribution is presented in statistical-tabular terms using a

Table 10.5 Constructing of 'Mainland visitors' as a consumer category and presentation of the sectors that gained from their activities

	Per capita spending	
	Overnight visitors (HKD)	Same-day visitors (HKD)
2004	3305	1644
2005	3829	1663
2006	4170	1985
2007	4978	2232
2008	5367	2517
2009	6511	2719
2008/09 (% change)	(21.3%)	(8.0%)

	Spending pattern in 2009	
	Overnight visitors	Same-day visitors
Hotel and boarding houses	8.3%	0.2%
Restaurants	7.9%	2.7%
Retail trade	77.8%	92.2%
Local transport	2.8%	2.9%
Other	3.3%	2.1%

Note: Sum of figures may not equal 100% due to rounding.

Source: Financial Secretary's Office, Economic Analysis and Business Facilitation Unit, Table 3, p. 3.

technology of measurement. It calculates their contribution in terms of, for example, number of visitors per year, per capita spending of visitors by place of residence in China, spending patterns of visitors, contributions of IVS to specific sectors and so on. Table 10.5 is extracted from this report. It presents the increasing spending power of this group between 2004 and 2009 and indicates thereby the benefits that it brings to the Hong Kong economy. The main beneficiaries were the retail trade plus hotel and boarding houses. Their combined benefit amounted to 96.1 per cent of the total spending coming from overnight visitors and 92.4 per cent from same-day visitors in 2009. Within the sectors that benefited, retail trade stands out as the big winner – with brand-name fashion, jewellery, gold watches and electronics (e.g. iPhones) said to be the most popular items.

Tensions (and later on struggles) emerged at the point of consumption when Mainland visitors and their spending power increasingly flowed across the border. Local people began to observe spatial changes in the Hong Kong urban shopscape with the arrival of these spenders. Borrowing from Schafer's idea of 'soundscape' (Schafer 1993; Kelman 2010), which denotes the relations among sound, place and meanings, this chapter sees shopscape in similar terms. Shopscape refers here to particular relations among shops, place and meanings for Mainland visitors and local residents. Meanings may differ and tensions may emerge.

Tensions in brands-land With the influx of *nouveaux riches* from the Mainland queuing for brand-name goods in the retail sector, local shops started to disappear from the main tourist areas such as Tsim Sha Tsui and Causeway Bay. These districts became bridgeheads for high-end brand shops (e.g. D&G, LV, Chanel, Prada etc.). In this brands-land, Mainland visitors are treated as a valued class of consumers and they are even offered specialized services (e.g. shop assistants who can speak fluent Mandarin, shoppers can pay in the Chinese currency and can shop in private for exclusive designs and vintage products). This brands-land is frequented by the nouveaux riches from the Mainland because visitors can purchase luxury goods 30 per cent cheaper than in the Mainland because of import duties in China. In addition, these goods carry the marks of authenticity (they are unlikely to be counterfeits) and of novelty – because certain versions are exclusively placed in Hong Kong to showcase its role as a 'Shoppers' Paradise'. Buying for authenticity, novelty and exclusivity becomes the hallmark of Hong Kong's shopscape and consumer identities of prosperous Mainland visitors.

The landmark clash emerged when locals sought to reclaim their pedestrian rights in brands-land on 8 January 2012. The Italian fashion house D&G (Dolce & Gabbana) set local residents apart from Mainland shoppers by banning the former from taking photographs of their shop front from the public pavement while allowing Mainlanders to do so. Organized via Facebook, a resistance group of local protestors opposed to brand hegemony called for a *'D&G Front Door Photo Shot'* and over 1000 people turned up at its Canton Road branch. They were armed with cameras and some held home-made banners such as *'D & Pig'* and 'D&GO Home'. They demonstrated against their alleged preference for Mainland shoppers, their discriminatory practices against the locals, the infringement of their rights to take photographs from the public pavement, the hegemony of 'luxury brands', their role in pushing up commercial rents and in driving out local independent stores.

Tensions in needs-land The shopscape, as a site of struggle, did not stop at the site of luxury brands. After Shenzhen allowed its permanent residents to apply for multi-entry permits in 2009, more Mainland visitors have crossed the border. According to the Tourism Board, Hong Kong received 28.1 million visitors from the Mainland in 2011, almost four times the city's population. Of this number, 14.5 million were day visitors and 6.17 million entered on multi-entry permits from Shenzhen. By December 2012, the total of Mainland visitors had increased to 35 million, a 23 per cent increase over 2011 (Hong Kong Tourism Board PartnerNet 2012). This increase in cross-border shoppers is producing further changes in Hong Kong's shopscape that affect not just brands-land but also needs-land. We use this latter term to refer to everyday shopping places (e.g. supermarkets, chain stores, dispensaries and grocery shops) that sell food and other daily necessities. In Hong Kong's needs-land, Mainland visitors are targeting household necessities (e.g. shampoo, toothpaste, nappies, medicated ointment etc.), cosmetics and food as their major purchases. These everyday shopping places are frequented by Mainland visitors, and locals struggle to secure their own supplies. In this regard, Hong Kong needs-land has become a new site of cross-border tensions.

There are several factors behind this change. They range from the appreciation of the renminbi (the Chinese currency, or RMB), high inflation in China, frequent scandals concerning food safety in China, high consumer taxes and the convenience offered by multi-entry permits. According to a survey conducted by the Shenzhen Retail Business Association in November 2012, 24 per cent of respondents said they had visited Hong Kong specifically to shop. Of these, almost 60 per cent said they bought household necessities and food, compared with just over 32 per cent in 2011. The number of people buying food rose from 14.6 per cent to almost 40 per cent (Nip 2013). In total, these visitors to Hong Kong spend 20 billion RMB per year on household goods (Tam 2012).

The appreciation of the RMB and Hong Kong's reputation for high safety standards are two important motives for visitors' cross-border shopping activities. More specifically, currency appreciation means that Mainland visitors can buy more Hong Kong goods with the same amount of RMB. Between 2009 and 2013, the exchange rate between the RMB and the Hong Kong dollar changed from 1 RMB = HK$1.10 to 1 RMB = HK$1.24. Thus, for Mainland visitors, prices of Hong Kong goods have fallen on average by 13 per cent. One Guangdong-based newspaper, *Yangcheng Evening News*, even described flippantly (but not mistakenly) Hong Kong as a 'big discount market with 20 percent off' (2012). This popular view in China of Hong Kong's shopscape as a 'big discount market' not only spurred the middle classes to come; it also stimulated a new class of traders to take advantage of the price differentials across the border. In the same piece in *Yangcheng Evening News*, the journalist even offered a manual on how best to gain from being a parallel trader, what to put into a trolley with a weight limit of 32 kg, and how to avoid being arrested by customs and excise.

This common Mainland view of Hong Kong's shopscape as a 'big discount market' with cheap and trustworthy daily necessities and food is behind syndicated and individual parallel trading. Syndicated networks organize at grass-roots levels via: (1) assigning some retired or freelance people to queue and/or buy products from supermarkets, chain stores and dispensaries; (2) buying in bulk and storing the goods in warehouses and car parks in or near border towns; and (3) distributing goods to punters who collect them at specific sites (e.g. mass transit railway [MTR] stations; industrial parks, housing estates, and even specific train carriages) and move them over the border.

Whether acting as couriers for syndicates or as individuals on their own account, this is a highly labour-intensive process. It relies on ant-like moving tactics to shift goods across the border. A Chinese newspaper, *Wenweipo*, reports that there were at least 6000 full-time cross-border parallel traders at work every day (2013). More than half are Mainlanders with multi-entry permits.[11] They make at least two return trips a day, but some may undertake four to five trips in 24 hours. They gain around HK$60 to 100 per trip. On obtaining these products, some resell them online or pass them on to other traders who can secure higher prices. It was reported that there are some 157 online stores that sold Hong Kong goods on the *Taobao* (Treasure Hunt) website in China (Fei 2012). Popular food items online and offline include imported infant-milk formula, Yakult probiotic drink, chocolates (especially Ferrero Rocher), lemon tea, wine, crackers, seafood and so on. Many of these products have special mythical or magical properties in China's consumer market (see Table 10.6).

Initially, these parallel traders gathered in Hong Kong border towns such as Sheung Shui. Its main streets are increasingly occupied by chain stores, cosmetic shops and pharmacies. Given the bulkiness of the goods that they convey, long queues form in the Sheung Shui MTR station. Transit and repacking activities block and litter streets and create health hazards. Local residents are agitated by the loss of public space and lament the closure of local shops that sell and cater for their low-cost everyday supplies. The influx of chain stores and pharmacies on the high streets also drives up rents and local prices. A *South China Morning Post* study (Wong and Nip 2012) showed that the average price of everyday goods in Sheung Shui, when they are available, was some 10 to 20 per cent higher than in nearby districts in Hong Kong's New Territories. It was

Table 10.6   Food targeted by parallel traders and their mythical stories in China

Food targeted	Mythical stories related to the products
Infant-milk formula	Better safety standards and good for babies
'Yakult' probiotic drink	Breast enhancement, anti-cancer properties
Chocolates ('Ferrero Rocher')	Best gift for loved ones
Lemon tea	Sexual enhancement for men
Wine	Consuming Western lifestyles A mark of sophistication and class

Source: Sum's own compilation based on various Mingpao news items and interviews.

reported that an ointment for joints cost HK$38 in Sheung Shui but only HK$28 in dispensaries further down the rail-track in districts such as Tai Po and Sha Tin. In short, local residents must either pay higher prices or search further afield for cheaper supplies.

Rise of reclaim movements and tensions   Tensions grew when some local residents organized a resistance meeting via Facebook. Naming themselves as Reclaim Sheung Shui, they arranged to meet near Exit C of its MTR station on 16 September 2012. Scuffles occurred outside the station with parallel traders, who were accused of inflating local prices and disturbing local tranquillity. Protestors raised placards and chanted slogans: 'Reclaim Sheung Shui, Protect our Homes' and 'Dead Locusts' (this is a common derogatory term for Mainland visitors). Some protestors even demanded that 'Chinese people return to China' and raised the colonial flag as a place-based resistance symbol. These efforts to reclaim local territory and a sense of place have triggered responses from pro-China groups and Mainland visitors alike. They insist that these activities are contributing positively to Hong Kong's economy and that any action against arbitrage would make a 'mockery' of Hong Kong's proud claim to be a 'free-market economy'.

The reclaim movement and the resulting debates have revealed the seriousness of the issue to the HKSAR government and the MTR administration. On 4 October 2012, under the codename 'Windsand', a joint operation by the Immigration Department and police raided several black-spots in Sheung Shui and arrested a few illegal workers and parallel traders. On 9 October 2012, the MTR administration started to impose a weight limit of 32 kg per passenger on luggage at four stations – Sheung

Shui, Fanling, Lok Ma Chau and Lo Wu.[12] These actions did not reduce the activities of parallel traders. Tensions have continued to grow in Hong Kong's needs-land as the buying spree has intensified and spread. Indeed, because the border town of Sheung Shui is in the limelight, some parallel trading has shifted to other districts along the same MTR line (e.g. Fanling, Tai Po and Tai Wo).

As for the food products that are being targeted, infant-milk formula was high on the list ahead of the 2013 Chinese New Year, when it is customary to stock up for the holiday. In addition, milk-formula products sold in Hong Kong are framed as 'safe' and 'good for babies' partly because of the 2008 milk scandal in China and partly as a result of advertising campaigns by wholesalers in Hong Kong. These campaigns do not follow the WTO's *International Code on Marketing of Breast-milk Substitutes* and formulas are marketed aggressively on TV and by some medical practitioners.

With the Chinese New Year approaching in 2013, Hong Kong's shopscape for infant-formula milk powder entered a new wave of struggle over meanings and resources. For local parents, the fear of shortage means that formula milk is a product with a use-value essential to protect their babies' health; for parallel traders, it is a product with an exchange-value that can be purchased in a free market and resold at a premium in China. Fear heightens and resources tighten whenever stocks of milk powder become scarce. Local parents search far and wide to secure supply. Supermarkets, chain stores and dispensaries declare the item as 'out of stock' or their customers must pay higher prices for the limited stock. According to a *Mingpao* report (2013b), prices of major brands have gone up from 19 to 61 per cent between 2010 and early 2013 in supermarkets and dispensaries (see Table 10.7).

Believing that infant formula is in short supply, local parent (and grandparents) brave rising (if not manipulated) prices and shrinking income. Some middle-class families chase across the needs-land to stockpile supplies, organize into mutual support groups to exchange milk-powder information, and advocate their position in public debates. Some working-class parents have shifted from powder milk to home-made rice porridge and other forms of nourishment. Fearful of continual shortages and upset by the government's and business groups' continuous support for the benefits of cross-border integration and tourist/retail trade, democrats and parent groups have begun movements to reclaim formula milk. Slogans such as 'Hong Kong milk for Hong Kong people' are being voiced to reinforce their efforts to reclaim their babies' right to milk. Looking for wider support and perhaps seeking to embarrass the Hong Kong (and even Chinese) governments into action, one anonymous person petitioned

Table 10.7 Price increases of major infant-milk formula in supermarkets and dispensaries, 2010–13 (in HKD)

Major brands	Supermarket prices		Dispensary prices	
	2010	2013	2010	2013
Frisolac No. 1	211.5	283.0 (34%)	199.0	320.0 (61%)
Mead Johnson No.1	243.5	294.0 (21%)	233.0	340.0 (46%)
Cow & Gate No. 1	209.9	252.0 (20%)	185.0	268.0 (45%)
Nestlé No. 1	225.5	268.3 (19%)	210.0	265.0 (26%)
Snow Band No. 1	192.9	249.9 (30%)	168.0	230.0 (37%)
Wyeth No. 1	222.9	297.9 (34%)	220.0	290.0 (32%)

Source: Adapted from *Mingpao*, 9 February 2013.

the We the People section of the Obama's White House website on 29 January 2013.[13] Framing the petition in terms of 'Baby Hunger Outbreak in Hong Kong, International Aid Requested', it communicated a sense of fear and frustration in the following way:

> Local parents in Hong Kong can hardly buy baby formula milk powder in drugstores and supermarkets, as smugglers from Mainland China stormed into this tiny city to buy milk powder and resell it for huge profits in China. Many retailers stockpiled milk powder and are reluctant to sell to local parents as the shops can sell their stocks, in big cartons, to Mainland smuggler for huge profits. Countries like Germany, the Netherlands, Australia and New Zealand have already exercised rationed sale to tourist buyers from China for milk powder. However, the HKSAR government simply framed the situation as a matter of free trade and refuse [sic] to exercise the law which is already there to stop cross-border smuggling. We request for international support and assistance, as babies in Hong Kong will face malnutrition very soon.

This declaration was cross-posted on Facebook, the UK government's epetition website, and elsewhere. Meanwhile, the Reclaim Sheung Shui group reorganized itself on 14 September 2012 as the North District Parallel Imports Concern Group and stepped up its activities. It called for another round of reclaim actions on Facebook on 3 February 2013. This time it went beyond Sheung Shui and organized: (1) protests in Tai Po and Fanling stations; (2) a vendetta-style art production clip voicing its counter-hegemonic views; (3) musical parodies on the parallel traders and their activities; and (4) a photographic competition on the social impact of parallel trade activities upon Hong Kong.

In response to the heightening of competitiveness–integration tensions in needs-land, the HKSAR government, under Leung Chun-Ying as the new CE, announced three measures on 1 February 2013 to ease the shortage and tensions. They were: (1) setting up a telephone hotline to enable parents to order and reserve seven brands of formula milk; (2) amending the Import and Export Ordinance to limit Mainland visitors to carrying two tins of infant milk powder (or 1.8 kg) across the border; and (3) capping the weight of luggage carried by rail to the Mainland from 32 to 23 kg. A subsequent amendment to the Import and Export Ordinance allowed the HKSAR government to impose a fine of HK$500 000 or two-year imprisonment for offenders. These measures lessened the pressure on Hong Kong parents but did not end parallel trade. Ordinary cross-border visitors (e.g. workers, tourists, housewives, children etc.) simply carry two tins and these are collected and exchanged for cash by syndicated traders as soon as they cross the border. Others pass through the border by concealing a few tins in rucksacks and two more in transparent plastic bags as distractors. Meanwhile, the search for milk powder continues and Chinese diaspora and extended families feed this demand by sending it from the Netherlands, Germany, New Zealand, Australia and the UK. Supermarkets in these countries have started to limit buyers to two to three cans (Tsang et al. 2013). Some producers in Australia and New Zealand even ride on this 'white gold rush' and export directly to China.

As for the restriction in Hong Kong, there were criticisms and heated dialogue across the border. Some Mainland media and public figures commented that it was a set of bad (and harsh) measures and compared it with a UN embargo; others remarked that it was too hasty and discriminated against 'needy Mainland compatriots', and violated Hong Kong's free-market principles; and questioned whether China's support for Hong Kong has turned it away from making money into a lazy and insensitive populace (*Mingpao* 2013a). Apart from critical remarks, other commentators call for more news on Mainland's food safety, and point to the consumption craze among the Chinese middle classes for imported goods, etc. Meanwhile, the dissident Chinese artist Ai Wei Wei created a map of China entitled 'Baby Formula 2013'. This used 1800 large tins of infant formula to highlight the food scandals and the tensions between Hong Kong and the Mainland.

Hong Kong commentators responded to these criticisms by saying that some are far-fetched and that parallel trade is illegal; dampening it by legal means is not an embargo. They also suggest that it is time to reconsider whether (1) the HKSAR government should stand up to the Mainland's showering of 'gifts' and search for global alternatives; and (2) the multi-entry permits are effective and Hong Kong can handle the vast number of IVS visitors and traders. Issues and debates of these kinds indicate the opening of deep social rifts that have been narrated as 'big gifts' from the centre. This gifts–rifts paradox highlights the rupture and continuity of the competitiveness–integration (dis)order. While some groups are capitalizing on these hope/gifts, others are struggling to come to terms with them.

Capitalizing hope and resort to localisms This cross-border competitiveness–integration (dis)order and its various hope objects are intensifying differential accumulation and inequalities in the region. The 'big gift' of IVS and the increasing number of Mainland visitors enhance profits from the marketing/selling of goods, services, places and experiences. Schemes of this kind are not neutral and are capitalized by strategic actors. In this case, the IVS has benefited the tourist and retail sectors as well as related suppliers (e.g. milk-powder manufacturers), property owners in brands-land and needs-land, networks of cross-border syndicated and individual parallel traders and so on. However, tensions and contradictions develop at the sites of consumption with the falling value of the Hong Kong dollar, the rise in price inflation, struggles for resources, shortages of everyday goods, long queues, loss of local consumer/communal spaces, and locals' rights to be equally treated in Hong Kong's shopscape. Some local residents are disturbed by these changes and seek to reclaim their places. Parents and working-class families are finding it hard with rising inflation, high rent and low interest to make ends meet. Fears and anxieties emerged and some local people organized to protect their interest via activities to reclaim pedestrian rights, local communities (e.g. Sheung Shui), and even infant-milk formula. It is obvious that IVS is not the only hope/gift object; there are others (see Table 10.4) with different service groups capitalizing on them – for example, the gift of 'renminbi business' in Hong Kong becomes an object in which cross-border trade enterprises, banks and hedge funds as well as small-time local speculators arbitrage between the interest spread of onshore and offshore renminbi (Sum 2013b).

Changing Relations of the Cross-border Rule: Norms, Baselines and Struggles

Looking at wider sites of Hong Kong's integration struggles, other sites of rupture and resistance include rising renminbi value (meaning imported inflation from the falling Hong Kong dollar), high property prices, Mainland pregnant women giving birth in Hong Kong, hospital beds, school places, displaced villages, the use of simplified Chinese characters, travelling habits, national education, universal suffrage by 2017, judicial independence, donation to Mainland charities, clean government and so on. These uneven and disjunctive changes have created hope, anxieties, fear, resentment and resistance. They create hope for those who self-guide by the integration logic and opportunities to capitalize from it. Competitive-integration symbols include 'big gifts', 'Pan Pearl River Delta', 'Qianhai Cooperation Zone', 'Guangzhou–Shenzhen–Hong Kong Express Rail Link', 'Shenzhen–Hong Kong One-hour Metropolitan Life Circle' and so on. These geo-coded imaginaries and related policy norms are guiding sensing, speaking and acting about the intensification of this order.

This speeding up of the integration project also opens deep social and political rifts and these are partly expressed in people's changing identity. According to a public opinion poll conducted in December 2011 by the University of Hong Kong as part of a series of half-yearly inquiries undertaken since 1997, 16.6 per cent of people living in Hong Kong identify themselves first as Chinese citizens, a 12-year low, while a majority of 79 per cent declared themselves first as Hong Kong citizens or Hong Kong Chinese citizens, and this was the highest in 10 years (Simpson 2012). This result was contested by Mainland officials; but nonetheless, it reflects people's shifting identities and anxieties towards integration and even competitiveness. In addressing these tensions and contradictions, responses range from organizing local reclaim movements to using Facebook to post resistance songs (e.g. *Hong Kong is Dying* as a way to mourn the 'end of the one country, two systems') to reinventing Hong Kong's 'core values' as well as seeking to protect the value of their Hong Kong savings from the appreciating renminbi and rising inflation and questioning the excessive drive for competitiveness.

As these tensions and contradictions have been bubbling away in the HKSAR, cross-border intellectual and social forces are intensifying the competitiveness–integration rhetoric to build alliances and remake the power bloc. Mainland and pro-China supporters are now playing a greater role in this regard. Official Chinese rhetoric avoids seeing the social ruptures noted in the preceding paragraphs as an important issue (an *urgence* or urgent problem) in Hong Kong–China integration. Instead, Mainland officials and pro-China voices continue to reach out to business and industrial factions as well as intellectuals and grassroots by reiterating the competitiveness–integration vision.

In this regard, the competitiveness–integration vision is restated as the coordination and cooperation of HKSAR with the Mainland's regional and national development norms so that China can continue to back Hong Kong's competitiveness drive and to share the dignity and glory of being Chinese nationals. This reiteration partly marks the shift from the softer politics of 'big gifts' to the more intensive use of Mainland-centred norms and baselines. These encompass a complex mix of national political standards (e.g., 'understanding of national conditions', 'national education for integration', 'democratic reform within the framework of national interests' etc.), and geo-coded economic imaginaries as exemplified above. On 24 March 2013, the Chairman of the National People's Congress Law Committee, Qiao Xiaoyang, thickened these reference points by stressing that the future CE needs to be 'patriotic' and not 'oppose the central government' (Pepper 2013). This nationalist-oriented genre chain is becoming broader and thicker – witness the Mainland's micro-discursive (re)framing of Hong Kong's time (as national time) and space (as national-regional space). These modes of framing are contributing to the normalization of the Mainland's standards with reference to which Hong Kong's actions, resistance and agency are judged and, if necessary, restricted and corrected. Some intellectuals such as Mainland officials, local spokesmen, business representatives, pro-China organizations and grass-roots groups (e.g. *Caring Hong Kong Power*) repeat these baselines and norms in public forums and the media as the new modes of knowing, sensing and denouncing. This new form of rule is not soft, and in certain ways it is more 'interventionist' than the 'big-gift' mode. At times, this even involves symbolic violence on both sides, especially through the use of abusive language (e.g. some Hong Kong people labelled Mainland visitors as 'locusts' and a Mainland scholar called Hong Kong people '(running) dogs') (*The Economist* 2012a) and even disruptions of public meetings.

These changing relations of rule and struggles to reorganize the power bloc have triggered some local attempts to voice alternatives and seek a different equilibrium of compromise. Some groups use the discourses on 'Hong Kong's core values' to renegotiate the future and/or resist these normative baselines. More specifically, the meaning attributed to these values varies as they are rearticulated with other signifiers: for example, the claim that Hong Kong's competitive edges stem from its cultures of entrepreneurship, freedom, justice and fairness that could steer China towards democracy or protect Hong Kong's local values could help to prevent the rising influence of Mainland's party-dominated nationalist integrationism. In the midst of these struggles to redefine Hong Kong's values and draw different political conclusions, a plan has emerged to speed up the 'universal suffrage' according to the Basic Law. Benny Tai, who is an associate professor at the University of Hong Kong, proposed a civil disobedience campaign to 'Occupy Central' to pressurize the Mainland to grant universal suffrage by 2017. With the support of two other proponents, they presented a detailed plan to mobilize 10 000 people for non-violent occupation of the Central financial district in July 2014.

This has taken all parties by surprise and the Mainland government (and its relays) was quick to restate its baselines. Specifically, 'Hong Kong's democratic progress, including CE [Chief Executive] and LegCo [Legislative Council] elections, must guarantee it will never undermine national interest and Hong Kong's healthy relationship with the central government' (*China Daily* 2013: 9). Potential losses to the economy, and thus competitiveness, are also highlighted as 'harming' Hong Kong. Concurrently, the pan-democrats have reacted by forming a new coalition, the Alliance for True Democracy, to rethink their longer-term strategy in the struggle for universal suffrage, with a 30-year time horizon. In a Gramscian sense, we can observe both a medium- to long-term war of position unfolding through these political struggles, the local reclaim movements, and the protest against plans for 'national education' as well as more long-term struggles, such as the 'Occupy Central' campaign, which nonetheless gave warning signs of rising future resistance. These struggles result from the contradictory conjuncture created as the (re)making of the competitiveness–integration (dis)order is intensified. The unfolding of contradictions within and between competitiveness and integration are opening spaces for potentially counter-hegemonic protests in Hong Kong's changing CPE.

CONCLUDING REMARKS

This chapter has examined two overlapping periods in Hong Kong's post-1997 transition. It seeks to capture the modes of selectivity and material–discursive moments involved in the (re)making of competitiveness–integration (dis)order between 1997 and 2013. Period one saw the structural selectivity of the colonial legacies and institutional set-ups that favoured the path-dependent continuation of the service mode of accumulation. In addition, agential, discursive and technological selectivities operated to influence and shape the nature of the service bloc via the activities of actors, institutions, forums, and reports. Harvard-related and business actors were active, well-coordinated and skilful in recontextualizing and coordinating the competitiveness knowledge brand despite the MIT challenge. The selectivity of the service–competitiveness genre chain, which included books, reports, conferences, speeches and discursive technologies (e.g. ranking, chaining and closing) helped to advance the competitiveness mode of knowing and sensing. These discourses, knowledging technologies, subjective modalities and institutions were gradually sedimenting service–competitiveness as a hegemonic project supported by a labile social bloc. This bloc remained unstable because of the heterogeneous demands from industrial groups and the rise of new conjunctures (e.g., China's WTO entry and the SARS crisis) that challenged Hong Kong's competitiveness.

Period two is more complicated as Hong Kong's service–competitiveness project is being articulated in various ways with the Mainland's national-integration strategy. At this juncture, the churning out of growth icons (e.g. CEPA, IVS) is mediating the rise of a regime of hope and new relations of rule. The discursive and technological selectivities of this new regime and related 'big-gifts' narratives operate to inspire integration energies and remake cross-border partnerships. However, this hope regime and its associated ensemble of social practices (e.g. Mainland shopping and parallel trading for everyday items) is also creating tensions and provoking resistance. As illustrated by the 'big gift' of the IVS, 'gifts' discourses and practices fuel anxieties and fear when Mainland visitors arrived in large numbers. They have changed Hong Kong's shopscape. Some visitors are treated as 'big spenders' in brands-land while others operate as parallel traders in needs-land. The mix of commercial and discriminatory practices in both cases has a very uneven impact: whereas tourist/retail sectors and property owners in the shopscape gain more from the IVS, others suffer from rising prices, supply shortages, loss of communal spaces and threats to pedestrian rights. This has encouraged counter-hegemonic reclaim groups to resist particular aspects of the cross-border integration project. At the time of writing, such fears and anxieties are not abating and Hong Kong's integration journey is changing from a politics of 'big gifts' to a more 'interventionist', more overtly disciplining use of Mainland-centred norms and baselines. This shifting conjuncture provides fertile soil for the growth of counter-hegemonic political forces such as reclaim movements, the 'Occupy Central' campaign, the rise of localisms, and so on.

Through its emphasis on different selectivities and competing strategies, a CPE approach can offer important insights into these paradoxes/limits, disclose the complex interaction between micro- and macro-power relations, and propose explanations adequate at the level of meaning as well as material causation. Thus this chapter has examined the micro-discursive power involved in the 'big-gift' discourses and outlined the uneven impact of specific 'big-gift' practices on socio-economic restructuring. Rising tensions are being exacerbated by the more interventionist approach of the Mainland to relations of rule. Advancing a counter-hegemonic discourse of protecting 'Hong Kong's core values', democratic groups are engaging in wars of position to make their voices heard. In short, the changing relations of rule are politicizing issues at the interface of four trends: Hong Kong's continuous drive towards renewal of its competitiveness in relation to the Mainland's national-integration project; the rise in cross-border contradictions and tensions that impact policies and everyday life;

democratic demands for universal suffrage; and the challenges of localisms and the post-90 generation. These intersecting trends in Hong Kong's changing CPE are hard to reconcile and will continue to prompt multiple conflicts and unstable compromises.

NOTES

1. Raymond Chin is the Chair of the Industrial and Technology Development Council and Henry Tang is the Chair of the Federation of Hong Kong Industries.
2. Victor Fung has a Harvard Business School PhD and taught there before returning to Hong Kong in 1974, when he became Chair of the Li and Fung Group – a major international subcontracting management firm for major brands and global retail chains. Chair of the Hong Kong Trade Development Council, 1991–2000, Fung chaired the Hong Kong University Council until 2009 and is still chairman of the Vision 2047 Foundation, which represents commercial, financial capital and related professionals.
3. The authors interviewed Mr W.K. Chan in 1997 and 2006 when he was the Secretary-General of HKCSI. His sudden death in 2008 was a shock and this chapter is dedicated to his memory.
4. Despite the popularization of service–competitiveness themes in the forums, some stakeholders in the Tripartite Forum challenged them on specific policy-administration areas (e.g. bureaucratic red tape, inconsistent immigration policies etc.). Different opinions were disguised as a 'Catalogue of Ideas'.
5. This brand of competitiveness truth was later extended to the Pearl River Delta by Enright, Scott and Associates, Ltd in a new book entitled *Regional Powerhouse: Pearl River Delta and the Rise of China* (2005).
6. Searches on its digital archive for 'competitive + competitiveness + Hong Kong' revealed 6349 news articles from 1 July 1997 to 20 December 2001; and 5730 articles between 1 January 2002 and 1 June 2006.
7. A hegemonic project exists when one group in society manages to convince a number of other groups that their interests will be well served by entering into a social coalition under the leadership of the hegemonic group.
8. The National Day Golden Week holiday is the week that falls on China's National Day between 1 and 7 October.
9. This piece had disappeared from the Savantas website no later than 28 January 2007.
10. Hong Kong's coloniality and 'Big Hong Kongism' was reinforced by a member of the Chinese Consultative Committee, Lau Nai-keung, in an article published in *Ta Kung Pao* on 24 November 2004. The same paper was republished on 24 January 2007 as 'Twelve Years Are Too Long for Development of the Border Area'.
11. *Shenzhen Daily* (2012) reported more than half of the parallel traders were from the Mainland. *Wenweipo* (2013) recorded the proportion as 6:4 between Hong Kong and Mainland visitors who are engaged in parallel trade.
12. It was changed to 23 kg on 4 February 2013.
13. On 12 February 2013, 24 000 people had signed. The number did not reach the 100 000 needed by 28 February to trigger a response from the Obama Administration.

PART IV

Financialization, financial crisis and reimaginations

11. Crisis construals and crisis recovery in the North Atlantic financial crisis

Crises are multi-faceted phenomena that invite multiple approaches from different entry-points and standpoints. This chapter deploys a CPE approach to explore how the recent crisis in the North Atlantic economies, still continuing at the time of writing in mid-2013, has been construed through different economic imaginaries. Of interest is the shock that crises gave to the prevailing economic wisdom and dominant policy paradigms, leading to the recovery of other economic perspectives as well as a search to imagine alternative economic and political paths to economic recovery. Key aspects of the retrospective interpretation and prospective envisioning of economic performance are actors' differential capacities for lesson-drawing and asymmetrical abilities to refuse to learn from their mistakes. Accordingly the following analysis considers the multi-faceted nature of the North Atlantic financial crisis and its global repercussions, the selection of some construals rather than others as the basis for economic responses and crisis management, and the transformation of a crisis that originated in private credit relations and securitization into a crisis of sovereign debt and public finances. Of special interest are two issues. One is the contestation between hegemonic neoliberal economic imaginaries and those that had been consigned to oblivion in recent decades as scientifically outmoded, historically superseded, politically disproven or ideologically unacceptable. The other is the capacity of those economic and political elites who are still committed to neoliberalism to reject alternative, possibly more accurate or adequate, readings of the crisis and maintain a neoliberal course in the face of economic and political resistance. Addressing these issues reveals the limits of a purely constructivist approach to political economy and the advantages of a more materialist cultural political economy (or CPE) account.

ON CRISES

Crises disrupt accepted views of the world and how to 'go on' within it and also call established theoretical and policy paradigms into question. Crises are objectively overdetermined yet subjectively indeterminate (Debray 1973: 113). In other words, while crises have multiple causes that interact to produce (hence overdetermine) a particular 'event' or sequence of events in a particular conjuncture, the crisis does not come pre-interpreted but is often profoundly disorienting, creating space for alternative, often contested, construals and crisis responses, with different subjects likely to adopt different stances. Objectively, crises occur when a set of social relations (including their connection to the natural world) cannot be reproduced (cannot 'go on') in the old way. They can be 'accidental' (triggered by exogenous causes) or structurally determined (i.e. rooted in system or structural logics). They may be manageable through routine forms of crisis management (including muddling through) or provoke a crisis in crisis management. A crisis is most acute when crisis tendencies and tensions accumulate across interrelated moments of a given structure or system, limiting manoeuvre in regard to any particular problem. Shifts in the balance of forces may also intensify crisis tendencies by weakening or resisting established modes of crisis management (Offe 1984: 35–64).

A crisis is never a purely objective, extra-semiotic event or process that automatically produces a definite response or outcome. Without subjective indeterminacy, there is no crisis – merely chaos, disaster or catastrophe, and, perhaps, fatalism or stoicism. Crises are a potential moment of intervention and transformation, where, rather than muddling through, decisive action can repair broken social relations, lead to change via piecemeal adaptation, or produce radical innovation. But we must also beware of manufactured crises, that is, creating crises where none exist (or exaggerating the nature, degree and import of a crisis) for 'political' motives. In short, crises are potentially path-shaping moments that provoke responses that are mediated through semiotic-cum-material processes of variation, selection and retention.

Similar arguments appear in a hybrid rational-choice, constructivist analysis by Mark Blyth (2002). He suggests that crises are moments of a-probabilistic uncertainty, that is, they cannot be modelled and thus addressed rationally because past expectations are no longer fulfilled due to the failure of institutions. This creates a space for 'entrepreneurs' (presumably ideational entrepreneurs) to diagnose what has gone wrong and what to do about it on the basis of the ideas 'lying around' at the time (the reference to ideas lying around is to Milton Friedman, 1962; see below). Very similar conditions can be associated with a huge variety of diagnoses, and hence potential institutional resolutions. But which construal (our term) 'wins out' is always underdetermined. As such, he concludes, which ideas 'win out' is best thought of as an emergent property of the moment rather than the quality of the idea or the structure of the situation (Blyth in Boyer and Labrousse 2008). The CPE approach offers more theoretical tools to explore these ideas regarding both the semiotic and structural dimensions of a crisis and, through its analysis of conjunctural overdetermination, also provides a way to examine the 'emergent property' (sic) of the crisis moment, including its periodization and development as different crisis tendencies and their effects unfold and interact, prompting rereadings of the crisis, learning effects, and the uneven impact of different attempts at crisis management.

Because they are never purely objective, extra-semiotic events or processes that automatically produce a particular response or outcome, crises offer a real-time laboratory to study the dialectic of semiosis and materiality. Ideas and imaginaries[1] shape the interpretation of crises and the responses thereto. Thus a CPE approach combines semiotic and structural analyses to examine: (1) how crises emerge when established patterns of dealing with structural contradictions, their crisis tendencies and strategic dilemmas no longer work as expected and, indeed, when continued reliance thereon may even aggravate matters; (2) how contestation over the meaning of the crisis shapes responses through processes of variation, selection and retention that are mediated through a mix of semiotic and extra-semiotic mechanisms. Those affected by crisis typically disagree both on their objective and subjective aspects because of their different entry-points, standpoints and capacities to read the crisis. The system-specific and conjunctural aspects of crises have many spatio-temporal complexities and affect social forces in quite varied ways. The lived experience of crisis is necessarily partial, limited to particular social segments of time-space. So it is hard to read crises. Indeed, if spatio-temporal boundaries are uncertain, if causes and effects are contested, can we speak of The Crisis? Resolving them into one crisis involves at best *strategic essentialism* rather than rigorous scientific practice (on strategic essentialism, see Chapter 3). But such simplifications may help to create conditions for learning lessons and taking effective action. This is why it is necessary to consider processes of learning in, about and from crises from the viewpoint of different actors or social forces – these aspects or processes may not coincide across all actors or forces (in part because the crisis will affect them differently in space-time as well as in relation to their different identities, interests and values).

Imaginaries shape the interpretation of crises and the responses thereto. At one end of a continuum, some crises appear 'accidental', that is, are readily (if sometimes inappropriately) attributable to natural or 'external' forces (e.g. a volcanic eruption, tsunami, crop failure). At the other end, there are form-determined crises, that is, crises rooted in crisis tendencies or antagonisms grounded in specific social forms (e.g. capitalism). Another useful distinction is that between crises *in* a given social configuration and crises *of* that configuration. Crises '*in*' occur within the parameters of a given set of natural and social arrangements. They are typically associated with routine forms of crisis management that restore the basic features of these arrangements through internal adjustments and/or shift crisis effects into the future, elsewhere, or onto marginal and vulnerable groups. This is exemplified in alternating phases of unemployment and inflation in the post-war advanced capitalist economies and their treatment through countercyclical economic policies.

Crises '*of*' a system are less common. They occur when there is a crisis of crisis management (i.e., normal responses no longer work) and efforts to defer or displace crises encounter growing resistance. Such crises are more disorienting than crises 'in', indicating the breakdown of previous regularities and an inability to 'go on in the old way'. They can cause social stasis or regression, attempts to restore the old system through *force majeure*, fraud or corruption; efforts at more radical social innovation for good or ill, leading in some cases to exceptional regimes (e.g. military dictatorship, fascism), or to attempts to break the power of such regimes. This is seen in the crisis *of* the post-war mode of growth, reflected in the declining effectiveness of Keynesian economic policies, which created the conditions for a neoliberal regime shift and a transition to a finance-dominated mode of growth. This produces a more or less acute crisis, a potential moment of decisive transformation, an opportunity for decisive intervention, or a moment when the dialectic of revolution–restoration favours restoration. This opens space for strategic interventions to significantly redirect the course of events rather than 'muddle through' in the hope that the crisis is resolved in due course or that the *status quo ante* can be restored by taking emergency measures to return to 'business as usual'.

In short, a crisis is a moment for contestation and struggle to construe it and inform individual and collective responses. This involves, among other issues, delimiting the origins of a crisis in space-time and its uneven spatio-temporal incidence; identifying rightly or wrongly purported causes (agential, structural, discursive and technical) at different scales, over different time horizons, in different fields of social practice, and at different levels of social organization from nameless or named individuals through social networks, formal organizations, institutional arrangements, specific social forms or even the dynamic of a global society; determining its scope and effects, assessing in broad terms whether it is a crisis '*in*' or '*of*' the relevant arrangements; reducing its complexities to identifiable causes that could be targeted to find solutions; charting alternative futures; and promoting specific lines of action for socially identified forces over differently constructed spatio-temporal horizon.

Crisis interpretations may address a more or less broad range of questions: the challenge of making sense of a 'crisis' (and its uneven development); attributing material, institutional, organizational and personal blame for the 'crisis'; deciding in broad terms whether it is a crisis *in* or *of* the relevant arrangements; charting alternative futures; and recommending specific lines of action oriented to different spatio-temporal horizons. In the present context, this poses crucial problems around delimiting the origins of a crisis in space-time, establishing whether it is purely economic or has broader roots and effects, and reducing its complexities to identifiable causes that could be targeted in the search for solutions (for a study of the 1997 'Asian' crisis in the Republic of Korea on these lines, see Ji 2006). Often, wider ideational and institutional innovation going beyond the economy narrowly conceived is needed, promoted and supported by political, intellectual and moral leadership. Indeed, as Milton Friedman (1962: 32) put it hyperbolically but tellingly: '[o]nly a crisis produces real change. When that crisis occurs, the actions that are taken depend on the ideas that are lying around.' It follows that preparing the ground for crisis-induced strategic interventions helps to shape the nature and outcome of crisis management and crisis responses. This preparation may include a new 'economic imaginary' linked to new state projects and hegemonic visions that can be translated into material, social and spatio-temporal fixes that would jointly underpin continued accumulation. Conversely, inadequate preparation (for whatever cause) will make it harder to influence struggles over crisis construal and management, however adequate, with hindsight, the crisis diagnosis may prove to have been.

It is a truism that getting consensus on interpretations about the crisis (or crises) and its (their) most salient features is to have framed the problem. Successfully to blame one set of factors and/or actors deflects blame from oneself and sets the stage for efforts to resolve matters. For example, when crisis management is reduced to issues of the best *policies*, defined through 'governing parties' and hegemonic forces (e.g. representatives of interest-bearing capital), opportunities for more radical solutions are marginalized. By limiting crisis management to the search for correct policies, one implies that crisis is due to incorrect policy rather than being rooted in deeper structural causes, linked to patterns of economic, political and social domination (cf. Wolff 2008). A focus on policy may be reinforced by the apparent 'urgency' of crisis. Here we can contrast the drawn-out structural crisis of Fordism in the 1970s with the 'month of panic' in September 2008 in the financial crisis. This holds not only for regional, national or federal political regimes but also for the international system, where the policies of major international institutions and forums are at stake (see below on the Bretton Woods institutions, United Nations agencies and other international groupings). Limiting crisis management to the search for correct policies also implies that the crisis is due to incorrect policy or inadequate regulation rather than being rooted in deeper structural causes that are linked to patterns of economic, political and social domination. This is particularly advantageous to newly elected governments committed to maintaining capitalism because they can blame the defeated government for its policy mistakes without delving further into more basic mechanisms or causes of capitalist crisis.

Whether a crisis is defined as one *in* or *of* a given set of social relations, conflicts occur over how best to resolve it and allocate its costs. Other things being equal, more resonant interpretations will get selected as the basis for action, whether this takes the form of restoration, piecemeal reform or radical innovation. But other things are rarely equal. There is many a slip between the discursive resonance of particular interpretations and proposals in a given conjuncture and their translation into adequate policies, effective crisis-management routines, durable new social arrangements and institutionalized compromises that can underpin new patterns of economic, political and social stability in a given spatial and temporal context. Crucial here is the correspondence, always limited and provisional, between new imaginaries and crisis solutions and real, or *potentially realizable*, sets of material interdependences in the wider natural and social world.

Forums matter too. Powerful narratives without powerful bases from which to implement them are less effective than more 'arbitrary, rationalistic and willed' accounts that are pursued consistently by the powerful through the exercise of power. This has proved important in the global crisis because some international institutions and some national states are clearly more important than others: even if the UN General Assembly had adopted an agreed position on the global crisis, it would have been less influential (even if more legitimate) than bodies such as the International Monetary Fund (IMF), the World Bank and the World Trade Organization (WTO), because of its slow-footedness in reaching agreement, its weak capacities to implement decisions, and the ability of leading states to block radical recommendations. Moreover, as the Stiglitz Commission demonstrates, UN deliberations are shaped by particular theoretical and policy paradigms as well as power plays that limit serious consideration of radical alternatives. At best, then, the UN family of organizations provides scope for developing sub-hegemonic narratives, that is, accounts that are widely accepted in regional forums and subaltern organizations, but do not challenge mainstream paradigms. This indicates the need to address the overall architecture of global, regional and national organizations and the differential capacity to jump scales to pursue solutions at the most effective scale(s) of action and intervention. The scope for pursuing counter-hegemonic narratives is even more limited within this institutional architecture and points to the increased importance of regional forums, local initiatives and social movements.

Timing and sequencing also matter. Because this crisis was not only 'made in the USA' but broke there, with contagion spreading first to other neoliberal, finance-led regimes, crisis interpretations and reactions were initially shaped by readings in these heartlands. Developed nations focused on their own financial market stability rather than addressing crisis-induced global repercussions. It was clearly harder in 2006-08 than in 1997-98 to blame East Asian 'crony capitalism' or the spread of contagion from indebted, incompetent or weak emerging economies. The reverse flow, from the centre to semi-peripheral and peripheral formations, developed mainly from October 2008. Even then some economies were relatively insulated because they were less exposed to the world market (for example, Brazil, India and Indonesia). Regarding the others, the impact began in developing economies with the most globally integrated financial sectors (notably in Eastern Europe). It was then relayed through trade relations as manufacturing and commodity prices and/or volumes dropped (notably in East Asia, sub-Saharan Africa and through ties to Russia and Central Asia). Subsequently, it was mediated through falling remittances from migrant workers and through other repercussions on the informal sector that affected the most vulnerable groups in many economies. And most recently, it has been intensified through its effects on public sector finances, which, even without the weak fiscal and institutional capacities that characterize many less developed economies, are limiting the scope to pursue countercyclical policies and cushion the impact of the crisis (see Oxfam International 2010). The impact outside the developed economies was often slower than in comparable crises in the 1980s and 1990s. This is reflected in the initial relative lack of mass upheavals or mobilization of radical social movements, especially where centre-left governments were in power and may have been vulnerable to hostility from right-wing parties and movements.[2]

Finally, power matters. Although we have already noted that not all discourses and their spokespersons are equal, it is particularly important during periods of crisis to recall Karl Deutsch's definition of power, namely, the capacity not to have to learn from one's mistakes (Deutsch 1963: 111). We shall see below that the asymmetries of power in the geo-economic and geopolitical field are especially significant in the selection of crisis interpretations and their translation into crisis responses. This helps to explain the reassertion of key elements in the neoliberal project despite the initial shock thereto from the form, timing, location and incidence of the current crisis.

Having power does not guarantee success – and can be a recipe for failure. Only crisis construals that grasp key emergent extra-semiotic features of the social world as well as mind-independent features of the natural world are likely to be *selected* and *retained*. Some of these construals in turn produce changes in the extra-semiotic features of the world and in related (always) tendential social logics. Construals can be assessed in terms of scientific validity, that is, evaluated in terms of scientific procedures and rules of evaluation according to specific scientific programmes and paradigms. They can also be judged in terms of their correctness, that is, their ability to read a conjuncture, provide ideas about potential futures, and guide action that transforms the conjuncture. This is mediated through language as well as through social practices and institutions beyond language. Indeed, crisis construal is heavily mediatized, depending on specific forms of visualization and media representations, which typically vary across popular, serious and specialist media. Correctness depends both on the limits set by the objective nature of a crisis conjuncture and on the capacities of strategic forces to win hegemony or, at least, impose their preferred construals, crisis-management options and exit solutions. The mechanisms of variation, selection and retention tend to eliminate 'arbitrary, rationalistic, and willed' construals in favour of 'correct' construals of the conjuncture. In these conditions, then, a 'correct' reading creates its own 'truth-effects'.

ON THE VARIATION, SELECTION AND RETENTION OF IMAGINARIES

Arguing that all social phenomena have semiotic *and* material properties, CPE studies their interconnections and co-evolution in constructing as well as construing social relations. This enables CPE to avoid both a structuralist Scylla and a constructivist Charybdis (Chapter 3). A significant feature of CPE regarding this 'third way' is the distinction between the sedimentation and repoliticization of discourses. These processes are contingent aspects of all social relations, with sedimentation giving rise to the appearance of their structural fixity and repoliticization in turn suggesting their socially arbitrary nature. Crises are particularly important moments in the general dialectic of sedimentation and reactivation because they often produce profound cognitive, strategic and practical disorientation by disrupting actors' sedimented views of the world. They disturb prevailing meta-narratives, theoretical frameworks, policy paradigms and/or everyday life, and open the space for proliferation (*variation*) in crisis interpretations, only some of which get *selected* as the basis for 'imagined recoveries' that are translated into economic strategies and policies – and, of these, only some prove effective and are *retained*. In this context we explore how semiosis and extra-semiotic factors vary in importance across different stages of economic crisis. (Similar arguments hold for other types of crisis.) We suggest that semiosis becomes more important in path-shaping when crises disrupt taken-for-granted discourses and generate unstructured complexity, provoking multiple crisis interpretations. Its scope is more restricted in the selective translation of some imagined paths to recovery into specific social responses. Extra-semiotic mechanisms matter most in the retention of some strategic responses as the basis for new, sedimented routines, organizations and institutions.

Moreover, when applied to the analysis of crisis, CPE provides a heuristic schema to understand why semiosis and extra-semiotic factors have varying weight across different stages of economic crisis and why only some of the many competing crisis construals get selected and why even fewer strategies are retained. This heuristic schema offers useful analytical distinctions based on hypotheses about the changing mix of factors involved in the variation, selection and retention of crisis construals. It does not derive from empirical observation.

Figure 11.1 depicts these hypotheses. One purpose of this heuristic schema is to avoid overemphasis on construal due to a one-sided focus on variation (where semiosis matters most) or on the structural determination of crisis responses due to a one-sided focus on retention (where materiality

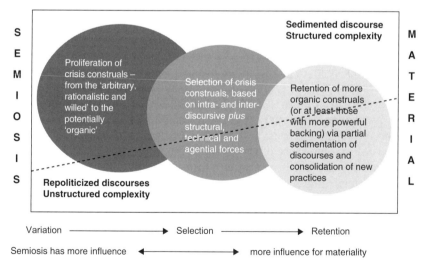

Figure 11.1 Schematic representation of variation, selection and retention

matters most). It represents an overlapping sequence of variation, selection and retention of crisis interpretations triggered by a crisis that sees the repoliticization (contestation) of sedimented discourses and the breakdown of established patterns of structured complexity (relative institutional coherence). The broken diagonal line indicates that the semiotic and material are always co-present but their weight varies by stage. As one crisis interpretation and its imagined recovery path are selected, discourse is resedimented and new forms of structured complexity are established (or old patterns restored). If stage three is not reached because the selected path is impractical, the sequence restarts at stage one or two.

The first phases of a crisis generally prompt massive *variation* in construals of its nature and significance, opening a space for the (re)politicization of sedimented discourses and practices. Many early accounts prove arbitrary and short-lived, disappearing in the cacophony of competing interpretations or lacking meaningful connections to the salient phenomenal forms of the crisis, and lacking long-term consequences for power relations and overall social dynamics. This holds for religious readings of the crisis as signs of divine retribution for moral degeneration, for example, as well as for the equally fanciful claims that the terminal crisis of capitalism was close. Overall, the plausibility of interpretations, strategies and projects depends on their resonance (and hence their capacity to reinterpret and mobilize) in a more or less complex social field with its own discursive and other selectivities (see next paragraph). Relevant aspects include the lived experiences of members of key classes, strata, social categories or other crisis-hit groups, diverse organizational or institutional narratives, and meta-narratives (on narratives, see Somers 1994).

While some narratives need to convince only a few key policy-makers or strategists, leading to more administered, indirect, market-mediated or molecular changes that involve limited participation from subaltern groups, others are effective only through their capacity to mobilize significant support from a broader range of social forces. Such transformative narratives connect personal experiences, the narratives of key stakeholders and organized interests, and grand narratives that provide a broader context for making sense of the crisis. In the latter cases, the plausibility of narratives and their associated strategies and projects depends on their resonance (and hence capacity to reinterpret and mobilize) with the personal (including shared) narratives of significant classes, strata, social categories or groups affected by the crisis. Moreover, although many plausible narratives are advanced, their narrators will not be equally effective in conveying their messages and securing support for the lessons they hope to draw.

For CPE, what matters is which of these many and diverse

interpretations get *selected* as the basis for private and public strategic and policy initiatives to manage the crisis and/or move beyond it. This is not reducible to narrative resonance, argumentative force or scientific merit alone (although each may have a role), but also depends on diverse extra-semiotic factors associated with structural, agential and technological selectivities. These include the prevailing 'web of interlocution' (Somers 1994) and its discursive selectivities (Hay 1996), the organization and operation of the mass media, the role of intellectuals in public life, and the structural biases and strategically selective operations of various public and private apparatuses of economic, political and ideological domination. That some institutional and meta-narratives resonate powerfully does not validate them. All narratives are selective, appropriate some arguments rather than others and combine them in specific ways. So we must study what goes unstated or silent, repressed or suppressed, in specific discourses. Nonetheless, if the crisis can be plausibly interpreted as a crisis *in* the existing economic order, minor reforms may first be tried to restore that order. If this fails or the crisis is initially interpreted primarily as a crisis *of* that order, more radical changes may be explored. In both cases conflicts are likely over the best policies to resolve the crisis and allocate its costs as different social forces propose new visions, projects, programmes and policies, and struggle over hegemony.

A third phase would occur when some accounts are *retained* and undergo theoretical, interpretative and policy elaboration leading to their eventual sedimentation and structuration. However, it is one thing to (re)politicize discourses in the face of crisis-induced unstructured complexity; it is another to move to sedimented (taken-for-granted) discourse and seemingly structured complexity. This raises the key issue of the (always limited and provisional) fit between imaginaries and real, or potentially realizable, sets of material interdependencies in the economy and its embedding in wider sets of social relations. This is where the distinction introduced in Chapter 4 between construal and construction becomes especially relevant. Proposed crisis strategies and policies must be (or seen to be) effective within the spatio-temporal horizons of relevant social forces in a given social order.

Generally, the greater the number of sites and scales of social organization at which resonant discourses are retained, the greater the potential for institutionalization. This in turn should lead to relative structured coherence across institutional orders and modes of thought, and to relatively durable patterns of social compromise among key actors (see Chapter 1). If this proves impossible, the new project will seem 'arbitrary, rationalistic and willed' rather than organic (Gramsci 1971: 376–7; Q7, §19: 868). The cycle of variation, selection and retention will then restart.

CRISIS, CRISIS CONSTRUAL AND CRISIS MANAGEMENT

Paraphrasing Baudrillard (1995) on the Gulf War, one could say '*the Crisis*' did not happen. Given its complexity and the wide range of possible entry-points and standpoints from which to read it, there are countless interpretations, explanations, strategic plans and specific policy recommendations. These range from early claims about the terminal crisis of capitalism through to the equally fanciful initial belief that it was a temporary blip in an otherwise well-functioning, self-correcting free market system. Even 'mainstream' interpretations, explanations, blame and proposed solutions reflect different regional, national and macro-regional economies' experiences of 'the' global financial crisis and its broader repercussions. A CPE approach explores which of these interpretations gets selected as the basis for private and public attempts to resolve the crisis. This is not reducible to narrative resonance, argumentative force or scientific merit (although each may have its role), but also depends on important structural, agential and technological selectivities. Critical here is that most accounts lack support from economic and political actors with enough economic, administrative, fiscal or legislative resources to offer 'necessary' institutional and policy solutions on the most relevant scales of action.

The dominant crisis interpretation in liberal market economies after the initial emergency measures is that this is a crisis *in* finance-led accumulation or, at most, *in* neoliberalism. As such it can be resolved through a massive, but strictly temporary, financial stimulus, recapitalization of the biggest (but not all) vulnerable banks, (promises of) tighter regulation, and a reformed (but still neoliberal) international economic regime. This will allegedly permit a return to neoliberal 'business as usual' at some unfortunate, but necessary, cost to the public purse, some rebalancing of the financial and 'real' economies and, in the medium term, cuts in public spending to compensate for the costs of short-term crisis management. One reason for the lack of popular mobilization against the crisis and these measures in the heartlands of neoliberalism may be the widespread belief that 'everyone' is to blame because of generalized 'greed' based on the financialization of everyday life in the neoliberal economies. This implies that the housing bubble and financial meltdown were due to excessive consumption rather than unregulated, profit-oriented supply of loans, and also distracts attention from the explosive growth in unregulated derivatives. A more significant account, especially in the USA, 'blames' China for its exchange rate policy, sweated labour, excess savings and so forth, and, accordingly, demands that it bears a significant part of the burden of economic restructuring in the immediate post-crisis period (A.M. Fischer 2011).

To labour the obvious, the crucial sites for crisis interpretation and crisis management following the outbreak of crisis in 2006-08 have been the USA and the international financial institutions (IFIs) that it dominates. Beyond this, we have seen advocacy of a G-2 (with its proposed membership having switched from the USA and the European Union to the USA and China) as the most appropriate and most effective partnership to lead crisis management and the redesign of international governance (e.g. Bergsten 1999, 2008). Although there have been many bilateral USA-China high-level dialogues, an effective working partnership is lacking. Hence the most heavily promoted forum for resolving the current financial and economic crisis has become the G-20, at first informally, then formally. This self-elected group of 19 key industrial and emerging market economies (plus the European Union, the IMF, the World Bank and other major IFIs) has become the *de facto* global crisis committee. This reflects growing recognition of the actual and potential influence of the 'BRIC' economies (Brazil, Russia, India and China) and the creditor position of major East Asian economies. Thus the G-20 Summit in November 2008 expanded the Financial Stability Forum to incorporate creditor nations, including China; and, in April 2009, it established a Financial Stability Board with a wider remit. This has integrated the leading 'Southern' economies into problem-solving and burden-sharing, thereby strengthening the leading IFIs, and has also reinforced an unsustainable growth-oriented global economy. But the informal, self-selected status of the G-20 means that it cannot replace the United Nations, IMF, WTO and other official bodies in crisis management, with their official status and, in some cases, significant strategic intervention capacities (Bello 2009).

A sometimes favoured alternative is the G-77, which comprises a loose union of developing nations. Despite its association with China, it lacks, however, clout in international decision-making. Yet its members are generally among the worst-affected victims of the crisis, due to contagion and/or spillover effects, and are also suffering from the longer-term and more wide-ranging effects of climate change produced over many decades by the developed economies. The G-77 has been a major voice calling for more concerted action to deal with world poverty and the Millennium Development Goals (MDGs), including a debt moratorium, enhanced IMF resources and increased official development assistance (ODA) (e.g. Ministerial Declaration 2009). It has also demanded that polluters pay for climate change, the stalled Doha Development Round negotiations be reactivated, mutually beneficial South-South trade arrangements and regional cooperation among developing economies be pursued, technology be transferred in ways that do not reproduce dependence on the developed economies, and the global South be more effectively integrated into global economic governance through reform of the international financial and economic institutions. This could also include new forms of international reserve (e.g. BRIC arrangements) as an alternative to the dollar, euro, yen and Special Drawing Rights. With fewer resources, however, many members of the G-77 have been forced to pursue procyclical monetary and fiscal policies, adversely affecting their economies.

Looking beyond the leading neoliberal economies and their house-trained IFIs, the crisis is more often read by leading forces in other capitalist regimes in one or both of two ways: (1) as a crisis *of* finance-led accumulation, prompting efforts to limit the influence of the financial sector through more radical reregulation, restrictions on the size and activities of banks, and greater investment in the 'real economy'; and/or (2) as a crisis *of* neoliberalism, which has led to efforts to roll back neoliberalism at home and impose more controls on market forces in supranational and international contexts. Even in more neo-statist or neo-corporatist advanced capitalist economies, however, this has not yet prompted leading forces to question the broader commitment to world market integration or to take seriously sub- or counter-hegemonic proposals from subaltern nations, institutions, agencies and social forces.

LEARNING IN, ABOUT, AND FROM CRISIS

Our concern in this section is the fourth key feature of the CPE approach. This is the dialectic of experience and learning or, on a certain reading, the spiral 'unity of theory and practice'. This dialectic is crucial both for sense- and meaning-making and for structural stabilization and transformation. Ontologically, learning is grounded in complexity reduction and its limits. In other words, every reduction (whether semiotic or structural) of complexity excludes aspects of the real world that are relevant to actors' ability to 'go on' within it on the basis of sedimented meaning systems and structured complexity. This leads to disappointed expectations that present opportunities to learn or, indeed, refuse to do so (see below). This is an everyday occurrence. It is especially significant during 'crises' when sedimented meanings and structured complexity are revealed as historically contingent and opened to repoliticization and in relation to what Foucault calls *urgences*, that is, unexpected 'problems' that prompt contested efforts to build new dispositives through a co-constitutive development that both confirms a problematization and consolidates a solution. We have addressed problematization elsewhere in terms of the co-constitution of modes of regulation (or governance) and objects of regulation (or governance) (Jessop and Sum 2006), and we have referred above to Foucault's analyses of dispositivization in response to *urgences* (Chapters 5, 7–10 and 12). In this chapter we propose, methodologically, that 'crisis' can serve CPE as an entry-point to explore learning *in*, *about* and *from* crisis. Likewise, in line with its critical vocation, a CPE approach would argue that learning occurs in contested fields with ideological effects and is shaped by uneven capacities to frame, impose or ignore lessons.

These are all fundamental issues and should not be confused with managerial discourses about learning, learning failure, organizational learning, strategic learning, resilience in the face of challenges and so forth. Indeed, from a CPE perspective, these discourses need to be criticized for their implication that problems are shared and can be resolved in ways that realize, at some scale, a collective interest. As noted above, strategic learning and crisis management have become major 'growth industries' as knowledge-intensive business services and knowledge brands compete for business (see Chapters 7, 8 and 10). And we have also observed the importance of 'learning' in the emergence of the knowledge-based economy imaginary, including notions such as the learning economy, the learning region, the learning organization, the 'smart state', lifelong learning and the learning society (see Chapter 7). More generally, there is now a broad literature on policy learning and transfer but it is rooted in cognitive, constructivist, governance, organizational and strategic management frameworks.

Learning is an important aspect of the evolutionary processes in and through which semiosis and structuration develop at all levels, from individual utterances and encounters through specific social practices to orders of discourse and social forms and up to the basic semantic systems and structural configurations of a social formation. This suggests in turn that learning processes (and, indeed, forgetting) can become significant sites and stakes for contestation at all scales, ranging from responses to disappointing social encounters through to the responses to organic crises of a social formation. One focus of contestation could be relevant past experiences (raising issues of alternative memories and the use of the past to make the future), another concerns the construal of present events that disturb routine expectations, and a third would involve conflict over alternative responses and scenarios to the events that are deemed to require lessons to be drawn. This matters especially in crises considered as overdetermined moments that are subjectively indeterminate, raising issues about policy and strategic learning in the face of crises (including crises of crisis management) and strategies and tactics of transformation.

Symptomatology, Experience and Learning

One way to develop CPE as a third way between the constructivist Charybdis and the structuralist Scylla is to appropriate (and transform) the distinction, introduced by St Augustine in *De Doctrina Christiana* (Augustine of Hippo, AD 389), between *signa data* and *signa naturalia*. The first are the conventional signs explored by Saussureans and social constructivists: they link *signum* (sign) and *signans* (signifier) and bracket the *signatum* (referent). The second are natural, indexical signs that can be interpreted as symptoms of something beyond the *signum–signans* relation. This relation is grounded in a causal nexus that connects an invisible entity to the visible signs that it produces. This relation is not immediately transparent or self-evident but requires interpretation because there is no one-to-one relation between event and symptom. This fits with CPE's critical-realist 'depth ontology', marked by its distinctions among the real (the invisible entity), the actual (an event) and the empirical (the visible sign). It also fits with the typical critical-realist mode of inquiry, that is, retroduction, which asks what the real world must be like for this event to have occurred and/or these symptoms to have existed (Bhaskar 1972). St Augustine's examples of natural signs include smoke (indicating fire) and animal tracks. One could add the symptoms of disease in medical diagnosis (with its link to the medical concept of crisis) or the symptoms of economic crisis (and the problems of interpreting their causal link to economic crisis tendencies).

Just as medical diagnosis requires knowledge based on careful observation, trial-and-error learning and successful retroduction, so does construal of the symptoms of economic crisis. For, while crises become visible through their symptoms, the latter have no one-to-one relation to crisis tendencies and specific conjunctures. This explains the subjective indeterminacy that attends the objective overdetermination of the crisis. In this sense, economic 'symptomatology' is challenging to social forces just as medical symptoms challenge physicians and surgeons. Indeed, crises are moments of profound cognitive and strategic disorientation. They disorient inherited expectations and practices; challenge past lessons and ways of learning; and open space for new lessons and ways of learning. Indeed, analogies with past crises may be misleading, especially when current crises display new symptoms. This provides the basis for a threefold distinction between learning in crisis, learning about crisis and learning from crisis (see Ji 2006).

Learning has a critical role in crises (including crises of crisis management), affecting the capacity to formulate imagined recoveries. It has the same selectivities (semiotic, structural, technological and agential) as semiosis more generally and also undergoes variation, selection and retention. A crisis does not automatically lead to learning: cognitive capacities may be lacking or the situation may be too unstructured (chaotic); or, again, lessons learnt are irrelevant because the situation is too turbulent to apply them. Learning depends on a dialectics of *Erlebnis* and *Erfahrung* that has its own temporalities, shaped by crisis dynamics.

- *Erlebnis* refers to *immediate experience* in the face of disorientation and associated attempts to make sense of disorienting events/processes. Lived experience is not an immediate reflection of an extra-semiotic reality but draws on semiosis as a 'meaning pool' that shapes personal and empathetic experience. It is grounded in *relationality* (lived relations to others), *corporeality* (the lived body), *spatiality* (lived space) and *temporality* (lived time). Some might add spirituality (lived relation to the spirit world through internal conversations with imagined others) (e.g. Archer 2003). Lived experience is linked to meaning-making schemes, categories, classifications, codes, frames, programmes and so on. These may be sedimented but can be dislocated, repoliticized and contested with a view to restoring, altering or overturning meaning.
- *Erfahrung* refers to the lessons learnt from this disorientation and sense-making. Importantly, it typically includes an element of the objective dimensions of the crisis – lessons must be adequate to the crisis, not just idiosyncratic reactions. Indeed, without some form of correspondence to the natural and social world as a 'reality check', the lessons drawn from crisis are likely to fail in one or another way (for discussions of learning failure, see, e.g., Birkland 2009; Murphy 2010; Weick 1995).

When crises throw established modes of learning into crisis, three stages in learning can occur: learning in crisis, learning about crisis and learning from crisis (Ji 1996). Each stage is likely to involve different balances of semiosis and structuration (see Figure 11.1). It can also involve different degrees of reflexivity, that is, learning about learning. This requires that actors recognize the need for new imaginaries because inherited approaches have not worked well in crisis situations and that they reorganize information collection, calculation and embodied and/or collective memory. Shifts in strategic learning and knowledge production often require a shift in the balance of forces in wider social relations.

Learning in Crisis

Crises of a given system, hence crises of crisis management, are especially likely to disrupt learnt strategic behaviour and lead to an initial trial-and-error 'muddling-through' approach. Learning in crisis occurs in the immediacy of experiencing crisis, considered as a moment of profound disorientation, and is oriented to the phenomenal forms of crisis. It involves attempts to make sense of an initial disorientation (at some level of everyday life, organizational and/or institutional and/or policy paradigms, disciplinary or theoretical framing, and meta-narrative) in order to 'go on' in the face of the crisis as it is experienced (*Erlebnis*). For those directly affected, it occurs via direct experience of its *phenomenal* forms. Lived experience will vary across persons, groups and organizations. How someone experiences and understands his/her world(s) as real and meaningful depends on their subject positions and standpoint. For those not directly affected, learning in crisis occurs through real-time observation of the *phenomenal* forms of crisis. This is often mediated through diverse forms of representation (serious and tabloid journalism, statistics, charts, econometric models, reports etc.) and can be highly mediatized (MacKenzie 2009; Engelen et al. 2011; Tetlock 2007; Pahl 2011; on mediatization, Hajer 2011, and, for a Swedish case study, Nord and Olsson 2013). In neither case does such learning dig beneath surface phenomena to deeper causes, crisis tendencies and so on.

Three points merit attention. First, social actors have different social, spatial and temporal positions as well as reflexive capacities and pasts, and will live the crisis in different ways. In this sense, actors' strategic learning does not come directly from the crisis as a whole, but from their own circumstances and crisis experiences. They also have different entry-points and different standpoints when approaching lesson-drawing, and crises will affect them differently according to their identities (on the latter, see Nishimura 2011). This can lead to different strategic responses (strategic variation); and their results vary in terms of success or survival under certain structural and conjunctural conditions (strategic selection). Second, actors vary in their capacities to 'read' the crisis and to respond to it in the 'short term'. At one extreme we find wilful blindness or repeated bouts of 'crying wolf' that lead to the dismissal of real crises; at the other extreme, crises may be manufactured (or crisis construals may be deliberately biased) to force decisions favourable to one's own interests. Lastly, in critical-realist terms, learning in crisis is more likely to address the empirical and actual dimensions of the crisis than to deal with its real causes (especially in terms of their spatio-temporal breadth and depth).

Learning about Crisis

Learning about crisis occurs as a crisis unfolds, often in unexpected ways, with lags in real time as actors begin to interpret the crisis in terms of underlying mechanisms and dynamics. It goes beyond the 'phenomenal' features of a crisis to its 'essential'[3] features in order to develop more effective initial responses and a more effective mid-term strategy. It is most likely where the routine crisis-management procedures adopted by actors prove, or seem to be, inadequate or inappropriate, with the result that policy-making and implementation must engage in experimentation. Crisis construal and management are now more experimental as actors seek to make sense of the crisis not merely at the phenomenal level but also in terms of underlying mechanisms and crisis dynamics. For those directly affected, this occurs when attention turns from phenomenal forms to deeper causes and dynamics and their bearing on crisis management. For 'outside' observers, it occurs when they focus on real causes, dynamics and effects, and monitor actors' trial-and-error attempts to solve the crisis and/or how other 'outsiders' seek to shape its course, costs and outcome. Not all actors or observers can or do move to this stage; it is typically highly selective, partial and provisional, as well as mediated and mediatized. In addition, retrospective learning about crisis may draw on contemporary accounts of those who have attempted to describe, interpret, explain and manage crisis.

This stage differs from learning in crisis because it takes more time to dig beneath phenomenal features (if it did not, then this would not be a 'crisis', that is, disturbs a theoretical or policy paradigm, and it would be possible to engage in routine crisis-management routines) and/or to scan the environment for analogous events in past or present. Social actors learn through 'trial-and-error' in specific conditions and, in this sense, through 'learning about crisis' they also embark on learning from crisis.

Learning from Crisis

Learning from crisis occurs after a crisis is (temporarily) resolved (or changes its form, e.g. from liquidity crisis to sovereign debt crisis or fiscal crisis) and includes preventive or prudential actions to prevent repetition, to improve crisis-management routines and so on. Whether one has directly experienced the crisis or 'merely' observed it in real time, learning from crisis occurs after 'it' ends. Learning from a crisis can also occur through institutionalized inquiries, based on reports from those who experienced it, observed it, and tried to describe, interpret and explain it. This is an important mechanism of policy learning for future crisis prevention and crisis management. It may lead to revisions in imaginaries, whether these take the form of meta-narratives, theoretical frameworks, policy paradigms or everyday expectations and routines. In this phase, strategic lessons are retained after the surviving social actors have had time to reflect on the new, post-crisis realities. Only then is overall strategic reorientation and path-breaking likely to be accomplished. This is an important mechanism of policy learning for future crisis prevention and crisis management. In contrast to learning in and about crisis, learning from crisis may happen much later, based on lessons drawn from other times and/or places. Such studies may be limited to iconic, high-profile or benchmark crises, or aim to be more comprehensive. Relevant comparators and appropriate lessons are often disputed, as demonstrated by the continuing debate on the 1930s Great Depression.

Learning from crisis may shape policy in two ways. First, lessons learnt by those directly affected can be conveyed in more or less codified terms to others who experience similar crises. This may lead to fast policy transfer, whether appropriate or not. Because learning and normal politics both 'take time', crises create pressure to take action based on unreliable information, narrow or limited consultation, and participation. Calls for quick action lead to shorter policy development cycles, fast-track decision-making, rapid programme rollout, continuing policy experiments, institutional and policy Darwinism, constant revision of guidelines and so on. An emphasis on speed affects the choice of policies, initial policy targets, sites where policy is implemented, and the criteria adopted for success. It also discourages proper evaluation of a policy's impact over various spatio-temporal horizons, including delayed and/or unintended consequences and feedback effects.

Second, lessons drawn by 'outside' observers may be conveyed to those directly affected as more or less codified guidance for managing future crises. This can backfire in this as well as in the previous case where codified knowledge is followed rigidly without regard to the tacit knowledge and improvisation that also shaped crisis management. The one-size-fits-all lessons of bodies such as the IMF illustrate this and can be contrasted with the very different lessons drawn from Iceland's handling of its disastrous liquidity and solvency crises – and, indeed, with the recent admission by the IMF that it had underestimated the impact of austerity on debt–default–deflation dynamics (on Iceland, see Sigfusson 2012; on the IMF, see Blanchard and Leigh 2013). Lessons from the past can be invoked in all three types of learning. Sometimes this involves seeking appropriate historical parallels as a basis for responding effectively to the crisis in real time – with the attendant risk of drawing false analogies and/or missing novel features of the crisis. Lessons from the past can also be deliberately invoked to steer crisis construal toward one rather than another set of crisis measures (on historical parallels, see Samman 2013).

Lessons from the Past

Lessons from the past are often invoked in the course of all three learning types. This involves the use of history to make history or, put differently, the effort to define appropriate historical parallels as a basis for responding effectively to the crisis in real time. Such lessons often interact with 'spatial' dimensions, such as policy transfer across different fields, sites, levels and scales of policy-making.

Learning Failure

In general, learning in, about and from crisis is relevant to the critique of political economy, to strategic and policy learning on how to prevent and/or manage crises, and to political learning. On this last point, it is worth recalling Karl Deutsch's aphorism that power is the ability not to have to learn from one's mistakes (1963: 111). This raises issues concerning structural and strategic asymmetries that bear on both policy and political learning. Learning may not be translated into new policies: there is a difference between 'identifying lessons' and 'acting upon them', and there are many possible intervening factors in this regard. Agents may lack the capacity (technologies, suitable leverage points or access to power) to act on lessons learnt; the powerful may block action where it hurts their interests. There are many ways in which learning may be ineffective: simplistic conclusions, fantasy lessons, falsely generalized lessons, turbulent environments that mean that lessons learnt are almost immediately rendered irrelevant, rhetorical learning, limits on learning due to prior policy/political commitments, politicized learning that reflects power relations, ideological barriers to learning, social barriers and rigidities that block active learning, and codified lessons that miss tacit, implicit lessons/practices.

ON FINANCE-DOMINATED ACCUMULATION

The so-called global financial crisis offers a good opportunity to test this approach. It is far more complex, multi-dimensional, and multi-scalar than its simple label implies, and has unfolded very unevenly around the globe – to such an extent, indeed, that one might ask whether it is truly global or whether this label merely offers an alibi to actors in the economic spaces where it emerged before spreading elsewhere through contagion.

It is probably better described as the North Atlantic financial crisis (hereafter NAFC) because it originated in the USA and the UK, spread through contagion effects elsewhere in North America and Europe and, in part, to China and to other export-oriented emerging economies, and, more recently, acquired a new dynamic through the eurozone crisis. The NAFC has a complex aetiology and, just as labelling it as global distracts attention from its origins in a particular accumulation regime in the world market, labelling it as financial distracts attention from other mechanisms that led to its complex overdetermination.

The NAFC began to develop well before it attracted general attention in 2007–08 and is a product of the interaction of at least five processes: (1) the global environmental, fuel, food and water crisis; (2) the decline of US hegemony, dominance and credibility in the post-Cold-War geo-political order; (3) the crisis of a global economy organized in the shadow of ongoing neoliberalization; (4) a range of structural or branch crises in important sectors (such as automobiles and agriculture); and (5) the crisis of finance-dominated accumulation regimes that emerged in a few but important economic spaces. Each process has its own spatio-temporal and substantive logic, each interacts with the others and, collectively, they are overdetermined by specific local, regional, national and macro-regional factors that ensure that crisis tendencies are always spatio-temporally and substantively specific rather than simple instantiations of global crisis tendencies. Lastly, there are unevenly distributed capacities for crisis management.

Nonetheless the specific form of the crisis is closely related to the extent of hyperfinancialization produced in and through the consolidation of finance-dominated accumulation (hereafter FDA) in the economic spaces that experienced neoliberal regime shifts. The FDA regime is not a simple inversion of Fordism because it involves different principal contradictions as well as different institutional and spatio-temporal fixes. The *principal* (or dominant) structural forms of finance-dominated accumulation are money and the (social) wage relation; the others are subordinated to these in potentially destabilizing ways – as the genesis and repercussions of the NAFC have amply demonstrated. This regime gained increasing influence in the variegated world market through the disembedding of financial capital and the importance of neoliberalism as the driving force in world market integration (Jessop 2010b). The continuing efforts to revive this model tell us something about the limits of the regulation approach in so far as it ignores the broader dynamics of class domination, the ability of those with power not to have to learn from their mistakes, and the growing turn to authoritarian statism and, indeed, repressive measures to maintain class power (on this, see, e.g., Duménil and Lévy 2004, 2011; Harvey 2005; Lapavitsas 2011) (see Table 11.1).

Table 11.1 Finance-dominated accumulation en régulation?

Basic form	Primary aspect	Secondary aspect	Institutional fixes	Spatio-temporal fixes
Money/capital	Fast, hyper-mobile money as general form (+ derivatives)	Valorization of capital as fixed asset in global division of labour	Deregulation of financial markets, state targets price stability, not jobs	Disembed flows from national or regional state controls; grab future values
(Social) wage	Private wage plus household credit (promote private Keynesianism)	Reduce residual social wage as (global) cost of production	Numerical + time flexibility; new credit forms for households	War for talents + race to the bottom for most workers and 'squeezed middle'
State	Neoliberal policies with Ordoliberal constitution	Flanking plus soft + hard disciplinary measures to secure neoliberalism	Free market plus authoritarian 'strong state'	Intensifies uneven development at many sites + scales as market outcome
Global regime	Create open space of flows for all forms of capital	Dampen uneven growth, adapt to rising economies	Washington Consensus regimes	Core–periphery tied to US power, its allies and relays

The primary aspect of money (as capital) in the finance-dominated regime is (world) money as the most abstract expression of capital and its disembedding in a space of flows (in contrast to the more territorial logic of Atlantic Fordism or a productivist KBE). The primary aspect of the wage form is its privatization or recommodification with growing resort to private consumer credit (sometimes called privatized Keynesianism) and the secondary aspect was handled via cutbacks in the residual social wage as a (global) cost of production (resulting in a lean welfare state). The secondary aspect of money (real assets) was secured through the neoliberal policy boost to post-tax profits – that was not always reflected, however, in productive investment in financialized neoliberal regimes. Indeed, the neoliberal bias towards deregulation also creates the basis for an institutional fix that relies on 'unusual deals with political authority', predatory capitalism and reckless speculation – all of which have helped to fuel the global financial crisis. An Ordoliberal framework, along the lines advocated in the German theory of the 'social market economy' (rather than the Chicago-style liberal market economy) would have provided a more appropriate institutional and spatio-temporal fix, including the embedding of neoliberalism internationally in a new, disciplinary constitutionalism and new ethicalism (Gill 1995; Sum 2010b; Chapter 9).

Separately and together, neoliberal measures (such as liberalization, deregulation, privatization, the use of market proxies in the residual state sector, internationalization, and the lowering of direct taxes) privilege value in motion, the treatment of workers as disposable and substitutable factors of production, the wage as a cost of (international) production, money as international currency (especially due to the increased importance of derivatives), nature as a commodity and knowledge as intellectual property. World market integration enhances capital's capacity to defer and/or displace its internal contradictions by increasing the global scope of its operations, by reinforcing its capacities to disembed certain of its operations from local material, social and spatio-temporal constraints, by enabling it to deepen the spatial and scalar divisions of labour, by creating more opportunities for moving up, down and across scales, by commodifying and securitizing the future, and rearticulating time horizons. This helps to free monetary accumulation from extra-economic and spatio-temporal constraints, increases the emphasis on speed, acceleration and turnover time, and enhances capital's capacity to escape the control of other systems in so far as these are still territorially differentiated and fragmented. This disembedding from the frictions of national power containers intensifies the influence of the logic of capital on a global scale as the global operation of the law of value commensurates local conditions, that is, renders them more easily subordinate to the same, dominant logic of profit-oriented, market-mediated accumulation, at the same time as it promotes the treadmill search for superprofits. Supported by a stress on shareholder value, this particularly benefits hypermobile financial capital, which controls the most liquid, abstract and generalized resource, and has become the most integrated fraction of capital, and enhances its abilities to displace and defer problems on to other economic actors and interests, other systems and the natural environment.

In the short term, financial accumulation depends on pseudo-validation of highly leveraged debt, but finance capital (let alone capital in general) cannot escape its long-term material dependence on the need for surplus-value to be produced before it can be realized and distributed. Nor can it escape its material dependence in this regard on the existence and performance of other institutional orders (e.g. protection of property rights and contracts, basic education, effective legislation, scientific discoveries). And, of course, it always remains a prisoner of its own crisis tendencies.

The overaccumulation of financial capital enabled by its dissociation from, and indifference to, other moments of the capital relation was a crucial factor contributing to the eventual bursting of financial bubbles around the world. But the crisis has a specific form due to the *hyperfinancialization* of advanced neoliberal economies and, in particular and most immediately, practices of deregulated, opaque and sometimes fraudulent financial institutions that still benefit from a corrupt relation with political authority. These features reflect the hybrid nature of FDA through its articulation with a predatory and parasitic political capitalism. Overall, the hierarchy of structural forms in this regime is generating an epic recession, and perhaps eventually, another great depression, which is based on the vicious interaction among debt, default and deflation (Rasmus 2010).

In contrast to the thought-experiment presented in Table 11.1, Table 11.2 presents the actually existing features of FDA in crisis. It can be seen that this crisis inverts many features of the ideal-typical institutional and spatio-temporal fixes that might have provided some partial, provisional and temporary stability for this regime. The neglect of investment in fixed assets and the emphasis on cost reduction to increase shareholder value produced a rising antagonism between interest-bearing capital (Wall Street, the City of London) and profit-producing capital (conventionally identified with industrial capital but more extensive than this). This is reflected in the USA's and the UK's increasingly urgent demands for infrastructural investment to support manufacturing (especially as current interest rates [2013] are effectively negative in real terms). Second, thanks to the credit crunch and rising unemployment or precarious employment, private Keynesianism is thrown into reverse, further contributing to the crisis through the effects of private financial deleveraging. When coupled with neoliberal and neoconservative calls for welfare retrenchment and other austerity measures, this has reinforced the debt–default–deflation dynamic because it leads to recession, increasing the public-debt-to-GDP ratio rather than reducing it. Indeed, recent econometric work by the IMF shows that the multiplier effect of government austerity is far greater than previously assumed and can prove counterproductive (Blanchard and Leigh 2013). This reinforces uneven development and is also likely to increase popular resistance, prompting harsher financial discipline and police action. This is associated with the trend to 'post-democracy' (Poulantzas 1978; Crouch 2004; Jessop 2013b).

Despite the neoliberal commitment to free trade and world market integration, the actually existing crisis of FDA has promoted growing calls

Table 11.2   Finance-dominated accumulation in crisis

Basic form	Primary aspect	Secondary aspect	Institutional fixes	Spatio-temporal fixes
Money/capital	Rising antagonism between 'Main Street' and 'Wall Street' (City of London, etc.)	Epic recession based on debt–default–deflation dynamics (D4)	Deregulation → crisis of TBTF predatory finance + contagion effects	Protectionism in core economies, growing resistance to free trade from periphery
(Social) wage	Credit crunch puts private Keynesianism into reverse	Austerity reinforces D4, leads to double dip recessions	Growing reserve army of surplus, precarious labour	Global crisis and internal devaluation → reproduction crisis
State	Political capitalism undermines Ordoliberalism	Austerity policies meet resistance, harsher discipline	Crises in political markets reinforce 'post-democracy'	Cannot halt uneven development at many sites + scales
Global regime	Unregulated space of flows intensifies 'triple crisis'	Multi-lateral, multi-scalar imbalances and race to the bottom	Crisis + rejection of (post-) Washington Consensus	Crisis of US hegemony, BRICS in crisis and disarray

for protectionism in the USA, reflecting the pathological co-dependence of the US and Chinese economies, and for renegotiation of the UK's relationship with the European Union (especially in the field of post-crisis financial regulation, which reflects a threat to the position of the City of London as the leading and remarkably deregulated international financial centre for international financial transactions). The crisis has also increased the reserve army of labour and created conditions for stagnant or falling wages and downward pressures on the social wage, which reinforces the debt–default–deflation dynamic in the absence of compensating public expenditure – a measure regarded as taboo by the neoliberal power bloc. The measures needed to manage the economic state of emergency have produced a further centralization of political power in the executive branch of government and in IFIs (national, European and international), reinforced the tendency towards 'unusual deals with political authority' in the bailouts of too-big-to-fail (TBTF), too-interconnected-to-fail and politically too-well-connected financial institutions. This leads to loss of political legitimacy (reflected in the 99 per cent mantra of the Occupy movement and declining support for mainstream parties) and to the growth of 'post-democracy' or authoritarian statism. Finally, we note *en passant* that the crisis has also produced problems in the legitimacy of the (post-)Washington Consensus, the search for post-neoliberal strategies in Latin America and elsewhere, and attempts to move to a more multi-lateral global order, based in part on increasing economic, trade and financial cooperation among the BRICS (Brazil, Russia, India, China, South Africa) economies.

CONSTRUING THE FINANCIAL AND ECONOMIC CRISES (2007–2012)

The symptoms of crisis have shifted from a credit crunch in subprime mortgage markets through a liquidity crisis in the financial sector, a solvency crisis in parts of the real economy as well as finance, a fiscal crisis resulting in part from the public bailout of banks and firms too big, too interconnected, or too well connected to be allowed to fail, and, eventually, in some cases, a sovereign debt crisis. This metamorphosis is reflected in successive phases in interpretations of 'the' crisis and is linked to different kinds of learning in, about and from crisis. Even this crude periodization reveals a theoretical and empirical challenge in crisis construal: is a crisis an event (and, if so, how would one identify its beginning and its conclusion), a contingent series of events distributed in time and space that are connected, if at all, because of earlier crisis responses that could have taken a different turn, an evolving conjuncture shaped by attempts at crisis management, or a series of events with an underlying tendential logic that therefore unfold as a relatively predictable, determinate process with its own logic? On the event–process problem and related issues in crisis management, see, for example, 't Hart et al. 2001; Forgues and Roux-Dufort 1998).

This question can be answered, and often is, in terms of alternative crisis construals. In other words, the crisis is defined through its construal and has no reality outside that construal. In contrast, for a CPE approach, contradictions, crisis tendencies, strategic dilemmas and material interdependencies also matter. Nonetheless, in steering a course between Scylla and Charybdis, CPE emphasizes that these features exist only in so far as they are reproduced through particular social practices.

This poses the twin issues of (1) the resonance of construals and (2) their material adequacy. Thus, as the crisis became more visible from mid-2007 (however far back its causes may be traced) and unfolded as a series of events that were regarded as a connected process, its extent, depth and complexities grew faster than economic and political leaders could grasp, let alone find time to agree upon a coherent, coordinated response. This was most remarkable in September–November 2008, with countless competing interpretations, explanations, strategic plans and specific policy recommendations. This is linked in turn to uneven learning in crisis as the NAFC seems to have transmuted from an allegedly containable crisis in the subprime mortgage market in a few economies into a broader liquidity crisis in the financial sector affecting more economies, next to a solvency crisis affecting many financial institutions and the 'real economy',[4] then to a fiscal crisis requiring major austerity packages to reduce public debt and/or a sovereign debt crisis requiring international rescue packages at the cost of more or less grudgingly accepted austerity programmes implemented through exceptional measures and policed by external economic and political bodies.

The NAFC has already led to countless interpretations, explanations, strategic plans and specific policy recommendations, and to several retrospective official inquiries. This has been accompanied by important disputes about the character, material causes and agential responsibility for the crisis. Construals have ranged from the terminal crisis of capitalism to a temporary blip in a free market system. Debates have also concerned whether the crisis symptoms are signs of a normal business cycle, a normal recession, an epic recession (as prelude to a great depression) or an actual great depression. This has been accompanied by important disputes about the character, material causes and agential responsibility for the crisis as different actors seek to draw lessons from the past and/or from elsewhere – does it involve a normal business cycle, a normal recession, an epic recession, a great depression and so on? Further, are the parallels to be found, for example, in Weimar Germany, the depression years in the USA, the crisis of the Atlantic Fordist accumulation regimes that became visible in the late 1960s and 1970s, Japan's 'lost decades' (1990–2010 and continuing), the Savings and Loan crisis in the USA, the so-called Asian crisis in 1997–98, the bursting of the irrationally exuberant dot.com bubble in 2000 and its wider repercussions, or in yet other cases of crisis? This illustrates the role of historicity, that is, efforts to identify historical parallels, construe the crisis in their terms, and thereby frame the correct business and policy responses. Given that different local, regional, national and macro-regional economies experienced the NAFC and its contagion effects differently, leading interpretations also varied geographically, with correspondingly different explanations, blame and proposed solutions. Moreover, as various official and unofficial inquiries into earlier features and dynamics of the crisis report and seek to understand and draw lessons, we can see efforts to learn from the crisis and shape how recovery may be conceived in future.

The crisis means different things to different actors and its interpretation beyond immediate lived experience is heavily mediatized, that is, filtered through information from various communication media. To labour the obvious, the crucial sites for crisis interpretation and crisis management following the outbreak of the crisis in 2007–08 have been the USA and the international financial institutions that it dominates with the UK and European Union as its junior partners. They have been slower to respond to the needs of 'social reproduction' in daily, life-course and intergenerational terms; and to take effective action on impending environmental, food and fuel crises.

The disorienting effects of crisis can be seen in the well-known confession by Alan Greenspan, Chair of the Federal Reserve (1987–2006), that he was in 'a state of shocked disbelief' over the crisis because it contradicted the efficient-market hypothesis, a key element in neoclassical economics, and the basis of his conviction that markets should be left to manage themselves (Greenspan 2008; see Chapter 4). This disorientation was widely shared in the economics profession and led many, in a state of denial, to blame the crisis on one or another form of state intervention rather than on predatory or imprudent activities enabled by deregulation.

Putting aside such blinkered, self-serving reactions, the crisis certainly opened the space for the recovery or reassertion of other economic imaginaries. Overall, taking account of responses across the broad spectrum of advanced capitalist economies, whether more or less neoliberal in orientation, economic and political elites have looked to solutions that involve variable combinations of the following:

- Marx's critique of the capitalist mode of production and its crisis tendencies, including his observations on the distinctive features of financial crises as well as the crisis tendencies inherent in the circuits of productive capital.
- Reassertion of different variants of Marxism, with conflicting interpretations focusing more or less one-sidedly on specific features of capitalism, imperialism and/or neoliberalism.
- The general Keynesian critique of 'casino capitalism' and the revival of the case for a government role in contra-cyclical demand management to avoid a spiral into recession and/or prevent a second downward dip.

- The rediscovery of Hyman Minsky, a financial Keynesian, whose most famous dictum is that 'stability is de-stabilizing'. Several commentators declared the crisis to signal a 'Minsky moment', that is, a point in financial cycles when even interest payments on loans could not be met from income because borrowers had gambled on continued asset appreciation. This reflects Minsky's account of a transition from prudent hedged finance to speculative and then Ponzi[5] financing, and is exemplified in (without being confined to) the role of subprime mortgages (on Minsky, see Jessop 2013c).
- The reassertion of Ordoliberalism, based partly on Austrian economics, with its emphasis on the necessity of a strong state (and/or strong regulatory framework) for the smooth operation of free and competitive markets. Ordoliberalism survived largely intact in the European Union's Rhenish heartlands and, indeed, on this basis, Germany initially experienced *Schadenfreude* over the Anglo-Saxon crisis. Conversely, in the USA, Ordoliberalism was revived through calls to return to New Deal regulatory principles, especially the desirability of separating retail from investment banking.
- Developmental state models also saw a revival because the East Asian economies had recovered from their own crisis through a careful mix of fisco-financial prudence, neoliberal reforms in selected parts of the private and public sectors, long-term investment and renewed competitive export-oriented growth. In addition, the charge of 'crony capitalism', once levelled against the Asian economies by the advocates of neoliberal reform, was redirected towards the Anglo-Saxon economies and the practices of their predatory financial and industrial capitalist institutions and tightly interwoven economic and political elites.
- Other recovered economic imaginaries have restated mutualist or cooperative visions about how to organize a sustainable economy based on solidarity rather than the anarchy of exchange or top-down planning. Ecological imaginaries have also been mobilized, focusing on various forms of 'green recovery' with a more or less strong commitment to de-growth rather than the renewal of the treadmill of competitive accumulation.

Most of these recovered imaginaries have been ignored by dominant (trans-)national economic and political elites as the basis for pursuing imagined recoveries. Marxist readings have won some intellectual attention and have shaped some responses within some radical left-wing parties, among some union militants, and among some social movements. But they remain marginal in the global North. The critique of casino capitalism has proved more resonant, but proposals to limit the scope for financial speculation and risk-taking have been diluted during the legislative process and are being further undermined through wars of attrition by vested financial interests, clever legal and accounting tricks, and continued expansion of shadow banking. Minsky had his own 'moment' in the early stages of the crisis but it has passed as far as mainstream economics is concerned and the policy responses advocated by Minsky and his followers (financial regulation, government spending, a state role as 'employer in the last resort' at the minimum wage, and community development banks) have been largely ignored or rejected.

Ordoliberalism has enjoyed a revival in Europe's coordinated market economies but Germany has applied these principles to its domestic economy in continuation of its neo-mercantilist export-oriented policies while choosing to back a neoliberal fiscal compact for the European Union as a whole and to impose austerity packages on Southern Europe in exchange for loans that are intended primarily to rescue insolvent or illiquid financial institutions in the wider North Atlantic region. The developmental state model has been re-evaluated, especially in the light of the continued competitiveness and quick recoveries of the East Asian economies, but it has not been translated into policies at supranational or national level in the North Atlantic economies. Mutualism and cooperation have also gained greater attention but are still largely confined to the margins of the leading economies as flanking or supporting mechanisms to soften the impact of the GFC rather than operating as agents of radical transformation. Finally, while ecological imaginaries have become more influential outside Australia, Canada and the USA (where climate-change denial has powerful economic and political backing), pursuit of green recovery remains marginal and/or is being integrated into neoliberal crisis packages by commodifying green policy measures.

Following the month of panic, the dominant construal in neoliberal market economies that was selected for crisis management is that this is a crisis in FDA that could be resolved through targeted, timely and temporary (but not tiny) stimulus measures, recapitalization of systemically important financial institutions, central bank swaps to protect the international monetary system (and the dollar's exorbitant privileges within it), a moderately tighter regulatory system (since further diluted), and repeated rounds of quantitative easing to maintain a near-zero official interest rate and protect private debt through an 'extend and pretend' strategy for private debt. This has been accompanied by a studied refusal to prosecute financial fraud (to maintain market confidence) and a manufactured crisis around the fisco-financial crisis attributable to 'profligate' entitlement programmes. These construals, which have more to do with the prevailing balance of forces than with any scientifically valid account of the dynamics behind this crisis in FDA or, again, with the practicalities of combining private sector deleveraging, deficits on trade, and public sector deleveraging without producing a double- or triple-dip recession.

Early construals of the crisis in these neoliberal economies that were marginalized on discursive, practical or political grounds included: a Keynesian critique of 'casino capitalism' coupled with calls to revive Keynesian policies to restore full employment levels of demand; a remoralization of capitalism in the name of corporate social responsibility and responsible competitiveness; and a 'Green New Deal' that would address the financial crisis, energy crisis and environmental crisis at the same time as promoting 'green jobs'. Many other accounts were also advanced but they were even more handicapped by the lack of support from economic and political actors with enough economic, administrative, fiscal or legislative resources to offer the 'necessary' institutional and policy solutions on the most relevant scales of action. No account of the crisis is innocent, of course, because each focuses on some factors or actors at the expense of others. This also holds for surveys of different explanations, which can never be comprehensive. In addition, as a crisis evolves, changes, is addressed, and lessons get learnt, the character of any survey is bound to change. A general survey of 38 largely mainstream causal explanations is provided by Davies (2010), but it gives most attention to issues of regulatory failure. (Other surveys from contrasting positions in the matrix of economic and political entry-points and standpoints include Allison 2012; Buckley 2011; Häring and Douglas 2012; Hein 2012; Heinrich and Jessop 2013; Macartney 2011; Sinn 2010; Smith 2011; and van Treeck 2012).

Following an initial wave of *Schadenfreude* at the discomfort of neoliberal, FDA regimes, the dominant construals in coordinated market economies affected through contagion from these regimes tended to highlight the systemic risks generated by unregulated financial capitalism divorced from the 'real' economy. This pointed to the strengthening of regulation and the reassertion of the virtues of Ordoliberalism and analogous approaches to macro-prudential *Ordnungspolitik* at the same time as steps were taken to preserve the functional coherence of the core sectors of each national economic space. The most effective approach in this regard came from the powerhouse of the European economy: the neo-mercantilist, export-oriented German model and its Rhenish counterparts.

This approach proved unsustainable on a wider European scale, however, because of the growing incoherence of the eurozone economies. The eurozone crisis is not just another Ponzi-finance-induced recession nor another crisis of competitiveness in individual economies (on Ponzi finance, which involves speculative borrowing in which not even interest payments, let alone capital, can be paid without asset price inflation, see Minsky 1982; for critical reviews on European competitiveness, see Becker and Jäger 2012; Bellofiore 2013). There are well-rehearsed crisis-management responses. Instead it is the result of pursuing the 'incompossible dream' of European monetary union without stronger fiscal and political integration – producing a short-term boom as credit flowed from Northern to Southern Europe and then a debt–default–deflation trap reinforced by internal devaluation as the contagion effects of the NAFC destabilized the Southern European economies and they could neither exit the eurozone nor boost exports in a weakened world market. Nonetheless, behind a nationalistic and rhetorical blame game targeted at the people, governing parties and governing class of the four PIGS (Portugal, Italy, Greece and Spain), and despite the political paralysis that has postponed effective coordination among member states, technocratic monetary and financial manoeuvres have enabled the unwinding of massive and potentially destabilizing cross-border private debt, the recapitalization of European financial institutions, and the temporary taming of speculation against the euro and the sovereign debt of the weakest member states. This has been combined with virtual coups d'état in Southern Europe to impose neoliberal austerity packages justified in the name of fiscal responsibility but, on the evidence to date (including that from the IMF), likely to boost debt–default–deflation dynamics (Blanchard and Leigh 2013; Lapavitsas 2012).

IMAGINED RECOVERIES

Looking beyond the revival of economic imaginaries that had been marginalized as neoliberalism became hegemonic, the NAFC has also been construed in the global North in one or both of two ways: (1) as a crisis *of* finance-led accumulation, prompting efforts to limit the influence of the financial sector through more radical reregulation, restrictions on the size and activities of banks, and greater investment in the 'real economy'; and/or (2) as a crisis *of* neoliberalism more generally, requiring efforts to roll back neoliberalism at home and impose more controls on market forces in supranational and international contexts, notably regarding finance and credit. Even in more neostatist or neocorporatist advanced capitalist economies, however, calls are being made for stricter regulation of *financial* markets in various supranational and international contexts. This has not yet prompted leading forces to question the broader commitment to world market integration through free trade in goods and services or to take seriously sub- or counter-hegemonic proposals from subaltern nations, institutions, agencies and social forces. In this sense, the neoliberal imaginary remains dominant and continues to shape imagined economic recoveries.

Overall, surveying responses across the broad spectrum of advanced capitalist economies, economic and political elites have proposed variable combinations of the following solutions in response to the renewed recognition that markets can fail:

- The restructuring, recapitalization and nationalization of banks, as well as isolating toxic assets in state-owned or state-supported 'bad banks'. This is a core plank of crisis management in all advanced economies and has been pursued behind a veil of secrecy through emergency legislation and executive discretion. It resulted in the nationalization and/or recapitalization of 'impaired' banks (notably in Iceland, Ireland, the USA and the UK, plus those Baltic States and Eastern and Central European economies that took a radical neoliberal turn and, *inter alia*, experienced real-estate booms). It is especially significant in the recent efforts to manage the sovereign debt crises in Europe.
- A turn to the typical state powers of sovereignty, command, planning, nationalization and subvention, taxation and public spending to restore stability, to stimulate growth, and to restructure public finances through a mix of modest tax rises and more or less savage spending tax cuts. This is reflected in a partially recovered Keynesian economic imaginary and in the shift, nationally, regionally or globally, from 'private Keynesianism' – where consumer debt sustained demand despite declining real wages – to the provision of short-term stimuli to some hard-hit industrial sectors plus massive quantitative easing in the North Atlantic economies most affected by the crisis. Such responses are handicapped because deregulation and liberalization have weakened state capacities ideationally and materially. This explains the resort to 'printing money' through quantitative easing, which, in the absence of public outcry, is one of the least demanding of state responses, and through continued reliance on historically low interest rates. The economic crisis has also intensified the loss of temporal as well as territorial sovereignty, and this is reflected in the resort to fast policy and the concentration of political power in few hands.
- These measures are nonetheless proving ineffective because of deficient demand for productive investment in a context of economic austerity. This is reflected in the accumulation of reserves by productive capital or their investment in emerging markets and in

the recycling of freshly minted money capital into the purchase of government debt and/or speculation.
- Efforts to redesign and reregulate markets so that they are less prone to predictable kinds of market failure. This is the preferred approach of neoliberal organic intellectuals and think tanks, financial lobbyists and unrepentant neoliberal politicians. This applies particularly to a medium-term strategy of reviving or reforming the Bretton Woods international financial architecture. But the conditions for such a strategy were removed with the crisis of Atlantic Fordism and the rise of finance-dominated accumulation.
- A medium-term strategy of restructuring the international financial architecture to realign it with the new financial realities. This is proving difficult to realize in a concerted and coherent way. It appears easier to introduce new institutions than reform old ones, which leaves the latter in place and in power. The displacement of the G-8 by the G-20 illustrates this well and the key players still seem to be committed to more free trade, deregulation and so on. The opportunity for tighter regulation seems already to have been lost when the semblance of 'business as usual' was restored – although this illusion is now shattered.
- Another imagined path of recovery is through the G-20. This self-elected group of 19 key industrial and emerging market economies (plus the European Union, the IMF, the World Bank and other major IFIs) has become the *de facto* global crisis committee. This reflects growing recognition of the actual and potential influence of the 'BRIC' economies and the creditor position of major East Asian economies (see Chapter 12). Thus the G-20 Summit in November 2008 expanded the Financial Stability Forum to incorporate creditor nations, including China; and, in April 2009, it established a Financial Stability Board with a wider remit. This has integrated the leading 'Southern' economies into problem-solving and burden-sharing, thereby strengthening the leading IFIs, and has also reinforced an unsustainable growth-oriented global economy. But the informal, self-selected status of the G-20 means that it cannot replace the United Nations, IMF, WTO and other official bodies in crisis management with their capacities for significant strategic intervention (Bello 2009). The rise of the BRIC economies has seen their redefinition as an exit strategy for mobile capital and a source of strength and hope for a global recovery. A sometimes favoured alternative is the G-77, which is a loose union of developing nations. Despite its ties to China, however, it lacks clout in international policy forums.

- Given that the amount of toxic assets far exceeded the immediate revenue-generating capacities of the states concerned, space opened for demands that government spending on 'entitlements' and social welfare be drastically cut. In this context the manufactured 'deficit hysteria' is an excellent (but disastrous) example of how economic imaginaries can shape crisis management. Attention has thereby been redirected from the crisis in the financial sector and the real (but private) economy to the public sector, framed in terms of accumulated government debt, unsustainable public spending and public sector employment. Another effect was the concentration and centralization of political power in the hands of economic and political elites, and the extent of agreement among the leading political parties has narrowed the space for democratic debate and accountability to a limited set of alternatives. This diverted attention from more basic questions of institutional design and, more radically, of the basic social relations that reproduce crisis tendencies and shape their forms.
- Measures to introduce further flanking and supporting mechanisms to maintain the momentum of neoliberal reforms – a sort of reinvigorated Third Way approach. This concedes that there are some problems with neoliberalism, especially in its earlier celebration of greed and its creation of distorted incentives as well as in its polarizing redistributive effects, with broad swathes of the middle classes as well as the industrial working class and 'underclass' losing out to financial elites, trans-national capital and political insiders. But Third Way policies are not intended to stop the further extension of a hopefully *remoralized* neoliberalism. Instead they are meant to provide greater compensation to those who lose from that extension within national frameworks or, in the EU case, in a European framework that nonetheless visibly reproduces centre–periphery relations.
- These policies also contradict the commitment to more 'austerity' to contain partly manufactured, partly real fisco-financial crises. The 'Tea Party' and 'Occupy' movements represent two responses to these changes. But the former is more of an artificial, 'astroturf' movement manipulated by moneyed interests than an effective grass-roots party; and the latter has certainly shifted the political agenda with its slogan of the '99 per cent' against the '1 per cent' but is subject to authoritarian policing and has hitherto had a largely local and weak economic impact.
- Another imagined route to recovery is the remoralization of capitalism in tune with corporate social responsibility (CSR) and

responsible, even 'green' competitiveness (see Chapter 8). This remains largely rhetorical and has had limited impact on the operation of the real economy and even less on the still dominant financialized sectors of regional, national and global economies.
- A Green New Deal, which is being heralded in many quarters as a 'magic bullet' (Brand 2009) – capitalism's best hope to create jobs, restore growth, deal with the problem of peak oil and limit climate change (e.g. NEF 2008). Little agreement exists, however, on how to proceed, let alone how to translate promised action into binding multi-lateral commitments, as shown by the 2009 Copenhagen Summit. It is associated with many different visions and strategies, with neoliberal, neocorporatist, neostatist and neo-communitarian inflections that prioritize, respectively, market incentives, social partnership, societal steering and solidarity. At stake, however, are the form, manner and likelihood of its retention as a powerful imaginary that can be translated into accumulation strategies, state projects and hegemonic visions. Currently, it seems likely that the Green New Deal will acquire a strong neoliberal inflection in the leading national economies whatever its form beyond them and/or at local level.

ALTERNATIVE VOICES AND SOLUTIONS

Much mainstream commentary has read the crisis from the viewpoints of capital accumulation rather than social reproduction, the global North rather than the global South, and the best way for states to restore rather than constrain the dominance of market forces. Such commentaries reflect government responses to the crisis, especially in the global North. Executive authorities reacted quickly with emergency measures to safeguard the monetary, banking and credit systems to prevent large banks and firms from going bankrupt, and to restore the conditions for capital accumulation. They have been slower to respond to the needs of 'social reproduction' in daily, life-course and intergenerational terms; and to take effective action on impending environmental, food and fuel crises. We will explicate these differences in terms of how competing narratives about the crisis framed policy responses, and how structures of economic, political and ideological domination enabled economic and political elites in key power centres to push the risks and costs of crisis management on to subaltern groups and developing countries. Thus, besides identifying the key responses from the global North, we examine developing countries' engagement through, for example, the G-20, the so-called Stiglitz

Commission established by the President of the 63rd General Assembly of the United Nations and the associated summit (United Nations General Assembly 2008; United Nations 2009a, 2009b), the G-77 and the People's Republic of China (hereafter China), and efforts at South–South cooperation. We also comment briefly on social movement and activist groups and post-neoliberal futures.

There are many other accounts of the crisis and proposals for reform, but they are not backed by economic and political actors with enough economic, administrative, fiscal or legislative resources to offer effective crisis-management solutions or long-term prospects for another type of global economic order. The attempt by the United Nations General Assembly to take a lead in the global debate on the crisis illustrates this well. In October 2008, the President of the General Assembly established a commission of experts with the mandate 'to review the workings of the global financial system, including major bodies such as the World Bank and the IMF, and to suggest steps to be taken by Member States to secure a more sustainable and just global economic order' (United Nations General Assembly 2008). The General Assembly also convened a three-day summit in June 2009 'to identify emergency and long-term responses to mitigate the impact of the crisis, especially on vulnerable populations, and initiate a needed dialogue on the transformation of the international financial architecture, taking into account the needs and concerns of all Member States' (see United Nations 2009a). These initiatives aimed to give a voice to the interests of developing countries, which are not fairly represented in the existing institutions of global economic governance.

But as the 'Stiglitz Commission' prepared its report, the main lines of policy response were already being set by the leading economies (the USA, the EU and China) and institutions of global economic governance. Furthermore, sharp differences of opinion emerged between the G-77 group of 130 developing countries that pushed for a major role for the United Nations in dealing with the crisis and backed a comprehensive set of reforms, and Northern countries, including the USA and the EU, which played a blocking game (Brettonwoodsproject 2009). Although the Commission's outcome report mentioned the disjunction between growing world market integration and the weakness of representative global economic governance, identified problems of institutional design and the inequities of the international reserve system, and the need for economic and social measures to protect the most vulnerable, the specific proposals that it actually recommended did not measure up to the critique (United Nations 2009b). The Commission failed to propose an alternative to finance-led growth (Amin 2009; Khor 2009) or question the basic logic of profit-oriented, market-mediated capital accumulation and its implications for the 'triple crisis' of finance, development and the environment.⁶

The challenges to neoliberalism have come primarily from social movements and some governments in the global South. It is possible to identify nine sets of sub- or counter-hegemonic discourses, projects and practices that have gained currency in the context of the crisis.

- A trend toward relatively autonomous regional solutions and/or multi-polar cooperation aimed at decoupling from the neoliberal dynamic of the global North with its inherent deflationary bias. Two prominent examples are the revival of proposals for an Asian monetary fund and the Bolivarian Alliance for the Americas (ALBA), which (following the withdrawal of Honduras) currently comprises eight Latin American and Caribbean member states. Instituted in 2004 by Venezuela and Cuba to promote South–South solidarity and fair trade as an alternative to neoliberalism, ALBA has nevertheless been weakened by the crisis and faces domestic opposition from right-wing populist groups and external neoliberal forces.
- Demands for a readjustment of the balance between capital and labour to boost demand, employment and decent work. This makes most sense in more developed economies without large informal sectors.
- Emphasizing the close connection between economic development and social protection, and the fact that measures of social protection should also contribute to economic recovery.
- Relatedly, neoliberal trickle-down policies are being rejected in favour of a trickle-up approach on the grounds that money 'invested in the poor' has an immediate economic stimulus impact and also contributes to social development. This policy can have a neoliberal inflection (witness the idea of 'the bottom billion' advanced by Collier 2007), or be aimed at promoting a social economy and social empowerment.
- A human rights approach is being advocated to economic development, environmental justice, global governance and transparency. This focuses not only on strengthening soft and hard law, but also on active citizenship and claims-making, which are seen as crucial for the realization of rights.
- There are demands for tax reform through closure of tax havens, clampdown on tax evasion, and imposition of a 'Robin Hood' tax on financial transactions to release billions of dollars for investment in poverty reduction and social infrastructure.

- The exhaustion of neoliberal theoretical and policy paradigms is complemented by the activities of the World Social Forum, its regional affiliates and similar bodies concerned to promote South–South cooperation, mutual learning and policy transfer on the basis of social movements and social activism with a strong emphasis on various anti-imperialist, anti-capitalist, feminist, environmentalist, anti-racist, socialist and autonomist alternatives.
- Many local and regional initiatives are pursuing alternative development strategies based on fair trade, a solidarity economy, local trading schemes, eco- and agri-tourism, slow food and so on.
- The benefits of revamped developmental states for a post-neoliberal world are being asserted – with grudging, half-hearted recognition from bodies such as the IMF and World Bank.

NEOLIBERALISM REDUX

Until the fiscal crisis of the state (including local and regional states as well as sovereign states) re-emerged in 2010, many individuals in the developed economies seemed to have accepted the crisis as a fact of life and turned to coping strategies, populist anger against 'banksters' and politicians seemed to have been defused, financial capital was blocking serious reform attempts, and a return to capitalist normality seemed to have occurred. In short, it seemed that a phase of normalization had been reached as the main lines of *national* and *international* response had been agreed and were being pursued. Indeed, one important general conclusion is that the overall project of neoliberalism has emerged stronger even if finance-led accumulation has been discredited. Initial worries about strong protectionist responses that would be hard to remove and slow the economy were not realized:

> For months, we've heard that the economic crisis would unleash protectionism, trade conflict and 'de-globalisation'. But far from unravelling, the world economy seems likely to emerge from the crisis more, not less globalised . . . the crisis has actually spurred more efforts to liberalise trade than restrict it, as a way of cutting costs, attracting investment and boosting competitiveness . . . So why didn't globalisation implode? One reason is that the international economic system has proved stronger than even its defenders had hoped. (Hancock and Greenhill 2009)

This observation is disingenuous because it suggests that the economic system is robust and independent of political institutions and state intervention. Of course, if the international economic system proved stronger than even its defenders had hoped, this had much to do with policy measures that flew in the face of the neoliberal doctrines that had been hegemonic in the years before the crisis.

Nonetheless, the overall trend emerging from crisis interpretation and practical response has been further strengthening of the neoliberal project at the cost of some modest (and capitalistically necessary) limits on FDA. With some differentiation reflecting specific economic, political and institutional locations and interests, the leading economic and political actors in neoliberalized economies have defined this as a crisis *in* finance-led accumulation or, at most, *in* neoliberalism. In the short term, generous (and often ill-defined) discretionary powers were granted to the executive, or its nominees, to solve the crisis (Scheuerman 2002). The authorities reacted quickly without much consultation and with timely, targeted and temporary emergency measures to safeguard the monetary, banking and credit systems and stimulate demand in vulnerable industrial sectors. In particular the aim was to rescue financial institutions that were deemed too big (or too interconnected) to be allowed to fail. These emergency measures were accompanied by recapitalization of the biggest (but not all) vulnerable banks, (promises of) tighter regulation, and proposals for a reformed (but still neoliberal) international economic regime. In addition, and crucially, excessively leveraged and indebted private giant industrial and financial concerns were enabled through crony capitalist connections to offload toxic assets to the state based on the capacity of states to create fiat money backed formally by their powers of taxation and monopoly of organized coercion.

The crisis *of* FDA regimes in the UK and the USA did not produce a crisis *of* neoliberalism. Indeed, the only example where this occurred was Iceland, where the weight of the hypertrophied financial sector was even more excessive than in the UK, and where radical measures were taken to impose the costs of crisis management on financial capital (Cyprus came later as part of the eurozone crisis). In the two Anglo-Saxon economies, however, while financial capital may have lost some credibility, it remained dominant in the accumulation regime, in the state apparatus and, for the USA, in the legislature. It was therefore able to exploit the crisis, making sure that it did not, in Rahm Emanuel's terms, 'go to waste'. Where FDA drives economic expansion and financial capital is a significant part of the economy (and strongly interconnected with other sectors), financial crisis becomes a source of problems that must be addressed to restore the logic of accumulation. If financial capital is well entrenched in the state apparatus, then the capacity to rescue 'too-big-to-fail' financial institutions also exists when states can create fiat money and engage in other credit manoeuvres to socialize toxic assets and losses. And when financial capital is also dominant in the power bloc, it can manoeuvre to delay, dilute and otherwise weaken attempts to reregulate its operations. The costs for this are passed to the state and this, in turn, provides the opportunity (also not to be allowed to go to waste) of doubling up on the neoliberal vilification of the state, to cut entitlement programmes, and roll out further austerity measures. In short, a crisis *of* FDA has been transformed into a drawn-out crisis in FDA accumulation. This was possible because the neoliberal project experienced only a temporary crisis *in* its onward march.

Despite the passing of the neoliberal high point and even after its contradictions came into play, as evidenced, *inter alia*, by the NAFC, which produced a new phase of 'blowback' neoliberalism, the project still dominates world society thanks to the path-dependent effects of policies, strategies and structural shifts that were implemented during that high point. This is seen in the continuing structural power of FDA and accumulation through dispossession.

These path-dependent effects are political and ideological as well as economic. This is related, first, to the weight of the US economy in financial and economic terms (linked to its pathological co-dependence with China) in the world market, in spite (and, indeed, because) of the many disproportions with which it is associated on a world scale. Second, it is related to the continued attraction of the dollar as a world currency in the unfolding crisis. And, third, it is related to the role of the US state in helping to displace and defer the contradictions of neoliberalism onto other spaces and times. This does not mean that the US case (itself heterogeneous and by no means confined, in any case, within US economic and political space) is paradigmatic – it means no more (but no less) than that it is dominant. The UK economy and state are not so privileged in these respects. The UK is more exposed financially, sterling lost its role as world money more than 80 years ago, and it lacks the military and other capacities to act as a global hegemon. In this sense, the UK remains the junior partner of the USA (even being encouraged by US economic and political interests to stay in Europe) and has less room to escape the constraints of the cumulative effects of FDA and its neoliberal regime shift.

Of course, these have not become hegemonic or dominant responses for the reasons explored above, but they have proved significant sources of local and regional resilience and have put social and environmental protection on the agenda away from the mainstream forums. There is widespread evidence that local solutions can be developed to address the short-term effects of the crisis in its various local manifestations, and the challenge is to establish ways to exploit this real-time experimental laboratory to find what works, for whom, when and why, as a basis for mutual learning and policy transfer among subaltern groups. But a global crisis cannot be solved at local level (even in a slower, less runaway world that is partly decoupled from the world market and that emphasizes local sustainability).

CONCLUDING REMARKS

We have again pursued two sets of objectives in this chapter. The first set was to outline a CPE approach to crisis construals and crisis management. Language and other forms of semiosis are central to CPE but it also stresses the contingent articulation of semiosis and structuration as complementary forms of complexity reduction. It does not reduce crisis to its construal(s) but argues that crises are objectively overdetermined and subjectively indeterminate. This opens space for studying the variation, selection and retention of crisis construals and policy lessons as crises develop. Crisis construals establish 'truth effects'; that is, the hegemonic or dominant meanings of crisis result from power relations. They are not the outcome of a cooperative language game with fixed rules but of a political struggle with variable rules and contested stakes (Lecercle 2006: 98). In this sense, construals are not simple *linguistic (re)descriptions* of a conjuncture but, when backed by powerful social forces, they lead to *strategic interventions* into that conjuncture. In this regard, the interaction of semiotic, structural, technological and agential selectivities and their mediation through the evolutionary mechanisms of variation, selection and retention produces particular 'modes of crisis management' that are not dictated solely by the objective overdetermination of the crisis, nor by 'arbitrary, rationalistic, and willed' construals of this, that, or another social force. At stake here is the production of 'truth effects' that are not so much scientifically valid as conjuncturally correct, that is, offer a sound objective analysis in terms of the correlation of forces as well as underlying causes and can gauge and guide the strategic horizons of action, organizing effective action and disorganizing opposition.

This chapter has addressed attempts to draw and implement appropriate lessons for economic and social governance and policy, and considered how they are constrained by the world market, the interstate system and global governance regimes, and an asymmetrical 'global civil society'. It has indicated, without fully being able to establish, the wide range of interpretations of the global economic crisis; and it has also indicated how, from the initial proliferation of interpretations, those more congenial to the leading social forces have been privileged for action.

This shapes the information flows and command lines among the actors and defines the focus and sequence of crisis management. In turn, this leads to the uneven 'distribution of crisis effects' among social forces. A key aspect of this are the ways in which crises reproduce centre–periphery relations. While some actors pay relatively low costs, other actors assume much higher burdens. This distribution has spatial and temporal as well as social aspects. This means that social actors experience the 'same' crisis differently from one another, and this affects capacities for learning in, about and from crisis. Thus the shifting balance of power and its resultant rounds of distribution of crisis effects have significant impacts on the capacity to define 'the truth' of a crisis and the most appropriate responses. Nonetheless there is always some scope for counter-hegemonic narratives and, notably, sub-hegemonic narratives, that is, accounts that are widely accepted in regional forums and subaltern organizations. This is the basis for that pessimism of the intellect, optimism of the will that motivates and justifies continued contestation of the hegemonic or, at least, dominant linguistic (re)descriptions of crisis symptoms and the elaboration of alternative construals, crisis-management options, and crisis-avoidance strategies.

This said, sub- and counter-hegemonic projects have proved significant sources of local and regional resilience, have put social and environmental protection on the agenda away from the mainstream forums, and offer a reservoir of alternative economic imaginaries and alternative paths to recovery that provide a standing critique of neoliberal mainstream theoretical and policy paradigms. There is widespread evidence that local solutions can be developed to address the short-term effects of the crisis in its various local manifestations, and the challenge is to discover ways to exploit this real-time experimental laboratory to find what works, for whom, when and why, as a basis for mutual learning and policy transfer among subaltern groups. Developments in the European Union in 2010–12 and the more general signs of a great recession around the world indicate that the global economic crisis has not disappeared, and that emergency measures produced only a temporary illusion of business-as-usual while downgrading the urgency of other moments of the multiple crises confronting global capital.

The second set of objectives was to analyse FDA along the same lines as we have previously analysed Atlantic Fordism and the KBE. Although we have presented the KBE and FDA as if they were simple alternatives, they actually coexisted as competing accumulation strategies in the same economic spaces and/or in closely connected economic spaces within a variegated world market. This itself could have caused additional problems because it made it less likely that either growth regime would be stable compared to the golden years of Atlantic Fordism: their coexistence made it correspondingly harder to secure their respective forms of embedding.

NOTES

1. Imaginary refers here to sets of cultural elements common to a given social group (or groups) that shape 'lived experience' and help to reproduce social relations.
2. On the Latin American case, see Petras and Veltmeyer (2009).
3. The scare quotes warn against a simple, fixed distinction between appearance and essence. At stake is strategic, not ontological, essentialism (see Chapter 4).
4. The real economy has long been monetized and depends on credit–debt relations.
5. Minsky (1986) distinguished three types of financial transaction: hedging occurs when payment of interest and repayment of principal are funded from routine business activities; speculation when interest payments are met from business activities but capital repayment depends on asset appreciation; and Ponzi finance when even interest payments depend on asset appreciation.
6. Regular updates on the crisis were posted at www.triplecrisis.com.

12. The North Atlantic financial crisis and crisis recovery: (trans-)national imaginaries of 'BRIC' and subaltern groups in China

This chapter explores discourses of crisis recovery scenarios advanced during the North Atlantic financial crisis (NAFC) and the selection of some of these for practical action. There is no lack of 'crisis-recovery' imaginaries (e.g. austerity measures, stimulus packages, debt reliefs etc.; see Chapter 11) and some of them are selected and pushed forward by national state-centred interest coalitions. Instead of examining imaginaries at this level, however, this chapter redirects attention to an imaginary that is being repeated, selected and promoted by (trans-)national and/ or (inter-)governmental forces as another road to recovery. Specifically, it focuses on how some major actors including economists in investment banks, economic strategists, politicians, officials in international organizations/intergovernmental agencies, think tank researchers and business journalists have (re)imagined the role of the BRIC (Brazil, Russia, India, China) economies as drivers of recovery in the context of the North Atlantic Financial Crisis.

The chapter has four sections. The first examines the roles of strategic (trans-)national actors in constructing, circulating and negotiating BRIC as an economic imaginary. This involves constructions of 'hope'/'strength' that have occurred in three overlapping stages: an investor narrative; then an investor–consumer tale; and, since 2009, an investor–consumer–lender story. The changing BRIC imaginary has both trans-national and national significance, and its resonance depends not only on developments in the 'financial' and 'real' economies but also on specific technological selectivities of discourses, practices and modes of knowledge. The second section addresses the conjuncture of the 2007 financial crisis when the BRIC discourses were circulated and popularized by private and public sector actors as sites that could facilitate 'economic recovery'. This imagined recovery was made more credible when the BRIC countries developed their own stimulus packages. China was seen as leader in this regard and its large national package was described by one international economist (Lardy) as '*gold standard*' (see below). The third section examines how this package intensified some deep-rooted tensions in central–local relations in China. More specifically, it posed tremendous fiscal challenges for local authorities, which rely heavily on land as a source of revenue and mortgage loans. The resulting intensified commodification of land has further inflated the 'property bubble' and stimulated more land dispossession/grabbing. This harms China's subaltern groups in various ways, illustrated below by the cases of 'house slaves' and the plight of migrant workers' children. Although some measures have been taken to dampen the property market, their impact has been limited and social unrest continues. The fourth section comments on CPE's contribution to the understanding of BRIC as an object of 'crisis recovery' and the struggles and unevenness of this process, especially at the national–local levels.

CONSTRUCTING HOPE/STRENGTH: THREE STAGES IN THE MAKING OF 'BRIC'[1]

The 'BRIC' imaginary recontextualizes the idea of 'emerging markets'. This latter notion was introduced in 1981 by fund manager Antoine van Agtmael of Emerging Markets Management. It mapped selectively some large Third World and post-socialist economies as sites of 'new opportunities' with 'high risks' but potentially high returns (Sidaway and Pryke 2000). 'BRIC' is a recontextualization that sounds promising and offers hope at particular conjunctures (see later). It was first coined by a Goldman Sachs team of investment strategists and was later popularized by consulting firms and business media as having high-growth potential and, hence, as a suitable target for increased investment after 9/11 in 2001. As a regime of hope (see Chapter 9), it emerged through three overlapping stages: as an investor narrative; an investor–consumer tale; and an investor–consumer–lender story (see Table 12.1). Shifting sets of actors were involved at each stage as nodal agents responded to new crisis symptoms emerged by elaborating new BRIC imaginaries. These processes are mediated by genre chains that restrict and extend the meanings of BRIC. The knowledge produced over time (re)constructs hope (partly) via micro-level apparatuses (e.g. reports, books and investment funds) and related governing technologies. These were oriented to creating new subjectivities for individuals and collective actions. They are shot through with the affective energy of capitalism (Chaput 2010: 4–8) in framing and pushing this strategy of crisis recovery.

Table 12.1 The production of 'hope'/'strength': three overlapping stages in the production of 'BRIC' knowledge

Stages	Major actors/institutions	Major discourses and knowledge instruments	Knowledging technologies
Stage 1 2001– present 'BRIC' as an investor story	International investment banks (e.g. Goldman Sachs) Chief economist (e.g. Jim O'Neill) and colleagues, fund managers, sales teams, financial journalists, rating agency etc.	• 2001 Invented the category in the report on *Building Better Global Economic BRICs* • 2003 Research report on *Dreaming with BRICs: The Path to 2050* • Other reports, books, webtours, indexes, etc. (see also Table 12.2) • BRIC investment funds (see also Table 12.3)	Technologies of identification and achievement Technology of investability
Stage 2 2004–present 'BRIC' as an investor–consumer story	Economists, investment consultants, business media (Bloomberg, *The Economist*, CNN, blogs etc.), international organizations (e.g. World Bank, IMF)	• Decoupling theses (The transatlantic economies are in recession due to the subprime crisis and its fallout. Other regions, especially the BRIC, continue to grow during this downturn – strong consumption) • 'Decoupling 2.0' article *(The Economist)*	Technology of identification
Stage 3 Late 2008– present 'BRIC' as an investor–consumer–lender story	International organizations (WB, IMF, G-20, BRIC summits etc.), national leaders, foreign policy analysts and mass media	• Subscribing to IMF Special Drawing Rights (e.g. US$50 bn by China in 4/9/09) • Shifting global economic and political governance (e.g. 'multi-polar world' from G-8 to G-20)	Technology of agency

First Stage in the BRIC Imaginary: 2001–Present: Investor Story

While most discursive objects have uncertain origins, we can clearly date the birth of the BRIC imaginary. With the security crisis of 9/11 and China's entry into the WTO in 2001, there were different responses from strategic actors to the former crisis and to fear of decline triggered by the latter. Transatlantic policy-makers reacted to the 'War on Terror' and investment bankers and strategists responded with the fear of recession that might dampen growth. Others reassessed the dominance of the USA and looked elsewhere. Jim O'Neill, then Goldman Sachs' chief economist, interpreted the destruction of the World Trade Center as signifying that further progress in globalization could no longer rely on US leadership and, indeed, must look beyond the Northern–Western world (Tett 2010). Problematizing it as related to the decline of American dominance and the rise of global China (and other emerging markets), a Goldman Sachs team selected some useful 'non-Western others' and narrated them as being low risk with high growth potential. By 30 November 2001, these 'others' were baptized as the 'BRIC' in Goldman Sachs Global Economic Paper No. 66, which was titled 'Building Better Global Economic Brics'.

Based on a mathematized model of demographic trends and productivity rates, it forecast that their combined GDP growth rates would range between 9 and 14 per cent in 2010. This new body of knowledge identified and constructed BRIC as a complementary group of economies that is 'set to grow again by more than the G7' (Goldman Sachs 2001: S.03). Within this group, while China and India were seen as having higher growth rates and emerging as dominant global suppliers of manufactured goods and services (see Chapter 9), Brazil and Russia would acquire dominance as suppliers of agricultural goods, raw materials and energy.

The creation of BRIC as a distinct site for investors initially met with mixed reactions. While Goldman Sachs' corporate clients, who were seeking new markets, liked this construction, it was not embraced by banks and investors because they deemed the BRIC vulnerable to political upheavals and falling commodity prices. Nonetheless, O'Neill's team continued to lead the dream by supplying their clients with 'hope' by focusing on expectations of high investment returns. In a 2003 report, *Dreaming with BRICs: The Path to 2050* (Wilson and Purushothaman 2003), two other economists in his team framed BRIC economic dynamics in terms of growth paths spurred by 'ingredients' such as sound macro-economic policies, low inflation, openness to trade and high levels of education (O'Neill 2012: 34–5).[2] The team forecast that, by 2050, the BRIC would catch up and become 'emerged' economies. By then, China's gross domestic product could be 30 per cent larger than that of the USA; India's could be four times that of Japan; and the figures for Brazil and Russia could be at least 50 per cent bigger than UK GDP. For the team, such achievements would rebalance the world economy with the BRICs' growth offsetting 'the impact of greying populations and slower growth in the advanced economies' (Wilson and Purushothaman 2003: 2).

Deploying the catch-up metaphor and highlighting prospective performance can be seen, in neo-Foucauldian terms, as technologies of identification and achievement in which the BRIC quartet is selected, made knowable and visibilized as a coherent set of 'emerging' economies embarking on high-growth paths with great potential for long-term investors (Table 12.1). The interdiscursive space created by these two documents set up the 'sales pitch' of Goldman Sachs and other fund managers and financial sales teams, and thereby facilitated the circulation of BRIC as a new 'dream' in this nodal investment network. As neoliberal globalization was consolidated (in part with China's entry into the WTO), more and more corporations and financial organizations were scoping new markets and profitable investment sites. New intellectual forces, which included corporate executives, investment bankers, fund managers and so on, began to endorse and reinforce the BRIC imaginary as a desirable object of investment and ground for strategic actions. After the 2003 paper, Goldman Sachs economists entered what O'Neill described as 'briclife' (Tett 2010) as clients (e.g. Vodafone, BHP Billiton, IKEA and Nissan) swamped their daily routines with inquiries. Indeed, some clients not only imbibed but also actively promoted the BRIC KoolAid as a refreshing object of investment hope and actions. The Goldman Sachs team had the capacity to keep this affective space alive by churning out more knowledge products. Between 2001 and 2012, to keep 'briclife' going,[3] it created 21 such products, including reports, fresh forecasts, books, videos and webtours (in different languages) to inspire hope (see Table 12.2).

The 'BRIC' imaginary continued to connect and circulate among economic strategists, investment consultants, sales teams, etc. Its appeal derived not only from the projection of 'hope'/'strength' of the individual BRIC economies but also from their purported complementarity and profitability as an asset/investment group. Major international banks such as HSBC and other investment banks/hedge funds began bundling stocks/shares/bonds and inventing funds marketed as new financial instruments under the BRIC brand, including 4-Year MYR HSBC BRIC Markets Structured Investment, Templeton BRIC Fund (Singapore), and the iShares MSCI BRIC Index Fund. In order to motivate investors, consultancies such as Investment U (2009) narrated these funds as highly investable (see Table 12.3).

Table 12.2 Major BRIC knowledge products constructed by O'Neill and the Goldman Sachs team

Name of the knowledge products	Nature of product (year/month)	Ways of constructing hope and strength
'Building Better Global Economic BRICs'	Report November 2001	• Invented the BRIC category • Outlining healthier outlook in BRIC economies than current forecast of 1.7% growth in global output for world
'Dreaming with BRICs: The Path to 2050'	Report October 2003	• Mapping out BRIC's GDP growth until 2050 • Postulating BRIC economies could be larger than G6 in 40 years' time
'How Solid are the BRICs?'	Forecast December 2005	• Updating the 2003 forecast • Arguing that BRIC grow more strongly than projection
Web Tour: The BRICs Dream (in English, Arabic, Chinese and Japanese)	Webtours May 2006	• A video on the BRIC • Dreaming about BRIC and the changing world after 9/11 • Contending that China would overtake the USA in 2050 • Arguing for growth of the middle classes in BRICs major consumers of cars and energy
'India's urbanization: Emerging opportunities'	Report July 2007	• Framing boom in city life • Identifying investment opportunities in urban infrastructure and fast accumulation of financial assets
BRICS and Beyond	Book November 2007	• Updating the 2001 report • Postulating increase in value of BRIC's equity markets • Moving beyond BRIC to other emerging economies (e.g. N-11)
Interview with Jim O'Neill	Video February 2008	• Maintaining BRIC's share of global GDP as 15% • Advising individual BRIC countries (e.g. India needs more FDI) • Arguing for the sustainability of BRIC • Increasing international role of these countries

446   *Towards a cultural political economy*

Table 12.2   (continued)

Name of the knowledge products	Nature of product (year/month)	Ways of constructing hope and strength
'Building the World: Mapping Infrastructure Demand'	Report April 2008	• Identifying increase in demand for infrastructure • Arguing that China will be the source of one-half to three-quarters of incremental demand in world market • Intensifying pressure on commodity markets
'Ten Things for India to Achieve its 2050 Potential'	Report June 2008	• Advising on improvement of governance and the need to control inflation • Promoting the liberalization of the financial market • Supporting improvement in agricultural productivity
'BRICs Lead the Global Recovery'	Report May 2009	• Arguing that BRIC can help to lead the stabilization of the world economy • Promoting BRIC as one of the driving forces in the export-driven recovery
'The BRICs as Drivers of Global Consumption'	Report August 2009	• Arguing that G-3 countries face slow and difficult recovery • Maintaining that BRIC can contribute to global domestic demand through higher consumption
'The BRICs Nifty 50: The EM & DM Winners'	Report and stock baskets November 2009	• Stating good consumption and infrastructural demand from BRIC • Identifying two BRIC Nifty 50 baskets to help investors to access the BRIC market
'BRICs at 8: Strong through the Crisis, Outpacing forecasts'	Video March 2010	• BRIC weathered the global crisis remarkably well • On pace to equal the G-7 in size by 2032
The Growth Map: Economic Opportunities of BRICs and Beyond	Book 2012	• A sole-authored book by O'Neill, reviewing the economic opportunities of BRIC and beyond

Source: Sum's own compilation based on materials from Goldman Sachs' Idea Website on BRIC.

Table 12.3 BRIC investment funds and their construction of strength and profitability

Name of recommended fund	Reasons for choice	Breakdown of Exchange-Traded Fund by country	Top 10 components consist of giant firms
iShares MSCI BRIC Index Fund First choice	A portfolio of about 175 stocks from the BRIC countries. Despite a gain in excess of 40% year-to-date, the fund is still down over 30% over the past 52 weeks, so valuations are still not back to pre-crisis levels in 2009	China and Hong Kong: 42%, Brazil: 32%, India: 13% and Russia: 13%	China Mobile, Gazprom, Reliance Industry, Petrobras, Vale, Itau Unibanco, HDFC Bank, China Life Insurance, Lukoil, and Industrial & Commercial Bank of China
Templeton Emerging Markets Fund Second choice	Managed by emerging market guru, Mark Mobius. Mobius has been with the Templeton since 1987 and has blazed the trail for emerging-market investors	China and Hong Kong: 23%, Brazil: 23%, India: 10%, Russia: 9%, Thailand: 8%, Turkey and South Korea: 7% each	Petrobras, Vale, Petrochina, Akbank, Denway Motors, Itau Unibanco, Sesa Goa, Banco Bradesco, Aluminum Corp of China and SK Energy

Source: Adapted from Invest U (2009).

Their investability was constituted in terms of the financial good practices of the fund managers as well as the qualities of the BRIC economies. These practices included: (a) a good risk spread via a broad portfolio (e.g. the iShares MSCI BRIC Index Fund invested in 175 stocks); (b) the placement of funds in bigger BRIC economies, above all China/Hong Kong; (c) investment in giant companies operating in 'strong' lines of business (e.g. telecommunications, resources); and (d) strong profit forecasts based on technical criteria (reversion to a pre-crisis mean) or the charismatic status of the 'emerging market' guru (Mark Mobius from Templeton) who managed one fund. In neo-Foucauldian terms, this technology of investability: (a) normalizes the BRIC countries as investment sites in contrast to previous worries about risk; (b) identifies BRIC stocks as a novel,

Table 12.4 Net inflows of portfolio equity to the BRIC economies, 2002–08 (USD billion)

Country	2002	2003	2004	2005	2006	2007	2008
China	2.2	7.7	10.9	20.3	42.9	18.5	3.7
India	1.0	8.2	9.0	12.1	9.5	35.0	−15.0
Brazil	2.0	3.0	2.1	6.5	7.7	26.2	−7.6
Russia	2.6	0.4	0.2	−0.2	6.1	18.7	−15.0
BRIC (total)	**7.8**	**19.3**	**22.2**	**38.7**	**66.2**	**98.4**	**−33.9**
Developing countries	5.5	24.1	40.4	68.9	104.8	135.4	−57.1

Source: Adapted from World Bank, *Global Development Finance 2008 and 2010.*

important and promising alternative asset class; and (c) encourages clients desirous of long-term, above-average profits to invest their money in these economies. In this regard, this technology selectively framed BRIC as an investment hope.

Energetic financial sales teams and other intermediaries marketed these products to potential punters, reaching them through advertisements, glossy brochures, financial journalism, phone calls, one-to-one meetings and so on. Coupled with the general search for new investment sites and asset classes, the flow of portfolio equity funds into BRIC increased by almost twelvefold between 2002 and 2007. Relatedly, the BRIC had a two-thirds share of all investment in developing countries between 2003 and 2007 (see Table 12.4). Within the BRIC group, China gained most in 2006 and India in 2007. In 2008, however, the global credit crunch markedly slowed inflows to the BRIC, apart from China, which received US$3.7 billion net.

Second Stage in the BRIC Imaginary, 2004–Present: Investor–Consumer Story

The BRIC story developed a consumption sub-plot from the mid-2000s. This was also started by the O'Neill-led team, which published a report on *The BRICs and Global Markets: Crude, Cars and Capital* in 2004. This time, it identified the increasing consumption potential of their 'emerging middle classes', especially in terms of demand for commodities, consumer durables and capital services. This part of the BRIC 'dream' was echoed by economic strategists such as Clyde Prestowitz. A former Reagan Administration official, Prestowitz relayed this 'dream' to a wider policy audience through his book, *Three Billion New Capitalists*, which projected that, by 2020, 'the annual increase in dollar spending by the BRIC will be twice that of the G6' (2005: 227).

This BRIC-as-consumer story gained more weight as the American subprime crisis spread within the USA and then to Europe's financial institutions via securitized banking. What started as a mortgage crisis in the USA has turned into a sovereign debt crisis in Europe. This wide and deep contagion effects and the fear of possible North Atlantic recession have energized the policy communities to seek new signs of 'hope' and objects of recovery. Among many such objects (e.g. the Green New Deal), the pre-existing BRIC story was selectively chosen and reworked to include a consumption dimension. This second stage in the BRIC imaginary (see Table 12.1) attributed a new 'locomotive role' to the BRIC on the grounds that their consumer-led demand would defer recession and offer recovery possibilities for recession-ridden advanced economies.

This narrative was enthusiastically circulated in the genre chain by economists, (business) media (e.g. Bloomberg, *Newsweek*, *Wall Street Journal* and CNN) and international organizations (e.g. the IMF) in terms of the 'decoupling thesis'. This asserted that the BRIC economies could expand on the basis of their own investment and consumption, despite recession in the USA and other advanced economies. Jim O'Neill was reported on Bloomberg as saying that 'the BRIC consumer is going to rescue the world' (Marinis 2008) and 'since October 2007, the Chinese shopper alone has been contributing more to global GDP growth than the American consumer' (Mellor and Lim 2008). This thesis can be interpreted as a redeployment of the technology of identification in which the strength of BRIC was that it was seen as a 'decoupled' object with autonomous consumption power that could save the world from recession.

By this time, O'Neill's timely imaginary was widely accepted; he was described in the business press as the world's first 'rock star' economist or 'Mr BRIC'. The lead story was further popularized by other actors such as top investment advisers (e.g. Peter Schiff) and fund managers (e.g. Todd Jacobson from Lord Abbett) (Shinnick 2008; Lordabett.com 2009) in the mass and Internet media. For example, Peter Schiff, author and President of Euro-Pacific Capital Inc., made a strong case that was echoed in many YouTube videos, blogs, articles and news items. A typical statement, from his book, *Little Book of Bull Moves in Bear Markets*, declared:

> I'm rather fond of the word decoupling, in fact, because it fits two of my favorite analogies. The first is that America is no longer the engine of economic growth but the caboose. [The second] When China divorces us, the Chinese will keep 100% of their property and their factories, use their products themselves, and enjoy a dramatically improved lifestyle. (Schiff 2008: 41)

The 'decoupling thesis' did not go unquestioned. Some financial analysts, economists and international/regional organizations, such as the World Bank and Asian Development Bank, noted a contraction rather than decoupling of trade. For example, in April 2008, citing reduced exports, the World Bank lowered its China growth forecast to 6.5 per cent. A different view was expressed in June 2008, when the IMF released *Convergence and Decoupling*. This study argued that decoupling could coexist with integration. Globalization since 1985 has stimulated greater trade and financial integration and this, in turn, has created tighter coupling of business cycles among countries with similar per capita incomes. But it also cited historical evidence that some (groups of) countries have decoupled from the broader global economy at certain periods.

Despite this mixed reception, the decoupling thesis continued to circulate and resonate. As Jim O'Neill noted in *Newsweek* in March 2009:

> Who said decoupling was dead? The decoupling idea is that, because the BRICs rely increasingly on domestic demand, they can continue to boom even if their most important export market, the United States, slows dramatically. The idea came into disrepute last fall, when the U.S. market collapse started to spread to the BRICs, but there's now lots of evidence that decoupling is alive and well.

This claim was endorsed in modified form on 21 May 2009 in a comment in *The Economist* magazine. In 'Decoupling 2.0', it reinterpreted decoupling as 'a narrower phenomenon, confined to a few of the biggest, and least indebted, emerging economies', such as China and India. These economies purportedly had strong domestic markets, prudent macroeconomic policies and growing bilateral trade. Thus this version of the BRIC-decoupling thesis filtered out the weak and attributed strength to China and, to a lesser extent, India. These now became 'useful consumers' thanks to their large foreign exchange reserves, buoyant fiscal positions and financial stimulus packages. In November 2009, after its previous pessimistic forecast, the World Bank raised its 2010 economic forecast for China's GDP growth to 8.4 per cent. These economies offered 'hope' through their solid investment markets, robust consumption from their rising middle classes, and relative large stimulus packages (see Table 12.5).

This narrowing of BRIC was reinforced within the policy circuit by Roger Scher in the Foreign Policy Blogs Network (2009). Questioning

Russian strength, he asked whether the story was now 'From BRIC to BIC ... or Even IC??' Marc Chandler (2009), a prominent foreign exchange market analyst with Brown Brothers Harriman, echoed this and suggested relabelling the BRIC as CRIB. This foregrounding of China resonated with an earlier view of Deutsche Bank Research's Markus Jäger, who described China as being 'in a class of its own' within the BRIC group (2008).

Third Stage in the BRIC Imaginary, 2008–Present: Investor–Consumer–Lender Story

Since late 2008, this revised decoupling thesis has provided the basis for the third stage of the BRIC story (see Table 12.1). As the crisis in developed countries deepened and reinforced the search for 'hope' or objects of recovery, more attention went to the BRIC quartet's geo-political significance. Policy-makers, international organizations, think tanks, foreign policy analysts and so on warmed to the BRIC imaginary (see above). Foreign policy rhetoric such as 'the rising power of BRIC', 'BRIC's challenges towards the "Washington Consensus"', 'Rise of "Beijing Consensus"' and 'post-American world' filled policy discussion papers, think tank reports and media commentaries. These new geo-economic and geo-political imaginaries became more credible when strategic policy actors in Russia held the first BRIC Leaders' Summit in Yekaterinburg in June 2009. This new layer of the BRIC imaginary was enhanced by subsequent summits hosted by Brazil and China in April 2010 and 2011 respectively. On China's recommendation, South Africa was included in the 2011 Summit and the BRIC quartet became BRICS. Subsequent summits were held in March 2012 in India and 2013 in South Africa. They operated (partly) as arenas for the BRIC leaders to: (1) perform and project their capacity as a bloc (despite their differences and competition); and (2) discuss their future cooperation in trade, investment and finance (on BRIC Development Bank, see below).

BRIC summits apart, the IMF and G-20 became important sites in which attention turned to the recovery potential of BRIC's lending capacities. For example, at the G-20 meeting in London in April 2009, the then UK prime minister, Gordon Brown, who was coordinating an IMF rescue package for the global economy, called for support from reserve-rich countries such as China. In response to demands to diminish the dollar's international reserve role, a new loan mechanism was proposed based on an increased Special Drawing Right (SDR) allocation, which amounted to US$250 billion. To this end, China pledged US$50 billion, and Russia, Brazil and India each promised US$10 billion. As the debt crisis deepened in the eurozone in 2010, the IMF renewed its call for a firewall against 'southern contagion' in March 2012. It proposed a euro bailout fund of US$430 billion. Risking domestic criticism for lending to countries with higher per capita GDP than themselves, China eventually agreed to contribute US$43 billion and Russia, Brazil and India committed to US$10 billion each in June. This was justified as protecting their own economies from contagion as well as gaining power in the IMF's governance structure (e.g. more voting rights, membership in the executive broad, inclusion of the Chinese renminbi in the SDR basket etc.).

These newly created lending mechanisms symbolically (re)affirmed the growing economic and political capacity of the BRIC quartet via: (1) the developed economies' recognition that they should be part of the solution to crisis management by subscribing to SDR-denominated bonds and bailout funds; (2) their bargaining power in pushing for changes in the IMF's governance structure; and (3) their specific demand for an uplift from 5 to 7 per cent of total voting shares in the IMF.

Despite these signs of 'hope'/'strength' in making a 'multipolar'/'post-American' world, some observers questioned whether these new arrangements would challenge dollar hegemony (e.g. Kelly 2009) and whether BRIC might just become a 'non-western body ... funnelling money to the west' (Chaudhuri 2012) to facilitate the recovery of finance capitalism.

In short, these three overlapping stages of (negotiated) construction of 'BRIC' discourses and practices (and their continued affective and cognitive reworking) have helped to constitute, naturalize and sediment BRIC as a multi-layered object of 'hope' in investment and policy common sense. Each stage in the development of the BRIC narrative has had performative effects: the BRIC economies have graduated from being 'emerging markets' with their own identities and are seen as 'emerging global powers' with new hopes invested in them, new practices developed, and new self-identities created. This discursive shift illustrates what neo-Foucauldians regard as a technology of agency (Cruikshank 1999), based on the coexistence of participation and control, this time in the international arena (see Table 12.1). The BRIC countries have been encouraged to participate as a 'we' in the new 'multi-polar world order', but this is accompanied by efforts to guide the manner of their engagement, for example as consumption engines, lenders to the IMF and so forth. The G-8 powers, transnational capital, and the leading international regimes thereby seek to control the mode of engagement and to induce the BRIC to play larger roles in crisis management, especially in remaking the post-crisis neoliberal global agendas.

This is not to say that the BRICS do not push their own agendas. For example, the proposed BRICS Development Bank was formalized in the Durban BRICS Summit in 2013. They signed a Contingent Reserve Agreement for around US$100 billion as an emergency bailout mechanism and fund for infrastructural projects. This proposal is largely framed within an understanding of development finance that owes much to a Bretton-Woods-style economic and financial imaginary – with the addition of large dose of hope. In other words, it offers a way to 'strengthen the global financial safety net and complement existing international arrangements as an additional line of defence' when financial crisis strikes (Dikshit 2013). This does not preclude appropriation by the dominant partner in the BRICS. Thus there are worries that China might use these initiatives to exploit the use of the renminbi (Chinese currency) in the bloc and to increase its exports to other BRICS countries at the expense of local workers (Hunter 2013). These changes do not represent a real threat to the dominant neoliberal order that is reinventing itself through the crisis. However, it does modify the pattern of variegation through the integration of the BRICS (see Chapter 6). The latter have adapted to and hybridized neoliberalism with developmentalism (Ban and Blyth 2013) and seek to negotiate the terms of their integration into this order based on their new-found strengths.

In short, these three stages in the remaking of the BRIC regime as object of 'hope' were created/negotiated/circulated by intellectual forces at the interface of (trans-)national civil and political societies (e.g. investment banks, economic strategists, think tanks, business journals, political leaders, international organizations etc.). They selectively formulated and prioritized this category. Narratives were sedimented and identities such as 'BRIC as consumers' and 'IMF lenders'/'financial safety net' were constructed. These drew on the affective energy of capitalism as well as rational calculation of the BRIC imagination. Knowledging technologies of identification, achievement, investability and agency selectively portrayed BRIC (especially China) as a cathectic object of horizon-expanding, crisis-transcending hope that opened the prospects of increased returns on investment, growing consumer demand, new sources of loans, and even, on these bases, global recovery. The making of this hope dispositive (in a Foucauldian sense) is far from a smooth and seamless process. The discursive boundary has been constantly challenged and reinterpreted by other actors who have emphasized the incoherent, discrepant and even 'hopeless' nature of the hegemonic BRIC discourse. Some global market strategists and economists asked why some emerging economies were excluded (e.g. South Korea) and others included (Russia). Some foreign policy analysts question the coherence of the quartet, leading one to use '*BRIC-à-Brac*' to convey their heterogeneous nature (Drezner 2009).[4] More prosaically, others warned of the potential 'BRIC bubble' (e.g. Sharma 2012) and one contrarian rephrased the BRIC acronym as 'bloody ridiculous investment concept' (Business Insider 2011), suggesting that those who entered this market should abandon hope.

Conversely, at the national level, BRIC discourse has been embraced and recontextualized to promote new and positive collective imaginaries. In India, the discourses of 'Chindia' (Ramesh 2005; Sheth 2007) have been linked to the 'BRIC' imaginary since 2005. In Russia and Brazil, official BRIC narratives are used to project their images as 'rising global players' (e.g. Lula da Silva 2011). In the Sinophone world, the appropriation of the term 'BRIC' is more complicated. It has been translated as 'bricks' and was reframed, initially by Taiwan's *Business Weekly* magazine (No. 901–4), as 'the four golden brick countries'. It appeals to China's nationalist project, which narrates China as a nation regaining international 'greatness-at-last' after a 'century of humiliation'. The 'golden' metaphor helps to signify a 'shining brick' eager to re-enter the world stage. One among many 'proofs' is China's self-narration as the 'second largest economy in the world' with large gold and forex reserves that could boost global growth.

STRUCTURAL CONTEXTS OF THE BRIC DISCOURSES AND CHINA'S 'GOLD STANDARD' STIMULUS PACKAGE

The intensification of the BRIC imaginary is not only a rhetorical process. It is related to the widening and deepening of neoliberal financialization since the 1990s in the name of free markets and financial innovation. The growth of FDA fuelled the creation of new investment products as well as powerful stock, credit and housing booms that ended in the NAFC. Governments in developed countries put together various financial bailouts and austerity measures that resulted in further support for the financial industry, more unemployment and threats to society (Crotty 2009). The deep-rooted and contradictory nature of this epoch has led to an energetic search for new horizons of action, and new objects such as BRIC were imagined, especially during the above-noted second and third stages. The BRIC economies, notably China and India, were repeatedly invoked as investment–consumer and, later, as lender sites that could alleviate the recession and facilitate global economic recovery. In 2008, this imagined recovery was made more convincing and materially credible by the BRIC governments' moves to launch stimulus packages according to

Table 12.5   BRIC's stimulus packages during the financial crisis, 2008–09

Country	Amount (USD billion)	Percentage of GDP
China	586	15.0
India	9	0.8
Brazil	20	1.2
Russia	62.5	4.1

Sources: On China: ILO (2009a: 1); on India: Kannan for ILO (2009: 3); on Brazil: ILO (2009b: 2); on Russia: ILO (2009c: 2).

their domestic circumstances and place in the world market. According to ILO country reports (2009a–c), China invigorated its economy with a vast infrastructural stimulus package amounting to US$586 billion. India committed US$9 billion in stimulus and reduced some excise duties. Brazil announced a US$20 billion fiscal stimulus and made cuts to interest rates several times. Russia proposed a US$62.5 billion Anti-Crisis Programme with numerous measures to upgrade its workforce (see Table 12.5).

China was seen as the leader in this bloc in terms of the size of its package (15 per cent of its GDP) both at home and abroad. Domestically, it was intended to maintain its 8 per cent growth rate as exports and investment fell with the onset of the crisis. Internationally, it was a way to alleviate the global crisis thanks to its 'fast and vast investment'. When this package was announced in the G-20 meeting in São Paulo in November 2008, it was widely welcomed. For example, it was reported by Reuters that Nicolas Lardy, a China expert and senior fellow at the US-based Peterson Institute for International Economics, described it as 'the gold standard on the stimulus package. It was early, large, and well-designed and it's already gotten very substantial results' (Baldwin 2009). A study by Song (2010) of the *New York Times*' coverage of the relevant measures between 20 January and 31 March 2009 showed that they were depicted as 'genuine efforts to stimulate the world economy' and led to a more positive reassessment of China's role in the global community. However, from a CPE viewpoint, such positive responses from global players to the stimulus package may not match the everyday experience of ordinary people at national or local level in the BRIC countries. Concentrating on China, the next section examines how this 'gold-standard' package of the leading BRIC country intensified some deep-rooted structural tensions within its local political economies.

CHINA'S STIMULUS PACKAGE, LAND-BASED FINANCE AND THE SUBALTERN GROUPS

With the onset of the financial crisis and economic recession in advanced economies, the Chinese central government stimulated its economy by providing support for ten major industrial sectors (e.g. steel, shipbuilding, electronics, petrochemicals etc.), building infrastructural projects (e.g. high-speed rail, electricity grids), boosting consumer spending, developing the rural economy, and encouraging education and housing. This strategy aimed to maintain GDP growth at '8 per cent' – a rate that is theoretically the minimum required to create enough jobs to maintain social stability as well as show the world that the 'Chinese brick is rising'. Although the stimulus package was well received at the global level, the rolling out of this package has aggravated central–local relations related to their mode of financing.

Land-based Finance and Rising Property Prices in China

Based on practices since the late 1990s, central government funded around one-third of this package; the rest was to come from municipal–local governments, governmental ministries and state-owned enterprises (see Table 12.6). To facilitate this funding, the central government loosened

Table 12.6 The central–local government shares of the stimulus package and sources of finance in China, 2008–10

Level of government	Amount (in trillion RMB)	Percentage of total	Major sources of finance
Central government	1.2	29.5	• Direct grants • Interest-rate subsidies
Local governments	2.8	70.5	• Loan-based finance – Policy loans – Local government bonds issued by the central government (around 200 billion RMB) – Corporate bonds (130 billion RMB were issued in Q4 2008) – Medium-term notes (25 billion RMB were issued in March 2009) – Bank loans

Source: *Window of China* (2009); Naughton (2009).

its credit policies, and encouraged state-owned banks to lend. When these measures were communicated to the ministries and local (including provincial, city, prefecture and county) governments, they welcomed this opportunity to get approval for pet projects (e.g. high-speed trains and dams) (Naughton 2009). Under the prevailing central–local fiscal arrangements, local governments must provide matching funds. This is hard because (1) they are expected to channel 60 per cent of their revenue to Beijing; (2) the economic downturn reduced business taxes; and (3) they have no formal mandate to borrow money without central government approval.[5] This produced a funding gap. Thus a 2009 National Audit Office survey reported that local governments in 18 provinces were failing to provide the expected-level matching funds, with the poorest performing province sending only 48 per cent of the amount due (Xi et al. 2009).

This shortfall can in principle be filled by financial resources coming from a mix of local government bonds issued by the central government (or with its approval), corporate bonds, medium-term notes and bank loans (see Table 12.6). However, as China's bond market is still developing, local governments mainly seek their own sources of finance. This section concentrates on the increasing commodification of land as a means to generate income. This is possible because China's land leasehold market was formally established in the late 1970s under Deng Xiao-Ping. Urban land is state-owned but the separation of ownership and land-use rights means that public and private actors can shape its disposition and utilization. Urban land-use rights could be leased for fixed periods (e.g. 70 years for residential housing) at a fee, and land-right leases are tradable at auctions. This development encourages local officials to acquire arable land for conversion and rezoning of rural towns as urban by compensating (at least in principle) the communities involved. In this regard, local governments engage in 'land-based finance'. This means that local governments derive extra-budgetary income from intensifying land-based commodification. The latter involves acquiring land, developing land, selling land-use rights, collecting fees, obtaining mortgage loans and acquiring land again (*Global Times* 2010).[6] Local governments can thereby generate 'land-transfer income' from auctions, land-rights licences, land-transfer fees, collateralize mortgage loans and so on. In 2009, this income accounted for 46 per cent of overall financial revenue of local governments compared with 35 per cent in 2001 (*Global Times* 2010). A complication is that the Budget Law prohibited local governments from raising loans directly. So they established government-run financial vehicles to borrow from large state-owned banks (e.g. Bank of China, China Construction Bank), using land as collateral. Close relations among local governments, their financial vehicles and state-owned banks made credit easily available between 2008 and 2010. During this period, local government debt rose tenfold from 1 trillion RMB (US$146 billion) to an estimated 10 trillion RMB (US$1.7 trillion) (Xinhua 2011). Concurrently, the Bank of China recorded a profit rate of 28 per cent year on year for 2010 (*Business Weekly* 2011).

This monopoly use of land (and land-use rights) for generating income and loans means that local governments, property developers and state-owned banks have strong interests in keeping land development active and property prices high. This land-based expansion is reinforced by emerging popular socio-economic attitudes that property ownership is a source of housing, economic security, hedge against inflation, social status, family safety net and personal pride. The business press, media and peer/family outlooks strengthen these views in everyday life. Indeed, sayings such as 'no car, no house, no bride' are common among women of married age (Offbeat China 2011).The desire for home ownership apart, low interest rates and the absence of a national property tax allowed for speculative property to be purchased and held relatively cheaply. In short, all these public and private land-based calculations have been propelling real-estate inflation and fears of a 'property bubble' have revived since 2009. According to Colliers International, residential prices in 70 large and medium-sized cities across China rose in 2009, with 50 to 60 per cent increases in Beijing and Shanghai. Such increases reduce housing affordability, with the conventionally calculated standard residential property price to average annual family income ratio for Beijing being 1:22. This compares with the UN's ideal figure of between 1:3 and 1:4 (Smith 2010; Powell 2010; FlorCruz 2009).

The inflationary rise of real estate and falling affordability of property have politicized the housing question. This was acknowledged by Premier Wen when he remarked on 27 February 2010 that 'property prices have risen too fast' and this 'wild horse' must be tamed. The central government leaders introduced regulatory measures in 2010 to dampen the market (e.g. tightening of credit, raising deposits for purchase of new land to 50 per cent; restricting the purchase of second and third homes, etc.). However, such stabilization measures have had moderate effects and property prices continue to rise in some provinces and cities. The reasons include: (1) banks find other ways to increase their credit (e.g. selling off mortgage loans to state-owned trusts and asset-management companies; turning loans into investment products and selling them to private investors etc.); and (2) local governments soften up these property investment restrictions and selectively implement local-level initiatives to maintain their land-based mode of accumulation.

Impact on Subaltern Groups in China

This way of organizing the local political economy does not imply unity of purpose among actors. It means only that, for their own particular purposes, they work together at this conjuncture. Specifically, this mode of accumulation generates 8 per cent (or higher) growth rates for the central government; jobs, perks and promotion for local officials; revenue, projects and growth statistics for ministries and local governments; profit/investment for state-owned banks and state-owned/private property developers; and, of course, benefits to property owners (Sum 2011). Such apparent advantages to central–local elites are not matched by benefits elsewhere in the economy and population. Indeed, rising property prices, wealth accumulation and regular land auctions coexist with social unrest related to land grab, affordability of housing, the plight of 'house slaves', conditions of migrant workers, inflationary pressures and corruption. These sources of unrest destabilize the society and have markedly uneven impacts upon the socio-economic positions of ordinary citizens and the subaltern groups. The incidence of protests, riots and mass incidents quadrupled between 2000 and 2010 (Orlik 2011). Given that land-grab issues and high-profile resistance cases (e.g. Wukan revolt) are already well reported in the academic literature (e.g. van Westen 2011; Jiang 2012) and on the Internet (e.g. Wikipedia, YouTube, etc.),[7] this section turns to two less well-known social issues related to everyday life: the life of 'house slaves' and the plight of migrant workers (and children) in rural towns.

First, the life of 'house slaves' was reflected and popularized in a TV serial entitled *Dwelling Narrowness* (*Snail House*) in 2009. It is based on a novel by Tu Qiao, an independent journalist and writer. The story highlights a couple's struggle to buy an apartment in the midst of rising property prices in a fictional city that could well be Shanghai. Specifically, the story concerns two sisters who have borrowed heavily to buy user rights to an apartment. To obtain the money, one sister begins an affair with a wealthy and corrupt official. He later falls from grace because of a scandal over the diversion of pension funds to finance property projects (He 2009). The story resonated among ordinary people and social critics especially regarding the impact of high property prices upon families and young couples, corruption and cronyism in real-estate markets, class disparities and the sexual economy of mistresses. In spite (or perhaps because) of its popularity, the serial was taken off the Beijing TV Youth Channel on 22 November 2009. It was subsequently criticized by the State Administration of Radio, Film and Television as sensationalizing 'sex and corruption for profit'. Nonetheless, its gritty urban realism continues to appeal and the serial is still available on the Internet and DVD. It has been viewed online and downloaded more than 100 million times on the Internet (Yu 2011) and government officials have admitted to having watched it.

Like most cultural products, this serial has been interpreted in many ways. One view is that it is a piece of social criticism that sharply depicted the painful everyday life of underpaid university graduates, 'stooges of real estate business' and 'house slaves' (Hung 2011: 165). For example, it signified a life dominated by numbers – the joy of payday, the pain of saving for a flat, and the daily distress of making ends meet. It seems as if these workers do not own their dwelling, but their dwelling owns them and dictates their working lives and family relationship as if it has enslaved them. The serial supplied material for countless newspaper columns, blog and forum discussions as well as appeals for action. Among many responses to this depiction, a Xiamen artist, Li Bing, constructed a 'house slave sculpture' that portrayed a man standing on his hands while his body was overloaded with many layers of bricks (Xiamen News 2010).

A second, but related, issue is the plight of migrant workers in rural towns on the periphery of cities. These workers comprise a significant part of the reserve army of labour that supports the Chinese export economy and high growth rates. While low and insecure income and lack of household registration entitlements (*hukou*)[8] prevent them becoming 'house slaves', they risk becoming displaced by the same property-boom dynamic. This accelerates land clearance in rural towns for real-estate projects, displaces workers and increases the rent for their accommodation. These effects are so rampant that it has triggered rising social unrest related to land appropriation, undercompensation for land/property seizure, inflation, corruption and so on. Apart from land-based peasant riots, resistance is also expressed through the Internet. An unusual and innovative example of everyday resistance emerged in October 2010. A blogger called 'Blood Map' used Google Map to chart the distribution of sites where there have been land conflicts, use of violence against residents, and people's resistance to illegal land grab and property demolitions in China.[9]

Land appropriation and clearance also affect migrant workers, especially their children. Migrant families have no *hukou* in urban areas and some children go to low-fee schools set up in slums in these rural towns. These provide inexpensive instruction with support from NGOs and community movements. Urban clearance means that this kind of affordable education is vanishing due to school closures. In Beijing alone, migrant schools have fallen from 320 in 2008 to 180 in mid-2012 (Meng 2012). These schools were categorized by the local authorities either as 'unsafe' or 'illegal' (making them ineligible in both cases for compensation on closure). As for the displaced children, a *Beijing News* survey (2012) showed that 53 per cent transferred to other migrant-children schools, 33 per cent returned to home villages (some for schooling), 13.6 per cent reregistered at government-run schools, and 0.4 per cent had parents who had not yet decided what to do. Those reregistered in government-run schools often face discrimination from permanent residents who do not want their children to have classmates whose parents 'sell fish or vegetables'. Children who were sent back to home villages become 'left-behind children' with social concerns related to living with ageing relatives or in school dormitories. These issues raise more general questions about the rights of migrant workers and a *hukou* system that creates second-class citizens in urban areas. Whereas the central government is eager for change, local governments are more reluctant because they must foot the welfare bills especially in times of shortfall. Nevertheless, some cities (e.g. Shanghai) conducted pilot programmes in 2009 to grant 'permanent resident permits' to migrants. Eligibility is narrowly based on a points system related to education, tax payment, criminal record and so on. This creates a stratified citizenship as less than 0.1 per cent of migrants qualify (Kong 2010).

In response to these socio-economic tensions, there are calls to stabilize growth and maintain social stability. Responses include controlling property prices by credit restrictions, lowering the targeted growth rates to 7.5 per cent, and reorienting policies for a social agenda (e.g. housing, education etc.). However, tightening of credit is hurting local governments (and related property interests) as their expansion is largely based on collateralized mortgage loans and rising property prices. A credit squeeze means a fiscal crunch for local governments with the result that they resort to heavy-handed means of collecting taxes and selectively modulating the economic and social agenda according to local priorities. As the North Atlantic financial crisis continues to deepen and the economy experiences slowdown, China, is currently (the first half of 2013) facing more intense struggles between central government, local governments and the people (especially the subaltern) over issues related to slowing growth, a shrinking stimulus package, rising local government debts, unemployment, controlling property prices, continuing land-based finance, rising social unrest and maintaining stability, and rebalancing the economy.

Although China may have been 'in a class of its own' in recent years, the BRIC quartet appeared to be proceeding towards slowdown in 2012 with the deepening of the crisis. This poses more questions for the widely circulated BRIC investment story and the 'decoupling thesis'. Bloomberg reported on 15 June 2012 that O'Neill himself said the situation in China and other BRIC members might be 'more worrisome than the Eurozone crisis' but he also refused to write off the BRIC (just yet). However, the backlash on the BRIC hope is gathering as more negative media headlines (e.g. 'O'Neill's BRIC risk hitting wall threatening G20 growth' and 'Broken BRIC') appeared. Apart from reimagining BRIC's future, Goldman Sachs and some of the business press are wasting no time in identifying new objects of hope: already the MIST bloc (Mexico, Indonesia, South Korea and Turkey) is on the discursive horizon. In February 2013, O'Neill announced his retirement as Chairman of Goldman Sachs Asset Management.

CONCLUDING REMARKS

This chapter has examined the emergence of BRIC as the object of crisis recovery. The CPE approach seeks to capture the modes of selectivity and material–discursive moments that are involved in the production of BRIC. In structural selectivity terms, BRIC was problematized in three overlapping stages, each of which was related to particular material conjunctures (e.g. the 9/11 attack and the 2007 financial crisis) and opportunities for meaning-making. In the first conjuncture, the Goldman Sachs investment bank team enjoyed a privileged agential role (agential selectivity) by being the first to identify '9/11' as an opportunity to reorient investment strategies and then continually supply the financial and business arena with their expert knowledge and knowledge products on BRIC. These have built up their intellectual leadership and followings (e.g. investment strategists, think tanks, international organizations, mass media etc.). Diverse actors in the BRIC genre chain produced reports, books, webtours and newspaper articles as well as activities such as interviews, speeches and official summits. They select and circulate BRIC as an object of 'hope'/'strength'. The social practices related to this hope object condense a multi-layered dispositive and regime of economic truth via an intertwining of discourses, knowledging technologies, subject positions, affective hope energies, institutions and so on. These practices created intellectual leadership that is continuously being negotiated within and beyond the investment-policy circuits. Nonetheless, the BRIC ways of seeing/speaking/acting have become the mainstay that could drive growth and recovery as investment sites, useful 'non-Western' consumers and lenders to the developed world. This is more than a rhetorical process as this imagination has been made more credible, materially, since the emergence of the second conjuncture, i.e., the financial crisis in 2007. The BRIC's efforts to introduce stimulus packages between 2008 and 2110 captured the attention of the investment and policy worlds. Within the globalized mode of BRIC knowing, BRIC was seen as challenging the 'Washington Consensus' and China was singled out as having a 'gold-standard' stimulus package in 2008. In a period of profound international economic and political challenges, the BRIC imaginary reinforced the commitment to global neoliberal integration, offered hopes of crisis recovery and of changing the pattern of variegated capitalism based on hope as well as the new-found strengths of BRICS.

However, a CPE approach is not only interested in 'how' the BRIC is constructed; it also inquires into the nature (the 'what') of the struggles and unevenness of this process, especially at the national–local levels. Using China as an illustration, this chapter noted that this 'gold-standard' stimulus package has intensified some deep-rooted tensions within central–local relations. It gave a central-government green light for local governments to bring forward pet projects. Given that these authorities are expected to provide 70 per cent of the fund, land is increasingly used to leverage loans and raise revenue. Land sales and property development become important investment and speculative activities with consequences such as a property bubble, forced displacement from land, peasant riots, state terror, dispossession of the already vulnerable (e.g. migrant children) and increasing inequalities. Such growing social tensions and unevenness characterize, in part, the dark side of the 'shining BRIC' as sites of investment, consumption and lending. Within the BRIC, China was seen as leader and its vast stimulus package was narrated as important for Western recovery and reinvigorated growth. However, such 'hope and energy' needs to be examined together with the 'fear and anger' of the subaltern groups at specific sites as well as the energy of (trans-)national networks turning up more hope objects such as MIST (i.e. Mexico, Indonesia, South Korea, Turkey). In this regard, a CPE approach aims to offer ideological critiques of hegemonic constructions (e.g. BRIC and possibly MIST) based on micro-technologies of power as well as to highlight tensions and contradictions in some local subaltern social sites (e.g. slum schools, and 'Blood Map'). These are often neglected and glossed over in globalized discourses and practices of imagining crisis recovery and socio-economic changes.

NOTES

1. Given the deepening financial crisis, a fourth stage has emerged: the construction of 'fear'. Apart from worries about China's and India's locomotive roles, this mainly concerns a feared loss of US competitiveness rooted in 'innovation deficits' aggravated by rising 'frugal innovation' in these countries (G. Schmidt 2010).
2. These growth ingredients evolved into a measurement tool known as the Growth Environment Scores (GES) Indexes by 2005 (for details, see O'Neill 2012).
3. On these products, see http://www2.goldmansachs.com/ideas/brics/index.html, accessed 8 October 2011.

4. Fundamental differences among the BRIC include diverse political systems, and dissimilar views on key policy issues such as free trade and energy pricing.
5. As local government debts grew, they were allowed to issue bonds from October 2011 until June 2012.
6. Wang Xiaoying, a researcher in the Chinese Academy of Social Sciences, described this process in 2010 as 'acquiring land, selling land, imposing taxes, mortgage and then acquiring land again' (see http://www.globaltimes.cn/business/china-economy/2010-12/606958.html, accessed 16 August 2012). My account clarifies this, builds on it, and gives more details.
7. Wikipedia lists 'Protests on Wukan' (http://en.wikipedia.org/wiki/Protests_of_Wukan) and a Google search on 2 March 2013 generated 103 000 hits for 'Wukan Revolt' on YouTube, international media and blog sites.
8. Most rural migrants have no *hukou* in urban areas and no rights to public housing, education for their children or local pension and health-care benefits.
9. For details of the 'Blood Map', see 'Elusive "blood map" founder speaks out', http://observers.france24.com/content/20101119-china-evictions-violence-blood-map-google-founder-speaks-out, accessed 14 March 2012.

PART V

Consolidating cultural political economy:
from pre-theoretical intuition to
post-disciplinary practice

13. Implications for future research in and on cultural political economy

This book began by reviewing some achievements of institutional turns in the social sciences and of cultural turns in political economy. It also offered critiques of these turns and identified possibilities for a CPE research agenda (see Part I). The next step was to introduce some useful concepts and analytical strategies from semiotic analysis (focused on semantics and pragmatics) and reception theory in cultural studies (especially literary theory) to underpin a synthesis of grand theory and grounded analytics for the further development of CPE. This enabled us to indicate how CPE can chart and navigate a path between a structuralist Scylla and constructivist Charybdis. Building on this synthesis we presented a heuristic schema for studying the production of hegemony that other researchers could adapt to their own purposes (Part II). As the title of this chapter indicates, this is an unfinished project. Our aim has been to map one path towards a trans-disciplinary CPE that draws on, *inter alia*, critical discourse analysis (CDA), cultural anthropology, cultural studies, institutional economics, political economy and sociology.

We also presented some case studies on changing accumulation strategies and modes of regulation in the (re)making of capitalism (see Chapters 6 to 12). These studies range from economic imaginaries and practices involved in building Atlantic Fordism and responding to its crisis, the knowledge-based economy, the governance of competitiveness, cluster-based accumulation, neoliberal developmentalism, Wal-Martization, finance-dominated accumulation, crises of crisis management, and crisis recovery imaginaries and strategies. In this light, we will highlight three major themes that can inform the future development of CPE. Although our case studies have not demonstrated this (and were not intended to do so), CPE can also be applied to non-capitalist economic and political orders by combining critical semiotic analysis with concepts suited to these topics. Finally, while the CPE approach has been applied mainly, as its name implies, in the field of political economy, broadly interpreted, it can be applied elsewhere by combining the same approach to semiotic analysis with concepts more appropriate to other social forms, institutional complexes and social practices.

PUTTING INSTITUTIONAL AND CULTURAL TURNS IN THEIR PLACE(S) AND MOVING ON

CPE provides a response to the institutional and cultural turns without losing contact with the lessons of critical political economy about the basic (material) features of capitalism, its foundational contradictions, its crisis tendencies and the dynamics of differential accumulation. In this sense, it offers a *via media* between 'soft economic sociology', which one-sidedly emphasizes the constructivist features of economic activities and their greater or lesser social embedding in wider sets of social relations, and 'hard political economy', which one-sidedly naturalizes and reifies the basic economic categories and 'laws of motion' of the profit-oriented, market-mediated economy. Our response to the institutional turn and institutionalism more generally aimed to demonstrate the relevance of general strategic-relational principles to institutional analysis and to show how institutions could be better described, interpreted and explained if they were put into their broader strategic-relational place (Chapter 1). And our response to different cultural turns has been directed at putting semiosis (sense- and meaning-making) in its place within a broader concern with structuration, social forms, social practices and, above all, the non-discoursal aspects of discursive practices (see Chapter 4).

Given that others have also developed approaches that seek to avoid the twin temptations of structuralism and constructivism, the distinctiveness of our approach can be found in its proposal to combine some core categories and analytical techniques of semiotic analysis with a radical, heterodox critique of political economy. We listed six features of CPE in the Introduction that, together, distinguish it from similar approaches that have taken a cultural turn in political economy and/or from similar approaches in critical discourse or semiotic analysis that have extended its characteristic techniques to economic and political themes. We now revisit these six features and offer some brief reflections on other issues relevant to CPE and its research agenda.

This project rests on our belief in the continued vitality of the Marxist tradition and other types of evolutionary and institutional political economy and in the potential for making it even more productive through creative articulation with other pre-, trans- or post-disciplinary approaches that can illuminate the co-evolution of the semiotic and material features of the capital relation, its contradictions, dilemmas and repercussions for wider social formations. In ending our previous book, we highlighted the potential of neo-Gramscian state theory and CDA in this regard, especially their role in highlighting the contingency of social imaginaries and their translation into institutions and social practices. This volume has cast the trans-disciplinary net wider and focused on the potentials of critical semiotics and Foucauldian analyses of technologies as well as on the ways that agency makes a difference.

In these regards, the present book builds on our past work in four main ways. First, more explicitly than before, it thematizes complexity and complexity reduction as complementary moments of the natural and social world. This is linked to the inclusion of semiotic and technological selectivities into the discussion of complexity reduction and our reflections on the dialectic of path-dependency and path-shaping. It is also related to our more systems-theoretical analysis of the conditions that facilitate the 'ecological dominance' of profit-oriented, market-mediated accumulation in an increasingly complex world society. This concept provides a much-needed alternative to the classical Marxist principle of economic determination in the last instance (on ecological dominance, see especially Jessop 2002, 2011; Jessop and Sum 2006: 284–8). This is another way to say that, while the tools that we have proposed for CPE can be applied in many contexts, we are especially interested in applying them to advance the critique of capitalist social formations.

Second, whereas our earlier work focused on specific imaginaries or specific types of imaginary (e.g. accumulation strategies, state projects, hegemonic visions), semiosis has now gained its rightful, foundational place in a critical-realist, strategic-relational approach alongside the moment of the always-already-relational, emergent structural–conjunctural properties of social interaction. This is grounded, as noted above, in the role of sense- and meaning-making in complexity reduction and its role as the basis for lived experience, social construal and social construction. In addition to its general relevance, this innovation has been significant for CPE analyses of crisis, where, as we have shown, structured coherence is weakened and sedimented meanings are liable to reactivation. On the assumption that crises are objectively overdetermined, but subjectively indeterminate (Debray 1973), CPE opens the space for studying the variation, retention and selection of crisis construals and policy lessons as crises develop and struggle to shape the hegemonic or, at least, dominant construals of the crisis and to translate them into present crisis-management and future crisis-avoidance strategies. At stake here, as noted several times above, is the production of 'truth effects' that are not so much scientifically valid as conjuncturally 'correct'.

This entails that further development of CPE (like the more general strategic-relational approach of which it is one instantiation and elaboration) depends, as in the past, on a spiral movement between general reflections on the overall approach and the specification and application of particular variants of CPE. Our chosen field for these activities to date has largely been historical materialist analyses of the capitalist state, the profit-oriented, market-mediated dynamics of capital accumulation, and the structural coupling and co-evolution of the economic and political in capitalist social formations. But this does not exclude other ways of developing the approach in these or other fields.

RECURSIVITY AND REFLEXIVITY IN CULTURAL POLITICAL ECONOMY

One feature of the institutional and cultural turns identified in earlier chapters is their recursivity and reflexivity. This has four aspects. First, turns are one moment in the development of scientific inquiry. They are staging posts or bridgeheads in the spiral movement of investigation into the natural and social worlds, and key aspects of what critical realists term the transitive as opposed to intransitive aspect of social inquiry. In this sense turns are recursive – once the benefits of a particular turn have been largely achieved (as far as these are reflected in new results and ready acceptance in relevant epistemic communities), it is almost natural to ask where to turn next. For example, in a special issue of *South Atlantic Quarterly*, concerned with the consolidation of one trans-disciplinary revolution, the editors, Janet Halley and Andrew Parker, asked contributors: 'What is it like to be doing queer theory *still*, to be working today in a tradition that has managed somehow to have acquired a past?' (Halley and Parker 2007: 428). One among several answers was the 'anti-social turn', another was the affective turn, and a third was to 'take a break'. In short, when it is time to write the history of a turn, it is also time to turn, turn and turn again! Or, at least, take a break and then return!

Second, perhaps equally vertiginous but for different reasons, a turn can be applied reflexively. Thus, just as first-order actors are more or less capable of monitoring their own actions, of learning from experience, of integrating social knowledge into their activities, and of programming their own development, so, too, can social scientists commit themselves to reflexivity. This also holds for reflection on the twists and turns in social scientific inquiry. Thus the institutional turn can be used to investigate the changing institutional conditions in which different institutional turns (rational-choice, historical, sociological and, even, as in the new 'fourth' variant, constructivist, discursive or ideational institutionalism) are proposed, selected, and retained – both from the viewpoint of changes in the natural and social world that 'irritate' social scientists (and the users of social science, including lay persons) and from the viewpoint of shifts in the institutional conditions in which social scientists operate. Likewise, the cultural turn can be applied, in one or other of its many variants, to the cultural turn itself. Under what conditions does it make sense to reflect on how forms of thought, modes of existence, particular modes of calculation, structures of feeling and so on have been sedimented and are now liable to reactivation? For example, how might one explain through one or another cultural turn perspective the growing interest in constructivist approaches in US political science, mainstream economics or realist international relations theory? How and why have narrativity, rhetoric, translation, post-colonialism and so forth travelled beyond their natural home domains in the humanities and cultural studies, and how are they transformed as they get 'translated' into new disciplines?

Third, combining recursive and reflexive turns can serve to slow or reverse the fossilization of scientific work, the temptations to overextend an argument beyond the limits of *theoretical playfulness* in order to promote *disciplinary imperialism*, and to reflect on the blindspots and asymmetries in one's own field of study that come from privileging one particular turn. The temptation to overextend is found in the so-called exorbitation of language that goes beyond a potentially useful mode of analogical reasoning (what might one discover if one considered social relations as if they were structured like language) to interpret them with linguistic tools as essentially linguistic phenomena. The same criticism can be levelled, of course, against the efforts of neoclassical economists to extend an unreflective, unquestioned model of *homo economicus* into all spheres of social life, reducing its dynamics to cost–benefit calculation. This is one reason why we refer to CPE as steering a course between a constructivist Charybdis and structuralist Scylla in critical political economy. And, regarding self-reflexivity, the complexity turn that we have made in CPE is a standing reminder that, like all other social practices, scientific work rests on enforced selection. It is therefore crucial to attempt 'to see what one cannot see' by switching perspectives. This requires a playful theoretical spirit, openness to other perspectives, a willingness – for a time – to reflect on what other thematic, methodological or ontological approaches might reveal about one's own theoretical objects. As noted above, this involves the risks of undisciplined eclecticism, wilful bricolage, or an anarchic 'anything-goes' attitude that is not merely 'anti-disciplinary' but radically disorienting and paralysing in the ratio of noise to information, interpretation, explanation and action-orientation.

Fourth, as indicated in our comments on inter- or trans-disciplinary projects and the appeal of post-disciplinary horizons, recursivity and reflexivity are crucial parts of CPE as an intellectual project. It has changed and will continue to do so. This reflects (and refracts) changes in its referents and relata in the real world and the theoretical challenges that come from engaging with a wide range of approaches and schools. This has prompted us to rethink old approaches, examine new ones, and consider how they might be linked. Stepping outside one's comfort zone and participating in conferences, workshops and research projects beyond one's discipline is not only challenging but can be intellectually productive. However, it is also important to recognize that the study of capitalist social formations continues to be an important entry-point for us into the variety of economic imaginaries and practices at global, regional, national and local levels. Thus we oppose reifying or fetishizing the national scale as occurs in much of the varieties-of-capitalism literature or examining accumulation regimes, modes of regulation and modes of growth without regard to modes of adhesion to – or extrusion from – the world market. Instead, in the spirit of the logical–historical approach that we adopt, one must be prepared to move beyond whatever scale or site of analysis with which one's initial research begins in order to see how this fits into smaller or larger scales of activity and/or involves various horizontal or transversal linkages within and across different social spheres. This is all the more important in so far as changes in these spheres are mediated by new and reinvented economic imaginaries that seek to reduce the complexity of the real world and/or build alliances across different sites and scales.

REVISITING AND CONSOLIDATING THE SIX FEATURES

We now focus on the broader significance of the theoretical foundations of CPE by revisiting its six distinctive features as outlined in the Introduction and discussed from Part II onwards (see Table 13.1).

Semiosis and Complexity Reduction

First, CPE takes semiosis seriously and gives it a foundational role in the description, understanding and explanation of social action. Indeed, this is why 'cultural' is included in the self-description of our approach. This foundational role is grounded in the existential necessity of complexity reduction through semiosis (sense- and meaning-making). Many other approaches in evolutionary and institutional political economy have taken one or another kind of cultural turn but none, as far as we are aware, has grounded the importance of such a turn (at least in political economy) in the necessity of complexity reduction. The theoretical benefit from this more foundational approach is that it places semiosis and structuration on an equal ontological footing in the development of CPE. On this basis,

Table 13.1   Six features of CPE and location in the book

Six features of CPE	Location in the book
Semiosis and complexity reduction	Chapters 1 to 5 and 13
From construals to construction	Chapters 2, 3, 6 and 7
Coupling and co-evolution of semiosis and structuration	Chapters 2, 3, 4, 5, 6, 8, 10 and 12
'Problems', 'crises' and learning	Chapters 3, 5 and 11
Discourse, dispositives, domination and hegemony	Chapters 3, 4, 5, 8, 9, 10 and 12
The critique of ideology and domination	Chapters 4, 5, 8, 9, 10 and 12

there is no *a priori* ground for privileging either semiosis or structuration as an entry-point in the analysis and critique of political economy and, hence, of introducing its 'complement' as a mere supplement or optional extra in the analysis.

From Construals to Construction

Second, like other currents in evolutionary and institutional political economy, and unlike generic studies of semiosis, CPE explicitly integrates the general evolutionary mechanisms of variation, selection and retention into its semiotic analysis. It opposes trans-historical analyses, insisting that both history and institutions matter in political economy (see Chapter 1). In this respect it is close to semantic conceptual history, pragmatic conceptual history, historical semantics, and the sort of cultural materialism developed by Raymond Williams and his associates (see Chapter 3). It aims to explain, for example, why only some economic imaginaries get selected and institutionalized and come to co-constitute economic subjectivities, interests, activities, organizations, institutions, structural ensembles, emergent economic orders and their social embedding, and the dynamics of economic performance. This does not entail the sort of *evolutionism* that posits predetermined sequences driven forward by some *telos*. Nor does it imply a master process of evolution that coordinates variation, selection and retention – each of these processes has its own contingencies that differ with the 'objects' of evolution. Indeed, we consider that these mechanisms operate with different mixes of selectivities, that the modalities of their operation evolve, and that their operation varies across different institutional spheres and social worlds (see Chapter 11).

This also requires attention to periodization. A strategic-relational approach to periodization should identify discontinuity in continuity and continuity in discontinuity, and explore different types of conjuncture where strategic interventions could make a decisive contribution to path-shaping in spite of path-dependent legacies (see Jessop and Sum 2006: 323–47). Thus the *evolutionary* turn in CPE highlights the dialectic of path-dependency and path-shaping that emerges within semiosis, within structuration, and in the contingent co-evolution of semiotic *and extra-semiotic* processes that make some meaningful efforts at complexity reduction more likely to be selected and retained than others. In this sense, the evolutionary turn directs attention more explicitly to the mechanisms of variation, selection and retention that generate the contingently necessary development of social practices, organizations, organizational ecologies, institutions, institutional orders and patterns of societalization. In addition, we note that modes of evolution evolve and that social forces may, in part, shape the modes of evolution.

Coupling and Co-evolution of Semiosis and Structuration

The third feature is the emphasis on the interdependence and co-evolution of the semiotic and extra-semiotic. The evolutionary turn in CPE was initially concerned with the mechanisms of selection, variation and retention that might help to explain the recursive selection and reproduction of an otherwise improbable 'structured coherence' of social relations within specific spatial-temporal fixes (or time-space envelopes) associated with zones of relative stability at the expense of the deferral and/or displacement of contradictions, dilemmas, crisis tendencies and conflictuality into the future and/or elsewhere (Chapters 1, 4, and 9 to 12). But it was soon also applied to the field of semiotics. We have since explored the coupling and co-evolution of the semiotic and extra-semiotic in terms of the contingent historical relationship between semiosis and structuration, orders of discourse and social forms, and the semiotic and 'material' aspects of social practices (see Chapter 4).

This calls for a shift from a mainly semiotic analysis of individual texts or discursive genres to concern with the diverse mechanisms that shape the variation, selection and retention of particular imaginaries such that some social construals are also vectors of social construction. This is consistent with a general trend in discourse analysis to move from the word or sentence as the basic unit of analysis to texts, intertextuality, interdiscursivity, discursive themes, discursive nodes, orders of discourse and discursive formations. The mechanisms that condition this variation, selection and retention are not purely semiotic but also include structural, agential and technological selectivities (see Chapter 4). This is why we see the multi-dimensional evolutionary approach to the movement from construal to construction as one of CPE's key defining features. Conversely, as a necessary complement to its interest in sense- and meaning-making as a form of complexity reduction, CPE also highlights the role of structuration. This cannot be separated, of course, from the questions of structure and agency. In addition, to avoid any misunderstanding, we also noted in Chapters 4 and 5 that semiosis, too, is structured. Indeed, the relation between semiotic structures and semiotic practices can be analysed in the same strategic-relational manner as the structuring principles of social relations considered in Chapter 1. Their structuring principles and their effects are nonetheless different precisely because semiosis and structuration reduce complexity in different ways.

Semiosis and structuration are potentially complementary but possibly contrary or disconnected mechanisms of complexity reduction in social relations. From a CPE perspective, the evolution of social order involves the coupling and co-evolution of meaning-making and structuration, with neither form of complexity reduction being reducible to the other. In so far as these mechanisms work in harmony, they generate sedimented meaning and structured complexity. Whether or not they work in harmony is another matter. This is why we have consistently emphasized the improbability of social order.

A concern with the co-evolution of semiosis and structuration modifies the typical concerns of discourse analysis from individual texts or discursive genres to a more explicit concern with the semiotic and extra-semiotic mechanisms that shape the variation, selection and retention of particular imaginaries in a continuing dialectic of path-dependent path-shaping. This is the basis for the potential rapprochement between CPE and established fields of historical inquiry and/or methods such as historical semantics, conceptual history, and Foucauldian genealogies of power-knowledge (see Chapters 3 and 4). In particular, this development opens a space for examining the contingent long-run correlation between the introduction of new social imaginaries and processes of structural transformation that provoke the search for new meanings, and help to select some social imaginaries rather than others, which, in turn, may play a constitutive role in the consolidation–contestation of still emerging institutions and structures (cf. Bartelson 1995; Koselleck 1972, 1982; Luhmann 1980, 1981, 1989; Skinner 1989).

This could mark a further step in developing CPE in so far as it provides means to link the genealogy of imaginaries with their role in consolidating distinct patterns of structured coherence, historical blocs and spatio-temporal fixes. It also opens the space for a more nuanced analysis of the relative weight of semiotic and extra-semiotic mechanisms in the different phases of evolution, with the working hypothesis that semiotic mechanisms have greater weight in the stage of variation and that extra-semiotic mechanisms are more important in the phase of retention (see Chapter 11). But this should be combined with the second working hypothesis that the relative weight of semiotic and extra-semiotic mechanisms will also vary with the type of social field, organizational ecology or institutional order in which new imaginaries emerge. Indeed, it requires no great leap of imagination to suggest that extra-semiotic mechanisms will play a smaller role in the fields of theology and philosophy than they will in those of technology and natural science, and that these semiotic mechanisms will be more significant in the former than in the latter. Nonetheless, given the importance of imaginaries in each field to the reproduction of systems of domination, semiotic and extra-semiotic mechanisms are at work in them all.

'Problems', 'Crises' and Learning

A fourth key feature is interest in the dialectic of experience and learning from routine communication and encounters through organized and instituted social practices to orders of discourse and social forms, and thence to innovation in the basic forms and content of semiosis and structuration. Thus, given its interest in the relation between semiosis and structuration, CPE investigates how learning depends on a dialectics of *Erlebnis* (immediate experience) and *Erfahrung* (lesson-drawing) – with the former more concerned with subjective sense-making, and the latter more concerned with the reinterpretation of the world, in its actual existence and deeper realities. Of particular interest are individual, organizational and societal learning in response to 'problems' or 'crises' and their role in the dialectic of semiosis and structuration and, by extension, of path-shaping and path-dependency.

Ontologically, we indicated how learning is grounded in complexity reduction *and its limits* in a double sense: first, learning contributes to the selection and retention of some modes of complexity reduction over others; and, second, because any reduction excludes aspects of the real world that are relevant to actors' ability to 'go on' within it, life is 'full of surprises' that disturb expectations and provide opportunities for learning. This is an everyday occurrence but is especially significant during 'crises' when sedimented meanings and structured complexity are revealed as historically contingent and/or in relation to *urgences*, that is, unexpected 'problems' that prompt contested efforts to build new dispositives. In all cases, but especially for crises and *urgences*, we argue that the construal of events and/or processes as constituting crises and problems involves both contestable signification and contestable crisis responses. Both have the same selectivities (semiotic, structural, technological and agential) as semiosis more generally and also undergo variation, selection and retention. Importantly, from a CPE perspective, effective learning is shaped by the objective as well as subjective dimensions of the learning experience: it cannot be arbitrary, rationalistic and willed.

We have also emphasized that learning refers in the first instance to actually existing learning and not to the discourses of learning that are integrated into some social imaginaries (e.g., the knowledge-based economy) or policy recommendations (e.g., the promotion of lifelong learning). Nonetheless these discourses could be important objects of CPE analysis in terms of their problematizations, practices and effects. Finally, in line with its commitment to critique, CPE argues that learning occurs in contested fields with ideological effects and is shaped by uneven capacities to shape, impose or ignore lessons. This approach could prove useful in reinterpreting the unity of theory and practice (Ji 2006; Chapter 11).

Discourses, Dispositives, Domination and Hegemony

Fifth, CPE explores the interaction of four selectivities – structural, discursive, technological and agential – in the remaking of domination and hegemony. Three of these were introduced in our earlier work on the strategic-relational approach and the significance of semiosis. The relatively new feature is technological selectivities, understood not only in the ordinary-language, Marxist or material-culture senses of technical and social relations of production, distribution and consumption, but also, and more significantly, in terms of Foucauldian technologies of discipline, normalization and governmentality, and their role in power/knowledge relations. Technologies refer here to the mechanisms involved in the governance of conduct and in the selection and retention of specific imaginaries in so far as they provide reference points not only for meaning-making but also for coordinating actions within and across specific personal interactions, organizations and networks, and institutional orders. These mechanisms are often overlooked in discourse analysis and heterodox political economy. In the former case, this occurs because of the temptation to explain semiotic properties in semiotic terms, in the latter because of the temptation to explain economic dynamics in economic terms. Yet, as we have shown above, these technologies have key roles in the selection and retention of specific meaning-making approaches and patterns of structuration. In particular, as Chapter 5 demonstrates, they are crucial in constructing, promoting, consolidating and contesting hegemonic, sub-hegemonic and counter-hegemonic imaginaries, projects, visions and so forth.

Thus we consider the interface between discourses, discursive technologies, dispositives, subjectivities, domination and hegemonies. We have drawn undogmatically on Marx, Gramsci and Foucault to examine how micro-technologies and other practices are assembled as dispositives and articulated to form more encompassing and enduring sets of social relations that are sedimented in *habitus*, *hexis* and common sense, and that also secure the substratum of institutional orders and broader patterns of social domination (see Chapters 5 to 8, and 10). In this context, after explicating the four modes of selectivity in social relations, we explored Richard Marsden's insight that Marx explains 'why' but cannot explain 'how'; Foucault explains 'how' but cannot explain 'why'. This insight is especially pertinent to the emergence of new targets of governmental intervention (in a broad, Foucauldian sense) and the effects of such intervention as it intersects with other forces and vectors in specific conjunctures.

In this regard, the risk of how/why disjunctions can be resolved by addressing two broad sets of questions. The Foucauldian set now comprises 'what' as well as 'how': (1) what governmental knowledging technologies are involved in constituting subjectivities and identities; and (2) how do these imaginaries, subjectivities and identities become normalized in everyday practices? The Marxian–Gramscian set adds 'when' and 'who' to the 'why' question, which is readily answered in terms of the contradictory and potentially antagonistic nature of the capital relation. The additional questions thus comprise: (1) when do particular economic imaginaries and their related networks or advocates in political and civil society begin to gain credence; (2) what contradictions are these networks seeking to disguise, harmonize or transcend in developing these imaginaries; (3) who is involved in the discursive networks that construct and promote particular objects of economic regulation and governance; (4) what additional ideas and practices are selected and drawn upon to recontextualize and hybridize the referents of these objects; (5) how do these objects become hegemonic, in so far as they do, despite the inevitable tendencies towards instability and fluidity in social relations; (6) who and what do they include/exclude in formulating a new 'general interest' or economic community of fate; (7) how do these changes impact different sites and scales (e.g. the lives of subaltern groups); (8) how are incompressible contradictions and uneven development negotiated and/or resisted in the rebuilding of social relations; (9) how do counter-hegemonic forces challenge routinized categories and naturalized institutions, generate new subject positions and social forces, and struggle for new projects and strategies; and (10) how are diverse forces continually balanced and counter-balanced in an unstable equilibrium of compromise?

The Critique of Ideology and Domination

Sixth, CPE critiques ideology and domination. It does not presuppose that any given sense- and meaning-making system is necessarily and always ideological nor that every social relation or social practice is necessarily and always entails domination. The biases in any communication or interaction must be established. In this sense we are sympathetic to the original definition of ideology proposed by Comte Destutt de Tracy in 1796 as the science of the formation of ideas (which prefigures the definitions of semiology and semiotics proposed some 100 years later by de Saussure and Peirce respectively). However, semiology and semiotics are quite acceptable names for this general science, and ideology can be preserved for aspects of sign-systems that are related to the legitimation and mystification of structured power relations.

While a fundamental critique of ideology should begin with the foundational categories of sense- and meaning-making, CPE analyses typically start with orders of discourse and discursive practices (the two intermediate semiotic categories in Table 4.1 on the dialectic of semiosis and structuration) as aspects of specific institutional orders and more or less instituted social practices. Although we have not demonstrated this here (but CDA theorists have), refined analyses can be conducted at the level of words, texts, paratexts or their equivalents in other modes of signification (including multi-modal signification). Indeed, this is where CDA began in the 1980s and 1990s with a view to critiquing the connections among language, ideology and power. At stake in all cases of ideological critique are the sources and mechanisms that 'bias' lived experience and imaginaries towards specific identities and their changing ideal and/or material interests in specific conjunctures. The 'raw material' of ideology is meaning systems, social imaginaries and lived experience. As we have indicated, actors can only 'go on' in the world because they adopt, wittingly or not, specific entry-points and standpoints to reduce complexity and make it calculable. This involves selective observation of the real world, reliance on specific codes and programmes, deployment of particular categories and forms of calculation, sensitivity to specific structures of feeling, reference to particular identities, justification in terms of particular vocabularies of motives, efforts to calculate short- to long-term interests and so forth.

As proposed in Chapter 4, a CPE-based critique of ideology involves four main steps: (1) recognize the role of semiosis as a heterogeneous pool of intersubjective meanings; (2) identify social imaginaries, that is, specific clusters of meaning (or semiotic) systems, and describe their form and content; (3) analyse their contingent articulation and functioning in securing the conditions for structured patterns of domination that serve particular interests; and (4) distinguish between cases where these effects are motivated and/or where they are effects of sedimented meaning. In short, a key issue is how basic categories and general social imaginaries come to more or less durably shape, dominate or hegemonize the world. One aspect of this is how far and how they are linked to 'lived experience', that is, how actors experience and understand their world(s) as real and meaningful seen from one or more subject positions and standpoints and also how they empathize with others. Lived experience never reflects an extra-semiotic reality but involves meaning-making based on the meaningful *pre*-interpretation of the natural-cum-social world. Lived experience may be sedimented but its form is not pre-given and this creates space for learning. Lived experience is open to dislocation, contestation, reactivation and struggle to restore, alter or overturn meaning systems, including those involved in diverse social imaginaries.

Only when the analysis reaches steps three and four could one demonstrate that specific sense- and meaning-making systems operate to legitimize the orders of discourse, social forms and social practices associated with particular hegemonic and/or dominant power relations. These systems are all the more powerful, the more it becomes part of common sense understood as sets of everyday social practices with their discursive and material aspects. As such, the ideological process refers to the contribution of discourses to the contingent reproduction of power relations, especially where this involves hegemony (political, intellectual, moral and self-leadership). One should not limit the critique of ideology to the form and content of beliefs – it must be related to their forms of 'inscription' (the field of sociologistics, mediology, of modes of communication) and to the structurally inscribed strategic selectivities that condition who gets the chance to engage in discourse. Whether a particular cultural ensemble has an 'ideological' moment depends on the form of (hegemonic) domination at stake: this could be capitalist, patriarchal, heteronormative, 'racial', national, regional and so forth. In this sense, a discourse could be ideological in regard to capitalism but non-ideological in relation to patriarchy (or vice versa). In short, *Ideologiekritik* requires an entry-point and a standpoint and must also be related to specific conjunctures rather than conducted *in abstracto*. In this sense, ideology is a contingent feature of culture and discourse that gets naturalized, articulated, selected and sedimented in the (re)making of social relations.

Turning to the critique of domination, CPE focuses on the effects of structuration but relates them to all four modes of selectivity. It stresses the 'materiality' of social relations, that is, their emergent properties, and highlights how these properties operate in strategically selective ways 'behind the backs' of the relevant agents. It is especially concerned with the structural properties and dynamics that result from such material interactions. Thus it views technical and economic objects as socially constructed, historically specific, more or less socially (dis)embedded in broader networks of social relations and institutional ensembles, more or less embodied ('incorporated' and 'embrained'), and in need of continuing social 'repair' work for their reproduction. Of interest is how the four selectivities are condensed to form specific dispositives that help to secure hegemonies and dominations. While discursive selectivities are especially relevant to *Ideologiekritik*, *Herrschaftskritik* pays more attention to structural and technological selectivities. At stake here is their role in reproducing specific semiotic, social, institutional and spatio-temporal fixes that secure the conditions for the reproduction of economic, political and social domination. We have illustrated this for accumulation regimes and modes of regulation, but the same approach is valid for other forms of domination (e.g. patriarchy, the apartheid state, heteronormativity, centre–periphery relations or national subjugation). This would help to disclose the location and mechanism of ideological effects that are often narrated in terms of meaning systems that are self-described as universal, rational, necessary and beneficial.

This focus on how social practices produce particular strategic logics, subjectivities, and events exposes the constructed nature of ideology, hegemonies and dominations. Instead of abandoning critique, however, CPE advocates *Ideologiekritik* and *Herrschaftskritik* that expose these self-naturalizing beliefs, for example national competitiveness as bringing prosperity, unequal class relations as socially harmonious, unjust policies as just and so on. It aims to disclose the micro-elements of these hidden beliefs and to identify how they express contradictory social relations so that emancipatory struggles become possible with regard to capitalism and other forms of domination.

PLACING CULTURAL POLITICAL ECONOMY IN POST-DISCIPLINARY RESEARCH

We conclude where we began – with some remarks on trans- and post-disciplinarity. Developing this general CPE agenda on this basis requires an aspiration towards post-disciplinarity. The latter is a horizon towards which one moves. It involves a commitment to crossing boundaries, smudging borders, emphasizing intersections and interconnections. But horizons retreat as one approaches them and the commitment to post-disciplinarity needs to be renewed continuously. Exciting as it is, such research poses the problem of how to link different disciplines, to integrate a broad range of theoretical stances, and to address a wide range of methodological problems without falling into free-floating eclecticism or, conversely, resorting to a compartmentalized approach in which different issues are addressed through different kinds of reasoning, different sets of concepts and different methods that, were they combined, would surely prove incommensurable or logically incoherent. Having a clearly defined real-world problem that is specified in relatively concrete–complex terms helps to avoid these risks. But this does not mean that we can ignore the meta-theoretical issues addressed in this and the preceding volume. Without attention to ontological, epistemological and methodological as well as substantive theoretical issues, there can be no road map for post-disciplinary research.

We stress this point because Sil and Katzenstein (2010) have presented a superficially similar approach to that proposed here. They label this 'analytical eclecticism' and declare, as we do, that research should be problem-oriented and choose concepts, theories and methods in the light of a particular research topic. But they also explicitly refuse meta-theoretical questions because they are insoluble (cf. Wodak and Mayer 2009: 26). They therefore advocate a self-consciously pragmatic mix of investigative tools. In practice, then, analytical eclecticism is more likely than not to produce precisely that free-floating, incoherent eclecticism that we oppose (for a critique along similar lines, see Reus-Smit 2011). In contrast, we argue that post-disciplinary research needs consciously to address, enter into dialogue, and selectively combine theoretical and substantive elements in other disciplines where these have been (or could be) shown to be commensurable, complementary and non-contradictory.

This is important because today we do not have the luxury of working in a pre-disciplinary age, but scholars can seek, as their work develops, to engage in trans-disciplinary inquiry and research with a view to breaking with the conceptual and epistemic constraints of disciplinary boundaries. This is why we sometimes describe our work as pre-disciplinary in inspiration, trans-disciplinary in practice (or perspiration!), and post-disciplinary in aspiration. But this mode of intellectual work is time-consuming and can only be realized over time – often in cooperation with fellow travellers heading in similar directions. We all have to start with a narrower perspective and broaden and deepen through our engagement with an intellectual project.

To avoid eclecticism and dispersion is, for us, effectively one and the same problem. Our theoretical and empirical work has developed in response to emerging theoretical and empirical challenges, sometimes rooted in the nature of the object, sometimes rooted in criticisms that have been addressed to the one-sidedness, the blind spots or the aporias in our work. Ultimately, a post-disciplinary aspiration involves not simply crossing boundaries and looking for interconnections, but also having a real-world problem as well as ethnographic details to think through the how, what, who and why questions. This is the agenda that we recommend for cultural political economy.

References

AccountAbility (with United Nations Industrial Development Organization) (2006), *SME Clusters and Responsible Competitiveness in Developing Countries*, available at: http://www.accountability.org/images/content/3/1/317/SME%20clusters%20and%20Responsible%20Competitiveness%20in%20Developing%20Count.pdf (accessed 12 March 2013).

Aglietta, M. (1979), *A Theory of Capitalist Regulation: The U.S. Experience*, London: NLB.

Aglietta, M. (1982), 'World capitalism in the eighties', *New Left Review*, **136**, 25–35.

Aglietta, M. (1986), *La fin des devises-clés: essai sur la monnaie*, Paris: La Découverte.

Aglietta, M. (2002), 'Problèmes posés par la régulation monétaire', in P. Jacquet, J. Pisani-Ferry and L. Tubiana (eds), *Gouvernance Mondiale*, Rapport du CAE, n° 37, Paris: La Documentation française, 375–92.

Aitken, R. (2007), *Performing Capital: Toward a Cultural Economy of Popular and Global Finance*, Basingstoke: Macmillan.

Albert, M. and Laberge, S. (2007), 'The legitimation and dissemination processes of the innovation system approach: the case of the Canadian and Québec science and technology policy', *Science, Technology & Human Values*, **11** (2), 221–49.

Albrecht, J. (1996), 'Neolinguistic School in Italy', in E.F.K. Koerner and R.E. Ascher (eds), *Concise History of the Language Sciences: From the Sumerians to the Cognitivists*, Oxford: Pergamon, 243–7.

Aldrich, H. (1999), *Organizations Evolving*, London: SAGE.

Allan, K. and Robinson, R.A. (eds) (2011), *Current Methods in Historical Semantics*, Berlin/Boston: Walter de Gruyter.

Allison, J.A. (2012), *The Financial Crisis and the Free-Market Cure: Why Pure Capitalism Is the World Economy's Only Hope*, New York: McGraw-Hill.

Althusser, L. (1965), *For Marx*, London: NLB.

Althusser, L. (1971), *Lenin and Philosophy and Other Essays*, London: NLB.

Althusser, L. (1999), *Machiavelli and Us*, London: Verso.

Altvater, E. (1993), *The Future of the Market: An Essay on the Regulation*

of Money and Nature after the Collapse of 'Actually Existing Socialism', London: Verso.
Amable, B. (2011), 'Morals and politics in the ideology of neoliberalism', Socio-Economic Review, **9** (1), 3–30.
Amable, B. (2009), 'Structural reforms in Europe and the (in)coherence of institutions', Oxford Review of Economic Policy, **25** (1), 17–39.
Amable B. and Palombarini, S. (2005), L'économie politique n'est pas une science morale, Paris: Raisons d'agir.
Amable, B., Guillard, E. and Palombarini, S. (2012), L'économie politique du néoliberalisme: le cas de la France et l'Italie, Paris: Editions Rue d'Ulm.
American Logistics Association, Exchange Roundtable (2005), 'What's leading edge with today's leading mass volume retailers?', Dallas, TX, 8 March, available at: http://www.hoytnet.com/HTML obj-315/ALA2005R3-FINAL_with_Pics_March_8_2005.ppt (accessed 11 September 2011).
American National Standards Institute and Global Competitiveness Council (2001), 'Proposed Draft American National Standard Knowledge Management – Vocabulary', Tucson, AZ: GKEC/ANSI.
Amin, S. (2009), 'A critique of the Stiglitz Report: The limits of liberal orthodoxy', Pambazuka News, available at: www.pambazuka.org/en/category/features/58453 (accessed 31 December 2010).
Andersen, N.Å. (2003), Discourse Analytical Strategies: Foucault, Koselleck, Laclau, Luhmann, Bristol: Policy Press.
Andersen, N.Å. (2011), 'Conceptual history and the diagnostics of the present', Management & Organizational History, **6** (3), 248–67.
Anderson, P. (1983), In the Tracks of Historical Materialism, London: Verso.
Angermüller, J. (2011), 'Heterogeneous knowledge. Trends in German discourse analysis against an international background', Journal of Multicultural Discourses, **6** (2), 121–36.
Ansell, C. (2006), 'Network institutionalism', in R.A.W. Rhodes, S.A. Blinder and B.A. Rockman (eds), The Oxford Handbook of Political Institutions, Oxford: Oxford University Press, 75–89.
Aranson, P.H. (1998), 'The new institutional analysis of politics', Journal of Institutional and Theoretical Economics, **154** (4), 744–53.
Archer, M.S. (2000), Being Human: The Problem of Agency, Cambridge: Cambridge University Press.
Archer, M.S. (2003), Structure, Agency and the Internal Conversation, Cambridge: Cambridge University Press.
Archer, M.S. (2012), The Reflexive Imperative in Late Modernity, Cambridge: Cambridge University Press.

Archer, M., Bhaskar, R., Collier, A., Lawson, T. and Norris, A. (eds) (1998), *Critical Realism: Essential Readings*, London: Routledge.

Arnold, C. (2010), 'Where the low road and the high road meet: flexible employment in the global value chains', *Journal of Contemporary Asia*, **40** (4), 612–37.

Arts, B. and Bahili, I. (2013), 'Global forest governance: multiple practices of policy performance', in B. Arts, S. van Bommel, J. de Koning and E. Turnhout (eds), *Forest and Nature Governance. A Practice Based Approach*, Dordrecht: Springer, 111–32.

Arts, B., van Bommel, S., de Koning, J. and Turnhout, E. (eds) (2013), *Forest and Nature Governance. A Practice Based Approach*, Dordrecht: Springer.

Asian Development Bank (2003), *Asian Development Outlook*, available at: http://www.adb.org/sites/default/files/pub/2003/ado2003.pdf (accessed 2 August 2012).

Augustine of Hippo (AD 389 [1995]), *De Doctrina Christiana*, trans. R.P.H. Green, Oxford: Oxford University Press.

Augustine, N.R. (2007), *Is America Falling off the Flat Earth?*, Washington, DC: National Academies Press.

Austin, J.L. (1975), *How to do Things with Words*, Cambridge, MA: Harvard University Press.

Babe, R.E. (2009), *Cultural Studies and Political Economy: Toward a New Integration*, Oxford: Lexington Books.

Bachmann-Medick, D. (2006), *Cultural Turns: Neuorientierungen in den Kultur-wissenschaften*, Reinbeck bei Hamburg: Rowolt.

Bakhtin, M.M. (1981), *The Dialogic Imagination*, Austin, TX: University of Texas Press.

Bakhtin, M.M. (1984), *Problems of Dostoevsky's Poetics*, Austin, TX: University of Texas Press.

Bakhtin, M.M. (1986), *Speech Genres and other Late Essays*, Austin, TX: University of Texas Press.

Baldwin, C. (2009), 'China: one bright spot of US companies' results', Reuter, 27 March, available at: http://www.reuters.com/article/2009/04/27/us-usa-earnings-china-analysis-idUSTRE53Q2DE20090427 (accessed 15 January 2013).

Balibar, E. (1992), 'Foucault and Marx: the question of nominalism', in T.J. Armstrong (ed.), *Michel Foucault, Philosopher*, London: Routledge, 38–56.

Ban, C. and Blyth, M. (2013), 'The BRICs and the Washington Consensus: an introduction', *Review of International Political Economy*, **20** (2), 241–55.

Barbieri, M. (2008), 'The code model of semiosis: the first steps toward a scientific biosemiotics', *The American Journal of Semiotics*, **24** (1–3), 23–37.

Barbieri, M. (2012), 'Life is semiosis: a biosemiotic view of nature', *Cosmos and History: The Journal of Natural and Social Philosophy*, **4** (1–2), 29–51.

Barnett, C. (1999), 'Culture, government and spatiality: reassessing the "Foucault effect" in cultural-policy studies', *International Journal of Cultural Studies*, **2** (3), 369–97.

Bartelson, J. (1995), *A Genealogy of Sovereignty*, Cambridge: Cambridge University Press.

Barthes, R. (1967), *Elements of Semiology*, London: Jonathan Cape.

Bartlett, T. (2013), *Analysing Power in Language: A Practical Guide*, London: Routledge.

Bartoli, M. (1925), *Introduzione alla Neolinguistica: Principi-scopi-metodi*, Geneva: Olschki.

Bartoli, M. and Gramsci, A. (1912–13), *Appunti di glottologia: Anno accademico 1912–1913*, Rome: Archive Fondazione Istituto Gramsci.

Basker, E. (2007), 'The causes and consequences of Wal-Mart's growth', *Journal of Economic Perspectives*, **21** (3), 177–98.

Baudrillard, J. (1995), *The Gulf War Did Not Take Place*, Bloomington, IN: Indiana University Press.

de B'Béri, B.E. (2008), 'Review essay & interview: Peter Ives on *Gramsci's Politics of Language*', *Canadian Journal of Communication*, **33**, 319–37.

Becker, J. and Jäger, J. (2012), 'Integration in crisis: a regulationist perspective on the interaction of European varieties of capitalism', *Competition & Change*, **16** (3), 169–87.

Beckert, J. (2003), 'Economic sociology and embeddedness: how shall we conceptualize economic action?', *Journal of Economic Issues*, **37** (3), 769–87.

Beijing News (2012), 'Closing Down of Migrant Children Schools: 30 Percent Children Returned to Home Villages', 27 August, available at: http://news.163.com/12/0827/02/89SNTI4N00014AED.html (accessed 13 March 2013) (in Chinese).

Belabes, A. (1999), 'Myth and Paradox of "U.S. Competitiveness" Debate from the End of World War II to Nowadays', available at: greqam.univ-mrs.fr/pdf/working_papers/1999/99c07.pdf (accessed 25 November 2007).

Béland, D. and Cox, R.H. (eds) (2010), *Ideas and Politics in Social Science Research*, New York: Oxford University Press.

Bell, D. (1973), *The Coming of Post-Industrial Society*, New York: Basic Books.

Bell, D. (1989), 'The third technological revolution', *Dissent*, **36**, 164–76.

Bello, W. (2009), *G20: Form, Not Substance*, Washington, DC: Foreign Policy in Focus, 24 September.

Bellofiore, R. (2013), '"Two or three things I know about her": Europe in the global crisis and heterodox economics', *Cambridge Journal of Economics*, **37** (3), 497–512.

Bendell, J. (2004), 'Barricades and Boardrooms: A Contemporary History of Corporate Accountability Movement, Programme on Technology, Business and Society', UNRISD Paper No. 13, Geneva: UNRISD.

Beniger, J.R. (1986), *The Control Revolution: Technological and Economic Origins of the Information Society*, Cambridge, MA: Harvard University Press.

Bennett, T. (1998), *Culture: A Reformer's Science*, St Leonards: Allen & Unwin.

Benveniste, E. (1966), *Problèmes de Linguistique Générale*, Paris: Gallimard.

Berger, S. and Lester, R. (1997), *Made by Hong Kong*, Hong Kong: Oxford University Press.

Bergsten, C.F. (1999), 'America and Europe: clash of titans?', *Foreign Affairs*, **78** (1), 20–33.

Bergsten, C.F. (2008), 'A partnership of equals: how Washington should respond to China's economic challenge', *Foreign Affairs*, **87** (4), 57–69.

Bernstein, B. (1996), *Pedagogy, Symbolic Control and Identity: Theory, Research, Critique*, London: Taylor & Francis.

Best, J. (2005), *Limits of Transparency*, Ithaca, NY: Cornell University Press.

Best, J. and Paterson, M. (eds) (2010a), *Cultural Political Economy*, London: Routledge.

Best, J. and Paterson, M. (2010b), 'Introduction', in idem (eds), *Cultural Political Economy*, London: Routledge, 1–25.

Bevir, M. and Rhodes, R.A.W. (2006), 'Interpretive approaches to British government and politics', *British Politics*, **1**, 84–112.

Bhaskar, R. (1972), *A Realist Theory of Science*, Leeds: Leeds Books.

Bieler, A. and Morton, A.D. (2004), 'A critical theory route to hegemony, world order and historical change: neo-Gramscian perspectives in international relations', *Capital & Class*, **82**, 85–113.

Biernacki, R. (1995), *The Fabrication of Labor: Germany and Britain, 1640–1914*, Berkeley, CA: University of California Press.

Birkenholtz, T. (2009), 'Groundwater governmentality: hegemony and technologies of resistance in Rajasthan's (India) groundwater governance', *Geographical Journal*, **175** (3), 208–20.

Birkland, T.A. (2009), 'Disasters, lessons learned, and fantasy learning', *Journal of Contingencies and Crisis Management*, **17** (3), 1–12.

Blanchard, O. and Leigh, D. (2013), 'Growth Forecast Errors and Fiscal Multipliers', IMF Working Paper WP 13/1. Washington, DC: IMF.

Bloch, M. (1973), *Royal Touch: Sacred Monarchy and Scrofula in England and France*, London: Routledge & Kegan Paul.

Blyth, M.M. (1997), '"Any more bright ideas?" The ideational turn in comparative political economy', *Comparative Politics*, **29** (2), 229–50.

Blyth, M.M. (2002), *Great Transformations: Economic Ideas and Institutional Change in the Twentieth Century*, Cambridge: Cambridge University Press.

Bode, R. (1979), 'De Nederlandse bourgeoisie tussen de twee wereldoorlogen', *Cahiers voor de Politieke en Sociale Wetenschappen*, **2** (4), 9–50.

Boje, D.M. and Rosile, G.A. (2008), 'Specters of Wal-Mart: a critical discourse analysis of stories of Sam Walton's ghost', *Critical Discourse Studies*, **5** (2), 153–80.

Bollier, D. (2002), *Silent Theft: The Private Plunder of Our Common Wealth*, London: Routledge.

Bonacich, E. and Wilson, J.B. (2006), 'Global production and distribution: Wal-Mart's global logistic empire', in S.D. Brunn (ed.), *Wal-Mart World: The World's Biggest Corporation in the Global Economy*, New York: Routledge, 227–42.

Boothman, D. (1991), 'Gramsci als Ökonom – Gramsci as economist', *Das Argument*, **185**, 57–70.

Boothman, D. (2004), 'The sources for Gramsci's concept of hegemony', *Rethinking Marxism*, **20** (2), 201–15.

Borg, E. (2001), *Projekt Globalisierung: Soziale Kräfte im Konflikt um Hegemonie*, Hannover: Eric Borg.

Boucher, G. (2008), *The Charmed Circle of Ideology: A Critique of Laclau and Mouffe, Butler and Žižek*, Melbourne: re.press.

Bourdieu, P. (1981), 'Men and machines', in K. Knorr-Cetina and A.V. Cicoure (eds), *Advances in Social Theory and Methodology*, London: Routledge and Kegan Paul, 304–17.

Bourdieu, P. (1988), 'Vive la crise! For heterodoxy in social science', *Theory and Society*, **17** (5), 773–87.

Bourdieu, P. (1994), *Raisons pratiques*, Paris: Le Seuil.

Bowman, P. (ed.) (2003), *Interrogating Cultural Studies: Theory, Politics, and Practice*, London: Pluto.

Boyer, R. (1990), *Regulation Theory: An Introduction*, New York: Columbia University Press.

Boyer, R. (1998), 'Hybridization and models of production: geography, history and theory', in R. Boyer et al. (eds), *Between Imitation and Innovation*, Oxford: Oxford University Press, 23–56.

Boyer, R. (2000), 'Is a finance-led growth regime a viable alternative to Fordism?', *Economy and Society*, **29**, 111–45.
Boyer, R. (2002a), 'Introduction', in R. Boyer and Y. Saillard (eds), *The Theory of Régulation: State of the Art*, London: Routledge, 1–10.
Boyer, R. (2002b), 'Is Régulation Theory an original theory of economic institutions?', in R. Boyer and Y. Saillard (eds), *The Theory of Régulation: State of the Art*, London: Routledge, 320–33.
Boyer, R. (2003), 'L'anthropologie économique de Pierre Bourdieu', *Actes de la Recherche en Sciences Sociales*, **150**, 65–78.
Boyer, R. (2004a), *Une théorie du capitalisme. Est-elle possible?*, Paris: Odile Jacob.
Boyer, R. (2004b), 'Pierre Bourdieu. Analyste du changement? Une lecture à la lumière de la théorie de la régulation', Paris: CEPREMAP, Couverture Orange 2004-01.
Boyer, R. (2011), *Les financiers détruiront-ils le capitalisme?*, Paris: Economica.
Boyer, R. and Labrousse, A. (2008), 'The secret life of institutions: on the role of ideas in evolving economic systems', interview with Mark Blyth, *Revue de la régulation*, **3** (4), available at: http://regulation.revue.org/document5833.html (accessed 24 April 2013).
Boyer, R. and Saillard, Y. (eds) (2002), *The Theory of Régulation: State of the Art*, London: Routledge.
Brand, U. (2009), 'Schillernd und technokratisch. Grüner New Deal als *magic bullet* in der Krise des liberal-imperialen Kapitalismus?', *Prokla*, **156**, 475–81.
Brand, U. and Görg, C. (2008), 'Post-Fordist governance of nature', *Review of International Political Economy*, **15** (4), 566–88.
Brandist, C. (1996a), 'Gramsci, Bakhtin, and the semiotics of hegemony', *New Left Review*, **216**, 94–110.
Brandist, C. (1996b), 'The official and the popular in Gramsci and Bakhtin', *Theory, Culture and Society*, **13** (2), 59–74.
Brettonwoodsproject (2009), *Economic Crisis: Rich Countries Block Reform at UN Summit*, available at: www.brettonwoodsproject.org/update/66/bwupdt66.txt (accessed 24 April 2013).
Brinton, M.C. and Nee, V. (eds) (1998), *The New Institutionalism in Sociology*, New York: Russell Sage Foundation.
Bristow, G. (2005), 'Everyone's a "winner": problematising the discourse of regional competitiveness', *Journal of Economic Geography*, **5** (3), 285–304.
Brown, P., Green, A. and Lauder, H. (2001), *High Skills: Globalization, Competitiveness, and Skill Formation*, Oxford: Oxford University Press.
Brown, N. (2006), 'Shifting Tenses – from "regimes of truth" to "regimes of

hope"', available at http://www.york.ac.uk/media/satsu/documents-papers/Brown-2006-shifting.pdf (accessed 8 July 2013).

Brunner, O. (1992 [1939]), *Land and Lordship: Structures of Governance in Medieval Austria*, Philadelphia, PA: University of Pennsylvania Press.

Bryant, A. and Charmaz, K. (eds) (2007), *The SAGE Handbook of Grounded Theory*, London: SAGE.

Bryson, J. and Ruston, G. (2010), *Design Economies and the Changing World Economy: Innovation, Production, and Competitiveness*, London: Routledge.

Buci-Glucksmann, C. (1980), *Gramsci and the State*, London: Lawrence & Wishart.

Buckel, S. and Fischer-Lescano, A. (eds) (2007), *Hegemonie gepanzert mit Zwang: zum Staatsverständnis von Antonio Gramsci*, Baden-Baden: Nomos.

Buckel, S., Georgi, F., Kannankulam, J. and Wissel, J. (2012), *Die EU in der Krise: zwischen autoritärem Etatismus und europäischem Frühling*, Münster: Westfälisches Dampfboot.

Buckley, A. (2011), *Financial Crisis: Causes, Context and Consequences*, Harlow: Longman.

Bührmann, A.D. and Schneider, W. (2008), *Vom Diskurs zum Dispositiv. Eine Einführung in die Dispositivanalyse*, Bielefeld: Transcript.

Bunge, M. (1961), *Causality*, Cleveland, OH: Meridian.

Burgess, S. (1999), 'Queer new institutionalism: notes on the naked power organ in mainstream constitutional theory and law', in H. Gillman and C. Clayton (eds), *The Supreme Court and American Politics: New Institutionalist Approaches*, Lawrence: University Press of Kansas, 199–218.

Burke, P. (1992), *History and Social Theory*, Cambridge: Polity.

Burkhardt, J. (1992), 'Wirtschaft', in O. Brunner, W. Conze and R. Koselleck (eds), *Geschichtliche Grundbegriffe. Historisches Lexikon zur politisch-sozialen Sprache in Deutschland*, Band 7, Stuttgart: Klett-Cotta, 511–95.

Burnham, P. (1991), 'Neo-Gramscian hegemony and the international order', *Capital & Class*, **45**, 73–93.

Burns, T.R. and Flam, H. (1987), *The Shaping of Social Organization: Social Rule System Theory and Its Applications*, London: SAGE.

Business Insider (2011), 'BRICs=Bloody Ridiculous Investment Concepts', available at: http://articles.businessinsider.com/2011-11-30/markets/30457741_1_bric-investors-markets (accessed 14 January 2013).

Business Weekly (2011), 'Bank of China Posts Record Profit, Drop in Bad Loans', 24 August, available at: http://www.businessweek.com/

news/2011-08-24/bank-of-china-posts-record-profit-drop-in-bad-loans. html (accessed 13 January 2013).
Busse, D. (1987), *Historische Semantik. Analyse eines Programms*, Stuttgart: Klett-Cotta.
Busse, D. (2000), 'Historische Diskurssemantik. Ein linguistischer Beiträg zur Analyse gesellschaftlichen Wissens', in *Sprache und Literatur in Wissenschaft und Unterricht*, **31** (86), 39–53.
Busse, D. (2013), 'Diskurs-Sprache-Gesellschaftliches Wissen: Perspektiven einer Diskursanalyse nach Foucault im Rahmen einer linguistischen Epistemologie', in D. Busse and W. Teubert (eds), *Linguistische Diskursanalyse: neue Perspektiven*, Wiesbaden: VS Verlag.
Bussolini, J. (2010), 'What is a dispositive?', *Foucault Studies*, **10**, 85–107.
Butler, J. (1990), *Bodies that Matter*, London: Routledge.
Butler, J. (1993), *Gender Trouble: On the Discursive Limits of Sex*, London: Routledge.
Buzan, B. (2001), 'The English School: an underexploited resource in IR', *Review of International Studies*, **27** (3), 471–88.
Cafruny, A.W. and Ryner, M. (2003), 'Introduction: the study of European integration in the neoliberal era', in A.W. Cafruny and M. Ryner (eds), *A Ruined Fortress? Neoliberal Hegemony and Transformation in Europe*, Oxford: Rowman & Littlefield, 1–17.
Calabrese, A. (2004), 'Toward a political economy of culture', in A. Calabrese and C. Sparks (eds), *Toward a Political Economy of Culture: Capitalism and Communication in the Twenty-First Century*, Lanham, MD: Rowman & Littlefield, 1–13.
Caldwell, R. (2007), 'Agency and change: re-evaluating Foucault's legacy', *Organization*, **14** (6), 769–91.
Callon, M. (ed.) (1998), *The Laws of the Market*, Oxford: Blackwell.
Calvert, R.L. (1995), 'Rational actors, equilibrium, and social institutions', in J. Knight and I. Sened (eds), *Explaining Social Institutions*, Ann Arbor, MI: University of Michigan Press, 57–93.
Campbell, D. (1992), *Writing Security: United States Foreign Policy and the Politics of Identity*, Manchester: Manchester University Press.
Campbell, J.L. and Pedersen, O.K. (eds) (2001), *The Rise of Neoliberalism and Institutional Analysis*, Princeton, NJ: Princeton University Press.
Candeias, M. (2005), *Neoliberalismus, Hochtechnologie, Hegemonie. Grundrisse einer transnationalen kapitalistischen Produktions- und Lebensweise*, Hamburg: Argument Verlag.
Candeias, M. (2011), 'Passive revolution vs. socialist transformation', Brussels: Rosa Luxemburg Foundation.
Carannante, A. (1973), 'Antonio *Gramsci* e i problemi della lingua italiana', *Belfagor*, **28** (5), 544–56.

Cardoso, G. (2008), 'From *mass* to *networked communication*: communication models and the information society', *International Journal of Communication*, **2**, 587–630.
Cardoso Machado, N.M. (2011), 'Karl Polanyi and the new economic sociology: notes on the concept of (dis)embeddedness', *RCCS Annual Review*, **3**, available at: http://rccsar.revues.org/309 (accessed 16 April 2013).
Carlaw, K., Nuth, M., Oxley, L., Thorns, D. and Walker, P. (2006), 'Beyond the hype: intellectual property and the knowledge society/knowledge economy', *Journal of Economic Surveys*, **20** (4), 633–90.
Carlucci, A. (2013), *Gramsci and Languages: Unification, Diversity, Hegemony*, Leiden: Brill.
Carroll, W.K. and Carson, C. (2003), 'The network of global corporations and elite policy groups: a structure for transnational capitalist class formation?', *Global Network*, **3** (1), 29–57.
Castoriadis, C. (1987), *The Imaginary Institution of Society*, Cambridge, MA: MIT Press.
Cerny, P. (1990), *The Changing Architecture of Politics: Structure, Agency, and the Future of the State*, London: SAGE.
Chan, A. and Unger, J. (2011), 'Wal-Mart's China connection', *The American Prospect*, 19 April, available at: http://prospect.org/article/wal-mart%E2%80%99s-china-connections (accessed 13 February 2013).
Chandler, M. (2009), 'BRIC or CRIB?', available at: http://seekingalpha.com/author/marc-chandler/comment/549887 (accessed 13 March 2012).
Chappell, L. (2006), 'Comparing political institutions: revealing the gendered "logic of appropriateness"', *Politics & Gender*, **2** (2), 223–35.
Chaput, C. (2010), 'Rhetorical circulation in late capitalism: neoliberalism and the overdetermination of affective energy', *Philosophy and Rhetoric*, **43** (1), 1–18.
Chaput, C. (2011), 'Affect and belonging in late capitalism', *International Journal of Communications*, **5**, 1–20.
Chartier, R. (1988), *Cultural History: Between Practices and Representations*, Cambridge: Polity.
Chaudhuri, P. (2012), 'Expert: why a group of BRICS has pledged cash to a wealthier West', *Asia Society*, available at: http://asiasociety.org/blog/asia/expert-why-group-brics-has-pledged-cash-wealthier-west (accessed 10 July 2013).
Chen, K.-H. and Morley, D. (1996), *Stuart Hall: Critical Dialogues in Cultural Studies*, London: Routledge.
Chesnais, F. (1986), 'Science, technology and competitiveness', *STI Review*, **1** (Autumn), 86–129.
China Daily (2013), 'No single standard on suffrage', *China Daily*,

Hong Kong edn, 18 April, available at: http://chinaelectionsblog.net/hkfocus/?p=549 (accessed 24 April 2013).

Cho, D.S. and Moon, H.C. (2000), *From Adam Smith to Michael Porter: Evolution of Competitiveness Theory*, Singapore: World Scientific Publishing.

Choi, T.-M., Liu, S.-C., Pang, K.-M. and Chow, P.-S. (2007), 'Shopping behaviors of individual tourists from the Chinese Mainland to Hong Kong', *Tourism Management*, July, available at: http://lms.ctu.edu.vn/dokeos/courses/KT321/document/LUOC_KHAO_TAI_LIEU/shopping_behavior_of_tourists_in_hong_kong.pdf (accessed 14 February 2013).

Chorus, S. (2012), *Care-Ökonomie in Postfordismus: Perspektiven einer integralen Ökonomietheorie*, Münster: Westfälisches Dampfboot.

Chouliaraki, L. and Fairclough, N. (1999), *Discourse in Late Modernity: Rethinking Critical Discourse Analysis*, Edinburgh: Edinburgh University Press.

Christopher, M. (2005), *Logistics and Supply Chain Management*, Harlow: Pearson Education.

Clark, T. and Fincham, R. (eds) (2002), *Critical Consulting: New Perspectives on Management Advice Industry*, Oxford: Blackwell.

Clarke, J. and Newman, J. (1997), *The Managerial State*, London: SAGE.

Clean Clothes Campaign (2005), 'Looking for a Quick Fix: How Weak Social Auditing is Keeping Workers in Sweatshops', available at: http://www.cleanclothes.org/resources/publications/05-quick-fix.pdf/view (accessed 14 February 2013).

Clean Clothes Campaign (2009), 'Cashing In: Giant Retailers, Purchasing Practices and Working Conditions in the Garment Industry', available at: http://www.cleanclothes.org/resources/publications/cashing-in.pdf/view (accessed 14 February 2013).

Coase, R.H. (1937), 'The nature of the firm', *Economica*, **4**, 386–405.

Collier, P. (2007), *The Bottom Billion: Why the Poorest Countries Are Failing and What Can Be Done About It*, Oxford: Oxford University Press.

Collier, S.J. (2009), 'Topologies of power: Foucault's analysis of political "governmentality"', *Theory, Culture & Society*, **26** (6), 78–108.

Collins, D. (2000), *Management Fads and Buzzwords: Critical–Practical Perspective*, London: Routledge.

Collins, P.H. (1998), 'It's all in the family: intersections of gender, race, and nation', *Hypatia*, **13** (3), 62–82.

Cornwall, A. (2007), 'Buzzwords and fuzzwords: deconstructing development discourse', *Development in Practice*, **17** (4–5), 471–84.

Cornwall, R. (1998), 'A primer on queer theory for economists interested in social identities', *Feminist Economics*, **4** (2), 73–82.
CorpWatch (2012), 'Greenwashing Wal-Mart', available at: http://www.corpwatch.org/article.php?id=15707 (accessed 10 March 2013).
Coté, M.E. (2007), *The Italian Foucault: Communication, Networks, and the Dispositif*, PhD dissertation, Burnaby, BC: Simon Fraser University.
Council on Competitiveness (2001), *U.S. Competitiveness 2001: Strengths, Vulnerabilities and Long-Term Priorities*, Washington, DC.
Council on Competitiveness (2007), *Five for the Future. Roadmap for Competitiveness in the 21st Century*, Washington, DC.
Council on Competitiveness (2009), '*Rebound*'. *Three Essentials to Get the Economy Back on Track*, Washington, DC.
Council on Competitiveness (2012), *Making Impact: Annual Report 2011–12*, Washington, DC.
Cousins, M. and Hussain, A. (1984), *Michel Foucault*, London: Macmillan.
Coward, R. and Ellis, J. (1977), *Language and Materialism: Developments in Semiology and the Theory of the Subject*, London: Routledge & Kegan Paul.
Cox, J., Mann, L. and Samson, D. (1997), 'Benchmarking as a mixed metaphor: disentangling assumptions of competition and collaboration', *Journal of Management Studies*, **34** (2), 285–314.
Cox, R.W. (1981), 'Social forces, states and world orders: beyond international relations theory', *Millennium*, **10** (2), 126–55.
Cox, R.W. (1983), 'Gramsci, hegemony and international relations: an essay in method', *Millennium*, **12** (3), 162–75.
Cox, R.W. (1987), *Production, Power and World Order: Social Forces in the Making of History*, New York: Columbia University Press.
Cox, R.W. (1992), 'Multilateralism and world order', *Review of International Studies*, **18** (2), 161–80.
Cox, R.W. (1995), 'Critical political economy', in B. Hettne (ed.), *International Political Economy: Understanding Global Disorder*, London: Zed Books.
Cox, R.W. (1996), 'Global "Perestroika"', in R. Cox with T.J. Sinclair (eds), *Approaches to World Order*, Cambridge: Cambridge University Press, 296–313.
Cox, R.W. with Schecter, M.G. (2002), *The Political Economy of a Plural World: Critical Reflections on Power, Morals and Civilization*, London: Routledge.
Craik, J. (1995), 'Mapping the links between cultural studies and cultural policy', *Southern Review*, **28** (2), 190–207.

Crampton, J.W. and Elden, S. (eds) (2007), *Space, Knowledge and Power: Foucault and Geography*, Aldershot: Ashgate.

Crocombe, G., Enright, M. and Porter, M. (1991), *Upgrading New Zealand's Competitive Advantage*, Oxford: Oxford University Press.

Crotty, J. (2009), 'The structural causes of the financial crisis', *Cambridge Journal of Economics*, **33** (4), 536–80.

Crouch, C. (2004), *Post-Democracy*, Cambridge: Polity.

Crouch, C. (2005), *Capitalist Diversity and Change: Recombinant Governance and Institutional Entrepreneurs*, Oxford: Oxford University Press.

Crowder, M. (1978), *Colonial West Africa*, London: Taylor & Francis.

Cruikshank, B. (1999), *The Will to Empower*, Ithaca, NY: Cornell University Press.

Cutler, C., Haufler, V. and Porter, T. (eds) (1999), *Private Authority and International Affairs*, Albany, NY: State University of New York Press.

D'Andrea Tyson, L. (1988), 'Competitiveness: an analysis of the problem and a perspective of future policy', in M. Starr (ed.), *Global Competitiveness, Getting the U.S. Back on Track*, New York: W.W. Norton, 95–120.

David, P. and Foray, D. (1995), 'Assessing and expanding the science and technology knowledge base', *STI Review*, **16**, 13–68.

Davies, H. (2010), *The Financial Crisis, Who is to Blame?*, Cambridge: Polity.

Davies, M. (1999), *International Political Economy and Mass Communications in Chile: Transnational Hegemony and National Intellectuals*, Basingstoke: Macmillan.

Davies, N. (2007), 'Corporate reputation management, the Wal-Mart way: exploring effective strategies in the global market place', Senior Honours Thesis, Texas A&M University, available at: http://repository.tamu.edu/bitstream/handle/1969.1/5687/Microsoft+Word+-+TEMPLATE.pdf?sequence=1 (accessed 24 February 2013).

de Certeau, M. (1984), *Practice of Everyday Life*, Berkeley, CA: University of California Press.

de Goede, M. (2003), 'Beyond economism in international political economy', *Review of International Studies*, **29** (1), 79–97.

de Koning, J. and Cleaver, F. (2012), 'Institutional bricolage in community forestry', in B. Arts et al. (eds), *Forest People Interfaces*, Wageningen: Wageningen Academic Publishers, 277–90.

de Jong, E. (2009), *Culture and Economics*, New York: Routledge.

de Vroey, M. (1984), 'A regulation approach interpretation of the contemporary crisis', *Capital & Class*, **23**, 45–66.

Dean, M. (1994), *Critical and Effective Histories: Foucault's Methods and Historical Sociology*, London: Routledge.
Dean, M. (1999), *Governmentality*, London: SAGE.
Debray, R. (1973), *Prison Writings*, London: Allen Lane.
Debray, R. (1991), *Cours de Médiologie Générale*, Paris: Gallimard.
Debray, R. (1996), *Media Manifestos: On the Technological Transmission of Cultural Forms*, London: Verso.
Debray, R. (2000), *Introduction à la médiologie*, Paris: PUF.
Degele, N. and Winker, G. (2009), *Intersektionalität: Zur Analyse sozialer Ungleichheiten*, Bielefeld: Transcript.
Deleuze, G. (1992), 'What is a dispositif?', in T.J. Armstrong (ed.), *Michel Foucault: Philosopher*, London: Routledge, 159–68.
Demirović, A. (1992), 'Regulation und Politik. Integrale Ökonomie und integraler Staat', in A. Demirović, H.-P. Krebs and T. Sablowski (eds) (1992), *Hegemonie und Staat. Kapitalistische Regulation als Projekt und Prozess*, Münster: Westfälisches Dampfboot, 232–62.
Demirović, A. (1999), *Der nonkonformistische Intellektuelle*, Frankfurt: Suhrkamp.
Demirović, A., Krebs, H.-P. and Sablowski, T. (eds) (1992), *Hegemonie und Staat. Kapitalistische Regulation als Projekt und Prozess*, Münster: Westfälisches Dampfboot.
Derrida, J. (1988), *Limited Inc.*, Evanston IL: North Western University Press.
Destutt de Tracy, Comte (1796 [1804]), *Eléments de l'idéologie*, Paris: Courcier.
Deudney, D. (2000), 'Geopolitics as theory: historical security materialism', *European Journal of International Relations*, **6**, 77–107.
Deutsch, K.W. (1963), *The Nerves of Government*, New York: Free Press.
Deyo, F.C. (2013), 'Addressing the development deficit of competition policy: the role of economic networks', in M.C. Dowdle, J. Gillespie and I. Maher (eds), *Asian Capitalism and the Regulation of Competition*, Cambridge: Cambridge University Press, 283–300.
Diebert, R.J. (1999), 'Harold Innis and the empire of speed', *Review of International Studies*, **25** (2), 273–89.
Dierse, U. (1982), 'Ideologie', in O. Brunner, W. Conze and R. Koselleck (eds), *Geschichtliche Grundbegriffe*, Band 3, Stuttgart: Klett-Cotta, 131–70.
Diettrech, B. (1999), *Klassenfragmentierung im Postfordismus: Geschlecht, Arbeit, Rassismus, Marginalisierung*, Hamburg: UNRAST Verlag.
Dikshit, S. (2013), 'BRICS Bank to focus on funding infrastructural development', *The Hindu*, 27 March, available at: http://www.thehindu.

com/business/Economy/brics-bank-to-focus-on-funding-infrastructure-development/article4554773.ece (accessed 4 April 2013).

DiMaggio, P. (1998), 'The new institutionalisms: avenues of collaboration', *Journal of Institutional and Theoretical Economics*, **154** (4), 696–705.

Diskin, J. and Sandler, B. (1993), 'Essentialism and the economy in the post-Marxist imaginary: reopening the sutures', *Rethinking Marxism*, **6** (3), 28–48.

Djelic, M.-L. (2010), 'Institutional perspectives – working towards coherence or irreconcilable diversity?', in G. Morgan et al. (eds), *Oxford Handbook of Comparative Institutional Analysis*, Oxford: Oxford University Press, 15–40.

Dollery, B.E. and Wallis, J. (1999), *Market Failure, Government Failure, Leadership and Public Policy*, Basingstoke: Macmillan.

Domain-b.com (2011), 'Bharti Walmart to More Than Double Wholesale Stores in India This Year', 24 May, available at: http://www.domain-b.com/companies/companies_b/Bharti_Enterprises/20110524_wholesale_stores.html (accessed 23 January 2013).

Dordick, H.S. and Wang, G. (1993), *The Information Society. A Retrospective View*, London: SAGE.

Dosi, G. and Soete, L. (1988), 'Technical change and international trade', in G. Dosi (ed.), *Technical Change and Economic Theory*, London: Pinter, 401–31.

Drahos, P. (1996), *A Philosophy of Intellectual Property*, Aldershot: Dartmouth.

Drezner, D.J. (2009), 'BRIC-à-Brac', available at: http://drezner.foreignpolicy.com/posts/2009/06/17/bric-a-brac (accessed 5 March 2013).

Du Gay, P. and Pryke, M. (eds) (2002), *Cultural Economy: Cultural Analysis and Commercial Life*, London: SAGE.

Dubet, F. (2002), *Le déclin de l'institution*, Paris: Seuil.

Ducatel, K., Webster, J. and Herrmann, W. (2000), 'Information infrastructures or societies', in K. Ducatel, J. Webster and W. Hermann (eds), *The Information Society in Europe*, Oxford: Rowman & Littlefield, 1–17.

Duggan, L. (1994), 'Queering the state', *Social Text*, **39**, 1–14.

Duménil, G. (1978), *Le concept de loi économique dans 'Le Capital'*, Paris: Maspero.

Duménil, G. and Lévy, D. (2004), *Capital Resurgent. Roots of the Neoliberal Revolution*, Cambridge, MA: Harvard University Press.

Dumez, H. and Jeunemaître, A. (2010), 'Michel Callon, Michel Foucault and the «*dispositif*». When economics fails to be performative: a case study', *Le Libellio d' AEGIS*, **6** (4), 27–37.

Dunning, J. (1992), 'The competitiveness of countries and the activities of transnational corporations', *Transnational Corporations*, **1** (1), 135–68.
Durkheim, E. (1938), *Rules of Sociological Method*, London: Collier-Macmillan.
Eade, D. (1997), *Capacity Building: An Approach to People-Centred Development*, Oxford: Oxfam.
Eagleton, T. (1991), *Ideology: An Introduction*, London: Verso.
Eco, U. (1976), *A Theory of Semiotics*, London: Macmillan.
Eco, U. (1984), *Semiotics and the Philosophy of Language*, Basingstoke: Macmillan.
Economic Times (India) (2012), 'Wal-Mart Looks to Source More Farm Items from India', 1 April, available at: http://articles.economictimes.indiatimes.com/2012-04-01/news/31270328_1_bharti-walmart-pvt-indian-farmers-source (accessed 23 January 2013).
Edenius, M. and Hasselbladh, H. (2002), 'The balanced scorecard as an intellectual technology', *Organization*, **9** (2), 29–73.
Egan, D. (2001), 'The limits of internationalization: a neo-Gramscian analysis on the Multilateral Agreement on Investment', *Critical Sociology*, **27** (3), 74–86.
Eggertsson, T. (1990), *Economic Behavior and Institutions*, Cambridge: Cambridge University Press.
Ehlich, K. (1983), 'Text und sprachliches Handeln. Die Entstehung von Texten aus dem Bedürfnis nach Überlieferung', in A. Assmann, J. Assmann and C. Hardmeier (eds), *Schrift und Gedächtnis. Beiträge zur Archäologie der literarischen Kommunikation*, München: Fink, 24–43.
Eisenstadt, S.N. (1968), 'Social institutions', in D. Sills (ed.), *International Encyclopedia of the Social Sciences*, New York: Macmillan and Free Press, **14**, 409–29.
Ekers, M. and Loftus, A. (2008), 'The power of water: developing dialogues between Foucault and Gramsci', *Environment and Planning D: Society and Space*, **26** (4), 698–718.
Eklund, M. (2007), *Adoption of the Innovation System Concept in Sweden*, Uppsala: Uppsala University.
Elden, S. (2007), 'Rethinking governmentality', *Political Geography*, **26**, 29–33.
Elder-Vass, D. (2007), 'Reconciling Archer and Bourdieu in an emergentist theory of action', *Sociological Theory*, **25** (4), 325–46.
Elson, D. (1979), 'The value theory of labour', in D. Elson (ed.), *Value: The Representation of Labour in Capitalism*, London: CSE Books, 115–80.
Elster, J., Offe, C. and Preuss, U.K. (1998), *Institutional Design in Post-Communist Societies: Rebuilding the Ship at Sea*, Cambridge: Cambridge University Press.

Engels, F. (1987) [1876], 'The part played by labour in the transition from ape to man', in *Marx–Engels Collected Works, Vol. 25*, London: Lawrence & Wishart, 452–64.

Engelen, E., Ertürk, I., Froud, J., Johal, S., Leaver, A., Moran, M., Nilsson, A. and Williams, K. (2011), *After The Great Complacence: Financial Crisis and the Politics of Reform*, Oxford: Oxford University Press.

Enright, M. (1998), 'Transcript of Professor Michael Enright's Response', Conference on 'Hong Kong's Competitiveness' organized by the Central Policy Unit of the HKSAR Government, available at: http://www.cpu.gov.hk/txt_en/events_conferences_seminars/conference_19980422.html (accessed 4 April 2013).

Enright, M., Chang, K.-M., Scott, E. and Zhu, W.-H. (2003), *Hong Kong and the Pearl River Delta: The Economic Interaction*, Hong Kong: The 2022 Foundation.

Enright, M., Scott, E. and Dodwell, D. (1997), *The Hong Kong Advantage*, Hong Kong: Oxford University Press.

Enright, M., Scott, E. and Ng, K.-M. (2005), *Regional Powerhouse: The Greater Pearl River Delta and the Rise of China*, London: John Wiley & Sons.

Enright, M. and Scott, E. & Associates (2007), 'The Greater Pearl River Delta', 5th edn, *InvestHK*, available at: http://www.investhk.gov.hk/UploadFile/GPRD_5th.pdf (accessed 15 February 2013).

Ensminger (1998), 'Anthropology and the new institutionalism', *Journal of Institutional and Theoretical Economics*, **154**, 774–89.

Esser, J., Görg, C. and Hirsch, J. (eds) (1994), *Politik, Institutionen und Staat. Zur Kritik der Regulationstheorie*, Hamburg: VSA.

Esser, K., Hillebrand, W., Messner, D. and Meyer-Stamer, J. (1996), *Systemic Competitiveness: New Governance Patterns for Industrial Development*, London: Cass.

Etzkowitz, H. (1994), 'Academic–industry relations: a sociological paradigm for economic development', in L. Leydesdorff and P. van den Desselaar (eds), *Evolutionary Economics and Chaos Theory*, London: Pinter, 139–51.

European Commission (1993), *White Paper on Growth, Competitiveness and Employment*, available at: http://europa.eu/documentation/offical-docs/white-papers/pdf/growth_wp_com_93_700_parts_a_b.pdf (accessed 8 July 2013).

European Commission (1995), *Green Paper on Innovation*, available at: http://europa.eu/documents/comm/green_papers/pdf/com95_688_en.pdf (accessed 8 July 2013).

European Commission (2000), *Lisbon Strategy for Competitiveness*, available at: http://europarl.europa.eu/summits/lis1_en.htm (accessed 8 July 2013).

European Commission (2012), *European Competitiveness Report: Reaping the Benefits of Globalization*, available at: http://ec.europa.eu/enterprise/policies/industrial-competitiveness/competitiveness-analysis/european-competitiveness-report/files/2012_full_en.pdf (accessed 8 July 2013).

Evans, P.B., Rueschemeyer, D. and Skocpol, T. (eds) (1985), *Bringing the State Back In*, Cambridge: Cambridge University Press.

Fagerberg, J. (1996), 'Technology and competitiveness', *Oxford Review of Economic Policy*, **12** (3), 39.

Fairclough, N. (1989), *Language and Power*, Harlow: Longman.

Fairclough, N. (1992), *Discourse and Social Change*, Cambridge, MA: Blackwell.

Fairclough, N. (1993), 'Critical discourse analysis and the marketisation of public discourse: the universities', *Discourse & Society*, **4** (2), 133–68.

Fairclough, N. (2000), *New Labour, New Language*, London: Routledge.

Fairclough, N. (2001), *Language and Power*, 2nd edn, London: Longman.

Fairclough, N. (2003), *Analysing Discourse*, London: Routledge.

Fairclough, N. (2005), 'Critical discourse analysis', *Marges Linguistiques*, **9**, 76–94.

Fairclough, N. (2006a), *Language and Globalization*, London: Routledge.

Fairclough, N. (2006b), 'Semiosis, mediation and ideology: a dialectical view', in I. Lassen, J. Strunck and T. Vestergaard (eds), *Mediating Ideology in Text and Image: Ten Critical Studies*, Amsterdam: John Benjamins, 19–35.

Fairclough, N. and Graham, P. (2002), 'Marx as a critical discourse analyst: the genesis of a critical method and its relevance to the critique of global capital', *Journal Estudios de Sociolinguistica*, **3** (1), 185–229.

Fairclough, N., Jessop, B. and Sayer, A. (2004), 'Critical realism and semologic', in J.M. Roberts and J. Joseph (eds), *Realism, Discourse and Deconstruction*, London: Routledge, 23–42.

Farrell, T. (2002), 'Constructivist security studies: portrait of a research program', *International Studies Review*, **4** (1), 49–72.

Favereau, O. (1997), 'L'incomplétude n'est pas le problème, c'est la solution', in B. Reynaud (ed.), *Les limites de la rationalité, tome 2. Les figurs du collectif*, Paris: La Découverte, 219–33.

Favereau, O. (2002a), 'Conventions and régulation', in R. Boyer and Y. Saillard (eds), *Régulation Theory*, London: Routledge, 312–19.

Favereau, O. (2002b), 'L'économie du sociologue ou penser (l'orthodoxie) à partir de Bourdieu', in B. Lahire (ed.), *Le travail sociologique de Pierre Bourdieu: dettes et critiques*, Paris: La Découverte, 255–14.

Febvre, L. (1979), *Life in Renaissance France*, Cambridge MA: Harvard University Press.

Fei, M. (2012), 'Bordering on madness', *People's Daily*, 13 October, available at: http://www.chinadaily.com.cn/hkedition/2012-10/13/content_15814816.htm (accessed 13 January 2013).
Ferguson, A. (1990), 'The intersection of race, gender, and class in the United States today', *Rethinking Marxism*, **3** (3–4), 45–64.
Ferguson, N. and Schularick, M. (2007), '"Chimerica" and the global asset market boom', *International Finance*, **10** (3), 215–39.
Ferguson, N. and Schularick, M. (2011), 'The end of Chimerica', *International Finance*, **14** (1), 1–26.
Feyerabend, P.K. (1978), *Against Method*, London: NLB.
Financial Secretary's Office (2010), '2010 Update of CEPA's Impact on the Hong Kong economy (Individual Visit Scheme)', available at: http://www.tid.gov.hk/english/cepa/statistics/files/individual_visit.pdf (accessed 13 January 2013).
Fine, B. (2001), '"Economics imperialism": a view from the periphery', *Review of Radical Political Economics*, **34** (2), 187–201.
Finnemore, M. and Sikkink, K. (2001), 'Taking stock: the constructivist research program in international relations and comparative politics', *Annual Review of Political Science*, **4**, 391–416.
Fischer, A.M. (2011), 'The perils of paradigm maintenance in the face of crisis', in P. Utting, S. Razavi and R. Buchholz (eds), *Global Crisis and Transformative Social Change*, Basingstoke: Palgrave, 43–62.
Fischer, C. (2011), 'Green Competitiveness', available at: http://ec.europa.eu/economy_finance/events/2011/2011-11-21-annual-research-conference_en/pdf/session032_fischer_en.pdf (accessed 10 April 2013).
Fischer, F. and Forester, J. (eds) (1993), *The Argumentative Turn in Policy Analysis and Planning*, Durham, NC: Duke University Press.
FlorCruz, J. (2009), 'Will the China Property Bubble Pop?', available at: http://www.cnn.com/2009/BUSINESS/12/30/china.property.bubble/index.html (accessed 14 February 2013).
Flores Farfán, J.A. and Holzscheiter, A. (2011), 'The power of discourse and the discourse of power', in R. Wodak, B. Johnstone and P. Kerswill (eds), *The SAGE Handbook of Sociolinguistics*, London: SAGE, 139–52.
Florida, R. (2002), *The Rise of the Creative Class*, New York: Perseus.
Florida, R. (2005), 'The world is spiky: globalization has changed the economic playing field, but hasn't levelled it', *Atlantic Monthly*, October, 48–51.
Foray, D. and Lundvall, B.-Å. (1996), 'The knowledge-based economy: from the economics of knowledge to the learning economy', in D. Foray and B.-Å. Lundvall (eds), *Employment and Growth in the Knowledge-Based Economy*, Paris: OECD, 11–32.
Forester, J. (1993), 'Learning from practice stories: the priority of practi-

cal judgment', in F. Fischer and J. Forester (eds), *The Argumentative Turn in Policy Analysis and Planning*, Durham, NC: Duke University Press, 186–212.

Forgacs, D. and Nowell-Smith, G. (1985), 'Introduction', in A. Gramsci, *Selections from Cultural Writings*, London: Lawrence and Wishart.

Forgues, B. and Roux-Dufort, C. (1998), 'Crises: events or processes', Working Paper 98-71, Hazards and Sustainability Conference, Durham, UK, 26–27 May, available at: http://cermat.iae.univ-tours.fr/IMG/pdf/CAHIER_1998-71_FORGUES_ROUX_DUFORT_crises_events_or_proces_.pdf (accessed 13 April 2013).

Foucault, M. (1970 [1966]), *The Order of Things: An Archaeology of Human Sciences*, New York: Pantheon.

Foucault, M. (1972), *Archaeology of Knowledge*, London: Tavistock.

Foucault, M. (1977 [1975]), *Discipline and Punish: The Birth of a Prison*, trans. A. Sheridan, London: Allen Lane.

Foucault, M. (1979), *History of Sexuality: Volume 1: Introduction*, trans. R. Hurley, London: Allen Lane.

Foucault, M. (1980), *Power/Knowledge: Selected Writings and Other Interviews 1972–1977*, trans. C. Gordon, L. Marshall, J. Mepham and K. Soper, Brighton: Wheatsheaf.

Foucault, M. (1984), Personal letter to Joe Buttigieg, 20 April, cited in J. Buttigieg (ed.), 'Introduction', in A. Gramsci, *Prison Notebooks, Volume 1*, New York: Columbia University Press.

Foucault, M. (1991), 'Governmentality', in G. Burchell, C. Gordon and P. Miller (eds), *The Foucault Effect: Studies in Governmentality*, London: Harvester Wheatsheaf, 87–104.

Foucault, M. (1996), 'The discourse of history', in M. Foucault, *Foucault Live: Collected Interviews, 1961–1984*, New York: Autonomedia, 19–32.

Foucault, M. (2003), *'Society must be Defended'. Lectures at the Collège de France 1975–1976*, New York: Picador.

Foucault, M. (2008a), *Security, Territory, Population, Lectures at the Collège de France, 1977–1978*, Basingstoke: Palgrave.

Foucault, M. (2008b), *The Birth of Biopolitics: Lectures at the Collège de France, 1978–1979*, Basingstoke: Palgrave

Fraser, N. and Bartky, S. (eds) (1992), *Revaluing French Feminism*, Bloomington and Indianapolis, IN: Indiana University Press.

Free, C. (2008), 'Walking the talk? Supply chain accounting and trust among UK supermarkets and suppliers', *Accounting, Organizations, and Society*, **33**, 629–62.

Freeman, C. (1982), *Economics of Industrial Innovation*, London: Pinter.

Freeman, C. (1995), 'The "national system of innovation" in historical perspective', *Cambridge Journal of Economics*, **19** (1), 5–24.

Frege, G. (1984 [1892]), 'On sense and meaning', in B. McGuiness (ed.), *Gottlob Frege: Collected Papers on Mathematics, Logic, and Philosophy*, Oxford: Blackwell, 157–77.
French, J.D. (2006), 'Wal-Mart, retail supremacy and the relevance of political economy', *Labour Studies in Working-Class History of the Americas*, **4** (1), 33–40.
Friedman, M. (1962), *Capitalism and Freedom*, Chicago, IL: University of Chicago Press.
Friedman, T.L. (2005), *The World is Flat: A History of the 21st Century*, New York: Farrer & Giroux.
Fung, V. (1998), 'Keynote Speech on "Adding value to Hong Kong's competitiveness"', Hong Kong Trade Development Council at the HKSAR Government Central Policy Unit Seminar, available at: http://info.hktdc.com/tdcnews/9804/98042201.htm (accessed 4 August 2012).
Gal, S. (1989), 'Language and political economy', *American Review of Anthropology*, **18**, 345–67.
Galbraith, J.K. (1967), *The New Industrial State*, Harmondsworth: Penguin.
Gardiner, M. (1992), *The Dialogics of Critique: M.M. Bakhtin and the Theory of Ideology*, London: Routledge.
Garud, R., Hardy, C. and Maguire, S. (2007), 'Institutional entrepreneurship as embedded agency', *Organization Studies*, **28** (7), 957–69.
Geertz, C. (1975), *Interpretation of Culture*, Chicago, IL: University of Chicago Press.
Gereffi, G. and Korzeniewicz, M. (eds) (1994), *Commodity Chains and Global Capitalism*, Westport, CT: Praeger.
Gereffi, G. and Ong, R. (2007), 'Wal-Mart in China: can the world's largest retailer succeed in the world's most populous market?', *Harvard Asia Pacific Review*, **9** (1), 46–9.
Germain, R. and Kenny, M. (1998), 'Engaging Gramsci: international relations theory and the new Gramscians', *Review of International Studies*, **24** (1), 3–21.
Gibson, J.J. (1979), *The Ecological Approach to Perception*, London: Houghton Mifflin.
Gibson, K. and Graham, J. (2008), 'Diverse economies: performative practices for "other worlds"', *Progress in Human Geography*, **32** (5), 613–32.
Gibson-Graham, J.K. (1995), *The End of Capitalism (As We Knew It): Feminist Political Economy*, Oxford: Blackwell.
Giddens, A. (1984), *The Constitution of Society*, Cambridge: Polity.
Gill, S. (1991a), *American Hegemony and the Trilateral Commission*, Cambridge: Cambridge University Press.

Gill, S. (1991b), 'Historical materialism, Gramsci, and international political economy', in C.N. Murphy and R. Tooze (eds), *The New International Political Economy*, Boulder, CO: Lynne Rienner, 51–75.

Gill, S. (1992), 'Epistemology, ontology and the "Italian School"', in S. Gill (ed.), *Gramsci, Historical Materialism and International Relations*, Cambridge: Cambridge University Press, 21–48.

Gill, S. (1995a), 'Globalisation, market civilisation, and disciplinary neo-liberalism', *Millennium*, **24**, 399–423.

Gill, S. (1995b), 'The Global panopticon? The neoliberal state, economic life, and democratic surveillance', *Alternatives*, **20** (2), 1–49.

Gill, S. (1997), 'Finance, production and panopticism: inequality, risk and resistance in an era of disciplinary neo-liberalism', in S. Gill (ed.), *Globalization, Democratization and Multilateralism*, Basingstoke: Macmillan, 51–76.

Gill, S. (1998), 'European governance and the new constitutionalism: economic and monetary union and alternatives to disciplinary neo-liberalism', *New Political Economy*, **3** (1), 5–26.

Gill, S. (2002), 'Privatization of the State and Social Reproduction? GATS and New Constitutionalism', paper presented at the Centre for the Study of Globalization and Regionalization Workshop on GATS: Trading Development, University of Warwick, Coventry, 20–21 September.

Gill, S. (2003a), 'The post-Modern Prince', in S. Gill (ed.), *Power and Resistance in the New World Order*, New York: Palgrave, 211–21.

Gill, S. (2003b), 'A neo-Gramscian approach to European integration', in A.W. Cafruny and M. Ryner (eds), *A Ruined Fortress? Neoliberal Hegemony and Transformation in Europe*, Oxford: Rowman & Littlefield, 17–47.

Gill, S. (2011), 'Leaders and led in an era of global crises', in S. Gill (ed.), *Global Crises and Crisis of Global Leadership*, Cambridge: Cambridge University Press, 23–37.

Glaser, B.G. and Strauss, A.L. (1967), *The Discovery of Grounded Theory. Strategies for Qualitative Research*, New Brunswick, NJ: Transaction Books.

Global Times (2010), 'Land Transfer Now Major Source of Local Governments' Fiscal Revenues: A Report', available at: http://www.globaltimes.cn/business/china-economy/2010-12/606958.html (accessed 26 January 2013).

Global Times (2012), 'Hong Kong Wants Mainland Tourists but not Too Many', available at: http://www.globaltimes.cn/content/737185.shtml (accessed 13 January 2013).

Glynos, J. and Howarth, D. (2007), *Logics of Critical Explanation in Social and Political Theory*, London: Routledge.

Godin, B. (2004), 'The new economy: what the concept owes to the OECD', *Research Policy*, **33**, 679–90.
Godin, B. (2006), 'The knowledge-based economy: conceptual framework or buzzword?', *Journal of Technology Transfer*, **31** (1), 17–30.
Goffman, E. (1961), *Asylums: Essays on the Social Situation of Mental Patients and Other Inmates*, New York: Anchor Books.
Goh, K.S. (1996), 'The technology ladder in development: the Singapore case', *Asian-Pacific Economic Literature*, **10** (1), 1–12.
Goldman Sachs (2001), 'Building Better Global Economic Brics', Goldman Sachs Global Economic Paper no. 66, available at: www.goldmansachs.com/our.../brics/brics.../build-better-brics.pdf (accessed 10 January 2012).
Goldman Sachs (2010), 'Idea' Website on BRIC, available at: http://www2.goldmansachs.com/ideas/brics/index.html (accessed 10 January 2012).
Goodin, R.E. (1996), 'Institutions and their design', in R.E. Goodin (ed.), *The Theory of Institutional Design*, Cambridge: Cambridge University Press, 1–53.
Goodin, R.E. and Tilly, C. (eds) (2006), *The Oxford Handbook of Contextual Political Analysis*, Oxford: Oxford University Press.
Goodstadt, L. (2005), *Uneasy Partners: The Conflict between Public Interest and Private Profit in Hong Kong*, Hong Kong: Hong Kong University Press.
Goodwin, M. and Painter, J. (1997), 'Concrete research, urban regimes and regulation theory', in M. Lauria (ed.), *Restructuring Urban Regime Theory*, London: SAGE, 13–29.
Görg, C. and Brand, U. (2002), 'Konflikte über "das grüne Gold" des Gene', *Prokla*, **129**, 631–52.
Gorz, A. (1980), *Ecology as Politics*, London: Pluto Press.
Gough, J. (1991), 'Structure, system, and contradiction in the capitalist space economy', *Environment and Planning D: Society and Space*, **9** (4), 433–49.
Gough, J. (2004), 'Changing scale as changing class relations: variety and contradiction in the politics of scale', *Political Geography*, **23** (2), 185–211.
Graça, J.C. (2005), 'Afinal, o que é mesmo a Nova Sociologia Económica?', *Revista Crítica de Ciências Sociais*, **73**, 111–29.
Grafstein, R. (1992), *Institutional Realism. Social and Political Constraints on Rational Actors*, New Haven, CT: Yale University Press.
Graham, P.W. (2001), 'Space: irrealis objects in technology policy and their role in a new political economy', *Discourse & Society*, **12** (6), 761–88.

Gramsci, A. (1971), *Selections from the Prison Notebooks*, London: Lawrence & Wishart.

Gramsci, A. (1975), *Quaderni del Carcere*, 4 vols, Turin: Einaudi.

Gramsci, A. (1985), *Selections from Cultural Writings*, London: Lawrence & Wishart.

Gramsci, A. (1995), *Further Selections from the Prison Notebooks*, London: Lawrence & Wishart.

Gray, H.P. (1991), 'International competitiveness: a review article', *International Trade Journal*, **5** (4), 503–17.

Gregg, M. (2006), *Cultural Studies' Affective Voices*, Basingstoke: Palgrave-Macmillan.

Greimas, A.J. (1958), 'Histoire et linguistique', *Annales*, **13**, 110–14.

Greenspan, A. (2008), 'Evidence given on 23 October 2008', Washington, DC: House Committee on Oversight and Government Reform.

Greenwood, R., Oliver, C., Sahlin-Andersson, K. and Suddaby, R. (eds) (2008), *The Sage Handbook of Organizational Institutionalism*, London: SAGE.

Grice, H.P. (1989), *Studies in the Way of Words*, Cambridge, MA: Harvard University Press.

Grint, K. and Woolgar, S. (1997), *The Machine at Work*, Cambridge: Polity.

Grossberg, L. (1993), 'Cultural studies and new worlds', in C. McCarthy and W. Crichlow (eds), *Race, Identity and Representation*, New York: Routledge, 89–95.

Grossberg, L. (2006), 'Does cultural studies have futures? Should it? (Or what's the matter with New York?)', *Cultural Studies*, **20** (1), 1–32.

Grossberg, L. (2010), *Cultural Studies in the Future Tense*, Durham, NC: Duke University Press.

Gulati, M. (1988), 'SME cluster development programme', in J.S. Juneja (ed.), *Small and Medium Enterprises – Challenges and Opportunities*, New Delhi: AIMA, Excel Books, 173–212.

Günther, H. (1982), 'Herrschaft', in O. Brunner, W. Conze and R. Koselleck (eds), *Geschichtliche Grundbegriffe. Historisches Lexikon zur politisch-sozialen Sprache in Deutschland*, Band 3, Stuttgart: Klett-Cotta, 101–202.

Hajer, M.A. (2011), *Authoritative Governance: Policy Making in the Age of Mediatization*, Oxford: Oxford University Press.

Hall, P.A. and Soskice, D. (eds) (2001), *Varieties of Capitalism: The Institutional Foundations of Comparative Advantage*, Oxford: Oxford University Press.

Hall, P.A. and Taylor, R.C.R. (1996), 'Political science and the three new institutionalisms', *Political Studies*, **44** (4), 936–57.

Hall, S. (1980), 'Cultural Studies: two paradigms', *Media, Culture and Society*, **2**, 57–72.

Halley, J. and Parker, A. (eds) (2007), *After Sex? On Writing Since Queer Theory*, Special Issue of *South Atlantic Quarterly*, Durham, NC: Duke University Press.

Hämäläinen, T.J. (2003), *National Competitiveness and Economic Growth: The Changing Determinants of Economic Performance in the World Economy*, Cheltenham, UK and Northampton, MA, USA: Edward Elgar.

Hancock, J. and Greenhill, R. (2009), 'News of globalization's death vastly exaggerated', *Toronto Star*, 6 December.

Hanfling, O. (2002), *Wittgenstein and the Human Form of Life*, London: Routledge.

Hang Seng Economic Focus (2011), 'The Tourist Industry', available at: http://www.hangseng.com/cms/tpr/eng/analyses/PDF/ecof_e_ 2011a pr.pdf (accessed 13 January 2013).

Harder, P. (2011), 'Conceptual construal and social construction', in M. Brdar, S.T. Gries and M.Ž. Fuchs (eds), *Cognitive Linguistics: Convergence and Expansion*, Amsterdam: John Benjamins, 305–42.

Häring, N. and Douglas, N. (2012), *Economists and the Powerful*, London: Anthem Press.

Harribey, J.-M. (1998), *Le Développement Soutenable*, Paris: Economica.

Harris, M. (1980), *Cultural Materialism*, New York: Random House.

Harris, M. (1988), *Culture, People, Nature: An Introduction to General Anthropology*, 5th edn, New York: Harper & Row.

Harris, R. and Watson, W. (1993), 'Three versions of competitiveness: Porter, Reich and Thurow on economic growth and policy', in J. Courchene and D. Purvis (eds), *Productivity, Growth and Canada's International Competitiveness*, Ontario: John Deutsch Institute for the Study of Economic Policy, 233–80.

Hartley, J. (2003), *A Short History of Cultural Studies*, London: SAGE.

Harvey, D. (2005), *A Brief History of Neoliberalism*, Oxford: Oxford University Press.

Haug, W.F. (1985), *Pluraler Marxisms*, Band 1, Berlin: Argument Verlag.

Hay, C. (1996), 'Narrating crisis: the discursive construction of the "Winter of Discontent"', *Sociology*, **30** (2), 253–77.

Hay, C. (2006), 'Constructivist institutionalism', in R.A.W. Rhodes, S.A. Blinder and B.A. Rockman (eds), *The Oxford Handbook of Political Institutions*, Oxford: Oxford University Press, 56–74.

Haynes, M. and Sharpe, S. (2009), 'Affected with joy: evaluating the mass actions of the anti-globalisation movement', *Borderlands e-journal*, **8** (3), 1–21, available at: http://www.borderlands.net.au/vol8no3_2009/hynessharpe_affected.pdf (accessed 5 March 2013).

He, B. (2003), 'Why is establishing democracy so difficult in China?', *Contemporary Chinese Thought*, **35** (1), 71–92.

He, H.-F. (2009), 'Rumours swirl as top TV series blacked out', *South China Morning Post*, 26 November, available at: http://www.scmp.com/portal/site/SCMP/menuitem.2af62ecb329d3d7733492d9253a0a0a0/?vgnextoid=1e7f639a40c25210VgnVCM100000360a0a0aRCRD&ss=China&s=News (accessed 12 February 2011).

Hearn, J. (1996), 'Deconstructing the dominant: making the one(s) the other(s)', *Organization*, **3** (4), 611–26.

Hein, E. (2012), 'Crisis of finance-dominated capitalism in the Euro Area, deficiencies in the economic policy architecture, and deflationary stagnation policies', Levy Economics Institute Working Papers 734, Annandale on Hudson, NY: Jerome Levy Institute.

Heinrich, M. and Jessop, B. (2013), 'Die EU Krise aus Sicht einer kulturellen Politischen Ökonomie. Krisendeutungen und ihre Umsetzung', *Das Argument*, **301**, 19–33.

Helsloot, N. (1989), 'Linguists of all countries. . .! On Gramsci's premise of coherence', *Journal of Pragmatics*, **13** (4), 547–66.

High Level Group Chaired by Wim Kok (2004), *Facing the Challenge: The Lisbon Strategy for Growth and Employment*, Luxembourg: Office for Official Publications of the European Communities.

Hindle, T. (2008), *Guide to Management Ideas and Gurus*, 3rd edn, London: The Economist Books.

Hirsch, J. (1995), *Der nationale Wettbewerbsstaat*, Hamburg: Edition Archiv.

Hirsch, J. (1998), *Materialistische Staatstheorie*, Hamburg: VSA.

Hirschkop, K. (2000), *Michael Bakhtin: An Aesthetic for Democracy*, Oxford: Oxford University Press.

Hjarvard, S. (2008), 'The mediatization of society: a theory of the media as agents of social and cultural change', *Nordicom Review*, **29** (2), 105–34.

HKCER Letters (1999), 'Hong Kong's competitiveness, or do we still have the Hong Kong Advantage?', *HKCER Letters*, **54**, January, available at: http://www.hkcer.hku.hk/Letters/v54/enright.htm (accessed 8 July 2013).

HKSAR, Central Policy Unit (2003), Baseline Study of Hong Kong's Creative Industries, available at: http://www.cpu.gov.hk/doc/en/research_reports/baseline%20study(eng).pdf (accessed 8 July 2013).

Hobson, J.M. and Seabrooke, L. (eds) (2007), *Everyday Politics of the World Economy*, Cambridge: Cambridge University Press.

Hodge, B. (2012), 'Ideology, identity, interaction, contradictions and challenges for critical discourse analysis', *Critical Approaches to Discourse Analysis across Disciplines*, **5** (2), 1–18.

Hodge, B. and Kress, G. (1974), 'Transformation, models and processes', *Journal of Literary Semantics*, **3**, 5–21.

Hodge, B. and Kress, G. (1993), *Language as Ideology*, 2nd edn, London: Routledge.

Hodgson, G.M. (1989), *Economics and Institutions: A Manifesto of a Modern Institutional Economics*, Cambridge: Polity.

Hodgson, G.M. (2001), *How Economics Forgot History*, London: Routledge.

Hodgson, G.M. (2002), 'Reconstitutive downward causation: social structure and the development of human agency', in E. Fullbrook (ed.), *Intersubjectivity in Economics: Agents and Structures*, London: Routledge, 159–80.

Hodgson, G.M. (2004), *The Evolution of Institutional Economics*, London: Routledge.

Hoggart, R. (1957), *The Uses of Literacy*, Harmondsworth: Penguin.

Holmes, T.J. (2001), 'Bar codes lead to frequent deliveries and superstores', *RAND Journal of Economics*, **34** (4), 708–25.

Hölscher, L. (1982), 'Kapital(ist), Kapitalismus', in O. Brunner, W. Conze and R. Koselleck (eds), *Geschichtliche Grundbegriffe*, Band 3, Stuttgart: Klett-Cotta, 399–454.

Holub, R. (1984), *Reception Theory: A Critical Introduction*, London: Methuen.

Hond, F. den, de Bakker, F. and Neergaard, P. (2007), *Managing Corporate Social Responsibility in Action: Talking, Doing and Measuring*, Aldershot: Ashgate.

Hong Kong SAR Government (1998), 'The Chief Executive's Commission on Innovation and Technology, First Report', available at: http://wwwitc.gov.hk/en/doc/First%20report%2098%20(eng).pdf (accessed 11 November 2008).

Hong Kong SAR Government (2007), 'Report on the Economic Summit on 'China's 11th Five-Year Plan and the Development of Hong Kong', available at: http://www.info.gov.hk/info/econ_summit/eng/action.htm (accessed 9 November 2008).

Hong Kong Tourism Board PartnerNet (2012), 'Research and Statistics', available at: http://partnernet.hktb.com/en/research_statistics/index.html (accessed 4 January 2013).

Höppe, W. (1982), *Karl Marx–Friedrich Engels: Sprache und gesellschaftliches Gesamtkomplex*, Bonn: Bouvier Verlag.

Horn, L.R. and Ward, G. (eds) (2004), *The Handbook of Pragmatics*, Oxford: Blackwell.

Howarth, D. (2013), *Post-Structuralism and After*, Basingstoke: Palgrave

Howarth, D., Norval, A.J. and Stavrakakis, Y. (eds) (2000), *Discourse*

Theory and Political Analysis, Manchester: Manchester University Press.

Huczynski, A. (1996), *Management Gurus: Who Makes Them and How to Become One*, London: Routledge.

Hudson, R. (2008), 'Cultural political economy meets global production networks: a productive meeting?', *Journal of Economic Geography*, **8** (3), 421–40.

Hung, R. (2011), 'The state and the market: Chinese TV serials on the case of Woju (Dwelling Narrowness)', *Boundary 2*, **38**, 157–87.

Hunt, L. (1986), 'French history in the last twenty years: the rise and fall of the *Annales* paradigm', *Journal of Contemporary History*, **21** (2), 209–24.

Hunter, Q. (2013), 'Banking on Brics economies', *The New Age Online*, 27 March, available at: http://www.thenewage.co.za/89390-9-53-Banking_on_Brics_economies (accessed 4 April 2013).

Husserl, E. (1954 [1936]), *The Crisis of the European Sciences and Transcendental Phenomenology*, Evanston IL: Northwestern University Press.

Hutchby, I. (2001), 'Technologies, texts and affordances', *Sociology*, **35** (2), 441–56.

Ifversen, J. (2003), 'Text, discourse, concept: approaches to textual analysis', *Kontur*, **7**, 60–69.

Ifversen, J. (2011), 'About key concepts and how to study them', *Contributions to the History of Concepts*, **6** (1), 65–88.

ILO (2009a), 'China's response to the crisis', *G20 Country Briefs*, available at: http://www.ilo.org/public/libdoc/jobcrisis/download/g20_china_countrybrief.pdf (accessed 11 March 2013).

ILO (2009b), 'Brazil's response to the crisis', *G20 Country Briefs*, available at: http://www.ilo.org/public/libdoc/jobcrisis/download/g20_brazil_countrybrief.pdf (accessed 11 March 2013).

ILO (2009c), 'Russian Federation's response to the crisis', *G20 Country Briefs*, available at: http://www.ilo.org/public/libdoc/jobcrisis/download/g20_russia_countrybrief.pdf (accessed 11 March 2013).

Improvement and Development Agency [I&DeA] (2008), 'Industrial Clusters and their Implications for Local Economic Policy', available at: http://www.local.gov.uk/web/guest/economy/-/journal_content/56/10171/3510371/ARTICLE-TEMPLATE (accessed 28 March 2013).

IMD (1989–), *World Competitiveness Yearbook*, Lausanne: IMD World Competitiveness Centre (annually since 1989).

Innis, H.A. (1950), *Empires and Communication*, Oxford: Oxford University Press.

Innis, H.A. (1951), *The Bias of Communication*, Toronto: University of Toronto Press.

Investment U (2009), 'Profit from the "New Decoupling"', available at: http://www.investmentu.com/IUEL/2009/July/decoupling-emerging-markets.html (accessed 15 March 2013).

Irwin, A. (2011), 'Social constructionism', in R. Wodak, B. Johnstone and P. Kerswill (eds), *The SAGE Handbook of Sociolinguistics*, London: SAGE, 100–112.

Ives, P. (1998), 'A grammatical introduction to Gramsci's political theory', *Rethinking Marxism*, **10** (1), 34–51.

Ives, P. (2004a), *Gramsci's Politics of Language. Engaging the Bakhtin Circle and the Frankfurt School*, Toronto: University of Toronto Press.

Ives, P. (2004b), *Language and Hegemony in Gramsci*, London: Pluto Press.

Ives, P. and Lacorte, R. (eds) (2010), *Gramsci, Language, and Translation*, Oxford: Lexington Books.

Ives, P. and Short, N. (2013), 'On Gramsci and the international: a textual analysis', *Review of International Studies*, **39** (3), 621–42.

Jackson, B. (2001), *Management Gurus and Management Fashions*, New York: Routledge.

Jacobsen, J. and Zeller, A. (eds) (2008), *Queer Economics: A Reader*, London: Routledge.

Jäger, M. (2008), 'BRIC as international investors: China in a class of its own', *Deutsche Bank Research, Talking Point*, available at: http://www.slideshare.net/soniabess/china-as-an-international-investor-in-a-class-of-its-own-presentation (accessed 12 March 2013).

Jäger, S. (1993), *Kritische Diskursanalyse. Eine Einführung*, Duisburg: DISS.

Jäger, S. (2001), 'Dispositiv', in M. Kleiner (ed.), *Michel Foucault. Eine Einführung in sein Denken*, Frankfurt: Campus, 72–89.

Jäger, S. and Diaz-Bone, R. (2006), 'Kritische Diskursanalyse: Zur Ausarbeitung einer problembezogenen Diskursanalyse im Anschluss an Foucault', *Forum Qualitativsozialforschung*, **7** (3), article 21.

Jäger, S. and Maier, F. (2009), 'Theoretical and methodological aspects of Foucauldian critical discourse analysis and dispositive analysis', in R. Wodak and M. Reisigl (eds), *Methods for Critical Discourse Analysis*, 2nd revised edn, London: SAGE, 34–61.

Jakobson, R. (1971), *Selected Writings: Word and Language*, The Hague: Mouton.

Jenson, J. (1989), '"Different" but not "exceptional": Canada's permeable Fordism', *Canadian Review of Sociology and Anthropology*, **26** (1), 69–94.

Jenson, J. (1990a), 'Different but not exceptional: the feminism of permeable Fordism', *New Left Review*, **184**, 58–68.

Jenson, J. (1990b), 'Representations in crisis: the roots of Canada's permeable Fordism', *Canadian Journal of Political Science*, **24** (3), 653–83.
Jenson, J. (1995), 'Mapping, naming and remembering: globalisation at the end of the twentieth century', *Review of International Political Economy*, **2** (1), 96–116.
Jessop, B. (1982), *The Capitalist State: Marxist Theories and Methods*, Oxford: Martin Robertson.
Jessop, B. (1990), *State Theory*, Cambridge: Polity.
Jessop, B. (1997a), 'A neo-Gramscian approach to the regulation of urban regimes', in M. Lauria (ed.), *Reconstructing Urban Regime Theory*, London: SAGE, 51–73.
Jessop, B. (1997b), 'The governance of complexity and the complexity of governance: preliminary remarks on some problems and limits of economic guidance', in A. Amin and J. Hausner (eds), *Beyond Markets and Hierarchy: Interactive Governance and Social Complexity*, Cheltenham, UK and Northampton, MA, USA: Edward Elgar, 111–47.
Jessop, B. (1999), 'Reflections on the (il)logics of globalization', in K. Olds, P. Dicken, P. Kelly and H. Yeung (eds), *Globalization and the Asia Pacific: Contested Territories*, London: Routledge, 19–38.
Jessop B. (2001a), 'Institutional (re)turns and the strategic-relational approach', *Environment and Planning A*, **33** (7), 1213–37.
Jessop, B. (2001b), 'Regulationist and autopoieticist reflections on Polanyi's account of market economies and the market society', *New Political Economy*, **6** (1), 213–32.
Jessop, B. (2002), *The Future of the Capitalist State*, Cambridge: Polity.
Jessop, B. (2004a), 'Critical semiotic analysis and cultural political economy', *Critical Discourse Studies*, **1** (2), 159–74.
Jessop, B. (2004b), 'Intellektuelle Eigentumsrechte', in F.W. Haug (ed.), *Historisch Kritisches Wörterbuch des Marxismus*, Band 6.2, Berlin: Argument Verlag, 1287–95.
Jessop, B. (2005a), 'Cultural political economy, the knowledge-based economy, and the state', in A. Barry and D. Slater (eds), in *The Technological Economy*, London: Routledge, 144–65.
Jessop, B. (2005b), 'Gramsci and spatial theory', *Critical Review of International Social and Political Philosophy*, **8** (4), 421–37.
Jessop, B. (2006), 'Spatial fixes, temporal fixes, and spatio-temporal fixes', in N. Castree and D. Gregory (eds), *David Harvey: A Critical Reader*, Oxford: Blackwell, 142–46.
Jessop, B. (2007a), Knowledge as a fictitious commodity: insights and

limits of a Polanyian analysis', in A. Buğra and K. Agartan (eds), *Reading Karl Polanyi for the 21st century*, New York: Palgrave, 115–33.

Jessop, B. (2007b), *State Power: A Strategic-Relational Approach*, Cambridge: Polity.

Jessop, B. (2007c), 'What follows neo-liberalism? The deepening contradictions of US Domination and the struggle for a new global order', in R. Albritton, R. Jessop and R. Westra (eds), *Political Economy and Global Capitalism: The 21st Century, Present and Futures*, London: Anthem, 67–88.

Jessop, B. (2008a), 'A cultural political economy of competitiveness and its implications for higher education', in B. Jessop, N. Fairclough, and R. Wodak (eds), *Education and the Knowledge-Based Economy in Europe*, Rotterdam: Sense Publishers, 11–39.

Jessop, B. (2008b), 'Zur Relevanz von Luhmanns Systemtheorie und von Laclau und Mouffes Diskursanalyse für die Weiterentwicklung der marxistischen Staatstheorie', in J. Hirsch, J. Kannankulam and J. Wissel (eds), *Der Staat der bürgerlichen Gesellschaft: zum Staatsverständnis von Karl Marx*, Baden-Baden: Nomos, 157–79.

Jessop, B. (2009), 'Cultural political economy and critical policy studies', *Critical Policy Studies*, **3** (3), 336–56.

Jessop, B. (2010a), 'Another Foucault effect? Foucault on governmentality and statecraft', in U. Bröckling, S. Krasmann and T. Lemke (eds), *Governmentality: Current Issues and Future Challenges*, London: Routledge, 239–48.

Jessop, B. (2010b), 'From hegemony to crisis? The continuing ecological dominance of neo-liberalism', in K. Birch and V. Mykhnenko (eds), *The Rise and Fall of Neoliberalism: The Collapse of an Economic Order*, London: Zed, 171–87.

Jessop, B. (2011), 'Rethinking the diversity of capitalism: varieties of capitalism, variegated capitalism, and the world market', in G. Wood and C. Lane (eds), *Capitalist Diversity and Diversity within Capitalism*, London: Routledge, 209–37.

Jessop, B. (2013a), 'Cultural political economy, spatial imaginaries, regional economic dynamics', in O. Brand, P. Eser and S. Dörhöfer (eds), *Ambivalenzen regionaler Kulturen und Identitäten*, Münster: Westfälisches Dampfboot (in press).

Jessop, B. (2013b), 'Finance-dominated accumulation and post-democratic capitalism', in S. Fadda and P. Tridico (eds), *Institutions and Economic Development after the Financial Crisis*, London: Routledge (in press).

Jessop, B. (2013c), 'The North Atlantic financial crisis and varieties of capitalism: a Minsky moment and/or a Marx moment? And perhaps

Weber too?', in S. Fadda and P. Tridico (eds), *Financial Crisis, Labour Markets and Institutions*, London: Routledge, 40–59.
Jessop, B. (2013d), 'Recovered imaginaries, imagined recoveries', in M. Benner (ed.), *Before and Beyond the Global Economic Crisis: Economics and Politics for a Post-Crisis Settlement*, Cheltenham UK and Northampton, MA, USA: Edward Elgar, 234–54.
Jessop, B. (2013e), 'Revisiting the regulation approach: critical reflections on the contradictions, dilemmas, fixes, and crisis dynamics of growth regimes', *Capital & Class*, **37** (1), 5–24.
Jessop, B. and Sum, N.-L. (2000), 'An entrepreneurial city in action', *Urban Studies*, **37** (12), 2290–315.
Jessop, B. and Sum, N.-L. (2001), 'Pre-disciplinary and post-disciplinary perspectives in political economy', *New Political Economy*, **6** (2), 89–101.
Jessop, B. and Sum, N.-L. (2006), *Beyond the Regulation Approach: Putting Capitalist Economies in their Place*, Cheltenham UK and Northampton, MA, USA: Edward Elgar.
Jessop, B. and Sum, N.-L. (2010), 'The development of cultural political economy: on logics of discovery, epistemic fallacies, and the complexity of emergence', *New Political Economy*, **15** (3), 308–15.
Ji, J.-H. (2006), *Learning from Crisis: Political Economy, Spatio-Temporality, and Crisis Management in South Korea, 1961–2002*, PhD Thesis, Sociology Department, Lancaster University.
Jiang, X. (2012), 'China's Land Grab Alchemy', available at: http://thediplomat.com/china-power/chinas-land-grab-alchemy/ (accessed 17 March 2013).
Jobert, B. (1989), 'The normative framework of public policy', *Political Studies*, **37** (3), 376–86.
Jones, G.S. (1983), *Languages of Class: Studies in English Working Class History 1832–1982*, Cambridge: Cambridge University Press.
Jones, G.S. (1996), 'The determinist fix: some obstacles to the further development of the linguistic approach to history in the 1990s', *History Workshop*, **42**, 19–35.
Jones, P. (2004), *Raymond Williams's Sociology of Culture: A Critical Reconstruction*, Basingstoke: Palgrave Macmillan.
Kabobel, J. (2011), *Die politische Theorien von Luhmann und Foucault im Vergleich*, Würzburg: Königshausen & Neumann.
Kalyvas, A. (2004), 'The stateless theory: Poulantzas's challenge to postmodernism', in S. Aronowitz and P. Bratsis (eds), *Paradigm Lost: State Theory Reconsidered*, Minneapolis, MN: University of Minnesota Press, 105–42.
Kannan, P. (2009), 'National policy responses to economic and financial crisis: the case of India', Report Prepared by the Centre for Development

Studies, Kerala for the ILO Regional Office in Asia, available at: http://www.ilo.org/wcmsp5/groups/public/---asia/---ro-bangkok/documents/meetingdocument/wcms_101591.pdf (accessed 19 March 2013).

Kaplan, D. (2003), 'Measuring our competitiveness – critical examination of the IDM and WEF competitiveness indicators for South Africa', *Development South Africa*, **20** (1), 75–88.

Katznelson, I. and Weingast, B.R. (2010), 'Intersections between historical and rational choice institutionalism', in I. Katznelson and B.R. Weingast (eds), *Preference and Situation: Intersections between Historical and Rational Choice Institutionalism*, New York: Russell Sage Foundation, 1–24.

Kelly, B. (2009), 'Brazil, Russia, India and China (the BRICs) Throw Down the Gauntlet of the International Monetary System', 28 June, available at: http://www.eastasiaforum.org/2009/06/28/brazil-russia-india-and-china-the-brics-throw-down-the-gauntlet-on-monetary-system-reform/ (accessed 14 March 2013).

Kelman, A. (2010), 'Rethinking the soundscape: a critical genealogy of a term in sound studies', *Sense & Society*, **5** (2), 212–34.

Kenway, J. (1990), 'Education and the Right's discursive politics', in S. Ball (ed.), *Foucault and Education*, London: Taylor & Francis.

Khor, M. (2009), 'Six key issues in the UN Conference on Economic Crisis', *South Bulletin*, **38**, 9–10.

Knorr-Cetina, K., Schatzki, T.R. and von Savigny, E. (eds) (2000), *The Practice Turn in Contemporary Theory*, London: Routledge.

Kohlmorgen, L. (2004), *Regulation, Klasse, Geschlecht. Die Konstituierung der Sozialstruktur im Fordismus und Postfordismus*, Münster: Westfälisches Dampfboot.

Kong, S. (2010), 'China's Migrant Problem: The Need for Hukou Reform', available at: http://www.eastasiaforum.org/2010/01/29/chinas-migrant-problem-the-need-for-hukou-reform/ (accessed 18 March 2013).

Koselleck, R. (1972), 'Einleitung', in O. Brunner, W. Conze and R. Koselleck (eds), *Geschichtliche Grundbegriffe. Historisches Lexikon zur politisch-sozialen Sprache in Deutschland*, Band 1, Stuttgart: Klett-Cotta, xiii–xxvii.

Koselleck, R. (1981), *Preussen zwischen Reform und Revolution. Allgemeines Landrecht, Verwaltung und soziale Bewegung von 1791 bis 1848*, Stuttgart: Klett-Cotta.

Koselleck, R. (1982), '*Begriffsgeschichte* and social history', *Economy and Society*, **11** (4), 409–27.

Koselleck, R. (1985), *Futures Past: On the Semantics of Historical Time*, Cambridge: MIT Press.

Koselleck, R. (1992), 'Vorwort', in O. Brunner, W. Conze and R. Koselleck (eds), *Geschichtliche Grundbegriffe: Historisches Lexikon zur Politisch-sozialen Sprache in Deutschland*, Band 7, Stuttgart: Klett-Cotta, vi–viii.

Koselleck, R. (1996), 'A Response', in H. Lehmann and M. Richter (eds), *The Meaning of Historical Terms and Concepts, New Studies on Begriffsgeschichte*, Washington, DC: German Historical Institute, Occasional paper 15, 64–7.

Koselleck, R. (2006), 'Crisis', *Journal of the History of Ideas*, **67** (2), 357–400.

Koselleck, R. (2011), 'Introduction and prefaces to the *Geschichtliche Grundbegriffe*', *Contributions to the History of Concepts*, **6** (1), 1–37.

Krätke, M.R. (2011), 'Antonio Gramsci's contribution to a critical economics', *Historical Materialism*, **19** (3), 63–105.

Kraus, B. (2006), 'Lebenswelt und Lebensweltorientierung – eine begriffliche Revision als Angebot an eine systemisch-konstruktivistische Sozialarbeitswissenschaft', *Kontext*, **37** (2), 116–27.

Kress, G. (2001), 'Sociolinguistics and social semiotics', in P. Cobley (ed.), *Routledge Handbook of Semiotics and Sociolinguistics*, London: Routledge, 66–82.

Kristeva, J. (1969), *Semiotiké*, Paris: Editions du Seuil.

Kristeva, J. (1975), 'The subject in signifying practice', *Semiotext(e)*, **1** (3), 19–26.

Krook, M.L. and Mackay, F. (eds) (2011), *Gender, Politics and Institution: Towards a Feminist Institutionalism*, Basingstoke: Palgrave Macmillan.

Krücken, G. and Drori, G.S. (2010), *World Society: The Writings of John W. Meyer*, Oxford: Oxford University Press.

Krugman, P. (1994a), 'Competitiveness: a dangerous obsession', *Foreign Policy*, **73** (March), 342–65.

Krugman, P. (1994b), 'The myth of Asia's miracle', *Foreign Affairs*, **73** (Nov/Dec), 62–79.

Krzyżanowski, M. (2010), 'Discourses and concepts: interfaces and synergies between *Begriffsgeschichte* and the discourse-historical approach in CDA', in R. de Cillia, H. Gruber, M. Krzyżanowski and F. Menz (eds), *Diskurs Politik Identität*, Tübingen: Stauffenburg, 125–36.

Kuhn, T.S. (1962), *The Structure of Scientific Revolutions*, Chicago, IL: University of Chicago Press.

Labrousse, A. and Weisz, J.-D. (eds) (2001), *Institutional Economics in France and Germany*, Berlin: Springer.

Laclau, E. (1977), *Politics and Ideology in Marxist Theory*, London: NLB.

Laclau, E. (1980), 'Populist rupture and discourse', *Screen Education*, **34** (Spring), 87–93.

Laclau, E. (1990), *New Reflections on the Revolution of our Times*, London: Verso.

Laclau, E. (2005), *On Populist Reason*, London: Verso.
Laclau, E. and Mouffe, C. (1981), 'Socialist strategy – where next?', *Marxism Today*, January, 17–22.
Laclau, E. and Mouffe, C. (1985), *Hegemony and Socialist Strategy*, London: Verso.
Lakatos, I. (1978), *The Methodology of Scientific Research Programmes: Philosophical Papers Volume 1*, Cambridge: Cambridge University Press.
Lakatos, I. and Musgrave, A. (eds) (1970), *Criticism and the Growth of Knowledge*, Cambridge: Cambridge University Press.
Lakoff, G. and Johnson, M. (1980), *Metaphors We Live By*, Chicago, IL: University of Chicago Press.
Lall, S. (2001), 'Competitive indices and developing countries: an economic evaluation of the Global Competitiveness Report', *World Development*, **29** (9), 1501–25.
Lam, W. (2004), 'Beijing's hand in Hong Kong politics', *China Brief*, 9 June, **4** (12), available at: http://www.jamestown.org/single/?no_cache=1&tx_ttnews[tt_news]=26643 (accessed 3 March 2013).
Landwehr, A. (2008), *Historische Diskursanalyse*, Frankfurt: Campus.
Langley, P. (2008), *The Everyday Life of Global Finance*, Oxford: Oxford University Press.
Lapavitsas, C. (2011), 'Theorizing financialization', *Work, Employment and Society*, **25** (4), 611–26.
Lapavitsas, C. (2012), *Crisis in the Eurozone*, London: Verso.
Larner, W. and Le Heron, R. (2004), 'Global benchmarking: participating "at a distance" in the globalizing economy', in W. Larner and W. Walters (eds), *Global Governmentality*, London: Routledge, 212–32.
Lash, S. and Urry, J. (1994), *Economies of Signs and Spaces*, London: SAGE.
Latham, M. (2000), *Modernization as Ideology*, Chapel Hill, NC: University of North Carolina Press.
Lauder, H., Brown, P. and Green, A.D. (2001), *Education and Training for a High Skills Economy: A Comparative Study*, Swindon: Economic and Social Research Council.
Leca, B. (2006), 'A critical realist approach to institutional entrepreneurship', *Organization*, **13** (5), 627–65.
Lecercle, J.-J. (2006), *A Marxist Philosophy of Language*, Leiden: Brill.
Lee, K.-H. and Ho, Y. (2008), 'Impact of individual visit scheme (IVS) and positive tourism policy', *Food for Thought Newsletter*, February, available at: http://www3.baf.cuhk.edu.hk/htm/news/news.asp?refNo=81 (accessed 15 January 2013).
Lemke, T. (2003), 'Andere Affirmationen: Gesellschaftsanalyse und Kritik

im Postfordismus', in A. Honneth and M. Saar (eds), *Zwischenbilanz einer Rezeption*, Frankfurt: Suhrkamp, 259–74.

Lévi-Strauss, C. (1958 [1972]), *Structural Anthropology*, Harmondsworth: Penguin.

Levinson, S.C. (1983), *Pragmatics*, Cambridge: Cambridge University Press.

Levy, D.L. and Scully, M. (2007), 'The institutional entrepreneur as modern prince: the strategic face of power in contested fields', *Organization Studies*, **28** (7), 971–91.

Lévy-Bruhl, L. (1923 [1922]), *The Primitive Mentality*, London: Routledge & Kegan Paul.

Li, T.M. (2007), *The Will to Improve: Governmentality, Development and the Practice of Politics*, Durham, NC: Duke University Press.

Li, T.T.T. (2011), 'UNIDO and CIEM Promote Cluster Development Policies of Vietnam', available at: http://www.un.org.vn/en/feature-articles-press-centre-submenu-252/1904-unido-and-ciem-promote-cluster-development-policies-for-viet-nam.html (accessed 5 March 2013).

Lichtenstein, N. (ed.) (2006), *Wal-Mart: The Face of Twenty-First-Century Capitalism*, New York: New Press.

Lieberman, P. (2006), *Toward an Evolutionary Biology of Language*, Cambridge, MA: Belknap Press.

Link, J. (1982), 'Kollektivsymbolik und Mediendiskurse. Zur aktuellen Frage, wie subjektive Aufrüstung funktioniert', *KultuRRevolution*, **1**, 6–21.

Link J. (1983), *Elementare Literatur und generative Diskursanalyse*, Munich: Wilhelm Fink Verlag.

Link, J. (1986), 'Noch einmal: Diskurs. Interdiskurs. Macht', *KultuRRevolution*, **11**, 4–7.

Link, J. (1997), *Versuch über den Normalismus. Wie Normalität produziert wird*, Göttingen: Vandenhoeck & Ruprecht.

Link, J. (2012), *Kritische Diskursanalyse: Eine Einführung*, 8th edn, Duisburg: Edition DISS.

Link, J. (2013), *Normale Krisen? Normalismus und die Krise der Gegenwart*, Konstanz: Konstanz University Press.

Lipietz, A. (1984), 'Imperialism or the beast of the apocalypse', *Capital & Class*, **22**, 81–109.

Lipietz, A. (1985), *The Enchanted World: Inflation, Credit, and the World Crisis*, London: NLB.

Lipietz, A. (1987), *Mirages and Miracles: The Crises of Global Fordism*, London: Verso.

Lipietz, A. (1988), 'Accumulation, crises, and ways out: some methodological reflections on the concept of "regulation"', *International Journal of Political Economy* **18** (2), 10–43.

Lipietz, A. (1992), 'Allgemeine und konjunkturelle Merkmale der ökonomischen Staatsintervention', in A. Demirović, H.-P. Krebs and T. Sablowski (eds), *Hegemonie und Staat*, Münster: Westfälisches Dampfboot, 182–202.

Lipietz, A. (1994), 'The national and the regional: their autonomy vis-à-vis the capitalist world crisis', in R.P. Palan and B. Gills (eds), *Transcending the State–Global Divide: A Neo-Structuralist Agenda in International Relations*, Boulder, CO: Lynne Rienner, 23–44.

Lipietz, A. (1995), *Green Hopes*, Cambridge: Polity.

Lo Piparo, F. (1979), *Lingua, intellectuali e egemonia in Gramsci*, Bari: Laterza.

Lodge, G. and Vogel, E. (1987), *Ideology and National Competitiveness: An Analysis of Nine Countries*, Boston, MA: Harvard Business School Press.

Lordabett.com (2009), 'Why Decoupling Should Benefit International Investors', available at: https://www.lordabbett.com/articles/wp_why_decoupling_should.pdf (accessed 17 July 2012 and no longer available on the worldwideweb).

Lordon, F. (1997), *Les quadratures de la politique économique: les infortunes de la vertu*, Paris: Michel Albin.

Lordon, F. (1999), 'Croyances économiques et pouvoir symbolique', Association Régulation et Recherche, *L'Année de la régulation*, **3**, 169–210.

Lordon, F. (2000a), 'La «création de valeur» comme rhétorique et comme pratique', *L'Année de régulation*, **4**, Paris, 117–68.

Lordon F. (2000b), 'La force des idées simples. Misère épistémique des comportements économiques', *Politix*, **13**, 52, available at: http://frederic.lordon.perso.cegetel.net/Textes/Textes_recherche/Textes_PolEco/Politix.pdf4 (accessed 24 April 2013).

Lordon, F. (2002), '*Régulation Theory* and economic policy', in R. Boyer and Y. Saillard (eds), *Régulation Theory*, London: Routledge, 129–35.

Lordon, F. (2008), *Jusqu'à quand? Pour en finir avec les crises financières*, Paris: Raisons d'agir.

Lordon, F. (2010), *Capitalisme, désir et servitude: Marx et Spinoza*, Paris: La Fabrique.

Lordon, F. (2011), *L'Intérêt souverain: essai d'anthropologie économique spinoziste*, 2nd edn, Paris: La Découverte.

Lowe, E.J. (1995) 'Ontology', in T. Honderich (ed.), *The Oxford Companion to Philosophy*, Oxford: Oxford University Press, 634–5.

Lowndes, V. (2010), 'The institutional approach', in D. Marsh and G. Stoker (eds), *Theories and Methods in Political Science*, 3rd edn, Basingstoke: Palgrave, 60–79.

Luhmann, N. (1980), *Gesellschaftsstruktur und Semantik. Studien zur Wissenssoziologie der modernen Gesellschaft*, Band 1, Frankfurt: Suhrkamp.
Luhmann, N. (1981), *Gesellschaftsstruktur und Semantik. Studien zur Wissenssoziologie der modernen Gesellschaft*, Band 2, Frankfurt: Suhrkamp.
Luhmann, N. (1987), 'The representation of society within society', *Current Sociology*, **35** (2), 101–8.
Luhmann, N. (1989), 'Staat und Staatsräson im Übergang von traditioneller Herrschaft zu moderne Politik', in N. Luhmann, *Gesellschaft und Semantik 3*, Frankfurt: Suhrkamp, 65–148.
Luhmann, N. (1990), 'Complexity and meaning', in N. Luhmann, *Essays in Self-Reference*, New York: Columbia University Press, 80–85.
Luhmann, N. (1995), *Social Systems*, Stanford, CA: Stanford University Press.
Luhmann, N. (2000), *Organisation und Entscheidung*, Wiesbaden: Westdeutscher Verlag.
Luhmann, N. (2008), *Ideenevolution: Beiträge zur Wissenssoziologie*, Frankfurt: Suhrkamp.
Luke, A. (2002), 'Beyond science and ideology critique: developments in critical discourse analysis', *Annual Review of Applied Linguistics*, **22**, 96–110.
Lula da Silva, L. (2010), 'The BRIC Countries Come into Their Own as Global Players', available at: http://www.huffingtonpost.com/luiz-inacio-lula-da-silva/the-bric-countries-come-i_b_539541.html (accessed 25 July 2012).
Lund-Thomsen, P. and Nadvi, K. (2010), 'Clusters, chains and compliance: corporate social responsibility and governance in football manufacturing in South Asia', *Journal of Business Ethics*, **93** (Supplement 2), 201–22.
Lundvall, B.-Å. (ed.) (1992), *National Systems of Innovation: Towards a Theory of Innovation and Interactive Learning*, London: Pinter.
Lundvall, B.-Å. (2006), 'Innovation systems between theory and policy', paper for the Innovation Pressure Conference, Tampere, March 2006.
Lundvall, B.-Å. and Johnson, B. (1994), 'The learning economy', *Journal of Industry Studies*, **1** (2), 23–42.
Lung, C.-M. (2006), 'Assisting Hong Kong firms in the PRD to solve problems', in *Ta Kung Pao*, 22 August, A 25 (author's translation from Chinese).
Lury, C. (2004), *Brands: The Logos of Global Economy*, London: Routledge.
McCarney, J. (1980), *The Real World of Ideology*, London: Harvester.

McCloskey, D.N. (1998), *The Rhetoric of Economics*, 2nd edn, Madison, WI: University of Wisconsin Press.
McLuhan, M. (1964), *Understanding Media: The Extensions of Man*, New York: McGraw-Hill.
Macartney, H. (2011), *Variegated Neoliberalism: EU Varieties of Capitalism and International Political Economy*, London: Routledge.
Macdonald, B.J. (2002), 'Marx, Foucault, genealogy', *Polity*, **34** (3), 259–84.
Mackay, F., Monro, S. and Waylen, G. (2009), 'The feminist potential of sociological institutionalism', *Politics & Gender*, **5** (2), 253–62.
MacKenzie, D.J. (2006), *An Engine, Not a Camera: How Financial Models Shape Markets*, Cambridge, MA: MIT Press.
MacKenzie, D.J. (2009), *Material Markets: How Economic Agents are Constructed*, Oxford: Oxford University Press.
MacKinnon, D., Cumbers, A. and Chapman, K. (2002), 'Learning, innovation and regional development: a critical appraisal', *Progress in Human Geography*, **26** (3), 293–311.
Magnusson, L. (1994), *Mercantilism: The Shaping of an Economic Language*, London: Routledge.
Maihofer, A. (1995), *Geschlecht als Existenzweise: Macht, Moral, Recht und Geschlechterdifferenz*, Frankfurt: Ulrike Helmer.
Maillat, D. and Kebir, L. (1999), '"Learning region" et systèmes territoriaux de production', *Revue d'Économie Régionale et Urbaine*, **3**, 430–48.
Malhotra, Y. (2000), 'Knowledge management and new organizational forms: a framework for business model innovation', *Information Resources Management Journal*, **13** (1), 5–14.
Malpas, J. and Wickham, G. (1995), 'Governance and failure: on the limits of sociology', *Australia and New Zealand Journal of Sociology*, **31** (3), 37–50.
Mandrou, R. and Duby, G. (1964), *Histoire de la Civilisation Française*, 2 vols, 3rd edn, Paris: Armand Colin.
Mao, Z. (1967 [1937]), 'On contradiction', in Z. Mao, *Collected Works of Mao Tse-Tung*, vol. IV, Beijing: People's Publishing House, 311–47.
March, J.G. and Olsen, J.P. (1984), 'The new institutionalism: organizational factors in political life', *American Political Science Review*, **78** (3), 734–49.
March, J.G. and Olsen, J.P. (1996), 'Institutional perspectives on political institutions', *Governance*, **9** (3), 247–64.
March, J.G. and Olsen, J.P. (2006), 'Elaborating the "new institutionalism"', in R.A.W. Rhodes, S.A. Blinder and B.A. Rockman (eds), *The Oxford Handbook of Political Institutions*, Oxford: Oxford University Press, 3–20.

Marginson, S. (1999), 'After globalisation: emerging politics of education', *Journal of Education Policy*, **14** (1), 19–31.
Marinis, A. (2008), 'BRIC consumers can't hold off world recession', *Livemint.com*, available at: http://www.livemint.com/2008/12/18211911/Bric-consumers-can8217t-hol.html (accessed 22 March 2013).
Marsden, R. (1999), *The Nature of Capital: Marx After Foucault*, London: Routledge.
Martin, R. and Sunley, P. (2003), 'Deconstructing clusters: chaotic concept or policy panacea?', *Journal of Economic Geography*, **3** (1), 5–35.
Martin-Barbero, J. (1973), *Communication, Culture and Hegemony*, London: SAGE.
Marx, K. (1967a [1890]), *Capital, Volume I*, London: Lawrence & Wishart.
Marx, K. (1967b [1893]), *Capital, Volume II*, London: Lawrence & Wishart.
Marx, K. (1967c [1894]), *Capital, Volume III*, London: Lawrence & Wishart.
Marx, K. (1970 [1859]), *Contribution to the Critique of Political Economy*, London: Lawrence & Wishart.
Marx, K. (1972 [1862–63]), *Theories of Surplus Value*, 3 vols, London: Lawrence & Wishart.
Marx, K. (1973 [1857–8]), *Grundrisse: Foundations of the Critique of Political Economy*, Harmondsworth: Penguin.
Marx, K. and Engels, F. (1976a [1845–46]), *The German Ideology*, in K. Marx and F. Engels, *Marx–Engels Collected Works*, vol. 5, London: Lawrence & Wishart.
Marx, K. and Engels, F. (1976b [1848]), 'Manifesto of the Communist Party', in *Marx–Engels Collected Works*, vol. 6, London: Lawrence & Wishart, 477–519.
Massey, D. (1994), *Space, Place, and Gender*, Cambridge: Polity.
Masuda, Y. (1981), *The Information Society as Post-Industrial Society*, Washington, DC: World Future Society.
Mauss, M. (2000 [1925]), *The Gift: Forms and Functions of Exchange in Archaic Societies*, New York: W.W. Norton & Company.
Mautner, G. (2005), 'The entrepreneurial university: a discursive profile of a higher education buzzword', *Critical Discourse Studies*, **2** (2), 95–120.
Mavroudeas, S. (2012), *The Limits of Regulation: A Critical Analysis of Capitalist Development*, Cheltenham UK and Northampton, MA, USA: Edward Elgar.
May, C. (2002), *The Information Society: A Sceptical View*, Cambridge: Polity.
May, C. and Nölke, A. (2013), 'Kritischer Institutionalismus in der

vergleichenden Kapitalismusforschung: Konzeptionelle Überlegungen und Forschungsprogramm', in I. Bruff, M. Ebenau, C. May and A. Nölke (eds), *Vergleichende Kapitalismusforschung: Stand, Perspektiven, Kritik*, Münster: Westfälisches Dampfboot, 103–18.

Mayntz, R. (1997), *Soziale Dynamik und Politische Steuerung: Theoretische und Methodologische Überlegungen*, Frankfurt: Campus.

Mayntz, R. (2001), 'Zur Selektivität der Steuerungsperspektive', Cologne: Max-Planck Institut für Gesellschaftungsforschung, Working Paper 01/2.

Mayntz, R. and Scharpf, F.W. (1995), 'Der Ansatz des akteurzentrierten Institutionalismus', in R. Mayntz and F.W. Scharpf (eds), *Gesellschaftliche Selbstregulierung und politische Steuerung*, Frankfurt: Campus, 39–72.

Megill, A. (2007), *Historical Knowledge, Historical Error: A Contemporary Guide to Practice*, Chicago, IL: University of Chicago Press.

Mehta, L., Leach, M. and Scoones, I. (2001), 'Editorial: environmental governance in an uncertain world', *IDS Bulletin*, **32** (4), 1–9.

Mellor, W. and Lim, L.-M. (2008), 'BRIC Shoppers Will "Rescue World" Goldman Sachs Says', available at: http://www.bloomberg.com/apps/news?pid=newsarchive&sid=a3aTPjYcw8a8 (accessed 17 March 2013).

Melton, J.V.H. (1996), 'Otto Brunner and the ideological origins of *Begriffsgeschichte*', in M. Lehmann and M. Richter (eds), *The Meaning of Historical Terms and Concepts*, Washington, DC: German Historical Institute, Occasional Paper No. 15, 21–34.

Melve, L. (2006), 'Intentions, concepts and reception: an attempt to come to terms with the materialistic and diachronic aspects of the history of ideas', *History of Political Theory*, **27** (3), 378–406.

Meng, L. (2012), 'Parents worry as migrant school faces shut down', available at: http://www.globaltimes.cn/content/717811.shtml (accessed 28 February 2013).

Messner, D. (1996), *The Network Society*, London: Cass.

Miettinen, R. (2002), *National Innovation System: Scientific Concept or Political Rhetoric*, Helsinki: Edita.

Miettinen, R., Paavola, S. and Pohjola, P. (2012), 'From habituality to change: contribution of activity theory and pragmatism to practice theories', *Journal of the Theory of Social Behaviour*, **42** (3), 345–60.

Miller, J.A. (1966), 'Suture: éléments de la logique du signifiant', *Cahiers pour l'analyse*, **1**, 37–49.

Miller, P. and Rose, N. (1990), 'Governing economic life', *Economy and Society*, **19** (1), 1–31.

Mills, C.W. (1959), *The Sociological Imagination*, Oxford: Oxford University Press.

Milner, A. (2002), *Re-Imagining Cultural Studies: the Promise of Cultural Materialism*, London: SAGE.

Milonakis, D. and Fine, B. (2008), *From Political Economy to Economics: Method, the Social and the Historical in the Evolution of Economic Theory*, London: Routledge.

Mingpao (2013a), 'Too Drastic A Law on Milk Powder', 5 March, available at: http://news.mingpao.com/20130305/gaa1h.htm (accessed 5 March 2013) (in Chinese).

Mingpao (2013b), 'Consumer Council: price difference can reach $ 93 in the same district', 9 February, http://news.mingpao.com/20130209/gga1.htm (accessed 9 February 2013) (in Chinese).

Ministerial Declaration (2009) adopted by the 33rd Annual Meeting of Ministers for Foreign Affairs of the Group of 77 (New York, 25 September), http://www.g77.org/doc/Declaration2009.htm (accessed 7 July 2013).

Minsky, H.P. (1982), *Can it Happen Again?*, Armonk, NY: M.E. Sharpe.

Minsky, H.P. (1986), *Stabilizing an Unstable Economy*, New Haven, CT: Yale University Press.

Møller, H.-G. (2006), *Luhmann Explained. From Souls to Systems*, Chicago, IL: Open Court.

Morçöl, G. (2005), 'Phenomenology of complexity theory and cognitive science: implications for developing an embodied knowledge of public administration and policy', *Administrative Theory & Praxis*, **27** (1), 1–23.

Morera, E. (1990), *Gramsci's Historicism: A Realist Interpretation*, London: Routledge.

Moreton, B. (2009), 'The soul of the service economy', *Enterprise and Society*, **8** (4), 777–83.

Moreton, B. (2011), *To Serve God and Wal-Mart: The Making of Christian Free Enterprise*, Cambridge, MA: Harvard University Press.

Morgan, G., Campbell, J.L., Crouch, C., Pedersen, O.K. and Whitley, R. (eds) (2010), *The Oxford Handbook of Comparative Institutional Analysis*, Oxford: Oxford University Press.

Morris, C.W. (1946), *Signs, Language, and Behaviour*, New York: Prentice-Hall.

Mouffe, C. (1979), 'Hegemony and ideology in Gramsci', in C. Mouffe (ed.), *Gramsci and Marxist Theory*, London: Routledge & Kegan Paul, 168–204.

Muller, P. (1995), 'Les politiques publiques comme construction d'un rapport au monde', in A. Faure, G. Pollet and P. Warin (eds), *La Construction du Sens dans les Politiques Publiques*, Paris: L'Harmattan, 153–79.

Murphy, C.N. (2010), 'Lessons of a "good" crisis: learning in, and from the Third World', *Globalizations*, **7** (1), 203–15.

Murphy, J. (2008), *World Bank and Global Managerialism*, London: Routledge.

Mutuc, J. (2006), 'Standards and standardization for SMEs and subcontractors', available at: http://www.bworld.com.ph/Downloads/2006/Outsourcing4.ppt (accessed 14 February 2010 and no longer available on the worldwideweb).

Myrdal, G. (1978), 'Institutional economics', *Journal of Economic Issues*, **12** (4), 771–83.

Nash, J.C. (2008), 'Re-thinking intersectionality', *Feminist Review*, **89**, 1–15.

National Development and Reform Commission (2008), *Outline of the Plan for the Reform and Development of the Pearl River Delta 2008–2020*, Beijing: National Development and Reform Commission (published in English by Intercultural Publishing, Beijing, in 2011).

Naughton, B. (2009), 'Understanding Chinese stimulus package', *Chinese Leadership Monitor, No. 28*, Spring, available at: http://www.hoover.org/publications/clm/issues/44613157.html (accessed 12 April 2013).

Naumann, T.M. (2000), *Das umkämpfte Subjekt. Subjektivität, Hegemonie und Emanzipation im Postfordismus*, Tübingen: Edition Diskord.

Naumann, T.M. (2003), 'Sozialcharakter zwischen Spätkapitalismus und Postfordismus', in A. Demirović (ed.), *Modelle kritischer Gesellschaftstheorie. Traditionen und Perspektiven der Kritischen Theorie*, Stuttgart: Metzler-Verlag, 266–89.

Nee, V. and Strang, D. (1998), 'The emergence and diffusion of institutional forms', *Journal of Institutional and Theoretical Economics*, **154**, 707–15.

Nelson, R.R. (1992), 'National innovation systems: a retrospective on a study', *Industrial and Corporate Change*, **1** (2), 347–74.

Nevalainen, T. and Raumolin-Brunberg, H. (2012), 'Historical sociolinguistics: origins, motivations and paradigms', in J.M. Hernández-Campoy and J.C. Conde-Silvestre (eds), *The Handbook of Historical Sociolinguistics*, Chichester: Blackwell-Wiley, 22–40.

New Economics Foundation (2008), *A Green New Deal: Joined-up Policies to Solve the Triple Crunch of the Credit Crisis, Climate Change, and High Oil Prices*, London: New Economics Foundation.

Nip, A. (2013), 'Shenzhen shoppers in Hong Kong buy food and daily items over clothes', *South China Morning Post*, 24 January, available at: http://www.scmp.com/news/hong-kong/article/1134668/mainland-shoppers-head-daily-items (accessed 12 February 2013).

Nishimura, K. (2011), 'Worlds of our remembering: the agent–structure problem as the search for identity', *Conflict and Cooperation*, 46 (1), 96–112.

Nisipeanu, E. (2013), 'The determinants of the national competitiveness advantage', *International Journal of Academic Research in Business and Social Science*, February, **3** (2), available at: http://www.hrmars.com/admin/pics/1646.pdf (accessed 22 March 2013).

Nord, L.W. and Olsson, E.-K. (2013), 'Frame, set, match! Towards a model of successful crisis rhetoric', *Public Relations Inquiry*, **2** (1), 79–94.

Norreklit, H. (2003), 'The balanced scorecard: what is the score?', *Accounting, Organizations and Society*, **28** (6), 591–619.

North, D.C. (1981), *Structure and Change in Economic History*, New York: Norton.

North, D.C. (1983), 'Prize Lecture: Economic Performance Through Time', available at: http://www.nobelprize.org/nobel_prizes/economics/laureates/1993/north-lecture.html (accessed 26 May 2013).

North, D.C. (1984a), *Structure and Change in Economic History*, New York: Norton.

North, D.C. (1984b), 'Three approaches to the study of institutions', in D. Colander (ed.), *Neoclassical Political Economy*, Cambridge, MA: Ballinger, 33–40.

North, D.C. (1986), 'The new institutional economics', *Journal of Institutional and Theoretical Economics*, **142**, 230–37.

OECD (1962), *The Measurement of Scientific and Technical Activities: Proposed Standard Practice for Surveys of Research and Development*, Paris: OECD.

OECD (1991), *Technology and Productivity: The Challenges for Economic Policy*, Paris: OECD.

OECD (1996), *The Knowledge-Based Economy*, Paris: OECD.

OECD (1997), *National Systems of Innovation*, Paris: OECD.

OECD (2002), *Dynamising National Innovation Systems*, Paris: OECD.

Offbeat China (2011), 'Leftover Women in China Speak Their Hearts Out "No Car, No House, No Bride"', available at: http://offbeatchina.com/leftover-women-in-china-speak-their-heart-out-no-house-no-car-no-bride (accessed 27 February 2013).

Offe, C. (1984), *Contradictions of the Welfare State*, London: Hutchinson.

Olssen, M. (2006), *Michel Foucault: Materialism and Education*, London: Paradigm Publishers.

O'Malley, E. and van Egeraat, C. (2000), 'Industry clusters and Irish industrial manufacturing: limits of the Porter's view', *Economic and Social Review*, **31** (1), 55–79.

O'Neill, J. (2009), 'The New Shopping Superpower', available at: http://

www.newsweek.com/2009/03/20/the-new-shopping-superpower.html (accessed 5 April 2013).

O'Neill, J. (2012), *The Growth Map: Economic Opportunity in the BRIC*, London: Portfolio/Penguin.

O'Neill, J., Lawson, S. and Purushothaman, R. (2004), 'The BRICs and global markets: crude, cars and capital', *CEO Confidential*, October, available at: http://www.goldmansachs.com/ceoconfidential/CEO-2004-09.pdf (accessed 8 July 2013).

Orlik, T. (2011), 'Unrest grows as economy booms', available at: http://online.wsj.com/article/SB10001424053111903703604576587070600504108.html (accessed 30 August 2012).

O'Rourke, D. (2002), 'Monitoring the monitors: a critique of corporate third-party labour monitoring', in J. Rhys Jenkins, R. Pearson and G. Seyfang (eds), *Corporate Responsibility and Labour Rights: Codes of Conduct in the Global Economy*, London: Earthscan, 196–208.

O'Rourke, D. (2003), 'Outsourcing regulation: analyzing nongovernmental systems of labour standards and monitoring', *Policy Studies Journal*, **31** (1), 1–29.

Orwell, G. (1945), *Animal Farm: A Fairy Story*, London: Heinemann.

Ostry, S. and Nelson, R.R. (1995), *Techno-Nationalism and Techno-Globalism: Conflict and Cooperation*, Washington, DC: Brookings Institution.

O'Tuathail, G. (1996), *Critical Geopolitics: The Politics of Writing Global Space*, Minneapolis, MN: University of Minnesota Press.

Overbeek, H. (1990), *Global Capitalism and National Decline: The Thatcher Decade in Perspective*. London: Unwin Hyman.

Overbeek, H. (2000), 'Transnational historical materialism: theories of transnational class formation and world order', in R. Palan (ed.), *Global Political Economy: Contemporary Theories*, London: Routledge, 168–83.

Overbeek, H. (2004), 'Transnational class formation and concepts of control', *Journal of International Relations and Development*, **7**, 113–41.

Oxfam International (2010), 'The Global Economic Crisis and Developing Countries: Impact and Response (Working Draft for Consultation)', available at: http://policy-practice.oxfam.org.uk/publications/the-global-economic-crisis-and-developing-countries-112461 (accessed 14 April 2013).

Oxley, L., Walker, P., Thorns, D. and Wang, H. (2007), 'Exploring the knowledge economy/society: another example of measurement without theory', Working Paper, University of Canterbury at Christchurch, New Zealand.

Pahl, H. (2011), 'Die Wirtschaftswissenschaften in der Krise:

vom massenmedialen Diskurs zu einer Wissenssoziologie der Wirtschaftswissenschaften', *Swiss Journal of Sociology*, **37** (2), 259–81.

Palmisano, S.J. (2005), *Innovate America: National Innovation Initiative Summit and Report*, Washington, DC: Council on Competitiveness.

Palombarini, S. (2001), *La rupture du compromis social italien. Un essai de macroéconomique politique*, Paris: CNRS Editions.

Palonen, K. (2004), *Die Entzauberung der Begriff: Das Umschreiben der politischen Begriffe bei Quentin Skinner und Reinhart Koselleck*, Münster: LIT Verlag.

Palonen, K. (2006), *The Struggle with Time: A Conceptual History of 'Politics' as an Activity*, Münster: LIT Verlag.

Parker, J. (2000), *Structuration*, Milton Keynes: Open University Press.

Pêcheux, M. (1982 [1973]), *Language, Semantics and Ideology: Stating the Obvious*, Basingstoke: Macmillan.

Peck, J.A. (2010), *Constructions of Neo-Liberal Reason*, Oxford: Oxford University Press.

Peet, R., Robbins, P. and Watts, M. (2010), *Global Political Ecology*, London: Routledge.

Peirce, C.S. (1992), *The Essential Peirce: Selected Philosophical Writings (1867–1893)*, Bloomington, IN: Indiana University Press.

Peltonen, M. (2004), 'From discourse to dispositif: Michel Foucault's two histories', *Historical Reflections/Reflexions Historiques*, **30** (2), 205–19.

People's Panel on West Kowloon (2007), 'Policy Feedbacks to the West Kowloon Cultural District Proposal', available at: https://www.mindvan.com/cgi-bin/ourdb/bdetail?share=contact@ppwk.org&template=758674850001&key=1 (accessed 15 March 2013) (in Chinese).

Pepper, S. (2013), 'Between the Lines: More on the Speech of Qiao Xiaoyang', available at: http://chinaelectionsblog.net/hkfocus/?tag=patriotism (accessed 15 April 2013).

Peters, B.G. (1999), *Institutional Theory in Political Science: The 'New Institutionalism'*, London: Pinter.

Peters, M.A. (2007), 'Knowledge societies and knowledge economies', in M. Peters (ed.), *Knowledge Economy, Development and Further of Higher Education*, Rotterdam: Sense Publishers, 17–30.

Petit, P. (1999), 'Structural forms and growth regimes of the post-Fordist era', *Review of Social Economy*, **57** (2), 220–43.

Petras, J.F. and Veltmeyer, H. (2009), 'Neoliberalism and the dynamics of capitalist development in Latin America', available at: http://www.globalresearch.ca/index.php?context=va&aid=16167 (accessed 28 March 2013).

Philo, C. and Parr, H. (2000), 'Institutional geographies: introductory remarks', Geoforum, **31**, 513–25.

Pierson, P. (2004), *Politics in Time: History, Institutions and Social Analysis*, Princeton, NJ: Princeton University Press.
Piore, M.J. and Sabel, C. (1984), *The Second Industrial Divide*, New York: Basic Books.
Pløger, J. (2008), 'Foucault's dispositif and the city', *Planning Theory*, 7 (1), 51–70.
Pocock, J.G.A. (1973), *Politics, Language, and Time: Essays on Political Thought and History*, New York: Athenaeum.
Pocock, J.G.A. (1975), *The Machiavellian Moment: Florentine Republic Thought and the Atlantic Republic Tradition*, Princeton, NJ: Princeton University Press.
Pocock, J.G.A. (1985), *Virtue, Commerce and History*, Cambridge: Cambridge University Press.
Pocock, J.G.A. (1996), 'Concepts and discourses: a difference in culture? Comment on a paper by Melvin Richter', in H. Lehmann and M. Richter (eds), *The Meaning of Historical Terms and Concepts: New Studies on Begriffsgeschichte*, Washington, DC: German Historical Institute, 47–58.
Polanyi, K. (1957 [1944]), *The Great Transformation: The Economic and Political Origins of Our Time*, Boston, MA: Beacon.
Polanyi, K. (1977), *The Livelihood of Man*, New York: Academic Press.
Polanyi, K. (1982), 'The economy as instituted process', in M. Granovetter and R. Swedberg (eds), *The Sociology of Economic Life*, Boulder, CO: Westview, 29–51.
Politics & Gender (2009), Special issue on feminist institutionalism, **2** (2).
Porter, M.E. (1980), *Competitive Strategy: Techniques for Analyzing Industries and Competitors*, New York: Free Press.
Porter, M.E. (1985), *Competitive Advantage: Creating and Sustaining Superior Performance*, New York: Free Press.
Porter, M.E. (1990), *The Competitive Advantage of Nations*, Basingstoke: Macmillan.
Porter, M.E. (2005), 'Building the microeconomic foundations of prosperity: findings from the Business Competitiveness Index', in M.E. Porter, K. Schwab and A. Lopez-Claros (eds), *The Global Competitiveness Report 2005–6*, New York: World Economic Forum and Basingstoke: Palgrave-Macmillan, 43–77.
Porter, M.E. and Kramer, M.R. (2011), 'The big idea: creating shared value', *Harvard Business Review*, Jan–Feb, 1–17.
Porter, M.E. and van der Linde, C. (1995), 'Green and competitive: ending the stalemate', *Harvard Business Review*, **73** (5), 120–34.
Posner, M. (1961), 'International trade and technical change', *Oxford Economic Papers*, **13** (1), 323–41.

Poulantzas, N. (1973), *Political Power and Social Classes*, London: NLB.
Poulantzas, N. (1974), *Fascism and Dictatorship: The Third International and the Problem of Fascism*, London: NLB.
Poulantzas, N. (1975), *Classes in Contemporary Capitalism*, London: NLB.
Poulantzas, N. (1978), *State, Power, Socialism*, London: NLB.
Powell, B. (2010), 'China's Property: Bubble, Bubble, Toil and Trouble', 22 March, available at: http://www.time.com/time/magazine/article/0,9171,1971284,00.html (accessed 22 July 2012).
Powell, W.W. and DiMaggio, P. (eds) (1991), *The New Institutionalism in Organizational Analysis*, Chicago, IL: University of Chicago Press.
Power, M. (1997), *The Audit Society: Rituals of Verification*, Oxford: Oxford University Press.
Pradhan, S. (2010), *Retail Merchandizing*, New Delhi: Tata McGraw-Hill Education.
President's Commission on Industrial Competitiveness (1986), *Global Competition: The New Reality*, Washington, DC: Government Printing Office.
Prestowitz, C. (2005), *Three Billion New Capitalists*, New York: Basic Books.
Przeworski, A. (1977), 'Proletariat into a class: the process of class formation from Karl Kautsky's *The Class Struggle* to recent controversies', *Politics and Society*, **7** (4), 343–67.
Pun, N. (2005), *Made in China*, Durham, NC: Duke University Press.
Ramachandariah, C. and Srinivasan, K. (2011), 'Special economic zones as new forms of corporate land grab: experiences from India', *Development*, **54** (1), 59–63.
Ramesh, J. (2005), *Making Sense of Chindia*, New Delhi: India Research Press.
Rasmus, J. (2010), *Epic Recession: Prelude to the Great Depression*, London: Pluto.
Ray, L. and Sayer, A. (eds) (1999), *Culture and Economy after the Cultural Turn*, London: SAGE.
Reichardt, R. (1998), 'Einleitung', in R. Reichardt and E. Schmitt (eds), *Handbuch politisch-sozialer Grundbegriffe in Frankreich 1680–1820*, I (2), Munich: Oldenbourg Wissenschaftsverlag, 139–48.
Reinert, E.S. (1995), 'Competitiveness and its predecessors – a 500 year cross-national perspective', *Structural Change and Economic Dynamics*, **6** (1), 23–42.
Reinert, E.S. (2007), *How Rich Countries Got Rich and Why Poor Countries Stay Poor*, London: Constable & Robinson.

Reisigl, M. and Wodak, R. (2001), *Discourse and Discrimination: Rhetoric of Racism and Anti-Semitism*, London: Routledge.

Reisigl, M. and Wodak, R. (2009), 'The discourse-historical approach (DHA)', in M. Reisigl and R. Wodak (eds), *Methods for Critical Discourse Analysis*, 2nd edn, London: SAGE, 87–119.

Rescher, N. (1975), *Theory of Possibility: A Constructivist and Conceptualist Account of Possible Individuals and Possible Worlds*, Oxford: Blackwell.

Rescher, N. (1998), *Complexity: A Philosophical Overview*, New Brunswick, NJ: Transaction Books.

Reus-Smit, C. (2011), 'The contours of analytical eclecticism', available at: http://pacs.einaudi.cornell.edu/system/files/ReusSmit-PKFest1.pdf (accessed 14 April 2013).

Rhodes, R.A.W., Blinder, S.A. and Rockman, B.A. (eds), (2008) *The Oxford Handbook of Political Institutions*, Oxford: Oxford University Press, 56–74.

Richter, M. (1990), 'Reconstructing the history of political languages: Pocock, Skinner and the *Geschichtliche Grundbegriffe*', *History and Theory*, **19** (1), 38–70.

Richter, M. (1995), *The History of Political and Social Concepts. A Critical Introduction*, Oxford: Oxford University Press.

Richter, M. (1996), 'Appreciating a contemporary classic: the *Geschichtliche Grundbegriffe* and future scholarship', in H. Lehmann and M. Richter (eds), *The Meaning of Historical Concepts*, Washington, DC: German Historical Institute, 7–20.

Ringer, F.K. (2000), *Max Weber's Methodology*, Cambridge, MA: Harvard University Press.

Roberts, J. (2004), 'Will the materialists in the Bakhtin Circle please stand up?', in J. Joseph and J. Roberts (eds), *Realism Discourse and Deconstruction*, London: Routledge, 80–110.

Robins, K. and Webster, F. (1989), *The Technical Fix: Education, Computers and Industry*, London: Routledge.

Robinson, W.I. (1996), *Promoting Polyarchy: Globalization, US Intervention, and Hegemony*, Cambridge: Cambridge University Press.

Robinson, W.I. (2004), *A Theory of Global Capitalism*, Baltimore, MD: Johns Hopkins University Press.

Roe, E. (1994), *Narrative Policy Analysis: Theory and Practice*, Durham, NC: Duke University Press.

Roelvink, G. (2010), 'Collective action and the politics of affect', *Emotion, Space and Society*, **3** (2), 111–18.

Roner, L. (2007), 'North America: Wal-Mart's ethical sourcing – green does not mean ethical', *Ethical Corporation*, 19 October, available at: http://www.laborrights.org/creating-a-sweatfree-world/wal-mart-campaign/news/11270 (accessed 15 March 2013).

Rose, N. and Miller, P. (2008), *Governing the Present: Administering Economic, Social and Personal Life*, Cambridge: Polity.

Rosiello, L. (2010 [1986]), 'Linguistics and Marxism in the thought of Antonio Gramsci', in P. Ives and R. Lacorte (eds), *Gramsci, Language and Translation*, Oxford: Lexington Books, 29–49.

Rothstein, B. (2005), *Social Traps and the Problem of Trust*, Cambridge: Cambridge University Press.

Röttger, B. (2003), 'Verlassene Gräber und neue Pilger an der Gräbestätte. Eine neo-regulationistische Perspektive', in U. Brand and W. Raza (eds), *Fit für den Post-Fordismus?*, Münster: Westfälisches Dampfboot, 18–42.

Ruedel, M. (1975), 'Gesellschaft, bürgerliche', in O. Brunner, W. Conze and R. Koselleck (eds), *Geschichtliche Grundbegriffe*, Band 2, Stuttgart: Klett-Cotta, 719–800.

Ruggie, J.G. (1982), 'International regimes, transactions, and change: embedded liberalism in the post-war economic order', *International Organization*, **36** (2), 379–415.

Rugman, A. (1991), 'Diamond in the rough', *Business Quarterly*, **55** (3), 61–4.

Rugman, A. and D'Cruz, J. (1993), 'The double diamond model: Canada's experience', *Management International Review*, **33** (Special Issue 2), 17–39.

Runciman, W.G. (1985), 'Grand theories', *London Review of Books*, **7** (18), 17 October, 18–19.

Rupert, M. (1993), 'Alienation, capitalism, and the inter-state system: towards a Marxian/Gramscian critique', in S. Gill (ed.), *Gramsci, Historical Materialism and International Relations*, Cambridge: Cambridge University Press, 67–92.

Rupert, M. (1995a), *Producing Hegemony: The Politics of Mass Production and American Global Power*, Cambridge: Cambridge University Press.

Rupert, M. (1995b), '(Re)politicizing the global economy: liberal common sense and ideological struggle in the US NAFTA debate', *Review of International Political Economy*, **2** (4), 658–92.

Rupert, M. (1997), 'Globalization and contested common sense in the United States', in S. Gill and J. Mittelman (eds), *Innovation and Transformation in International Studies*, Cambridge: Cambridge University Press, 138–52.

Rupert, M. (2003), 'Globalising common sense: a Marxian–Gramscian (re-)vision of the politics of governance/resistance', *Review of International Studies*, **29**, 181–98.

Rustemeyer, D. (2006), *Oszillationen: Kultursemiotische Perspektiven*, Würzberg: Königshausen & Neumann.
Rutherford, M. (1994), *Institutions and Economics: The Old and New Institutionalisms*, Cambridge: Cambridge University Press.
Rutherford, M. (2011), *The Institutionalist Movement in American Economics, 1918–1947: Science and Social Control*, Cambridge: Cambridge University Press.
Ryner, M. (2002), *Capitalist Restructuring, Globalization and the Third Way: Lessons from the Swedish Model*, London: Routledge.
SACOM (2007), 'Wal-Mart's Sweatshop Monitoring Fails to Catch Violations: The Story of Toys Made in China for Wal-Mart', June, available at: http://sacom.hk/wp-content/uploads/2008/07/walmart-reportsacomjun2007.pdf (accessed 14 March 2013).
Samman, A. (2013), *Re-imagining the Crises of Global Capital*, PhD Thesis, Department of Politics and International Studies, Birmingham University.
Sayer, A. (1995), *Radical Political Economy: A Critique*, Oxford: Blackwell.
Sayer, A. (1999), 'Valuing culture and economy', in L. Ray and A. Sayer (eds), *Culture and Economy after the Cultural Turn*, London: SAGE, 53–75.
Sayer, A. (2000), *Realism and Social Science*, London: SAGE.
Sayer, A. (2001), 'For a critical cultural political economy', *Antipode*, **33** (4), S. 667–708.
Sayer, A. (2002), 'Moral economy and political economy', *Studies in Political Economy*, **61**, 79–103.
Sayer, A. (2005), *The Moral Significance of Class*, Cambridge: Cambridge University Press.
Sayer, A. (2006), 'Language and significance – or the importance of import: implications for critical discourse analysis', *Journal of Language and Politics*, **5** (3), 449–71.
Sayer, A. (2009), 'The injustice of unequal work', *Soundings*, **43**, 102–13.
Sayer, A. (2012), 'Power, causality and normativity: a critical realist critique of Foucault', *Journal of Political Power*, **5** (2), 179–94.
Sayer, A. and Walker, R. (1992), *The New Social Economy: Reworking the Division of Labour*, Oxford: Blackwell.
Schabas, M. (2006), *Natural Origins of Economics*, Chicago, IL: University of Chicago Press.
Schafer, M. (1993), *The Soundscape: Our Sonic Environment and the Tuning of the World*, Rochester, VT: Destiny Books.
Scharpf, F.W. (2000), *Interaktionsformen. Akteurzentrierte Institutionalismus in der Politikforschung*, Opladen: Leske + Budrich.
Schecter, M.G. (2002), 'Critiques of Coxian theory: background to a con-

versation', in R.W. Cox with M.G. Schecter, *The Political Economy of a Plural World*, London: Routledge.

Scher, R. (2009), 'From BRIC to BIC ... or Even to IC??', available at: http://risingpowers.foreignpolicyblogs.com/2009/06/08/from-bric-to-bic%E2%80%A6or-even-ic/ (accessed 19 March 2013).

Scherrer, C. (1995), 'Eine diskursanalytische Kritik der Regulationstheorie', *Prokla*, **100**, 457–82.

Scheuerman, W.E. (2002), 'Rethinking crisis government', *Constellations*, **9**, 492–505.

Schiff, P. (2008), *Little Book of Bull Moves in Bear Markets*, Chichester: Wiley.

Schmidt, G. (2010), 'Erasing Our Innovation Deficit', available at http://www.washingtonpost.com/wp-dyn/content/article/2010/02/09/AR2010020901191.html (accessed 27 July 2012).

Schmidt, V.A. (2008), 'Discursive institutionalism: the explanatory power of ideas and discourse', *Annual Review of Political Science*, **11**, 303–26.

Schmidt, V.A. (2010), 'Taking ideas *and* discourse seriously: explaining change through discursive institutionalism as the fourth "new institutionalism"', *European Political Science Review*, **2** (1), 1–25.

Schmidt, V.A. (2012), 'Discursive institutionalism: scope, dynamics, and philosophical underpinnings', in F. Fischer and H. Gottweiss (eds), *The Argumentative Turn Revisited*, Durham, NC: Duke University Press, 85–113.

Schroeder, J. and Morling, S. (eds) (2005), *Brand Culture*, London: Routledge.

Schumpeter, J. (1934), *The Theory of Economic Development*, Cambridge, MA: Harvard University Press.

Scott, J.C. (1977), *Moral Economy of the Peasant*, New Haven, CT: Yale University Press.

Scott, J.C. (1985), *Weapons of the Weak: Power and Resistance*, New Haven, CT: Yale University Press.

Scott, J.C. (1990), *Domination and the Arts of Resistance: Hidden Transcripts*, New Haven, CT: Yale University Press.

Scott, L. (2005), 'Wal-Mart CEO credits consumers' "negotiating power" in creating savings that are improving lives', available at: http://news.walmart.com/news-archive/2005/02/23/wal-mart-ceo-credits-consumers-negotiating-power-in-creating-savings-that-are-improving-lives (accessed 7 July 2013).

Seabrooke, L. (2007), 'Varieties of economic constructivism in political economy: uncertain times for disparate measures', *Review of International Political Economy*, **14** (2), 371–85.

Sedgwick, E. (1990), *Epistemology of the Closet*, Berkeley, CA: University of California Press.
Selenu, S. (2009), 'Ives and Gramsci in dialogue: vernacular subalternity, cultural interferences, and the word-thing interdependence', *Rethinking Marxism*, **21** (3), 344–54.
Sen, S. (2008), *Globalization and Development*, New Delhi: National Book Trust.
Senellart, M. (2008), 'Course context', in M. Foucault, *Security, Territory, Population*, Basingstoke: Palgrave, 369–401.
Senge, K. (2011), *Das Neue am Neo-Institutionalismus. Der Neo-Institutionalismus im Kontext der Organisationswissenschaft*, Wiesbaden: VS Verlag.
Sharma, R. (2012), *Break Out Nations*, Harmondsworth: Penguin.
Sheller, M. (2006), 'Towards a Carribean cultural political economy', *New West Indian Guide*, **80** (1–2), 91–5.
Shenzhen Daily (2012), 'Parallel Traders a Growing Problem', 18 September, available at: http://szdaily.sznews.com/html/2012-09/18/content_2208357.htm (accessed 11 January 2013).
Shepsle, K.A. (2006), 'Rational choice institutionalism', in R.A.W. Rhodes, S.A. Binder and B.A. Rockman (eds), *The Oxford Handbook of Political Institutions*, Oxford: Oxford University Press, 23–38.
Sheth, J. (2007), *Chindia Rising*, New Delhi: Tata McGraw-Hill.
Shi, L.-W. (1999), 'To develop high technology, take employment seriously', *Wenhuibao* newspaper, 6 May (in Chinese).
Shinnick, R. (2008), 'Decoupling Thesis Intact', available at: http://seekingalpha.com/article/63886-decoupling-thesis-intact (accessed 12 March 2013).
Shionoya, Y. (ed.) (2001), *The German Historical School: The Historical and Ethical Approach to Economics*, London: Routledge.
Shiva, V. (1997), *Biopiracy: The Plunder of Nature and Knowledge*, Foxhole, Dartington: Green Books.
Shonfeld, A. (1995), *Modern Capitalism*, Oxford: Oxford University Press.
Sidaway, J. and Pryke, M. (2000), 'The strange geographies of "emerging markets"', *Transactions of the Institute of British Geographers*, **25** (2), 187–201.
Sigfusson, S. (2012), 'We Reacted Immediately to Symptoms of Crisis' (Interview with Iceland's Economy Minister), in *Der Spiegel*, 26 November, available at: http://www.spiegel.de/international/europe/icelandic-economy-minister-explains-reaction-to-finance-crisis-a-869351.html (accessed 31 January 2013).

Sil, R. and Katzenstein, P.J. (2010), 'Analytical eclecticism in the study of world politics: reconfiguring problems and mechanism across research traditions', *Perspectives on Politics*, **8** (2), 411–31.

Simpson, P. (2012), 'China Slams Survey that Shows Rising Hong Kong Resentment', available at: http://www.telegraph.co.uk/news/worldnews/asia/china/9010457/China-slams-survey-that-shows-rising-Hong-Kong-resentment.html (accessed 10 February 2013).

Sinclair, T.J. (2005), *The New Masters of Capital: American Bond Rating Agencies and the Politics of Creditworthiness*, Ithaca, NY: Cornell University Press.

Sinn, H.-W. (2010), *Casino Capitalism: How the Financial Crisis Came About and What Needs to be Done Now*, New York: Oxford University Press.

Skinner, Q. (1969), 'Meaning and understanding in the history of ideas', *History and Theory*, **8**, 3–53.

Skinner, Q. (1978), *The Foundations of Modern Political Thought I–II*, Cambridge: Cambridge University Press.

Skinner, Q. (ed.) (1985), *The Return of Grand Theory in the Human Sciences*, Cambridge: Cambridge University Press.

Skinner, Q. (1989), 'The state', in T. Ball, J. Farr and R. Hanson (eds), *Political Innovation and Conceptual Change*, Cambridge: Cambridge University Press, 90–131.

Slater, D. (2002), 'Markets, materiality and the "new economy"', in S. Metcalfe and A. Warde (eds), *Market Relations and the Competitive Process*, Manchester: Manchester University Press, 95–114.

Slaughter, S. and Leslie, L.L. (1997), *Academic Capitalism: Politics, Policies, and the Entrepreneurial University*, Baltimore, MD: Johns Hopkins University Press.

Smart, B. (1985), *Foucault*, London: Tavistock Press.

Smith, C. (2010), 'Global Economy's Next Threat: China's Real Estate Bubble', available at: http://www.dailyfinance.com/story/global-econ omys-next-threat-chinas-real-estate-bubble/19302329/# (accessed 18 January 2013).

Smith, D. (2004), 'Ideology, science and social relations: a reinterpretation of Marx's epistemology', *European Journal of Social Theory*, **7** (4), 445–62.

Smith, K. (2010), 'Gramsci at the margins: subjectivity and subalternity in a theory of hegemony', *International Gramsci Journal*, **1** (2), 39–50.

Smith, Y. (2011), *E-conned: How Unenlightened Self Interest Undermined Democracy and Corrupted Capitalism*, Basingstoke: Palgrave Macmillan.

Snowdon, B. and Stonehouse, G. (2006), 'Competitiveness in a globalized world: Porter on the microeconomic foundation of competitiveness of

nations, regions and firms', *Journal of International Business Studies*, **37**, 163–75.
Sohn-Rethel, A. (1978), *Intellectual and Manual Labour: A Critique of Epistemology*, Basingstoke: Macmillan.
Somers, M. (1994), 'The narrative constitution of identity: a relational and network approach', *Theory and Society*, **23** (5), 605–49.
Song, Y. (2010), 'Framing China under global financial crisis', paper for Annual Meeting of the International Communication Association, Singapore, 22 June 2010, http://citation.allacademic.com/meta/p_mla_apa_research_citation/4/0/3/4/8/p403482_index.html (accessed 25 March 2013).
South China Morning Post (2000), 'Hong Kong's loss of competitiveness', *Letters to Editor*, 12 December, 10.
Spector, R. (2005), *Category Killers: The Retail Revolution and its Impact on Consumer Culture*, Boston, MA: Harvard Business School Press.
Spence, L. et al. (eds) (2011), *Ethics in Small and Medium Sized Enterprises*, Dordrecht: Springer.
Spitzmüller, J. and Warnke, I.H. (2011), 'Discourse as a "linguistic object": methodical and methodological delimitations', *Critical Discourse Studies*, **8** (1), 75–94.
Spivak, G.C. (1987), *In Other Worlds: Essays in Cultural Politics*, London: Routledge.
Springer, S. (2010), 'Neoliberal discursive formations: on the contours of subjectivation, good governance and symbolic violence in post-transitional Cambodia', *Environment and Planning D: Society and Space*, **28**, 931–50.
Steger, M.B. (2002), *Globalism: The New Market Ideology*, Oxford: Rowman & Littlefield.
Steinmetz, G. (1994), 'Regulation theory, post-Marxism and the new social movements', *Comparative Studies in Society and History*, **36**, 176–212.
Stoddart, M. (2005), 'The Gramsci–Foucault nexus and environment sociology', *Alternative Routes*, **21**, 26–40.
Stone, D. (1988), *Policy Paradox and Political Reason*, Glenview, IL: Scott Foresman.
Stones, R.A. (1991), 'Strategic context analysis: a new research strategy for structuration theory', *Sociology*, **25** (3), 673–95.
Stones, R.A. (2005), *Structuration Theory*, Basingstoke: Palgrave Macmillan.
Stopford, J. and Strange, S. (1991), *Rival States, Rival Firms*, Cambridge: Cambridge University Press.

Stråth, B. (ed.) (2000), *Myth and Memory in the Construction of Community, Historical Patterns in Europe and Beyond*, Brussels: Peter Lang.

Streeck, W. (2010), 'Institutions in history: bringing capitalism back in', in G. Morgan, J.L. Campbell, C. Crouch, O.K. Pedersen and R. Whitley (eds), *The Oxford Handbook of Comparative Institutional Analysis*, Oxford: Oxford University Press, 659–86.

Sum, N.-L. (1995), 'More than a "War of Words": identity politics and the struggle for dominance during the recent political reform period in Hong Kong', *Economy & Society*, **24** (1), 68–99.

Sum, N.-L. (1996), 'The NICs and competing strategies of East Asian regionalism', in A. Gamble and A. Payne (eds), *Regionalism and World Order*, Basingstoke: Macmillan, 207–46.

Sum, N.-L. (1999), 'Rethinking globalization: rearticulating the spatial scales and temporal horizons of trans-border space', in K. Olds et al. (eds), *Globalization in the Asia Pacific*, London: Routledge, 129–46.

Sum, N.-L. (2000), 'Globalization and its "Other(s)": three new kinds of Orientalism and the political economy of trans-border identities', in C. Hay and D. Marsh (eds), *Demystifying Globalization*, Basingstoke: Palgrave, 105–26.

Sum, N.-L. (2004), 'From integral state to integral world economic order: towards a neo-Gramscian cultural political economy', Working Paper on Cultural Political Economy, available from the author on request.

Sum, N.-L. (2005), 'From the regulation approach to cultural political economy', Workpackage 1, Discussion Paper on the EU Framework 6 DEMOLOGOS project, available at: http://www.lancs.ac.uk/cperc/publications.htm (accessed 13 February 2013).

Sum, N.-L. (2009), 'The production of hegemonic policy discourses: "competitiveness" as a knowledge brand and its (re-)contextualizations', *Critical Policy Studies*, **3** (2), 184–203.

Sum, N.-L. (2010a), 'A cultural political economy of transnational knowledge brands: Porterian "competitiveness" discourse and its recontextualization in Hong Kong/Pearl River Delta', *Journal of Language and Politics*, **9** (4), 546–73.

Sum, N.-L. (2010b), 'Wal-Martization and CSR-ization in developing countries', in P. Utting and J.C. Marques (eds), *Corporate Social Responsibility and Regulatory Governance*, London: Palgrave and Geneva: UNRISD, 50–76.

Sum, N.-L. (2011), 'Financial crisis, land-induced financialization and the subalterns in China', in C. Scherrer (ed.), *China's Labour Question*, Berlin: Springer-Verlag, 199–208.

Sum, N.-L. (2013a), 'A cultural political economy of crisis recovery:

(trans)national imaginaries of "BRIC" and the case of Subaltern Groups in China', *Economy & Society*, **42** (4), in press.

Sum, N.-L. (2013b), 'A cultural political economy of crisis responses: a turn to BRIC and the case of China', in M. Benner (ed.), *Before and Beyond the Global Economic Crisis: Economics and Politics for a Post-Crisis Settlement*, Cheltenham UK and Northampton, MA, USA: Edward Elgar, 173–96.

Sum, N.-L. (2013c) 'Challenges of Renminbi internationalization: global and local responses', Rosa Luxemburg Foundation Workshop Lecture, Institut für Gesellschaftsforschung, Rosa Luxemburg Foundation, Berlin, 7 March.

Sum, N.-L. and Pun, N. (2005), 'Globalization and ethical production chain: corporate social responsibility in a Chinese workplace', *Competition and Change*, **9** (2), 181–200.

Swedberg, R. (1996), *Max Weber's Economic Sociology*, Princeton, NJ: Princeton University Press.

't Hart, P., Heyse, L. and Boin, A. (2001), 'New trends in crisis management and crisis management research: setting the agenda', *Journal of Contingencies and Crisis Management*, **9** (4), 181–8.

Tam, F. (2012), 'Rich buys basics in Hong Kong', *South China Morning Post*, 4 May, available at: http://www.scmp.com/article/1000042/shenzhens-rich-buy-basics-hk (accessed 7 December 2012).

Tang, C.C. (2007), 'Struktur/Ereignis: eine unterentwickelte, aber vielversprechende Unterscheidung in der Systemtheorie Niklas Luhmanns', *Soziale Systeme*, **13** (1–2), 86–98.

Tauheed, L.F. (2013), 'A critical institutionalist reconciliation of "contradictory" institutionalist institutions: what Is an institution?', *Journal of Economic Issues*, **47** (1), 147–67.

Taylor, C. (2004), *Modern Social Imaginaries*, Durham, NC: Duke University Press.

Taylor, M. (1999a), 'Professors say Cyberport will boost creativity', *South China Morning Post*, 24–25 March.

Taylor, M. (1999b), 'SAR sinks to third in competitiveness', *South China Morning Post*, 26 July.

Teichler, U. (1998), 'The role of the European Union in the internationalization of higher education', in P. Scott (ed.), *The Globalization of Higher Education*, Buckingham: Open University Press, 88–99.

ten Brink, T. (2007), *Kapitalismus und Staatenkonkurrenz. Ansätze eines analytischen Rahmens zur Erklärung imperialistischer Phänomene*, doctoral thesis, Frankfurt University.

Tetlock, P.C. (2007), 'Giving content to investor sentiment: the role of media in the stock market', *Journal of Finance*, **60** (3), 1139–68

Tett, G. (2010), 'The Story of the Brics', available at: http://www.ft.com/cms/s/2/112ca932-00ab-11df-ae8d-00144feabdc0.html (accessed 14 April 2013).

The 2022 Foundation (2003), 'Hong Kong and the Pearl River Delta: the economic interaction', available at: http://www.2022foundation.com/index.asp?party=reports (accessed 11 June 2007 and this report is no longer available on the worldwideweb).

The Economist (2012a), 'Dogs and Locusts', 4 February, available at: http://www.economist.com/node/21546051 (accessed 14 April 2013).

The Economist (2012b), 'Monitor's End', 14 November, available at: http://www.economist.com/blogs/schumpeter/2012/11/consulting (accessed 4 April 2013).

The White House *We The People* website (2013), 'Baby Hunger Outbreak in Hong Kong, International Aid Requested', available at https://petitions.whitehouse.gov/petition/baby-hunger-outbreak-hong-kong-international-aid-requested/xVSGJNN1 (accessed 15 March 2013).

Thelen, K. (1999), 'Historical institutionalism in comparative perspective', *American Review of Political Science*, **2**, 369–404.

Thomas, G.M., Meyer, J.W., Ramirez, F.O. and Boli, J. (eds) (1987), *Institutional Structure: Constituting State, Society, and the Individual*, London: SAGE.

Thomas, P. (2003), 'Recontextualization of management', *Journal of Management Studies*, **40** (4), 775–801.

Thompson, E.P. (1963), *The Making of the English Working Class*, London: Gollancz.

Thompson, E.P. (1971), 'The moral economy of the English crowd in the eighteenth century', in E.P. Thompson, *Customs in Common*, London: Merlin Press, 259–351.

Threadgold, T. (2003), 'Critical theory and critical discourse analysis: histories, remembering and futures', *Linguistik online*, **14**, 2/03, 1–33.

Thurow, L. (1990), 'Competing nations: survival of the fittest', *Sloan Management Review*, **32** (1), 95–7.

Thurow, L. (1992), *Head to Head*, New York: Morrow.

Thwaites, T., Davis, L. and Mules, W. (1994), *Tools for Cutural Studies*, Basingstoke: Palgrave-Macmillan.

Toffler, A. (1980), *The Third Wave*, New York: William Morrow.

Torfing, J. (1999), *New Theories of Discourse. Laclau, Mouffe and Žižek*, Oxford: Blackwell.

Tribe, K. (1978), *Land, Labour and Economic Discourse*, London: Routledge & Kegan Paul.

Tsang, A., Lucas, L. and Hume, N. (2013), 'Baby formula rations aim to stop smugglers milking Chinese frenzy', *Financial Times*, 8 April, 1.
Turner, S.P. (1994), *The Social Theory of Practices: Tradition, Tacit Knowledge and Presuppositions*, Cambridge: Polity.
United Nations (2009a), United Nations Conference on the World Financial and Economic Crisis and Its Impact on Development, 24–26 June, available at: www.un.org/ga/econcrisissummit (accessed 26 April 2013).
United Nations (2009b), *Report of the Commission of Experts of the President of the United Nations General Assembly on Reforms of the International Monetary and Financial System*, 21 September, New York: United Nations, available at: www.un.org/ga/econcrisissummit/docs/FinalReport_CoE.pdf (accessed 26 April 2013).
United Nations General Assembly (2008), *Report by the Office of the President of the General Assembly on the Inter Active Panel on the Global Financial Crisis*, 30 October, New York: United Nations, available at: www.un.org/ga/president/63/interactive/gfc/report_gfc101108.pdf (accessed 26 April 2013).
United Nations Office Vietnam (2011), 'UNIDO and CIEM promote cluster development policies for Viet Nam', available at: http://www.un.org.vn/en/feature-articles-press-centre-submenu-252/1904-unido-and-ciem-promote-cluster-development-policies-for-viet-nam.html (accessed 07 July 2013).
United Nations Industrial Development Organization (UNIDO) (2001), 'Tanzania: Sustainable Industrial Development and Competitiveness', available at: http://www.unido.org/fileadmin/user_media/Publications/Pub_free/Tanzania_sustainable_industrial_development.pdf (accessed 22 March 2013).
van Apeldoorn, B. (2002), *Transnational Capitalism and the Struggle over European Integration*, London: Routledge.
van Apeldoorn, B. (2004a), 'Theorizing the transnational: a historical materialist approach', *Journal of International Relations and Development*, 7 (2), 142–76.
van Apeldoorn, B. (2004b), 'Transnational historical materialism: the Amsterdam International Political Economy Project', *Journal of International Relations and Development*, 7 (2), 109–241.
van Apeldoorn, B. (2009), 'The contradictions of 'embedded neoliberalism' and Europe's multi-level legitimacy crisis: the European Project and its limits', in B. van Apeldoorn, J. Drahokoupil and L. Horn (eds), *Contradictions and Limits of Neoliberal European Governance: From Lisbon to Lisbon*, Basingstoke: Macmillan, 21–43.

van der Pijl, K. (1984), *The Making of the Atlantic Ruling Class*, London: Verso.
van der Pijl, K. (1998), *Transnational Classes and International Relations*, London: Routledge.
van Dijk, T.A. (1977), *Text and Context: Explorations in the Semantics and Pragmatics of Discourse*, London: Longman.
van Dijk, T.A. (1998), *Ideology, A Multidisciplinary Approach*, London: SAGE.
van Dijk, T.A. (2013), 'CDA is NOT a method of critical discourse analysis', available at: http://www.aediso.org/debate/115-cda-not-method-critical-discourse- analysis (accessed 13 March 2013).
van Heur, B. (2010), 'Beyond regulation: towards a cultural political economy of complexity and emergence', *New Political Economy*, **15** (3), 421–44.
van Leeuwen, T. (2008), *Discourse and Practice: New Tools for Critical Discourse Analysis*, Oxford: Oxford University Press.
van Treeck, T. (2012), 'Did inequality cause the financial crisis?', Institut für Makroökonomie und Konjunkturforschung Working Paper 91, Düsseldorf: IMK.
van Westen, A.C.M. (2011), 'Land in China: reform and struggles', *Development*, **54** (1), 55–8.
Vernon, R. (1966), 'International trade and international investment in the product cycle', *Quarterly Journal of Economics*, **80** (2), 190–207.
Vidal, M. (2012), 'Reckoning with the Waltonist growth regime', *New Political Economy*, **17** (5), 543–64.
Vidal, M. and Peck, J. (2012), 'Sociological institutionalism and the socially constructed economy', in T.J. Barnes, J. Peck and E. Sheppard (eds), *The Wiley-Blackwell Companion to Economic Geography*, Chichester: Wiley-Blackwell, 595–618.
Vijsysbaskar, M. (2011), 'Global Crisis, Welfare Provision and Coping Strategies of Labour in Tirupur', available at: http://re.indiaenvironmentportal.org.in/files/file/Tiruppur.pdf (accessed 12 April 2013).
Vološinov, V.N. (1973), *Marxism and the Philosophy of Language*, Cambridge, MA: Harvard University Press.
Wæver, O. (2004), 'Discursive approaches', in A. Wiener and T. Diez (eds), *European Integration Theory*, Oxford: Oxford University Press, 197–215.
Wagner, P. (1994), 'Dispute, uncertainty and institution in recent French debates', *Journal of Political Philosophy*, **2** (3), 270–89.
Wainwright, J. (2010), 'On Gramsci's "conceptions of the world"', *Transactions of the Institute of British Geographers*, **35**, S 507–21.

Wal-Mart (2003), *Factory Certification Report*. March 2003–2004, available at: http://www.walmartstores.com/Files/FactoryCertificationRep ort2003.pdf (accessed 15 October 2007 and this report is no longer available on the worldwideweb).

Wal-Mart (2006), *2006 Report on Ethical Sourcing*, available at: http:// walmartfacts.com/reprots/2006/ethical_standards/documents/2006Rep ortonEthicalSourcing.pdf (accessed 14 February 2010 and this report is no longer available on the worldwideweb).

Wal-Mart (2007), *Wal-Mart 2007 Annual Report*, available at: http:// walmartstores.com/media/investors/2007_annual_report.pdf (accessed 11 September 2011 and this report is no longer available on the worldwideweb).

Wal-Mart (2010), *Wal-Mart Annual Report 2010: We Save People Money, So They Can Live Better*, available at: http://cdn.walmartstores.com/sites/AnnualReport/2010/PDF/WMT_2010AR_FINAL.pdf (accessed 11 March 2013).

Wal-Mart (2011), *Building the Next Generation Walmart . . . Responsibly*, available at: http://walmartstores.com/sites/ResponsibilityReport/2011/ (accessed 11 March 2013).

Wal-Mart Watch (2005), *New Wal-Mart Lobbying Document Reveals Company's Nonconcern Over Loss of American Jobs*, available at: http:// walmartwatch.org/press/new-wal-mart-lobbying-document-reveals-company%E2%80%99s-nonconcern-over-loss-of-american-jobs/(accessed 11 September 2011 and this document is no longer available on the worldwideweb).

Wallerstein, I. (1975), *The Modern World System II: Mercantilism and the Consolidation of the European World-Economy, 1600–1750*, London: Academic Press.

Wallerstein, I. (1980), *The Modern World System III: The Second Era of Great Expansion of the Capitalist World-Economy, 1730–1840*, London: Academic Press.

Wallerstein, I. (1996), *Opening the Social Sciences. Report of the Gulbenkian Commission on the Restructuring of the Social Sciences*, Stanford, CA: Stanford University Press.

Wallerstein, I. (2001), *The Essential Wallerstein*, New York: Free Press.

Wallis, R. (1985), 'Institutions', in A. Kuper and J. Kuper (eds), *The Social Science Encyclopedia*, London: Routledge, 399–401.

Walmart Canada (2007), 'Sustainability Progress to Date 2007–2008', available at http://www.walmartstores.com/sites/sustainabilityreport/2007/communityEthical.html (accessed 8 July 2013).

Walmart Canada (2009), 'Responsible sourcing: being socially and environmentally responsible', Mississauga, ON: Walmart Canada.

Walsh, J.I. (2000), 'When do ideas matter? Explaining the successes and failures of Thatcherite ideas', *Comparative Political Studies*, **33** (4), 483–516.
Wang, J. and Mei, L. (2009), *Dynamics of Labour-intensive Clusters in China: Relying on Low Labour Costs or Cultivating Innovation?*, Geneva: International Institute for Labour Studies, available at: http://www.ilo.org/wcmsp5/groups/public/---dgreports/---inst/documents/publication/wcms_193157.pdf (accessed 15 March 2013).
Wang, X.-W. (2003), 'Beijing has final say on Hong Kong's constitutional reform', *South China Morning Post*, 6 December, 6.
Warner, M. (1993), *Fear of a Queer Planet: Queer Politics and Social Theory*, Minneapolis, MN: University of Minnesota Press.
Warner, M. (2012), 'Queer and then?', *The Chronicle of Higher Education*, 1 January.
Webb, D. (1999), 'Cyber Villas by the Sea', 22 March, available at: http://www.webb-site.com/articles/cybervillas.asp (accessed 7 July 2013).
Webb, D. (2004), 'Cyberport Secrets', 24 October, available at: http://webb-site.com/articles/cybersecrets.asp (accessed 8 July 2013).
Weber, M. (1949), *The Methodology of the Social Sciences*, Glencoe, IL: Free Press.
Weber, M. (1965), *General Economic History*, New York: Collins.
Weber, M. (1978), *Economy and Society*, 3 vols, Berkeley, CA: University of California Press.
Weick, K.E. (1995), *Sensemaking in Organizations*, London: SAGE.
Weimer, D.L. (ed.) (1995), *Institutional Design*, Dordrecht: Kluwer.
Wenweipao (2013), 'Sixty Percent Parallel Traders Are from Hong Kong, Better Border Control Would be Effective', 20 January, available at: http://trans.wenweipo.com/gb/paper.wenweipo.com/2013/01/20/HS1301200006.htm (accessed 14 March 2013) (in Chinese).
Wickham, G. (1987), 'Power and power analysis: beyond Foucault?', *Economy & Society*, **12** (4), 468–98.
Wickramasinghe, D. and Hopper. T. (2005), 'A cultural political economy of management accounting controls', *Critical Perspectives on Accounting*, **16** (4), 473–503.
Wikipedia (2013), 'Irrealis', available at: http://en.wikipedia.org/wiki/Irrealis_mood (accessed 23 March 2013).
Williams, R. (1971), *Communications*, 2nd edn, Harmondsworth: Penguin.
Williams, R. (1973), 'Base and superstructure in Marxist cultural theory', *New Left Review*, **82**, 3–16.
Williams, R. (1974), *Television: Technology and Cultural Form*, London: Fontana.

Williams, R. (1980), *Problems in Materialism and Culture*, London: Verso.
Williams, R. (1985), *Keywords: A Vocabulary of Culture and Society*, 2nd edn, Oxford: Oxford University Press.
Williams, R. (1993), *Keywords: A Vocabulary of Culture and Society*, Oxford: Oxford University Press.
Williams, R. (1997), *Problems in Materialism and Culture*, London: Verso.
Williamson, O.E. (1994), 'Transaction cost economics and organization theory', in N.J. Smelser and R. Swedberg (eds), *The Handbook of Economic Sociology*, Princeton, NJ: Princeton University Press, 77–107.
Williamson, O.E. (1996), *The Mechanisms of Governance*, Oxford: Oxford University Press.
Willke, H. (1997), *Der Supervisionsstaat*, Frankfurt: Campus.
Wilson, D. and Purushothaman, R. (2003), 'Dreaming with the BRICs', Global Economic Paper No. 99, Goldman Sachs Global Economic Research Website, available at: http://www.goldmansachs.com/our-thinking/archive/archive-pdfs/brics-dream.pdf (accessed 22 April 2012).
Wilson, J. and Stapleton, K. (2007), 'The discourse of resistance: social change and policing in Northern Ireland', *Language in Society*, **36** (4), 393–425.
Window of China (2009), 'China updates details of stimulus fund', 21 May, available at: http://news.xinhuanet.com/english/2009-05/21/content_11415559.htm (accessed 7 July 2013).
Winnubst, S. (2012), 'The queer thing about neoliberal pleasure: a Foucauldian warning', *Foucault Studies*, **14**, 79–97.
Wissel, J. (2007), *Die Transnationalisierung von Herrschaftsverhältnissen. Zur Aktualität von Nicos Poulantzas' Staatstheorie*, Baden-Baden: Nomos.
Wodak, R. (ed.) (1989), *Language, Power and Ideology: Studies in Political Discourse*, Amsterdam: John Benjamins.
Wodak, R. and Mayer, M. (2009), 'Critical discourse analysis: history, agenda, theory and methodology', in R. Wodak and M. Mayer (eds), *Methods of Critical Discourse Analysis*, 2nd rev. edn, London: SAGE, 1–33.
Wolff, R. (2008), 'Policies to "avoid" economic crises', *MR Zine*, 6 November, available at: http://mrzine.monthlyreview.org/index061108.html (accessed 28 March 2013).
Wong, C. and Nip, A. (2012), 'Sheung Shui Prices Soar as Mainland Traders Buy in Bulk', *South China Morning Post*, 17 September, available at: http://www.scmp.com/news/hong-kong/article/1038591/sheung-shui-prices-soar-mainland-traders-buy-bulk (accessed 13 January 2013).
World Economic Forum (2004–12), *Global Competitiveness Reports* available at: http://www.weforum.org/en/initiatives/gcp/Global%20Competitiveness%20Report/index.htm (accessed 5 February 2013).

Worth, O. (2009), 'Beyond world order and transnational classes: the (re)application of Gramsci in global politics', in M. McNally and J. Schwarzmantel (eds), *Gramsci and Global Politics: Hegemony and Resistance*, London: Routledge, 19–31.

Xi, S., Zhang, X.-D. and Cheng, Z.-Y. (2009), 'Mitigating debt bomb for Chinese local governments', *Economic Observer*, 1 June, available at: http://www.eeo.com.cn/ens/finance_investment/2009/06/01/138892.shtml (accessed 27 April 2013).

Xiamen News (2010), 'House Slave Sculpture in Xiamen Street Sparks Heated Discussion', available at: http://www.whatsonxiamen.com/news14866.html (accessed 14 April 2013).

Xinhua (2011), 'China's local government debts exceed 10t Yuan', available at: http://www.chinadaily.com.cn/bizchina/2011-06/27/content_12786826.htm, (accessed 23 March 2013).

Xue, H. (2011), 'Outsourcing in China: Wal-Mart and Chinese Manufacturers', in A. Chan (ed.), *Wal-Mart in China*, Ithaca, NY: Cornell University Press, 34–53.

Yangcheng Evening News (2012), 'Falling HK/RMB exchange rate: what is the best strategy?', 26 October, available at: http://finance.people.com.cn/stock/BIG5/n/2012/1026/c222942-19399581.html (accessed 13 January 2013) (in Chinese).

Yanow, D. (1995), 'Built space as story: the policy stories that buildings tell', *Policy Studies Journal*, **23** (4), 407–29.

Yip, S.-F. (2012), 'There must be a limit to Mainland visitor numbers', 10 December, available at: http://www.scmp.com/comment/insight-opinion/article/1101593/there-must-be-a-limit-mainland-visitor-numbers (accessed 15 March 2013).

Yonay, Y.P. (1998), *The Struggle Over the Soul of Economics: Institutionalist and Neoclassical Perspectives in America between the Wars*, Princeton, NJ: Princeton University Press.

Young, J.A. (1988), 'Technology and competitiveness: a key to the economic future of the United States', *Science*, **241**, 313–16.

Yu, H. (2011), 'Dwelling narrowness: Chinese media and its disingenuous neoliberal logic', *Continuum: Media and Cultural Studies*, **25** (1), 33–46.

Zadek, S. (2005), *Responsible Competitiveness: Reshaping Global Markets through Responsible Business Practices*, London: AccountAbility.

Zadek, S., Sabapathy, J. Dossing, H. and Swift, T. (2003), 'Responsible Competitiveness: Corporate Responsible Clusters in Actions', available at: http://www.accountability.org/images/content/1/0/107/CR%20Clusters%20-%20Full%20Report.pdf (accessed 14 February 2013).

Zafirovski, M. (2000), 'Extending the rational choice model from the economy to society', *Economy & Society*, **29** (2), 181–206.

Zheng, T.-X. (2006), 'On the marginalization of Hong Kong', *Singtao* (newspaper), 11 September (in Chinese).
Ziltener, P. (2001), *Strukturwandel der Europäischen Integration*, Münster: Westfälisches Dampfboot.

Name index

Aglietta, Michel 10, 70, 82, 200, 246, 253, 257
Althusser, Louis x, 83, 111, 121, 165, 249, 252
Andersen, Niels-Åkerstrøm 40, 111, 113, 133, 207
Anderson, Benedict 173
Angermüller, Johannes 115, 140
Apeldoorn, Bastiaan van 86
Archer, Margaret 64, 195
Augustine of Hippo 410

Bakhtin, Mikhail M. 104–7, 123, 163, 171, 205, 319
Balibar, Etienne 212
Barbieri, Marcello 152,195
Bartoli, Matteo 74, 103, 130
Bernstein, Basil 205, 306
Best, Jacqueline 18
Bevir, Mark 54, 134
Bloch, Marc 121, 130, 143
Blyth, Mark 53, 54, 56, 69, 84, 397
Bourdieu, Pierre 19, 36, 51, 57, 82f
Boyer, Robert 45, 72, 81, 82–3, 84, 176, 200, 249, 252f
Braudel, Fernand 121f, 130, 142
Brunner, Otto 44
Buci-Glucksmann, Christine 67
Bührmann, Andrea 111, 113
Busse, Dietrich 116
Butler, Judith 17, 62

Cafruny, Alan 80, 85
Callon, Michel 19, 83, 217
Candeias, Mario 87, 92–3
Castoriadis, Cornelius 171
De Certeau, Michel 115, 142
Chartier, Roger 121f, 142, 143–4
Chouliaraki, Lilie 127
Coase, Ronald 40
Commons, John R. 39

Côté, Mark 113, 142,
Cox, Robert W. 76–80, 85, 200, 201–2, 347
Crouch, Colin 36, 37, 419

D'Andrea Tyson, Laura 298
Dean, Mitchell 48–9, 111, 123, 205
Debray, Régis 118, 138, 395–6, 469
Demirović, Alex 82, 87, 91
Derrida, Jacques 127, 131
Deutsch, Karl W. 283, 401, 415
DiMaggio, Paul 42f, 46f, 67
Diskin, Jonathan 179
Djelic, Marie-Laure 39, 46, 68–9
Drahos, Peter 294–5
Duby, Georges 122, 142
Du Gay, Paul 19, 182
Duke, Michael 350
Dumez, Hervé 66, 82, 217
Durkheim, Emile 43, 122

Eagleton, Terry 24, 153
Eco, Umberto 3, 24
Egan, Daniel 79
Eklund, Magnus 272
Elden, Stuart 208, 212
Elder-Vass, Dave 51
Emanuel, Rahm 453
Engels, Friedrich 117, 168–9, 188, 258–9
Enright, Michael 353–6, 359–64
Etzkowitz, Henry 292

Fairclough, Norman xi, 124–7, 130, 153–4, 158, 165, 184, 205, 216, 291
Favereau, Oliver 81, 84
Febvre, Lucien 121f, 130
Florida, Richard 268, 297
Foucault, Michel xi, 5, 20, 22, 51–2, 62, 80, 101, 111–16, 123, 127, 130, 132, 143, 163, 196–7, 201, 205–13, 217, 219, 238, 342, 350f, 360

549

Friedman, Milton 396
Fung, Victor 325, 359, 361

Galbraith, John K. 257
Geertz, Clifford 5
Gereffi, Gary 297, 312, 331ff
Germain, Randall 76
Giddens, Anthony 49f, 150
Gill, Stephen 76, 80, 200–2, 329, 347, 350, 418
Godin, Benoît 272, 274ff, 279ff
Goodin, Robert 34, 37, 47
Gramsci, Antonio x, xi, 1, 19, 22, 52, 72–76, 77f, 82, 92–3, 95, 100, 102–4, 109, 130, 171, 174, 196–202, 204, 205–11, 215, 219, 222, 290, 350ff, 366
Greenspan, Alan 190–1, 423

Habermas, Jürgen 128, 130
Hall, Peter A. 35, 42, 44, 46, 234
Hall, Stuart 19, 80, 119
Hay, Colin 56, 59–60, 71n, 405
Hegel, Georg W.F. 16
Hirsch, Joachim 86, 267
Hodge, Bob 123, 142
Hoggart, Richard 19, 116, 119
Hudson, Ray 20
Husserl, Edmund 130, 143

Ifversen, Jan 107, 110
Innis, Harold 19, 118, 142, 194
Ives, Peter 75, 77, 100, 102ff, 121, 142, 164

Jäger, Margarete 114
Jäger, Siegfried 29, 70n, 112, 114–15
Jenson, Jane 56, 87, 89
Jessop, Bob 5, 66, 95, 150, 166, 186, 196, 205, 213, 258, 264, 284, 416
Jeunemaître, Alain 66, 82, 217
Ji, Joo-Hyoung 410, 439, 477
Jones, Gareth Stedman 156
De Jong, Elke 19

Kenney, Mike 76
Koselleck, Reinhart 58, 100, 107–10, 135, 143
Kress, Gunther 124, 142, 149, 152f

Kristeva, Julia 153
Krugman, Paul 266, 298
Krzyżanowski, Michal 128
Kuhling, Carmen 79
Kuhn, Thomas 39, 130

Labrousse, Agnès 72, 81
Laclau, Ernesto 90, 126, 129–31, 143, 153, 177–80, 188
Lakatos, Imre 39, 294
Lash, Scott 19, 177, 182
Lemke, Thomas 212
Lévi-Strauss, Claude 153
Lévy-Bruhl, Lucien 122
Link, Jürgen 114–15,137
Lipietz, Alain 16, 87, 88–9, 93, 246, 249, 256
Lo Piparo, Franco 102
Lordon, Frédéric 82, 83–4
Luhmann, Niklas 100, 134–5, 142, 143, 149
Lundvall, Bengt-Åke 272, 277, 297
Lury, Celia 304

McCarney, Joe 168–9
McLuhan, Marshall 118, 142
Machiavelli, Niccolò 121, 202
Maier, Florentine 29, 115
Maihofer, Andrea 163
Malpas, Jeff 66
Mao, Zhe-Dong 249
March, James G. 42f, 53, 66
Marsden, Richard 197, 206–7, 209, 211–12, 238
Marx, Karl 1, 5, 7, 18, 75, 85, 117, 130, 168–9, 179, 183, 187f, 195, 197, 199, 206–7, 209, 212f, 233f, 238–40, 243, 245, 258–9, 263, 288, 423
Mayntz, Renate 37, 60–1
Melve, Leidulf 121, 134,137–8, 143
Meyer, Michael 125, 128, 482
Miettinen, Reijo 51, 272, 277–8
Miller, Jacques-Alain 133
Miller, Peter 205
Mills, C. Wright 99
Minsky, Hyman P. 424–5, 427, 439
Mouffe, Chantal 90, 126, 129–31, 143, 153, 177–80, 188

Morris, Charles W. 4
Myrdal, Gunnar 39

Nietzsche, Friedrich 130
North, Douglass C. 35, 42, 55–6, 69, 288

Offe, Claus 396
Olsen, Johan P. 42f, 53, 66
O'Neill, Jim 442–50, 461
Orwell, George 163
Overbeek, Henk 85

Palonen, Kari 110
Palombarini, Stefano 84
Paterson, Matthew 18
Pêcheux, Michel 111, 153
Peirce, Charles Sanders 4, 11, 479
Peltonen, Matti 13, 142
Peters, B. Guy 46
Peters, Michael 273
Petit, Pascal 251
Pierson, Paul 46, 47, 62
Pocock, John 119–20
Polanyi, Karl 43–4, 45, 154, 175, 195, 263, 284
Porter, Michael E. 266, 296, 299–308, 311, 319–22, 349, 360
Poulantzas, Nicos x, 67, 71n, 109, 183, 419
Prestowitz, Clyde 449
Przeworski, Adam 187

Rasmus, Jack 419
Ray, Larry 183
Reinert, Erik S. 266, 296f
Reisigl, Martin 126, 128f, 143
Rescher, Nicolas 110, 235
Rhodes, Roderick 54, 134
Ricardo, David 73, 76, 179, 212
Richter, Melvin 100, 108
Robinson, William I. 76f, 200
Rose, Nik 205
Röttger, Bernd 183, 251
Runciman, W. Gary 99
Ruggie, John 320
Rupert, Mark 76, 78, 169–70
Ryner, Magnus 80, 84f

Sachs, Jeffrey 307
Sala-i-Martin, Xavier 307–8
Sandler, Blair 179
Saussure, Ferdinand de 11, 54–5, 108, 159, 215, 479
Sayer, Andrew 7–8, 19, 162, 183, 184, 286
Scharpf, Fritz W. 60–1
Scherrer, Christoph 66, 87, 89–91, 133, 276
Schmidt, Vivien 55, 56–78, 215
Schmitt, Carl 130
Schneider, Werner 111, 113
Schumpeter, Joseph A. 298
Scott, James C. 115
Scott, Lee 339
Shiva, Vandana 287
Short, Nicola 77
Sinclair, Timothy 80
Skinner, Quentin 99–100, 119, 121
Smith, Adam 16, 212, 297
Smith, Dorothy 20, 168–9
Somers, Margaret 404f
Soskice, David 45, 234
Spitzmüller, Jürgen 58, 97, 116, 154
Spivak, Gayatri Chakravorty 188
Stapleton, Karyn 58
Stiglitz, Joseph A. 432
Stråth, Bo 110
Streeck, Wolfgang 46, 233
Sum, Ngai-Ling 196, 205, 318, 353, 360, 387, 459

Taylor, Charles 165, 171
Taylor, Rosemary M. 35, 36, 42, 44, 46
Thompson, Edward P. 7, 19, 116
Threadgold, Terry 58
De Tracy, Comte Destutt 479
Tsang, Donald 359, 368

Urry, John xi, 19, 177, 182

van Dijk, Teun 101, 124f
van Leeuwen, Leo 124f
van der Pijl, Kees 85–6
Veblen, Thorstein 39
Vološinov, Valentin 104, 105

Wallerstein, Immanuel 11, 234
Walton, Sam 331

Warnke, Ingo 58, 97, 116, 154
Waxman, Henry 190–1
Weber, Max 39, 83, 132, 233, 251
Wickham, Gary 66, 186, 195
Williams, Raymond 19, 80, 116–20, 121, 136, 173, 177, 194
Wittgenstein, Ludwig 130

Wodak, Ruth xi, 124ff, 128–9, 143, 482
Wolff, Rick 399–400
Worth, Owen 77, 79, 80

Zadek, Simon 320, 347
Žižek, Slavoj 132–3

Subject index

Page numbers in bold indicate places where the relevant index item is defined or discussed more fully.

abstract–concrete 7–10, 23, 41, 46, 88, 482
  see also logical–historical, simple–complex
academic–policy–consultancy circuit 296, 319, 321–2, 352, 358
accountAbility 320
accumulation regime (and mode of regulation) 27, 34, 52, 61, 76, **81–2**, 87ff, **89–91**, 173, 182, 200, **235–8**, **246f**, 251–3, 258, 265, 472
  and contradictions **235–8**, **246–50**
  and crisis **249**, 253–5
  en régulation 81, 91, 251–4, 257, 261ff, 284, 417f
  and spatio-temporal fixes **248f**, 250, 258
  see also accumulation strategy, Atlantic Fordism, Fordism, Green New Deal, knowledge-based economy, finance-dominated accumulation, spatio-temporal fix, Wal-Martization, Waltonism
accumulation strategy 87, 181f, 185, 203, 209, 226, 247f, 258, 291, 293, 317, 338, 350, 355–8, 366ff, 431, 438, 469
activity theory 51
actor-network theory 217, 219, 230
advocacy 203ff, 344, 354, 359, 407
aestheticization 19
affect 202, 210, 214, 222f, 305, 317, 366, 371, 441, 448, 452–4, 462, 470
  see also desire, hope/fear, hope/strength
affordance 9, 29

agency x, 26, 33, 36, 41, 48–51, 63, 86, 89ff, 100, 106, 132, 137f, 174, 177, 182, **187–90**, 191, 202, 219–21, 229, 242–3, 245, 252, 258, 304–5, 316f, 358–64, 440
  see also selectivity (agential), strategic-relational approach
agent-centred institutionalism **60–2**
ALBA (Bolivarian Alliance for the Americas) 433
'*Always Low Prices*' 324, 331
Americanism 73–9, 198ff, 226
Amsterdam School 80, **84–6**, 246
anatomopolitics 208–9, 218
Anglo-Foucauldian approach to governmentality 66, 205, 213, 346
Annales School **121–3**, 129, 143f
antagonism 105, 177f, 187, 195, **252–3**, 259
anti-disciplinary approach 14–15, 471
anti-essentialism 90, 132, 189
apartheid 481
apparatus 34, 51f, 70, 163, 208
  coercive 199, 210
  discursive 222, 296, 317, 360, 364f, 368f, 374, 442, 452–3, 462
  economic 73, 405
  ideological 210, 405
  hegemonic 86, 201, 210
  knowledge 222, 306–9, 322, 341, 343, 360, 362, 441
  logic 113, 210, 216
  state 205, 210, 405, 435
  technological 222
  see also dispositive
appareil, *see* apparatus
archaeology 100f, 111ff, 123, 130

553

argumentation 16, 26, 57, 69, 121, 128, 130, 135, 193, 405f
articulation 72, 90, 131–4, 178f
ASEAN countries 270, 302, 314
Asia Competitiveness Institute (Singapore) 301–3, 311, 314
Asian Development Bank 301–2, 306, 311, 314, 322, 450
Asia Development Outlook 306, 311
assemblage 150, 208, 211, 218, 224, 317, 350
   see also apparatus, dispositive
Atlantic Fordism 200, 246, 251–2, **253–7**, 261f, 270, 277, 290f, 296, 299
   see also Fordism
audit 325, 339–43, 349
   see also '*Beyond Audit*' approach
austerity 245, 414, 419–20, 422, 425, 427–30
authorial intention 57, 98, 107, 111, 119, 121, 124, 134, 136ff
   see also reception

Bakhtin Circle **104–7**, 171, 205
base (economic) 92, 114, 117, 132, 143, 178,199
   see also economism, superstructure
baselines 387, 390–1
basic concept (*Grundbegriff*) 107–10
Begriffsgeschichte 135, 137
   see also semantic conceptual history
Beijing Consensus 451
benchmarking 167, 227, 279, **307–11**, 322, 336, 341ff, 362
best practice 222, 296, 304, 310, **315–17**, 322, **344–7**
'*Beyond Audit*' approach 325, 343–7, 389, 391
'*Big gifts*' discourses 353, 368–75, 389, 391
biopiracy 287
biopolitics 209, 218
biosemiosis 152, 195
body politics 322
Bretton Woods 254ff, 399, 429, 453
BRIC (Brazil, Russia, India, China) 226, 228, 255, 289, 407f, 420f, 429, **440–64**
   three stages in BRIC discourse, 440–54
BRIC summits 451
bricolage 33, 36, 66, 150
bubbles 357, 406, 419, 422, 441, 454, 458, 463
business schools 203, 301, 319, 325, 366

calculation 12, 26, 35f, 54, 62, 166f, 176, 181, 183, 191, 211, 334ff, 342, 471, 479
   strategic 6, 49ff, 63, 114, 203f, 217, 370
Cambridge School (pragmatic conceptual history) 119–21, 128f, 130, 137
capacity-building discourses and practices 312–13, 315–16, 344–6
capital as object of regulation **241–4**
capital as a social relation **238–40**, 246, 251
capitalism 61, 233f
   academic 292f
   commonalities of **237**
   variegated 234–5
   varieties of 182, 234–5
   see also accumulation strategy, cell form, class, commercial capital, commodity, competition, competitiveness, contradiction, fictitious commodity, finance-dominated accumulation, financial capital, fix, interest-bearing capital, labour, labour market, market economy, market forces, mode of regulation, money, productive capital, profit, profit-oriented-market-mediated accumulation, profit-producing capital, structural form, world market
capitalist mode of production 74, 169, 178, 234, 237–40, 263, 423
capitalist social formation 23, 44, 141, 212ff, 237, 472
catch-up competitiveness 289, 296, 306, **310–18**
catch-up metaphors 311, 444
categories 75, 155, 169, 171, 175–7

Subject index

category management 324, **334–5**, 350
causation 3–4, 9, 143, 155, 158
cell form **238–9**
centre–periphery 4, 236, 270, 401, 417, 420, 430, 438, 481
   linguistic 103, 120
chain discourses and metaphors 296, 306, 312–18
   see also cluster discourses
chambers of commerce 301, 359, 366, 368
Charybdis 22
   see also constructivism, Scylla and Charybdis
Chimerica 5, 436
China 266, 276, 281, 294, 352f, 369, 406f, 416, 429, 432, 440–63
   and Hong Kong 352–90
   pathological co-dependency with USA 5, 426
Christian free enterprise 331
civilization 79–80
civil society 16, 107, 173, 198, 200f, 207, 209ff, 290, 320, 354, 357, 364f, 437
   see also lifeworld
class 80, 85f, 121, 126, 168, 178, 223, 404
   agency 86
   alliance 77, 85, 189
   compromise 85, 209, 255f, 317
   domination 84f, 102, 105f, 118, 168, 190, 206f, 416
   fraction 77f, **84–5**, 203, 223, 236, **243**, 248, 418
   identities and lines of conflict 223, 229, 241, 297
   identity 79, 86, 179, 188ff, 194
   interest 86, 189f
   powers 71, 198, 416
   relations 259
   relevance 79, 188–90
   struggle 91, 105ff, 183, 187ff, 241, 286
   subaltern 106f, 201
   transnational 77
class analysis 74, 121, 179
closure, incomplete 90, 192
cluster discourses 296, 300–1, 306, 312–17, 360–1

cluster observatory 315, 326, 328
cluster plans and programmes 304, 313–17
cluster policy and methodologies 315–18
coercion 77f, 198ff, 201, 206, 210, 224, 435
co-evolution 5, 23, 37, 52, 103, 113, 135, 140, **184–6**, 202, 464, 470, 474f
collective symbols 114f
commercial capital 358ff, 361, 367, 374, 379, 392f
   see also financial capital, service bloc
commodification 241
commodity 237, 238f, 284
   see also fictitious commodity
commodity form 237, 239, 263
common sense 201, 206f, 211, 222, 229, 319, 353, 366, 378–90, 454–5, 463, 480
competition 35, 237, 240, 234, 237, 242, 259, **261–80**, 286f
   units of 266–7
competition state **267**, 285
competitiveness 202, 211–13, 216, 226, 266, 275ff
competitiveness clusters 324–9
competitiveness discourses 202, 211–13, 216, 226, 262, 266f, 275, 287, 292, **296–318**, **352–92**
   'industry standard' 304
   three stages 296–305, 325
   see also catch-up competitiveness, green and responsible competitiveness, chains, clusters, 'diamond model', indexes, knowledge brand, neoliberal competitiveness, policy paradigm, theoretical paradigm
competitiveness integration (dis)order 352–9
complexity 3, 13–15, 21
   reduction 3, 23–4, 110, 130, 140, **147–51**, 153, 155, 158, 164, 170, 172–3, 180f, 188, 191f, 194, 197, 213f, 247, 317, 350, 408, 437, 469, 472–6
   structured vs unstructured 52

compossibility **3–5**, 24, 148f, 150–1, 160–1, 168, 192, **235–6**, 259, 427
compromise, institutionalized 33, 81–4, 89, 91, 149, 177, 185, 248–50, 257, 400
   see also unstable equilibrium of compromise
concept of control 85–6, 176
consensus 56, 92f, 109, 118, 277f, 399
   see also hegemony, ideology
conjunctural analysis 197, 204, 219, 317
   see also strategic-relational approach
conjuncture 121f, 187, 217
conscience collective 43, 122
'constitutive outside' 130, 131, 173, 247, 261
construal 4, 29, 112–15, 149, 157, 265, 281, 283, 437, 474–5
   vs construction 4, 29, 147, **161–3**, 165, 184, 473–5
   see also crisis, construal
construction 203–4, 210, 216, 221–30 passim 265, 270, 283, 296, 306–9, 342–4, 352–5, 368–71, 374–7
constructivism 18, 26, 40, 47, 54ff, 62, 65, 71, 84f, 105, 127, 143, 157, 177–181, 226, 395–6, 410, 467f, 470ff
consultancy firms 301, 343, 354
consultancy knowledge 299, 304–18
consumption/consumers 19, 20, 81f, 91, 199, 246, 254ff, 380, 386f, 442, 446–51, 453, 458, 463
context 4, 97f, 107, 125, 128, 138
   spatio-temporal 174, 248, 400, 427
contingency 132, 178f, 468
contingent necessity 5, 41, 264, 474
contradictions 61, 66, 69, 85, 88ff, 92, 141, 150, 155, 182f, 186f, 192, 212, 223, 226, 229, 233–7, 242f, **244–51**, 258, 262, 289, 319, 397, 416, 478
   and crises 397
   and Foucault 213
   aspects 249ff, 251f, 254ff
   of neo-liberalism 436
   principal 249, 251, 254, 284f, 416
   secondary 249, 254
   socio-ideological 106f
   and world market 418
   see also institutional fix, semantic fix, social fix, spatio-temporal fix
contradictory consciousness 222–3
conventions, economics of 19, 53, 82ff
corporate form 264
corporate social responsibility 226, 319–22, 339–50
Corporate Watch 338
'correct' construals 402, 432, 469
Council on Competitiveness 276, 299
counterconcept 109
counter-hegemony 165, 173f, 197, 201, 203, 214, 218f, 223–4, 265, 273, 283, 318, 353, 358, 390f, 401, 427, 433, 438, 468, 477f
credit 239, 244, 251, 255ff, 395, 417, 420f, 427, 431, 435, 454, 458
   crunch 419ff, 448, 461
crisis 23, 25, 75, 88, 90, 107, 130, 245, 173, 184, **396–400**, 469
   Accidental vs systemic 397
   Asian 354, 356, 399
   blame 399, 406
   construal 282, **398–400**, 403–4, 415, 421–2, 425–6, 437–40, 469
   of crisis-management 5, 252f, **398**, 413
   CPE approach 397–8
   economic 249
   as event or process 421
   in eurozone 426–7
   of finance-dominated accumulation 418–20
   of Fordism 399
   in versus *of* a system 249, 398, 400
   organic, of neoliberalism 92
   recovery 226, 440, 454, 463
   SARS 358, 367–8
   subprime 449
   see also North Atlantic Financial Crisis
crisis-tendency 141, 186, 233
critical discourse analysis 20f, 59, 101ff, 115, **124–6**, 127f, 197, 203–5, 219
critical institutionalism 35, 48, 61–2
critical realism ix, 2, 6, **8–10**, 20–1, 28, 48, 51–2, 100, 126, 197, 241, 267, 410, 412, 470
critique 4, 7, 128, 164

of domination 4, 150f, 164f, 191, 197, 230, 240, **479–81**
of ideology 4, 151, 165, 168–70, 197, 230, 240, **479–81**
cultural economy 18–19
culturalization 19, 177, 182
cultural materialism 80, **116–19**, 120, 136, 177, 473
  in anthropology 117, 142
cultural political economy **18–19**, **23–5**, 47, 72, 124, 129, 130ff, 139ff, 147ff, 158, 181ff, 186–90, 192–3, 206f, 218ff, 229–30, 233ff, 293–4
  vs constructivism 226
  and critical realism x, 1, 6, 8–10, 28, 48, 98, 129, 197, 214, 241, 267
  and disciplines 1
  differs from neo-Foucauldian approaches 226, 229, 299
  Gramsci as proto-CPE analyst 72–6
  heuristic schema 214–29
  and institutionalism 36, 45, 54, 56
  meso-level research agenda 196–229
  and regulation approach 82–7
  seven discursive–material moments 219–29
  six key themes 8, 23, 147, 196–8, **472–6**
  as social science 2
cultural studies 16–19, 73, 80, 118–19, 136, 467, 471
cultural turn, *see* turns
culture viii, 5, 117
  and meaning making viii
cultural vs social 155

databases 304, 333–6
debt 256, 395, 407, 413f, **418–22**, 425, 427ff, 435, 439, 449f, 458
deinstitutionalization 69
Denkformen (forms of thought) 98, 163
depoliticization 224
desire 83f
determinism,
  economic 178, 181
  structural 46, 90, 132, 180
developmentalism 318–19, 322

development discourses 221, 311–19
development outlooks 304, 306, 322
diagram of power 208, 210
  see also dispositive
'*diamond model*' 299–301, 304–5, 317
  see also competitiveness discourses
differential accumulation 239ff, 252, 264, 387, 468
dilemmas 61, 66, 69f, 141, 182f, 199, 237, 242f, **245–50**, 251ff, 258, 397, 421
  methodological 41–3
discipline 13, 34, 477
disciplinary technology 80, 201, 211ff, 336, 477
discoursal 59, 124ff, 153f, 158, 160
discourse 97, **151–3**, 201, 204, **207–11**
  discourse analysis 16, 58–9, 96, 132
  forms of 104–5, 153, 160
  orders of 158, 208
  see also critical discourse analysis, intellectuals
discourse coalitions 203, 205
discourse and dispositive analysis 101, **111–16**
  see also dispositive
discourse historical approach 124, 127, 143
discursive ability 57f, 215, 412
discursive competence 215
discursive economy 111ff
discursive formation 1, 16, 101, **111–15**, 130, 155,194, 205f, 210, 215, 474
discursive–material 214–16, **219–29**, 306, 390
discursive node 115
dispositive 25, 34, 51–2, 113, 138, 142, 160, 208, 211, 216, 246f, 317, 350, 364–5, 368, 453, 462
  in CPE **208**
  Foucault on 113f
  Jürgen Link on 114
dispositivization 223, 242
domination 8, 21, 23, 28, 80, 101ff, 107, 114f, 125f, 148, 162, 171f, 190, 201, 206, 238, 246, 399f, 405, 431, **477–9**
Duisburg School 115, 126

eclecticism 67, 94, 159, 471, 482
ecological dominance **235–6**, 253, 262, 469
ecological imaginaries 87, 258, 424f
economic imaginaries 1, 23, 81, 87, 94, 141, 147, 166, 186, 196, 252, 261–5, **283–4**, 296, 355ff, 472ff, 478
economism 73, 94, 131, 175–7, 477
education 276–8, 284–5, **290–5**
embedded liberalism 254
emergence 155, 167, 396f, 481f
emerging markets 277, 301, 428f, 441–44, 452
Enright, Scott and Associates Ltd 301, 303, 311, 314, 324–5
entrepreneurship 237, 269, 282, 292, 298, 310–18, 396
entry-point 7, 21, 27, 38, 42, 142, 170, 182, 187, 214, 220, 265, 271–2, 397, 472
environmental sustainability 318
episteme 111, 116, 123, 130, 163, 173, 212
epistemic community 55, 67, 203, 470
epistemic fallacy 24
epistemic grammar 222, 306–18, 322, 364
epistemology 2, 5–6, 8, 10, 13–15, 20, 41, 116, 125, 132, 168, 194, 278–9, 482
  see also truth regimes
Erfahrung 170
  see also learning
Erlebnis, see lived experience
essentialism 132, 178f
  strategic **187–9**, 223, 397, 439
Essex School 126
ethico-political 12, 199
  see also new ethicalism
ethics 1, 7–8, 111
  standards 338–43
  see also moral economy
European Union 4, 80, 85f, 266, 270, 275, 319, 407, 420, 423ff, 429, 438
eurozone 5, 84, 235, 416, 426f, 435, 449, 452, 461
everyday life 8, 18–19, 58, 70, 101, 104–5, 122, 163, 312, 317, 322, 353ff, 364ff, 378, 381f, 387, 391, 402, 406, 412ff, 455, **458–61**, 480

evolutionary mechanisms, *see* variation–selection–retention
evolutionary turn 22, 98f, 161, 474
exchange-value 85, 230, 237, **243–4**, 259, 384
  vs use-value 237, **243–4**, 269
  see also neoliberalism
exorbitation of language 127, 139f, 153, 471
expertise 154, 221–2, 287, 317, 343, 359, 462
explanation 3, 7, 9–10, 25, 27, 54f, 59, 65, 100, 132, 142, 155, 158, 233, 391, 490
exploitation 165, **179**, 189, 195, **240**, 242, 248, 331, 333
explosion (of antagonisms, contradictions) 252
export-orientation 311–12, 316, 333
extra-discoursal 131
extra-discursive 28, 45, 110ff, 124, 132, 147, **155ff**, 162, 178, 182, 194, 215, 247, 305
extra-economic 33, 67, 76, 167, 173ff, 181ff, 191f, 238, 241ff, 262–75, 281ff, 293, 418
extra-linguistic 59, 102, 108, 128
extra-semiotic 4, 23ff, 75, 134, 141, 147, 156, 163f, 167, 172ff, 177f, 180f, 185ff, 193, 208, 238, 265, 396f, 402f, 411, 474ff, 480

facticity 149, 191, 195
factor-driven growth 266, 301
factory-rating system 341–2, 350
feeling, structure of 120, 122, 218, 471, 479
feminism 10, 17, 47f, 62, 434
fetishism 12, 62, 88, 132, 169, 175f, 207
fictitious commodity 44f, 154, 179, 211, 237–40, 245, 259, 263, 271, 284, 287, 290
finance-dominated accumulation 200, 261–2, 264, 269, 398, **415–21**, 425f, 429, **435–6**, 454, 467
finance-led growth 200, 432
financial capital 236, 332, 359, 392, 416–9, 426f, 434f, 452
financialization 18, 264, 297, 406, 416f, 419, 454

Subject index 559

fix
  see institutional fix, semantic fix, social fix, spatio-temporal fix
flexible specialization 200
flexicurity 245
Fordism 74f, 78, 87, 198ff, 226, 331
  see also Atlantic Fordism
foreign direct investment 311, 316–18, 322
form analysis 90, 158, 246
formation analysis 111
forum, policy 352, 360, 363, 400
Foundation 2022 325
Foundation of MSME Clusters (India) 303, 315
Frankfurt School 91f, 128
functionalism 93, 99, 123
fund managers 228, 441–2, 444, 447, 449

G-2 407
G-8 429, 452
G-20 407, 429, 442, 451, 455
G-77 329f, 429
GATS 324, 329, 331, 347–9
GATT 256
Gegenbegriff (counter-concept) 107
  see also semantic conceptual history
genealogy 100, 111ff, 130, 132, 475
general intellect 284
general theory 98–99, 111
genre **104**, 128, 475
genre chain 127, 155, 205, 216ff, 221, 230, 294, 296, 304, 322, 326, 338f, 360, 389f, 441, 449, 462
German historical school x, 10, 39, 72
German regulation approach 86–7
Germany 91, 107, 422ff
global capitalism 324–5, 349
global commodity chains 264, 297, 312, 317–18, 322, 333, 336ff
  see also world market
Global Compact 320, 347
Global Competitiveness Index 306–9, 322
Global Competitiveness Reports 306–9, 322
globalization 78, 127, 175, 221, 255, 262–6, **269**, 290, 296f, 299, 312, 324, 347, 443f, 450

  see also global commodity chains, world market
glocal partnerships 324, 331f
'going on' in the world **21–2**, 24, 147f, 158, 165f, 169–73, 188, 191, 195, 265, 395, 408, 412, 476, 479
Goldman Sachs 441–7, 462
good governance 11, 16, 282
governance 11, 70, 166, 243, 246, 446, 478
  chronotopic 63
  collaborative 320–1
  different from régulation **246**
  at a distance 371
  economic 166, 182ff, 212, 408f, 467
  global economic 11, 432, 437
  international 407, 442
  multi-scalar 284f
  object(s) of 166, 210, 212f, 220, 226, 311
  see also regulation, governmentality, régulation-cum-governance, service governance, spatio-temporal fix, technologies
governmentality 11, 101, 130, 166, 201, 210, 213–14
  see also technologies
governmentalization 197, 201, 206–11
  see also dispositives, knowledging technologies
grand theory 1, 10, 41, **99–100**, 102ff, 111, 123, 139, 467
  allegedly inoperationalizable 128
  see also Annales School, Bahktin Circle, Cambridge School, cultural materialism, discourse and dispositive analysis, historical semantics, semantic conceptual history, vernacular materialism
green competitiveness 319–22
Green New Deal 274, 319, 321, 426, 431, 449
Grenoble School 246
grounded analytics **123–4**, 139, 467
  see also critical discourse analysis, discourse historical approach, post-Marxism, reception theory
grounded heuristics viii
grounded theory 123, 128

Growth and Business Competitiveness
    Index 306–8
Grundbegriff, see basic concept
gurus 204, 221, 304–5

habitus 36, 51, 282, 478
hard political economy 132, 175ff, 187,
    193, 223, 468
Harvard Business School 296, 299,
    301, 304, 311, 325, 349, 359
    see also Asian Competitiveness
        Institute, Institute for Strategy
        and competitiveness
Harvard–Porterian brand 324–5, 352,
    354, 358–61, 364
hegemonic bloc 198
hegemonic project 28, 86, 92, 182, 186,
    204, 214, 219, 223ff, 248, 296–7,
    353, 358, 366, 390, 392f, 438
hegemony 23, 69, 74, 76ff, 85ff, 89, 92,
    101, 120, 131, 149, 206–7, 208,
    214ff, 221–9, 358–65
    in production 196, **198–200**, 206,
        229f
    production of 196, **200–30**, **296–318**,
        357, 364, 462
    struggles over 92, 165, 171, 289, 354,
        357
heteroglossia 104ff, 152, 222
heteronormativity 62, 481
hierarchization in fixes **248ff**
historical bloc 77f, 171, 196–9, 207, 475
    Transnational 200
historical discourse analysis 127
historical materialism 102, 117, 195,
    470
historical semantics 100, 122, **134–6**
historicity
    as historical situatedness 5, 115
    as use of history to make history 63,
        414–15, 422
hollowing out 352, 354, 356, 358
homo economicus 12, 36, 39, 175,
    471
Hong Kong 314, **352–92**
    as colony x
hope/fear 353, 366, 368–70, 375–6, 385,
    387, 453, 462–3
hope/strength 440–6, 449–50 452–4,
    462–3

horizons of action 4, 49, 62ff, 68, 109,
    143, 150, 157, 172, 174, 190, 215,
    218, 238, 245f, 282, 398f, 405, 414,
    418, 437, 454
how/why questions 124, 205ff, 209,
    226–7, 478, 483

Iceland 414, 428, 435
idealism 108, 117
ideas 76ff
ideational abilities 57f, 215, 412
ideational institutionalism, *see*
    institutionalism
Ideologiekritik 23, 115, **164–5**, 196, 240
ideology 43, 55, 105, 110f, 125, 142,
    164, **168–72**, 188, 286ff, **479–80**
    vs imaginary 170
    vs science 169
identity 170, 174, 187f, 194, 210
idiographic analysis 41
illocution 121
imagined economy 167
imaginary 26, 87, 90, 130, 141, **164–6**,
    204, 226, 261, 278, 296–7, 353,
    356, 360, 368, 389, 414, 440, 449,
    451, 453–4, 463
    competitiveness 262, 364f, 368f, 374f
    hegemonic 166, 261–2, 265, 395
    and ideology **168–72**
    Neoliberal 395
    political 23, 81, 94, 141, 147, 166,
        186, 196, 261f, 296, 451
    social 23, 27, 29, 56, 75, 96, 147,
        170–1, 262, 468, 475, 477–80
    spatial 166
    vs semiosis 165
    see also accumulation strategy,
        ecological imaginaries,
        economic imaginaries, regional
        spaces
IMF 221, 400, 407, 429, 432, 434, 442,
    451–3
imperialism, classical 264ff
imperialism, disciplinary 471
improbability 191–2, 213, 239, 247
India 315, 327–7, 330, 448, 450, 454–5
indexes 222, 279ff, 304, 306–10, 317,
    362
Individual Visit Scheme 353, 370,
    378–87

Subject index

industrial capital, *see* productive capital
information economy 274–5
   see also knowledge-based economy, knowledge economy
innovation-led growth 266, 298–9, 301, 356–7
Institute for Competitiveness (Barcelona) 301–2, 366
Institute for Development Studies 313
Institute for Management Development 306, 362
Institute for Strategy and Competitiveness 301
instituted economy 168
institution 25–6, 34, 108, 223, 246, 365, 390, 462
   definition 34f
   and organization 35, 45
institutional coherence 66
institutional complementarity 37, 150, 252
institutional design 36f
institutional embeddedness 36–7, 43–4
institutional entrepreneurship 36
   see also bricolage
institutional fix 27f, 46, 76, 141, 149f, 168, 192, 200, 213, **247f**, 250, 253f, 284f, 417–20, 481
institutional form 160, 252
   see also structural form
institutionalism 26, **33–6**, 42, 47f, 85, 468
   actor-centred 60–1
   critical 48
   feminist 47f, 70
   fourth (constructivist, discursive, or ideational) 33, 47, **54–9**, 67, 69, 71, 139, 159, 470
   historical 42, 44ff, 59f, 65, 67
   network 47
   new vs old 10, 39, 47, 219, 46, 65f, 68, 219
   organizational 35, 45, 47
   queer 47
   rational choice 17, 36, 40ff, 45f, 52, 59f, 65–7, 70, 83f, 470
   sociological 42, 45f, 67
institutional isomorphism 37
institutionalization 65, 159, 366
integral analysis 1, 159, 206

integral state 359
intellectual 74, 79, 91, 174–5, 200–1, 207, 219–20, 224, 286
   see also organic intellectual
intellectual commons 279, 285–6, 288
intellectual labour 286
intellectual property rights 154, **284–9**, 292, 294
interdisciplinarity 105, 472
interdiscourse 115, 128, 278
interdiscursivity 98
interest 170, 187f
   general 85
   ideal vs material 170, 189f
interest-bearing capital 239, 244, 262, 399, 419
international political economy 200
   see also Italian School, world market
international regimes 11
intersectionalism 17, 189
intertext 4, 97f, 101, 104ff, 112, 119, 121, 124ff, 128, 135
intertextuality 4, 97, 105, 128, 138
intransitive dimension of science 6
InvestHK 325–6
investment 443–8, 453, 463
investment banks 422–4, 453
investment-driven growth 266
irrealis x, 3, 215
Italian School 72, 76–80, 84, 95, 200–2
Italy 74–5, 77, 202

Japan, lost decade 274f

Keynesian welfare national state 245, **254–6**, 269, 291, 398
keywords 117f
knowledge 111, 244, 285ff
   as fictitious commodity 240, 244, 271, 285–6, 290
   division of 286
   scientific 9
   traditional 287f
knowledge bank 315, 317
knowledge-based economy 200, 213, 240, 261f, 269f, 292f, 356–7, 364, 477
knowledge brand 229, 267, 274, 296, 304–5, **352–65**, 368, 390

knowledge economy **270–3**, 279, 355–6, 360
knowledge interests 35
knowledge/power, *see* power/knowledge
knowledge practice 91
knowledge society **271–3**, 284
knowledging technology, *see* technologies

labour 160, 243, 318
  Abstract 237, 244,
  concrete 237, 243, 244
  and language 160
labour market 79, 179, 195, 239–40, 255–6, 290–1, 365
labour power 212, 237, 263, 276
  as fictitious commodity 239f, 263
labour theory of value 263
land 244, 318, 441, 456–9
land-based finance 457–8
language 75, 102, 107, 120, 124, 215
  as medium of ideology 126
  ideology and power 103, 124
  see also langue
language politics 108, 215
langue 106, 108, 119, 138, 161, 192, 215
law of motion 88, 91, 178, 181, 206–7, 242, 259, 468
law of value **241–2**
learning 23, 51, 55, **64**, 161, 170f, 184, 194, 204, 253, 344, 397, 470, 473, **476–7**, 480
  and complexity reduction 476
  in, about, from crisis 397, **408–15**
  and power 283, 401
learning, discourses of 270–3, 277, 284f
learning economy 263, 270f, 277, 280, 284
lending 451–3, 463
lifeworld 19, 143, 147, **173–5**, 181
  see also civil society
linguistic innovation 103, 161
linguistic meaning x, 3f
linguistic reductionism 97f, 153, 215
linguistics 10, 11, 54f
  core 4, 111,125, 152
  corpus 116
  critical 16

discourse 115f
external vs internal 159
historical 103, 130
spatial 74, 103, 130
structural 104, 119, 157, 161
lived experience 88, 171, 479f
local government debts 458, 461
logic of capital 182
logical–historical method 2, **7**, 472
  see also critical realism

Mainland and Hong Kong Closer Economic Partnership Agreement 353, 370–1
management consultancies 203, 287, 298f, 314, 362
marginalization discourses 353, 375–8
market 221, 263–5
  failure 234, 241, 245, 295, 321, 406, 428f
  financial 83, 319, 417, 427, 446, 454
market economy 44, 46, 175f, 178, 236, 240, 269, 276, 284, 297, 383ff, 406f, 417, 422
  social market economy 418
market forces 183, 192, 234ff, 238–42, 249, 252, 264, 267f, 284, 293, 298, 321, 342, 408, 427, 431
mass media 58, 167, 174, 301, 358, 360, 364, 442, 449, 453, 458
Marxianization of Foucault 197, 206f, 212ff
Marxism x, 10, 17–18, 132, 187, 212f, 468
  Western 82
material culture 118f
material force 4, 122
material provisioning 44, 166, 173, 175, 195, 265
material vs semiotic 154f
meaning 109, 111, 118, 131f, 156
meaning context 57, 108, 111
meaning-making, *see* sense- and meaning-making
media studies 16–17
media technology 118, 138, 152
mediatization 412f
mental equipment 122, 185
mental model 43, 55
mentalities 121ff, 130

Subject index 563

mercantilism 266
mercato determinato 73–5, 206
meso-level agenda 196
metaphors 5, 29, 75, 222, 306, 311–13, 355, 360, 444
methodological cultural turn 82
methodological holism 40f
methodological individualism 40f, 98
methodological institutional turn 41–43, 47, 69, 87
methodological nationalism 95, 472
methodological relationalism 50
methodology 2, 7, 20–1, 40, 59, 125, 204, 209, 226–7
micro-economic 300, 307f, 318
micro-finance 316, 318
micro-firms 315, 326ff
micro-foundations 40f, 59–60, 68, 82, 300
micro–macro relations 41f, 59f, 68, 82, 99, 167, 183, 195, 209, 217, 219f, 391, 472
micro-management 324, 331, 336, 342, 348, 441
micro-power 42, 208–9, 219, 222, 224, 336, 350, 362, 441, 463
middle classes 381, 384, 386, 430, 445, 448, 450
migrant labour 257, 333, 345, 353, 353, 401, 441, 459–61
Ministry of MSME (India) 326
MIT 352, 354–8, 363, 390
mode of growth 251, 163, 265
mode of regulation 81–2, 89–91, 235–8, 246f
   see also accumulation regime
Modern Prince 202
money 45, 237, 243f, 254ff, 259, 417ff, 427f
   see also finance-dominated accumulation, financial capital, financialization
Monitor Group 301
moral economy 7–8, 105
MSME/SME cluster development 313, 315–16, 322, 326, 328
multi-accentuality 106f
multi-modal communication 97, 152f
multinational firms 264, 311, 317, 322, 326

national economy 68, 246, 251, 253–6, 269, 281
national state 68, 77, 246, 253ff, 269f, 280, 400
national system of innovation **277–8**, 279, 299
naturalization (reification) 12–13, 115, 132f, 164, 169, 175ff, 187, 191, 240, 317, 352, 468, 478,
nature 87f, 166, 218, 240, 248, 257, 319, 418
Nebenbegriff 107, 109
   see also semantic conceptual history
neoclassical economics 12, 17f, 39f, 45f, 52f, 55, 70, 82, 423, 471
neo-Gramscian approach 77, 79, 87, 196, 201–2, 215, 329, 347, 468
neo-liberalism 45, 61, 80, 83–4, 86f, 92f, 175, 202, 235f, 255, 261f, 266, 269, 284, 288, 291, 296ff, 329f, 347ff, 395, 398, 401, 417f, 423ff, 429f, 444, 454
   crisis in/of 92–3, 406, 408, 427, 435, 453
   developmentalism 317–22, 467
   disciplinary 80, 200, 329, 418
   ecological dominance of 235f, 269, 282
   embedded 80, 86
   periodization 346ff, 416, 436
   regime shift 261, 398, 416ff, 428, 436
   shadow of 236, 282, 416
neolinguistics 74, 95
neomercantilism 274
new constitutionalism 200, 329, 347–8, 418
new ethicalism 28, 325, **346–50**, 418
newly industrializing countries 311
NGOs 223, 313, 318–19, 325, 337, 345–50
nodal actors 204, 220, 224, 227f, 354, 364, 441
nodal link metaphor 312
nodal point 131ff, 229, 305
non-discoursal 126, 154, 158, 160, 468
non-discursive 114, 129, 131, 139f, 155f, 163, 193
   see also extra-discursive
nonsense 161
normalism 115

normalization 82, 201, 205f, 207, 222, 226, 284, 343, 353, 365, 389, 447, 477f
normal science 39, 133
norms 221, 387–9, 391
North Atlantic Financial Crisis 269–70, 416–17, 421–7, 434–5, 440, 454, 461
number order 309, 362
numbers and rankings 222, 309–10

object 203, 208, 215–16
  and subjects 204, 213, 216f
objectification 282
objectivation 112, 114, 163, 197, 206, 208, 218, 222
OECD 167, 262, 270f, 274, **282**, 299
OntheFRONTIER Group 301
ontological turn
  cultural 80, 87–94
  institutional 43–5, 87, 96
ontologization 178–9
ontology 1, 3–5, 8f, 13–15, 21, 23–25, 38ff, 43ff, 73, 80ff, 86ff, 102, 132, 140, 155, 211, 408, 476, 482
  depth 9, 410
  empty 211
  relational 217
order of discourse 127
Ordoliberalism 417f, 420, 424ff
organic intellectuals 200, 202, 219, 354, 364, 444, 453
  and discourse **201–3**, 219, 322, 364
organizational ecology 35
organizational institutionalism 35, 45
original equipment manufacturing 311, 356
orthodox economics 176f
overdetermination 9, 132, 253, 307, 410, 416
overgeneration 58
own-brand manufacturing 311, 356
own-design manufacturing 311, 356

Panopticon 208, 331, 333–8, 342, 362
  cost-squeezing 336
  paper 309–10
pan-politicism 133f, 178
pan-semiosis 152
paradigm, societal 176

para-institutionalism 36f
paratext 97, 126, 138, 479
Parisian School 246, 251ff, 257f
parole 119, 138, 215
passive revolution 74, 120, 130, 215, 347f, 351
path-dependency 3, 37, 55, 70, 107, 113, 132, 185, 201–15, 218, 390, 469, 474
path-shaping 3, 114, 203, 218, 390, 469, 474f
patriarchy 62, 481
Pearl River Delta 301, 314, 325–7, 352–4
People's Republic of China 353–92, 440, 443, 448, 450–61
  see also BRIC, China
performativity 62, 127, 273–4, 283, 474f
  see also construction
periodization 129f, 474
philology 1, 120
  and Gramsci 1, 74f
  see also linguistics, semiosis
philosophical anthropology 11
philosophy 75
plebeian instincts 213
pluralism, theoretical 7, 10–11
pluri-disciplinarity 12–13, 67, 77
policy paradigm 37, 57, 263, **267–74**, 277, 282f, 294, 296ff, 299, 321, 395f, 402, 412ff, 434, 438
political capitalism 419f
political ecology 16
political economy 11
  classical 15–16, 33
political parties 86, 92, 167, 174, 203–4, 210, 399, 401, 421, 424, 427, 430
political, primacy of 132
political science 177
population 210, 216, 306, 316–17, 322
post-disciplinarity 14–15, 33, 67, 471f, 481–3
post-discursive 156f
post-fordism 87, 261
post-industrialism 271, 275, 291
post-institutionalism 36, 47
post-Marxism 129, **131–3**, 139, 188
post-modernism 136
post-neoliberalism 421, 433f

Subject index

post-structuralism 10, 29
poverty reduction 221, 306, 311–12, 316
power 35, 69, 71, 126, 169
   capillary 209
   disciplinary 201, 207
   structural 435–6
   symbolic 125
power/knowledge 22, 100, 114, 116, 134, 197, 205f, 208f, 213, 221–2, 326
practice 127, 158, 169, 179, 195, 222, 313–15, 317, 336, 343, 352–3, 365–6, 377–8, 391, 447, 462
   discursive 97, 131f, 154ff, 160, 193f, 210
   social 97, 131f, 154ff, 160, 202
   see also best practice
practice theory 157
pragmatic conceptual history, *see* Cambridge School
pragmatics 16, 97, 112, 121, 128, 130
pre-disciplinarity 10–13, 15ff, 30, 33, 482
pre-discursive 156f
price competitiveness 255, 267, 331, **333–8**, **342**, **383**
price form 44, 46, 88, 183, 193, 236, 239, 242, 287, 297, 385, 417
primitive accumulation 287, 436
prioritization in fixes **249f**
problematization 61, 150, 202, 208, 313, 355–6, 443, 462, 476
productive capital 243f, 254, 284, 352, 355, 366f, 428
   see also profit-producing capital
productivism 85
profit 44, 240, 242, 244, 255, 264, 286, 288, 334f, 387, 453
   of enterprise 244f
   equalization 242, 287
   monopoly 74, 289
   super 240, 286f, 289, 418
   surplus 212, 259
   rate 199, 259, 286, 290, 448, 458f
profit-oriented, market-mediated accumulation 61, 154f, 175, 195, 206, 233, 237, 293, 406, 418, 432, 468ff
profit-producing capital 262, 419

pro-poor growth 313, 322
property 367, 441, 458f, 461
proto-concept of control 85

queer theory 17, 62, 470

'*race to the bottom*' 268, 285, 318–19, 325
rational choice approach 187, 396
   see also institutionalism
rationality 40, 44, 54f, 175f
   bounded 36, 53, 60
real-concrete 7, 9
real estate development and speculation 205, 215, 296, 301, 306–18, 324, 352, 359, 441
reception 27, 107, 134, 136,
reception theory 136–8, 143, 467
recontextualization 28, 59, 98, 104f, 109, 114f, 119f, 122, 127, 133f, 137, 192, 205, 215, 220f, 296, 301, **306–18**, 322, 352ff, 359, 441, 454
recruitment, selective 185
recursivity 22, 36, 41, 50ff, 64, 174, 470ff
redistribution 44
reductionism 61, 92, 98, 108, 122, 131, 159, 215
referent 24, 108f
reflexivity 38, 50–2, 62ff, 73, 111, 161, 470f
regional spaces 315–17, 322
regularization 211, 223, 296
regulation approach 19ff, 22, 26f, 34, 39, 44, 61, 72f, 76, 80–7, 89, 93f, 126, 176, 182, 200, 233, **251–3**, 238, 331, 416
   see also Amsterdam School, German School, Grenoble School, Parisian School
régulation-cum-governance 72, 81, 94, 213, 237f, **246**, 249–50
remoralization 224, 350
repoliticization 223, 348
reports
   Benchmarking 305–9
   consultancy 304, 314, 317, 352, 355, 359, 361, 441, 444–6
reputational risk management 339–47
resilience discourses 312, 318–19, 322

resistance 33, 66, 105f, 113ff, 167, 171, 179ff, 207, 213f, 223, 289, 318f, 321–2, 337, 350, 380–2, 385, 390, 459ff, 463f
resonance 223–4, 279, 282–3, 305, 317, 440
responsible competitiveness 318–20, 322
retail chains 324
Retail Link 333–5
retention 282–3
  see also variation–selection–retention
retroduction 9, 25, 410
risk assessment 315–16
ruling class 168f

scale 198, 223, 270, 276, 282, 284, 296, 302–3, 305–18, 322, 352, 365
Schumpeterian Workfare post-national regime 284f
scoreboards 222, 304, 324, 334–7, 350
Scylla 22
  and Charybdis 108, 141, 150ff, 159, 175ff, **181**, 193, 196f, 229, 233, 467, 471
sedimentation 90, 105f, 132f, 143, 150, **163–4**, 170f, 211, 222f, 262, 317, 322, 452, 476, 478
selectivities 75, 96f, 120, 134, 165, 184, 191, 194, 203ff, 208, 213f, **218–19**, 226ff, 296, 321, 349, 355–66, 390, 398, 405f, 437, 477, 481
  agential 25, 64, 96, 137–8, 197f, **203–4**, 216, **217**, **219–20**, 227f, 304, 321–2, 349, 355, 358, 360–5, 366, 390, 403, 444, 462, 477
  discursive 68, 109, 137, 204f, 210, 215f, 218, 220–2, 227–8, 405
    (extra-discursive dimensions 215f)
  spatio-temporal 215
  structural 68, 185, 203, 208, 214–15, 218, 227–8, 355, 357–8, 366, 390
  technological 96, 196f, 203–4, 208, 211, 216–19, 221f, 227f, 306–18, 321, 350, 355, 366, 390, 448, 453
  weight of selectivities 197, 212, 214
  see also strategic-relational approach

self-governance 208, 310
self-leadership 201, 222, 224
self-reflexivity 70, 471
self-responsibility 201, 291, 317–18, 348–9, 365
semantic conceptual history 44, 58, 100, **107–11**, 117, 130, 137, 473
  and discourse historical approach 128
  see also Cambridge School
semantic fix 79, 105f, 149f, 194, 200, 237, 246f
semantics 97, 107f, 112, 135
semiologistics 138, 142, 185, 216
semiosis 1, 3, 24, 29, 85, 120, 135, 148ff, 152f, 156f, 204, 241, 469, 472f
  and ideology 164
  see also sense- and meaning-making
semiotics 11, 16
sense- and meaning-making viii, x, 1, 3f, 89, 97, 135f, 140, 152, 157, **160–2**, 204, 354, 441
service bloc 365–7
service governance 352, 353, 358–65
service sector 358–70, 373, 387
shopscape 353, 358–75, 391
sign 24, 75
signified 24, 131f
signifier, empty 132
signifier, floating 34, 132
sign-value 19
skill 243f, 254, 268, 271, 276, 290–2, 316
small and medium enterprises 315, 320, 322, 326
social entrepreneurs 320
social fix **246f**
social forces 203–4
social form 158, 160
social history 110, 118
social movements 204, 223
societal paradigm 81f, 89
societalization 10f, 61, 70, 74, 90, 92, 115, 124, 134, 149, 172, 175, 187ff, 208, 211ff, 241, 263, 474
sociolinguistics 29, 53, 58, 97, 111, 125, 128, 152, 215
soft cultural economics 177ff, 182f, 233, 468

Subject index 567

sovereignty, temporal and territorial 428
space 12, 167
space economy 234, 259
spatiality 111, 268
spatialization in fixes 250
spatio-temporal fix 27f, 46, 63, 76, 130, 133, 141, 149f, 167, 172, 183f, 186, 192f, 200, 213, 223, 235ff, **247–50**, 252, 257f, 261, 283ff, 399, **416–20**, 474f, 481
spatio-temporality 62, 215
Staatswissenschaft 11
standpoints 3, 7, 149, 165f, 169–72, 214, 220, 265, 397, 406, 412, 479f
state 170, 207, 209, 244, 254f, 260, 264–5, 267, 288, 293, 430, 435
  see also national state, EU
state power 109, 260, 435
state project 203, 209
Stiglitz Commission 400, 431–3
stimulus packages 440, 454–8, 462
strategic context 52, 62, 64ff, 67, 98, 104, 204
strategic line 113, 210, 212
strategic-relational approach x, 24–5, 28, **48–50**, 67, 70, 100, 109, 114, 150, 197, 203–29, 204f, 246, 252f, 468, 475
  and institutionalism 53
  and language 53–4
strategic selectivity 22, 28, 50–1, 63, 67f, 114, 203, **213–19**
  see also selectivities
'strategy without a subject' 210, 212
structural coupling 235
  see also co-evolution
structural form 34, 44, 46, 251
structuralism 34, 98, 468
structuration 3f, 24, 97, 149–50f, 191, 197, 475
structuration theory 49f, 61
structured coherence 50, **52**, 66, 74, 150f, 172, 184f, 247, 283, 405, 469, 474ff
subalterns 223–4, 456, 459–62
sub-hegemony 173, 202, 214, 218, 223
subject 66, 111
subjectivation 111ff, 138, 148, 179, 187, 197, 204–8, 211, 217, 222f, 318, 365

subjectivities 203, 207–11, 216, 222–3, 296, 371, 374, 441
  see also standpoints
superprofit 287
superstructure 92, 104, 117, 132, 197
supply chain clusters 324, 326–8, 333, 349
supply-side interventions 296, 316
supratext 97f, 104, 126, 136, 138
surplus meanings 156, 223
sustainability 221, 307f, 315, 319f, 322, 335ff, 343–4, 346–7, 356, 407, 424, 432
suture 132f, 223
sweatshops 326, 337–9, 342
symptomatology 75, **410ff**
system relevance 172–4

tactics of the weak 224
taxation 64, 245, 433
technical assistance 314, 317
technical–managerial 296, 313–16, 347–50
  see also best practice, benchmark, cluster methodologies, indexes, reports, scorecards, technical assistance, training courses
technologies (knowledging and governmental) 194, 205–11, 213, 218, 221–2, 304, 306–18, 360–5, 371, 390
  of agency 306, 316, 322, 374, 442, 452–3, 462
  of boundary protection 362–3
  of control 342
  of differentiation 377
  of domestication and combinability 371–4
  of identification and achievement 442, 444, 449, 453
  of investability 442, 444, 447–8
  knowledging 5, 207ff, 221f, 272
  of performance, judgement, and gap 306–10, 322, 362–3
  of positive chaining 362–4, 366
  of self 211, 343–6, 348
technology-driven growth 298–9, 355–6
temporalization in fixes 249f
  see also STF

tendencies (in capitalism) 7, 88, 172, 199, 241, 259, 286, 290
  crisis-tendencies 37, 66, 183, 192, 233ff, 249ff, 253, 396f, 410, 416, 419
  doubly tendential nature of tendencies 66, 175f, 180–4, 234, 258, 421
thematic cultural turn 18, 55, 73, 80–2, 87, 93, 96
thematic institutional turn 37–41, 47f, 68f
theoretical paradigm 39, 57, 267, **271f**, 297f, 321, 395f, 400, 413
think tanks 203, 301, 325, 354, 358–9, 361, 366, 368, 440, 451, 453, 462
time 12, 109, 121f, 167, 172
  abstract 237
  political economy of 237, 241, 245, 284
  reproduction time 240
  turnover time 239f
time-space compression 297
totalization 10, 90, 99
training courses 296, 304, 310, 313–14, 322
transaction costs 40f
trans-disciplinarity 12–16, 17, 19, 21, 28, 33f, 67, 100, 126, 196f, 203ff, 229f, 467ff, 481f
trans-discursive terms 278f
transitive dimension of science 6, 471
transnational historical materialism, *see* Amsterdam School
transnational symbols 305
TRIMS 329
TRIPS 289–90
truth effects 437, 469
truth regime 5f, 202, 207–11, 216, 222, 317, 364
turn,
  complexity 21, 134, 197, 471
  cultural 4, 16–18, 22ff, 26f, 30, 55, 69, **72–3**, 79–83, 90, 94, 140, 183, 188, 193, 204, 468
  evolutionary 96, 474
  hermeneutic 72, 81
  institutional **37–9**, **45–8**, 68–70, 196, 468, 470

linguistic 132, 156
practice 157f
pragmatic 69
reflexive 64, 161
self-reflexive 70, 87
spatial 69

underspecification 58, 97
uneven development 47, 62, 108, 236, 249, 254, 259, 290, 417ff, 420, 478
United Kingdom 298, 416, 419, 428, 435
United Nations 432
United Nations Industrial Development Organization (UNIDO) 301–2, 306, 313–15, 320, 326
United States Agency for International Development (USAID) 301, 303, 311
universities 291–4
unstable equilibrium of compromise 94, 100, 209, 223, 226, 247, 253, 317, 347, 367, 389, 392, 478
urgences 202, 208, 217, 238, 476
  see also problematization
USA 5, 256, 276–8, 292, 298, 309, 331, 401, 406f, 416, 419, 422–5, 428, 432, 435f, 443
  pathological co-dependency with China 5, 420, 436
use-value 19, 85, 230, 237, 240ff, 259, 384
  vs exchange-value 237, **243–4**, 269

valorization 92, 241, 264, 268
value 88, 212
  exchange-value vs use-value 237, 243
value theory of labour 263f
variation–selection–retention 25, 59, 96, 105, 129, 134, 136, 138, 140, 151, 159, 161–2, **184–5**, 197–8, 202f, 223, 238, 273, **282–3**, 397
variegated capitalism 37, **233–6**, 252f, 416, 438, 453, 463
varieties of capitalism 41, 45, 67, 85, 233–6, 245, 472
Vergesellschaftung, *see* societalization

vernacular materialism 100, **102–7**, 119, 130
Vienna School, *see* discourse historical approach
Vietnam 313–14
visibilization 324–5, 342, 376, 444
vulgar materialism 102, 117, 120

wage form 239f, 244, 252, 254f, 285, 417f
Wal-Mart 317, 321, 324–5, 329–50
Wal-Martization 226, 325, 331–8, 349–50
Waltonism 200, 331
  retail-led model 200
war of manoeuvre 215
war of position 109, 120, 204, 215, 390
Washington Consensus 417, 420f, 451, 462

working class 195, 199, 239ff, 253ff, 259, 266, 318, 321f, 337f, 340ff, 345 384, 387, 420, 430
  see also capital relation, class, migrant labour, wage form
World Bank 11, 167, 270, 400, 407, 429, 432, 434, 442, 450
World Economic Forum 301–2, 307–10, 319, 322, 362, 366–8
world market 155, 175, 233, **234ff**, 240, 246f, **258f**, 262ff, 268, 282, 289, 293, 312, 317f, 401, 408, **416ff**, 427, 432, 437f, 446, 472
World Social Forum 434
World Trade Organization 221, 329, 346ff, 353, 370, 384, 400, 443–4

zone of relative stability 27, 141, 235
  see also fix, spatio-temporal